LITERATURE AND PULPIT IN
MEDIEVAL ENGLAND

LITERATURE AND PULPIT
IN MEDIEVAL ENGLAND

A NEGLECTED CHAPTER IN
THE HISTORY OF ENGLISH LETTERS & OF
THE ENGLISH PEOPLE

by
(GERALD Robert)
G. R. OWST

Fellow of Emmanuel College and Emeritus
Professor in the University of Cambridge

OXFORD
BASIL BLACKWELL
1966

PRINTED IN GREAT BRITAIN
BY THE COMPTON PRINTING WORKS (LONDON) LTD., LONDON, N.1
FOR BASIL BLACKWELL & MOTT LTD.
AND BOUND BY
THE KEMP HALL BINDERY, OXFORD

TO MY BELOVED WIFE
MAY

ἀλλὰ τὰ μωρὰ τοῦ κόσμου ἐξελέξατο ὁ Θεὸς ἵνα τοὺς σοφοὺς καταισχύνῃ, καὶ τὰ ἀσθενῆ τοῦ κόσμου ἐξελέξατο ὁ Θεὸς ἵνα καταισχύνῃ τὰ ἰσχυρά, καὶ τὰ ἀγενῆ τοῦ κόσμου καὶ τὰ ἐξουθενημένα ἐξελέξατο ὁ Θεὸς καὶ τὰ μὴ ὄντα ἵνα τὰ ὄντα καταργήσῃ· ὅπως μὴ καυχήσηται πᾶσα σὰρξ ἐνώπιον αὐτοῦ.

1 Cor. i, 27–9.

PREFACE TO SECOND EDITION

THIS book—in the words of the original preface—the first attempt made to estimate comprehensively the debt of English literature to the message of her medieval Church, as preserved in sermon and tractate, was written thirty years ago and has been out of print for twenty. Since the study was completed, very naturally fresh information has come to hand from time to time and more than one set of medieval homilies used in its construction, formerly available only in manuscript, has been published in this country, notably through the enterprise of American editors. Wherever the process of reproduction has allowed, corrections and additions have been made to this new issue; but some things have had to stand which to-day the author would have preferred to express differently. Even in the matter of names, for example, the form "Brunton" (for a certain Bishop of Rochester) has had to be left unchanged, although Sister M. A. Devlin of Illinois has now proved conclusively that it should be "Brinton". The interested reader may like to be reminded that a wealth of further illustrative examples for almost every page can be found in the *Destructorium Viciorum* of Alexander Carpenter, on the subject of which the present writer published a Durham lecture,* eight years ago, with the sub-title "A Fifteenth-century Sequel to *Literature and Pulpit in Medieval England.*" Finally, he would like to thank Sir Basil Blackwell and Mr H. L. Schollick for so readily undertaking the re-publication of so lengthy a work, long "even for the well-brought-up, accustomed to sermons."

G. R. OWST

St Valentine's Day
GREAT WILBRAHAM
CAMBRIDGE

* S.P.C.K. (for the Church Historical Society), 1952

CONTENTS

CONTENTS

CHAPTER I

Introductory influences, linguistic, romantic and realistic.

To the average man a study of the influences of preaching upon the general development of literature must seem a singularly futile and wearisome task. From that century in which the author of *Hudibras* mocked the beatings of "the pulpit, drum ecclesiastic", down to our own, it has made but few noteworthy contributions to current thought and literary expression. Here and there, the sermons of a greater Butler, a Wesley, or a Robertson may still claim to be read for their special philosophic or doctrinal content, those of a Jeremy Taylor or a Donne for their charm of style. Otherwise, with the ages of Religion passed, and now with this latest decay of the old oratorical eloquence even in Parliament, the utterances of the pulpit are so ephemeral, so drab and commonplace, for the most part, that the beatings of its drum attract little more attention from men of letters than the drum of some forlorn-looking showman in a side street. Like unwilling listeners of an earlier age, they "weenen that it is an ydil thinge", and turn from it with a sigh or a smile to more vital and picturesque affairs.

The student of ancient literatures knows, however, that the religious discourse once played a far more distinguished part in this very sphere. Even in pre-Christian times, literature owed much for its actual beginnings to the inspired declamation of the priest, the fearless denunciations by prophets from the hills, the sacred odes and recitations of the festival. Turning to the history of our own national literature, at an early date we are made familiar with a mass of Anglo-Saxon and Middle-English homilies and religious treatises which for some centuries seem to constitute wellnigh all that remains to us of "ancient relics of the language". For some considerable time to come, they continue to play a prominent part in the entertainment as well as the education of the people. Even the history of Christian Art tells us a similar tale. For, the themes of painter and sculptor are the themes of the pulpit. And, to take but a single example of the more direct influence of the latter, it was that same Franciscan preaching revival which produced the Saint's own *Canticle of the Sun*, and the ardent *laude* of Jacopone da Todi among the earliest vernacular gems of Italian literature, that led also to the birth of a brilliant age of Italian painting and sculpture, freed from the bondage of Byzantine formalism.

In England, the first epoch of what may be called a national literature eventually passes away with the triumph of a foreign invader. We may leave, therefore, to more competent hands the task of deciding, from the limited material that is available, how far the work of the Christian pulpit in those far-off Saxon days may be held responsible for the poems of a Caedmon and a Cynewulf, or even for the appearance of that still more remarkable literary phenomenon in the vernacular known as the *Anglo-Saxon Chronicle*.[1] The present study will be mainly concerned with the literature that proceeds from the vernacular renaissance of the fourteenth century; that which, though yet essentially medieval, is linked more directly with our own. It will seek to re-examine that literature in the light of contemporary sermons and religious treatises of English origin, such as are not unnaturally to be found in increasing numbers in the last two medieval centuries, thus to establish what relations it can between them. At the same time, however, it will be necessary continually to have recourse to earlier works of the kind, wherever the age of a particular sermon manuscript may throw doubt on the priority of the pulpit tradition. For here we shall discover again and again that the latter almost invariably represents a tradition older by centuries than the actual writing before us. Our homilists of the fourteenth and fifteenth centuries speak and write the language of earlier generations of preachers. They borrow wholesale their phrases, their maxims, their arguments, even their illustrations. As was indicated in the present author's original volume,[2] and as will be reindicated

---

[1] See here J.-Th. Welter, *L'Exemplum dans la Litt. Rélig. et Didact. du Moyen Âge*, p. 21, n. 28.

[2] Cf. *Preaching in Med. Engl.* pp. 54, 303, etc.

here, reference to the homilies of St Bernard and his fellow-orators on the continent, to treatises like the *De Contemptu Mundi* of Bernard of Morlaix or the *Elucidarium* of Honorius of Autun, and yet earlier still to the homilies of such Fathers and Doctors as Augustine, Chrysostom and Gregory the Great, will swiftly destroy the appearance of originality in many a later disciple. It is nevertheless through the latter that these living voices of the past continue to speak to men's hearts and minds. Hence, in a medieval world where to the end books and book-learning remained pre-eminently the privilege of churchmen, we shall often be justified in crediting the pulpit, even where the evidence is not wholly conclusive, with the initiation of some new literary conceit. It is only in a modern world that it lags so sadly behind, frequently hiring its fashionable vesture ready-made and all too "shop-soiled" from the cheapest secular markets. Once it was a real power in the land, speaking at its highest with the authority of the prophet, even at its lowest with something of the learning of scribes. Thus, as our study progresses, we shall understand more clearly how that "main stream" of scholastic and ecclesiastical literature, which Courthope distinguishes from the Romantic or Chivalrous in the Middle Ages, irrigated the soil of Allegory, Satire and Drama in this country; and why in the latest pre-Reformation period the two streams finally merge and flow on together. For, in that prime work of irrigation it was the pulpit that provided the necessary channels by which the characteristic thought and expression of the churchmen flowed into the popular mind and were turned to secular advantage. No study therefore of the literature of medieval England can ever claim to be complete, until it has taken into its purview these much-neglected records of the preachers themselves.

The first point to be made in estimating the literary contribution of our preaching is its early influence upon the development of the language. It is surely no extravagance to speak of the activities of the Mendicants in this respect, when, as Dr Little has reminded us, "for a century and a half" before Wycliffe, "men versed in all the learning of their time had been constantly preaching to the people in the vulgar tongue,

in every part of the country".[1] Even before their coming, in
a polite and official world of Latin and French, the pulpit alone
had maintained a regular public use of the English tongue by
educated men from the days of the Conquest.[2] In no other
way, so it seems, could a language otherwise virtually aband-
oned to the common uses of common folk have been preserved for any future cultural revival. A long thin line of
homilies and kindred metrical paraphrases, dull enough though
important for this very reason, holds the fort for our English
tongue from the days of Aelfric and Wulfstan to those of
Rolle and Mannyng, until a more brilliant relief arrives, and
the siege is raised. Their very existence is enough to give the
lie to Professor Fawtier's absurd deduction from the slipshod
phrase of a chronicler, that the peasantry (!) of England, prior
to the Black Death, habitually spoke in French, and that
that language was therefore the regular medium of popular
preaching.[3] Until the second half of the fourteenth century,
indeed, French remained the invariable tongue of the gay
"chanson de geste", the tongue of the English law courts and
of polite society in general, with Latin, of course, as the official
language of the clergy. But, if the mass of "Englisshe men",
prior to this time, were as bilingual as M. Fawtier would have
us believe, why, we may ask, for example, did the thirteenth-
century author of the *Ormulum* write in English "thatt mann
birrth spellenn to the follc", or Robert Mannyng of Brunne
trouble to translate the *Manuel des Pechiez* in the year 1303?

> For lewde men y undyrtoke
> On englyssh tunge to make thys boke.

By pointing, then, to the work of such homilists, it is possible
to explain not merely the preservation of English as a worthy
medium of expression, but, further, its gradual fusion with
those Latin and Gallic elements from without, which helped
to fashion the English of Wycliffe and Chaucer. The sacred
discourse, though still written out and preserved as a rule in

[1] *Grey Friars in Oxford*, p. 64.
[2] On the survival and use of English as a language for preaching, even
in the twelfth century, cf. e.g. Prof. Jo. Vising, *Anglo-Norm. Lang.
and Lit.* (World's Manuals), p. 14.   [3] *Rev. d'hist. francisc.* iv, 522.

clerical Latin, had yet to be spoken in the vernacular to "lewde men". With the advent of the friar, a host of missioners spread through the land, most of them foreigners at the first and not a few trained in the schools of Paris, bringing with them minds reared amid the riches of continental civilization and learning, but now forced to adapt themselves to the ways and expressions of the people they came to instruct. The friar, where faithful to his task, was committed, moreover, to a life of evangelism spent among the common folk, the lower orders of society, intimate enough in its turn to teach him all that the foreign traveller may still learn of strange oaths, quaint sayings and ideas, and quainter local customs in foreign parts.[1] Like his modern counterpart, he too learnt to make use of this new knowledge to assist him in the popular presentation of his message. Thus the preacher becomes, in due time, the chief mediating influence through which "the mixed culture of medieval Christendom" permeates the thought and expression of the land he has adopted. "The medicine, the science of the time were in their hands", wrote Stopford Brooke, forty years ago, with little exaggeration, "and from 1220 they mixed themselves up, both by preaching and in society, with the crafts of the merchantmen; and, interlarding all their speech with French words, made these words common among the crafts and the middle class, till they stole in even into the Creed and the Lord's Prayer...."[2] Through constant repetition in homely sermons to the masses and in daily conversation by the way, such words at length became familiar to the ears of the most ordinary Englishman. No great flights of imagination therefore are needed to picture the process at work, where direct historical evidence may be sparse. For we are all aware of the influence exercised in quite modern times by a William Carey or a Stewart of Lovedale upon the linguistic development of the more primitive peoples among whom they toiled. Medieval England therefore owed much to her more educated

[1] Cf. the Italian (?) friar's reminiscence of an English rustic, in MS. Add. 27336, fol. 64 b ("Quidam frater de ordine predicatorum...asseruit et dixit se vidisse in Anglia...").

[2] *Engl. Literature* (1891), p. 35.

missionaries of "the cosmopolitan Orders", as Ten Brink calls them, men like friar Brito in Syria, in the thirteenth century—"in linguis pluribus optimus praedicator".[1]

So, too, at length, with the English friar preacher, himself trained in the learning of the Church, whether at Paris or in the medieval Universities of his own land. Differences of dialect within the mother country must have been gradually modified by such contact, as "limitor" and licensed preacher changed their districts from time to time like the travelling vendors and other comrades of the road, and the wandering scholar returned to his own "vineyard". The itinerant friar, to-day preaching in Newcastle, will be preaching later at Lichfield, at Melton or at Lynn, like Nicholas Philip.[2] Around Bury St Edmunds in an earlier century the friars come and go even from day to day—"qui cotidie hic veniunt et recedunt".[3] So, Archbishop Fitzralph of Armagh, their distinguished rival in the pulpits, has harangued scattered audiences "in vulgari" in many parts of the kingdom.[4] It is precisely such activity which is needed to explain "the mixture of dialects" which Courthope discovers in *Piers Plowman's Vision*—a typical product of the preacher's art as we shall see—"raising the presumption that the intercourse between the different parts of the country must have been frequent".[5] The little popular idioms of speech, the alliterative and proverbial phrases, the snatches of vernacular verse that still meet the eye in manuscripts of Latin sermons,[6] thus preserved for ready repetition, are vivid

---

[1] Or Ivo of Brittany (13th cent.) (see Quétif et Échard, *Script. Ord. Praed.* vol. i, p. 131, col. 2: cf. the further evidence in *Calendar of Papal Registers*, passim, etc.).

[2] Cf. MS. Bodl. Lat. Th. d. i, fols. 5, 38b, 90, 113, 162, 165, 43b, 170b, etc.; and cf. my *Preaching in Med. Engl.* p. 59, etc.

[3] MS. Add. 11284, fol. 20 (*Speculum Laicorum*, cap. xx, ed. Welter, p. 30).   [4] Cf. *Preaching in Med. Engl.* pp. 12–3, 225, etc.

[5] *History of Engl. Poetry*, vol. i, p. 243.

[6] Cf. examples in my *Preaching in Med. Engl.* pp. 231, n. 1, 272, etc.; in Prof. Carleton Brown, *Engl. Relig. Lyrics of the 14th Cent.* passim; and MSS. Harl. 7322, fol. 92, etc. ("reuthe et treuthe"; "resoun eciam tresoun"), fol. 163b ("Of thi lif non litil lete: for thou art tornid to wormis mete"), etc.; Bodl. 649 passim; Jo. Rylands, Manch. 367, fol. 299b, etc.; and John Felton's *Sermones Dominicales*.

enough evidence of such linguistic intercourse on a much larger scale.

In the development of secular literature an important stage is reached when the traditional rhymes of the more primitive gleeman, hitherto handed down, presumably by word of mouth, from generation to generation of minstrels, pass into the written verse of the later Romance-books. So, in a measure, we may behold a striking parallel development in the history of medieval preaching, when the spoken vernacular of the pulpits, hitherto preserved in an "unknown tongue", the "mystery" of a privileged class, no longer remains unrecorded for the literate layman. The contents of the sermon at length lie open on the manuscript page for all who can read English. Though the friar himself apparently did little to make his Latin homilies and treatises thus generally readable, apart from vernacular verse, others were not wanting to undertake this task of popularization.[1] Recluses, canons, monks and others, notably in the fourteenth and fifteenth centuries, thus became the authors of a new literature in "ynglych tonge", created mainly out of the more popular and vivid pulpit material of earlier Mendicants. The anecdote, the fable, the symbolic figure, so brilliantly utilized by the latter, could now be enjoyed in literary form, along with all the paraphernalia of sacred exposition, by the enterprising layman even in the circle of his own home, provided that he could secure some reader or else manage to read the treasured manual for himself. As the outstanding figure of this movement, if for no other reason, Richard Rolle, the hermit of Hampole, deserves the title bestowed on him by Horstmann, that of "the true Father of English Literature". It was clearly a similar union of gifts that had made David of Augsburg father of the German tongue long before Luther,[2] and Francis of Assisi a father of the vernacular in Italy. Not to epic and romance, but to the love-passion and moral fervour of the Christian homilist these great native literatures owe their vital impulse.

[1] See *Preaching in Med. Engl.* pp. 116, 227, 285 et seq.
[2] Cf. Preger, *Gesch. der Deut. Mystik im Mitt.* Bd. i, p. 275, n. 4. ("in declamandis sermonibus ad populum excellentis ingenii").

But to return, through this scattering of the written word, the influence of the pulpit upon our language and the dissemination of its characteristic expressions and ideas obviously widens and deepens still further. The little manuscripts themselves, passed on from hand to hand, transcribed again and again from one remote dialect into another, only increased the pace of this general linguistic interpenetration and consolidation. Nowadays, each new Middle-English text of the kind, that makes its appearance in print, gives us fresh insight into the eager demands that must have been made for copies of these works, and the amazing distances which they travelled.[1] Thus, each helped in its turn to create a new reading or listening public, hitherto left untouched by the delicate French Romance or the works of chronicler and theologian, as yet innocent of the joys alike of modern newspaper and novel. Historians and haughty men of letters may continue to pour scorn on the literary achievements of the fifteenth century. In similar fashion Caxton himself has been condemned by them for the "mean and frivolous things" which he chose to print in place of the classics. The fact remains, however, that these despised tracts and crude homiletic poems led to a popular Renaissance as well as to a popular Reformation; and the fifteenth century has an importance all of its own, not indeed as a period of brilliant authorship, but one of slow and steady self-education for the middle classes in the art of reading and literary appreciation.[2] Under its own roof-trees and by its own firesides, as a study of contemporary wills reveals to us[3] along

[1] Two recent publications which I would cite in this connection are Miss H. E. Allen's invaluable and learned *Writings ascribed to Rich. Rolle*, New York and Oxford, 1927, and Miss Frances Foster's edition of *The Northern Passion*, E.E.T.S. O.S. no. 147 (cf. here pt. ii, p. 2: "The poem ['written with the purpose of instructing the laity in matters of religion'—see p. 1] had already made its way from the north to the south of England during the first third of the fourteenth century, and before 1350 it was expanded and in part rewritten", etc.).

[2] Cf. here C. L. Kingsford, *Prej. and Promise in 15th cent. Engl.*, cap. ii, and *Engl. Hist. Lit. in the 15th cent.*, cap. i.

[3] I may here be permitted to refer the reader to my recent article, "Some Books and Book-owners of 15th cent. St Albans", in the *Transactions of the St Albans and Herts Archaeol. Soc.* for 1928, pp. 176–195.

with the surviving literature itself, a fresh part of the nation went silently to school. And that strange Providence that often delights to order the ways of men so differently from the history-books and the wise conceits of *littérateurs* ordained for its "primers" of study, not the learned tomes of the Classical Revival, but these same little works of devotion and moral instruction. The fact that they and kindred trivialities figure so largely in Caxton's list only goes to prove, of course, how far they had already become the true literature of a people, for whom Reformation was to mean more than Renaissance, and character more than wit. It may well seem at first sight from the modern text-books that "sixteenth-century England, until then so backward, suddenly assimilated its inheritance in the Bible and in classical antiquity, and burst out into the richest drama in Europe".[1] But it was not so. More than a century before any English Bible or any English edition of the classics had issued from a printing press, the work of assimilation had been proceeding silently and steadily. Even further, in the pages that follow it will be part of the reader's chief task to discover, if he has not already discovered it for himself, that in these same queer works of devotion both large and small there lurks more than one germ of future Elizabethan greatness. In some cases it becomes positively clear that the laurels have been awarded too hastily to the heroes of Classical Humanism. For, in the above lurk not only the germs of a future Protestantism, but germs of artistic realism, germs of satire and literary humour, germs of the popular drama itself, and of the Englishman's solid independence and love of compromise in social affairs,—even crude smatterings of classical and scientific lore at least calculated to awaken the imagination of the multitude. Much, indeed, has been written about William Shakespeare and his times. But we shall never understand him or his audience aright while we continue to ignore this literary upbringing of the immediate generations that produced them. The coarse and vicious scenes in his plays, for example, like many of the Shakespearean stories and moralizings, are often

[1] G. G. Coulton, *Art and the Reformation*, p. 9. Dr Coulton himself here does not overlook the slow preliminary development.

obviously reminiscent of similar scenes conjured up in the medieval homily-books. Yet it has been possible for a distinguished critic and modern man of letters to say that they were written merely to amuse the foolish, the brutal and the filthy of the poet's own day.[1] In one direction, at all events, there is in a recent remark of Mr Belloc a certain profundity of truth which has still to be explored: "The plays of Shakespeare were written by a man plainly Catholic in habit of mind, and for audiences in the same Catholic mood".[2]

It is time now to turn from consideration of these more general aspects of the subject to the actual sermons and treatises which are to engage our attention in the present study. At the outset, we may well stop to ask what our English preachers have to say, in the last two medieval centuries, about the descendants of earlier *trouvère* and minstrel, the initiators of that other great body of traditional literature represented by the secular lyric and the Romance. The attitude of the thirteenth-century Church to the minstrel has been set forth in adequate detail in the learned pages of Sir Edmund Chambers.[3] Coming to the century following, we shall not be surprised to find the London clerk, John of Mirfield, repeating in his *Florarium Bartholomei* the warning remarks of St Thomas Aquinas—"Si qui autem superflue sua bona vel cum vane glorie appetitu in tales consumunt, vel eciam sustentant histriones illos qui illicitis ludis utuntur, peccant quasi eos in peccatis foventes".[4] The attitude of the preachers themselves may best be described, perhaps, as one alternating between open hostility and ill-restrained contempt. Two picturesque sermon stories, older than the fourteenth century, occurring in the same manuscript, help to explain and illustrate this characteristic mood.[5] One

[1] The late Dr Robert Bridges, *The Influence of the Audience on Shakespeare's Drama*, in *Collected Essays*, etc. Oxford, 1927.

[2] *How the Reformation Happened* (1928), p. 13.

[3] *The Medieval Stage*, vol. i, pp. 58–62.

[4] MS. Camb. Univ. Libr. Mm. ii. 10, fol. 258b. (Cf. *Summa Theol.* pt. ii, § 2, qu. 168, art. 3, as given in continuation of footnote, p. 59 of Chambers, as above.)

[5] MS. Add. 27336, fols. 45 and 61 (Ital. prov.). Cf. further Hauréau, *Notices et Extraits de Quelques MSS. Lat. de la Bibl. Nat.* vol. ii, pp. 287–8.

tells how St Bernard was once disturbed in his preaching by the harping of a *histrio*. The other relates the reply of a girl who was urged to marry and enjoy herself while still young, postponing piety to old age. She will not make a *jougleur* of God, she says; for men give old clothes to *jougleurs*! Here our "*joculator*" may well be one of the least reputable type of a fast-decaying race of entertainers. Yet, whether it is "histrio", or "mimus", or "menestrallus"[1] who is being mentioned in our sermons, the tale is almost invariably the same, be he in the halls of the nobility or in the street. The Dominican Bromyard speaks bitterly, in his *Summa Predicantium*, of *histriones* performing before the mighty, who, like the lap-dog and the prostitute, get rich food and presents when they ask for them, while the poor go empty away.[2] "At the feasts of kings and other great lords", he tells elsewhere how those guests who seek their favour bestow upon their minstrels (*menestrallus*) gifts of robes in their honour.[3] "For largess! for largess!" is the insatiable cry of the *histrio*.[4] Assuredly, to give to such persons, adds the preacher, "is not largess, but vice".[5] The *mimus* is described by Bromyard as performing a task similar to that of *herraldus* and *menestrallus*, namely the glorification of the deeds of noble knights.[6] More than once, however,

[1] In his *Troubadours and England* (Cambridge, 1923), Mr Chaytor takes all these words to mean simply—the minstrel (p. 7), following the learned Appendix B in Chambers' *Medieval Stage*, vol. ii, pp. 230–3, q.v.

[2] *S.P.* s.v. "Eleemosyna". (Cf. again—"Non dicit (i.e. Esaias lviii, 7) mimum vel joculatorem, sed nudum pauperem".) Similarly in a vernacular sermon, MS. Linc. Cath. Libr. A. 6.2, fol. 21b: "Then commythe mynstrells and cowrtyers, and thei schall have grete 3yftes".

[3] s.v. "Nativitas". (Apparently the *mimi* got so many gifts of garments that they were in the habit of selling them: cf. s.v. "Eucharistia".) Similarly MS. Harl. 45, fol. 164; MS. Salisb. Cath. Libr. 103, fol. 113 (unpublished *Jacob's Well*): "mynstrallys and iaperys"; etc. Cf. *Piers Plowman*, B Text, pass. xiv, l. 24, and C Text, pass. xvi, ll. 202–4.

[4] Cf. here, Chaucer, *Hous of Fame*, bk. iii, ll. 1308–9.

[5] s.v. "Furtum". Cf. here, *Piers Plowman*, C Text, pass. viii, ll. 108–20.

[6] s.v. "Audire verba Dei" ("...in ore tantum, sicut mimi habent facta proborum militum, et herraldi."); and "Locutio". Cf. further Robert Rypon, MS. Harl. 4894, fol. 27 ("ministralli et alii adulatores"), and for denunciation of heralds, *Jacob's Well* (E.E.T.S. ed.), p. 134; *Ayenbite of Inwyt*, E.E.T.S. ed. p. 45; etc.

his complaint is of their shameful words and oaths, their indecent stories and comments that provoke laughter at the
banquet table.[1] The *mimus* is therefore unmistakably a "jester"
not only in the original but also in the more modern sense of
that word. As in the case of the *histrio*, who in his turn does
not escape a similar identification with the speakers of "verba
dissolutionis" in these same pages,[2] we must believe that the
rude jokes and coarse detraction were becoming ever more
popular at the expense of the more elevating matter. The
thirteenth-century English author of the *Speculum Laicorum*
tells the story of how one of their number narrowly escaped
death at the hands of King Henry III, for the blasphemies
which he had uttered.[3] When we reach the age of Bromyard,
we find that it is repeatedly spoken of as an age of growing
worldliness and dissipation, in which the old refinement and
knightly virtues seemed threatened with extinction, even in
their ancient strongholds. Little wonder, then, that the earnest
preacher, ever seeking to call men's attention to more serious
and enduring affairs, felt in the entertainments of these triflers,
whether actually indecent or not, a deadly threat to the pro-
clamation of the Cross of Christ.

> Lo sirs, the place that we be in stereth us more to wepynge than to ioye.
> For, and we consceyve well, we be in the vaile of wepynge....For the
> tyme that now is, is the tyme of wepynge for oure synnes; and the tyme
> here-aftur shall be the tyme of lawtur for oure reward in hevene. But
> suerly, evell levers perverteth thise tymes, makynge the fest afore the
> even.[4]

A massed array of jesters, jugglers, minstrels, heralds, revellers,
witches, dancing-women, prostitutes, and even miracle-players
were leading a careless world to the Devil and the crack of

[1] s.v. "Laus"; "Locutio" ("tam mimi quam alii trufatores"). Bromyard here tells of their labours in preparing foul and scandalous remarks,
and also of their pleasure at the laughter that greets their scurrilities and
indecent stories; "Servire" ("Heraldi et mimi sua vel aliena peccata
jactantes...narratores turpium gestorum"); etc.

[2] s.v. "Audire...".

[3] MS. Add. 11284, fol. 6 (ed. Welter, p. 10).

[4] MS. Roy. 18. B. xxiii, fol. 144. Cf. Bromyard *S.P.* s.v. "Chorea"
("Locus iste in quo sumus est locus lachrimarum et non chorearum,
miserarum et non cantilenarum"), etc.

Doom. Let all such therefore be denounced relentlessly. Nicholas Bozon, the Franciscan, accordingly exhorts young men to flee minstrelsy as the hare flees at the sound of the huntsman's horn.[1] Likewise, the vernacular sermon-writer in English utters his warning note: "ȝif thou be a menstrall, a bourdour, and schewyst bourdefull woordys and many iapys for wynnyng, so honeste be savyd, it is venyall synne". If done "for delyȝt of dyssolucyoun", it is deadly sin.[2] Yet another links the minstrel with such "yvel lyvynge men" as "harlottes", "flaterers" and "glosers".[3] William of Nassington in his *Speculum Vitae* gives us the milder objection on the ground of mere idle vanity:

> I warn yow frust at the begynnyng,
> That I will make na vayn carpynge
> Of dedes of armys, ne of amours,
> As dus mynstralles and jeestours
> That makys carpyng in many a place
> Of Octovyane and of Isambrase
> And of many other jeestes,
> And namly when you come to festys.
> Ne of the lyfe of Buys of Hampton
> That was a knyght of grett renown;
> Ne of Sir Guye of Warwyke.
> All if it myght sum men lyke,
> I thinke my carpyng sall nott be,
> ffor that I hold bot vanite.[4]

If our English preacher thus poured his disdain or invective upon the minstrel and the Romance, did any stray themes of the latter yet find their way in amongst the mass of illustrations and examples in his discourse? As pointed out in my previous study, the preacher's net was cast very wide in his search for these goodly pearls of adornment, and the tales of chivalry remained popular. Bromyard himself refers to the zest with which listeners still heard and believed those reading to them

---

[1] See J. A. Herbert, *Cat. of Romances in the MS. Dept. of the B.M.* vol. iii, p. 105 (no. 47).

[2] *Jacob's Well* (E.E.T.S. ed. p. 136; and again, in MS. Salisb. Cath. Libr. 103, fol. 106b: "mynstrallys that usyn fals talys and lesynges").

[3] MS. Harl. 45, fol. 164b.

[4] MS. Roy. 17. C. viii, fol. 2b.

"cronicas vel romancias seu gesta de Karolo et Rolando";[1] and stories from such healthy romances would appear nowadays far more suitable for moralization to our ears than many of the then current pulpit *exempla*. Indeed, a vernacular homilist confesses: "Many men deliten moche to heren of other mennys famouse dedes; and the more worthi that such dedis ben, the more men profiten bi such ensaumplis".[2] It is somewhat strange, therefore, to find what singularly little use is made in actual sermons of this material. The fact can only be accounted for by that very opposition to the secular minstrel which has just been described, and by a natural preference therefore for Biblical heroes and saints.[3] In earlier homily-books like the *Gesta Romanorum*, however, that great storehouse of sermon-tales told in the feudal manner, there is an echo of the minstrel's enchantment with the fairyland of nature. The songs of birds still exercise a little of their ancient charm in a world of stern moralizing so devoid of aesthetic appreciation. We listen occasionally to "the swete songe of the nyghtyngale", or to "the brid that sang so murely in the top of the tre", which "is thi conscience". Here, like Siegfried's friendly songster, she, too, has a warning note, bidding the sinner, in the language of Dick Whittington's fairies—"Turn agayne; turne agayne".[4] Similarly, in the *Summa Predicantium* of Bromyard we may come across some pleasing reference to the singing of birds

[1] *S.P.* s.v. "Fides"; cf. again, s.v. "Audire" ("sicut multi [habent in libris] facta antiquorum in romanciis"), and "Feriaé seu Festa" ("...aliquorum qui romancias legendo probos laudant milites, factaque commendant armorum"). See further Hauréau, *Not. et Extr.* vol. iii, p.317, and vol. iv, pp. 24–5 (Robert de Sorbon, Gérard de Liège, etc.).

[2] MS. Harl. 2276, fol. 55. Cf. again, MS. Harl. 7322, fol. 49. (One who is left unmoved by the story of Christ's Passion read in the Gospel for Holy Week, is stirred to tears when the tale of Guy of Warwick is read aloud to him.)

[3] Often treated, however, in a thoroughly feudal and romantic manner. See below, in Chap. III.

[4] Cf. *Gesta Rom.* E.E.T.S. ed. Engl. version, pp. 58, 443, etc.; and MS. Harl. 5259, fols. 22, 95b, etc. (In Hauréau, *Not. et Extr.*, will be found a sermon excerpt comparing the preacher himself to a nightingale attracting passers-by with its sweet song, although so small a bird.)

that greets the first appearance of dawn;[1] or, in the earlier *Speculum Laicorum*, for example, the story of the canon-regular in Kent who dreamt that he was listening enraptured in a churchyard to birds chanting an Antiphon.[2] According to another *exemplum* given in several English collections, even a monk could become so entranced as to listen to a song from one of them for the space of two hundred years.[3] Nevertheless, these tales strike the ear as mere stray echoes of an art foreign to the preacher's mind, too intent on more solemn instruction to discover new joys for itself in the beauties of nature. Among stories of knights and their ladies in the *Gesta Romanorum*, of which that concerning "the Bloody Shirt"[4] is an example of peculiar charm and beauty, there are again echoes of the knightly Romances. The poem of "Sir Isumbras"[5] and the "Romance of Sir Guy of Warwick",[6] though scorned by the moralist Nassington as we have seen, here show their influence at work upon the older compilers of pulpit narrations—narrations therefore that are likely to have still coloured more than one English discourse in Nassington's own day.[7]

[1] s.v. "Maria". Cf. further, e.g. in Myrc's *Festial*, E.E.T.S. ed. p. 127 (the magic grove of birds), and in so unexpected a place as his *Manuale Sacerd.* (unpubl.), lib. v, caps. xvii and xviii: "Exemplum Philomene et Sagittarii" and "De Proprietatibus Philomene, que in solitis locis dulcius cantat quam in aliis".

[2] MS. Add. 11284, fol. 40 (ed. Welter, p. 62, no. 301).

[3] Odo of Cheriton, MS. Arund. 231, ii, fol. 6b; *Spec. Laic.* s.v. "Gaudium..."; *Les Contes mor. de N. Boȝon*, ed. Smith and Meyer, pp. 267–8 (*Metaphs.* Engl. ed. J.R. cap xc, p. 123); MS. Harl. 2391, fol. 189b (*Engl. Metr. Homs.*); MS. Egerton 1117, fol. 186b; etc. This is the tale that occurs in Longfellow's *Golden Legend*.

[4] E.E.T.S. ed. p. 23; also in Felton's Sermons (cf. MS. Harl. 4, fol. 25). See further, Hauréau, *Not. et Extr.* vol. iv, pp. 25–6. Cf. the beautiful and romantic story of the forgiving knight kissed by a crucifix, which occurs, e.g., in a sermon—"de passione Christi", in MS. Worc. Cath. Libr. F. 10, fol. 18 and frequently elsewhere; or "the 3 Shields in the Castle" (from the *Gesta Rom.*) in a sermon in MS. Linc. Cath. Libr. A. 6. 2, fol. 1b; etc.

[5] MS. Harl. 5259, fol. 30. (See important references in Herbert, *Cat. of Romances in B.M.* vol. iii, p. 203). Cf. *Gesta Rom.* E.E.T.S. p. 463.

[6] MS. Harl. 5259, fol. 87b. Cf. *Gesta Rom.* ibid. p. 529.

[7] The tale of Guy of Warwick and the Dragon actually appears, e.g., in Felton's Sermons (cf. MS. Harl. 4, fol. 31; etc.).

Professor Courthope declares that he has detected "the alchemy of Norman poetry transmuting the metrical homily"[1] in the introduction of anecdotes from lives of saints and from other quarters into such compositions, early in the fourteenth century. But when we recall the regular appearance of *exempla*, however few, in homilies and homiletical matter from the ninth-century days of Bishop Werferth's translation of Gregory's *Dialogues* onwards,[2] and in the really important English collections of the thirteenth century, there seems little point in his remark. The sermon story indeed has an antiquity of its own even greater than that of the Anglo-Norman lay. None the less it is true that, in their struggle with the secular entertainer for the attention of popular audiences, the preaching friars were driven more and more to resort to artifices similar to those of their old rivals. Thus the number and variety of pulpit anecdotes rapidly increase. They develop a more vivid and often a more ribald character. This much may have been due to contact and rivalry with secular influences. But the fact remains none the less that the medieval preachers had for long been making the short moralized story a peculiar province of their own, collecting them for themselves from religious and scholastic sources or fashioning them from personal reminiscences of their preaching careers.[3] The nearer we get to the Reformation, the less do we hear in English sermons of the actual themes of the *jougleur.*

The development of sermon *exempla* will be dealt with in one of the chapters that follow. But there is an interesting feature of this rivalry with secular minstrelsy which is here worth a passing notice. It illustrates how the homilist, when properly inspired, could fashion for himself a melodious instrument of his own. In its first beginnings, indeed, the religious love-lyric in this country may well have been a direct product of homiletic fervour, rather than a mild imitation of worldly

[1] *Hist. of Engl. Poetry*, vol. i, p. 140.
[2] See here J. A. Mosher, *The Exemplum in the Early Relig. and Didactic Literature of Engl.* pp. 24 et seq.
[3] Cf. here my *Preaching in Med. Engl.* pp. 80–3, and 299–304.

love-songs.[1] As such, then, we have a right to claim it as our
first triumphant example in post-Conquest England of the influence of preaching upon literature. Apart from famous
orators of the Church like Anselm, there are sermons on the
Assumption of the Blessed Virgin, setting forth her grace and
other charms, by his contemporary, Herbert de Losinga, Bishop
of Norwich,[2] and by the unknown author of a set of twelfth-
century homilies in English preserved in the library of Trinity
College, Cambridge.[3] But, at all events, as time went on and
the art of the *chanson courtoise* developed, it is clear that this
praise of the Queen of Heaven in homily and sacred poem was
definitely fostered—by the Mendicant in particular—to counter-
act the popularity of the *trouvère*'s secular love-themes.[4] The
sacred love-passion itself only waited for a touch of genuine
mysticism, never for long without a home in the heart of some
Christian homilist or hymn-writer, to kindle it into the ecstasy
of song and peroration. Here St Francis and his followers took
up the favourite theme of St Bernard and the Victorines in an
earlier age.[5] In the thirteenth century, the wealth of Mary
legends, hymns and orisons to the Blessed Virgin, *contes dévots*
and the like, is paralleled by similar outbursts of devotion in
sermons proper. Our English *Speculum Laicorum*,[6] in setting
forth her mercy, speaks of Our Lady as Star of the Sea,

[1] See here Ten Brink, *E. E. Lit.* vol. i, p. 200 ("Divine love in the
medieval sense became a new theme in English literature before secular
love-poetry...could take root there"). Examples will be found in *Old
Engl. Homs.* etc. 1st Ser. E.E.T.S. O.S. 34, pp. 205 et seq. (*On Lofsong
of Ure Lefdi*, etc.); *Old Engl. Misc.* O.S. 49, passim; etc.

[2] See ed. Goulburn and Symonds, *Life, Letters and Sermons of Bp.
H. de L.* vol. ii, pp. 328–57 (possibly preached *in vulgari*, cf. p. 425).

[3] See edit. Morris, E.E.T.S. O.S. no. 53, 2nd Ser. pp. 159 et seq.

[4] Cf. Douce, *Illustrations*, vol. ii, p. 338. A similar attempt to counter-
act secular "songes of fowle rebawdry and of unclennes" at Christmas
with the Church's "songes of lawde and preysyng, in honour and worchype
of cristes blessid burthe", the sacred carols and hymns, is indicated in our
sermons: cf. MS. Linc. Cath. Libr. A. 6. 2, fols. 23 b, 30; MS. Glouc. Cath.
Homilies, Sermo Dom. i. Septuag. as given below, in Chap. VIII, p. 483.

[5] For twelfth-century preaching on this subject, see Bourgain, *La
Chaire franç. au xiie siècle*, Chap. VI, pp. 348–61.

[6] Cap. li, "de Misericordia B.V.M." Cf. the yet more delicate tones
of the *Ancren Riwle*, pt. vii, a homily on the loving of Christ.

directing those who behold her in their guilt to the Port of Pardon. Thus, she is Lady of Tribulation rescuing the sinners and the straitened, and the glorious Luminary. She is to be honoured first "for her admirable beauty", secondly "for her incomparable sweetness", thirdly "for her inconsumable plenitude". No less than eighteen illustrative anecdotes garnish the author's argument. In this country the pulpit had to wait for its school of literary mystics until the age of Richard Rolle in the century following, to tell of love-longings for Jesus, of mystic unions with the Queen of Heaven, or of the wooing of our Lord. For, like another Francis, it was "he who rediscovered Love, the principle of Christ. He re-installed feeling, the spring of life".[1] When once that influence had asserted itself over the religious poets[2] and sermon-writers of the following generation, the preacher might again hope to outvie the minstrel, with his description of a lady more lovely and gentle than the loveliest dame in Camelot, of a queen more potent alike in her conquests and her miracles than the wisest of earthly kings and magicians.[3] Unfortunately, however, the English preachers of that day, like their own race, are not much given to this loftier type of mysticism, and their tone usually remains harsher than that of the religious love-poet. After all, perhaps, we have no right to expect that the rare poetic spirit of a Rolle should descend like a prophet's mantle upon the ordinary vernacular homilist who happens to come after him. Yet we can trace a survival of the older and more formal sacred-romantic tendencies in many of the sermons which these latter have left to us. Let us take some examples from a very typical fifteenth-century manuscript. In a sermon on the Blessed Virgin for the Feast of the Assumption, our simple preacher chooses his theme from the mystical *Song of Songs*: "*Quam pulchra es, et (quam) decora carissima in deliciis*" (Cant. vii, 6).

Thyse wordes in latyn were seid to oure lady of goddes own mouȝthe, and ben thus muche to sey in Inglish to your undirstondynge,—"thou most gracious in plesaunce, how comly art thou of persone, and of what

[1] Horstmann, *Yorkshire Writers*, vol. ii, p. xxxiv.
[2] Cf. here especially the exquisite verse of the Vernon MS. (E.E.T.S. O.S. no. 117, etc.).   [3] See *Preaching in Med. Engl.* p. 257.

bewte in sowle!" In thise wordes ben meved 4 questions, the wiche towcheth oure lady. The first is of hur comlynes—*Quam pulchra*; the secound is of spirituall bewte—*decora*; the third is of goostly delites—*deliciis*; the fowrte is of her charite—*carissima*.[1]

As the theme develops according to the conventional treatment, familiar figures, such as were used for separate subjects of discourse in the thirteenth-century *Rosarium* of Robert of Ware,[2] and again in the fourteenth century by John Bromyard,[3] reappear in the sermon-books. She is the moon "amonge the steres of heven", and "the sonne, the wiche is choson the cheff of all the seven planetys". The story of her miraculous birth is thus retold with a regular wealth of Biblical imagery:

An huge figure other a gret token apered in heven, a woman clothed in the sone, and the mone undir hur fete, and upon hur hede a crowne of 12 steres....Allmy3thy god 3ave this signe and token whan that she apered in presence of man....This gret signe and token strecheth don into the depnes of helle; for alle the dewels ther dredys the name of this glorious virgyne and ben subdewed to hur power, and she letteth hem to tempte hur servaundes to the uttrest entente of here malice. This token also strecheth in to heven; for she is ther emprys, syttyng aboven all ordres of angels,...and also by hur hevenly conversacion she maketh erthely men to be the cyte3yns of heven....

There is also a correspondingly fulsome and vivid account of the glories of her Assumption, well calculated to stir the hearts of the devout:

The goynge of this maide was mesured with-owte dissolucion, hur eyen declarynge all chastite, hur face full of delites and amyabull to angels. The wordes that she spake was full swete and full esye, ever sowndynge to the thankynge of god....

In another sermon of the series, she is compared to the Paradise of *Genesis*; and, like Esther, "she was wondurly faire,

[1] MS. Roy. 18. B. xxiii, fol. 136 (the scribe has written "chastite" for "charite" here).

[2] MS. Gray's Inn Libr. 7: cf. no. 3—"Sol egressus est super terram" (Gen. xix, 23); no. 4—"Fecit lunam in tempora" (Ps. civ, 19). For an account of this work and its author, see my art. "Some Franc. Memorials at Gray's Inn", in the *Dublin Review*, vol. 176, April–June, 1925, pp. 280–4. For another Engl. *Mariale*—of *Sermones super Ave Maria et alia* (14th cent., Fountains Abbey, Yorks.), cf. MS. Jo. Ryl. Libr. Manch. Lat. 365. See also F. J. E. Raby, *Hist. of Christian-Lat. Poetry*, Oxf., cap. xi, § 4.

[3] *S.P.* s.v. "Maria", mentioning "the man in the moon" ("sicut in luna plena apparet imago quasi hominis onus portantis spinarum").

fayrer than I may tell, and she was luffyng and gracious in every mans sight."[1] In yet another sermon, the chosen symbol is "the *flouredelice*", as "som clerkes calleth itt":

> Who is the rote of the lilie of heven but this mayden, that is the modere of the floure of heven; ffor she hath colours of all floures of heven...(i.e. vertewes of all creatures of heven)....And, shortely for to speke, ther is no vertewe founden in no creature but she hath itt fully in hure, ne no vice in man but ther aȝeyn she hath bote salve and remedie; and therfore she may sey well to all men thise wordes, Mt. XI^mo: "*Venite ad me omnes qui laboratis....*" "Commeth to me all ȝe that traveyll or ben charched with synne, and I shall refressh you."[2]

This insertion in the mouth of His mother of what are perhaps the most cherished and intimate words of Christ recorded in the Gospels is eloquent testimony of the place which she has come to fill in popular religion. This very preacher requests his audience to "make oure ladye to be mene betweyn god and the".[3] With much the same emphasis, another enjoins his clerical readers to "teche thy paryssch, next after god, to serve oure ladye devoutely, gretynge hure with the holy '*Ave*'".[4] One further point of importance follows from this cult. The harsh treatment of woman usually meted out by the medieval pulpit must have contrasted ill at all times with the finer ideal of chivalry. Here, then, in their mystical devotion to this lady Queen of the Skies, both preacher and poet sometimes found justification for a kindlier view of the sex. Of this we have interesting evidence in the manuscript first quoted:

> And therfore oure ladie amended that was amys, that woman shuld not be ashamed in that she made Adam trespace; therfore thorowe Crist Adam was amended. *For no man shuld have woman in despite*; for it is no wisdam to dispise that god loveth.[5]

---

[1] MS. Roy. 18. B. xxiii, fol. 169 b–71 (see Esth. ii, 15, Vulg. version).

[2] Ibid. fol. 118. Cf. here Bozon, e.g. *Metaphs.* cap. xlv ("He towards whom Our Lady turns cannot be lost...").

[3] Fol. 170. (The last 9 pages here take the B.V.M. as their theme.)

[4] MS. Harl. 2403, fol. 188 b (three short sections on the *Ave Maria*, following a version of Myrc's *Festial*).

[5] MS. Roy. 18. B. xxiii, fol. 98 b. For the same sentiment in verse, cf. "Of Women cometh this Worldes Weal", in *Minor Poems of Vernon MS.* pt. ii, E.E.T.S. O.S. no. 117, pp. 704–8; *The Southern Passion* (homil.), E.E.T.S. O.S. no. 169, pp. 70–1; Chambers and Sidgwick, *E. Engl. Lyrics*, pp. 197–8; and Vising, *Angl.-Norm. Lang. and Lit.* p. 65.

The Virgin herself indeed is type of the Perfect Woman, combining the two ideals of the Old and New Testaments.[1]

Where the love-passion of the homilist is directed toward Christ Himself, there the love-notes usually ring truer, the mystic mood is more genuinely spontaneous, the wilder extravagances of imagery are left behind. In their detailed descriptions of the agony on the Cross or the earlier Passion scenes, in which the suffering Redeemer is made to appeal direct to the audience,[2] our English preachers of the fourteenth and fifteenth centuries approach nearest to the tender sweetness of the love lyric. "Turne aʒen and set ti love e Crist, longe and desir as a lover after his blisse."[3] Well may they contrast the calm and security which this love of "Heaven's King" brings to His devotees, with the restless fever of earthly passions as sung by the *trouvère*:

> I ne wot quat is love,
> Ne i ne love ne lovede nouth;
> But wel i wot wo so lovet
> He brennet harde in his youth.
>
> I ne wot quat is love,
> Ne love me never bond;
> But wel I wot wo so lovet
> Reste havet he non.[4]

Such lines from the Sermon Note-book of the Franciscan John of Grimston merely echo typical sentiments expressed in the early thirteenth-century verse-homily known as *Hali Meidenhad*,[5] and in the *Luve Ron* of Thomas of Hales,[6] an earlier member of the same Order with a poetical gift of his own. Again, the vision of God and His saints in glory may call forth a similar strain of exaltation in the prose of the homily, as when Dr William Lichfield, of London, ponders

[1] *S.P.* s.v. "Maria" (viz. O.T.-Fecundity and N.T.-Virginity).

[2] Cf. examples in my *Preaching in Med. Engl.* pp. 120–1 and 346–8, and further below, in Chap. VIII, pp. 507–9.

[3] MS. Worc. Cath. Libr. F. 10, fol. 45 b.

[4] MS. Adv. Libr. Edinb. 18.7.21, fol. 17b–18. See further verses on the Passion here, fols. 116–26. With the above lines cf. the preaching husband in Chaucer, *Cant. Tales, Wife of Bath's Prol.* ll. 371–7.

[5] See E.E.T.S. ed. O.S. no. 18.

[6] See Morris, *Old Engl. Misc.* pp. 93 et seq.

"the swet blyse of hevene", inspired by a mystical theme from the *Song of Songs*.[1] But, at the most, these blissful passages—alas!—are but rare oases in the dreary desert of English pre-Reformation preaching. The note of gloom and repression easily predominates. Perhaps no modern commentator yet has hit upon the real significance of that remarkable Old-English poem known as *The Owl and the Nightingale*. Is it not, after all, intended to be an allegory of the age-long rivalry in the preaching of medieval Christendom between those who upheld the gentler themes of love and bliss and an ever-forgiving Redeemer, and those who preferred on the other hand to thunder of sin and Judgment and the Wrath to come?[2] There is certainly evidence that this very problem was continually weighing upon the minds of contemporary churchmen.[3] In the pulpits, at all events, the note of the Owl is heard most often. And it is to the bitter realism and the sad complaint of the pulpit, not to its random love-themes, that we must look for its abiding influence in English letters, when the pristine glories of *chanson courtoise* and sacred love-lyric have passed away.

The mystic love-theme, the moral tale and the allegory may have been growths on the soil of religion as independent in their way as the literature of chivalry in the courts of nobles. Yet all alike drew their sustenance directly from earlier sources in the literature of the race. Their roots run back to the mystic Dionysius and the Neo-Platonic tradition, to Aesop and the Eastern story-tellers, to the fragments of classical history and literature and primitive legend surviving in early medieval times. But there is a further feature in the adornment of our sermons which, though it is as old as the Founder of Christianity Himself, yet compels the word-painter to go ever afresh to current life and nature for his models. In brief, it is that

[1] MS. Roy. 8. C. i. fol. 127 et seq. ("Rise, my luf, my spouse, hiȝe up and come to me", Cantic. ii, 10). Cf. also Bromyard's analogue from the bliss of earthly lovers, *S.P.* s.v. "Beatitudo", and Bourgain, *La Chaire franç*. pp. 239–42.

[2] Rather than between the secular minstrel and the preacher, as has been suggested, or one Order of the Church and another.

[3] See my *Preaching in Med. Engl.* pp. 334 et seq.

type of verbal illustration which describes everyday things as seen by the shrewd observer, and may be called "realistic". From it in due time springs, as we shall see, the relentless and often witty satire which colours much verse and prose from the second half of the fourteenth century onwards. To it is due not a little in the development of the national self-consciousness, and wellnigh all in the characteristic Reformation and Renaissance temper of the sixteenth century in England. One who has at least reminded us (though without any mention of the pulpit) that "not to schools or courts need we look for the explanation of this revival of native art", thus describes a fifteenth-century version of the Romance *Morte Arthure*:

> The poet delights in realities and solid facts. . . . He puts all his strength into his pictures of stirring multitudes. . . . There is an observance of common things, sympathy with men in their daily occupation, and a grasp of fact. . . .

Just where we should expect the romantic spirit to flourish still as of old, we are informed—"the story is almost untouched by romance".[1] The same love of the commonplace is equally striking in the work of Chaucer and his school. Now, it is over the wide field of sermon literature that we must study the growth of this realistic treatment; for it is there that it seems most likely to have originated. Indeed, at the time of its first appearance no other field existed to offer the same scope. As Professor Haskins has reminded us, the thirteenth century, which saw this development, while not an age of poetry, was essentially an age of preaching.[2] Here literature springs, then, directly out of the fundamental requirements of moral instruction, full of the raw and simple facts of daily life, with little restriction of style—direct, candid, forceful. The pulpit, and not the revival of classical studies, will thus prove itself to be the true parent of a revived literary Realism.

[1] M. M. Banks, pp. 124–5, edition of *Morte Arthure* (Longmans, 1900) from Robert of Thornton's MS. Lincoln Cath. Libr. (This Yorkshire copyist is also apparently responsible for some well-known homiletical pieces in the same MS.: cf. edits. by Perry in E.E.T.S., Horstmann in *Yorkshire Writers*, etc.)

[2] See art. in the *American Hist. Review* (1904), vol. x, p. 2.

Though this actual employment of "common things" to point a moral is far older in the history of Christian evangelism, yet, once again, it is the friar, often learned in the schoolmen and the works of natural science, yet equally well versed in the thoughts and ways of ordinary men, who extended and popularized this mode of pulpit illustration in the Middle Ages. With a few deft touches he reproduces the everyday sights and sounds of town and country, "sede tyme and hervest, somyr and wyntyr", the appearance of familiar social types, their chatter, their arguments, the things they do and the things they deal in. Every preacher who followed this method may be said consciously or unconsciously to have been teaching his unlettered flock far better than any *mimus* the rudiments of a folk-literature and a philosophy of everyday existence, bidding them stop awhile to look at the passing show of life around them, to reflect upon it, to shape their thoughts in English, to discriminate, to criticize, and even to enjoy. It is in the vernacular sermons of the age of Chaucer onwards that we can best recapture to-day the naïve and picturesque language in which these preachers tricked out their pleasant little similes. The older sermons are as a rule recorded in Latin. Yet, these latter have a special value in that they bear witness to the antiquity of the practice, allowing us to realize what even older generations than that of Langland once listened to and enjoyed in their own native tongue.

If we begin with the fourteenth-century *Summa Predicantium* of John de Bromyard, omitting for the present its more elaborate satirical portraits, we shall find a mass of such homely scenes and characters. Not a few of them, indeed, are traceable to continental homily-books of a century earlier, from which they have been obviously borrowed by the compiler. Yet they represent types and haunts of human or animal nature equally true of Bromyard's own day and generation,[1] many of them changing but little through all the centuries. Everyday scenes of the streets give us such vivid characters as the tattered pedlars who cry through the villages " Old pots to mend!" and the like, whose own clothes and pots, as our

[1] Cf. his own—"Frequenter videmus..." (e.g. s.v. "Anima", etc.).

preacher observes, seem to need mending most of all;[1] the jugglers, with their clever performing dogs "that jump or dance or do whatever they tell them",[2] who can turn sticks or straws into serpents,[3] and magically empty a well-stocked hat;[4] or again, a race of swindlers whose habit it is to invite men to drink with them in the tavern, then invent some excuse for withdrawing in a hurry, as though to return before their guests are done, thus leaving them in reality to bear the full expense of the refreshments.[5] We behold the astute innkeepers running to meet the pilgrims of the road, jovially welcoming them in with promises of the good fare in store, "talking and gaming with them until the time comes for reckoning up the bill", when the mock friendship is promptly transferred to newcomers.[6] At the horse-fairs we are introduced to raucous horse-dealers called "corsours", false middlemen who will not hesitate, when opportunity occurs, to dupe one or both of the parties to the bargain they are to negotiate, blinding them at the start with fair words and solemn oaths of friendship, protesting later, when exposed, that their sly winks and nods were not properly heeded at the time.[7] Little familiar features of

---

[1] s.v. "Correctio". Cf. friar Jacques de Lausanne (early 14th cent.) on the clothes-menders, in Hauréau, *Not. et Extr.* vol. iii, p. 128.

[2] s.v. "Adulator".

[3] s.v. "Detractio", "Electio" ("...assimilantur capello subtili prestigiatoris,...sub quo, cum nihil creditur nisi palea, invenitur ut videtur serpens"), "Mors" ("sicut incantatores qui faciunt festucam apparere serpentem"), etc.

[4] s.v "Avaritia". Cf. further the magic "blow-mill", in MS. Harl. 268, fol. 34b (14th cent.).

[5] s.v. "Caro" ("ad modum truttanorum..."). Cf. "le hoqueleeur", in a thirteenth-century sermon, in Hauréau, *Not. et Extr.* vol. iv, p. 158.

[6] s.v. "Amor" (see further below, p. 31). If the customer is unable to meet the bill, the hot-tempered taverner will spoil him of some of his clothes (cf. s.v. "Mundus", and *Gesta Rom.* E.E.T.S. ed. p. 36).

[7] s.v. "Falsitas". An illustration follows: "Unde de tali quodam fertur quod modo uni parti faciem vertendo ei annuere solebat oculo et caput inclinare, quasi diceret—'Valet pro vobis!' Alteri vero solebat idem facere. Quando vero unus sensit se deceptum, malum suum secum plangere solebat et dicere—'Nonne feci tibi signum quod non fuit pro vobis? Illud enim signum quod feci tibi fuit quod non valuit pro vobis'. Si vero unus de mercatione sua guadebat, secum gaudere solebat, asserens

town life catch our eye again, like the inn signs,[1] the weather-cock upon the belfry,[2] or the crosses upon walls and gates that denote a Religious house,[3] the lowly packhorses in the lane,[4] some passing criminal led to the gallows, whose handsome looks command the pity of the onlookers,[5] the excitement over a conflagration, frequent enough in these narrow timbered rows,[6] or over a thief or murderer who has managed to evade his guard and is now taking sanctuary.[7] Perchance, for once in a way, streets have been carefully cleansed to welcome the sovereign. Houses are decorated, tapestries and festoons of cloth are hung out, the citizens themselves are dressed up for the occasion.[8] A few simple strokes, and the picture is almost as vivid and complete as in some illuminated masterpiece of the age.[9]

None knew better than our much-travelled Dominican the homes of rich and poor alike. Thus, he points us to the un-glazed windows of the more modest dwelling through which the winds and the swallows nesting within it freely come and go;[10] to the sparks and smoke flying out through the openings

sibi fecisse signum ut sic faceret...". These "corsours" appear in Sermon no. 57 of the *Sermones Vulgares* of Jacques de Vitry (early 13th cent.). Cf. also the "romongours of hors" in dan Michel of Northgate's *Ayenbite of Inwyt*, E.E.T.S. ed. p. 44 (A.D. 1340).

[1] s.v. "Luxuria": cf. further below, p. 27, n. 11.

[2] s.v. "Adulator" and "Consilium". Cf. *Ayenb. of Inwyt*, p. 180.

[3] s.v. "Crux": cf. s.v. "Ipocrisis", and the painted janitor as given below, p. 240, n.

[4] s.v. "Mundus" ("in nocte...panno vili cooperti in domo foe-tida...").

[5] s.v. "Compassio" ("Heu! quod tam pulchrum corpus debet sic mori!", they cry).

[6] s.v. ibid. "Feriae" ("in istis magnis villis ignis multa destruit aedi-ficia"), "Predicatio", "Mors" ("sicut domus de paleis est in periculo"—and, when on fire, is a danger to the rest in the row). Cf. also in my *Preaching in Med. Engl.* p. 88.

[7] s.v. "Confessio" (accordingly, those escorting criminals to the gallows are particularly alert when approaching churches), "Crux", "Eucharistia" and "Pœnitentia".

[8] s.v. "Adventus".

[9] Cf. here, e.g. in MS. Bibl. Roy. Brussels 9244, as reproduced in Salzman, *Engl. Life in the Midd. Ages*, p. 273.

[10] s.v. "Cogitatio".

of the chimney that discolour and blacken the rude paintings on its walls;[1] the garden with its flowers and carefully trained fruit trees.[2] Within, we may watch the mother and her children in a dozen moods,[3] the boiling pot over the fire,[4] the caged birds that learn to sing or talk as they hear men speak in English or French,[5] the ubiquitous house-dog, now chased out of the kitchen with a bowl of hot water,[6] now fighting over a bone,[7] now lying stretched out in the sunlight with the flies settling on him,[8] or eagerly watching the diners "until he gets what he wants, whereupon he turns his back" to enjoy the coveted morsel.[9] We are privileged also to visit the stately homes of feudal lords, travelling with them from manor to manor,[10] staying with them *en route* at the inn which now flaunts the lordly coat-of-arms,[11] dine at their banquets and

---

[1] s.v. "Dedicatio" and "Dilectio".

[2] s.v. "Ornatus" (viola, rosa, solsequium, lignum, herbae, etc.) and "Obedientia". Cf. further, s.v. "Visitatio", § 55.

[3] Cf. s.v. "Confessio" (the mother says to her child when it wants to play with one of her jewels: "Manus tuae turpes sunt valde! Lavate manus, et tunc tibi tradam; aliter non!"); s.v. "Labor" ("sicut etiam mater filio de labore redeunti necessaria preparat. Ipsum, cum tempus adest prandendi, reficit, filio vagabundo et famulis otiosis cum ribaldis tabernas excercentibus sine preparatione vel refectione cum asperis verbis ejectis."); etc.

[4] s.v. "Gratia".   [5] s.v. "Consilium".

[6] s.v. "Dimissio"; cf. s.v. "Avaritia".

[7] Ibid.   [8] s.v. "Accidia" (old dogs).

[9] s.v. "Adulterium" (cf. further "Conscientia"—the dogs barking at the moon, etc.). These and similar little sketches appear frequently in continental sermons of the thirteenth and fourteenth centuries (cf. Hauréau, *Not. et Extr.* vol. iii, p. 124, etc.).

[10] s.v. "Mors" (2). When their belongings have been sent on to the next manor, the owners apologize to their visitors, saying—"Talia et talia hic non habemus, quia illa praemisimus ad locum quo ituri sumus", etc. Again, e.g. when the courteous lord himself calls on a friend, we are told, he does not burst in suddenly upon him, but sends a messenger in advance, or else if entering unheralded will cough or give some other warning sign to the inmates that a visitor has arrived (s.v. "Adventus").

[11] s.v. "Anima" and "Crux" (the serf flies from the inn where he sees exhibited the arms of king or nobleman—"per vexillum extra fenestram pendentem vel per arma super ostium picta"—showing who is occupying it).

listen to the fashionable conversation,[1] see them entertaining
a king in their castle,[2] even penetrate to the royal chamber
itself with its curtains and upholstery,[3] and the royal banqueting
hall with its painted figures, where conquerors are hailed with
feasting and rewards.[4] At the king's court we find the sons of
noblemen who are there in boyhood to keep the king's son company, those who enjoy the special affection of their sovereign,
those welcomed for their personal beauty or charm of manners,
those who preside over the king's affairs, his table, or his
chamber. Others are there for their strength and bravery in
war; others, for their wisdom, whose counsel is freely sought;
others, for the large gifts which they bestow, and so forth.[5]
No corner of medieval life seems unrevealed to us, from that
in which the rustic squats to eat his frugal porridge of beans
or pease with a fragment of bread for his spoon,[6] or snores con-
tentedly in the open,[7] to the University schools where scholars
"determine" and conduct their arguments,[8] the prisoner's
dungeon,[9] or the places where folk play at bear-baitings on
holidays,[10] and other amusements,[11] while the more privileged
joust or hunt with dog and falcon.[12] The landscape is wellnigh

[1] Cf. below, pp. 448–9, and, e.g. s.v. "Dilectio" ("cibus preciosus in
fine prandii post alia cibaria ante dominum positus, omnibus commen-
salibus secundum personarum valorem ordinate distribuitur".); etc.

[2] s.v. "Dilectio".   [3] s.v. "Conversatio".

[4] s.v. "Correctio".

[5] s.v. "Gloria". Cf. the baronial officers, s.v. "Ministratio".

[6] s.v. "Ministratio" (finally, the "spoon" itself is eaten).

[7] s.v. "Mors". Cf. "Divitiae", the pathetic figure of the hungry and
thirsty poor dreaming in their sleep that they have become rich, then
waking to find it untrue.

[8] Cf. s.v. "Divitiae" (the Trick of the 2 Premises), "Humilitas",
"Lex", "Locutio", etc.

[9] Cf. s.v. "Confessio", "Consuetudo", "Correctio", "Damnatio"
("sicut in carcere mundi unus alio profundiorem locum tenet", etc...), etc.

[10] s.v. "Feriae seu Festa". Similarly in Hauréau, *Not. et Extr.* vol. iv,
p. 136.

[11] Cf. s.v. "Consilium", "Gloria" (the game "Botecoraye"?), "Mors",
"Mundus", etc. Cf. further, below, pp. 33, 176, 418, 444, 510, etc.

[12] Cf. s.v. "Ludus", "Bellum", "Consuetudo", etc. Similarly Bromyard pictures the miser, the lunatics, the lepers, the highway robbers,
the physician, the notaries, the schoolboys, and many other types; also
such trivial everyday incidents as wiping specks from one's face or crumbs

illimitable. To these scenes of current activity must be added
every kind of inanimate object, as diverse as the scarecrow in
the fields,[1] the mason's rule,[2] the shipman's "needle" and
"stone",[3] the ship's gangway,[4] or the ship's biscuit,[5] harbour
lights,[6] the medieval money-box,[7] clocks,[8] books, seals, charters,
letters of credit, coins, and a hundred other trivialities of daily
life. Little wonder that Master Robert Rypon, in one of his
sermons, declares of our encyclopaedic author—"Verba doc-
toris sunt diffusa".[9]

Other sermon-collections of the period, compiled in Latin
by English homilists, exhibit, though hardly to an equal degree,
the preacher's fondness for these same homely comparisons.
Master Rypon of Durham, for example, just mentioned, a
contemporary of Chaucer, who quotes now and again from
the *Summa Predicantium*,[10] borrows a figure of the kind from
the earlier homiletic writings of Bishop Grossetête of Lincoln.
A material town or manor, says he, has houses, streets and a
population, with a lord and lady to rule over it, and town
officials and servants to do their bidding.

> To such a town or manor *Lincoln* compares Man, whose body is as
> it were a town, in which his bodily members are like the houses, his
> mouth, eyes and ears like the town gates, through which the populace
> enters and goes out.... The lord of this town is the Soul or Intellect,
> his lady the Will, which, according to Augustine is queen in the realm
> of the Soul. Memory is the hall or chamber in which guests are received.

from one's lap at meals, extracting a fly from one's eye, smothering a
dangerous fire, etc. (all in "Confessio").   [1] s.v. "Correctio".
   [2] s.v. "Judices". [3] s.v. "Discretio". Similarly MS. Bodl. 649, fol. 63.
   [4] s.v. "Confessio".
   [5] s.v. "Eucharistia" ("sicut ergo volentes per mare ad Terram Sanctam
vel ad patriam propriam transire secum panem bis coctum pro viatico
accipiunt; quia illius auxilio melius in mari sustentantur et ad portum
perducuntur, quia non cito putrescit"). This occurs also in Hauréau,
Not. et Extr. vol. iv, pp. 171–2.
   [6] s.v. "Discretio" ("duo luminaria infra vitrum inclusa super altas
columnas..."). Again in "Gratia".
   [7] s.v. "Usura" (with key lost).
   [8] s.v. "Gula" (the *horologium*, and its *cavilla*). Again in "Adulator".
   [9] MS. Harl. 4894, fol. 54.
   [10] Cf. MS. Harl. 4894, fols. 33 b, 54 ("Doctor Bromyarde in Summa sua
Predicantium, in vocabulo *Servire*, docet per magnum processum..."), etc.

The chief sovereign of this town is God Himself, who resides in the Reason, as a lord in the principal place of his township. Officers and servants of this town are the Interior and Exterior Senses....[1]

On another occasion, Rypon compares his fellow clergy "to messengers or couriers" of the times. The courier, he reminds his audience, has to travel swiftly on foot to fulfil his mission. "Again, it is the courier's duty to carry a box painted with the arms and insignia of his lord, containing his lord's letters sealed and enclosed in it.[2] He has, moreover, his special credential to deliver by word of mouth."[3] In yet another sermon of the series we listen to a long disquisition upon the symptoms and causes of fevers—"secundum medicos". Each "species" of the ailment is carefully distinguished in turn— ephemeral, tertian, quartan and paralysis.[4] Then hydropsy is subjected to similar analysis, followed by leprosy. Finally the physician himself is brought on the scene to administer "first a digestive medicine, secondly a purgative, thirdly a sanative".[5] Another preacher describes to us in equally detailed fashion the state of the leper.[6] A third, the learned friar John Waldeby,

[1] MS. Harl. 4894, fol. 170. Cf. *Old Engl. Homs.* (12th cent.), 2nd ser. E.E.T.S. O.S. no. 53, p. 55; dan Michel's sermon, in E.E.T.S. O.S. no. 23, p. 263; and the "Castellum", as below, pp. 77–85.

[2] Cf. here Chaucer, *Hous of Fame*, bk. iii, ll. 2128–9 ("Currours, and eek messangeres with boistes").

[3] MS. Harl. 4894, fols. 208b–9. The application here is typical: "Pixis moraliter est anima sacerdotis, que pixis depingitur armis et insigniis Christi Jhesu, viz., virtutibus theologicis; in qua pixide includi debent littere Christi mittentis, scil., scientia litterarum Novi et Veteris Testamentorum, et sigillari sigillo Christi...", etc., etc. The messenger's credential is also in Bromyard, s.v. "Oratio"; and *Ayenb. of Inwyt*, p. 211.

[4] Fever in general is defined as follows: "est calor innaturalis in calorem igneum mutatus, et generatur ex uno humore vel pluribus humoribus indigestis qui remanent in canalibus cordis vel in venis circa cor, et ibidem putrefiunt...." "Effimera" is the type "que solum durat per diem" (like some men's anger). Paralysis is a prolongation—"pro perpetuo"—of the Quartan, involving continuous shivering.

[5] MS. Harl. 4894, fols. 23b–5.

[6] MS. Add. 21253, fol. 26 (specifying, amongst other things, the foul breath, the "raucous" voice, which forces the leper to speak "submisse", and his "ponderositas"). Another figure of the kind here (fol. 45) compares the Devil's tactics to those of the raven, which, when wishing to seize a hare in the valley, first plucks out the eyes of its prey, so that it cannot see to defend itself.

S.T.P. of Oxford, revives a typical scene which "schoolmen knew all about, who had been at Oxford or Cambridge": "When the Master in Theology has to incept, first he is put in the chair, then a pillion is placed on his head, and at length he reads one lecture, and after the lecture will dispute one Question".[1] Yet a fourth will choose for his simile the current procedure in the Courts of King's Bench and Common Bench.[2]

If the word-pictures of Latin homilists are thus able to hold the reader's attention, he is likely to be even more attracted by the vivacity and directness of those preserved in the vernacular. Doubtless, the medieval audience, then, fell likewise under their spell. Here, in such harangues, we find Bromyard's *hospitiarii* again, described in homely English, almost to the very phrase:

...We see well that osteleres in many places thei will renne gladdely a3eyns pilgryms to prey hem to com to ther Innes, and draweth hem by the honde, and behoteth hem many delycate thinges. Fayre the[i] speke with hem, and eteth and drynketh with hem, and lawy3th and makes gret chere, unto that thei shall com to acounte, in the wiche acounte thei will nowthe for3eve. But whan that thei be goye, 3iff that thei see newe, anon thei renne to the newe, and of the firste thei recke no more of. And on the same wise thei do to the newe, when thei have acounted, as thei dud to the firste.[3]

[1] MS. Caius Coll. Camb. 334, fol. 172 b. Waldeby continues: "Spiritualiter loquendo, Christus, filius Dei, isto tempore loquebatur discipulis suis, dicens—'Vos vocatis me "magister" et "domine", et bene dicitis: sum etenim' (Jo. xiii). Et hodie, ut magister, primo est ingressus cathedram crucis, et ergo isto die in signum sue inceptionis fuit pilum spicarum positum super caput ejus. Lectio quam loquebatur in ista cathedra fuerunt septem verba que loquebatur in cruce pendens".

[2] MS. Camb. Univ. Libr. Ii. iii. 8, fol. 147 (Wimbledon?) ("Rex celorum habet in regno suo duos justiciarios, sicut habet rex Anglie, et sunt Misericordia et Justicia. Justicia sedet in bancho communi; sed Misericordia sedet in bancho regis. Et si homo inveniat nimium rigorem coram justiciario de bancho communi, adhuc potest appellare ad altiorem judicem et salvari infra certum tempus..."). Cf. further, Bromyard, s.v. "Confessio", etc.

[3] MS. Roy. 18. B. xxiii, fol. 80. With this cf. the original Latin of Bromyard: "Illi enim hospitiarii in multis partibus hilariter occurrunt peregrinis, et eos ad hospitia sua diligenter invitant et trahunt, et multa eis delicata promittunt. Pulchre loquuntur, comedentes et bibentes, ridentes et ludentes cum eis usque veniatur ad computum, in quo aliqui

In place of the travelling tinkers, Dr Lichfield will point us to the "pore peddre", that "makith oft more noise to sel his sother[1] and his nedyll than doithe the ryche marchaunte with al his dere worthy ware".[2] John Myrc mentions the royal courtiers again in a similar reference to the Court of Heaven.[3] And we may even complete the Dominican's picture of the royal visit, from a sermon on the Second Advent given else-where: "as whan a kyng cometh to any of his owen citees, the hooste goth before beryng sygnes and the kynges baners, and with goyng aboute of araiyng and with armes, shewyng that the kyng is in-comyng".[4] Here, too, are the "pore beggers, that sitteth by the weie and preyeth of help for her lyflode of hem that cometh by hem, whiche, for to be the bettir herde and the sonner sped of that thei asketh, scheweth to hem of that thei asketh of her sores and her mescheves, to sture hem to have reuthe on hem of pitee".[5] Some of them sitting thus, or "in gatys of oure ladyes cherche with othere folk", perchance are merely "faytours, that getyn mete and monye of pyteous folk wyth wyles, as to makyn hem seme crokyd, blynde, syke, or mysellys, and are noȝt so".[6] Little wonder, then, that "whan pore men askyn hem owȝt", the well-to-do sometimes "be ryȝt vyleus, and clepe hem faytours and trowauntys, mycherys and thevys!".[7] In the homily-series known as *Jacob's Well* will be found what is surely one of the most brilliant little sketches of the tramp in literature.[8] Hardly less vivid are the slight touches which reveal the habit of the medieval housebreaker who, very naturally, "will the sonest

illorum nihil dimittunt quod habere possunt, et, ipsis procedentibus, amplius de eis non curant. Sed novis occurrunt, et idem eis faciunt quod fecerunt prioribus".

[1] = thread.   [2] MS. Roy. 8. C. i, fol. 124b.
[3] *Festial*, E.E.T.S. ed. p. 153.   [4] MS. Harl. 2276, fol. 5.
[5] MS. Harl. 45, fol. 106. Cf. MS. Roy. 8. C. i, fol. 139 b: (..."men of gret kyn ber not on hem pakkes ny bagges, as beggers done"); Bromyard, s.v. "Ordo Clericalis" (beggars at the church door and those who sit at city gates directing strangers who pass in); *Ayenb. of Inwyt*, p. 135; etc.
[6] *Jacob's Well*, E.E.T.S. ed. p. 134.
[7] Ibid., MS. Salisb. Cath. Libr. 103, fol. 106b (*Ayenb. of Inwyt*, p. 194).
[8] E.E.T.S. ed. p. 134. See below, p. 372.

breke in" "where the howse is ffebulleste and the wall lowest".[1]
"If thefes here berkyng of houndis, thei castith hem brede or
flessh, and so thei leve berkynge. And so the thef entrith the
hous and holdith men by the throtis, that thei cry not for
help, and doth oute the fire unto the tyme thei have sped
of her pray", and so forth.[2] Among denizens of the streets
and open places we meet again with the "jogoloure, that
werkyth be the devyl",[3] the "harlots" "makyng iapys aforn
folk, in pleying at the spore, at the bene, at the cat, in ledyng
berys and apys",[4] the wrestlers,[5] the dice-players,[6] "the cacche-
polis", to whose duty it may fall to draw convicted offenders
"upon the pavement, at the tailles of hors",[7] the "wacchemen"
of the night,[8] the "wrethe" or "karppynter" building a house,[9]
"a man goyng in a fayre",[10] and many such more. Perhaps no
group of sermon similes is so delicate and charming as that

[1] MS. Roy. 18. b. xxiii, fol. 127b.

[2] *Gesta Rom.* Engl. version, E.E.T.S. ed. p. 64. Cf. also MS. Harl. 45,
fol. 66; *Ayenb. of Inwyt*, p. 179; MS. Add. 21253, fol. 58b ("Quando
latrones...hostem suum capiunt, vertunt ei caputium ne possit eos videre,
et ponunt aliquem nodum in ore ejus ne possit loqui"); and many in
Bromyard, cf. s.v. "Audire verba Dei" ("Latronibus intrantibus domum
ad occidendum et spoliandum, socii illorum custodiunt portas et vias,
ne adjutorium eis veniat; et intrantes, vel faciem suam abscondunt, vel
lumen extinguunt,...et latenter curiam vel domum ingrediuntur,...et
guttur et os obturant ne spoliati clament" etc.); or "Cogitatio" ("sicut
latrunculus, per fenestram secretius intrans, magnis aperit latronibus").
When the hue and cry is raised, the escaping thief will sometimes himself
cry—"Catch thief!" to elude the pursuers by pretending that he is one
of their number (s.v. "Consilium").

[3] *Jacob's Well*, E.E.T.S. ed. p. 263.   [4] Ibid. p. 134.

[5] Cf. ibid. pp. 78, 141, 296, etc.; MS. Harl. 45, fol. 138; MS. Add. 41321,
fol. 103, etc.

[6] Ibid. pp. 100 and 135. See quotations in my article in the *Holborn
Review*, Jan. 1926, pp. 38 and 42, and below, pp. 372, 418, 430, 444, etc.

[7] *Gesta Rom.* adding—"til tyme that the pavement have i-frett the
fleshe fro the bones". E.E.T.S. ed. pp. 81 and 142. Here, too, is the
"Jabette" with swinging corpse, a prey for the birds.

[8] Ibid. p. 93. (N.B. "in the tyme of the nyght,...wacchemen come
blowyng hir hornes", etc.).

[9] MS. Roy. 18. B. xxiii, fol. 96b.

[10] Ibid. fol. 132 ("ther the shoppes be shitt, ther he is not stered to
by no ware. But when he seys it opon to is siȝthe, anone he chepeth
the ware").

which illustrates child life in the Middle Ages, those little
people that delight in every age—

With flouris for to jap and playe,	[flowers]
With stikis and with spalys small	[bits of wood]
To byge up chalmer, spens and hall;	[build] [chamber] [buttery]
To mak a whicht horse of a wand,	[white]
Of brokin breid a schip saland,	[bread] [sailing]
A bunwed tyll a burly spere,	[ragwort stalk] [to]
And of a seg a swerd of were,	[sedge] [war]
A cumly lady of a clout,	
And be rycht besy thar about	
To dicht it fetesly with flouris	[make] [elegantly]
And luf the pepane paramouris.[1]	[doll]

Here is a passage of the kind that occurs in more than one
collection:

The properte of a ʒong childe is that he can not be maliciusly disposyd,
ne bere no rancowre ne wrathe to tho that bete hym never so sore, as it
fallythe for a chylde to have dew chastisyng. But a none, aftyr as thou
hast bett hym, then schewe to hym a feyre flowre or ellys a feyre redde
appull; then hathe he forgeton all that was done to him be fore, and then
he wyll come to the, rynnyng, withe his clyppyng armys, for to plese
the and to kysse the.[2]

The fact that "a chyld ʒevyth largely of his breed to his felawys,
and to houndys and to cattys"[3] is another lesson drawn by
the homilist from this instinctive generosity of childhood. No
less tender and compassionate are references to the medieval
mother heart: "A wyman that hath a childe, in wynter, when
the childes hondes ben a colde, the modur taketh hym a stree
or a rusche and byddeth hym warme ith, not for love of the

---

[1] From the moral treatise *Ratis Ravyng*, E.E.T.S. ed. bk. i, pp. 57–8.
[2] MS. Linc. Cath. Libr. A. 6. 2, fol. 27. Also in MS. Camb. Univ.
Libr. Gg. vi. 16, fol. 39, etc. With this cf. e.g. Bromyard's sketch (s.v.
"Gloria") of the bereaved children, innocent of the meaning of death,
playing cheerfully with the silken pall that covers their dead parent's
body. See further, *Ayenb. of Inwyt*, pp. 84, 93–4, 208, etc.
[3] *Jacob's Well*, E.E.T.S. ed. p. 309. Cf. in Latin, MS. Add. 21253,
fol. 61 ("Certe, si pueri libenter dant de pane suo canibus..."). See
also, in this connection, the beautiful story of the child who wished to
share his bread with an image of the infant Christ ("Fair companion,
eat with me!"), retold by Bozon, *Metaphs.* cap. cxx.

stree to hete itt, but for to hete the childes hondes".[1] If her precious charge fall ill, then "the modyr for here syke chylde makyth a candell, and makyth a vowe in prayere".[2] Godless adults, on the other hand, who will not keep their fast on fasting days "to the none of the day", as Holy Mother Church enjoins, the preacher compares to "wantoun children, that woleth alwey have brede in here hond".[3]

A peep within the domestic hall, itself "blakyd wyth smoke",[4] shows us the hall fire that now "brennyth fayr and lyȝt togedyr", now "qwenchethe and smokethe",[5] "the catte, that sitteth nyhe the fyre" and "brenneth ofte hire hippes",[6] the floor "with grene rusches and swete flowres strawed all aboute" each eastertide,[7] or straw-covered in winter. We learn there the mysteries of house-cleaning—"like as a woman clenseth hur hous. She taketh a besom and dryveth togethur all the unclennes of the household; and, lest that the duste ascende and encwmber the place, she spryngeth it [with] water; and whan that she hath gadred all to-thethur, she casteth it with gret violence owte of the dore".[8] As every modern housewife knows, it is a task that is never ended: "For, on Saturday at afternone, the servauntes shall swepe the hous and caste all the donge and the filth be-hynde the dore on an hepe. But what than? Cometh the capons and the hennes and scrapeth it abrode, and makethe it as il as it was before".[9] We watch those at work on "the lynnen cloth, that furst is ybete, after-ward y-guyde, and thanne y-sponne, and thanne at the laste with gret travayle in waschynge to make it whyȝt";[10] or the "lawnder", who "in weshynge of clothes worcheth on this

[1] MS. Roy. 18. B. xxiii, fol. 83b (the straw would be picked from the floor-covering). Cf. in Bromyard (s.v. "Infirmitas"), the mother who holds her child's scorched hand to the fire, so that the heat of the latter may expel the heat of the burn (a true homœopathic treatment!).

[2] *Jacob's Well*, p. 191. Cf. the "norice", in *Ayenb. of Inwyt*, p. 161.

[3] MS. Harl. 45, fol. 139 (from *Ayenb. of Inwyt*, p. 52).

[4] Myrc's *Festial*, E.E.T.S. ed. p. 129.   [5] Ibid. p. 162.

[6] MS. Harl. 45, fol. 124b.   [7] *Festial*, p. 129: cf. p. 39.

[8] MS. Roy. 18. B. xxiii, fol. 145b ("in the siȝth of thi soule, make a spade of thi tounge, and cast all owte afore the prest; ȝe, oute of the dorre of thi mouthe").   [9] Ibid. fol. 167.

[10] MS. Harl. 2398, fol. 37b. Sim. MS. Harl. 45, fol. 130.

wiʒe: First, she taketh lie and casteth [the] clothes thérin, and suffurs them to be longe ther. Aftur, she draweth hem owte, turneth, betes, and washes hem, and hanggeth hem up, and so is the clothe clene. This lie is mad with askes and watur", and eventually there is used "freshe water to washe thi clothes owte of this lie".[1] Our fifteenth-century homestead doubtless will not escape its share of domestic woes. Sickness may invade its occupants, bringing sleepless nights when the "sike man in bodi, that liʒ[e]t in niʒt gretli tormentid in his disese,... herkeneth and desireth ever more after the crowynge of the cok; and, as tyme as he hereth hym, he is gretli confortid, for thanne he hopeth the dai be nyh".[2] Then, indeed, the "ffesicyan commythe", as in Master Rypon's discourse, "and is in full purpose for to gyfe hym medycyns, the whiche scholde be cawse of his helthe. ffyrste he ʒevithe hym a preparatyffe, secundary a purgatyfe, and aftyr that a proper sanatyff",[3] washes the wound with a "leyghe" of ashes and water like that used by the "lawnder", or lets his blood,[4] as the case may be.

[1] MS. Roy. 18. B. xxiii, fol. 144 (the beating is done with a "malle"). The laundress and her task are old and favourite topics of the medieval preacher. Cf. *Old Engl. Homs.* (12th cent.), 2nd ser. E.E.T.S. O.S. no. 53, p. 57. The same figures are to be found in twelfth-century sermons in France: see Hauréau, *Not. et Extr.* vol. iv, pp. 236 and 243. Hence their use in *Piers Plowman*, e.g. C Text, pass. xvii, ll. 329–32, B Text, pass. xv, ll. 181 et seq. Her soap is in MS. Laud Misc. 511, fol. 74.

[2] MS. Add. 41321, fol. 11. Also in MS. Camb. Univ. Libr. Gg. vi. 16, fol. 39, and MS. Linc. Cath. Libr. A. 6. 2, fol. 26.

[3] MS. Linc. Cath. Libr. A. 6. 2, fol. 90b. Cf. MS. Harl. 2247, fol. 49b, and Rypon—as above, p. 30—who gives "digestive" for "preparative".

[4] *Jacob's Well*, pp. 195 and 196. Cf. again, p. 143 ("lechys fysyk"), p. 178 ("the scharp corryzie", and the "drawyng salve"), p. 190 (the physician's reward, etc.). So, in MS. Roy. 18. B. xxiii, fol. 94b: "as the grett fecicions and leches don; when that thei com owte of a farre countrey, thei aspie where that other leches have fayled, and thether thei goy, and ʒeven here medecyn for to shewe here conynge"; fol. 75: "the fallynge ewill"—"for who so is in that sekenes, he leses all is witt, and hath no knolache of nothinge; and therfore he reche not whethure that he fall in fyre or watere"; MS. Camb. Univ. Libr. Gg. vi. 16 (the loving physician who first tastes and essays his patient's medicine, to encourage him); MS. Harl. 2398, fols. 22b (the man with the "dropesye") and 51b; etc., etc.

Familiar sounds of the English countryside crowd in upon us from her ancient pulpits: cries of the village slaughterhouse;[1] cry of the "wepynge babe" from a cottage door, presaging the endless sorrows of the race—"Welaway! Why was I resceyved in anny womans barme?";[2] cry of the "cuckow that evere syngeth his owen name";[3] cry of the "carte-qweel, drye and ungrecyd", that "cryeth lowdest of othere qwelys";[4] roar of the "smythes chymnye, in whiche chymnye is gret blowynge of belyes with wynde, and gret brennyng of fyir";[5] flap of "the fleyl" that "puryth the corn out of the huske";[6] gulp of the "gredy sowe in the draffe stoke";[7] peal of the village tocsin, "bellis" that sometimes, we are told, "may not wele be yronge, for thei beth bounde so strongly to a tre that they may not be ymeved".[8] We behold, in the fields, the "balkis", the "plough" and "the harwe",[9] the "byrdes" that "flyethe besyly aboute the seede when it is caste up-on the londe",[10] the vine-dressers,[11] "the good herdman"[12] and his "schep", and the "bestes when they go up on a grene pasture" that "kepen hemself from fley3en with here tayles".[13] Along country lanes, again, we fall in with the hissing geese that frighten the

[1] MS. Harl. 2398, fol. 25 b ("as a swyn hath compassion of another swynes cry, other an oxe hath compassion of the blod of an other ox that is slawe"). Cf. Bromyard, *S.P.* s.v. "Mors".

[2] MS. Roy. 18. B. xxiii, fol. 143 b ("the prophete of wrechednes"). Similarly, *Old Engl. Homs.* (12th cent.), E.E.T.S. O.S. no. 53, p. 181. See further below, pp. 533 and 536.

[3] *Jacob's Well*, p. 263. From the *Ayenbite of Inwyt*, see p. 22. Cf. Bromyard, *S.P.* s.v. "Simonia" and "Sortilegium" for other interpretations; and further below, p. 310.

[4] *Jacob's Well*, p. 260. Cf. *S.P.* s.v. "Avaritia".

[5] *Jacob's Well* (unpubld.), MS. Salisb. Cath. Libr. 103, fol. 134.

[6] Ibid. fol. 103 b.

[7] MS. Roy. 18. B. xxiii, fol. 85.

[8] *Gesta Rom.* Engl. version, E.E.T.S. ed. p. 64.

[9] MS. Add. 41321, fols. 74b–75.

[10] MS. Linc. Cath. Libr. A. 6. 2, fol. 71. Cf. the scarecrow, in Bromyard, *S.P.* s.v. "Correctio", etc.

[11] Ibid. fol. 67b; also in MS. Add. 41321, and Bromyard.

[12] MS. Roy. 18. B. xxiii, fol. 99.

[13] MS. Linc. Cath. Libr. A. 6. 2, fol. 81b, and MS. Harl. 2398, fol. 56 ("So a man schal kepe him from temptacioun of the worlde by thenkynge of his owene"—end!—i.e. death). Sim. Michel Menot in France.

children,[1] the patient "asse, that hath as leef to bere whete as
barly, rye as gold—he goth as faste for the smale as for the
grete",[2] the "bocherys dogge" with a "blody mowth",[3] the
ugly, boorish labourers moving with "gret dyne and hevy
tramplyng", their coarse eyes "twynklyng, and lokyng, and
staryyng abowtyn", from their mouths "uncurteys woordys
and lowde cryinge", with "leyȝhyng, mowyng, and lowde
dyne and noyse, and grennyng and schewyng of the teeth".[4]
All appear as in some contemporary miniature of the seasons. To
these homilists of the open road the face of nature is as familiar
as the faces of men. Her changing moods, her sun and wind,
her storm and calm, the unending solicitude of the farmer
provide them with a rich store of apt and forceful similes.
Thus, for example, one of their number compares the fate of
the bare sapling with that of the heavily laden fruit tree—"rith
as it farith be grete wyndes and grete tempestes". In the case of
the former—that "ha[th] noyther fruit nor bowes upon hym"—

b[l]owe the wynde never so blist, haild it never so harde, thrundre it
never so oribiliche, we[l] a stont stille, nothyng grevid nor disesid with
hem. But an t[h]is be a vair tre vul of fruit, bewtewus of bowes, loveliche
al abowte and lusti of levis, the sowthrenwynd schaketh hym o the to[n]
side, the northynwynd blasteth hym on the tother; ȝe, he is so vor-puffid
and so vorblowyn, that unnethe a may kepe his bowes hole to-gedder.

Yet, even so, if well rooted, it shall not be utterly cast down:

but ȝit, thei it be so that a lest overwhile a bow or a tweyene, ȝit for
the most part, and a be wel rotid, the rotis abide evermor stedvastliche
e the grownde but ȝif the wynde be the greter.[5]

There is likewise a true touch of the natural artist in that
other preacher who speaks of "cloudes [that] letteth nouȝt the
siȝt of the sunne; but anon after that thei have ȝeve hire reyn,
the sunne bersteth up ful cleer, and ofte...as men seen al dai

[1] *Jacob's Well*, p. 107 ("as a chylde that dare noȝt passe, for the goos
hysseth at him"). Cf. *Ayenb. of Inwyt*, p. 32.
[2] Ibid. p. 246 (*Ayenb.* p. 141).
[3] Ibid. p. 262. The butcher's dog figures (A.D. 1367) among the
ordinances of the Great Guild Book of Beverley (Yorks.). See *Beverley
Town Documents*, Selden Soc. vol. xiv (1900), pp. lvi and 29 ("of the
Custody of Butchers' Dogs").
[4] Ibid. MS. Salisb. Cath. Libr. 103, fol. 131, etc.
[5] MS. Worc. Cath. Libr. F. 10, fol. 44b. (See again below, p. 454.)

how it reyneth and schynethe bothe at ones".[1] Contemporary
field sports naturally furnish many a useful comparison. Several
homilists describe the practice of "men of worship" that have
gentle hawks, when they have let them fly after the game and
desire to call them to hand again. When they will not readily
come, we read, the master that keeps the hawks has a Reclama-
tory to call with, all made bloody, or else a part of the raw
flesh of some beast or fowl, to bring the bird down.[2] Bozon
makes frequent reference to incidents in the hunting of stags,
hares and foxes.[3] Another homilist in a single sentence mentions
how—"hunteris hunteth dyverse maneres of preies in diverse
maneres,...summe with bowes, summe with houndes ren-
nynge with open mouth, and summe with grehoundes, and
summe also...with prevee nettes".[4] Yet another selects the
"fyschere", that "huntethe after a fysche. Furst he stureth the
water and woreth it, that the fysche may nouȝt y-se...".[5]
Finally, as the Latin sermon-writer included inanimate objects

[1] MS. Add. 41321, fol. 13. Cf. again in an early fourteenth-century
sermon, in Latin, for the same imagery, MS. Heref. Cath. Libr. P. 5. 2,
fol. 75 b.
[2] MS. Camb. Univ. Libr. Gg. vi. 16, fol. 36. Sim. in a sermon of Robert
Holcot, MS. Roy. 7. c. i, fol. 112 b (*Convertimini*... series). Cf. the
"iesse", in MS. Harl. 45, fol. 161: "Right as men withholdeth the faucon
with the iesse, that he fle noght at his owne wille...and so falle in the
grennes and panteres of the fouler...".
[3] Cf. *Metaphs.* cap. xxi–ii, xxviii, xxxvi, xliii, cxlvi, etc. Such evidence
serves to show how the typical argument of literary scholars may be
entirely disproved by study of this sermon literature: cf. the late Sir I.
Gollancz on the author of the *Pearl* as "certainly no priest" (ed. 1921,
Med. Libr. p. xlii) because of his knowledge of woodcraft, elaborate descriptions of the hunting of deer, boars and foxes, etc.
[4] MS. Add. 41321, fol. 107b ("to conforte in this werke his houndes,
he blowith his horn with a blast" (fol. 109); "his grehoundes...renneth
not with open mouth, but pursueth ful stilli, and scharpeli rennen at
the bac" (fol. 110)). Cf. also the "boor of the wode" described on fol.
68b; and "the yonge grihound" in *Ayenb. of Inwyt*, p. 155.
[5] MS. Harl. 2398, fol. 16b; similarly in a late thirteenth-century sermon,
in Hauréau, *Not. et Extr.* vol. iv, p. 156 ("piscatores qui turbant aquam
ut possint melius capere pisces"). Cf. also, the fowler in MS. Roy. 18.
B. xxiii, fol. 125 b ("ȝiff a birde be taken in a nette, the more he wyndeth
hym therin, the wers may he goy owte; the mo ffeders that he leseth,
the wers he may flye to helpe hym selfe awey").

in his purview, so also does he who both preaches and writes in English. Nothing can be too trivial for him—"the pott boylyng over the fyir",[1] as in Bromyard, on which no flies will settle,[2] the cobbler's "brystell",[3] the over-dirty shirt,[4] the mirror and the candle,[5] the "gunne" and the "engyne-ston",[6] or the various domestic uses of oil.[7]

Many more examples of these lively little descriptions will be found in the pages that follow. But enough has been said already to make clear that we need not look far beyond the English pulpit and its records to account for the Realism which blossoms so freely in Langland and Chaucer. Courthope's attempt to explain this "revived principle of the direct imitation of nature, so long buried under the allegorical modes of interpretation", by attributing it to a new study of classical literature, is therefore quite gratuitous. Where, indeed, have we any signs of the latter in a realistic Jacques de Vitry or Robert de Sorbon? Nor again must the examples just given of this "direct imitation of nature" in our sermons be confused even with the more formal "text-book" *exempla* that will figure in a later chapter,[8] drawn by the preachers from written sources alone, of things often never seen and as often quite wrongly imagined and recorded. Such marvels and portents from the Histories, whether of the natural or human variety, introduced on the authority of some "great clerk" or other, are in marked contrast to the former. We may complete our survey of these vivid native elements in the contemporary preaching with a word or two concerning the many proverbs

[1] *Jacob's Well*, MS. Salisb. Cath. Libr. 103, fol. 109b (three ways for preventing it "rennyng ovyr").
[2] MS. Harl. 2398, fol. 28.   [3] *Jacob's Well*, p. 241.
[4] Ibid. p. 185.   [5] MS. Harl. 45, fols. 130–1.
[6] *Jacob's Well*, p. 267.
[7] MS. Harl. 2398, fol. 26b (eight uses, e.g.—"qyencheth fyr in a stok, and noryscheth fyre in a flynt", "kepyth metal fro rustynge", "maketh thynges that beth yfroyed savery and ly3t", etc.). Cf. similarly, MS. Lansd. 379, fol. 9 (the "good orderynge of sesenyng" for food); MS. Linc. Cath. Libr. A. 6. 2, fol. 109b (the "litil postrene 3ate"), or fol. 73 (the tally-stick); and Bozon, on the knot tied in the girdle to aid the memory, *Metaphs.* cap. lxxix; etc.
[8] i.e. Chap. IV.

and wise sayings that find their place in it, "the deep but humorous philosophy of our own people", as the philologist Kemble styled them.

In a little book published in the year 1910, Professor Skeat suggested somewhat tentatively that "one of the ways in which proverbs were formally popularized was by their use in sermons delivered in the vernacular".[1] The reading of Old English homilies of the twelfth century and certain familiar religious treatises, then in print, apparently led him to this conclusion. Two further observations that he makes have a significance for our study. Emphasis is laid in the first place upon the marked paucity of examples in much English verse of the thirteenth and fourteenth centuries, as contrasted with the richness of Chaucer.[2] Later, the Professor goes on to stress the very extensive use to which these same proverbs were put by Shakespeare and his fellow-dramatists.[3] Now, with characteristic industry, wellnigh twenty years before Skeat's essay appeared, M. Hauréau in France had already produced ample evidence from manuscripts in the *Bibliothèque Nationale* that even Latin sermons sometimes abounded in these current popular sayings, and that Parisian preachers of the thirteenth century were wont to make use of collections of both Latin and vernacular proverbs especially compiled for the purpose.[4] What, then, is the evidence of our own neglected sermon

[1] *E. E. Proverbs*, Oxford, p. vii, etc.

[2] "The Chaucerian examples...considerably exceed in number all the rest" (p. xi).

[3] Fifty-five in Shakespeare; sixty-four in other dramatists (p. xii). Cf. here Dr M. P. Tilley's recent work on *Eliz. Proverb Lore*, 1926.

[4] Cf. *Not. et Extr.* vol. ii, pp. 96–9 and 278–84; vi, pp. 62 and 68–72; etc. (Nicolas de Biard, Robert de Sorbon, etc.). Such collections of proverbs and epigrams are to be met with in Engl. MSS., some of which were obviously compiled for homiletic purposes, as is clear, e.g., in the case of MS. Arund. 507, fols. 69 et seq., and 54 (following Gaytryge's *Sermon*), etc., printed in Horstmann, *Yorksh. Writers*, vol. i, pp. 420–35; MS. Linc. Cath. Libr. 1. 7. 2, fols. 252–62; etc. Mr W. A. Pantin, in his recent art. on "A Mediev. Collection of Latin and Engl. Proverbs and Riddles, from the Rylands Lat. MS. 394", in *Bulletin of Jo. Ryl. Libr.* vol. xiv, no. 1, Jan., 1930, pp. 81–114, has overlooked this further use of works of the kind. For Bibliogr., etc., see also J. E. Wells, *Manual of M.E. Writ.* pp. 374 et seq.

manuscripts in this country? Turning first to the Latin *Summa*
of John Bromyard, we find, in like manner, a mass of proverbial
saws in both Latin and French scattered in its pages. Many
of those given in Latin are such familiar household sayings
of to-day as—"Many hands make light work",[1] "Enough is
as good as a feast",[2] or—in its more succinct Latinized form—
"to run with the hare and hunt with the hounds".[3] Some echo
the native wisdom of the market-place—"cum ergo proverbium
sit—'Bonum forum trahit denarium de bursa'";[4] others of the
law courts—"in proverbio dicitur—'Oportet quod illorum
inunguas manus!'", a proverb that one unfortunate female
litigant apparently once took all too literally.[5] Characteristic
French proverbs give us the favourite cry now of the medieval
gourmand,[6] now of the devotee of Paris:[7] others satirize such
current follies as the prattle of the empty-headed bore,[8] the
jealous rivalry of the proud,[9] or the diabolical anger of women.[10]
In a Latin sermon by Master Rypon of Durham, again, we
find the earlier equivalent of the saying "Pride goeth before
a fall", here illustrated by the story of Cinderella—"juxta commune proverbium—'Superbia precedit, et confusio sequitur'".[11]

[1] s.v. "Caritas".   [2] s.v. "Ebrietas".
[3] s.v. "Adulatio" ("Ita tales qui volunt omnibus placere, qui volunt
esse de parte leporarii et leporis"). Also in *Jacob's Well*, p. 263.
[4] s.v. "Eleemosina". Cf. Hauréau, *Not. et Extr.* vol. ii, p. 193.
[5] s.v. "Judices". (The story, here repeated by Bromyard and to be
found in Odo of Cheriton (see Hervieux, *Les Fabul. Lat.* vol. iv, p. 301),
also MS. Add. 18344, fol. 138b, is of the poor widow who thus greased
the prelate's hand.)   [6] See below, p. 449.
[7] s.v. "Honor" ("Mieulx vault ung bonvenant [?] de Paris que toute
la feste de Chartreez").
[8] s.v. "Locutio" ("Grainge voide venteuse").
[9] s.v. "Gloria" ("sicut pulchrius Gallice dicitur,—'Duo magni unum
asinum equitare non possunt; quia unus vult esse ante, et alius non vult
esse retro'").
[10] s.v. "Ira" ("...quoddam allegantes proverbium Gallicum, quod
Scriptura confirmat, *Ecclesiasticus*, xxv—'Non est ira...super iram
mulieris'"). Cf. Alex. Barclay, *Ship of Fools*, ed. Edinb. 1874, vol. ii,
pp. 1–11. See another, s.v. "Judicium Humanum".
[11] MS. Harl. 4894, fol. 27. The same occurs in Engl. vernac. sermons,
e.g. MS. Add. 41321, fol. 101b ("as it is seid in comen proverbe—'Pride
goth bifore, and schame cometh after'"); *Jacob's Well*, p. 70, etc. For
another saying in Rypon, see below, p. 435.

An anonymous sermon-writer in the same language repeats an equally favourite maxim alike of the medieval pulpit and the modern pew, which has been attributed to St Bernard: "He, who loves me, loves my dog".[1]

It is in the many proverbs preserved in English in our homily-books, however, that we seem to hear, as perhaps nowhere else in contemporary literature, the cry of an over-burdened, almost despairing peasantry that loves to shake off its sorrows and its fears with these quaint pessimistic folk-utterances.[2] They are the "Kismet" of the toiling medieval herd, eloquent of feelings stifled and long pent-up, sighs, gestures of helplessness and perhaps tears that turn suddenly to a bitter laughter. How else shall the toiler be reconciled to his lot, the long unending round of services and fines upon the feudal estate? Here are a random dozen of the kind:

For men seith on olde Englisshe—"So longe the potte goth to the water, that at the laste it cometh home broken; and so longe fleeth the butterflye aboute the fyre, that at the. laste he falleth amydde and is brent".[3]

Yf hope were not, herte shulde breke.[4]

Selde comet the lattere the betere.[5]

Whan the rofe of thyn hous lithe on thi nese,   [nose]
Alle the worldis blisse ys nouth worthe a pese.[6]

As it is seide in olde proverbe—"Pore be hangid bi the necke; a riche man bi the purs".[7]

It is an olde sawe—"Swych lord, swyche meyne".[8] [household]

[1] MS. Harl. 7322, fol. 95 b (cont.—"ita qui diligit Deum, diligit pauperes ejus"). Also in S.P. s.v. "Amor" (referring to the Ethics of Aristotle); and cf. Hauréau, Not. et Extr. vol. ii, p. 96; vol. iv, p. 170; vol. vi, p. 71. Other English proverbs appear in the above MS. fols. 92–6b, etc.

[2] Cf. here Prof. E. Westermarck's recent Frazer Lecture, 1928.

[3] MS. Harl. 45, fol. 103b. Sim. Ayenb. of Inwyt, p. 206. The first part appears twice in the Bk. of the Kni. of La Tour-Landry, Engl. version, E.E.T.S. pp. 82 and 90: see also below, p. 489.

[4] Gesta Rom., Engl. version, E.E.T.S. p. 228. Again in the Pricke of Conscience, ed. Philog. Soc. p. 196, ll. 7263–6, and S.P. s.v. "Damnatio".

[5] Odo of Cheriton (Serm.), MS. Arund. 292, fol. 13; etc.: see Herbert, Cat. of Romances in B.M. vol. iii, pp. 35 and 38 and Wright, Lat. Stories, Percy Soc. no. 51. (As in Shakespeare, Kg. Rich. III, Act ii, Sc. 3: "Seldom comes the better".)

[6] MS. Camb. Univ. Libr. Ii. iii. 8, fol. 166 (Latin text).

[7] MS. Add. 41321, fol. 86.

[8] MS. Salisb. Cath. Libr. 103, fol. 102b (unpublished Jacob's Well).

Stroke oule and schrape oule, and evere is oule oule.[1]
Trendle the appel nevere so far, he conyes fro what tree
he cam.[2]   [knows]
    Schrewe on, schrewe other.[3]   [one]
    Clym, clam! Cat lep over dam![4]
    ffor it is seyd—"He that fool sendyth, fool abydeth".[5]
And therfore hit is seide in proverbe that he, that best is, most loweth
him.[6]   Flatrie flourithe, treuthe pleurith.[6a]

Further proverbs remind us how the female sex has its own
particular burden to bear of ridicule and reproof at the hands
of layman as well as preacher. John Myrc quotes, for example,
the "old Englysch sawe" in one of his sermons—"A mayde
schulde be seen but not herd".[7] A popular saying about the
"iii claterars"—a pie (magpie), a jay and a woman, such as
we find recorded among the cipher-puzzles in the Brome MS.,[8]
becomes a solemn pulpit warning to women-folk, not "to be
ever jangelynge as a pye, other a jay".[9] It is possible to detect
at least a third distinctive type of proverb in use, one that
reflects the growing anti-clericalism and hostility to religious
observances in a most remarkable way. No longer will the
layman invariably take a rebuke from his spiritual superiors
in meek and silent fashion. He has ready a pert reply—"as
when ʒe do synne and speke lewdely, when on chaluns you,
than it is a comon seynge of the pepull—'ʒe latt God and
me alone!'"[10] Likewise, when reminded of his absence from
church and bidden to hasten thither, the insolent fellow will
now retort—"The cherche is non hare: there men leve it they
may fynde it!"[11] "But there is many that carythe not for the

---

[1] N. Bozon, *Metaphs.* cap. xvii (French text).
[2] Ibid.   [3] Ibid. cap. lv.
[4] Ibid. cap. cxxii (see the fable for meaning). See another, cap. xiv.
[5] MS. Salisb. Cath. Libr. 103, fol. 124b. Sim. *Ayenb. of Inwyt*, p. 211.
[6] MS. Harl. 45, fol. 155. [6a] Brunton. MS. Harl. 3760, fol. 62.
[7] *Festial*, p. 230.
[8] See *A Commonplace Bk. of the 15th cent.* ed. L. T. Smith, p. 12. See
further below, p. 387.
[9] MS. Harl. 2398, fol. 10b. Cf. in Horstmann, *Yorksh. Writers*, vol. i,
p. 144 ("Our Daily Work"). Cf. further an Anglo-Norman poem by
Nich. Bozon (Jo. Vising, *Anglo-Norm. Lang. and Lit.* p. 65).
[10] MS. Roy. 18. B. xxiii, fol. 75.
[11] *Jacob's Well*, p. 141. Also in Bromyard, *S.P.* s.v. "Accidia".

preste, ne for the chyrche. For thei wil sey—'it is no wilde
catt, ne it wyll not flee'. And so thei sett not by the chyrche,
ne by the kepers there-of".[1]

From our sermons come also undignified sayings of the
people which, while often quite inoffensive, are yet so artless
and trivial that one can scarcely honour them with the name
of proverb. Indeed, so trivial are they that one is left amazed
that the preacher should deign to recognize and repeat them
in the sacred discourse. For that very reason, however, we
must be grateful to him. For they reveal, sometimes with
almost startling effect, the unchanging psychology of our race,
the eternal sameness of conversational topic, the similarity of
outlook and the similarity of impression, even an identity of
phrase throughout the centuries. Nowhere else in contemporary literature but here shall we find so many of these trite
little remarks. Thus Bromyard informs us that folk loved to
say in his day precisely as in our own, when a child was very
like his parent,—"'He is his father's son!' or 'His father
couldn't deny him!'; or of the daughters—'As the mother,
so is the daughter: foolish mother, foolish daughter!'"[2] As
for the irascible, the French call them "allumaylles", because
they resemble inflammable material,[3] and so forth. The same
author delights, whenever he can, to repeat the arguments and
excuses of the guilty, however shallow, that he may proceed
to demolish them forthwith.[4] Then as now, another preacher
would remind us, the world was fond of an old excuse: "as
many fooles seyn—'When that othur do so, why may not I
do so?'"[5] Then, as not unoften nowadays, "he that is a
ffracer,[6] a braser,[7] a grete bragger, a grete swerer or a grete
fyȝtter, soche men ben callyd 'manly men'....He that is a
ryatour and a grete hawnter of tavernys or of ale howsys,
and a grete waster of his goodes, then is he callyd 'a good

[1] MS. Linc. Cath. Libr. A. 6. 2, fol. 68b. See further below, p. 489.
[2] S.P. s.v. "Filiatio" (cf. Ezek. xvi, 44).   [3] s.v. "Ira".
[4] Cf. below, pp. 256, 301, n. 3, 324, 336, 357, etc.
[5] MS. Roy. 18. B. xxiii, fol. 74b. Cf. Handlyng Synne, ll. 2385–6.
[6] = disturber of the peace (not in N.E.D.).
[7] = an impudent fellow (not in N.E.D.).

felaw'".[1] Says yet another preacher, in the course of his quaint address:

Sir, thou myght haske me this question, that "of what craft are most men of?" And it is a common seynge—"that of leches". For thou seest well that ȝiff a man mete anothur in the weye, what so that he be, and he see that he have anny sekenes, be it in is hede, eyen or in is hele, the tothur shall tell hym a medecyn, ȝiff it do hym no more good to is hede than to is honde.[2]

Clearly, human nature changes not at all, either in its love of conundrums or its faith in private remedies! So much, then, for this modest contribution of folk-lore to our sermons. If now we consider it along with the mass of everyday scenes and characters which we have found the pulpit employing, whilst excluding from our view those maxims and epigrams which may have been borrowed direct from classical antiquity, one main fact seems to emerge. It was neither poet nor dramatist, neither novelist nor chronicler, who first condescended to take notice of these things with a view to including them in his own compositions, there to be preserved as vivid reflections of current life. Before ever the day of such literary realism and humanism had dawned, it was the homilist who first stooped to raise them from the level of the dusty commonplace and set them on high amid the wider concerns of the human mind, thus "making their dust fat with fatness". He it was, as we shall see, who clothed them for the first time with a deep spiritual and social significance for the ordinary man, who linked them in his more polished speech with great religious themes and moral principles, with the majestic struggle of humanity between Right and Wrong, with the fate of Christendom, with the solemn issues of Life and Death, Judgment and the Hereafter, in short, the whole impressive

[1] MS. Glouc. Cath. Libr., 15th cent. Homilies, *Sermo Dom. V post Trin.* (cf. elsewhere—"a joly felowe", "a stowte revelour"). Similarly Bromyard, s.v. "Falsitas" ("Luxuriosi et gulosi qui malas diligunt societates et tabernas...vocantur boni socii").

[2] MS. Roy. 18. B. xxiii, fol. 120b. Cf. *Gesta Rom.* E.E.T.S. ed. p. 65, and below, p. 167, n. 2. (Cf. further in this MS. fol. 108: "Itt is a comone proverbe, bothe of clerkes and of laye men—'ȝounge seynt, old dewell'"; etc.)

revelation of the Church. In his discourses and treatises, they fall into line with the sacred romances of saint and martyr, the marvels of nature and the horrors of hell. They appear on the same stage with the greater Vices and Virtues, lending liveliness and colour to the drama of Bethlehem and Calvary, even at length playing the very parts of the Vices and Virtues themselves. Thus, what was originally introduced as mere homiletic warning and example came in due time to have an aesthetic value of its own. Henceforth their place in secular literature is assured.

It may not be wholly out of place, now that the aesthetic has been mentioned, if we close our introductory survey with a word concerning the general attitude of English homilists to contemporary Art. The subject has a direct bearing upon our future discussions. Moreover, it derives added interest and importance from the recent publication of a learned work by Dr Coulton,[1] in which he examines at considerable length the relations between medieval art and religious instruction, and thereby furnishes some pertinent criticisms of the thesis of M. Émile Mâle. In this present short section and in the chapters which follow, the reader will be left to make his own judgment upon the fresh evidence here put forward. It is sufficient to add, where space allows no full debate, that the author, if challenged, would incline to a position somewhere perhaps mid-way between those who argue for the intimacy of these relations and those who deny them. But first a word upon the purely aesthetic side of the question. While admitting at the outset that beauty in art can never be expected to figure amongst the first concerns of the Christian pulpit, we are surely justified in looking for some very clear response to it from those perpetually haranguing in the shadow of Gothic cathedral and parish church. In a rude and turbulent world like that of the Middle Ages, the more sensitive in the preacher's audiences might well be tamed and uplifted, nay, even educated by

[1] *Art and the Reformation*, Blackwell, Oxford, 1928. The present study will be found to amplify the information given in Appendix 23 of that work.

frequent references to the appear of the beautiful around them, where such was often so lavishly displayed. But the pulpit, as we have already remarked, was not much given to the kindred emotions of love and sweetness. It preferred generally the themes of denunciation and terror. Moreover, it is possible to discern another influence working in the opposite direction. If we turn to discussions of *Pulchritudo* in the homily-books, of which there are many, we find that the preacher is thinking exclusively of human beauty—"una corporalis, alia spiritualis". Buildings, sculpture, painting, landscape, apparently, do not come within his purview. But what has he to say to us of this corporal beauty? "Beauty", says the author of the *Speculum Laicorum*, for example, quoting Vincent of Beauvais, "as saith Secundus the Philosopher, is an outward form of little duration, a withered flower, carnal felicity, human concupiscence." It is to be shunned, first because it is vain and transitory; secondly, because it is false and deceptive; thirdly, because, unless well controlled, it is receptive of the divine curse.[1] "Wheresoever Beauty shows upon the face", adds Master Rypon, "there lurks much filth beneath the skin."[2] Bromyard shall conclude the argument for us: "If, lynx-eyed, men's vision could penetrate obstacles, after a sight of the entrails of beauties, would not the body seem most vile?"[3] This orthodox homiletic view of the Beautiful arrayed in human form and fair vesture is really part and parcel of a much larger doctrine: that which denounces every form of outward show, everything that tended to feast men's eyes upon the mere surface, all that either thus cloaked a falsehood or else

[1] Cap. lxx (ed. Welter, p. 95). The quotation is from the *Spec. Hist.* cap. lxxi. Bozon's quotation of Ecclesiasticus ix, 8–9—"Turn away thine eye from a beautiful woman....For many have been deceived by the beauty of a woman" (*Metaphs.* cap. liii) shows the direct influence of Scripture here.   [2] MS. Harl. 4894, fol. 180.

[3] *S.P.* s.v. "Pulchrit.", referring to a passage in the *Consol.* of Boethius, bk. iii, adducing 'Aristotle': "Si linxeis oculis uterentur homines ut eorum visus obstacula penetraret, nonne, inspectis visceribus pulchritudinum, corpus turpissimum videretur?" (See here, Coulton, *Five Cent. of Relig.* vol. i, pp. 176 and 528–9, indicating Aristophanes, etc.). Also in *Ayenb. of Inwyt*, p. 81.

failed to lead swiftly and unerringiy to some spiritual reality beneath.[1] It is this central doctrine that is vital to our understanding of the whole problem. For, on the one hand, it gives us, as we shall see, the one true and faithful clue to the preacher's doctrine of Images, his view, that is to say, of the sacred statues and pictures of the saints. On the other hand, it explains why, with almost the same breath, he will denounce "the fair polished and painted stone" of noble tombs, telling of the evil putrefaction at work within them,[2] or "the gay pawmentis for mennes feet and peyntid roofis above", made merely "to stony mennes wittis gapynge a-loft, undoinge the materes of mennes craft".[3] In the first case, we deal with something which is to be approved, *in so far as* it directs men's thoughts without false let or hindrance to the spiritual personality which it mirrors. In the second, we deal with something which is to be reprobated, because it is found, when thus probed to its spiritual core, to stand merely for human pride and self-seeking, because, to the preacher's relentless eye, it so often represents only the wickedness of those who have spoiled or neglected the poor "to clothe timber and stones" with such idle adornment.[4] But, in *both* cases, it is equally clear that the outward *beauty* of effigy and ornament themselves is of no concern for our pulpit. This, indeed, is the root of the whole matter. It sets in their right perspective both what Dr Coulton has called "the Puritan Revolt" of orthodox reformers in the Middle Ages, and also the heretical iconoclasm of the Lollard. It explains further why so little here divides them. It also sets forth the *idea* of medieval Catholicism regarding the subject, as something perfectly clear, perfectly logical, perfectly self-contained, however much we may choose to disagree with it; one moreover that was at least as lofty and spiritual as that of subsequent Protestantism, however much it may have collapsed in the practice of individuals.[5]

[1] Cf. here, e.g. Clement of Alexandria, *Stromata*, lib. iv, cap. xviii (Migne, *Patr. Graeco-Lat.* vol. viii, cols. 1324–5).
[2] Bromyard, *S.P.* s.v. "Luxuria", etc.   [3] MS. Add. 24202, fol. 27.
[4] See here *Preaching in Med. Engl.* pp. 162–3.
[5] I must here confess, with all my love and admiration for its author, that I have looked in vain in Dr Coulton's *Art and the Reform.* for any

How little, indeed, seems often to divide the best minds of these two parties!

Pure aesthetic appreciation and preaching are thus theoretically divorced in our period. To this extent, at least, Dr Coulton's contention is fully maintained. But are we to say that the preachers themselves were wholly insensible to the glories of current art? On the contrary, their very sermons show us sometimes that the man is bigger than his message. Bromyard, the Dominican doctor, will refer, in the course of his argument, to "the beauty of a House of Religion, which arises out of the fair arrangement of its cloister and other buildings"; or again to the beauty of a church, consisting partly in its fair paintings and images, partly in its symbolic orientation, such as "the fairer part and the fairer window looking eastwards, through which the whole church is lit up and adorned". He may even go so far as to add mention of the contributory beauty of its library treasures—"in proof of which, he, who shows others over a convent or church, sometimes in commending the beauties of the place shows its books also".[1] At another time, he may allude further to the practice of painters, who strive to combine in one masterpiece of their own the various features of beauty which their study of the masterpieces of others has revealed to them.[2] Similarly, to illustrate some point in passing he may throw out a hint at the beauty of the lily, "which is the fairest of flowers", set "in church before the image of God, or of Mary his Mother".[3] This, also, has not escaped his eye. Again, he will borrow a simile from the artistic value of the lead binding in stained-glass

clear appreciation or statement of this very fundamental point of view. He invariably gives us the impression, I think, that the voices of the Church were *always* "at sixes and sevens" when dealing with this and kindred topics. The bold discordances in orthodox medieval religion are indeed a *most* important feature of the times. But here there does seem to be a real underlying unity, in theory at all events.

[1] s.v. "Conversatio".

[2] s.v. "Exemplum". Cf. again s.v. "Luxuria" ("sicut pictores volentes picturarum addiscere experientiam...").

[3] s.v. "Munditia". (N.B., however, the point of the reference is purely practical: "Qui vult lilium...diu in pulchritudine sua custodire, ponit stipitem in terra lutosa vel humida...".)

windows,[1] or the advantages of a white ground for the artist's colour-scheme.[2] In like manner, on much rarer occasions, sermon-writers in the vernacular, too, may refer us to the "pynnaclis of a material temple other chirche", that "maketh hit feire to the siȝt of men",[3] or to the "colours with the wiche holy houses beth y-peynted".[4] But that is the full extent to which they will go. The beauty in all these things is certainly never their main theme. It slips casually into the discourse "to point a moral or adorn a tale" of theology, not of aesthetics. Its presence in this form merely serves to indicate that, at best, the best of them were at least conscious of its appeal.

The claims of external beauty and the solemn tasks of homiletics might be divorced to their full extent, and yet other links might obtain between the art of the sacred orator and that of the craftsman. So far as it concerns the relations between the sermon and the sacred images of the saints, this subject will be dealt with in our study of saint-lore. Let it suffice here to say that we shall be wise to look not so much for iconographic allusions in the former as for the concentrated influence of that hallowed place where "faces and voices met, a sort of spiritual market-place",[5] the parish church or church-yard. There we shall discover in due course an "essential unity of expression" in what is to be seen and heard—such, as Professor Huizinga rightly reminds us, does not reveal itself to mere documentary evidence[6]—crystallized most perfectly in certain common forms of Realistic treatment. It is, however, in the sphere of satiric representation that we might best expect

---

[1] s.v. "Nativitas" (a value, incidentally, that is akin to that of the heavy black outline given to figures in contemporary MS. illumination).
[2] s.v. "Munditia". [3] MS. Add. 41321, fol. 92. [4] MS. Harl. 2398, fol. 26b.
[5] (Coulton, *Art and the Reform.* p. 326.) On p. 317, Dr Coulton, perhaps, hardly does justice to the influence of Myrc's *Festial* (as indeed reference to his own Appendix 23 will show!). I now discern approximately a dozen allusions in these sermons (cf. below the additions on pp. 145–6). If then we consider even these few in the light of the popularity of the work as a model compendium for preachers (the fact that Caxton, Wynkyn de Worde and Pynson, between them, made themselves responsible for at least ten editions speaks also of its earlier popularity in MS., of which there is additional evidence), we have clearly at least the *initiation* of a pretty general practice. [6] *History*, July, 1929, p. 141.

to find common ground between the Realism of preacher and artist. This raises a question of even greater interest and complexity. Did the use of satire in ecclesiastical art first encourage pulpit satire, or *vice versa*? The answer must wait until we have had time to consider the evidence, in suitable conjunction with the whole subject of literary satire. That there is obviously much common ground between them no one will deny who is familiar with the carvings of misericord and corbel. One final word may here be added in support of Dr Coulton's contention that medieval art and religion remained largely separate growths. Apart from sacred portraiture and landscape, wherever we find the preachers actually referring to artistic symbolism, they seem to introduce it as something curiously independent of their own sphere of religious activity. It witnesses, of course, to some vital truth of religion that they happen to be expounding; but it is rather as the detached and corroborative witness of the stranger from without, of the lay things of the world, of the studio and not the sanctuary.[1] Among all the sermon-collections of English preachers which the present author has studied, with the single exception of the *Festial*, there is only one which even suggests that its author may have had a definite interest in pictures. What, then, are the pictorial topics which this pulpit orator of the reign of King Henry V chooses to bring to the notice of his listeners? Are they of some appropriate masterpiece of the Madonna, of the Crucified Redeemer, the saints and martyrs that still inspire the noblest efforts of contemporary artists? On the contrary, without exception, they are pagan portraits, as painted "apud veteres" and described in classical literature. Thus we have the Picture of Faith, "ut recitat Tullius Cichero, *de Officiis*", an image "set up by the ancients next to that of Jove in the Capitol, whose likeness was that of a crowned queen holding a sceptre in her left hand, and a shield in her right";[2] and along with

[1] Cf. examples given below, pp. 238–9.
[2] MS. Bodl. 649, fol. 180 (inscribed "*Pictura Fidei*" in the margin). Cf. the moralization here: "ad designandum quod fides bona debet esse regulatrix in simplicitate quia regina dominatrix, in magnanimitate quia coronata, triumphatrix in adversis ratione clipei, et premiatrix in meritis ratione sceptri".

it a kindred portrait of Wisdom, "a lady reclining on a couch", with appropriate circumscription.[1] Later, we meet with the Four Virtues—Prudence with jocund face, as described by Juvenal, Justice according to Socrates, Temperance according to "Ypocrates", and Fortitude after "Tullius" again.[2] On the very next page "the Picture of Lust" confronts us: "Venus", so the preacher informs his audience, "was painted in the form of a nude woman floating upon the waves of the sea; and she carried roses with thorns and had a bodyguard of doves".[3] Each detail of the picture is then duly moralized as in the case of the others.[4] Drunkenness is next portrayed "in the likeness of a boy with a horn in his hand and a crown of vine-leaves on his head". Other figures follow, such as the strange phantasy with three bodies and three faces, of which two weep while the third laughs, here said to be derived from "Dion Agellius [= Aulus Gellius], in a little book on the Armenian War";[5] and finally, the figure of Death.[6] Of Christian iconography, strange to say, we find not a word, where we should most expect it. The symbolic art of the churches excites no comment from our homilist, even by way of natural contrast. Ignoring the more obvious and homely material for moralization that lies close at hand, his mind roams rather to the "curiositates et declarationes philosophorum" which even so

[1] fol. 182b ("veteres ymaginem sapientie pre foribus omnium templorum depingere [solebant], cuius circumscriptio erat versus—'Me genuit, me peperit memoria: homines stultos ego odi...'").

[2] fol. 185b. Cf. here a *Pictura Justitie*, described from the *Noctes Atticae* of Aulus Gellius, in Holcot's Sermons (*Convertim.* series) and in a Coblentz MS. of his *Moralitates* (dated 1422, i.e. contemporary with our MS. Bodl. 649). See Herbert, *Cat. of Romances in B.M.* vol. iii, p. 119, No. 7; and further below, p. 594.

[3] fol. 186 (*Pictura Luxurie*). Cf. MS. Roy. 12. E. xxi, fol. 44b.

[4] "Venus, ergo, scil. Luxuria, depingitur nuda, quia, licet ad tempus poterit celari, non tamen diu, quia, quacumque sit inchoatio occulta et privata, ventre se elevante, patescet; ideo nichil occultum quod non revelatur...."

[5] fol. 188b. Another classical author here quoted by this preacher is "Sextus Julius", i.e. Frontinus.

[6] fols. 207b–9 (*Pictura Mortis*): "depingitur in hac forma—cum veste lacerata, cum telo infestata, cum pedibus ligata, cum manibus truncata, cum causis agitata et amicis orbata...".

learned a Dominican as John Bromyard had denounced as a snare of the pulpits of his time.[1] We are tempted to discern here the new taste of the Classical Renaissance displacing the glories of Gothic Christian Art in the very citadel of the Faith. Without honour in its own house and thus neglected of its own kindred, the artists of the sacred rostrum, little wonder that that art was doomed to extinction.

We come, then, by this somewhat devious route to the end of our preliminary survey. Mere aesthetic appreciation, as we have seen, is not for the preacher. He must deal with sterner methods and affairs. An evil world must be driven to contemplate the stark realities of current life and the ominous hereafter—sin, disaster, death and hell pains. His favourite pictures will depict the tragedy of Fortune's wheel[2] or the still greater tragedy of Devildom. Thus Gothic Art itself in the sear and yellow leaf of the closing centuries, smitten by the same wintry blasts, withers and dies. "With its autumnal flora, a leafage shrivelled, wrinkled, jagged",[3] it shares a common fate with the wrinkled foliage of Scholasticism and other shoots of the medieval tree which drew their nourishment from the same parent stem. Orthodox "great clerks" of the day themselves set no high example of noble and courageous thought to the man in the pulpit. Too often, like Plato's "boorish debaters", "they strive only for victory. For they, when they debate about anything, are not concerned where the truth of a matter lies; but their anxiety is merely for the impression which their arguments make upon their audience". Nor were the preachers slow to copy their heavy, pedantic phrases and arid theological conclusions, when it suited them. On its purely doctrinal side, then, the English pulpit of the waning Middle Ages has little inspiration to offer. "I have seen all the works that are done under the sun; and behold, all is vanity and vexation of spirit", saith the Preacher.[4] His influence here, therefore, upon the rising generations was almost

---

[1] *S.P.* s.v. "Predicatio".   [2] See further below p. 239.
[3] Fr. Funck-Brentano, *The Middle Ages* (Engl. ed.), p. 231.
[4] Cf. Bromyard, quoting this passage from the Book of Ecclesiastes (i, 2), *S.P.* s.v. "Mors", § 143; and *Ayenbite of Inwyt*, pp. 164–5.

invariably morbid. Fortunately, however, the preacher, unlike the schoolman, had direct and continuous contact with
Life. In the sermon as organ of a virile, picturesque speech
and a keen, critical view of society, as medium for vivid
illustration, lively anecdote, homely portraiture, witty and
ruthless satire we have to deal with something of a very different
order. Here, at all events, speak living voices. Here, at all
events, the spring of a new Renaissance had already blown
upon the Church, making the old sap of moral purpose
rise once again within her. We shall be fully justified, therefore,
if, in the pages that follow, we lay aside the dull mass
of theological argument and concentrate solely upon these
excrescences of the preaching. At the root and heart of the
tree now lay decay and disintegration. The more random
outgrowths here and there, the brighter fruit and flowers of
its branches bore within them the seed of a new, vigorous
life for both literature and society. As scholars of the future
awake to their importance, it is safe to say that a revolution
will be effected in our knowledge of English letters, the like
of which has not been seen since the days of Thomas
Warton[1].

[1] Already, the positive utterances of some of our most reputable
literary historians appear absurd in view of them. Thus, for example,
the late Prof. C. H. Herford remarks of the influence of the *Ship of
Fools* in England (*Lit. Relations of Engl. and Germany in the 16th cent.*
pp. 324–5): "It helped to bridge over the difficult transition from the
literature of personified abstractions to that which deals with social types.
It helped to substitute study of actual men and women at first hand for
the mere accumulation of conventional traits about an abstract sub-
stantive; to turn allegory into narrative..." etc. Again (p. 333)—"It
was destined to become one of the main starting-points of modern
satirical portraiture." As our pages now show, all this had been comfortably achieved in England at least a century and a half before
(cf. further below, p. 232). Likewise, Miss Grace Hadow, where she
attributes to Chaucer (*C. and his Times*, p. 78, etc.)—"a new development in literature—the study of the commonplace."

CHAPTER II

Scripture and Allegory

IN his discussion of the topic "Misericordia", John Bromyard, the Dominican, proceeds to show how nature provides us with numerous "Examples" of the mercy of God, in things above, in things below, and in things around. Such were the Examples or *Figures* which engaged our attention in the previous chapter. Although the practice of selecting them in this fashion had become so easy and so obvious a mode of pulpit moralization, our preachers of the fourteenth and fifteenth centuries still realized that it was from Holy Scripture that the mode received its supreme sanction. There, for example, in the words of one of them, "the lyf of man is likenid nowe to a flour,[1] nowe to hete or warmnes,[2] and nowe to a fleinge shadowe,[3] and nowe to a messager that rynnithe or ridithe afore, and nowe to an arowe[4] shote to a marke".[5] Even so commonplace a metaphor as the Echo applied to the case of flatterers is drawn by a simple homilist apparently from an obscure passage in the Book of Wisdom,[6] or at any rate thus clothed with the authoritative mantle of "holy wrytt". The homilist may prefer on other occasions to mingle natural and Biblical *figures* together to illustrate his point.[7] We have now to examine the influence of current modes of expounding Scripture in a more formal and systematic fashion. For it is here that we find a source, not merely of the naturalistic type of *example*, but also of the animal

---

[1] Cf. Job xiv, 2 (referred to again in the *Pricke of Conscience*, ed. Morris, Philog. Soc. 1863, p. 20).   [2] Cf. Job vi, 17.
[3] Cf. Job xiv, 2; 1 Chron. xxix, 15.   [4] Wisd. v, 12.
[5] *Gesta Rom.* E.E.T.S. ed. p. 235. Cf. here the long Scriptural *Index de Allegoriis* in Migne, *Patr. Lat.* vol. ccxix, cols. 123–242.
[6] See Wisd. xvii, 19. *Jacob's Well*, p. 150.
[7] Cf. Bromyard, *S.P.* s.v. "Gloria" ("Sicut absconditur candela quae in vento portatur, ne exstinguatur, quae tamen, cum ad hospitium portata fuerit, secure ostenditur et non ante; sicut parentes Moysi eum absconderunt, quia elegantem ipsum viderunt usque ad tempus,—ita...", etc.).

satire and similitude, of marvellous narrations and devil stories, and certain lively allegoric features common alike to the later religious drama and to such famous allegories as *The Vision of Piers Plowman* and *The Pilgrim's Progress*. We may begin then by reviewing the four authoritative senses of Biblical interpretation current in the Middle Ages in a sermon of about the year 1400 by Master Robert Rypon, the sub-prior of Durham. But before doing so, it may be well to re-emphasize somewhat more precisely what our study of the allegoric method in these later homilies has and has not to do.

Scholars have long been familiar with the pre-Christian origins of allegory and sacred symbolism.[1] They have known likewise that there are links between pagan and early Christian symbolic art, and the carvings and paintings of the later Middle Ages. They have traced the development of scholastic imagery to its crowning glory in the *Divina Commedia* of Dante, and compared that earlier vision with the *Vision of Piers Plowman*. They have even pointed to supposed indications of the influence of De Guileville in the post-Reformation masterpiece of Bunyan. With this distant ancestry—pagan or patristic— and these broad similarities of treatment, we have therefore little concern. What remains yet to be explained satisfactorily is the way in which the symbolic language of a privileged and exclusive class became part of the common inheritance of the people—in short, the later links in the long chain of this religious tradition. Mr G. C. Druce, for example, will show us the direct influence of the Bestiaries upon the designs of carved bench-end and door-moulding.[2] But we are not shown from contemporary evidence how this animal symbolism came to influence the minds of ordinary folk who rarely or never could have handled an illuminated Bestiary in their lives, much less have read one for themselves. M. Jusserand knows well enough that both Dante and Langland are heirs to the same

[1] Cf. the admirable article by Prof. Geffcken of Rostock on "Allegory", in Hastings' *Encycl. of Relig. and Ethics*.
[2] See his valuable articles on "The Medieval Bestiaries, and their Influence on Ecclesiastical Decorative Art", in the *Journ. of the Brit. Arch. Assoc.* N.S. vols. xxv, p. 41, and xxvi, p. 35.

great body of Catholic doctrine; but he cannot explain how the comparatively simple English poet obtained his special knowledge, without crediting him with a scholarship he certainly never possessed. In similar circumstances Bunyan's distinguished biographer was actually compelled to reject the idea of his tinker hero's acquaintance with any of the medieval versions of the *Pilgrimage of Man*, in spite of its resemblances. Nothing appeared to bridge the chasm. So, too, there is equal room for some better explanation of the growth of naïve scenes of a non-Biblical character in the miracle-plays, clearly the work neither of learned apocryphal scholars on the one hand, nor of mere popular *ribaldi* on the other. It is just here that a study of this much-neglected literature of the pulpit may give us some valuable light.

The sermon of Master Rypon, of Durham, which discusses the actual question of traditional expositions of scripture in our period, deals with the Gospel story of the Loaves and Fishes.[1] In the opening passages of the prologue we meet with an example of that favourite concordance of Old and New Testament types, so often reflected in the stained-glass windows and sculpture as well as in the literature of the day.[2] Rypon begins by pointing out that the "refectio corporalis" of the Gospel story signifies the spiritual refreshment of the Word of God.

By the five loaves, doctors understand the five Books of Moses which are aptly compared to a barley loaf; for a barley loaf on its outside is rough, in part, and harsh (*hispidum*), yet within it is full of the purest flour. Likewise the Books of Moses, too, are rude when considered historically (*quoad historiam*); nevertheless within they are full of moral senses and doctrines, useful alike to the preacher and to his audience.

[1] MS. Harl. 4894, fol. 114, et seq. (sermon for the 4th Sunday in Lent).
[2] Cf. Bromyard, *S.P.* "Lex", etc. (the Law of Moses and the Law of Christ are compared to the light created on the first day of Creation and the sun created on the fourth, or again to the prophetic staff of Gehazi (see 2 Kings iv), and that of Elijah respectively). For a vernacular example, cf. MS. Worc. Cath. Libr. F. 10, fol. 42b: "And i schulde openliche declare 3ow to what entente seynt Poul seyde this word, i most tel 3ow sumwhat the effecte of the pistel of this same day; and tervor 3e schul undirstonde that Genesis, te virste book of holi writ, make mynde be a long prosses how that a good rithwus man that was clepid Abraham hadde of twey wommon twey children...".

The two small fishes have to do duty for a more complex analogy:

By the two fishes are signified the Prophets and Psalms, and the Book of the Apocalypse of the New Testament, which, taken in their literal sense, are more difficult and obscure than the aforesaid books, but none the less in their mystical senses are far more fruitful. So it is with the Gospels and the Canonical Epistles of Paul; for as fishes lie hid in the waters, so the moral senses lurk hidden in these books. Wherefore it is clear that Holy Scripture is not merely to be understood according to its literal or grammatical sense, but with equal truth according to the mystical or moral sense.... It is to be observed [the preacher goes on, now broadening out into a more general discussion] that, according to the doctors, there are four senses of Holy Scripture, namely, the literal or Historical; the allegorical, or Allegory; the tropological or Tropology, that is, the moral; the anagogical, or Anagogy.[1] Concerning these senses there are two such verses as the following:

"Littera gesta docet; quid credas, allegoria;
Moralis, quid agas; quo tendas, anagogia".[2]

Rypon's explanations of the four senses, enriched with characteristic false etymologies,[3] are best reproduced in their original Latin. Thus, the first sense, the *Literal* or *Historical*:[4]

—docet gesta seu facta, i.e. quid credas. Nam historias sacre scripture oportet credere et supponere tanquam fidem. Immo, sicut fides est fundamentum conversationis sacre, ita etiam historialis sensus scripture est ejus fundamentum.

Allegoria[5] dicitur ab "alle", quod est "alienum", et "gore"—"sententia", i.e.—aliena sententia; nam allegoria est quando aliud dicitur et

[1] Cf. the exposition in a vernacular sermon of our period of these "foure maner undirstondynges" of Holy Scripture, in MS. Harl. 2276, fol. 32b–33 ("These as it were foure feet beren up the bord of goddis lawe"), and in MS. Linc. Cath. Libr. A. 7. 2, fol. 265b (a 15th-cent. sermon-book). For the early history of the Four Senses see art. by H. Caplan, in *Speculum*, U.S.A. July, 1929, pp. 282–90.

[2] Quoted also by Nicholas of Lyra (see art. by H. Caplan, in *Speculum*, vol. ii, no. 3, July, 1927, p. 292). Cf. similar verses used for summarizing the principles of sermon dilation, in my *Preaching in Med. Engl.* pp. 323–4.

[3] Cf. ibid. pp. 38, 327, 328, for other examples from Rypon.

[4] Cf. MS. Harl. 2276, as above: "sence historial"—"whan a man understondith the story that spekith of a bodili doynge even aftur the lettre sowneth".

[5] Ibid. "sence allegorik"—"whan a man understondith bi a bodili thyng that he redith of in story an other gostli thyng that is bitokened therbi".

aliud intelligitur. Et iste sensus secundus scripture est quasi lignum seu
arbor procedens ex radice, de qua arbore crescunt et pullulant duo sensus
alii quasi flores et fructus. De isto sensu est exemplum planum in epistola
hodierna, ubi dicit Apostolus Abraham habuisse duos filios, unum de
libera et alium de ancilla, viz. Ysaac de Sara uxore Abrahe libera, et
Ysmael de Agar ancilla Abrahe concubina. Que omnia dicit Apostolus
per allegoriam dictam, quia secundum ipsum duo signant testamenta,
que, ut constat, sonant et notant longe alia quam historia resonat
antedicta.

Tropologia[1] dicitur a "tropos", quod est "virtus", et "logos"—
"sermo", i.e. "sermo de virtutibus"; et hec est quando sensus historialis
seu allegoricus secundum aliquam proprietatem ydiomatis littere refertur
ad virtutes. Cuius sensus est exemplum in epistola antedicta ibi—"Itaque
fratres non sumus ancille filii, sed libere, qua libertate Christus nos
liberavit". Super quo glosa—"Libertas est qua liberati sumus a peccato...".

Anagogia[2] dicitur ab "ana", quod est "sursum", et "goge"...; et
notandum quod anagogia sive sensus anagogicus est quando sensus
literalis, allegoricus seu tropologicus transfertur ad celestia, sicut in dicta
epistola, ubi supra,—"Non sumus filii ancille, sed libere", etc. Glosa—
"Non servi peccati seu legis, sed filii libere", i.e. celestis Ierusalem, de
qua scribitur in eadem epistola—"Ierusalem, que sursum est, libera est
mater nostra". Cuius Ierusalem figura fuit ipsa famosa civitas terrena
Ierusalem....[Thus the name "Jerusalem" comes to signify: tropologically—each good Christian man; anagogically—heaven.]...Ex hiis
premissis sequitur evidenter quod capiens sensum scripture sacre solum
ad literam frequenter incidit in errorem, quia, viz., non intelligit dictos
sensus.

Our preacher, thus armed, now seizes the opportunity to
apply this conclusion of his argument to the two leading theological controversies of the day. For Rypon, as a Benedictine
monk and a preacher of some importance, feels himself naturally
called upon to take the field against the heresy of the Lollards
concerning the Sacrament[3] of the Altar. He must also attack

[1] Ibid. "sence tropologik"—"whan a man redith a story that spekith
moche of myȝti dedis or of gode worchyng, and understondith that he
shuld have stronge gostli dedis of holi lyvyng" (MS. Linc. version—
"that bitokneth wit of vertues").

[2] Ibid. "sence anagogik"—"whan a man undirstondeth an hevenli
thyng bi a bodili thyng seid in story", as, e.g., "Austyn's" heavenly
Jerusalem (MS. Linc. version—"that bitokneth thyng to hope in
blis".

[3] See Preaching in Med. Engl. pp. 137-8 (with quotation from Rypon,
p. 138, n. 1).

the deadly fallacy of the Mendicants concerning Holy Poverty which struck at the *religiosi possessionati* as well as the *curati*, that fallacy, indeed, with which Archbishop Fitzralph of Armagh had wrestled so conspicuously in the pulpit, forty years before.[1] Although the two groups of rivals are not mentioned here by name, we recognize their tenets without any difficulty.[2] Our Benedictine, then, traces the error in both arguments, Lollard and Mendicant alike, to a fatal preoccupation with the literal sense of Scripture. Biblical literalism, therefore, was clearly the mother of heresy. The Letter killed. It was only the Spirit that made alive.[3]

Historic controversies of this kind do not concern us at the moment. But the significance of Master Rypon's argument lies in its triumphant reassertion of the superiority and safety of the allegoric method. Little wonder that the orthodox preachers of his day, sharing this view, maintained a very riot of imagery in their expositions. "Glosyng" of this kind became "a ful glorious thing", as Chaucer's *Sompnour* observed, and a literalist

---

[1] See ibid. pp. 13, 89.

[2] "Qua etiam de causa multi moderni, scripturam sacram nimis grammatice intelligentes, asserunt corpus Christi in altari esse panem materialem, non intendentes ad allegoriam qua ipsemet Christus vocat se panem spiritualem et vivum. Quidam etiam asserunt Christum Jhesum fuisse naturaliter mendicum hominem, quia propheta (Psalm. [cix, 16]) dicit de se—'Persecutus est hominem inopem et mendicum', non videntes quod multa dicuntur de Christo in membris suis quae ipsemet non potuit personaliter exercere, immo nec ad suam personam quomodo libet pertinere, perinde mixtim in scripturis et psalmis et quandoque in eodem psalmo loquitur de sua persona propria, plerumque de suis membris, sicut patet in psalmo, ubi accipitur dictus textus, scil. 'persecutus est, etc.'...", etc., etc.

[3] These passages just given from Rypon's sermon should be of some interest to historians, because they constitute apparently the first evidence, direct from the lips of a contemporary *orthodox* English preacher, substantiating a famous complaint of the Lollards. Hitherto, from the *orthodox* side, so far, we have had only the University *Determinatio* of Master Wm. Butler, actually contemporary with the above (see Miss Deanesly, *Lollard Bible*, pp. 417–8), and the well-known remark in Chaucer's satirical account of the friar's sermon, in the "Somnours Tale" (l. 1794: "For lettre sleeth, so as we clerkes seyn"). See, e.g., Trevelyan, *Engl. in the Age of Wycliffe* (ed. 1920), App. p. 361, and Workman, *John Wyclif*, vol. ii, p. 152.

like Wycliffe might thunder his complaints in vain upon unwilling ears:

Thes wordes of Crist ben scorned of gramariens and devynes. Gramariens and filosophris seien that Crist knewe not his gendris, and bastard dyvynes seien algatis that thes wordis of Crist ben false, and so no wordis of Crist bynden but to the witt that gloseris tellen. But here we seien to these trowauntis that thei blaiberen thus for defaute of witt.[1]

There was certainly nothing to prevent the most divergent interpretations of the same passage, following the current development of Biblical *distinctiones* in the schools from the twelfth century onwards, little better than the improper "fablis" and "narraciouns" criticized in others. Examples in our sermons are all too numerous. An anonymous preacher of the period chooses the same theme[2] as that of Rypon which we have just discussed: "There is a lad here which hath five barley loaves and two fishes".[3] What, then, asks the preacher, first, does the "lad" signify, secondly, "the loaves and fishes", thirdly, "the twelve baskets of fragments"? The "lad" signifies Christ (!), first for his purity of life, secondly for his truth, thirdly for his kindliness. The "loaves" represent either the five wounds of Christ, or David's five smooth stones from the brook, wherewith Goliath was slain. The "two fishes" are the Blessed Virgin and the penitent thief on the cross. The "twelve baskets" are either the twelve Articles of the Creed or the twelve Apostles—"whichever you like". Then follows the Tropology: "Moraliter per istum puerum signatur quilibet justus, qui debet esse sicut puer propter illa tria predicta...". The bread, in its turn, is "hard and austere" like the barley loaf, and must be broken and given to the people by priest and prelate, each of the five loaves symbolizing a separate sacrament or religious act.[4] Similarly, the fishes are subjected

[1] *Select Engl. Works*, ed. Arnold, vol. i, p. 376 (Sermon CXI).

[2] MS. Add. 21253, fol. 60, et seq. Yet another exposition of this theme will be found in a sermon of the vernacular *Festial* of John Myrc, E.E.T.S. ed. p. 103, ll. 26–35.

[3] John vi, 9.

[4] Cf. again, here, fol. 54: The woman who came out of the borders of Tyre and Sidon used as a figure of the soul coming out of sin ("de peccato solo non debet egredi, sed etiam *de finibus* peccati et occasionibus...", etc.).

to a symbolic analysis of their special properties. John Bromyard, amongst all too many specimens of the art,[1] makes highly
satirical use of a famous passage in Isaiah, which, if not quite
so tedious as the former, is no less shocking to the senses.
Corrupt lawyers, he says, fulfil that prophecy of Isaiah: "They
shall beat their swords into ploughshares, and their spears into
pruning-hooks". First, because, instead of using the sword
or spear of justice, which are "straight" weapons—sparing
neither friend nor foe, poor nor powerful, acting with strict
impartiality, moved neither by love nor hate—they choose
"curved" instruments, designed for "earthly" use and for
temporal gain—ploughshares and hooks. So, too, as the curved
reaping-hook, though held in the right hand, is actually manipu-
lated by the "left" (*sinistra*), with this they seek to reap a
"lucrative" harvest, by "crooked" methods. So, again, like
ordinary reapers, you can never move them to take action,
until they see a "harvest" ready waiting for them![2] There is
a certain sensation of amusement to be gained as we watch the
preacher developing his *figure* with the agility of an acrobat
in a circus; but, indeed, little spiritual edification. Absurdity
reaches its monstrous climax with the better-known *Nemo*
sermons, apparently an invention late in the thirteenth century.[3]
It is an absurdity which does not seem to stop short of blas-
phemy at times. The homilist, with an industry that far out-
shines his good taste, collects from a concordance every manage-
able text of Scripture that he can find containing the word
"Nemo" ("No-man" or "No-one"), treats the latter as though
it were the proper name of a person, then strings the texts
together to produce a solemn discourse on his preposterous
imaginary hero, an abstraction thus literally created out of
Nothing! A version of this pulpit monstrosity appears in at
least one English manuscript of our period, along with what is
apparently a University sermon delivered at Cambridge, and

---

[1] Cf. further below pp. 261, 326 n. 2, 403, etc.
[2] *S.P.* s.v. "Justitia".
[3] See here the illuminating Note in Coulton, *From St Francis to Dante*,
App. A, p. 407 n. 13, quoting Denifle, *Archiv für Litt. und Kircheng.
Mitt.* vol. iv, p. 330, and tracing this sermon to one Radulphus, etc.

other homiletic matter of a serious nature.[1] The speaker begins, in equally serious vein, by reminding his learned audience that the greater part of the day has been spent in idleness and vacuity. He now proposes, therefore, to occupy what is left with the word of exhortation:

> There was, beloved, in the days of King Emmanuel, the conqueror of Jerusalem, a certain man outstanding in merits called Nemo by his own people, who, being co-eval with God himself, was—if it may so be said— made equal with Him in power and virtue through all things. For in creation of worldly substance he was most like unto his Son, as being neither created nor born, but proceeding forth....

So, in the course of his amazing career, Nemo ascended into heaven,[2] and visited the Almighty,[3] beholding the hidden mysteries—"secundum illud scripturae testimonium,[4] 'Nemo novit patrem', et ibidem—'Nemo novit filium'". On the testimony of that distinguished prince of the Jews, Nicodemus, we have it that Nemo could do the signs which Christ did,[5] and more marvellous still to relate—dared to do contrary to his Maker, for—"Deus claudit et nemo aperit, et Deus aperit et nemo claudit!"[6] Were it not for the subsequent history of this absurdity and its continued appearance, as here, in unexceptionable company, we should conclude that it was merely a piece of Rabelaisian buffoonery by some coarse satirist of the pulpit, of which examples are to be found even in pre-Reformation England.[7] To such a pass had this juggling with the sacred Text at length brought its devotees.

---

[1] MS. Caius Coll. Camb. 230, fol. 34 et seq. ("Pars Sermonis de Nemine").

[2] John iii, 13 ("Nemo ascendit in cœlum").

[3] Cf. John i, 18 ("Deum nemo vidit").

[4] Matth. xi, 27; Luke x, 22.

[5] John iii, 2 ("Nemo enim potest haec signa facere, quae tu facis").

[6] Apoc. iii, 7.

[7] It may be of interest to compare an English burlesque of this kind —in a MS. of the Adv. Libr. Edinb., printed in Wright and Halliwell, *Reliq. Antiq.* vol. i, p. 81—with the opening of one of our serious sermons:

Burlesque (MS. Adv. Libr. Edinb.): "The helpe and the grace of the grey gose...and all the salt sawsegis that ben sothen in Northefolke upon Seyturdaye, be with hus now at oure begynnyng, and helpe hus

Sermons recorded in the vernacular follow as usual the pattern of those in Latin, although the elaboration of forced expositions is correspondingly rarer, in keeping with their generally less sophisticated character. Favourite incidents naturally reproduce the favourite concordances and moralizations "after the exposition of seynte Gregore"[1] or some other divine. Thus, the "wondirful story" of the Burning Bush pertains to "the moderhed and virginite of oure blessed ladye": "the busche...betokens the moder and maiden enflamed with the speciall grace of the holy gost in consceyvyng and bryngynge forthe oure cheff soveran and lorde god and man".[2] The theme "Abiit Jhesus trans mare Galilee" produces the following typical schema:

> Goostely for to undirstond, Galile is as myche to sey as a passynge here, and be the see is undirstond the world that is fullfilled with many perels. Jhesus Crist "passed the see", for ther touched hym never no synne....And therfore he dud avey oure synnes; and tha[t] is well betokened by the hill that he wente up on; ffor he is worthy to ascende and to clyme, that can amend othur men of ther trespase....[3]

In another sermon of the same series, the creation of Adam, the Nativity of Our Lord, and His Second Coming at the Doom provide "three great Comings", typifying first, "the making of man"; second, "the buying [back] of man"; and third, the Judgment or "demyng" of man.[4] Other examples will be found with ease in the published portion of *Jacob's*

in owre endyng and quyte you of blys and bothe your een, that never schall have endyng. Amen".

Sermon (MS. Roy. 18. B. xxiii, fol. 65): "The helpe and the grace of Almyghty God thorowght tho3 besechynge of ys blessed modur and maydene oure ladye seynt Mary, be with us now at oure begynnynge, helpe us and spede us in alle oure lyvynge, and brynge us to that blis that never shall have endynge. Amen".

Cf. also, Folly's Sermon, in Sir David Lyndesay's *Ane Satyre of the Thrie Estaits*, E.E.T.S. ed. pp. 542–8.

[1] MS. Harl. 2398, fol. 180.

[2] MS. Roy. 18. B. xxiii, fol. 128b. See the interesting little collection of printed references to this figure in general literature of the period made by Miss Morrill, in her edition of the *Spec. of Gy de Warewyke*, E.E.T.S. Ext. S. no. 75, p. cxxi; and F. J. E. Raby, *Hist. of Christian-Lat. Poetry*, p. 369.   [3] fol. 104.   [4] fol. 168 et seq.

Well.[1] A final instance, which still lies buried in manuscript, may be worth adding to our list, with its curious interpretation of a direful passage of the Psalms, now occasionally omitted from the services of the English Church:

Beatus, inquit, qui tenebit et allidet parvulos suos ad petram,[2] that is to seye, "Blessed be he that schal holde and knocke his smale or his ȝonge children to a stoon". ffor ȝe schulle understonde that a mannes workes and his dedes beth as his children, gete and ybrouȝt forthe of his body and his soule to-gedere. Thes beth ycalled smale and ȝong children, while they beth withynne conceyved and not ybrouȝt nor fulfilde out in dede. And than blessed be he that, whan any styrynge of synne cometh into his soule, holdeth hem, that they go no ferre to the dede. But also blessed be he that taketh styrynges, that beth as smale children, and anoon knocketh hem to that ston of ryȝtwysnesse that is Crist Jhesu, the whiche is also stedefast as any stoon, and the which for oure sake was peersched and thurled upon the crosse with scharpe spere.[3]

Who can wonder that such allegorizing provoked in due time not merely the indignation of Reformers, but also the mocking laughter of the Renaissance wits!

So much, then, for the actual method of the expositors. The sacred page had clearly fallen, in the general decadence of preaching, to the mere level of any hand-book of collected Narrations or moralized Properties of Things. Its living historic continuity of thought and action was being ruthlessly ignored. Its various characters and objects were being wrenched from their context, distorted or mutilated into mere passive conveniences for moral dilation, a mere lifeless framework to be set up and arranged, as the preacher pleases, to suit the formal superstructure of his discourse. The reader may well be wondering what feature of such a building could possibly impress the minds of contemporary men of letters. But he must exercise patience a little longer. For the answer is not

[1] Cf. E.E.T.S. ed. p. 228 (interpretation of the Egyptian slain by Moses, and hid in the sand); p. 252 (interpretation of Christ's Ascension from Olivet), etc.
[2] Psalm cxxxvii, 9.
[3] MS. Harl. 2398, fol. 184b: cf. again, in the sermons of MS. Camb. Univ. Libr. Gg. vi. 16, e.g. fol. 56 (what is signified by the "Woman of Canonee", and her daughter, vexed with a devil and delivered by Christ).

far to seek. It will be already clear that one favourite device of this exposition was to select some particular object or objects of the Scripture narrative, and to concentrate on their allegoric significance, irrespective of the part which they play in their particular episode. Thus Bromyard, as we noticed in a previous passage, turned aside to develop the natural symbolism of the ploughshares and pruning-hooks, discussing their shape, their regular usage and their users.[1] Elsewhere we may find him arbitrarily amplifying the symbolic armoury of St Paul's Epistle to the Ephesians[2] to include arrows, spurs, and bit, or developing a curious parallelism of sacred numbers for a like purpose: "As Christ was forty weeks in His Mother's womb, and fasted forty days, and preached forty months, and was dead forty hours, so for forty days after His resurrection He appeared to [His disciples] and continued the teaching which He had given them for forty months by many arguments, being made immortal for forty days" (!).[3] Numbers, indeed, always seem to have exercised a fascination upon the preacher,[4] who thus found convenient *divisions* for his address, with ample scope for his fancy, in twelve symbolic gates of Paradise,[5] five symbolized porches of the pool of Bethesda,[6] or the seven devils expelled from the Magdalene.[7] Jacob's ladder is picked out of its context and discussed allegorically according to its two sides and its seven rungs, its length and height.[8] In the Gospel story of Christ on the Sea of Galilee, after a general interpretation of the meaning of the ship, the sea and the winds, the first-

---

[1] An excellent example will be found, from a late 13th-cent. Franciscan sermon, in Hauréau, *Not. et Extr.* vol. iv, pp. 251–2. Cf. also Bourgain, *La Chaire franç.* pp. 216–19 and 256–8, for 12th-cent. examples.

[2] Ephes. vi, 11–17; *S.P.* s.v. "Arma".

[3] Ibid. s.v. "Ascensio".

[4] See *Preaching in Med. Engl.* p. 322, n. 1.

[5] MS. Add. 21253, fol. 166 ("XII portae—Baptismus, Observatio Mandatorum, Confessio Peccatorum, Penitentia Tribulationum, Fidelitas Credentium, Humilitas Sanctorum, Misericordia Piorum, Puritas Bonorum, Caritas Proximorum, Virtus Justorum, Obedientia Subditorum, Devotio Orationum").

[6] *Jacob's Well*, E.E.T.S. ed. p. 224 (= "V gostly wyttes").

[7] Ibid. p. 185 (= "VII dedly synnes").

[8] Cf. MS. Harl. 2398, fol. 26.

named of the three is selected to undergo this curious treatment: "This ship, namely Penance, should be specially constructed of four kinds of timber, which are—cedar, cypress, palm, and olive-wood". The cedar signifies "Luctus (de peccatis)", because it grows near water; the cypress "Humilitas", because it grows high, that is, it exalts the soul. The palm signifies "Dilatatio (caritatis)", because of its spreading branches; the olive "Opus (pietatis et miserie)", ever "fruitful in the House of God".[1] This type of moralization is therefore recognizable, in every case, as an interesting compound of the purely naturalistic *example* illustrated in the previous chapter, and the Biblical *example* adhering more or less strictly to the narrative of Scripture. It takes its rise from the latter, but develops freely on its own account in accordance with ordinary life and experience.

The symbolic *Ship* will serve, as well as any other of these popular homiletic *figures*, to show how the pulpit here comes eventually to influence the vernacular poet in the construction of his verses. This developed nautical simile, like others of its kind, has had a long and honoured career in medieval preaching. We find it at least as far back as the eleventh century in the preaching of St Anselm.[2] A sermon of twelfth-century date, probably by Master Achard, Abbot of St Victor and later Bishop of Avranches,[3] compares the sea to this present world, salt and bitter, restless, swelling and foul. "To cross that sea we must have a ship, mast, sail, etc. The ship signifies the Faith; the sentences of Holy Scripture are its planks, and the authorities of the Holy Doctors its rudder. The ship is narrow in prow and stern, and broad in the middle; so is the Faith." For it was narrow at the beginning, in the days of Abraham and the Patriarchs; it broadened out at the advent of Christ, and will be narrow once more at the coming of Antichrist;

---

[1] MS. Add. 21253, fols. 29–30. Cf. again, the "Tree of Life", in the *Ayenbite of Inwyt*, E.E.T.S. ed. p. 95, with root, wood, sap, flowers, fruit, etc. and the whole treatment of the well, in *Jacob's Well*.

[2] See J. M. Neale, *Med. Preachers*, pp. 82 et seq. For the Fathers, cf. Tertullian, Hilary of Poitiers, Cassiodorus, Gregory the Great (*Moral.*), etc. (Migne, *Patr. Lat.* i, 1323; ix, 957; lxx, 772; lxxvi, 28).

[3] See Hauréau, *Not. et Extr.* vol. iii, p. 38 (d. 1171).

and so forth. In anonymous English homilies of the same century this imagery of the sea is used again and again,[1] and the ship—where it is mentioned—"is Holy Church, which is in this water of which I speak, that is this wretched world; and it is fast encompassed by storms which are our foul sins and many other tribulations".[2] Repeated use of the theme can be traced in subsequent sermons[3] until we come to the era of recognizable English homilists of the thirteenth and fourteenth centuries like the Oxford Thomist, Thomas Sutton, preaching upon it at the Dominican Friary there in November of the year 1292,[4] or the Dominican orator, John Bromyard, in the following century.[5] The Sea remains invariably "the Sea of this World".[6] But the Good Ship signifies sometimes, as in the case of Bromyard, a type of the Good Man—"good, not because it is painted with gay colours, not because its prow is silvery or golden, nor because it is laden with a royal treasure; but because it is steady and firm, compact and watertight, solid and swift, to meet the oncoming sea".[7] Frequently it becomes again the Ship of the Church, manned by the Prelates.[8] Sometimes—and here we touch a point of future significance—"by the shippe that bereth men up fro the see is undirstond *the gret men of this world*, the wiche supporteth and susteyneth othur in the see of this world, that susteyneth her owne men to overloke and overlede the smale fishes, the trewe pore peple that

---

[1] *Old Engl. Homs.* ed. Morris, E.E.T.S. O.S. no. 53, 2nd Ser., cf. pp. 43, 143, 161, 175–9.

[2] Ibid. p. 43: probably derived from Anselm (cf. above).

[3] Cf. Hauréau, *Not. et Extr.* vol. iv, pp. 171–2, 232, etc.

[4] MS. New Coll. Oxford, 92, fols. 57–9 ("Dedisti in mari viam", cf. Isa. xliii, 16).

[5] Cf. also John Felton, MS. Roy. 6. E. 1, fol. 31b; etc. (15th cent.).

[6] E.g. *S.P.* s.v. "Judices", etc.

[7] *S.P.* s.v. "Homo". Cf. also Rolle's *Psalter* (c. 1326?), ed. Bramley, p. 364, *v.* 27.

[8] Cf. Bromyard, *S.P.* s.v. "Accidia"; MS. Camb. Univ. Libr. Ii. iii. 8, fol. 145 (Thos. Wimbledon?, fl. 1388), as quoted in *Preaching in Med. Engl.* p. 37; *Engl. Metr. Homs.* (mid. 14th cent.), ed. J. Small, Edinb. pp. 135–6; and further below (Alkerton), p. 178. From this use, of course, is developed the idea of the famous *Ship of Fools* of Brandt, Barclay and others.

leveth in the watur of disase".[1] There is one English preacher,
whose name unfortunately cannot be known for certain, but
whom, from the internal evidence of his own quaintly macaronic
discourses, we can safely identify as a monk in the reign of
King Henry V,[2] who for some reason exhibits a peculiar
fondness for this same nautical *figure*. In a sermon upon the
text "*Abiit trans mare*",[3] for example, we have the contemporary ship bravely set forth, with its *forcastel* as the Fear
of God, its body, that is the widest part, as the huge Mercy
of God, its *hynde castel* the Divine Justice, its steersmen the
Clergy—"prelates, clerks and incumbents who have taken
upon them the care of souls".[4] In another, on the theme
"*Dies mei transierunt quasi navis*",[5] the preacher reverts to the
subject of Man. This "great high or grand" ship, that in full
sail "*aȝeynes the tide* of death" "goes *a gret sped, hyyth fast
and abid noȝt*", has Youth for its forecastle, Middle Age for
its "topcastel", and Old Age for its hindcastle. From each of
the latter a banner flies with appropriate device: "And for a
sign that he [Death] is lord and master of this ship, [he] *hath
pich*[6] *upon his baneres* in each castle".[7] Let us now look a
little more closely at yet another of these "naval" discourses,
if only for its own sake. Its theme is taken from a passage in
Ecclesiasticus xliii, 26—"Let them that sail on the sea tell the

---

[1] MS. Roy. 18. B. xxiii, fol. 142 (here referring to Prov. xxx, 19). The
italics are mine. The latter part of the passage is certainly influenced by
Old Engl. Homs. 2nd Ser. (as before), p. 179.

[2] Possibly Jo. Swetstock. In the sermon which is quoted above at
some length, he refers to the Hero of Agincourt as still on the throne,
and also mentions as a recent event the death of (Thomas) Duke of
Clarence (fol. 131: "cuius anime propicietur Deus!"), killed at the
battle of Beaugé, 1421. The discourse, therefore, must be dated c. 1421–2
(cf. also his frequent allusions to the death of Oldcastle, 1417). For his
monastic status, see below p. 84.

[3] MS. Bodl. 649, fols. 60b et seq. (text—John vi, 1).

[4] fol. 62b. Cf. also, fol. 63, "the nedel and the ston" moralized.

[5] fols. 119b et seq. (text—Job ix, 25–6).

[6] I.e. *black* flags.

[7] fol. 121b. That in the hindcastle of Old Age is the celebrated
Vexillum Mortis of the homilists. Finally the *anchor* of Hope in God
is mentioned (fol. 123b). Much of the other imagery is repeated in the
sermon fully quoted in my text.

dangers thereof".[1] "Ur maryner [i.e. Christ] that oftyn hat sailid the see", says our homilist, "clepid us to tell us qwer perelis be."

The great sea that Our Lord passed over is this unstable and turbid world, which like the sea is for ever restless and unstable, full of tempest and storm, strife, dissension *and debates*, full of wind and straits, toil and tribulation, misery and grief. Now it flows through *welth*, riches and prosperities: now it ebbs through *woo, siknes and adversite*: in it there is no assurance, in it no stability; but now *calme*, now *stormy*, now war, now peace, now honour, now *velony*, now *helth*, now infirmity, now *myrth*, now sadness, now *weel*, now *woo*, now *frende*, now *foo*. *Alle bodili myrthes* are mingled with sorrow; all the world's honours are sprinkled with bitterness; *the hier astate, the grettur charge; the hier dignite, the more drede*. In no worldly grade *is ful ioy, quiete and rest*.[2] *Qwo so hath asayed the bitturnes* of this world *may telle of care and soroo*: *qwo so oftyn seilid* upon that sea *may wel tel of perlys*.[3] . . .

What then in short must the sailors do, that they may "*the more saveliche oversaile* the perils of this sea"? Our homilist replies—"Let each one hasten to his ship, while time lasts! Set up within yourself the mast of a Constant Faith and Credulity, *tacle yt to the schip* of Holy Conversation with the ropes of a Good Hope and Compunction of Heart, *wynd up the sail* of a Perfect Love and Charity, *set on the bonettes*[4] of Penance and Almsgiving, as far as you can, *a ful blower of grace*"! Moreover, "let each take the oar of Devout Prayer, *and let us alle roe to-gedir* beseeching that Lord whom the winds and sea obey that he *stirre ur shippe* in the turbid sea, save us from the perils of the world and bring us to the port of Heaven. . . ." This long-winded but picturesque *prologus* develops still further into a lengthy description of the "two arms" of this great sea— one, "welth and prosperite", the other "woo and adversite". So close together do they lie, that the unlucky mariner all too often slips "ffro wele in to woo". The great peril of the former is "the wind of Pride and Ambition"; that of the latter, "the

---

[1] fols. 128b–133 ("Qwo sailet opon the see may oft telle of perlys"). Yet another discourse of the kind appears on fols. 145 et seq. ("Ascendens Jesus in naviculam, transfretavit", Matth. ix, 1).

[2] Cf. below p. 239 (the Wheel of Fortune).　　　[3] = perils.

[4] = small sails. This whole passage occurs also on fol. 119b, in another sermon.

maelstrom of Grief and Despair". To avoid these twin dangers, then, one must "*strike seil* in the first sea" to avoid over-turning, "*and cast ankur* in the second". At last we come, after further amplifications and repetitions, to the core of the whole discourse.[1] The *Ship*, it will be observed, refers no longer to Mankind in general, nor to the Universal Church: it is now the realm of England. And the preacher takes on an aggressively national tone in full keeping with the atmosphere of the times, yet one, as we shall see, that is equally characteristic of much English preaching in the previous century:

A great ship which sailed for many a day in the sea of Prosperity is that plenteous realm, the realm of England. May God, for his Passion's sake, save and preserve it! The forecastle of this ship is the Clergy—prelates, Religious and priests; the hindcastle is the Barony (*baronia*)—the king with his nobles; the body of the ship is the Commons—merchants, craftsmen and labourers. These three are essential parts of the ship: none can afford to be without the other....[2] *Tho topcastel* of this ship is the Saints at rest in this kingdom, by whose alms, merits and prayers she is time and again rescued from perils.... She was formerly a fair and gallant ship; a fair ship she was! Her forecastle, the Clergy, *was pavysid*[3] *with perfeccioun and helines.*[4] *In the hyndecastel, the baronie, was pizt*[5] *a stondard of bodile myzt and hardines.* The body of the ship, the Commons, *was ful frawt* with a great abundance of riches. When our ship *was ful taclid, the thre castelles ful apparailid with stremores and pavys,*[3] *hit was a faire vessel to loke opon, it was a faire schippe!* It was also so stout that the stoutest ship *of toure* upon the sea did not dare to await it. The swift *galeis* of Spain, if they had sighted it upon the sea, would have wanted to have taken flight and to have declined *to abay.*[6] The brave *turyeres* [or *curyeres?*] of Scotland, *as fer as thai myzt se hir* upon the sea, would have wanted [to] a[7] *strike sail* and honoured her. The whole of Christendom once feared and honoured the English for their bravery, their good realm and the good life which they led. While our ship *was stirid* by the helm of Virtue, we sailed the sea *of welth* and *prosperite.* Fortune *was oure frend.* Our honour increased. But immediately that Virtue ceased and Vices began to reign, Fortune changed her countenance. Our honour began to decrease. Our ship *was so feble, so litel oure enmys set of us,* that *the litel fischeres bote of Walis* was on the point *to overseile us.*[8] *Thus, thoroo*

[1] fol. 129 b.

[2] Plutarch is here quoted. For the social grouping, see below in Chap. ix.

[3] I.e. with palisading of shields.   [4] = holiness.

[5] = pitched.   [6] = offer battle.   [7] = have.

[8] I.e. the successes of the Welsh under Owen Glendower, in the reign of Henry IV.

pride and synne, from *prosperite* we sailed *in to* wo. *Mech wo and tribulacion* was in this realm *for synne: many mishappis mownt up* among us: stormes and *debate and dissencion piryyd up fast.* Our ship *was so hurlid and burlid* amid the winds and straits that she was in great peril and often on the point of perishing. She was in great peril when the Commons rose against the Lords:[1] she was in great peril when the lords quarrelled amongst themselves: she was in great peril *at the scharp schowre* of Shrewsbury:[2] she was in great peril when the Lollards rebelled and arose against God and the King *to a*[3] *distroyed him and holichirch.*[4] Our ship was in so great a peril that unless our noble King [had] *set honde on the rather*[5] *and stirid* our ship at the right moment, our ship *had scha[r]plich to a*[3] *go al to wrek. Qwo-so hath seilid the see and a-bidde thes bittur stormys, he may savele telle our schip hath be in perlis:* it was in perils *with-inne,* in perils *with-oute, in perles of oure-selve, in perlis* of enemies, in perils of the high sea, in perils of port. . . .

A long digression follows, based on a famous incident of the Roman siege of Syracuse,[6] when, only by a clever manœuvre on his part, the Roman general managed to free his ships from a great chain drawn by the enemy across the harbour mouth which they had entered.

The great and strong chain which confined *our* ship in port [continues the preacher] is our enemies, the French, the Normans, the Scots, and the Genoese, and their friends in alliance. . .linked against us, like *linkes* in a chain. The chain was cast before our port. Our foes were masters of the sea for many a day, and kept watch so strictly on our port that *ful* few of our mariners chanced to go out for merchandise *or manhad.* Thus the ship of England was shut in for several years, from the time of the last Edward to the time, now, of our own King.[7] Few warlike acts, few *iournays* of honour *wer do opone oure enmys.* And no wonder! for the ancient warriors *were almost weret out;* a tender knighthood had not the use of arms; few lords were left *that my3t knowe and dorst be cheveteyns of an host. Thus we stode destitute* of captains, and honour decreased, until our noble King now took upon himself the steering of the ship, by means of his noble government and prudence. Our ship which for long was shut up in port *sailed out at large.* . . .

So dawns the golden day of relief and victory. With the

[1] The Peasants' Revolt, 1381.
[2] The Battle of Shrewsbury, 1403, following the Revolt of the Percies.
[3] = have.　　　　[4] 1414.　　　　[5] = rudder.
[6] "Sextus Julius [i.e. Frontinus], *de Re Militari, li. primo*".
[7] I.e. from the end of the reign of Edward III to that of Henry V. This would represent roughly the span of the preacher's own life and personal memories.

prayers, litanies and processions of the clergy supporting it, the great campaign at length begins:[1]

The great *carrikkes of Geene*[2] were spoiled upon the sea...[our King] *oversailid* by conquest *the faire barge* of Normandy....At the fierce battle of (*de*) *Achyncourt* he wellnigh oversailed (*supervelificavit*) *the gret cogge* of France. To many dangers our *perles*[3] *prince* exposed himself *for ri3t* of the realm. *Mani bittur stormys hath he abide; many scharp schrowres* hath he sustained for the salvation of our ship; and in all perils God hath preserved him....As he confided in prayers, so did he progress: as *he hath qwyt* God, so God hath recompensed him....In that sea of Prosperity *our maister mariner, oure worthi prince hath sailet many wyntur. He hath be qwirled* upon the wheel of Honour: *much worschip and glory hath fallen to him in a breve tyme.* Many glorious princes *and worthi werrours* were rulers of our ship before the conquest and after. But none with so few folk *passid so terful* a war with the palm of victory as he, at the fierce storm of *Achyncourt*....[4]

But alas! military prowess abroad, apparently, does not go hand in hand with peace and prosperity at home. As usual, the England of the present looks all too dark and degenerate, beside the splendours of her past. When "*we sailid* the high sea *of welth and prosperite,* then there flowed in the realm *a spring flod* of riches...." But now:

qwo-so take hede of the world, *oure qwele is sumquat turned,...oure wele is sumquat wastid. Many myscheves a*[5] *mowntid up* in our days, *also many stormys, dissenciouns hath piriyd up* amongst us. Pestilence and poverty *hath almost overseild us. The stuf* of our ship *is nee delivered.* The riches of our realm are almost *at a grunde ebbe.* And why, think you, is our wheel of Prosperity turned backward? Assuredly, because our spirit goes ill.... The love of the people is turned away from God: devotion *is withdrawe* wellnigh in every rank. Neither Regular nor Secular lives as he ought. Our conversation and mode of living is not as it was. The cloth is of another hue. Our life is not like the life of our fathers of old. *Many brekkes* are in every part of the ship. Neither clergy, nor barony, nor commons can excuse themselves of sin. *Ful slak* many of them were in their life; and therefore *a*[5] *slakid her gode* health and wealth....If sin continues, the ship *goth to wrek*....[6]

[1] So devout is this sovereign that—"cordialius nunquam orabatur pro Christiano principe quam pro ipso, durante tempore guerre".

[2] = galleons of Genoa.

[3] here = peerless, of course (not "perilous", as before).

[4] fol. 132. For the evidences of his piety, we are here told—"Sic ipse augmentavit cultum Dei per fundacionem locorum sanctorum et destructionem lollardorum".

[5] = have.   [6] fols. 132b–133.

Thank God! our sovereign, at all events, has given us the right lead:

> Therefore the master mariner, *oure sovereyn lord*, . . . desiringe from his heart the *wele* and honour of us all, *besied him* by great means to repair *the brekkes* of our ship, *and rere up aȝen* our spirit to God, *that hath stalkid fro him mony day* through vices and sins. . . . Our ship, *ful repaired* through virtue, according to its own desire can *crosse sail* when it pleases, and *savelich* take the sea. . . .
>
> God, *sovereyn lord of lordes, spede him in his iourne,*[1] preserve him from perils, and *increce* his honour, and give us glory so to repair our ship by increase of virtue that *we mow passe* the perils of the sea *and saile* a true course to the port of Heaven. To that port, etc. Amen.

Side by side with this lengthy pulpit effusion, let the reader now consider a poem "on the Death of Edward III", printed among the *Political Poems and Songs* edited by Thomas Wright.[2] This song, composed presumably during the reign of Richard II, has obvious features in common with the much later discourse that we have just been studying. Not only its chosen allegorical *figure*, but its melancholy view of the present and its laudatory view of the past are the same. The poet begins, like the homilist, by deploring a world where "alle thing weres and wasteth away", though here it is the fickleness of human friendship and gratitude that most disturbs him. England was once a great ship:

> Nobel hit was, and heih of tour;
> Thorw al Christendam hit was drad,
> And stif wold stonde in uch a stour, [battle]
> And best dorst byde a scharp schour
> And other stormes smale and grete. . . .[3]

Indeed, our preacher would seem to have these particular verses in mind, since he twice borrows, as we have seen, the phrase "scharp schour" for his own narrative.[4] Knighthood is now significantly reminded of its former prowess against France. With the deceased sovereign as its rudder, "this gode comunes" as its mast, Duke Henry of Lancaster its "barge", and "gode preȝeres" as a following wind in its sails, the ship

[1] Is this a reference to the opening of Henry's third and last campaign in France, in June 1421?
[2] Rolls S. vol. i, pp. liv–v and 215–18.
[3] p. 216.   [4] Cf. above, pp. 73 and 74.

weathers every storm. Now alas! with devoutness and "gode dedes" as forgotten things of the past, a feebler generation holds the national fortunes in its hands.

What, then, are we to gather from a study of the main allegoric element in these two compositions? Had we nothing further than the two to guide us, we might well assume that here was the obvious example of an original piece of secular poetic imagery borrowed to enrich a sermon. The reverse, however, is the truth. All too scarce indeed, as a rule, are the surviving links in the long chain of homiletic tradition; and to-day we cannot choose our evidence just where we please. Nevertheless, in the case of this particular *figure* of the Good Ship, with its long history and its varying paraphernalia through five centuries of preaching, there is evidence enough to dispel the suggested illusion. Holy Scripture and the pulpit, we see, were the real first parents of the whole idea as developed alike in poem and in sacred discourse.[1] The political poet, who, as we shall find later, is often none other than the professional homilist himself, goes naturally to the fountain-head, not of elegant Romantic imagery meet for aristocratic ears, but of the popular imagery employed in the current preaching. Here, to return to our specific example, the "Good Ship" had already proved its seaworthiness in the world long before either our poet or his particular heroes had been dreamt of. The fourteenth-century songster and the fifteenth-century homilist are alike in their debt to this typical product of sacred allegory. Furthermore, we have to note that its vogue in medieval verse of the kind is not limited to a single example. The "Ship of State" reappears in the poem of *Richard the Redeles*,[2] and becomes the main theme of yet another political rhyme of the year 1458, re-adapted in similar fashion to the circumstances of the day.[3] In short, our acquaintance with the literary and secular penetration of the sermon has now begun.

[1] The Ship of State in Horace (*Odes*, i, 14) may have influenced early expositors, or Cicero (*pro Sestio*, 20, 46, etc.), or the like.

[2] See ed. Skeat, E.E.T.S. O.S. no. 54, pp. 502–3, ll. 71–82 (cf. especially e.g. l. 72: "...they bente on a bonet, and bare a topte saile", etc.).

[3] Printed in *Archaeologia*, vol. xxiv, 1842, pp. 326–30. (For date and appreciation, see Kingsford, *Engl. Hist. Lit. in the 15th cent.* p. 245.)

There is a yet more favourite allegoric *figure* of the kind in contemporary literature, which has grown in like fashion from the sacred page and its authoritative exposition. This is the Castle, or Fort. Secular romances might conceivably have suggested the likelihood of its popularity with sermon audiences at one time or another. But the word *castellum*, from its place in the Gospel text of the Vulgate version[1] from which the symbol is drawn, leaves no possible doubt as to its Scriptural origin. Its subsequent development in the sermon is no less grotesque and arbitrary than the manner of its birth. From one of the two texts most freely quoted—"Intravit Jesus in castellum"[2]—there springs at an early date the idea of the Blessed Virgin as a Castle, into which the Saviour entered at His Incarnation, a feudal stronghold protecting Him from the Devil[3] in an otherwise defenceless world. We find this curious imagery employed again as far back as the eleventh century in a noted sermon by St Anselm.[4] Abbot Serlo of Savigny, amongst others, supplies us with a typical example in the twelfth.[5] In the century following the whole idea is further worked out with greater elaboration in the *Chasteau d'Amour* of our own Bishop Grossetête of Lincoln, a work which had an abiding influence on the English pulpit of the last two pre-Reformation centuries.[6] Hence, while other interpretations of the Castle come to hold the field in the later period, this narrower and perhaps older interpretation still makes its appearance in English homilies. Myrc, for example, in a sermon *in die Assumpcionis* in his *Festial*,[7] tells how this Fortress of the Blessed Virgin had for its moat her Meekness, filled with the water of Compassion. Its drawbridge is Discreet Obedience,

[1] Where now we read in A.V., etc.—*village* (ἡ κώμη), the Douai version has *town*.

[2] See Luke x, 38 (the home of Martha and Mary).

[3] Derived from interpretation of Cant. iv, 4 (*Turris David*), etc.

[4] Cf. MSS. Worc. Cath. Libr. F. 132, fol. 118; F. 41; etc.: Hauréau, *Not. et Extr.* vol. ii, pp. 313–4; and Migne, *Patr. Lat.* vol. clviii, col. 644.

[5] See Bourgain, *La Chaire franç.* pp. 254–5 (d. 1158). Cf. Godefridus Admont. *Homil. Festiv.* lxiv (fl. 1137), in Migne, *Patr. Lat.* vol. clxxiv, col. 964, and Ailred of Rievaulx in vol. cxcv, col. 303 (d. 1167).

[6] Cf. here the *Castel of Love*, a 14th-cent. Engl. version, ed. R. F. Weymouth, Philog. Soc. pp. 30–40.   [7] E.E.T.S. pp. 228–30.

its outer rampart Wedlock or Patience, its inner wall Virginity, its gate Faith with the tower of Charity above. The captain of this Castle is the Holy Ghost, and its soldiery the angels. It is significant, however, that Myrc here, like our "nautical" homilist aforementioned who begins a discourse in the same strain,[1] branches off suddenly into a more general application of the simile. The Castle, viewed tropologically, becomes once more the residence of Mary and Martha, now treated as a symbol of Contemplative and Active Life respectively. The author of MS. Bodl. 649, for his part, chooses to convert his Fortress into "the pure and clean Conscience of a man or woman", their virtuous life and honest conversation, a Castle of Virtue, in which the Blessed Mary herself lived, having three symbolic towers, each with its own symbolic gateway.[2] So, indeed, Grossetête himself, apart from the imagery of his *Chasteau d'Amour*, employs the same figure in one of his homilies—delivered appropriately "to the pastors in synod"[3] —for the Sacraments of Holy Church, which "are as the most safe protection of a castle", around whose walls of Confession and Penance flow the waters of Baptism, from whose midst rises the mighty Keep of the Holy Sacrament of the altar, with its seven ascending steps.[4] "With these defences, therefore, you who are spiritual kings, defend your subjects strenuously against the spiritual powers of wickedness, with fasting and alms, offering up, without ceasing, lauds and spiritual hymns. . . ."[5]

---

[1] MS. Bodl. 649, fols. 124 et seq.

[2] fol. 127: "Vis et fortitudo huius castelli in turribus stat tribus. Prima turris est *lownes of hert and mekenes*; 2a turris, *deedes of mercy and almes*; 3a turris, *charite wt-out dowbulnes*. In qualibet turri est porta ad intrandum illud castellum. Porta in turre humilitatis est donum sciencie—*inward knolich of thi self*, consideratio *of thyn owne frelte* . . .", etc.

[3] MS. Bodl. 830, fol. 43.

[4] For this latter, cf. *Castel of Love*, as above, p. 33.

[5] In MS. Harl. 1706 (containing matter attributed to Rich. Rolle) I find mention of a book "cleped *Toure of all Toures*". With the above examples should be compared the well-known *Abbey of the Holy Ghost*, which Miss Allen attributes to the school of Rolle, cf. *Writings ascribed to R. R.* pp. 335–43. An edition (MS. Thornton) will be found in Horstmann, *Yorks. Writers*, vol. i, pp. 321–37. Another in *Rel. Pieces*, ed. Perry, E.E.T.S. O.S. no. 26, pp. 48–58.

Thus far, our symbolic Fortresses have been invariably strongholds of Virtue, a *Civitas Dei* of one kind or another, set up like that of Augustine in a hostile world.[1] Why should not the World itself or Man in his natural state then be likened to a fortress? The allegoric exposition of another text gives us these complementary developments of even greater significance for subsequent English literature. Although, again, as old as St Bernard[2] and current throughout the intervening centuries,[3] Master Rypon shall give us the typical *dilatatio* in question.[4] It springs from a favourite theme for the Palm Sunday sermon: "Ite in castellum quod contra vos est".[5] Here, by interpretation, Christ commands the preacher to go and loose the ass, that is the evil man "bound in the Devil's chains". The "Castellum" signifies "the Castle of Evil Community", says the homilist, or else Man himself in his naturally evil state, with his five senses represented by five gates of the fortress (in which latter circumstance "the ass" stands for the evil soul within it). In other words, then, our Castle is now collectively The World, individually Man, or Mansoul. Some details of its architecture, in the first case, may be gleaned from another sermon of the period:

This castel that he [i.e. Christ] bad hem [the apostles] goo in too, whiche he seith is overe aʒens hem, bitokeneth the falce wor[l]deli men of whiche John speketh in his gospel, seyinge thus—"*Et mundus eum non cognovit*" (Joh. i)....This world mai wel be likenyd to a castel; for rith as a castel is a stronge hoold maad of stones ioyned with lym to kepe oute men with-oute forth, so wickide men confederid to gidir with falce love and evele wille ben strengthid in her malice and kepeth evere goddes word oute of hire soules and hateth the true prechoures therof. The depe diche of stondyng watir that compaceth aboute this castel mai wel be the foule unordynat love that thei hav in her evele....The

---

[1] The Church as *Castle* or *City of God* appears in Bromyard, cf. s.v. "Bellum", "Avaritia", etc.

[2] Cf. Hauréau, *Not. et Extr.* vol. ii, p. 19 ("Mundus est Castellum..."), and *Pricke of Consc.* as referred to below, p. 80, n. 5.

[3] Numerous examples will be found in Hauréau, as above: cf. Nicholas de Aquavilla (13th cent.) in vol. v, p. 41.

[4] MS. Harl. 4894, fol. 1b. Cf. further *Old Engl. Homs.* (12th and 13th cent.), E.E.T.S. O.S. no. 29, p. 7; MS. Add. 21253, fol. 73; etc.

[5] Matth. xxi, 2.

enbatelynge aboute above the walles that maketh hit fair to mannes
siȝte mai wel be her feyned holynesse....[1]

John Bromyard's first conception of the Castle, on the other
hand, is that of the sanctified soul of each individual Man, as
the Castle (*Castrum*) of God. This use of the *figure* of the
"Castle of Mansoul" in English preaching can actually be
traced back to a sermon of the so-called *Lambeth Homilies*
compiled approximately at the end of the twelfth century.[2]
Here Man's five senses represent the defending garrison, and
the Devil manages to creep in through a breach in the walls
which symbolizes Sin. In kindred literature now generally
referred to the same period, the idea is suggested again here
and there in the *Ancren Riwle*[3] and in the "graceful homily"
Sawles Warde.[4] In the fourteenth century it reappears in the
Pricke of Conscience.[5] According to Bromyard the foundation
of the fortress is Faith; its outer wall is Charity; its lofty keep
is Hope; its inner ramparts, the other virtues; its gates, the
Five Senses; its hidden postern, the thoughts of the Heart; its
janitor, the Will; its castellan or constable, the Reason.

I have said, thus, the janitor is the Will, because, whatever may knock
at the gate of Sight or Hearing or the other senses the Will is immediately
on the spot to let in or shut out, that is, what should be shunned or
avoided.[6] If a good thing comes up and the Will desires it, the gate is

[1] MS. Add. 41321, fol. 3.   [2] See E.E.T.S. O.S. no. 29, pp. 22–3.
[3] Cf. pars ii, cap. i (the 5 Senses: the battlements of the Castle; etc.).
For the relations of this work to the *Lambeth Homs.*, see Miss H. E. Allen,
Publ. of Modern Lang. Assoc. of Amer. vol. xliv, Sept. 1929, pp. 679–80.
[4] See *Old Engl. Homs.* 1st Ser. pt. ii, E.E.T.S. O.S. no. 34, p. 249.
Cf. also pp. 127, 153, etc. of the same series.
[5] Definitely here quoting "Saynt Bernard" (*Bonum castrum custodit
qui corpus suum custodit*): ed. Philog. Soc. p. 158, ll. 5820–9. Again, in the
Ayenbite of Inwyt, pp. 154, 157, 204 (quoting St Gregory), 249, etc.
[6] With this treatment of the "Castle" should be directly compared
that of the *Abbey of the Holy Ghost* aforementioned—its symbolic cloister,
chapter-house, frater, chapel, dorter, infirmary, cellar, etc., and its lady
Abbess (Charity), prioress (Wisdom), sub-prioress, chantress, reader,
almoner, purveyor, cellaress, etc., etc. Here the lady janitor, or porter,
is "Dread"—"that kepis besyly the cloyster of the herte and of the
conscience, that chases owte alle unthewes, and calles in alle gud vertus,
and so speres the ȝatis of the cloyster and the wyndows that none evylle
hafe none ingate to the herte, thorowe the ȝatis of the mouthe, ne thorowe
the wyndows of the eghne, nere of the eris..." (ed. Horstmann, pp. 329–
30; ed. E.E.T.S. p. 53).

opened to God; if evil, and the Will desires that, the Devil is let in. And therefore the gate should not be opened too hurriedly. But as, when anyone knocks at gate or postern and may not be recognized—especially in time of war—the janitor runs to the guard of the castle to find out if he ought to open it or not, so when Pleasures or Delights or things Angry or Vengeful present themselves to the Will, whether at the gate of the Senses, or the postern of the Heart, the Will ought not to open immediately, in seeking that thing or showing agreement with it or desire for it. For this is exceedingly dangerous, in time of spiritual warfare. For many traitors knock, and enemies of the Soul, desiring to capture the Castle of the Soul and shut God out, and hand it over to the Devil.... So, too, I called the postern the thoughts of the Heart, because, as in a castle or city, when the great gates are shut and guarded, sometimes the way in or out lies open at the postern, where the city is either defended and guarded or lost, so when the other external senses and actions are in suspense, good thoughts or evil enter the Castle of the Soul secretly, by way of the Heart. Whence sometimes the Soul is defended and fortified, sometimes lost. That castle God created so strong, and placed officers in it so well, that neither Hell, nor the World, nor demons, nor men can capture or conquer it, unless it is betrayed from inside.[1]

Bishop Repingdon, in his turn, provides another little sketch of the Castle gate, equally vivid in its way.

The gateway of the Soul [he says] has two doors and a postern. The first door is Lack of the Divine Vision, the second is Punishment of Eternal Damnation, the postern the Worm of Conscience which dies not. Therefore, when the enemies of the Soul attack, that is, the Devil with his army of Vices, Fear does the work of the porters and shuts up those gates to prevent the enemies of the Soul from entering, saying—"On no account shall you enter; lest perchance my lord, through you, be deprived of the Vision of God and be tortured by eternal fire". Thus "*The fear of the Lord driveth out sin*", Ecclesiasticus i [*v*. 27].[2]

God then, like any medieval monarch of the times, has his chain of fortresses scattered through the land. His old enemy, the Devil, therefore must have his strongholds also. Having described the "Castle of God", Bromyard proceeds to give us an equally detailed account of "the Devil's Castle", "which has many castellans, and many more hastening thereto". In this fort stands the tower of Vanity and Pride, bristling with

---

[1] *S.P.* s.v. "Anima". Cf. again *Jacob's Well*, p. 292: "He is a tretour, for he betrayeth god whanne he ʒeldyth to the feend, that is goddys most enmye, that castel of his herte the whiche god took hym to kepe".
[2] MS. Jo. Ryl. Libr. Manch. Lat. 367, fol. 240.

occupants. These can be recognized at once by their bodily appearance and distinctive clothing. They wear the long fashionable beards and "dagged" garments[1] of the period, "such as are seen at tournaments, and the like". The office of justiciar in this fortress is held by Anger; for there, in all matters of justice and revenge there is more of Anger than Reason, as the dependents of the rich know to their cost. The treasurer is the sin of Greed,[2] like the manorial officials beloved of lords, "who know well how to get much and give little in return, how to give tallies for food and extort heavy compensation". Gluttony holds the office of Master of the Kitchen[3]—"and he is a wondrous cook, because he poisons many. For more die of his food than by the sword, as from 'late suppers', and irregularities of the like". Lust holds great hospitality in this fortress, and its chamberlain is the sin of Sloth, "who draws the curtains and makes men lie for long in wantonness,[4] and makes priests to celebrate after midday, fearing more to give offence to their lords than to God". To this realistic picture of the fortress, our homilists add each their own little naïve touches. It was clearly a subject that gave scope for the growing realism of their style.

> But now I intend [says one of them] to tell you about the Devil's Castle, which he is building in our realm with the help and favour of these aforesaid [sinners]. And it is a fortress of wondrous magnitude and strength, and impregnable. Its walls are of sinners hardened in their vices; for the walls of this fortress are thus constructed, as it were, of the hardest stone.... The cement with which its stones are joined together is the colligation of Impiety.[5] And that cement is put on quickly, heated, that is to say, in the fire of Inordinate Affection. The moat sur-

---

1 "In vestibus ex transverso scissis." Cf. below, p. 408.
2 In the *Abbey of the Holy Ghost*, the treasurer is Discretion.
3 In the *Abbey*, the cook is Penance.
4 MS. Roy. 7. E. iv version uses the French word *paylarder* here.
5 Similarly in MS. Jo. Ryl. Libr. Manch. Lat. 367, fol. 199b ("Muri ex obduracionibus in malicia constituuntur....Cementum vel bitumen est colligacio impietatis vel turpis amor..."). With this, contrast the *Abbey of the H.G.* with its river site, its stone walls made of "almes dedes and werkes of mercy and holy werkes, that sall be bowndene togedir with qwyke lyme of lufe and stedfaste byleve" and "syment" of the Love of God and True Belief.

rounding the fort is Avarice.... The water which flows in it around the fort is of great quantity, foul and perilous; and it is the water of Carnal Lust. And in the middle of the fortress is a very lofty tower, namely the tower of Pride.... Within this castle resides the Prince of Darkness with a great army. At that castle all traitors of king and country have refuge, all false perjurers, yea, and all transgressors of the law. From that castle, the King of Pride sends forth from day to day his infernal knights and also his mercenaries, namely, the false Christians of our country, who become his mercenaries and servants. And these encompass our realm, plundering and destroying....[1]

Another supplies, for example, some further details about the castle moat. The frogs croaking in its "filthy water" are the gluttons, the lustful and other ribalds. Into it, we are informed, tumble a large part of the invading host sent to capture the fortress, there to be miserably drowned. Such are the prelates of the Church who "live more delicately and more voluptuously than secular princes". "The mound on which this fortress is built is the ground and matter of the state of pride, such as riches, honours and the like."[2] So, then, the relentless tide of warfare rolls between stronghold and stronghold. The world itself is a mere battleground for the forces of Good and Evil; and the din of the fighting rises even to the very gates and towers of Heaven. The Celestial Fortress itself suffereth violence. But "neither men nor demons can reach it by any artifice. None-the-less the saints set up the machines of Thoughts, shoot out the arrows of their Sighs, despatch the messengers of their Prayers, hurl forth the stones of Good Works, and thus wound the phalanxes of the skies".[3]

To illustrate every use to which this ever popular *figure* was put in the sermons of our period would be an overwhelming and unnecessary task. As will be seen already, the range of its possible applications, for the homilist, was wellnigh inexhaustible. Thus, in a sermon to Religious, the Castle of Righteousness can become conveniently enough "the Castle

[1] MS. Camb. Univ. Libr. Ii. iii. 8, fol. 150 (Wimbledon?).
[2] MS. Jo. Ryl. Libr. Manch. Lat. 367, fol. 199b (Repingdon). Cf. further, *Ayenb. of Inwyt*, as below, p. 438.
[3] MS. Winch. Cath. Libr. xi, Sermon for the 23rd Sunday after Trinity, dealing with the Holy War (*Sermones de temp.* 15th cent.).

of Religion", in the narrower, monastic sense of that term.[1] The Devil's Fortress, on the other hand, by the kindly fortune of History, provides excellent scope for an attack on the iniquities of current heresy. "The Castle of Sin and Misery, the Devil's Castle" is now—

Oldcastell and his sect,[2] who were leagued in malice and were united against the Lord God, against our noble King and the ministers of Holy Church. *The sowdioures* of this *synful* fortress made many sharp attacks upon the fort of God. First, they shot the arrows of many wicked words at the poor friars. They slandered and rebuked their poverty and the Order which the Church approves, concerning which many excellent clerics, many perfect priests and virtuous men say that it is a great charity to succour and support them—whatever Lollards may gabble (garriant) to the contrary. Afterwards, *thai cast a myne* at the tower of the Possessioners; they dug deep for the Church's treasure; they made terms with temporal lords to take away our livelihood; they toiled beyond their strength to seize our possessions;[3] they made light of the Church's excommunications and censures, they threw conscience to the winds[4].... They hurled the machines of their malice at the fortress of Christ in this realm, but much more disastrously around *Prage* in the Kingdom of Bohemia, so it is said.... The strength and valour of this sinful castle terrified the hearts of many brave men. It began to be so strong in this kingdom that, if our liege lord had not made a timely and a manly attack upon it, it would in very truth by that time have either conquered or plundered the realm, according to men's reckoning.[5]

In the fourteenth and fifteenth centuries, such symbolic Castles were clearly nothing less than commonplaces of the pulpit. Here, then, we have before us at last the true prototype, not only of Langland's "Toure" of Truth and "Castel of Care" (or Falsehood) in the first *Vision of Piers Plowman*, but also of his "Castel of Kynde" in *Dowel*, and further, amongst

---

[1] MS. Add. 21253, fols. 146 et seq. (text—Luke xvii, 12: cont.—"In castellum religionis...qui vult venire ad visionem fraterne pacis debet intrare. Muri istius castelli sunt bona opera, ut vigilie, abstinentie, orationes devote et lacrime; et huius castelli custodes sunt angeli Dei..."). Similarly, the *Ship* in the *Pèlerinage* of De Guileville becomes the Ship of Religion, i.e. of Monastic Life.

[2] I.e. the Lollards, of course. Punning upon names was a recognized device of the medieval pulpit. Cf. *Preaching in Med. Engl.* p. 329 etc.

[3] It is these phrases that suggest that our preacher was a monk.

[4] Literally here—"to the cock" (*ad gallum*).

[5] MS. Bodl. 649, fol. 125. Cf. also the Castle of Lechery, *Hand. Synne,* p. 243; and the Castle of the Tavern, as below, p. 438.

miracle and morality plays, of "Maudelyn" Castle in the
Digby Mysteries and the *Castell of Perseverance* itself.[1] Likewise, there is actually extant a vernacular poem of the period
"against the Lollards", treating the name Oldcastle in precisely
the same punning fashion as in the sermon just quoted.[2] In
later post-Reformation times, the figure reappears as Bunyan's
"Mansoul" in *The Holy War made by Shaddai upon Diabolus*;
and its influence may possibly be traced in the Palace Beautiful
of his more famous *Pilgrim's Progress*. In the Middle Ages,
at all events, writers of popular allegoric verse and drama went
to no exalted sources, to no elegant *trouvère* or hoary commentator for their apparatus and ideas. To trace their Castles
and their Ships to the *Roman de la Rose* or some other work
of romance is wholly gratuitous and absurd.[3] They drew them
naturally, let it be repeated, from the very phrases of popular
homiletic discussion circulating around them, whence came,
as we shall see, much else that is characteristic of their
repertory.

Beings in human form, as well as inanimate objects, may
play their part as the centre of interest in these expanded
allegoric scenes. Accordingly, two curious outgrowths from
Scripture of this other kind now call for our attention, before
the subject of religious allegory is left. For they, too, are equally
responsible in their way for some well-known allegorical scenes
in the literature that has been mentioned. When Courthope
informs us that Langland and the author of the *Coventry
Mystery* are "the first to adopt a style of allegory" in which
"real personages are represented under the guise of abstrac-

---

[1] Cf. further, e.g., the allegoric Castle in Barclay's (?) *Castell of Labour*,
Wm. Nevill's *Castle of Pleasure* and Gavin Douglas' *Palice of Honour*,
and the House of Temperance in Spenser's *Faerie Queene*.

[2] Printed in Wright, *Pol. Poems and Songs*, Rolls S. vol. ii, pp. 244–5.

[3] Sir Edmund Chambers' quandary in his *Med. Stage* (vol. ii, p. 151,
n. 4) is here most illuminating. He strives to argue for the influence of
the Romances, but is forced to admit—"There is not much direct imitation of the *Roman de la Rose* in the moralities...". Equally pointless,
of course, are the attempts of Jusserand (*Piers Plowman*, p. 40) and
Courthope (*Hist. of Engl. Poetry*, vol. i, pp. 238–9, following Skeat)
to argue that Langland derived the allegoric *figures* of his poem from
medieval religious drama. The witness of the sermons explains both cases.

tions",[1] we must not take his words too seriously. He means, of course, what every historian of our literature means, namely —first among the writers of his own particular acquaintance. We have already had examples from the pen of Bromyard of Moral Senses and Vices introduced to us in the very real and lively persons of the Castle Porter, the Castle Constable, the Castle Chamberlain, the Castle Cook, and so forth. These in their turn clearly hark back to an earlier homiletic usage of the kind, corresponding to the inmates of Rolle's(?) *Abbey of the Holy Ghost* and the early thirteenth-century *Sawles Warde*, two works that alone serve to refute the Professor's statement. Into the early history of the personification of different Virtues and Vices it is unnecessary to enter here.[2] We notice with interest, however, in passing, the continued popularity of "Boyicius, the grete clerke in hys time",[3] in our later sermons. We recall that Alain de Lille, "Doctor Universalis", who, with the aforenamed, figures in the pages of Courthope[4] as one of the parents of medieval allegoric personification, was a leading master of the pulpit in his own day, and exercised an undying influence upon it throughout the Middle Ages by means of his ever popular *Summa de Arte Predicatoria*.[5] We notice even a reference by name to the primitive "Prudentius, in sua Sicomachia"—"the first poetical product" of the new type of Christian allegory—in a vernacular Worcester homily of the fifteenth century.[6] The pulpit is closely concerned with them all. No doubt, it was not the Bible in the first instance, but some deeper and more ancient racial attachment to folk-lore and pagan demonology that gave rise to these spiritual abstractions, and endowed them with a history of their own. When

---

[1] *Hist. of Engl. Poetry*, vol. i, p. 423.
[2] For classical influences of the kind active in our literature, cf. above, pp. 52–3, and below, p. 184, n. 6, p. 450, n. 1, etc.
[3] MS. Linc. Cath. Libr. A. 6. 2, fol. 176.
[4] *Hist. of Engl. Poetry*, vol. i, pp. 46–7. Alain's work here referred to, the *De Planctu Naturae*, will be found quoted in Bromyard (cf. s.v. "Munus", § 11; etc.).
[5] Cf. Bourgain, *La Chaire franç.* p. 88, etc., Hauréau, *Not. et Extr.* vol. i, pp. 274, etc., and my *Preaching in Med. Engl.* p. 315.
[6] MS. Worc. Cath. Libr. F. 10, fol. 48.

the Christian homilist points us to some passage of Scripture for their justification, we need not consider that he is pointing us to their real birth-place; any more than in the case of Durandus who expounds so convincingly in his *Rationale* the symbolic basis of the Christian architectural plan. Both expositors are waxing wise after the event. Nevertheless, that subsequent development of the allegoric abstractions in our native literature, in which the abstract figure is made to appear as a living, realistic personality, can safely be attributed to the influence of the pulpit.

The realism of sermon portraiture has already been emphasized. Writers of pulpit manuals and treatises, from the thirteenth century onwards, were accustomed to illustrate each separate "branch" of Vice or Virtue, treated in turn, with precisely such vivid little sketches of contemporary men and women and their ways. Thus grew up a natural tendency to identify topic with illustration, and blend them into one. At length, with the increasing popularity of sermon satire and realism, the Abstraction itself became a living person, known and recognised by all men. The Vices themselves now strutted upon the scene as well-known types and characters of the tavern or the market-place. The Virtues appeared in the guise of noble women of the times.[1] The growth of the former in this fashion from the homilist's page has a peculiar significance for the study of Langland's famous *Vision*. For it gives us a fresh clue to the poet's method of working; and thereby, from his own quaint efforts in verse, further insight into the history of this literary feature at an interesting stage in its career. Langland begins by adopting as his leading allegoric characters of Evil precisely those which were already fashioned and familiar in the homily-books. His next task is to apply them, in the time-honoured fashion, to the various classes of society for which they were held to be peculiarly appropriate. This he does in two distinct ways. The more conservative plan that he pursues for some characters is to make them visit in turn and consort with the different peoples in question. The

[1] On rarer occasions, *men* of the ruling class: cf. Bozon, *Metaphs.* cap. iii, and fonts at Stanton Fitzwarren and Southrop.

activities of the Lady *Mede* and of *Wrath* are two outstanding illustrations of this category. With others, however, he goes a step further, making instead the characters themselves play the part of the evil folk who are concerned with them in real life. But, as though this more original step proved too difficult an undertaking for the pioneer at so experimental a stage, Langland finds himself compelled apparently to leave some of these characters quite inadequately harmonized or unified, in the latter case.[1] Now it is a curious fact that not even Professor Skeat has realized how alternating are the personalities of some of the Seven Deadly Sins as thus portrayed in the *Vision*.[2] Whereas he imagined, for example, that *Sleuthe* is and remains a priest throughout the section devoted to *Accidia*, careful inspection of the verses will show that such a view is impossible.[3] Here, indeed, the Vice first comes before us as a layman, then transforms himself without warning into the slothful parson, and as quickly returns back later into his

---

[1] A more or less *successful* example can be seen, I think, in the case of *Coveytise* (*Avaritia*). Here a passage (C text, pass. vii, ll. 267–71) which in the homilies concerns the labouring husbandman (cf. below, p. 367) is worked into the life history of one who is clearly a merchant. Even here it is a rough and ready way of solving the problem (as though so wealthy a merchant prince—cf. ll. 247–52—would do his own ploughing!). Lady *Mede* really belongs in part to *both* categories. The one dazzling achievement in this *second* category is the creation of *Piers Plowman* himself, impersonation of the Virtues (see below, pp. 571–4).

[2] The case which Skeat *has* noted, of course, is that of *Pride* in the C text version, where the first part concerns a female character (Pernel Proud-heart), and the second a male character (a kind of sustained Haukyn). See his *Notes to Texts*, E.E.T.S. ed. pt. iv, § 1, pp. 103–4. Here, too, the poet is really individualizing or "personifying" two different characteristic types of homiletic treatment of the subject (cf. below in Chaps. VI and VII).

[3] Skeat's view is definitely set forth in his own Preface, q.v. Let us now look at the Poem itself here, e.g. B text, pass. v, ll. 392–468. From ll. 399 to 421, at all events, Sloth must be a layman: cf. l. 401—"as *the prest* it syngeth" (the layman had to know how to say his Paternoster correctly), l. 405—"as *the prest* me hi3te", etc. And would the parish priest "go to the freres", indeed? From ll. 422 to 428, he is clearly a priest. Then probably from ll. 429 onwards he is a layman again; at all events as a Penitent. For, cf. l. 460—"And *heren* matines and masse" (this is not the faithful parish priest's duty: he has to *say* them).

original form. It is an interesting case where the imagination of the artist is not yet fully freed from the formal didactic procedure of the homily-book which he thus clumsily adopts.[1] For we can actually trace these very changes in a typical specimen of the latter, as its homilist-author proceeds to deal in turn with the several "ramifications" of Sloth.[2] The butterfly has not yet emerged fully from its chrysalis. We are in fact actually watching the process of emergence. Finally, the old moralized animals of the Bestiary—itself "meines Erachtens aus der allegorischen Erklärung der Bibel erwachsen"[3] clearly lent their influence in the same direction. The particular beast and the particular Vice or Virtue reflected in its nature had but to change their respective positions upon the page, as it were, and the Vice or Virtue itself became a beast. In the *Ancren Riwle* this transformation has already taken place.[4] Had not the very Scriptures themselves lent weight to the idea of such a metamorphosis, when, at the divine command, evil spirits became swine? While it remains true to say that the more or less free and unstilted type of allegoric being is not prominent in our literature before the second half of the fourteenth century, it must have been already familiar enough in the pulpits when John Bromyard set about the compiling of his *Summa Predicantium*.[5] In another of his little graphic dilations, he depicts the sinner as a horseman galloping to Hell from stage to stage of the journey of Life: and the Vices are his steeds. When one Vice has been exhausted, the rider leaps upon the back of another ready waiting for him, and is

[1] And throws a remarkable new light on the famous "confusions" or "discursiveness" of the poem. For the sources of some other characters in the *Vision*, see below, pp. 278–9, 371–2, etc.

[2] MS. Harl. 2398, fols. 27–27b. The relevant passages will be found quoted (in part) below, on pp. 278, n. 2 and 436–7. After referring to typical lay sins of "men and women" that "synnyth in sleuthe", the homilist goes on—"Sleuthe maketh a man of holy churche...". Having concluded this passage, he continues again—"Sleuthe maketh wor[l]dliche men for3eme...", etc.

[3] A. Ebert, *Allgem. Gesch. der Liter. des Mittelalters*, bd. iii, p. 76.

[4] Pt. iv, ed. Jas. Morton, King's Classics, pp. 148–58.

[5] Animal types are exceedingly common here.

off again. "When the horse of Gluttony is weary, Lust takes its place; and so Theft and Homicide" and the rest, to the journey's end.[1] The reader will have to wait until the chapters on Sermon Satire for the full story of this achievement, so widely reflected in the *Summa*.

There is a well-known verse in the Book of Psalms (lxxxv, 10), reading as follows: "Mercy and truth are met together; righteousness and peace have kissed each other", in which the personification of Virtues seems to find an unmistakable place in the very pages of Holy Writ. Early allegorists and commentators of the Middle Ages must have seized upon it with delight, as a valuable stimulus for the development of their fancy along these same lines. At all events, by the twelfth century, this apparently innocent outburst of Jewish poetic fervour had been expanded into an elaborate disputation between the four Sister-Virtues in the presence of God, concerning the Fall of Adam and the plan of future redemption for mankind through Christ, following an example already set by the Jewish *Midrash*. Thus we find it in a commentary by Hugh of St Victor;[2] in twelfth-century sermons attributed to St Bernard,[3] Werner von Ellersbach,[4] Peter Comestor[5] and Stephen of Tournay;[6] also in an English tract on *Vices and Virtues*,[7] and in two twelfth-century pieces of French dramatic verse, at least one of which has been ascribed to another distinguished preacher, Archbishop Stephen Langton.[8] With the addition of a footnote reference to Bishop Grossetête's *Chasteau d'Amour*, however, these two French metrical pieces

[1] S.v. "Adulterium" (cf. "Ambulo").
[2] *Adnot. in quosdam Psalmos David*, cap. lxiii (Migne, *Patr. Lat.* vol. clxxvii, cols. 623–5).
[3] *in Festo Annunc. B.M.V.* A.D. 1140 (Migne, clxxxiii, 383–90).
[4] c. 1121 (Abbot of St Blasien). See Miss Hope Traver, *The Four Daughters of God...*, Bryn Mawr Coll. Mon. vol. vi, 1907, p. 12.
[5] *de Adv. Dom.* (Migne, cxcviii, 1736–7).
[6] See Hauréau, *Not. et Extr.* vols. iii, p. 260, iv, p. 6, v, p. 137.
[7] c. 1200. E.E.T.S. ed. O.S. 89, pp. 112–6.
[8] The theory of Stephen Langton's authorship, repeated by Chambers, is probably due to a confusion, I think, with the Stephen of Tournay above-mentioned. See, in this connection, Hauréau, *Not. et Extr.* as above. Cf. MS. Arund. 292, fol. 25.

are the only sources which Sir Edmund Chambers mentions[1] in his account of what appears eventually as an episode of the *Ludus Coventriae*. Once again, then, both the homiletic origin and also the vital link—or "special channel", to use Chambers' own phrase—between early exposition and later morality-play appear to have been entirely overlooked. For the prevalence of this quaint scene is due to the pulpit. Homiletic favourites of the thirteenth and fourteenth centuries, like the aforesaid *Chasteau d'Amour*, the *Meditationes Vitae Christi*, once attributed to St Bonaventura, and the *Cursor Mundi*,[2] all helped in the work of popularizing this allegoric "interlude" of the Four Virtues for the benefit of English sermon audiences. As we shall find in the case of the still more curious allegoric expansion that follows, certain marked variations of the original developed scene occur, as it circulates in the sermon-books from generation to generation. There is eventually discernible a tendency to secularize the allegory, making it appear as an incident in history or in fable wholly unconnected with its Scriptural origins. Thus, in the Anglo-Latin versions of the popular *Gesta Romanorum*, the four celestial sisters "contend for the fate of a criminal, and their brother Usyas releases him from prison".[3] In a Latin sermon for the Third Sunday in Advent, occurring in an English series of the fifteenth century,[4] the story takes a somewhat similar turn. A late example of the full "Disputation" scene, however, in its purer and more theological form, will be found in a Scottish homiletic treatise on the Lord's Prayer, Ave, and Creed, known as the *Meroure of Wyssdome*, completed in the year 1490 by one John Irlande.[5] Herein, then, lies the clue to its still more noteworthy reappearance in literature which has for long commanded the

---

[1] *Med. Stage*, vol. ii, p. 152.
[2] See E.E.T.S. ed. Morris, pp. 548–60. Cf. further, MSS. Harl. 5235, fol. 122, Add. 34763, fol. 63 (14th cent.); etc.; and in France, the *Summa* of Peter of Poitiers (?), 13th cent., MSS. Bibl. Nat. Paris 14886 and 5556, as quoted in Hauréau, *Not. et Extr.* vol. iii, pp. 260–3.
[3] J. A. Herbert, *Cat. of Romances in B.M.* vol. iii, p. 205, describing MS. Harl. 5259, fol. 46b.   [4] MS. Roy. 8. F. vi, fol. 4b.
[5] See the Scottish Text Soc. ed. vol. i, chaps. IX and X, and my Notice in the *Mod. Lang. Rev.* for Oct. 1927, pp. 459–60.

attention of scholars. For it is also the famous allegoric "interlude" of Passus XXI of *Piers Plowman's Vision*, of the *Coventry Cycle* of Plays and the *Castell of Perseverance*, of Lydgate's *Court of Sapience*, *Life of St Mary* and poem on *The Prospect of Peace*. In performances of the *Castell of Perseverance*, we are told, "the iiii dowters schul be clad in mentelys, Mercy in wyth, Rythwysnesse in red al togedyr, Trewthe in sad grene, and Pes al in blake, and they schul pleye in the place al togedyr, tyl they brynge up the sowle".[1] The Virtues of St Bernard's homily have thus become figures upon the stage as vivid and resplendent as Brunnhilde and Fricka in Wotan's heavenly courts. Indeed, the early fourteenth-century *Alphabetum Narrationum* of Arnold of Liège, a work held in the highest esteem by our English preachers, tells how a certain scholar at Bologna had actually beheld the good ladies in a vision, a century earlier, and in his extremity had been advised by one of them to become a Dominican.[2] Such vivid personalities had they developed already in the first years of mendicant preaching!

That primitive instinct which still led men to dwell, in the Middle Ages, upon a celestial hierarchy, in which not merely apostle and martyr, archangel and angel, saint and preacher in glory now have their appointed place, but even apparently a "Nemo" and the very Virtues in human form, sustained interest also in a diabolic hierarchy, with its corresponding "feudal" orders of evil spirits. Whatever may be said of their pagan origin, as the English preachers remind us, it was Holy Scripture itself that justified belief in the strange power of these monsters over men and the beasts. While Bromyard can speak upon the authority of St James of the one good trait which devils possess, namely, that they "also believe and tremble",[3] others refer to the indisputable Gospel evidence of the herd of swine, that at Our Lord's command, "with grette myghte

[1] For pictorial representations of the four Sister-Virtues in medieval *Art*, see Émile Mâle, *L'Art relig. de la fin du moy. âge*, pp. 43–6. (M. Mâle dates their prominent appearance in MS. illuminations from about the beginning of the fifteenth century.)

[2] MS. Harl. 268, fol. 150. Also in Bromyard, *S.P.* s.v. "Misericordia."

[3] *S.P.* s.v. "Obedientia" (see Jas. ii, 19).

of the fendes, ranne in-to the see".[1] "In signe", explains one, "that of hem that are lyche hoggys in glotonye, the feendys have powere to dwellyn in hem, and to drenchen hem in the se of helle."[2] Nowhere are the effects of this extravagant but familiar dualism more clearly visible than in the sermons before us. God has his Castle; so then must the Devil, as we saw. God has his apostles; the Devil therefore must have his "twelve", as our study of Satire will reveal. God has his faithful "hounds"; so also has the Devil.[3] God has his churches where he is worshipped with hymn and rite. The Fiend has his church, too, the tavern, whither the musician's drum or viol summons his worshippers to their strange rites of intoxication, and so on.[4] From the four symbolic Daughters of God, therefore, the preacher will proceed as naturally to the corresponding progeny of the Evil One, as indeed from Virtue to corresponding Vice. In an article in the *Journal des Savants*[5] Barthélemy Hauréau has made some observations on an allegoric narration concerning the Daughters of the Devil which frequently occurs in French sermons of the thirteenth century. He traces it to an apocryphal legend which tells how Satan, before his exclusion from Heaven, married Iniquity. We should imagine that this female abstraction, original Queen of Hell, "Babylon the Great", became the mother of Anti-Christ; and, no doubt, she did, where a more ruthless clerical wit did not prefer to say that that personage would be born of a nun and a friar![6] However, in the legend in question, she gave birth to daughters, the number varying, according to different accounts, from six to nine. These were the Vices, Deadly Sins and others—Pride, Simony, Hypocrisy, Rapine, Usury, Fraud,

[1] MS. Roy. 18. B. xxiii, fol. 84.
[2] *Jacob's Well*, p. 141. Cf. also, the "Marye Mawdelen" incident referred to, p. 185 (see Luke viii, 2).
[3] The version given by Nicholas Bozon in his *Metaphors*, cap. xxii, of the eight hunting dogs of the Devil, representing eight Vices which pursue various classes of society, offers a curious parallel to the Devil's daughters about to be described.
[4] Cf. below, p. 438.   [5] Vol. for 1884, pp. 225–8.
[6] "He xulde be begotyn of a frere and born of a nune, as folkys have tolde." MS. Stowe, 953. Cf. also, Wright, *Hist. of Caric.* p. 252.

False-service, Sacrilege, Lust. The final stage of the story is concerned with the marriage of these ladies to various appropriate classes of society. Thus, Usury is usually wedded to the burghers, Fraud to the merchants, Sacrilege to the peasants, and so forth. The earliest reference to this legend which M. Hauréau was able to find occurs apparently in the *Speculum Ecclesiae* of the Welshman Giraldus Cambrensis.[1] As a matter of fact the same story is given in his *Itinerarium Cambriae*[2] also. Good master Fulk de Neuilly, annoyed at the persistent refusal of King Richard I of England to come to terms with the King of France, says to the stubborn monarch: "King, you have three daughters who, as long as they are in your company, will never allow you to have the grace of God, namely Pride, Lust and Avarice". King Richard, after a minute's reflection, replies: "I have already given those daughters in marriage, the first and foremost, namely Pride, to the Templars, the second, namely Lust, to the Black Monks, the third and last, namely Avarice, to the White Monks". There we must take leave of M. Hauréau, who gives no hint in his valuable references of any Scriptural origin—real or imaginary—for this extraordinary tradition. Undoubtedly older than the accounts given by Gerald of Wales is the elaborate version of the story which is to be found in a twelfth-century sermon by Stephen of Tournay.[3] Indeed, we can easily believe that a medieval monarch like King Richard would enjoy flinging back at his clerical critic an allusion to a sermon allegory in which the rôle which he now took upon himself was originally played by his Satanic Majesty. However, for a possible link with Scripture we must turn to the records of our own national pulpit. In a sermon delivered at Paul's Cross in the year 1388, one Thomas Wimbledon speaks as follows:

And what vengeance falleth of this sinne of covetise I may see by figure in holy writ, when the angel sayd to prophet Zacharie,[4] "Rere up thine eien, and see what is that goeth out". And the prophet said, "What is it?" Then the angell saide, "This is the potte going out; this is the eiȝe [= resemblance] of hem on all the earth". And there was a weight of lead i-bore, and there was a woman sitting in the middle of

---

[1] See *Gir. Camb. Op.* Rolls S. vol. iv, p. 54.   [2] Ibid. vol. vi, p. 44.
[3] For this and other 12th-cent. examples, see Bourgain, *La Chaire franç.* pp. 220-2.   [4] Zech. v, 5-11.

this pot: and the angell saide, "This is Impietie". And he tooke her, and cast her into the middle of this pot; and he tooke the gobbette of lead and cast it into the pot's mouth. And the prophet lift up his eie, and he saw two women cumming out, and spirits in her wingis, like two kytes other gledes; and they care(r)id up this pot betweene heaven and the earth. And than the prophet spake to the angell, "Whider wol these beare this pot?" And he saide, "Into the lond of Sennaar". This pot is covetise; for right as a pot hath a wide open mouth, so covetise gapeth after worldlie good.... The woman that sat in the pot is Vnpittie, as the angell saide, that followeth unrighteousnesse and avarice.... The twoe women that bare up this pot are Pride and Lust of Flesh, that be cleped in holie writ, "the twey daughtren of the water-leche, crying, bring, bring".[1] ... Beware, I rede, that ye nought have to doe with this pot, ne with the woman therein; and, on all maner, *that ye be nought weddid to hir*, for than ye must be both one. This thilke foule lecherous woman *the kinges and marchauntis of the earth have done leacherie with, and of her vertue they haveth be made rich.*...[2]

Wimbledon's sermon seems to suggest, then, if we mistake not, that these mystical figures of women in Old Testament Scripture[3] were identified by the homilists with this strange apocryphal legend of the Devil's Daughters, the typical she-devils of primitive lore, much as in the previous case of the four disputing Virtues of the Book of Psalms. Be that as it may, there can be no doubt of the vogue which the legend itself enjoyed in the pulpits, from the thirteenth century on-wards, as already indicated by Hauréau.[4] In our English sermon manuscripts, subsequent to the day of Wimbledon, it persists again as an ordinary secular "fable" or "narration":

The devyl, *secundum fabulas*, hadde 7 dow3tres, Pride, Govyl, Wast, Raveyn, Symonye, Ipocrisye and Lecchere. The devyl hath maryid Pride

---

[1] See Prov. xxx, 15. Sim. Peter Cantor, Migne, *P.L.* vol. ccv, 76–7.

[2] *Acts and Mons. of Jo. Foxe*, Ch. Hist. ed. vol. iii, pt. i, pp. 298–330 (cf. Bourgain, p. 220, n. 3).

[3] Cf. a similar interpretation (Jer. xxxiv, misquoted) in *Jacob's Well*, pp. 81–2, probably of the two daughters of Ezek. xxiii, 2.

[4] See his *Not. et Extr.* vols. iii, pp. 72–3 and iv, 135–7. Preachers mentioned include our English Odo of Cheriton (MS. Bibl. Nat. Paris, Lat. 2593, fol. 93), Jacques de Vitry, and Adam de la Vacherie. Cf. also M. Paul Meyer in *Romania*, vol. xxix (1900), p. 57 ("Le Mariage des filles du diable est devenu tellement un lieu commun pour les clercs"), p. 61, a version in Anglo-Norm. verse (by Bp. Grossetête?), etc.; *Ancren Riwle*, ed. King's Classics, p. 163; and Miss H. E. Allen, *Writings ascribed to R. R.* p. 378. The legend appears in Bromyard, *S.P.* s.v. "Falsitas" (and "Peccatum").

to wommen; for wommen settyn all here stodye in pride of aray of here hed and of here body, to lokyn in myrrourys, in kemyng here heed, in here hornys, in peerlys, in other ryche aray abowte the heed, in ryngys, in brochys, in hedys, in longe trayles. Govyl is maryid to burgeysys of cytees and to lumbardys and to marchauntys. The feend hath maryed Wast to ryotours, and Raveyn to kny3tes and to men of lawe, and Symonye to byschopys and prelatys and clerkys, and Ypocrysie to frerys, and Leccherye to alle astatys.[1]

Other preachers introduce the legend under the form of an anecdote about a man who had seven daughters with ugly names, who was unable to get them married until he had renamed them: "So gostly to oure purpose, by this man that had the vii dow3tters is understonde the devyll, and by his vii dow3tters is understonde the vii dedely synnys". The Devil is likewise driven to have his daughters renamed for matrimonial purposes. Thus, the first and eldest was called Pride. "And for by cawse that the fende wolde marry hyr to the pepull of the worlde, he hathe sett on hyr a gay name and now sche is callyd 'Honestye'... Be well ware that 3e marry not with the dow3tter of the devyll!..."[2]

By this time the reader has probably guessed the reason for this somewhat detailed history of a further group of allegoric impersonations in our sermon literature. For, although strangely overlooked by Professor Skeat and other learned commentators hitherto, this legend provides us with the source from which William Langland must have drawn the idea of his Lady Mede, daughter of Falsehood or the Evil One who is Master of "the Castel of Care",[3] also of the elaborate arrangements for

---

[1] MS. Salisb. Cath. Libr. 103, fol. 196b–197 (unpublished *Jacob's Well.* N.B. this is a strongly *anti*-Lollard work).

[2] MS. Gloucester Cath. Libr. (15th-cent. Homilies), Sermon for the 5th Sunday after Trinity (unpaginated): the remaining six Deadly Sins are then dealt with in the same fashion. Cf. again *Serm. Dom. Quinquag.*: "The secunde dragon... is the foule synne of envy, the devyls worthi dow3ther, for sche foloweth the condiscions of hyr fader". See also Bromyard, s.v. "Falsitas", as before.

[3] There seems some confusion in the poem over the relationships here. Lady Holy Church explains distinctly of the Lady Mede—"fals was hire fader, that hath a fykel tonge", yet she is to be married "to one fals fikeltonge, a fendes bi3ete" (pass. ii, ll. 25 and 39–40 (B text)). It is interesting to note that Miss D. L. Owen is driven to admit (*Piers Plowman*, pp. 88–9) that she can find no parallel to the story in French allegory.

her marriage, of which more will have to be said in a subsequent chapter. Later again in the same century the story makes prominent reappearance in verse in Gower's *Mirour de l'Omme*, or *Speculum Meditantis*;[1] while the Lady Munera of Spenser's *Faerie Queene* is a noteworthy instance of its survival in Tudor times.[2]

To follow up the influence of all these allegoric sermon figures in the poetical works of the fourteenth and fifteenth centuries, and on, past the limit of the Middle Ages, into the era of Reformation and Renaissance, is here an unnecessary task. It can be traced at the reader's leisure in a voluminous literature already in print. There is, however, a still later English allegory, of purely religious character, which deserves some further attention where the influence of medieval preaching is being discussed. For, in spite of the fact that it accords so perfectly with the allegoric methods of the latter, critical scholarship has more or less felt itself driven to reject any medieval origin for its conceptions. In his brilliant and authoritative life of the author of *The Pilgrim's Progress*, the Rev. John Brown, though himself no medievalist, has been at some pains to consider all the possible prototypes of Bunyan's famous allegory, from *Le Pèlerinage de l'Homme* to *The Pilgrimage of Dovekin and Willikin to their Beloved in Jerusalem*.[3] He has noted the "several ideas in common between Bunyan and De Guileville", including for example the wicket-gate, the house of Grâce-Dieu and the pilgrim's armoury. Nor has he overlooked the fact that old English translations of De Guileville's work existed for two centuries before Bunyan's day. However, with his survey complete, Brown decides that the imprisoned tinker could hardly have had access to such literature when he wrote; still less was he likely to be a reader of "Caxtons" at any time of life. "The endeavour to hunt up recondite sources for Bunyan's inspiration has, in truth, been a little overstrained."

[1] ll. 751 et seq. ed. G. C. Macaulay; also described in *Camb. Hist. of Engl. Lit.* vol. ii, p. 140.

[2] Bk. v, canto ii: cf. especially st. x, l. 3: "That many Lords have her to wife desired".

[3] *John Bunyan: his Life, Times, and Work*, vol. ii, pp. 38–45. See also Dunlop, *Hist. of Fiction*, 3rd ed. p. 301.

The tinker's own protestation has a right to be heard in the matter: "Manner, and matter too, was all mine own". For the rest, a common source of inspiration in Holy Writ is quite sufficient to account for all similarities in the works of earlier and later allegorist. But can the problem be allowed to remain here as finally settled? We think not. A study of popular medieval English sermon literature reveals too many parallels to the characters and similitudes of Bunyan's greatest allegories. And it is through the mediation of the pulpit that we may best be able to find a way of explaining this medieval contact, without having to accuse the Puritan of deliberate dishonesty, or conscious misstatement.

Have we any right to believe that Bunyan may have listened to sermons in his youth of a typically medieval character? We do know that at one stage of his spiritual career he "fell in very eagerly with the religion of the times, to wit, to go to church twice a day, and that too with the foremost". We know, too, from his own testimony, that he was then a regular sermon-hearer at his parish church of Elstow, where the vicar, at least one of whose sermons—on a typical medieval theme—made a great impression on his mind, was apparently no Puritan.[1] But, in view of the profound gulf which is supposed to divide the religion of Protestantism from that of the pre-Reformation era, no one seems to have realized that the style and even the matter of pulpit exposition had changed but little, even in Bunyan's own day. Yet, such is the case. Less than a century before the tinker of Bedford was born, Bishop Hugh Latimer, the outstanding preacher of the English Reformation, came to his tragic end.[2] It is only a complete ignorance of medieval preaching in England that has hitherto prevented

---

[1] See *Grace Abounding*, §§ 16 and 20 ("But one day (amongst all the sermons our parson made) his subject was to treat of the Sabbath day, and of the evil of breaking that, either with labour, sports or otherwise;...wherefore I fell in my conscience under his sermon,...and so went home when the sermon was ended, with a great burthen upon my spirit..."). For medieval sermons on this subject see my *Preaching in Med. Engl.* p. 194, esp. n. 2, and my article in the *Holborn Review*, Jan. 1926, pp. 32–45. For Bunyan's vicar, see Brown, as above, vol i, p. 56 (Rev. Chris. Hall).   [2] Oct. 16, 1555.

editors and critics of his sermons from realizing that they follow directly the style of homely vernacular discoursing employed in the pulpits of the fourteenth and fifteenth centuries. His racy anecdotes and snatches of reminiscence, his simple directness of speech, his use of popular proverbs, his outspoken denunciation of corrupt judges, "unpreaching prelates", deceitful merchants and cloth-workers, or servants who defraud their masters are all too precisely given in the medieval style to allow of any doubt as to where that manner of speech was learnt. His choice and development of the playing cards as a *figure* for the famous "Sermons on the Card", which seem to have caused the modern commentator some ingenious search for an explanation,[1] will hardly surprise those acquainted with a Moralization of the Game of Cards made in the year 1377 by the Dominican John of Reinfelden,[2] or the endless moralizations of chess which find a place in English homilies of the same century.[3] Dean Beeching has the misfortune to choose as another characteristic example of the good bishop's method of address a passage which turns out to be an almost verbal repetition of statements made by English homilists of the fifteenth century, following a famous Letter of St Bernard.[4]

[1] Cf. Dean (then Canon) Beeching's Preface to the Everyman ed. of *Latimer's Sermons*, p. ix ("Probably by such a trick he caught the ear of the undergraduates of the day, who were younger then than now").

[2] Cf. MS. Egerton 2419.

[3] See my *Preaching in Med. Engl.* p. 326, esp. n. 3.

[4] Everyman ed. as above, p. x. Cf. with this, MS. Add. 24202, fol. 26; MS. Harl. 2398, fol. 83 b; etc.:

Latimer: "While they thus preached to the people that dead images not only ought to be covered with gold, but also ought of all faithful and christian people ...to be clad with silk garments, and those laden with precious gems and jewels...; whereas in the meantime we see Christ's faithful and lively images, bought with no less price than with his most precious blood, (alas, alas!) to be an-hungred, a-thirst, a-cold, and to lie in darkness, wrapped in all wretchedness...".

Early 15th-cent. Sermon on Images: MS. Add. 24202: "And ȝit men erren foul in this crucifixe makyng; for thei peynten it with greet cost, and hangen myche silver and gold and precious clothis and stones ther onne and aboute it, and suffren pore men, bouȝte with cristis precious blode, to be by hem nakyd, hungry, thursty, and in strong preson bounden, that shulden be holpyn by cristis lawe with this ilke tresour that is thus veynely wastid on thes dede ymagis...".

For St Bernard, see the transl. of his *Letter to Wm. of St Thierry*, given in Coulton, *Art and the Reform*. App. 26, p. 573. The whole is apparently derived from St Clement. See further below, pp. 143–4.

The very next excerpt which he quotes concerning practical almsgiving and the attitude of souls in purgatory might have fallen from the lips of "dan Michel" himself.[1] If Master Latimer is so essentially the disciple of medieval preaching, what then can be said of preachers of an even later day? From a little-known volume which has found its way into the author's hands dealing with *Pulpit Oratory in the time of James the First, considered and principally illustrated by Original Examples,* A.D. 1620–22,[2] it is equally clear that the same traditional methods persisted. The editor here emphasizes at the outset of his Preface that his selected examples from the manuscript of an unknown preacher "may at least be considered authentic specimens of village sermons more than two centuries ago", and are not to be confused with the sermons "of eminent divines and theologists" of the period, "who wrote with a view to publication" concerning more momentous questions of state.[3] He goes on to point out what to us are still the recognizable features of medieval preaching—"the indiscriminate use of sacred and profane (especially classical) allusion, quaint phraseology and homely metaphor", "the number of divisions and perplexing ramifications of the sub-divisions", the attacks on current fashionable vices, "the authority of the venerable Fathers of the Church to be repeatedly and largely cited". This latter custom, our editor tells us, "was discontinued soon after the revolution".[4] In addition we note for ourselves further medieval features surviving, such as the use of terms of formal Logic,[5] satirical phrases like that of "the Devill's false glasses",[6] elaboration of the properties of natural *figures* in the Scripture text,[7] and so forth. In a recent article on John Donne it has been stated likewise that the sermons of his day "were still, in spite of the dogmatic changes of the Reformation, cast in the iron mould of medieval theology. The Fathers, the Schoolmen, the mystical and allegorical torturing of scriptural texts were as frequent on the lips of the Caroline preachers as on

[1] Cf. e.g. *Ayenb. of Inwyt*, p. 195.
[2] By the Rev. J. H. Bloom, London and Norwich, 1831.   [3] p. 2.
[4] pp. 37–8.   [5] Cf. pp. 41, 161, etc.   [6] p. 126.
[7] Cf. the sermon on "Good Ground", pp. 195 et seq.

those of the medieval friars. Their riddling interpretations, their legalistic subtleties of distinction, the spell-like efficacy with which they invested isolated words or syllables of Holy Writ, the deliberate quaintness and whimsicality of their antithetical style are of a piece with fretted screens and gargoyles".[1] Clearly then the pre-Reformation tradition was by no means extinct in the rural pulpits of Protestant England when John Bunyan appeared.

A further question follows naturally. Was a district like that of Bedfordshire—"more than usually receptive of the new ideas", so we are told—likely to be amongst those which retained such traditional features of the old religion? Brown himself suggests that it was.[2] He shows how yeomen and farmers of the country, in particular, kept to "the old wellworn modes of religious thought, even while diligently attending the services of a Reformed Church"; still commending their souls to the Blessed Virgin and the saints in their wills, still suffering excommunication and penances for the old preReformation sins.[3] Indeed, his valuable excerpts from the Act-books of the Archdeaconry of Bedford in the early years of the sixteenth century read for all the world like another chapter of the rustic Middle Ages. Furthermore, in his lectures on *Puritan Preaching in England* he tells us of just such a preacher as we have indicated, one Thomas Adams, "the Shakespeare of the Puritans", who, in the year 1612 was "a preacher of God's Word at Willington", a village in Bedfordshire, four miles from Bedford and but "about half an hour's walk" from Bunyan's own home at Elstow. An outline given of one of his sermons reveals a thoroughly medieval spirit, and in some passages an amazing likeness to Bunyan's own

[1] Tercentenary Leading Article on Doctor Donne, in *The Times*, 1931.
[2] See esp. *John Bunyan*, vol. i, pp. 2–8.
[3] E.g. having dealings with, or assisting excommunicates; typical Lollard offences; consulting witches and "exercising the magic art"; failing to go to mass, or to observe such customs as "making two torches"; defiling the churchyard or church; women "not coming in a vaile" to church "as other honest women", etc.; clergy failing to "sprinkle holy water on the parishioners", or playing "lord of misrule at Christmas", or allowing bear-baiting in the holy place, etc.

treatment of the characters and scene of Vanity Fair. Curiously enough, however, this latter point is not remarked upon by the writer.[1] Again, among the books which Bunyan's own sainted wife brought with her to the new home, and one which he himself "would sometimes read with her",[2] after the manner of brother Whitford's advice to the medieval "Householder",[3] was *The Plain Man's Pathway to Heaven*, a little seventeenth-century treatise obviously based on pre-Reformation models.[4] For here, again, is the typical use of homely dialogue for the discussion of Vices and Virtues, the proverbial racy sayings, the satire of dress and finery, and that favourite medieval reference to the Doom, when we must "give an account of our Baily-wicke". This, then, in effect is the general conclusion to which our argument leads. Bunyan may not have consciously set out to reproduce any of the medieval versions of the Pilgrim story, when he put pen to paper and wrote his *Pilgrim's Progress*. The actual *Pèlerinage* of De Guileville he need never have seen or even heard of. But he must, nevertheless, have carried away with him to his prison-house stored memories of sermons or readings drawn from the ancient homily-books which he may very well have studied for the preparation of his own Sabbath-day discourses.[5] Returning, though now unrecognized, they kindled his imagination afresh, an imagination able to soar unimpeded in the enforced leisure and loneliness of the jail. Like the immortal allegorist of *The Vision of Piers Plowman*, he seemed "to lay him down in the wilderness of this world to sleep, and dreamed a dream".[6] But again the Vision welled up in reality from the dreamer's own half-conscious mind, influenced naturally enough

[1] Lyman Beecher Lectures, Yale, 1897 (publ. 1900), pp. 89–94.
[2] See *Grace Abounding*, § 15.
[3] "At every mele, or at the leest ones a daye" (*Werke for Householders*).
[4] By the Rev. Arthur Dent, of Shoeburyness, 1601 (see Brown, vol. i, pp. 52–4).
[5] It is again suggestive to find that there are links between the Lollards and the early sectaries in respect of hand-books of religion, such as the pre-Reformation Lollard MS. found amongst the records of the old Congregational Church at Sudbury (see W. H. Summers, *Our Lollard Ancestors*, p. 51).
[6] *Pilgrim's Progress*, Inc. See further below, p. 108.

by things often pondered and preached aforetime, or learnt in the company of those "talking of the things of God".[1] Let us see what our simple vernacular sermons of the Middle Ages have to say in the matter.

If Bunyan developed the story of his *Pilgrim's Progress* after his own fashion, the initial scene of the allegory at all events is a commonplace on the lips of English preachers of the fifteenth century—

for als mykell as ilk man, whils he lifs here in this worlde, and is a pilgrem, ilke day of hys lif travaylyng a dayes jorne towarde the place where he shall dwelle ay with-oute ende....And therfore, syn it is so that the kepyng and the fulfillynge of goddes commaundmentes es the hye wey to the blisse of heven, and no man may kepe the way bot so be that he knawe itt, therfore I thynke with the grace of God all mighty to teche ȝowe the commaundementes, so that ȝe may in this pilgremage here opon erth forsake the perlieus waye that ledes to the payn, and for to walke to the way that ledes to the blysse of heven.[2]

In a *Myroure for lewde men*, the pilgrim is described as moving towards either Jerusalem, the City of Peace, or Babylon, the City of Confusion.[3] Another homilist approaches yet nearer to Bunyan in making his pilgrim flee from a City of Destruction in which he already finds himself, namely, "the state of dedely synne"—"a plase and stede of grett perill. It is of so gret perill that it slethe mans sowle goostely".[4] Like Bunyan, again, he pictures the pilgrim's original parlous state and his acute anxiety of mind:

ffor the matere of my sermon at this tyme, ȝe shall undyrstonde that we shall goye ffor thre skylles: ffirste, for here to stonde is unpossible; the seconde and it is perlous to turne aȝeynewarde; and the thride is ffor he that goyth here in this world wurthelye, he shall com to the liffe that evermore is lastynge....Also by a nothur reson I may shewe you that we muste nedis goye and not to stonde here in this worlde. ȝe see well

[1] Cf. *Grace Abounding*, § 37.
[2] MS. Harl. 2250, fol. 88. Cf. also, *Pricke of Consc.*, ed. Philog. Soc. p. 39.
[3] MS. Harl. 45, fol. 1 ("Fore hit is so that alle mankynde in this world nys but in exile and wildernesse out of his kyndely contre, or as is a pilgrym or a weyfaringe man in a strange londe, where he may in no manere abide. But nedely every day, every houre and every tyme is passynge on his way...").
[4] MS. Roy. 18. B. xxiii, fol. 76.

that pilgrymes and weyfferynge men be not comonly stondynge, but evermore spedynge hem in here weyes, and therfore as the gospell [sic!] of Seynt poule seyth,..."We be called pilgrymes, and comen of an othur contre".¹ Wherefore every man sey of hymselfe as david seyth in the sawter boke—"*Advena ego sum, et peregrinus*", "I am a pilgryme and comen of an othur contrey". Wherefore all suche men muste spede hem in hure weyes, not lettynge, ne longe stondynge.

Richard Alkerton, in a sermon delivered in London, in the year 1406, describes the pilgrim taking leave of his neighbours and settling his affairs before setting out:

And ich gode cristin man oweth to be a pilgrime goinge into hevenly Ierusalem....But it is to witte that he that be a pilgrime duely owith first to paie his dettis, aftirwarde to sette his hous in governaunce, and aftirwarde to aray himself and take leve of his neiȝboris, and so go forthe....Whan the dettis been thus paied, and the meine is thus sette in governance, the pilgrime schal arraie himself; and than he owith first to make himself be marked with the cros, as men been wont that schul passe to the holy londe....Aftirwarde the pilgrime schal have a staf, a sclavein² and a scrippe.

With the staff he is to defend himself from the dogs of Hell; the "sclavein" is the "cloth" of Charity, without which no man shall enter the heavenly Jerusalem. Out of the scrip "shall be drawn victuals"—alms and works of Mercy.

Whan thes thinges ben doon, nothyng is left, no, but take leve of thi freendis and take thi iorney; for now thou moste goon out of thi fadir hous and out of thi kynred, and seie fare wele to hem.³

The most remarkable parallel of all to the opening scene of the *Pilgrim's Progress*, however, has yet to be mentioned. It appears in a vernacular treatise on the *Weye to Paradys*⁴ which is to be found in a Harleian Manuscript⁵—unfortunately incomplete—written about the end of the fourteenth century, or the beginning of the fifteenth, and illustrated with somewhat

¹ Hebr. xi, 13?   ² = a pilgrim's mantle.
³ MS. Add. 37677, fols. 57–8 (see Gen. xii, i, here quoted).
⁴ This work is clearly an English offspring of the better-known French family of medieval treatises known as *La Voie de Paradis*, inaugurated probably by Raoul de Houdenc's *Voie d'Enfer*, thirteenth-century ancestors of De Guileville's *Pèlerinage de l'Homme* (cf. Gaston Paris, *Med. French Lit.* 1903, p. 89; etc.).
⁵ MS. Harl. 1671. My discovery of this source was first announced in a letter to *The Times* of Nov. 24, 1928, q.v.

crude drawings of the period, in the English style. At a first inspection of the manuscript, the present writer happened to notice an illustration showing a man crossing an abyss by means of a wooden plank, with a large bulging sack on his right shoulder.[1] Reference to the text[2] soon proved that this was none other than our immortal Pilgrim, bearing his "great burden" of sins, and hastening towards the Celestial City. Strangely enough, there appeared also, in the same place, mention of the "Slough" into which Bunyan's pilgrim was in danger of falling, not indeed here called the Slough of Despond but the Slough of Hell:[3]

A man that is charged with synne is leke to hym that is in a fol streyt wey so that wyth peyne he may unnethe set his foot, and hath a gret sak up on his schuldres on the ton syde, and on the tother part of his weye is so gret depnes that hyt semeth al watres and swolewes. And he bere longe this sak, that he is in peryl to falle down, of whiche he hath gret drede, ȝif he kepe hym not wel and wyth good wylle castyth down hys sak. Ryght so hit is of hym that is charged wyth synne in this world that is not but a fowle, woful or a caytyf passage. For he that is charged with synne wot never whiche parte to torne, ne on the ryght side, ne on the left syde,[4] ȝif he bere longe the sak of synne and he susteyne hit tyl he be ded, and that he falleth down in to the swolwe of helle.[5] And ȝif [he] behelde wel the depnes, he schuld hav gret drede and with goode wylle caste down his sak, that he schulde not falle in this grete swolwe. No man may put down this saak of synne but oonly by confession....

The history of this famous allegorical scene would appear to provide us with yet one more typical illustration of the medieval

[1] fol. 5.   [2] fol. 4b–5.

[3] Cf. also the "very dangerous quag" of the Valley of the Shadow of Death: "The pathway was here also exceeding narrow, and therefore good Christian was the more put to it; for when he sought, in the dark, to shun the ditch on the one hand, he was ready to tip over into the mire on the other...".

[4] Cf. here the words of Bunyan: "I saw also that he [Christian] looked this way, and that way, as if he would run; yet he stood still, because (as I perceived) he could not tell which way to go".

[5] Cf. Bunyan's Christian: "I fear this burden that is upon my back will sink me lower than the grave, and I shall fall into Tophet". And, later—"They drew nigh to a very miry slough, that was in the midst of the plain; and they being heedless, did both fall suddenly into the bog....And Christian, because of the burden that was on his back, began to sink in the mire".

expansion of recondite Biblical imagery. For the whole idea
is to some extent anticipated by a passage in the Second Book
of Esdras.[1] Thus, the original pathway of Oriental tradition,
between "a fire on the right hand, and on the left a deep water",
became transformed by the Christian pulpit into a medieval
causeway running across the marshes.[2] In this modest old
English version of *The Way to Heaven* we have at last laid
bare the missing link between De Guileville and John Bunyan.[3]

The good and evil abstractions of the *Pilgrim's Progress*
who fall in with the heavenly footman on his way we have
seen already anticipated in a measure in the personified Vices
and Virtues of our pre-Reformation homilies and poems. In
the *Weye to Paradys* the pilgrim, here at length mounted on
horseback for his journey, encounters similar groups in his
path: "The seven dedly synnes arn the theves that assayled
the ryght man that is on hors back, and that dyspoylen hym
of his goodes, ʒif god ne helpe hym not".[4] Closer to the
characters of Bunyan's allegory are the special advocates, four
Vices in human form, whom the Devil here sends to argue
with this pilgrim, and so mislead him. In another religious
treatise, recorded in a manuscript of the same date,[5] good
company also waits to be encountered upon the road—Belief
and Love—as well as the lurking mischief-makers:

> He that is a pilgrym comen into a strange land where many theves
> and robboures beth, that nyght and day awayteth suche pilgrymes to
> robbe hem of all here godes and slee hem. Him nedeth busiliche studie
> and thinke how he myghte scape her hondes.... Good pilgrymes...
> thinketh noght elles but to make her iournees nyght and day til thei come
> to that contre aforseid that is her right heritage.... Such pilgrymes, if
> thei wole passe sikerliche, thei putteth hem all wey in good companye
> of stedfast byleve and parfite love. ffor bileve scheweth hem the wey,[6]
> and love bereth hem forth,[7] til thei come home into her contre and
> rightfull heritage, on whiche thei setten her thoght and desire so sadliche
> that the wey thiderward greweth hem noght.

[1] I.e. 2 Esdr. vii, 6–10. See a letter from Dr L. P. Jacks, in *The Times*,
Nov. 27, 1928, and my reply (ibid. Nov. 29); also below, p. 594.
[2] Cf. further here, N. Bozon, *Metaphs.* cap. xxix (the "narrow and
dangerous bridge" across the waters); and the Bridge in Hawes' *Exple.
of Vertue*; etc.   [3] See above, p. 104, n. 4.   [4] fol. 9.
[5] MS. Harl. 45, fol. 160b. Sim. *Ayenb. of Inwyt*, p. 254.
[6] Cf. Bunyan's "Evangelist".   [7] Cf. Bunyan's "Charity".

Richard Alkerton warns his pilgrim to flee occasions of sin "in al the cuntre", which, though not actually personified in his discourse, are vices which our seventeenth-century Puritan would single out as typical of the evil company of the road: Idleness, Delicate Meats, Much Speech, Folly Speech, Evil Fellowship, Sight of Vanities, Hearkening of Dishonest Things, Speaking of Ribaldry, and so forth.[1] The preacher goes on— "But for no man in this worlde may passe the wey for enemies, no, but this gode lorde lede him and defende him, therfore it is neede that thou and they that schul go with thee preye this lorde" for succour. When "it drawith toward niʒt...thanne weigoers dredyn moste perelis". How then shall Christian fare safely in the Valley of Shadows or face to face with Apollyon, if he go not armed? Says yet another of our homilists: "As we that ben everyday walkyng a iorney towarde the londe of lyghte amonge all oure enmyes,...therefore...cloth we us in armoure, oure enmyes to mete, that we may wythstonde the dynt of the devele".[2] God, yet another reminds us, "ʒaf the bothe armur, and wepens mithiliche for to defende it, ʒe the armur of cristendom...and the wepens of the ten commaundementes".[3] Here, then, is foreshadowed the visit of Bunyan's hero to the armoury of the Palace Beautiful, that Palace with its zealous Porter which recalls to us so vividly the "Castle of God" or "The Abbey of the Holy Ghost", and its four fair damsel Virtues so reminiscent of the four Sisters of our medieval *Sawles Warde*. Once we accept the homiletic theory of Bunyan's indebtedness, it is as idle to look abroad for archetypes in *Perceforest* as in *Le Pèlerinage de*

[1] MS. Add. 37677, fol. 58b. Cf. here the good and bad company of the road of Life in Barclay's (?) *Castell of Labour* (from the French of Pierre Gringore, ed. A. W. Pollard, Roxburgh Cl. 1905).

[2] MS. Roy. 18. B. xxiii, fol. 153b.

[3] MS. Worc. Cath. Libr. F. 10, fol. 49. Cf. the Christian's armour in *Old Engl. Homs.* (12th cent.), 1st Ser. E.E.T.S. O.S. no. 34, pp. 241–3; and in *Jacob's Well*, p. 292; also a sermon by Master Ralph of Acton, in MS. Jo. Ryl. Libr. Manch. Lat. 367, fol. 184: "*Sint lumbi vestri precincti et lucerne ardentes* (Luke xii, 35). Hiis verbis, fratres karissimi, nos armat dominus contra mala huius temporalis vite, que sunt tria. Est enim via huius temporalis vite lubrica, tenebrosa, insidiis plena...".

L'Homme itself. The giants of Bunyan's allegory, like that Giant Maul slain by Greatheart who "did use to spoil young pilgrims", may well have been suggested to him by echoes in sermon and treatise of the "fowr stronge geauntes" of the *Psychomachia,* such as we find in a Worcester manuscript of sermons.[1] Casual passages in the same literature, like that which describes "Veyn glorie" as "the money that the devel chaffareth with in the feyre of this worlde and profreth it to alle manere men",[2] call up other familiar episodes like that of Vanity Fair. Even Bunyan's exquisite picture of the innocent shepherd-boy with his little song seems strangely anticipated by a sermon story of the great St Bernard, who always saluted shepherd-boys, we are told, in order that he might receive a blessing from their innocent mouths.[3] Lastly, there is the introductory device of the Dream-vision itself. Apart from its survival in the *Pilgrim's Progress,* this well-known feature of such medieval allegoric verse as the *Roman de la Rose, Pearl* and the *Vision of Piers Plowman* provides a final illustration of the main theme of our chapter. For its history has been traced back to Biblical origins, notably in the prophetic visions of the Old Testament and the Johannine Apocalypse, by way of later homiletic tales of the revelations of the dying or of the miraculously-returning dead.[4]

---

[1] MS. Worc. Cath. Libr. F. 10, fol. 48. Cf. the "dragons of the pit" of Bunyan's Valley of the Shadow of Death with the "dragons" of MS. Gloucester Cath. Homilies, *Serm. Dom. Quinquag.,* and Bunyan's various "hop-goblins and satyrs" with various descriptions of the devils in Myrc and other typical homily-books, as below, pp. 511–5.

[2] MS. Harl. 45, fol. 38b. Again in MS. Add. 41321, fol. 99b: "Veyn-glorie is the peny that the fend hath redi ever to eche mannes harme in the feire of this world, to bie with al hire dedis"; and *Ayenb. of Inwyt,* p. 23.

[3] MS. Harl. 463, fol. 23b (Jacques de Vitry: printed in Crane's ed. of his *Exempla,* p. 120, no. 286). A correspondent (Rev. R. Ridge) mentions in *The Times* of Nov. 29, 1928, an old Shropshire carol, with a medieval tune, "which bears a striking resemblance to the Little Room full of dust in the House of the Interpreter".

[4] See Ernest Langlois, *Origines et Sources du Roman de la Rose,* Paris, 1891, pp. 55–9 ("un emprunt nouveau [de la littérature chrétienne]"...). So, doubtless, the allegoric *Castle* of the Romances originated from our Biblical and homiletic *Castle.*

The reader must be left to decide for himself whether the particular explanation here offered of Bunyan's apparent indebtedness to the Middle Ages is likely to be right or not. If, however, the repetition in the *Pilgrim's Progress* of all this medieval imagery is to be considered nothing more than a coincidence, what are we to believe, when, turning to his other masterpiece, the *Holy War*, we find the same amazing similarity of ideas? In view of what has been said already about the medieval *Castellum Animae* and its relentless sieges, nothing need be added to explain its significance in the case of Bunyan's "Mansoul". Here it is again in early fifteenth-century English guise, an accepted commonplace of the pulpit:

> I myth, mannes sowle, ha saide tanne am a cite defended and beseget; ȝe, i-beseget al abowte o the devel and of his knythtes, but i-strenthed and defended be the vertuus wepenes that God hath ȝyv me; nor me nedeth nevere to ben afered, for God himsilf is my constable and my defendur.... The castel...sikyrliche as me thyngȝ hath gret nede o strong defens and also o wis governaile....[1]

Whether or not the dreamer of Bedford jail was consciously or unconsciously building up his themes from such earlier homiletic models, in spite of his Protestantism he is at all events a typical child of the pre-Reformation piety, steeped in its atmosphere of homely imagery and practical mysticism. No one mirrors more clearly than he the mind and method of our English sermon-allegorists of the later Middle Ages, and the influence of their message upon subsequent generations of Englishmen. From their favourite mode of scriptural exposition we have watched the emergence of certain conspicuous *figures* and abstract impersonations. We have now to consider an important parallel development from the sacred text which gave to its more authentic *personae* a new realism and human interest.

1 MS. Worc. Cath. Libr. F. 10, fol. 48. The *Castellum Anime Humane* also appears in the contemporary *Destructorium Viciorum* of Alex. Carpenter, pars. v, cap. 12.

CHAPTER III

"The Heavenly Host"

"IT is characteristic of the primitive mind that it finds a difficulty about universals and is most at home with particulars", says Miss Evelyn Underhill.[1] "The Catholic peasant may find it easier to approach God through and in his special saint, or even a special local form of the Madonna. This is the inevitable corollary of the psychic level at which he lives; and to speak contemptuously of his 'superstition' is wholly beside the point." To some extent it is already true to say that the characteristic features of English medieval preaching so far revealed in our study exhibit this same desire to escape as far as possible from the abstract and the universal in religion, and to be "at home with particulars". That special devotion to the person of a romantic Queen of Heaven exhibited it in our first chapter. So also does the impersonation of Vices and Virtues, and the whole emphasis upon familiar concrete *figures* and illustrative scenes, which have just been noticed. Yet, while we must attribute some of these features, no doubt, to the influence of a more educated than plebeian taste, and discern them as the product of scholastic and clerical minds following their own favourite expository bent, there remains a further element in our sermons which is essentially for the crowd, nakedly and undisguisedly popular. Study of this element in preaching and exposition of Scripture will repay our attention. For it will bring us very close to those familiar interludes in the contemporary religious drama which pave the way for the yet more vulgar, homely and comic scenes of the greater Elizabethan dramatists.

In at least three directions it is still possible to trace the survival of primitive, pagan folk-ideas and tastes in the popular religious instruction of fourteenth- and fifteenth-century England. The naïve interest shown in the characters of

[1] *The Life of the Spirit*, p. 141 et seq.

Holy Writ and the holy men and women canonized by the Church reflects a pre-Christian attitude to the gods, goddesses and heroes of ancient Teutonic legend or the classical pantheon. Where Hercules, Perseus or Beowulf do not actually reappear in person, duly moralized[1] as the sign of their conversion to Christian usage, medieval preacher and sculptor make easy the transition of popular fancy from these mythological figures to an equally mythological Christ harrowing hell or, like a spiritual Hercules, rending the diabolic "Nemean" lion.[2] Sainted rescuers from dragons[3] and other scourges, monkish or episcopal combatants with devils in every form, some gracious Queen-Mother of the skies, working her miracles or interceding like Brunnhilde for the sons of men, before an awful Wotan armed with thunder—

> Father, take back the word that thou hast spoken;
> For thy heart loveth Siegmund!

—all these maintain the old themes with but a very superficial change of setting. As far back as the tenth century in Saxon England, the English preacher thus bids his audience entreat the aid of St Michael and his angels "against the hell-fiends", and gives as part of a Vision of St Paul, what Dr Morris discovered to be a passage taken from the poem of Beowulf.[4] In the later medieval centuries that concern us, we shall watch the popular mind still dwelling with affection upon the eccentric appearance of its favourite saint, still seeking the drollest particulars about his life or person, eager as a child to listen over again to the preacher's oft-repeated "notabyll story" of his doings. But, secondly, we seem carried back to an even more

---

[1] Cf. the moralized tale of the infant "Herculesse" wringing the snakes' necks in his "cradell", in a sermon of MS. Linc. Cath. Libr. A. 6. 2, fol. 164; and the killing of the Chimaera in Holcot's *Moralitates* (MS. Arund. 384, fol. 86); etc.

[2] The medieval comparison is really with Samson, as suggested by a sermon of St Augustine (*De Samsone*, 1): cf. also 1 Peter v, 8, and the carved bosses at Exeter Cathedral (3), and Hayles Abbey, Glos., etc.; also the border illustration in MS. Linc. Cath. Libr. C. 4. 6, fol. 50b.

[3] Cf. *Engl. Metr. Homs.* MSS. Add. 22283, fol. 12, Harl. 2391, fol. 214b; Latin sermons in MS. Add. 6716, fol. 54 (Engl. 15th cent.); etc.

[4] *Blickling Homs.* E.E.T.S. ed. O.S. no. 73, Pref. pp. vi–vii.

primitive stage in the development of religion with the ceaseless descriptions and stories of the devils themselves in sermon literature. They still "flye above in the eyer as thyke as motis in the sonne",[1] dropping "unclene maters" from the sky,[2] leaving storm and ruin in their path,[3] transforming themselves into a dozen shapes in as many different situations, now a swine, now a dog, now an ape, now a black horse, now a spider, now a fair damsel, now some innocent-looking parish clerk, manorial servant, or even well-known neighbour:[4] now perched on a lettuce-leaf,[5] now riding on a rich lady's train[6] or a "night-mare",[7] now haunting the chambers of the dying, now "sittyng in the stockis",[8] now presiding at the altar—"in habitu ponti-ficali",[9] or escaping in confusion from the church door.[10] Even in roundly condemning the "dyvynacions, or destynees, other eny maner enchantements" of popular superstition forbidden by Holy Church, the preacher is by no means prepared himself to deny their power to promote such disorders. Enchantments, he will say, "diverselyche and sotellyche beth y do by wor-chynge of certeyn fendes. ffor as the prophete seyth—'alle godes of folke beth fendes, and they beth y-cleped strange godes, other alyen godes'".[11] Besides thus lending credence to

[1] MS. Linc. Cath. Libr. A. 6. 2, fol. 133; and cf. Myrc, *Festial*, E.E.T.S. ed. p. 150; Bozon, *Metaphs.* cap. lxxxii; etc. Cf. *Piers Plowman*, A text, pass. i, l. 114.
[2] Cf. *Jacob's Well*, E.E.T.S. ed. p. 227.
[3] Cf. Bozon, *Metaphs.* cap. lxxxvi; MS. Linc. Cath. Libr. A. 6. 2, fol. 126b ("bare awey an ende of the howse", as in Dunbar's *Visitation of St Francis*, st. x); and *Gesta Rom.* E.E.T.S. ed. p. 421; etc.
[4] Cf. the *Festial*, pp. 277, 174, 9; MS. Add. 33956, fol. 83, col. 2; MS. Roy. 7. D. i, fol. 83; MS. Add. 11284, fol. 64; MS. Linc. Cath. Libr. A. 6. 2, fol. 125b; MS. Roy. 18. B. xxiii, fol. 117, and *Spec. Laic.* ed. Welter, p. 51.
[5] MS. Harl. 463, fol. 12, etc. (from Jacques de Vitry).
[6] Cf. below, p. 398.
[7] See Haupt and Hoffmann, *Altdeutsche Blätter*, vol. ii, p. 76.
[8] *Gesta Rom.* Engl. version, E.E.T.S. ed. p. 420.
[9] Cf. Rypon, MS. Harl. 4894, fol. 65.
[10] Cf. Bromyard, *S.P.* s.v. "Dedicatio", and Myrc, as quoted in my *Preaching in Med. Engl.* pp. 270–1.
[11] MS. Harl. 2398, fol. 80. So also Myrc, in the *Festial*, pp. 236, 275, etc. It is worth noting that our preachers are careful to denounce all worship

the ubiquity of devils, our homilists help also to maintain a
popular belief in ghosts and fairies. One speaks quite solemnly
in his sermon of "alle suche [that] been led al ny3t with gobelyn,
and erreth hider and thider" "after the sunne is downe, and
the ni3t is come".[1] Another tells of the "mony that walketh
aftyr that thay ben ded and buryet yn holy plase; (but that
is of no wexyng of the fend, but of grace of God)".[2] Likewise,
"3e may see here that aungeles to schrewed men beth wonder
ferdful; bot to goed men and wommen they beth wonder con-
fortable".[3] It is, indeed, a world filled with savage mystery
and primitive fears. One step further into the darkness finally
brings us to the fierce and mysterious Teutonic heart of nature
herself. Here, in the yawning chasm of hell-mouth with its
"fuyre and brymston", its "venemous wormes and naddris",
its "oribull rorynge",[4] "a sound like the grunting of many
hogs, so horrible that it seems that heaven and earth crash
together at the sound",[5] in the sudden humiliation and mystery
of Death,[6] or in the awful natural prelude to the Day of
Judgment[7]—all continually on the lips of these same preachers
—we behold "wild, original horrors created by the half-savage
brain and heart", a veritable *Inferno* of "cave men", unrelieved
by any sense of poetic tragedy or delicate religious feeling.
It is Dante's *Inferno* as it might be staged for a vulgar music-
hall, or "screened" for a film, short, nasty, brutish, with even
now a vein of rude comedy apparent to any sceptical onlooker.
Stories of saints and devils, lively episodes of Scripture and
of an apocryphal heaven and hell told in the vernacular, these,

of the fiends, and sorcery of this kind: e.g. Rypon, MS. Harl. 4894,
fol. 32 ("Ipse ydolotrat contra fidem qui quovis modo diabolum
adorat..."). For this view even amongst fourth-century Christians,
cf. T. R. Glover, *Life and Letters in the fourth cent.* p. 48.

[1] MS. Add. 41321, fol. 10.
[2] The *Festial*, p. 281. Similarly, Bromyard, *S.P.* s.v. "Mors".
[3] MS. Harl. 2398, fol. 177 (*Sermo in die Pasche*). Cf. further *Old Engl.
Homs.* 2nd Ser. E.E.T.S. O.S. no. 53, p. 11; and *S.P.* s.v. "Tentatio".
[4] See quotations and references given in *Preaching in Med. Engl.*
pp. 336–8.
[5] *Spec. Laic.* ed. Welter, p. 14.
[6] See *Preaching in Med. Engl.* pp. 341–4.
[7] Ibid. pp. 338–40.

then, constitute as we shall see a typical contribution of English medieval preaching to popular thought, full of the elemental passions and instincts of a thinly disguised folk-lore. To borrow Miss Underhill's phrase, "it is the art work of the folk-soul in the religious sphere", comparable to the rude contemporary sculpture and paintings of the churches, which the pulpit here transmits to the literature of posterity.

Once again, as in the previous discussion of formal symbolic exposition, it will be well to start our quest for evidences of this naïve sacred realism in sermons from the pages of Scripture, and the current modes of interpreting them in this particular fashion. For there again, undoubtedly, the practice took its rise. Illustrations of the breezy and forceful speech in which vernacular preachers could recount the more familiar Biblical narratives to their listeners need not detain us long. They will be found in sufficient number in the published edition of Myrc's *Festial*; as, for example, in the accounts there given of Noah's Ark, the sacrifice of Abraham, Joseph in Egypt, or Adam and Eve in Paradise.[1] It is enough to notice in passing that these same topics constitute favourite episodes of the miracle-plays. A point of greater interest to be observed is the way in which the homilists are often wont to "feudalize" scenes and characters of the sacred text. With a deft touch here and there they bring them "up to date", reclothing them, like the ancients of the *Gesta Romanorum* or the sacred figures in early painting, in garments of the period, giving them contemporary titles and ranks, thus making them vivid and familiar to common English folk of the Middle Ages. The practice was by no means a novelty. In Caedmon's Anglo-Saxon paraphrase of Scripture, Abraham had already appeared as "the bold earl", and Satan had rallied his heroes or retainers (*comitatus*) like any chieftain of the times. The author of the *Cursor Mundi* at the beginning of the fourteenth century had continued this same usage in speaking, like a poet of chivalry, of "Sir Judas", "Sir Caiaphas" and "Sir Pilate". So, the unpublished sermons of an unknown homilist, a century later,

[1] pp. 66, 72, 77, 97–8. Cf. here the homiletic poems *Cleanness* and *Patience*, E.E.T.S. O.S. no. 1, pp. 38–104.

present us with lively pulpit descriptions current when the passion for English miracle-plays must have been still at its height. Moses, to his eye, is a "grett" and "curious philosofre" of the schools, seeking to probe the mystery of the Burning Bush,[1] and that "glorious felyshippe" of Old Testament writ bearing the name Jesus, *Jhesus filius Naue*, the worthy duke that brow3the the childeren of Israel in to the londe of beheste", "*Jhesus Josedek*, the worthye Bysshope and holy man", "*Jhesus filius Sirac*, the noble clerke and morall man that made *Ecclesiasticus*, the noble boke of Wysdom".[2] Job, although admittedly "Kynge of Edom", is clearly no other than a typical worthy "frankelein" of Chaucer's England, "amonge gentilmen of wurshipp"—"a gentilman...clere in fey3the, excellent in mekenes, *a nobull housholdere*, ease to be tau3th, large in almes, riche in money, plentewous in children".[3] Jezebel's portrait is that of some tyrannic medieval queen, nobler in her blood and bearing than in her character:

And therfore take hede what thinge in this world is au3th worth with-owten grace. 3iff we speke of lordshipp or riches, who was a gretter conqueroure in erthe than kynge Alisaunder? And 3itt in ys most rialte he was poysond, and never after myght none of ys eres rewysen the furthe parte of is lordshippe.... 3iff we speke of bewte, who was gayer, or more joly richelier arayed than was Jesabell the qwhene?....[4]

Bromyard, in referring to her, has in mind the cruel lady of the manor as well as the cruel medieval queen. Commenting upon her evil part in the death of Naboth, where her husband merely sulked like a balked child, the preacher adds—"And this same thing I have seen done in my own times. Again, if the lord says—'You shall be beaten, or imprisoned!', his spouse says—'Let him be killed!'" Just as there is no more compassionate creature than a good woman, "so there is no beast more cruel than a wicked one", who will incite her lord and his household to cruelty, and fleece the tenants on her

[1] MS. Roy. 18. B. xxiii, fol. 128 b ("as he that was a curious philosofre considred this merveyll a3eyns the common cours of kynde, and was desirous to have had knolage how this bushe brenned with-owten anny wastynge,..as the maister of the stories seyth [i.e. the *Historia Scholastica* of Peter Comestor]...").

[2] fol. 51 b–52.   [3] fol. 138 b.   [4] fol. 173 b.

own account.[1] The "magi" of the Nativity story in their turn, as we shall see later, are the University "masters" of distant Persia, or Parthia.[2] In the sermons of John Myrc, Potiphar is "the maystyr of the kyngys knyghtys", the High Priest— "the byschop of the Jewes lawe", and St Paul—"a gret gentylman". "Pylat" is Herod's "lefetenant, undyr hym, of all his lond of Jury".[3] In yet another homily-collection, the Roman soldiery of Christ's crucifixion are "the knyhʒtis that putt hym on the crosse".[4] The various ranks and professions are precisely those already familiar to us in the miracle-plays. Thus at the awful Doom, God the Father himself is regularly pictured "as chefe-justice, sittyng in his mageste all this worlde demyng";[5] while, according to a previously cited homilist, the twelve apostles are ranged before him as a "queste", twelve heavenly gentlemen of the jury who "will present trowthe," as each soul appears before its Maker for final verdict.[6] "For god is suche a domes-man, that ʒe may not flee from hym."[7]

As with the actual characters of Holy Writ upon the lips of the homilist, so is it sometimes with their actions. It was "thurgh fastynge and bedys-byddynge", we are told, that "Josue...temprede the course of the sunne and of the mone".[8] The story of the householder who planted a vineyard, let it out to husbandmen, and went away, is that of a "man that ʒede a pilgrymage".[9] The Betrayal in the Garden was "Judas loveday".[10] An excellent illustration of the way in which a Scripture parable could be made not merely intelligible but

[1] S.P. s.v. "Mundus".

[2] See below, p. 506.

[3] Festial, pp. 98, 81, 190, 121, respectively.

[4] MS. Camb. Univ. Libr. Gg. vi. 16, fol. 54. Cf. Bromyard, quoted below, p. 336.

[5] MS. Linc. Cath. Libr. A. 6. 2, fol. 82b.

[6] MS. Roy. 18. B. xxiii, fol. 143.

[7] fol. 75. Cf. again the Pricke of Consc. ed. Philog. Soc. ll. 5178, 6120–4; etc.

[8] MS. Harl. 2398, fol. 34.

[9] fol. 28b. With this cf. the Good Samaritan riding to a joust at Jerusalem, in Piers Plowman, C text, pass. xx, l. 50: similarly B text, pass. xvii, l. 51.

[10] MS. Roy. 18. B. xxiii, fol. 96b.

vivid to a simple audience by such slight "modernization", is provided in the following:

But frendes, that thou spekest with thi mouthe thou must nedis thenke itt with thin herte. . . . Ensampull hereof I rede in the gospell of seynte luke (Luc. xviii)[1] that ther com a pharisew and a pupplicane into the tempull. . . . The phariseu, as sone as he com into the churche, he fell downe on ys knees amonge all the pepull oponly, and this was is preyour—"Now, lord god, thou knawiste my liff. I am no robbere, ne revere, ne no theff, as othur men are, ne no lechoure, ne proude man, ne noon extorcionere as this pupplicane is; and also I pey well my tythes, and fastes ii daies in the weke for thi love". And when that he had seid all this, he thanken god. . . .[2]

These sermons bring home to us how living and real many incidents of Scripture must have seemed to ordinary folk in the Middle Ages, which now, through changed social conditions, have lost much of their force, and are clearly events of a dim past. Take, for example, the appeal of this medieval preacher expounding the parable of the Ten Virgins: "Ther is noon of you all that had a lorde and were from home, and ʒe supposed that he wold com home to-nyʒthe, but ʒe wold wake and kepe is commynge. And therfore criste seys in the gospell—'Wake ʒe!' . . ."[3] Again, according to another, "Poule seyth, Eph. V°., 'Chyldryn, obeyith to ʒoure prelatys and to ʒoure curatys, and submytte ʒow to hem; thei wakyn and prayen for ʒow, as for to ʒeldyn acountys for ʒoure soules afore the doom of crist'".[4] Similarly, the Wedding Garment is made easily intelligible as "the weddynge levere",[5] and the Wedding Feast is a medieval bride-ale with appropriate marshalling of the guests: "Ther wern thre degrees of syttyng in this place of this bridale to folk that comen to this feest, in token that in this world among cristen puple sholden be thre degrees of holi lyvers".[6] Finally, as every medievalist knows, at

---

[1] Verses 9–13.
[2] MS. Roy. 18. B. xxiii, fol. 106 (cf. again, fol. 144b: "Let them be hold how that the theffe was saved on goode ffryday. Sirs, this theffe had an evell man all the daies of is liff. . . ").   [3] fol. 65b.
[4] *Jacob's Well*, p. 270. Apparently a confusion of Eph. vi, 1 with Hebr. xiii, 17 (see Douai version).
[5] MS. Roy. 18. B. xxiii, fols. 56b, 143. See Matth. xxii, 1–14.
[6] MS. Harl. 2276, fol. 35.

a court festivity of King Herod "Herodias douȝter...was a
tumbestere, and tumblede byfore him and other grete lordes
of that contre",[1] in true medieval fashion.

That the vernacular preachers could be equally practical and
picturesque with the moralization of Scriptural incidents, as
with the actual narrative itself, there is ample evidence: "Haa,
good lord!" cries one, "Where is the feyȝth of Abraam, the
good hope of Isaak, the prudens of Jacob; where is the chastite
of Joseph, the paciens of Moyses, the gret zele of Finees?...
Where is be-com the sadness of sent Petre, the charite of seynt
Poule, the holynes of Jacob, oure lordes brothur, and the
hevenly wisdom of seynt John the evangelist?...Lo, than, I
se well, ȝiff that I be not begiled, that in men of holy churche,
nothur in gentilmen, nothur in the comon peple, but the old
holines is goyn from hem".[2] Rebuke for the vices of women
was ever a solemn duty of the medieval pulpit. Here the Old
Testament Scriptures offered many admirable examples for the
purpose:

> Dowteles muche pepull is stered oft, ȝe, and assenteth to lechery by
> the nyse aray of women....For confirmacion her-of I rede in scripture[3]
> how when the prince Oliferne, the wiche had in is ost an hundreth
> thowsand and xxᵗⁱ of fote men, and of hors men xxᵗⁱ thowsand, and
> had overcom muche of the contre of the Est, he applied is ost to take
> the cite of Israel called Bethulia. Than was ther a wedow dwellynge in
> the cite, a ryght bewtewous woman and comly. She thoȝthe to begyle
> and to distrowe this prince, and so dud she. [She] mad hur selfe as freshe
> as she cowȝth be in aray, and ȝede owte of the cite in purpose to be
> take unto this prince. And so she was....[Thus came her chance to
> smite off his head with his own sword]....She broȝth this hed with hure
> thorow-owte the ost to the cite, and sett itt uppon the walles; and whan
> the ost on the morow se that prince was ded, anon thei flewȝ, and ther
> enmyes sewed hem and put many of hem to dethe. Loo sirs, here may
> ȝe see how that a prince, that wanne a grett parte of the world, myȝth
> not overcom, but was distrowed by the nyce aray and atyre of a woman.
> And atrowthe it is to drede that in thise dayes many men ben overcom
> spiritually and slayen in ther own soules....[4]

If this episode in the life of Judith was a shocking example of
the bad influence of fashionable dames, her normal behaviour

[1] MS. Harl. 2398, fol. 8.   [2] MS. Roy. 18. B. xxiii, fol. 138.
[3] See Book of Judith, chaps. vii–xv.
[4] MS. Roy. 18. B. xxiii, fols. 132 b–3.

as a widow, on the other hand, was a pattern to the preacher's eye of what medieval widowhood should be:

And thre thinges specialliche longeth to hem that beth in that estate of wedowhode and disposeth hem to kepe hit in clennes and chastite. One is that thei schulde kepe hem in pryve as moche as thei myghte out of grete companye and the sighte of men, and noght busye hem to moche aboute the world. Her-of is ensample in holy writt of the noble womman Judith, that was a faire womman and a clene wedowe, and sche held hir priveliche in clos in hir hous with hir women and wolde noght goon out, but schoned sight of men and los[1] of the world.... Also hit falleth to wedowes for to use symple and comune clothinge of mene colour and noght gay ne starynge, ne of queynte and sotil schap, and take ensample of the holy wedowe Judith, of whom holy writ maketh mynde, that anone whan hir housbonde was deed sche lefte all hir gay attyre and apparaile bothe of hir body and of hir heed, and toke mekeliche clothing and attyre that longed to a wydowe, to schewe doel of her herte and to eschewe veynglorie for the love of God. And to kepe hir wedow-hode in chastite and clennes, ffor sche was fayre and zonge, sche used grete penaunce of fastynge and wered the heyre[2] nexte hir body. Right so schulde wedowes lyve....[3]

Likewise, to the gay "society" girl of medieval England, the careers of Dinah, Jephthah's daughter and Eve were held up as a warning of the fate to which social ambitions and gadding about would inevitably lead:

as Dyna, Jacobes douzter, that walkede out of her ynne to se women of the contre that sche wonede ynne, and was yravesched and enforced and lost here maydenhode. Nyce[4] maydenhode is ylyckened to Jeptes douzter, that walkede aboute in the monteynes twey monthes for to wepe her maydenhode. So doth nyce maydenes that walketh aboute in medes and in fayre places ledynge daunces and syngynge, as it were schewynge hem self to lese her maydenhode, and makynge sorwe that they have ybe so longe maydenes. ffor it byfalleth to maydenes to be in stilnesse and in cloos, as oure lady seynte Marie was whenne the angel come to hure and fonde hure in a pryvy chambre and nouzt stondynge ne walkynge by stretys.... This maydenhode is as the erthe with-oute corne, other a lampe with-oute oyle, a pors withoute selver, a note[5] with-oute curnel, a tonne with-oute wyne, an yze with-out syzt, a body with-out soule. Eve was a nyce mayde and a proude; for sche byleved to the wordes of the serpent and wende[6] to haven be evene to godes knowynge,...and

[1] = honour, praise. [2] I.e. a hair shirt.
[3] MS. Harl. 45, fol. 121. Cf. similarly, MS. Harl. 2398, fol. 37 ("for Judith the wydewe putte an here next her flesche", etc.); MS. Salisb. Cath. Libr. 103, fol. 118; *Ayenb. of Inwyt*, pp. 226–7; etc.
[4] = foolish. [5] = nut. [6] = thought.

was unbuxom to godes hestes;...and thurgh that trespas were yschut aȝenst ous the ȝates of paradyse.¹

The preacher's typical moralizing here upon the case of Jephthah's daughter and her kind is, to say the least of it, not a little uncharitable and disheartening. However, another homilist has discerned in the Gospels a record more complimentary to the sex. For, in spite of their little weaknesses, "women in time of cristes deth...were nouȝt so flyttynge in the beleve as were the aposteles".² Men and women, after all, are both much alike where the commoner vices are concerned; and the pulpit is well aware of the fact. Another of our expositors in the mother tongue quaintly comments thus upon the theme of Israel sojourning in Egypt, that is, the land of darkness, or deadly sin: "And truliche, sirs, and we loke wel a-bout, I trew ther be bot ryght few of us all bot that he as ben this ȝer be-for in egypt, ȝe, and this derknes and tys sorw of synne. vor let everiche of us all enserche wel hys owne consciens and loke vor³ he havat prowd in rament, in beryng, or ell en any vertu that god have sent hym".⁴ In another sermon, he faces an imagined objection to his unsparing condemnation of gluttony and drunkenness. Scripture again appears on the scene, its interpretation in this naïve way a decisive factor in the dispute:

But, peraventur, this man or this womman, that tus doth, wil sey— "ser, whi may not i ete and drynke and be at feste with-owte trespas, syn god amythte made feste to vive thowsynd, as te gospel makȝ mynde that was red tis day?" Truliche, her-to ich answar the and sei that the maist lawfulliche i-now and with-owten synne be at feste, ȝe[f] the miserabiliche ete thi mete and drynke no more than wil be suffisiaunt to nor[i]sche thi kynde. vor Crist, e that feste that te gospel of this day makȝ mynd of, vedde vive thowsund of folk with twei vissches and fi barliloves, and hardeliche her i trow was but litel excesse. Vor ther was no bodi that we rede of that fil in ani glotenie or any other disese be-cause of this feste, and ȝit everi man hath inow and miche mete left after: but

¹ MS. Harl. 2398, fol. 39 b. Cf. *Gesta Rom.* Engl. version E.E.T.S. ed. p. 70, and below, Chap. VII. For similar treatment of these characters in earlier homiletic literature, cf. *Ancren Riwle*, ed. J. Morton, 1907 (King's Classics), p. 44.

² Cf. MS. Roy. 18. B. xxiii, fol. 98.   3 wer?

⁴ MS. Worc. Cath. Libr. F. 10, fol. 42.

for to declare ȝe how and o what maner, it wold aske a longe processe, and also it is but litel to the purpos a tis tyme, and tervore i pas over.[1]

There is one Gospel incident or group of incidents, concerned with the Nativity of our Lord, which called for little explanation but much naïveté of speech from those whose delight it was to concentrate upon them. Preachers and people alike clearly love to dwell upon every minute detail of the Christmas scene for its own sake. The romance and epic grandeur of Judith's story may be entirely missed by the medieval expositor, but here there is exposition sometimes quaint, sometimes almost lyrical in its beauty, a beauty rarely or never equalled elsewhere save perhaps in pathetic treatment of the Passion. As these scenes are intimately linked, however, with equally favourite scenes of the miracle-plays, they will be illustrated by some interesting specimens of vernacular homiletic art in one of the chapters that follow. Enough has been given, for the present, from these long-buried sources, to prove that a distinct tradition of homely, vigorous exposition persisted in our centuries, apart altogether from dry and formal scholastic modes of handling the Scriptures. To appreciate for the first time what this tradition means in the larger history of our national literature, we have only to glance, for example, at Mr G. C. Macaulay's estimate of the author of the *Confessio Amantis*. Gower, he says, "not seldom gives a fresh turn to a well-known story, as in the Bible instances of Jephthah and Saul, or makes a pretty addition to it".[2] But was *he*, after all, the true innovator? That spirit of realism in the pulpit which loved to play with examples from ordinary life had for long been equally active with the men and women of the Bible. Already, on the lips of the preachers they lived and moved again in the contemporary scene, with all the cheerful intimacy and local colour of a Dutch canvas.

Naïve curiosity and a characteristically childish interest in personal detail, sufficiently active to make "lewde men...aske prestes dyverse questyons of thynges" and argue with them, for centuries had encouraged preachers to embroider the

[1] fol. 43 b.
[2] *Camb. Hist. of Engl. Lit.* vol. ii, p. 151.

Scriptural record with quaint apocryphal matter. Into any full examination of the influence of uncanonical Scripture upon the sermons of our two centuries it is impossible to enter here. The sources still drawn upon are, as a matter of fact, those familiar to students of earlier periods of church history. English manuscripts of the fifteenth century accordingly continue to reveal translations of the ever-popular Gospel of Nicodemus,[1] of "the History of the thirty Pieces of Silver", for which Judas betrayed Our Lord, "from the time when they were coined by Terah, the father of Abraham",[2] and other curious excerpts like "the Obyte of Pylat",[3] or the 'Infancy' narratives, which the popular homilist might use. By means of them he could explain how Christ "wente into helle in soule and delyevered Adam and Eve and oure forme fadres",[4] or even tell the name of that "holy woman" of Scripture who cried—"Beatus venter qui te portavit, et ubera quae suxisti", "qwhen owre suffereyn lorde God preched upon a tyme unto the pepull". In the latter case, for example, wise "doctours" informed him that "this womanis name was Marcella, the servaunt off Martha", with a history of her own; and the information was passed on to the sermon-audiences accordingly.[5] So, in the Gospel incident of the woman taken in adultery:

But now som clerkes hasketh what Crist wrotte on the erthe, and clerkes seyth—*et est quidam postillator*—that Crist mad iii sercles in the erthe. In on he wrote the Jewes synnes, that acused the woman. In the seconde he wrote the woman[s] synnes; and in the iii sercle he wrotte is ryghtfull dome. And when thei sawe here synnes passed hogely the womans synnes, than the[i] were ashamed...and went avey.[6]

From legends of men and women of the Scriptures it is but a natural step to legends and descriptions of the saints.

[1] Cf. in Cath. Libraries, e.g. MS. Worc. Cath. Libr. F. 172 (15th cent.), and a Latin version in MS. Q. 51 (13th cent.).
[2] See MSS. Add. 34276, fol. 33b, and Laud Misc. 622 (cf. Dr G. F. Hill, *The Medallic Portraits of Christ*, Oxf. 1920, pp. 91–103).
[3] See MS. Harl. 149, fol. 280b; cf. also Myrc on the history of Pilate, *Festial*, sermon no. 28, p. 120 (and M. R. James, *Apoc. N.T.* pp. 157–61).
[4] MS. Harl. 2398, fol. 47b. Cf. *Ayenb. of Inwyt*, pp. 12–3, etc.
[5] MS. Camb. Univ. Libr. Gg. vi. 16, fol. 47 (see Luke xi, 27–8).
[6] MS. Roy. 18. B. xxiii, fol. 119 (see John viii, 1–11).

If the reader has had to be content with very meagre examples of the former, still less can be given him in illustration of saint-lore in English homiletic sources, proportionate, that is to say, to the mass of anecdotes, marvels, and histories surviving in collections of *exempla*, festival sermons and the like. Once again, our immediate purpose is merely to show that it was the pulpit that kept alive a keen human interest in these heroes and heroines of the Church on the widest scale, and that neither picturesque saint-dramas nor pious "contes dévots" in verse are isolated or even original phenomena of contemporary literature. Both of the latter, indeed, appear to be the natural and inevitable outcome of this pulpit propaganda. An unpublished English *Speculum Sacerdotale* of sermons upon the saints, apparently of the early fifteenth century, thus restates the preacher's special task in this direction:

> The olde fadres afore-tymes made fro bigynnynge the festyvites of holy apostles and martires whiche were before hem to be lovyd and halowed, as it [is] iseen. And specially in entent that we the herers of here blessid commemoraciouns, whiche ben in tymes of here fastes redde and songen, my3te be stired for to folowe hem in the same wey; and also that we my3te throu3 here prayers and medes be in here everlastynge fellaschip and holpen here in erthe....
>
> And therfore we worschepen martires with the same worschipynge of religion and felawehede as are other holy men and holy lyvers worschippid with here, the while they are in erthe, whos hertes we knowe to be redy for sothfastnes, 3if nede were, un to syche passiouns as they suffred. But 3it with a more tristefull devocion we commende and worschipen hem whiche ben passed, sythen we ben more seker of here hertes and passiouns then of tho that ben lyvynge.

The human as well as the pious aspect of the subject are thus both clearly set forth in the speaker's preface. He goes on later:

> Among alle other holy customes of holy churche, the whiche oweth to be worschipid with a soverayn devocion, this semeth right comendable and to be kepid with a good diligence and desire: that is to say, that in alle the chirches of the worlde the prestes of hem, whiche are sette to the governaunce of the parishenes, aftur the redyng of the gospel and of the offertorie at masse, turne hem unto the peple and schewe openliche unto hem alle the solempnitees and festes which shall falle and be hadde in the weke folowynge. And, afturwarde that they make hem to pray for pees to be grauntyd and for the clergie, for the peple, and alle the good doers of the parishe churche, also for the seke of the parishe, 3if ther be eny ther-inne, ffor goers on pilgrymage and hem that passeth

and ben over the see, ffor frutis of the erthe, that god kepe hem mercifully unto his trewe peple, and so at the laste for the lyvynge and dede—the whiche prestes owe for to do aftur the grace that god hath yeven hem, resonably, semyngly and devowtly. ffor the honestelier and holier that they make here proclamacion unto the peple, the more they stere and shuld stere the peple to that that they bydde hem. They schulden comende and prayse the solempnitees of god and of his seyntes excellentely with all here myghtes, and the cause wherfor they ben ordeyned openly to schewe and for to declare schortly some myracles that perteyneth unto the festes, that the peple of god may be lyghtenyd with, unto the knowlige of sothfastnes and to the love therof be inflamyd and styred.[1]

Such exposition of the saints, then, if faithfully performed, would picture them as no awful and misty haloed figures remote from human affairs as the sacred occupants of a clerestory window, but vivid and toil-stained flesh and blood. Thus they appear in the vernacular homilies before us. The reader has only to turn the pages of a popular festival-book, like that of Myrc, to see how the very grotesqueness and apparent irreverence of the speaker is but a natural result of the realistic, homely way in which he looks at his heroes. It is their humanity that delights him, as well as their virtue. His fresh Olympus of Apostles and New-Testament saints has an intimate family history of its own, relating to their earthly days. St Andrew was formerly an old disciple of John the Baptist, he tells us.[2] "Mary Mawdelen", of "Mawdelen-castell", was apparently once upon a time engaged to be married to "Jon the Evangelyst", before Christ called him into His service, and the Devil entered into her.[3] The Blessed Virgin confided the secrets of the Annunciation and the years of Christ's youth at Nazareth, in person, to St Luke, "for encheson that he was clene maydon" like herself, and was wont to visit her in the early period of her Son's ministry on earth.[4] Even Judas

[1] MS. Add. 36791, fols. 1 et seq. Cf. further, C. Horstmann, *Altenglische Legenden*, neue folge, Heilbronn, 1881; etc.
[2] Cf. *Festial*, p. 6. [3] pp. 31, 203.
[4] p. 262. Cf. again, MS. Roy. 18. B. xxiii, fol. 170: the B.V.M. was created by "the fadur of heven" to be "a mayden for hym-selfe, a modur for his sonne, a wiff for the holy gooste" (from "Seynt Barnard, in a sermon that he mad of hur"); fol. 38 b—"Seynte Jon the evangeliste"; etc.

"was somtyme so myghty goostely and so grete with God that he reysed men from dethe to liff, he caste oute ffendes fro men and heled mesels".[1] Little peculiarities of their personal habits or appearance—often absurd enough—are eagerly gleaned from the *Legenda*, and held up to sermon-audiences as evidence of extraordinary piety. Thus, "the harde here[2] of Seynt Edmunde of Abyngdon" now excites interest, or "the mekenes of Seynt Marie Egypcian",[3] like the more historical virtues of the Old Testament heroes previously alluded to. Even when "he was sowkynge" as a babe, says another, St Nicholas "begane to liffe an holy liffe and a good, and to use grett abstinence. For (as) we rede in ys liffe that every Wedenesdaye and Frydaye he wold souke but ons on the daye, and so helde hym contente".[4] St James (the Less), forsooth, had knees "soo thekke of ylle that fhey weren boched lyke a camele", because "he vset forto knell soo moche yn hys prayers". "Thys was the fyrst man that ever song masse yn vestementys, as prestes now dothe(!)."[5] St Clement's "ʒeftes, that God ʒeves for hym, ben ofton knowon and receved amonge us; inspeciall for perell of fure and watre it is knowon to you well inoʒthe."[6] Archbishop Fitzralph of Armagh, in his more dignified volume of Latin sermons, adds a note at the end of his report to remind him doubtless of useful material of this kind for some future occasion:

Then, on account of the Feast of the Blessed Apostle Andrew, an anecdote (*narratio*) was given concerning a bishop who was devoted to him,... as it is written in his life in the *Flowers of the Saints*, up to the end of the Legend; and so the sermon was brought to an end.[7]

However marvellous they might be, such miracles from the *Legenda* were definitely presented as true history, not to be confused in the popular mind with lighter forms of pulpit

[1] MS. Roy. 18. B. xxiii, fol. 119b (according to St John Chrysostom).
[2] = hair shirt.   [3] MS. Harl. 2398, fol. 19.
[4] MS. Roy. 18. B. xxiii, fol. 69 (probably from the *Aurea Legenda*, q.v.). Cf. *Altengl. Leg.* p. 11.   [5] *Festial*, pp. 139–40.
[6] MS. Roy. 18. B. xxiii, fol. 53 (a story of a woman follows, who made a pilgrimage to a chapel of St Clement "that stondeth in the see", and whose son was miraculously restored to life, after drowning).
[7] MS. Lansd. 393, fol. 80. See *Altengl. Leg.* pp. 8–10 for this story.

illustration: "This is no fabull that I sey ȝow. It is every woke songe and rad in holy church, in remembrance of the good ladies kyndenes and grace".[1]

The national hero among the saints of the English pulpit was clearly the martyred St Thomas of Canterbury.[2] Sermons in honour of his Feast are plentiful. Noted preachers like Bishop Brunton of Rochester and Archbishop Fitzralph[3] afford several examples in their homily-books. If we turn not to these, but to a collection of Latin sermons which appear to belong to the early years of the fourteenth century, preserved in the library of Hereford Cathedral,[4] we shall find interesting indication in one of them of the numerous sources for such an address which lay at the preachers' disposal, and of the elaborate efforts which the more scholarly and dignified among them were sometimes willing to expend upon its preparation. The speaker takes his text from the Book of Lamentations (v, 16)—"The crown is fallen from our head". His first concern is to exalt his hero to the front rank of the Church's saints and martyrs in all ages, and to meet certain arguments and unfavourable comparisons that have been made in disparagement of such a view. "Concerning these I say that the sacrifice of this day which Thomas offered excelled all others, as it seems, in all the five aforesaid conditions" (namely, in degree, person, place, time and cause). "Assuredly this high priest entered into the temple on this day to offer a sacrifice. 'Not with the blood of goats and calves, but through his own blood entered he into the holy place, having obtained eternal redemption', as it is

[1] MS. Roy. 18. B. xxiii, fol. 140b (concerning "the most synnefull man Theophile", who made a pact with the Devil, and afterwards repented and was forgiven through the intervention of the B.V.M.). Cf. here, the Lollard *contempt* for these legends of the saints (Wilkins, *Concil. Mag. Brit.* vol. iii, pp. 496–503; etc.).

[2] Cf. here Ten Brink, *E. Engl. Lit.* vol. i, pp. 273–4.

[3] Cf. MS. Lansd. 393, etc. nos. 67 ("Princeps maximus cecidit hodie in Israel", 2 Sam. iii, 38), N.D.; 71, A.D. 1335?; 76 ("Contempnit timorem, nec credit gladio", Job xxxix, 22), 1344; 84, N.D. Cf. another by John Wessyngton, prior of St Cuthbert's, Durham, in MS. Laud 262, fols. 33–6 (14th cent.). For sermons abroad see Hauréau, *Not. et Extr.* vol. iv, pp. 241 and 249 (Franciscan, 13th cent.).

[4] MS. Heref. Cath. Libr. P. 5. 2, fol. 99b–107.

said of Christ, in the Epistle to the Hebrews (ix, 11–12)".[1] He was "a lamb before the throne of God without blemish". In respect of "time", we are told that "the evening sacrifice was the most acceptable (to God) in the Old Law. But this same sacrifice of Thomas was made at the evening hour, according to history, when the monks were celebrating Vespers". So the panegyric proceeds from point to point, its author apparently not hesitating to apply the most exalted imagery of Scripture concerning Christ to his own favourite saint. Then the orator reveals to us at least one of the reasons for this gross exuberance of language.

For certain persons strive to extol other martyrs above Thomas, as for example Peter of Milan[2] and the like, on account of the cause of his martyrdom. "And the latter died for the Faith (they say); but Thomas, for the liberty of the Church. And since the Faith is more important than the Liberty of the Church, and the cause makes the martyr, one martyr exceeded the other in merit as in reward." But this argument is vain. For, since it is of greater excellence, as has been said, to give counsel rather than to make precepts, for counsel cannot be given without precepts, much more excellent is it to die for counsels given rather than for mere precepts.

Thus, the various objections to the supremacy of St Thomas are dealt with and dismissed in turn. An interesting objector mentioned here by name is our own chronicler William of Newburgh.[3]

And it is to be noted that the opinion of William of Malmesbury, Canon of Newburgh, breaks down in this respect. For, although he reckoned Thomas a glorious saint, yet he was unable to approve the cause of his martyrdom. Wherefore, in the Second Book of the *Gesta Anglorum*[4] which he wrote, he gives other reasons for this. For he says that Thomas had the zeal of the Law, "but not according to knowledge"; as the apostle saith,—Romans x [2]—concerning certain, "that they have a zeal for God, not according to knowledge". For his judgment is that no

---

[1] fol. 100b.   [2] I.e. St Peter Martyr, Domin. (+ 1252).
[3] fol. 101. The art. "Wm. of Newburgh" in *D.N.B.*, by Miss Kate Norgate, gives no mention of his association with Malmesbury. But is not the title mentioned here from Leland—"Gulielmus *Parvus*"—to be explained as a device for distinguishing him from his earlier namesake, the chronicler Wm. of Malmesbury (d. 1143?)?
[4] I.e. *Historia Rerum Anglicarum*. See *Chronicles of the Reigns of Stephen, Henry II, and Richard I*, Rolls S. vol. 1, pp. 142–3 (cap. xvi).

useful purpose could have been served by the language in which Thomas contradicted the king, save that the royal anger would be kindled. Therefore he does not praise his cause, although he commends the zeal of the man.... He adduces the authority of Amos the prophet, who says thus—capit. v [13]—"A prudent man shall keep silence in such a time; for it is an evil time". This is what this William alleges. But, in truth, that opinion was invented according to the wisdom of this world, which God hath accounted foolishness.[1] For, beyond doubt, "not his Father which is in heaven, but flesh and blood hath revealed it unto him".[2] ...

References follow, a little later in the discourse, to Bede's account of the pagan customs of the English surviving after their conversion,[3] to Anselm, to Lanfranc[4] and to an earlier Archbishop of Canterbury, St Alphege, and the Danes. Then the preacher takes up a further point of interest in the tragic story of St Thomas—"which I have read in a certain book written about his life, at Oseney".[5] This concerns the saint's refusal to sanction an uncanonical union proposed between William of Anjou, brother of the king, and the widow of the Earl Warenne; on the ground that the Empress Matilda, William's mother, and Stephen, parent of the countess's first husband, were cousins.[6] The speaker proceeds to tell how this refusal naturally enraged King Henry II as well as his brother, already annoyed as he was at his stubborn archbishop's opposition to him in matters of state. Hence later, when Richard Brito, one of the four knights concerned in the murder at Canterbury, struck the archbishop with his sword, the story goes that he cried out that he did it as vengeance "for love of my lord William, the king's brother!" Our preacher's own comment is

---

[1] Cf. 1 Cor. iii, 19.   [2] Cf. Matth. xvi, 17.

[3] MS. Heref. Cath. Libr. P. 5. 2, fol. 101 b.

[4] "Anselmus Cantuarensis de Bekko, et Lanfrancus."

[5] fol. 102 (Osney Abbey, near Oxford). This book was probably the *Vita S. Thomae* by Wm. Fitzstephen. See *Materials for Hist. of Thomas Becket*, Rolls S. vol. iii, p. 142. The incident occurs also in the *Draco Normannicus* of Etienne de Rouen. See *Chrons. of the Reigns of Stephen, Henry II, and Richard I*, Rolls S. vol. ii, p. 676.

[6] "Stephanus autem et Matilda erant consobrini, illa genita de fratre Henrico, scil. primo, rege Anglie, et ille Stephanus natus de sorore Henrici primi." For this Earl de Warenne (d. 1160), see art. "Matilda of Boulogne", in *D.N.B.*, and *Chrons. of the Reigns of Stephen, Henry II, and Richard I*, Rolls S. vol. ii, p. 676, n. 2.

that thus Thomas was martyred in an even nobler cause than that for which John the Baptist was done to death ("always saving the greater sanctity of John"). "For John merely prohibited an act of adultery which is always unlawful"; but Thomas not only prohibited this, but also declared unlawful by statute of the Church a marriage "which nevertheless could have been legalized by dispensation". Who can wonder then, he goes on,[1] at the disasters which ultimately befell the realm of England, under King John, a son of Henry II? Assuredly they were a punishment sent from heaven for the murder of the saint:

In the time of King Henry the Second, whose knights slew Thomas, the power and dominion of the realm of England were at their height. For that same Henry also acquired the duchy of Aquitaine. He, too, acquired Ireland and its kingdom. He was also the chief lord of Scotland, and King William the Scot did homage to him for his land of Scotland. Wherefore his sway extended from the end of the earth towards the North, and from the ends of the earth towards the West, from Ireland up to the end of Europe in the South, as far as the mountains of the Pyrenees upon the confines of Europe and Africa.

Under King John, however, the territory, we are told, was broken up and diminished—"almost to the very midst". William of Newburgh's account of King Henry's abject penance for the murder[2] leads our preacher to observe that, although no one would dare to repeat that murder nowadays, "notwithstanding, there may not be lacking such as have dared as much in public as in private to attempt such deeds". How many of the rich and mighty of to-day, "who adorn the tomb of Thomas with gold and silver and precious stones", would not have been guilty of a share in the blood of this martyr, if they had lived in the times of their ancestors? he asks. The human heart and human vice change but little through the centuries. The speaker goes on to point the significance of "the Statutes promulgated at Clarendon", and further disasters that befell King John, notably the great defeat inflicted on him by the French "in Poitou" (*in Pictavia*), a

[1] MS. Heref. Cath. Libr. P. 5. 2, fol. 102b.
[2] fol. 103.

divine vengeance for this same murder.[1] At length, a mystical prophecy is quoted from the *De Oneribus Prophetarum* of pseudo-Joachim of Fiore,[2] to the effect that the English people would suffer at the French king's hands—"because the son of Barachiah is slain again in Thomas". This leads to a fresh comparison between the saint and "Zechariah, son of Barachiah", slain between the sanctuary and the altar.[3] Subsequently,[4] the fulfilment of another prophecy is observed, in what is here spoken of as though it were a comparatively recent event "concerning which Henry the archdeacon speaks very fully in his *Chronicles*, in Book VI":[5] "A certain holy man shortly before the coming of the Normans had foretold to the English", besides lasting humiliation from France for their crimes, "that the Scottish people also, whom they were wont to repute most vile, would master them to their well-deserved confusion. Thus saith the archdeacon". Our preacher now sees the verification of this prophecy in the battle of Bannockburn.[6] "What wonder therefore", he cries, "that our

[1] Reference is also made to *Cronica ffrancorum*, concerning the great victory of Philip (Augustus) of France over the Germans, "apud pontem bovum apud Duacum", i.e. the battle of Bouvines, nr. Tournay (July 27, 1214).

[2] fol. 104: "Abbas iste Joachim de Flore in Calabria scripsit unum librum quem intitulavit *de Oneribus Prophetarum*. Hoc est de oneribus de quibus prophete loquuntur; et in illo libro, in capitulo quod intitulatur 'onus in Arabia', dicit hec verba—'Onus hoc Britannos mutuo respicit...'".

[3] See Matth. xxiii, 35, and Luke xi, 51.

[4] Other quotations (fol. 104b) from Bede (*de Gestis Anglorum*), Josephus, and "Magister Epiphanius Ciprius, qui secundum Ieronimum erat expositor Sacre Scripture". See below pp. 139 and 594.

[5] fol. 105. For this reference to Henry of Huntingdon, see *Henr. Archid. Huntend. Hist. Anglorum*, Rolls S. ed. T. Arnold, p. 173.

[6] This I take to be the Scottish victory here referred to, won on St John Baptist's Day (June 24) 1314. The preacher remarks further: "Et similiter milites huius temporis eodem modo male observant istam religionem militarem quam instituit Johannis, et ideo transgredientes ordinem committunt in patronum ordinis scil. Johannem Baptistam". This reference to the battle gives some rough indication of the date of these sermons. Cf. again in a "Sermo pro salute regis", fol. 80b, references to the Scottish Wars then proceeding—"Et certe in casu isto iustam habet pugne causam [rex]. Tres enim sunt cause iuste pugne, pro fide, pro iure,

knights have suffered confusion and ignominy on St John the Baptist's Day, and this from a people for whom they had the utmost contempt, namely the Scots." Divine retribution is the chief lesson of history drawn by these homilists of the later Middle Ages. He who speaks here has yet more to say of historic events, notably of the insults offered to St Thomas by Gilbert (Foliot), Bishop of London, and Hilary of Chichester,[1] also of a discussion between King John and the Papal Legate Pandulph, at Northampton.[2] But we must pass over these matters, as well as an allusion to the birthday of the saint, with a miracle accompanying it, which, our preacher declares—"I read in a certain book of his Life, at York".[3] For its length as well as for its industry, this sermon is certainly a most remarkable specimen of the art. But it is remarkable for a further reason. For in it we behold the English pulpit as the mouthpiece of the new national spirit, even where clearly an audience of clergy is concerned, all too suspicious of their lay fellow-countrymen.[4] St Thomas, troubler of his king, is yet lauded here as the special head and protector of the clergy of *England*.[5] His title is stoutly defended against all comers. That same spirit of national pride and national ambition, so quickly nettled at foreign interference with the sacred lands and liberties of England, is to be seen again in the sermons of Archbishop

et pro patria, que quasi omnes certe, si bene considerentur, locum habent in facto Scocie, sicut illi qui veritatem sciunt plenius possunt enarrare.... Certe illi sunt regis peiores inimici quam Scoti, quia illi extranei et ante faciem, isti domestici et a tergo...". With such passages should now be compared the order given to Dominicans, in 1315, to preach sermons against the Scots in the churches of their own and other convents, in parish churches, etc. See *Letters from Northern Registers*, Rolls S. pp. 238–9. Huntingdon's prophecy is also in MS. Roy. 12. E. xxi, fol. 44 b.

[1] MS. Heref. Cath. Libr. P. 5. 2, fol. 105 b.

[2] fol. 106 b.   [3] fol. 106.

[4] Cf. here, fol. 107, "Laici [in] oppido sunt infesti clericis sicut lupi ovibus".

[5] See esp. fol. 107. For the preacher's *national* feeling, even as a cleric of the Church addressing clergy, cf. again fol. 89 b: "Prelati...sunt fratres preterquam cognacione et natura, gente quidem quia *Anglici*". Again, fol. 115 b: "...ad salutem animarum et utilitatem ecclesie *Anglicane*", fol. 45; etc. On fol. 107 b, another sermon follows the above—"In translatione Sancti Thome Cantuar. Archiep. Sermo".

Fitzralph and Bishop Thomas Brunton.[1] Clearly then, the new patriotic sentiment in English literature of the fourteenth and subsequent centuries also owes something to the influence of her indefatigable preachers.

This patriotic instinct is equally in evidence when we turn from the learned oration in Latin to humbler and more picturesque homilies on the same saint in the vernacular. Though presented, in the following excerpt, as the loyal servant of that old enemy of English liberties, "our holy fader the pope", Becket is nevertheless declared to be dying for "the welfare of yngelonde":

> ... Ther were iiii knyghtes in this lond, of cursid lyvyng; and for to have a rewarde and a thanke of the king of yngelonde, they made an othe upon the halydam that with one consent thei shuld sle and distroy holy Thomas, one hight Reynalde beyrson, an other William Trasy, the third Sir Richard Bryton, the iiiith Sir hew morvile. So, upon childremasse day in Cristemas weke, al-moste at nyght, these iiii knyghtes cam to Caunterbery in to the hall of the bisshoppes paleis. Then Sir Reynolde Beyrson, for he was most cursid of kinde, without any salutyng reverens he said thus un to seint Thomas, "The King that is be-yonde the see send us to the, commaunding and bidding the that thou assoyle all the bissopis that thu haste do acursid". "Syrres", quod seint Thomas, "I do you to wille thei be acursid be auctoryte and power of our holy fader the pope, but in no wise bi me, and I may not assoile them that our holy ffadir the pope hath acursid with-oute auctorite of hym." "Well", quod Reynolde, "then we se thou woll not do the kynges commaundementes. By God thou shalt dye!" Then cried the other knyghtes, "Sle, sle!" And then thei yede oute of the halle and toke their counselle, and concluded for to sle hym. So thei armyd theim in alle haste, and in the mene tyme prestes and clerkes and other that were with hym drowghe holy Thomas in to the chirch and lokkid the dore and barrid it fast to hym. But whan seint Thomas perceyved that the iiii knyghtes were sparrid oute and wolde have cum in, and myght not, he went to the dore and unbarrid it. Then he toke a knyght by the hand and seid, "It is not semyng for [to] make holy cherche as a castell or a place of defence. Cum in my childre in goddes name". Than it was so derk that thei myght not wele se nor knowe seynt Thomas from a nother man, but cried and seide, "Ubi est proditor?"—"Where is this traytour?" "Nay", quod seint Thomas, "no traitour but Archbissop is here. I cum not to fle but to abide and take my dethe for goddes sake and holy chirche right." Then sir Reynold beyrson stroke at hym and smote of half his croun.

---

[1] See in my *Preaching in Med. Engl.* pp. 202–8, and below, p. 225. For a fifteenth-century example, cf. above, pp. 72–5.

Then an other knyght stroke in the same place and smote of the sculle. Then fell down holy Thomas on his knees and seid thus—"*Commendo deo, beate marie et sancto dionisio meipsum et ecclesie causam*". "I commende to god, to oure lady seint marye, and to seint dionyse my cause and the ryght of holy chirche"; and so he dyed. Then the thrid knyght stroke at hym, and halfe the stroke felle upon a clerkes arme that helde up seint Thomas, and so down unto seint Thomas hand. Then the fourth knyght smote his swerd up on the paviment and brake the poynte of his swerde, and seid, "He is dede. Go we hens!" But when thei were at the dore outeward, one of hem, Robert broke, went ageyn and sette his fote in his nek, and with his swerde shed oute the braynes on the pament. Thus toke holy Thomas of Cauntebery his dethe full mekely, for right of holy chirche and the welfare of yngelonde.[1]

The quaint dramatic fashion in which these preachers love to describe the martyrdom of their national hero is illustrated again in a sermon of the unpublished *Speculum Sacerdotale* already alluded to. Its popularity as a pulpit theme is reflected in the numerous wall-paintings of the Martyrdom which once adorned the interior of English parish churches, happily not all yet swept away.[2] Each picture has its own little characteristic differences.

So far this blessid creature Thomas hadde thus lyved in turmentis vii yere, by the forsaide iniuryes, wordis and dedes, stryves and myscheves. At the ende of the vii yere throuʒ prayer of pope Alexander and of Lodewyke, that tyme beynge kyng of ffraunce, he hadde as in worde frenschip of the forsaide Harrye, kyng of Engelonde. And forthy he turned home aʒen into his see, where he was resayved of the peple as he hadde ben an aungel for gladnes; that for ioye the peple songe and seyde, "Benedictus qui venit in nomine Dei". Nevertheles, withyn a lytel while aftur, *scilicet* the V day of Christenmasse, there come fowre knyʒtis, *scil.* Hughe Morvilla, Richard Bruto, William Tracye, Reginald the bere-son; the whiche men was seyde to be comen of gentel kynde, but withyn a litel while aftur they were more famosid with malice and wickydnes. ffor these persones armyd entreden in to the mynistere of the trinite, and cryed alowde, as the monkys were at evensonge, and seide, "Where is the Erchebischope, where?" And he metynge and commynge to hem, seyde thus: "Lo, here I am", he sayde, "what wolle ye?" Thenne seide one of the knyʒtus, "Now thow schalt be dede". Then seide he, "I am redy to die for crist and his riʒtwisnes, and fredome of holy chirche. But I forbede you in godis behalf and on peyne of cursyng that ye do non harme to non other then to me". And for the blessid martire sawe

[1] MS. Harl. 2247, fol. 23 b.
[2] Cf. Preston Church, Sussex (near Brighton), North Stoke, Oxfordshire, Pickering, Yorks, etc.

the swerdes drawen oute, he inclyned hym and his hede in maner of praying, and seide these laste wordes: "I commend me-self and the cawse of holy chirche to god and to his blissid modir marie and to the holy patrones of the chirche and to seynt Dynyse". And anon the wrecchide manquellaris sett the swerdis into his hede, and kyttyd sorowefully the holy crowne, that the brayn ranne oute amonge hem.[1]

Quaintest of all is the eulogy of John Myrc.[2] In his eyes, Thomas the "chaunseler", before he became archbishop, is clearly the great English patriot and gentleman of the age, expeller of the rascally foreigners,[3] repairer of the royal manors and "the kyngys palyce yn London", restorer of peace in the land, "manful" in the French wars, "manful" in his array of rich clothes and furs, horses and equipment, "manful" in his fare and household—"that hys hall was yche day of the ӡere new strawed, yn somyr wyth grene rosches and yn wyntyr wyth clen hay, forto save knyghtys clothys that setton on the flore for defaute of place on the benche". His hearers must have enjoyed the story of king and favourite minister having a merry tussle on horseback in the streets of Cheapside. Then comes the sudden and equally dramatic change in manner of life when the chancellor becomes archbishop, a change to "harde heyre" (-shirt), plenty of vermin, and a beating on the back "al bare" twice a week for penance, with much else of a like nature. So to his dramatic end, that was no end after all. For the inevitable miracles follow.

The excerpts hitherto passed in review have emphasized that vivid, human side of the preachers' treatment of the saints which was calculated to promote imitation of their holy lives, as well as to stimulate devotion to the persons of the saints themselves:

Thanne what schal we wrecchis seie, that heeren red the lyves of seintis, whiche weren brent with fier and roostid, and virgyns the brestis drawen of, and in many othere turmentis; of whiche turmentis thei went to god ioiynge and syngyng and in herteli taukyngis?...[4]

---

[1] MS. Add. 36791, fol. 9.   [2] *Festial*, p. 38 et seq.

[3] "For what tyme he was made chaunseler, thys lond was full of Flemyngys, and so oversette wyth hom that a man myght not goo bytwyx townes for hom unrobbet. But yn a schort tyme Thomas...drof hom out of thys lond,..." etc.

[4] MS. St Albans Cath. fol. 43.

The homilist who thus reminds his hearers of those continually set before them as patterns of right conduct to their own lasting shame and condemnation, elsewhere, in speaking of images, bids men "make these holi seintis her meenys bi-twix god and hem".[1] The saints themselves thus become objects of prayer and veneration, active celestial beings, in turn able by their own intercessions to help the earthly pilgrim along his road. We can judge of the popularity of saint-worship in our centuries, if in no other way, by the preachers' frequent warnings against excessive zeal in this direction, and the taunts of Lollardy which, no doubt, drove them the more earnestly to deal with it. A compiler of sermons devoted to the memory of the saints, namely the author of our *Speculum Sacerdotale*,[2] is scrupulously careful to explain the limits to which this zeal may be allowed to go:

Nevertheles we moste be warre that in the tymes of here festes we mene no3t that the offeryngis and sacrifises, the whiche we maken for here worschipynge at here autèrs and chapels made of hem, ben don unto the seyntis, apostels and martires, but to hym that is god of hem and of us bothe. ffor ther is no prelate ne preste which stondeth at eny of here auteres at his masse that seith, "Lo, we ofere unto the, Petyr; or to the, Poule; or to the, Ciprian". But that, the whiche is offred, it is offred unto God that hath corounde martires and [is] worschiped. And so the sacrifice is made in here festis and stedes, that the affection and charite may rise by the love of the places in to the sowles of the peple, so that they may folowen here holy fadres in goodnes and wisdome.... And therfore be warre, for they don ydolatre that dothe sacrifise in offerynge or triste to martir, seynt or angel as to hym [i.e. the Godhead], and punyschable, 3e, and dampnable. Ne seyntis ne angels wold not take it.... And sires, therfore martirs are to be worschipid for meditacion and folowyng of here good wayes that they have made to us, and for charite, but not for servitude or power.

Practical imitation, then, remains the chief object of this veneration. Indeed, it is only fair to the orthodox side of the argument to say that even the simplest homilists were regularly wont to give such warnings when they preached. Says one of them, after commending the miraculous virtues of St Clement:

For, on this wize thu shalt pleze this seynt, and thu wolte furste worshippe god, the rather be cause of hym.... For all that thu doste in the

[1] MS. St Albans Cath. fol. 10.   [2] MS. Add. 36791, fol. 1 et seq.

worshippe of anny seynt, loke that thin entent be to worshippe god principally and to pleze hym. So every good dede that thu dost in the worshippe of anny seynt othere offrynge, lat it be do principally to god, secundarie to the seynte, or to that ende that god be worshippe[d]. And than youre offrynge is well do, and then god will quyte youre mede, and the seynte will preye for you that ʒe so worshippe.[1]

On the other hand, a homilist whom we have reason to suspect of Lollard tendencies, while not disparaging the idea of the saints' intercessions in heaven, yet argues that the sinner's prayers thus directed to them are superfluous:

Whanne we maken our praioris herteli oneli to God for thyng that is due, other able to be praied fore, thouʒ we make no special praieris to the seyntes, ʒet natheles alle the seyntes that ben in hevene ben redi to praie for us to god. Here also we mai lerne that if a man kepe the commaundementes of god and lyve vertuousli, thenne alle praieris of seyntes bothe of hevene and of erthe ben ordeynd and god accepteth hem as menes to his helpe, thouʒ his praieris ben not dresset immediat to seyntes.[2]

The call to imitation and worship, then, in their varying degree, still drew both preachers and people alike to study the features of these holy but once very human saints. Little wonder therefore that there were many amongst the former who were prepared to justify the images of them in churches against the attacks of Lollards in our period. He who declares from the pulpit that "we ought to see Job sitting in the dung-heap, and John the Baptist clad in camels' hair fasting in the desert, and Peter on the gallows of the cross,...and James falling upon the sword of Herod",[3] is surely arguing in favour of any kind of representation which will bring them vividly yet reverently before the eyes of unlettered men, whether in pictures and carvings, or in the less permanent but more lively fashion of sacred drama. We may well be surprised that more preachers did not follow the example of Myrc and attempt occasionally to explain the sacred portraits and statues themselves in their sermon hand-books. Rude enough, of course, many of these figures were—as Rypon himself hints in a sermon, when he confesses that if St Peter or St Paul were to stand alongside the images representing them in churches, they

[1] MS. Roy. 18. B. xxiii, fol. 53b.
[2] MS. Add. 41321, fol. 114b.
[3] MS. Add. 21253, fol. 15.

would appear very unlike them.[1] Nevertheless, these "remote
likenesses", as he carefully styles them,[2] when regarded with
veneration by simple folk in the light of such pulpit instruction
as they might receive, and used by the educated as aids to a
more spiritual devotion, were to be heartily commended. For,
in the words of Bishop Brunton, repeating a classic phrase of
St Gregory—"ymagines et picturae sanctorum, et precipue
crucis Christi, sunt libri laicorum".[3]

The contribution of English pre-Reformation preaching to
this subject of pictures and statuary of the saints is in its way an
interesting little contribution to the slender literature of the times
dealing with early English Art, hitherto strangely neglected.
We are therefore justified in considering it in some detail, as
a fitting conclusion to our study of sermon hagiography. One
would like to believe, indeed, that these pulpit discussions
played their modest part in the encouragement of a more
realistic and lively skill in the work of the medieval artist. We
can at least say confidently that they helped to maintain the
popularity of that work for a time. A fourteenth-century
treatise "in defence of Images" compiled from patristic sources
by Walter Hilton, canon of Thurgarton and author of the
well-known *Scale of Perfection*, remains still unpublished.[4]
Many of our preachers appear to have borrowed from it in
their day. "What Scripture conveys to clerks", says Hilton,[5]
"that a picture is wont to exhibit to layfolk". "So, by looking

[1] MS. Harl. 4894, fol. 19b ("Sicut patet de ymaginibus in ecclesiis,
quarum quedam representant Petrum, quedam Paulum...".
[2] "Sunt igitur tales vocate ymagines solum similitudines remote, non
ymagines rerum vere et propinque." (This preacher favours the language
of logic, it will be recalled.)
[3] MS. Harl. 3760, fol. 305. Cf. Hoccleve and Lyndesay, as below.
[4] MS. Roy. 11. B. x, fols. 178–83b: "Contra eos qui volunt eas in
ecclesiis dei collocatas destruere"—from the *Explicit*. (This MS. contains, in addition, John de Burgo's *Pupilla Oculi*. See my *Preaching in
Med. Engl.* p. 298.) The arguments and quotations that I here put forward
from Hilton and others have additional importance in view of the wholly
adverse picture supplied in Dr Coulton's recent *Art and the Reformation*.
They suffice to emphasize once more that there was at least a nobler
ideal amongst the instructed, however gross the general degeneration.
[5] MS. Roy. 11. B. x, fol. 180.

at images laymen can recall to memory the Incarnation of our Lord, and His Passion", etc. After dealing with the significance of miracles worked by images in churches, he goes on to argue for their retention from the evidences of Old Testament Scripture. Thus the Cherubim and other carved representations in the ancient Temple, and God's instruction to Moses to make all as he had been shown on the Mount are indications of the divine will in this matter. God actually prohibited the people of Israel from making images of Him at that time, because of the evil example of neighbouring Gentiles "seduced by illusions of demons", who might with good reason have misinterpreted a "divine cultus" paid to such sacred figures. To-day, however, no such impediment exists. Images, then, are of value because they call back the wandering mind to spiritual and divine things, "because they arouse from vain and worldly thoughts to more intent and frequent meditation upon unseen things and the desire for them". They are also placed in the churches "as commemorative tokens of the departed". This constitutes their real significance for "the lettered, the learned and the pious laymen". For, realizing that they are wood or stone and nothing else, "when they kneel before the images that are as it were a reminder, they forget them, and utter their prayers to God and his saints". Such is termed an "explicit intention", as contrasted with the "implicit intention" of "simple lay-folk, who observe the rite of image-worship according to the form and intention of the church, implicitly". None the less, neither do these latter "sin in their adoration, although their mind is actually fixed on the images themselves and not on God, as simple folk are wont to do when they see a fair image artificially painted and lavishly adorned.... By a certain carnal reverence their mind is stirred to adore with bodily humiliation that image rather than any other. Yet their intention is habitually directed towards God, in whose name they do worship to such an image". Hilton's view is that this "sensual and carnal emotion" is a necessary first stage in the religious education of ignorant men. He realizes rightly that their whole thought about God, whether in the presence of images or not, is thoroughly anthropomorphic. "They judge", he says, "of divine things from the analogy of corporeal things, imagining, for example, that God in his own nature has the body of a man like their own, thinking that the three persons in the Trinity are separate beings like three men", and so forth. After all "they believe that they are acting according to the custom and intention of the church; and if they knew better they would want to *do* better". It is this same general doctrine which the poet Hoccleve repeats in some lines of his *Regement of Princes*, facing the well-known portrait of Chaucer.[1]

So much then for Master Hilton.[2] The sermons of Master Rypon of Durham that deal with the same topic show that he has the Lollard heresy directly in mind. The question to be decided is "whether images should be made and set up in the churches for the purpose of worship—which all Lollards and others deny".[3] His first Authority for the defence is Bishop Grossetête of Lincoln, and the first opposing argument to be demolished by him is the prohibition of images in the Mosaic Decalogue, "which we Christians are held to observe more strictly than were the Jews of that time". An incident recorded, he says, in an epistle of Epiphanius to John of Constantinople[4] appears to support the argument. For it tells of a "dyed and painted veil hanging on the church doors, bearing a portrait of Christ or of some saint", which had been torn down at a prelate's instigation, and given as a winding-sheet for a poor man's burial. Lincoln, he points out, however, has triumphantly answered this main objection by pointing to the different

---

[1] *Works*, E.E.T.S. ed. Ext. S. vol. lxxii, pt. i, p. 180.

[2] He mentions specifically the Altar crucifix (fol. 181 b), and the familiar medieval representation of the Trinity, as described again by a Lollard preacher in the text here, below, p. 143 (fol. 182 b), in the course of his arguments.

[3] MS. Harl. 4894, fol. 31 b. Cf. again, Hoccleve, as above (p. 181):

"Yit summe men holde opynyon and seye
That noon ymages shuld made be.
They erryn foule and goon out of the weye;
Of trowthe hav they scant sensibilitie."

[4] "quam epistolam transtulit beatus Ieronimus, et est inter epistolas Ieronimi 53." See further below, p. 594.

circumstances of those times,[1] and he further quotes Gregory to the effect that such images ought not to have been destroyed. "Therefore pictures should be had in churches, in order that those who are ignorant of letters, should at least read with their eyes upon the walls what they are not able to read in books." For the rest of his sermon Master Rypon follows the arguments of Hilton already given. A story is told from John Damascene, that earlier authority on the same subject among the Fathers of the Church:

A certain king despatched a painter to paint a portrait of Christ from the life. When, on account of the brilliance of Christ's face, he was unable to do it, Christ himself placing a cloth to his own face imprinted upon it a portrait of himself, and sent it to the king. The same Damascenus says again—"We learn that Luke the Evangelist painted Our Lord and His mother".

Finally, "the universal usage of the Church approves the erection of images of the saints in churches; therefore it is permissible to make them". In a later sermon of the same series,[2] the sub-prior argues equally relentlessly against the making and worshipping of pictures or sculpture of "angels or demons", grotesques and imaginary figures. Yet another conspicuous preacher of our period, Archbishop Fitzralph of Armagh, has left us his opinions on the vexed question at issue. In a sermon delivered—"apud Datyngtoun"—on the Feast of

---

[1] I.e. by pointing out, as above in Hilton, that in those days there was a general tendency to idolatry, from contact with surrounding paganism. This does not apply to later times, he argues. Such earlier legislation was for the benefit of those—"ad errorem ydololatricum proclivi".

[2] fol. 67 (discussing the 1st Commandment: "non habere deos alienos, ubi prohibetur adorare spirituales creaturas pictas, angelos vel demones; non facere sculptile, in quo prohibetur facere ymaginem fictam ad adorandum, que ymago nullius rei naturalis vel supernaturalis simili-tudinem representat, ut si pingatur ymago hominis forma corporis humani et capitis leonis, vel huiusmodi; non habere similitudinem rei naturalis ut adoretur, dicens—'neque omnem similitudinem', i.e. ymaginem rei naturalis representationem, cuius sunt ymagines in ecclesia, ita scil. quod adorentur propter se, sed solum adorentur propter prothotipum [sic!], i.e. propter illud quod representat ymago". Damascene is again quoted. Images are only to be adored—"sicut litere regie sigillate adorantur", etc.).

All Saints, in the year 1356,[1] after lending approval to the proper veneration of the saints, in accord with the honour which God himself pays to them, Fitzralph goes on to speak of "a certain danger from the veneration of images which some frequently and wrongfully call by the name of those they are intended to represent, such as St Mary of Lincoln, St Mary of Walsyngham, St Mary in the Newarke,[2] and so forth; since St Mary, the Mother of God, is above in heaven, and never in those places or others like them here on earth. Wherefore those who venerate such images for their own sake and make offerings to them to procure healing or benefits of some kind appear to be true and potent idolators...." Subsequently, he denounces "the oblations which are offered to such images on account of the false and fabricated miracles wrought by their ministers".[3] Quite clearly, therefore, the love of saints inculcated by the pulpit had led to some undesirable results.

Of greater interest than the words of Hilton, Rypon or Fitzralph, however, is an anonymous treatise on the Decalogue, which discusses the same matter in vigorous English under the heading of the Second Commandment:

"Thou schalt nouȝt make the an ymage grave by mannes honde." Here by this commaundement sume men peraunter weneth that it beo forbode to make eny ymages. Bot of this speketh the noble clerke Bede in exponyng the temple of Salomon, where he seyth thus: "It is to knowe", he seyth, "that ther beth sume men that weneth that it be by the lawe forbode, that we scholde nouȝt grave ne peynte lyknesse of men or of bestes, other lyknesse of eny other thynges, in churche, for as muche as in the ten hestes it is commaunded that thou scholdest make to the non ymage ygrave, ne no lykenesse;—the whiche scholde nouȝt trowe that forbode, yf they toke to mynde the werke of Salomon. ffor Salomon in temple of the olde lawe made dyverse peyntynges and graves bytoknyng ymages that we haveth nowthe in holy churche, as dyde Moyses in the tabernacle by heste of God; and as Moyses by Godes heste also made a brasen serpent for that the peple that by other wylde fyry serpentes were envenmed byholdynge him scholde be heled and lyve. By moche more it is lausom to ous to have the ymage of Crist in the cros, that we in havynge mynde on the deth of Crist mowe overcome the temptaciouns and the venym of the fende, the olde serpent. And answeryng to the xii ymages of the xii oxen and to other thynges that entyred the temple,

[1] MS. Lansd. 393, fol. 105 b (Davington Priory, Kent?).
[2] I.e. at Leicester ("sanctam Mariam in novo opere").   [3] fol. 106.

it is lausom to peynte in holy churche ymages of the xii apostoles and of other seintes as we doth worschep fullyche and presabyllyche in holy churche. Wherefore if we dylygentlyche take hede of the wordes of this commaundement, we mowe wel y-knowe that we beo nou3t forbode to make ymages.... "Ellys for sothe", seyth this grete clerk Bede, "Crist Jhesu oure sauyour seynge the ymage of Cesar the emperoure on a peny scholde nou3t have y-hote—'3ylde to Cesar thynges that beth his', but rather have reprehended the ymage of Cesar, by cause of ydolatrie that my3te be to the image in a peny".

But here we schal understonde that ymages mowe be occasion of goed and also of yvel. ffor a gret clerk seyth that ymages mowe be maked wel and eke ylle: wel to ly3te and haunte and to styrye other meue the soules of goede cristene folke for to the more bysyloker and devouteloker worschepe her God; and ylle, whenne that by occasion of ymages men erreth fro the sothenysse of feyth, so that thylke ymage be worscheped as god; as yf eny body tryste endelyche to be holpe or relyved by hem in eny sykenesse or in eny other nede or dysayse, and therfore offere and praye to hem with worschep that is onlyche y-propred to god and to no mo. Therfore techeth seynt Gregorye in a lettere that he wrot to a Byschop and seyth thus: "Leve brother, late it was y-schewed to ous that thou seynge some folke worschepynge ymages wherfore thou breke the ymages and casteth hem out of churche. The whiche zele or love that thou haddest that thate, that was y-maked with mannes hondes, scholde nou3t be worscheped, we preyseth. Bot that thou scholdest nou3t have y-broke hem, we demeth." For Gregorie seyth here—"fore peynture ys maked in churche that thay namelyche that cunneth no letterure scholde rede in walles thate that they mowe nou3t in bokes. And so if a clerk schal worschepe his boke, thanne may another man worschepe an ymage". In another lettre the same Gregorie seyth, "Who so wole make ymages, let him nou3t bot in alle manere schone hem to be worscheped, and warne alle men bysyliche that they take hete and charite that is love of compunccioun by the sy3te of thyng y-do, that they be put adoune other that they knele adoune in to the worschepe of onlyche trinite. Herefore seyth a gret clerke, "I worschepe nou3t the ymage of Crist, for that it is tre, nother for it ys the ymage of Crist; but ich worschepe Crist byfore the ymage of Crist, for it is the ymage of Crist and meneth me to worschepe Crist".

And so whenne we cometh into eny churche, mekelyche we scholde knele upon the grounde;...and whanne thou seyst the cros, thenke with gret sorowe and compunccioun of heorte what dethe he suffrede for man-kynde; and so byfore the cros that meveth the to devocion worschepe thou Crist with al thy my3t. And thus by images and peynture y-maked by mannes honde thou mayste y-se and knowe how holy seyntes of hevene lovede almy3ty god, and how grete and dyverse passiouns they suffrede for love that they hadde to him—as by the ymage of *seynte Laurence* that is y-peynte or y-grave holdynge a gredel in his honde bytoknyng and schewyng how Laurence was y-rosted upon a gredel, and also by ymage of *seynte Kateryne* that ys ypeynt holdyng in here hond a whel and a swerd, schewyng what passioun the holy virgyne Katryne suffrede; and so by ymages of other seyntes thou myst somdel y-knowe what passioun they suffrede for love that they hadde to almy3te god.[1] And thus by sy3te of thes thynges y-seye, as Gregorye meneth byfore, we schul putte ous adoune into worschep of onlyche trynyte; and this scholde be grete worschep to the seyntes in hevene, for as muche that by the sy3te of here ymages oure devocioun ys y-meved the more devoute-loker to worschepe god.

And yf we do offrynge and worschep, that is onlyche y-propred to god, to here ymages, we nou3t onlyche thenne offendeth god, brekynge his heste, but also we offendeth alle the holy seyntes of hevene. For they hateth, as wytnesseth seynt Austyn, if suche thynges be do to hemself, for they wolleth nou3t usurpe to hem suche thynges that beth onlyche y-propred to god. Thenne muche more hy hateth yf suche thynges be do to here ymages that beth bot here schadues y-maked of tre or stone. ffor holy wryt wytnesseth how the angel of god wolde nou3t suffre Jon the Evangeliste to worschepe him, bot bad him worschepe God. And yf thou wolt worschepe in his trewe ymage, do after the conseile of Thobye, "and ete thou thy bred with hungry and nedy", that is to mene, 3yf parte of thy sustenaunce after thy power to hem that nedeth, and namelyche to the meke trewe poure man, that ys the trewe ymage of god, and moche may helpe the with his prayere. . . .[2]

The foregoing quotations have shown very clearly the official attitude to images as set forth by the orthodox pulpit. One specimen of Lollard preaching upon the controversy, and one only, must be given to illustrate the views of the other side. The following extracts are particularly interesting for their criticism of the actual mode of representing the sacred figures in current ecclesiastical art. They thus serve to make clear the main grounds of the Lollard objection, namely that, as a matter of *fact*, it was the outward sensuous appeal of the images that alone gripped the popular mind; and that that appeal was not even calculated to give a true impression of the commemorated themselves:

For first men erren in makyng of ymagis, whanne thei maken ymagis of the godhed, as of the trinite, peyntyng the fadir as an olde man, and the son as a 3ong man on a crosse, and the holy gost comyng furthe of

[1] Cf. further in this same MS. (*Memoriale Credentium*), fol. 38 b ("the ymages of holy seyntes y-peynted to ensaumple of ous").

[2] MS. Harl. 2398, fols. 81–2 b. Cf. the much briefer discussion in MS. St Albans Cath. Treatise on the Decalogue, fol. 10; also Myrc, *Festial*, p. 171, etc.

the faders mowthe to the son, as white dowfe. For, in the olde testament, god commaundid that no man shulde make ony ymage or lickenesse of hym. . . .

But sythen Crist was makid man, it is suffrid for lewid men to have a pore crusifix, by the cause to have mynde on the harde passioun and bittere deth that Crist suffrid. . . .[1] And 3it men erren foul in this crucifixe makyng; for thei peynten it with greet cost, and hangen myche silver and gold and precious clothis and stones theronne and aboute it, and suffren pore men bou3te with Cristis precious blode to be by hem nakyd, hungry, thursty and in strong preson bounden, that shulden be holpyn by Cristis lawe with this ilke tresour that is thus veynely wastid on thes dede ymagis.[2]

And syth thes ymages ben bokis of lewid men to sture hem on the mynde of Cristis passion, and techen by her peynture and veynglorie that is hangid on hem an opyn errour a3enst Cristis gospel, thei ben worthi to be brent or exisid, as bokis shulden be and if thei maden mencion and tau3ten that Crist was naylid on the crosse with thus myche gold and silver and precious clothis, as a breeche of gold endentid with perry, and schoon of silver and a croune frettid ful of precious iewelis; and also that Jon Baptist was clothid with a mantil of gold and golden heer, as sum men peynten hym; and so of ymagis of pore apostolis of Crist and other seyntis, that lyveden in povert and gret penaunse, and dispiseden in worde and dede the foul pride and vanyte of this karful lif. For thei ben peyntid as thoghe thei hadde lyved in welthe of this world and lustus of their fleysche as large as ever dide erthely man. . . .

And now men shulden be more gostly and take lesse hede to siche sensible signes, as dyden the apostlis of Crist, that by schort tyme and rewlis of goddis hestis and charite ledden men to hevene with-outen siche newe peyntyngis schewid by manes craft. For oure lord god dwellis by grace in gode mennes soulis, and, with-oute comparesone, bettere than alle ymagis made of man in erthe, and bettere than alle bodies of seyntis, be the bones of hem never so gloriously shreynyd in gold. Also men erren myche in offrynge to these ymagis. For to the gayest and most rychely arayed ymage ratheest wil the puple offur, and nou3t to no pore ymage stondyng in a symple kirk or chapel, but 3if it stonde ryaly tabernaclid with kervyng and peyntid with gold and precious iewelis, as byfor is seyd[3]—and 3it with inne a mynster or a greet abbey where litil nede is or noon to help by siche offeryng. . . . Dere lord, what almes

---

[1] This is interesting evidence of how far the Lollard was actually prepared to go in the matter of images. He will allow the retention of an unadorned crucifix for the benefit of the unlettered, then.

[2] Curiously enough, Dr Workman (*Jo. Wyclif*, vol. ii, p. 17) in quoting a similar passage as characteristic of the later Lollard position, has not realized its orthodox origins. See above, p. 99.

[3] Cf. again, here: "Where is most richessis aboute a stok, there wil the blynd puple most offur".

is it to peynte gayly dede signes and rotun stokkis with sich almes that is pore mennes good and lyfelode... [1]

In the course of an attack upon pilgrimages, the same homilist is equally illuminating on the same subject. Here, indeed, his testimony agrees with that of Archbishop Fitzralph whom we quoted:

> Summe lewid folc wenen that the ymagis doun vereyly the myraclis of hemsilf, and that this ymage of the crucifix be Crist hym-silf, or the seynt that the ymage is ther sett for lickenesse. And therfore thei seyn—"the swete rode of Bromholme", "the swete rode of grace", "the swete rode at the northe dore", "our dere lauedy of Walsyngham", but nou3t "our lauedy of hevene", ny "oure lord of hevene"; but cleven sadly, strokande and kyssand these olde stones and stokkis, layyng doun here grete offryngis, and maken avowis ri3t there to thes olde ymagis to come the nexst 3eer agayn, as 3if thei weren Crist and oure lauedy and Jon Baptist and Thomas of Caunterbery and siche other. [2]

Apart from the Lollard and his kind, then, there is a chorus of approval from the English preachers for these pictorial aids to devotion, when not openly abused. Pulpit reference to "seynt petres croys, seynt laurence gredyre, the huldynge of seynt Baltolmew" (that "ne beth nou3t bot a schadewe a3enst the peynes of purgatorye"),[3] or to those that "schulen be punischid in the balaunce of seint my3hel, that her yvel dedis schulen be of greet wei3te ther-ynne",[4] must have gained fresh significance in their company. The tone of pulpit realism itself was thereby heightened. Under the Austin canon's guidance, simple audiences took the greater "hede how that Crist, wher that he syttythe, he hath Petyr on that on syde and Powl on that other syde, and he hath hys wondys opyn and bledyng".[5] The figures depicted upon rood and window, upon screen and wall-surface came down from their places and lived and moved again amongst men. Folk understood now "wherfore Powle hath a sworde, and Peter hath the keys of Hevyn",[6] or Laurence "a grydull".[7] They knew why "Margret ys payntyd othur carven, wher scho ys, wyth a dragon undyr her fete and a cros

---

[1] MS. Add. 24202, fols. 26 et seq.
[2] fol. 28. [3] MS. Harl. 2398, fol. 45 b–46.
[4] MS. St Albans Cath. fol. 36. [5] *Festial*, p. 187.
[6] Ibid. [7] pp. 219–220.

yn her hond".[1] The evangelistic symbols no longer led them
to believe that the evangelists themselves "wern suche bestys,
and not men".[2] Moses with his "two hornes",[3] the reason
why, "wher that any ymage of [Oure Lady] ys, ever scho hathe
hure sonne Jhesu on hur arme wyth hur",[4] "the potte and the
lyly...sette bytwyx our lady and Gabryell" in the familiar
Annunciation scene,[5]—all became vividly intelligible. Myrc
himself has no doubts as to the value of these representations:
"I say boldly that ther ben mony thousaund of pepull that
couth not ymagen in her hert how Crist was don on the rood,
but as thai lerne hit by sy3t of ymages and payntours".[6] The
sermons, too, in their turn show the effects of this naïve
realism, joint product of pulpit eloquence and artistic execution, upon the minds of simple laity. Bromyard[7] tells us of a
rustic whose arm was once broken by the fall of a crucifix
insecurely fastened up in the church where he was wont to
worship. For a whole year the injured man kept away from
his church, as a result of this unwarranted onslaught. At length,
when his neighbours begged him to return, saying that he
would be burnt as a heretic if he continued his non-attendance,
he grew afraid and relented so far as to come to the church.
Peeping in "with one eye", he espied the crucifix restored to
its place. "I shall be able to genuflect, bow my head and adore
you all right", said he, "but good love and faithful friendship
between us there will never be again".[8] In more solemn vein,
the vernacular homilist has now to reprove

alle thoo that, for any siknesse or sorwe that hem eileth, bihoteth and
renneth fro cuntre to cuntre to ymage 3oten or graven with mannes
hondes of gold or sylver, of tree or of ston, wenyng and tristynge that
ther be any dyvyne vertu in hem, or that thei moun any thyng helpen,
or oon more than an other, for any maner affeccion or fairenesse or coste.
...If thei seyen that thei bileeven not that ther is any vertu therynne but

---

[1] *Festial*, p. 201.   [2] p. 261.   [3] p. 102.   [4] p. 247.
[5] p. 109. Cf. in contemporary Engl. MS. illustration, MS. Add. 22720,
fols. 15 and 54b.   [6] *Festial*, p. 171. Cf. below, p. 509.
[7] *S.P.* s.v. "Adoratio". Cf. the story told here of the man who
regularly set a candle before a picture of the Devil in his church.
[8] This tale appears to be the source of a *facetia* of Lodovico Domenichi
(see E. Storer, *Facetiae of Poggio and others* (Broadway Translations),
p. 39, no. viii). Also in *Shakespeare Jest-Bks.*, vol. i, p. 94.

oneli in god, that loveth more and worcheth in oo place than in another, it wole seme [as] if it be provyd that thei lien falseli. For if men stele aweie that ymage that thei seche, thei wolen cese of hire pilgrymage in a schort tyme. And ȝet is god as myȝti as he was, and the place there stille. And thus thei proven bi hire deddis hire trist was in that ymage.[1]

For a last living contact with the holy dead through wonder-working relic and shrine, our medieval preachers also must take their share of the responsibility. Was it not they who regularly helped to popularize the miracle of St John the Baptist's finger that once pointed to Christ[2] or of the ring of St John the Evangelist preserved at Westminster,[3] the marvels wrought by "Thomas hond",[4] or by St Winifred's bones in "the abbay of Schrewsbury"?[5] Was it not they who even delivered special sermons for "Relike Sonday"?[6] In the eyes of a theologian like John Bromyard the record of marvellous happenings in Holy Writ gave ample justification for a belief in modern miracles of divine retribution and succour.[7] Why, then, should not an innocent preacher believe and still declare to his people—

ffor this blessed martyre [St Clement], oure lorde god shewyth many dyvers myracles, bothe be watur and by londe, and in specyall for perell of watur and fure, so farre forth that who that preyeth devoutely to god and to this holy martyre seynt Clement ys ofte delyvered fro suche deseses. ...Gloriose marter, thi name ys at us in helpynge; thou faylyste us not in ȝeftes ȝevynge!..."*Adest nomen tuum*", ut supra.[8]

The all-too-superstitious rustic might thus be induced at length to give up his pagan charms and witchcrafts for St "Colum-kille" as protection against fire, or for St "Appolonea" as a cure for the toothache.[9] Thus, too, "and a wife lose a keye

---

[1] MS. Add. 41321, fol. 85 (possibly Lollard).
[2] MS. Roy. 18. B. xxiii, fol. 172 ("Ecce agnus Dei...").
[3] Myrc, *Festial*, p. 149 ("Then whoso lust to have this prevet sothe, go he to Westmynstyr; and ther he may se the same ryng that was seven ȝere yn paradys").   [4] p. 20.
[5] pp. 100–1, 178–80.   [6] See my *Preaching in Med. Engl.* pp. 350–1.
[7] *S.P.* s.v. "Exemplum".   [8] MS. Roy. 18. B. xxiii, fol. 51b.
[9] See MS. Add. 37788, fol. 181, etc. ("Si aliqua domus ardeat, isti verbi sequentes jaciantur inter partem ardentem et partem non ardentem, et statim ignis cessabit, versus..."). St Apollonia, with forceps and tooth, appears frequently on painted rood-screens in Norfolk and occasionally in Devonshire (see Keyser's *List*, and *Suffolk and Norfolk* by Dr M. R. James). Cf. also, Lyndesay, *Monarche*, bk. ii, ll. 2295–6, 2365.

of valew of thre pens, anon she wil hete to seke seynt Sithe,
and spende a noble or ten schilyngis in the iurney".[1] It is
the author of *Dives and Pauper* who reminds us of others less
innocent, who were ready to make profit in the pulpits by this
popular credulity in miracles and saint-lore—

fals prechourys, which stale awey [God's] wordis fro the peple, and told
not the truthe as god bad them; butte only sayde such thynges that schal
please the peple, and so deseyved the peple with lesynges and with false
myracles, as men do these dayis, feynyng myracles of ymagis,...to
maynteyn ydolatrie for lucre of offerynge and false myracles of wicked
lyvers, and sey that god dothe myracles for them, and so blynde the peple
in falsnesse.[2]

Likewise, a Lollard evangelist calls to witness how image-
makers "stiren the symple puple to offur here litil catel to these
deede ymagis";[3] while the orthodox *Cilium Oculis Sacerdotis*
in its turn significantly warns parish clergy to "instruct their
people not to venerate or frequent places and relics of saints
unapproved by the church".[4] The preachers had themselves
largely to blame. The very brilliance of their own achievements
in the field of popular oratory is reflected in all these complaints.
Largely through their efforts the gods of the old Valhalla had
died at last: but a new race of deities and heroes, of good and
evil spirits had come to people the earth and dwell with men,
often strangely reminiscent of the former. So homely, so
fascinating, so *real* had the pulpit made these curious ancient
figures that blossomed everywhere upon the medieval fane—

patriarckes, prophetes, apostelles, martirs, confessours and virtuous
virgins, and other holy and devoute men and women.[5]

The effect of this teaching upon our literature will be patent
when we come to deal with the topic of Sermon and Drama.

---

[1] MS. Add. 24202, fol. 28 (for St Sithe, see Coulton, *Art and the
Reform.* p. 292). Cf. Lyndesay, *Mon.* bk. ii, ll. 2359 et seq.
[2] Prec. vii, cap. iii. Cf. further, *Piers Plowman*, C text, pass. i, ll. 96
and 119, and Chaucer, *Hous of Fame*, bk. iii, ll. 1265–70.
[3] MS. Add. 24202, fol. 26b. Cf. *The Complaint of the Ploughman*,
in Wright, *Pol. Poems*, Rolls S. vol. i, p. 331.
[4] MS. Harl. 4968, fol. 43b.   [5] MS. Harl. 2247, fol. 170b.

CHAPTER IV

Fiction and Instruction in the Sermon Exempla

THREE distinctive types of medieval sermon-illustration have already been noticed and discussed, more especially from the point of view of their literary influence, in the chapters preceding. We have seen brief illustrations drawn from men and things in the current everyday scene. We have had examples of the allegoric *figure* of speech, often Scriptural in origin but non-Scriptural in its development; and in addition we have had occasion to observe the part played by Biblical hero and saint in the pulpit legend. There remains yet the commonest type of *exemplum* to be considered, the moralized anecdote, whether historically true or fictitious, drawn from sources both ancient and contemporary, secular as well as religious. Of all the aforementioned types it is certainly this latter that has attracted the greatest attention hitherto from students of literature. For in it they have long recognized the medieval parent alike of the novel, the household fairy-tale, and some of the dramatic plots of the oldest and greatest school of secular English drama. To this extent, then, their labours in this field will have lightened our present task, namely, that we need only examine the actual uses to which typical *exempla* are put in the sermons of the period, studying the varieties with somewhat greater care and precision than has been possible hitherto in more limited surveys. Most of the stories themselves in some shape or form have been made accessible already in collections and catalogues by learned editors and archivists of modern time.[1] But the sources so far drawn upon have been almost entirely the better-known Example-books, compiled solely for the clerical reader.

---

[1] A sketch of the more important literature of the subject will be found in my *Preaching in Med. Engl.* pp. 299–302, etc. An important addition has now to be made to the list of published works there given, viz. M. J.-Th. Welter's new study—*L'Exemplum dans la Litt. Relig. et Didactique du moy. âge*, Paris, 1927. See esp. Part II for types and sources.

We have now to observe how these same tales and wonders were actually disseminated from English pulpits in the concluding centuries of the Middle Ages. For in this way alone could they become part of the literary heritage of a people blessed as we have seen with but few books and little or no means at the first of reading those that existed. The pulpit that concerns us here is again essentially a mere intermediary or handmaiden of letters, a modest teacher of other men's learning, with much industry but little original genius of its own. Nevertheless, the seed which it thus sowed was destined to bring forth in due time a rich harvest for others to garner. Does not Boccaccio, the very father of Renaissance wits and humanists, justify the license of his own more scandalous *novelle* by calmly pointing to the vogue of preachers like Gabriel Barletta—*et "qui nescit Barlettare, nescit praedicare"*.

"And so I may shewe to you by story, and also be ensampull of kende, and also of gestes", says a fifteenth-century preacher, discoursing to his congregation upon the Pride of Life.[1] For the first illustration he is content with an excerpt from "this grete clerke", Chrysostom. Dealing with the second—"the example in kind, or Nature"—he begins: "thu seest well that when floures and frutees ben sett uppon hie in tree toppes, ʒiff ther com a grett wynde, thei will sone wagge and fall down...." For the third type of illustration, the "geste", he proceeds as follows:

Also I rede *in cronicis romanorum* that, when Gaius was mad Emperour of Rome, it was not inought to hym that he was made lorde over all men but also he wolde be worshipped as a god, and sende over all abowte into every citee and countree an ymage of is likenes and that shulde be worshipped in the worshippe of hym, of all men. Beholde now this prowde man; ffor this was ryght a prowde dede. But listen what fell hereof, qwhen that he was moste in ys pride. The thride ʒere of is rialtee he was slayn in Rome [it]selfe, and as an hounde he was cast owte of Rome. Now goostely to speke, be this prowde emperor Gayus I undirstonde thise mysproude men that never will withedrawe hem from the synne of pride; and therfore I am aferde that itt shall fare by hem as itt dud by Gayus the emperor....So shall these proude men be slayn in the most of here pride, and as an hounde thei shall be caste in to the pitt of hell with-owten end....

[1] MS. Roy. 18. B. xxiii, fol. 124b.

Later, the homilist adds "also liknes in ffigure", from the book of Daniel,[1] to his other examples of sermon embroidery. In a modern essay on *The Exemplum in the Early Religious and Didactic Literature of England* by an American student,[2] the attempt has been made to give precise definition to these current terms of formal moralization—"example", "narration", "fable", "figure" and the like. It is clear, however, that with the possible exception of the "fable", which normally denotes a tale of animals, no such restriction of usage seems to have existed, even among the latest medieval homilists.[3] Mr Mosher himself has illustrated adequately their appearance in earlier homiletic works, from the printed sources at his command. Unpublished treatises and sermons of our period only emphasize the confusion. Thus, the words "exemplum" and "narratio" appear together as purely alternative descriptions for the story of a woman who converted her misbelieving husband, in a *Myrour for lewde men and wymmen*,[4] here followed by a "grete ensample" from Our Lord's own life: likewise, in the case of Myrc's *Festial* of sermons[5] and *Jacob's Well*.[6] But the treatise known as *Memoriale Credentium* employs the term "exemplum" for such typical "figures" as the stake in the stream,[7] and other natural objects treated symbolically. As for the "figure", in its turn, we find the phrase "this is wele figuryd" used to introduce the story of the creation of Man and Woman from the Book of Genesis[8] in a vernacular sermon, in contrast to its usual naturalistic application elsewhere—as in the discourse where "mans lyffe" is "well fygurde by roosis",[9]

---

1 "I rede that when Baltasar the kynge...." (Dan. v: Vulg. version).
2 J. H. Mosher (Columbia Univ. Press, 1911), chap. i.
3 See also here the important note by Welter, quoting further definitions offered by MM. P. Meyer, T. F. Crane, A. Piaget, G. Paris and G. Frenken (*L'Exemplum*, pp. 1–2).
4 MS. Harl. 45, fol. 84.
5 Cf. E.E.T.S. ed. pp. 56, 111, etc.
6 Cf. E.E.T.S. ed. p. 87, n. 4, etc.
7 MS. Harl. 2398, fol. 19b. Cf. also in MS. Camb. Univ. Libr. Gg. vi. 16, MS. Gray's Inn Libr. 15 (Staunton), etc.
8 MS. Camb. Univ. Libr. Gg. vi. 16, fol. 5.
9 MS. Linc. Cath. Libr. A. 6. 2, fol. 5. See below, p. 534.

or in the Prologue to Chaucer's *Canterbury Tales*.[1] Similarly,
in the aforementioned *Myrour* its author speaks "in figure,
qwerof it is red (4 Regum xxv) that Nebuzardan, that is
to mene the 'prince of cokis', destroyed the wallis of Ierusalem",[2]—another "example", that is to say, in the form of
Scripture narrative, not of animate or inanimate nature. The
best use of these terms that can be devised in the circumstances,
therefore, is to treat the word "Example" as the general all-
inclusive term for any kind of homiletic simile or illustration,
while reserving the "Narration" for stories of men and women,
the "Fable" for animal tales, and the "Figure" for similitudes
from natural objects. With this understanding, we can now
proceed to study some specimens of all three types, in detail,
from the sermon page.

It is Master Robert Rypon among the preachers of England
who reminds us once again that the record of Holy Scripture
is to be considered as parent authority for moralization in the
shape of anecdotes, whether historical or fictitious: this, too,
as set forth more particularly in the method of teaching adopted
by Christ Himself. "In various *parables* and *examples*, He in-
stigated the people, both Jewish and Christian, to abstain from
vices and pursue virtues. And this is what is said in Mark iv [2]—
'He taught them many things in *parables*' ".[3] English preachers
in especial, familiar as they must have been with a sermon story
of their own countrymen repeatedly on the lips of continental
fellow-preachers[4] before the century of Bozon and Bromyard,
had an additional good reason for respecting such *exempla*.
For the Venerable Bede had told in his *Historia Anglorum* how
a "very subtle and learned" bishop sent to convert the English
had failed miserably in the task "with his subtlety in sermons";
but how a less literate successor with his anecdotes and *examples* "converted well nigh the whole of England".[5] Such

[1] l. 499 (the *Persoun*).   [2] MS. Harl. 2398, fol. 128.
[3] MS. Harl. 4894, fol. 215 b. Cf. further the significant reference to the
Fable of the Trees, as given in the Book of Judges ix, 8–15, in *Ovidius
Moralizatus* (cf. Coulton, *Five Cent. of Relig.* vol. i, App. 25, p. 543).
[4] Cf. Jacques de Vitry, Etienne de Bourbon, etc.
[5] Cf. the version (English) in *Alphabetum Narrationum*, E.E.T.S. ed.
vol. i, p. 217: "St Bede tellis *in Gestis Anglorum* how when England was

even in those days was the power of a good story to hold the
attention of Englishmen, and make a popular favourite of the
raconteur:

> Than telle I hem ensamples many oon
> Of olde stories, longe tyme agoon:
> For lewed peple loven tales olde;
> Swich thinges can they wel reporte and holde.[1]

Robert Mannyng, in his *Handlynge Synne*,[2] speaks of this desire
to hear "talys" on the part of the common people, "yn gamys
and festys and at the ale". A passage of the Anglo-Latin *Gesta
Romanorum* tells further how they would sit around the hearth
on winter evenings after supper, listening to the ancient *gesta*.
In English sermons recorded in the vernacular, a regular practice can be detected of ending the discourse of the day with
one or two *narrations*,[3] eagerly looked forward to, no doubt,
by weary listeners with no "swetnesse...in heryng goddys
woord". In some Latin collections of sermons where the
exempla lie scattered at random, the preacher is reminded to
look up his source-books beforehand for the tale that will both
lighten and enliven his oration. Thus the story of "Perys" the
"toller", from the *Vitas-Patrum*, related in full as a sermon
ending by the author of *Jacob's Well*,[4] is merely indicated in
an anonymous series of *Sermones de tempore* elsewhere: "There
was a certain beadle in a certain city, named Peter. Look for
this narration in *Legenda sancti Johannis eleemosynarii*".[5] Again,
odd stories from such *Exemplaria* as the *Gesta Romanorum* will

oute of the belefe, the pope sente into it, to preche, a bisshop that was a
passing sutell clerk and well-lettered. And he usid so mekull soteltie and
strange saying in his sermons, that his preching owder litle profettid or
nought. And than ther was sent a noder that was les of connyng of
literatur than he was; and he usid talis and gude exsample in his sermon,
and he with-in a while convertyd nere-hand all England".

1 Chaucer, *Cant. Tales*, Pardoner's Prol. ll. 435-8.
2 E.E.T.S. ed. p. 3; cf. in MS. Harl. 45, fol. 143, a reference to the
English love of "veyn tales".
3 Cf. *Engl. Metr. Homs. of the 14th cent.* (ed. Small), Myrc's *Festial*,
Jacob's Well, MS. Roy. 18. B. xxiii, etc., passim.   4 See below, p. 156.
5 MS. Winchester Cath. Libr. xi (unpaginated): "Erat quidam bedellus
in quadam civitate, nomine Petrus...". Cf. Migne, *Patr. Lat.* vol.
lxxiii, col. 356.

sometimes be found added as a postscript to sets of homilies or didactic treatises of the day,[1] thus further indicating their value for the pulpit and their popularity with its audiences. Let us begin our survey with a contemporary reminder of the three great types of original sources upon which the medieval homilist could thus draw at pleasure. Excerpts "de sanctorum patrum ac doctorum legendis et scriptis" represent, in the first place the great majority of such *exempla* in common use. Those "de temporum preteritorum ac modernorum quibusdam eventibus" call to mind the contributions made by ancient chronicle and contemporary reminiscence. Those culled "de exemplis naturalibus" provide a third class of illustrations, for which the homilists were indebted to books of moralized animals and properties of things.[2] A work like the *Gesta Romanorum* already has been found to contain at least forty moralized tales used later in the *Summa Predicantium* of Bromyard, and thirteen or more in the *Sermones Dominicales* of the Oxford vicar John Felton. When the stories are related in the course of a sermon, some hint of their origin is usually given. But the task of identifying them may often be made harder by the absurd mistakes to which medieval preacher and copyist are alike prone. Thus one manuscript attributes the favourite story of the accursed dancers, who disturbed divine service in a church and were compelled to keep dancing till many of them fell dead, to the classical "Tullius".[3] Another manuscript, whose writer was apparently unacquainted with the priories of Shropshire, converts the Abbot of "Lilsull" (Lilleshall), into the Abbot of "Basil" in a narration from Myrc's *Festial*.[4] Mr J. A. Herbert has detected a curious error by which an author's

---

[1] Cf. MS. Glouc. Cath. Engl. Homs. (15th cent.), five folios at end; MS. St Albans Cath. Treatise on the Commandments, fol. 45: "*Narratio* —I rede in the gestis of romaynes that the Emperoure sent a worthi man to a lond, to be a iustice over hem...".

[2] MS. Add. 17723, fol. 1 (*Spec. Laic.*).

[3] MS. Salisb. Cath. Libr. 103 (unpubl. *Jacob's Well*), fol. 132. The mistake arose, apparently, from confusion with the name of the priest in the story. Cf. MS. Harl. 268, fol. 96b (*Alphab. Narrat.*): "Tullius presbiter ecclesie sancti Magni martyris". *Spec. Laic.* cap. xxi has: "in diocesi Tulliana...".   [4] MS. Rawl. A. 381, fol. 106b.

name, that of the Dominican Humbertus de Romanis, has actually intruded into his own narrative and become the name of its chief character.[1] The preacher himself was clearly not overmuch concerned at times with the source or even the veracity of his motley narrations. "Whether it is the truth of history or fiction doesn't matter", cries Bromyard, "because the *example* is not supplied for its own sake, but for its signification."[2] On the whole there is amazingly little originality in the choice of tales. The old favourites are repeated again and again, as though there was no risk of creating boredom with their perpetual staleness.[3] An interesting feature to notice, however, in much vernacular preaching, is the way in which many stories are enlivened in the process by touches of local colour and a contemporary setting. One version of the ever-popular tale of the prostitute converted in church thus amplifies the scene at the very outset: "So itt befell that ther was a feyre in a countrey ther beside the cite....And as she wente, she com by a churche, and att the stile stode the curate of the churche and is parischens with hym...."[4] There is an obvious pictorial sense in this preacher's handling of his narrative, simple and "unlettered" though he confesses himself to be. So, the English version of the *Gesta Romanorum*[5] makes vivid and homely to the minds of simple Englishmen a story of "Plebeius", the Emperor of Rome, "the whiche ordeynid for a lawe that wacchemen shulde eche nyght go aboute the cete and visite eche house, that there was no misgovernayle there-in, wher-by the city mygth peril or harm, and that there were no manslauter ne sodeyn deth in eny house...". The night-watchmen, thus described by the medieval preacher, would

---

[1] See the *Library*, v Ser. vol. vi, 1905, pp. 97–9. Another typical error of the kind—in the case of N. Bozon ("Barleam conte en son livre...")—is indicated by Mosher, *The Exemplum in Engl.* p. 103.

[2] *S.P.* s.v. "Avaritia". Cf. further s.v. "Dedicatio" (the Story of the Ass buried in the Churchyard, as below, p. 254): "Istud non adduco pro veritate hystoriali—quam [fabulam] non credo veram; sed pro tanto valet ad propositum quia...".

[3] Cf. here M. Meyer's Introd. to *Les Contes Moralizés de N. de Bozon*, pp. xv, xvi.

[4] MS. Roy. 18. B. xxiii, fol. 108 b.   [5] E.E.T.S. ed. p. 93.

be figures as familiar to a contemporary audience of townsfolk as the aforesaid Petrus Telonarius when depicted as "a tollere ... wondyr ryche, to the pore unmercyfull, non almes zevynge, but the pore dyspysing and hem betyng or cacchyng out at his gatys wyth his doggys".[1] Likewise with one deft word of interpretation, an ancient and time-worn story could be made to point a very up-to-date, useful moral: "I fynde in cronycles that ther was somtyme a worthy woman, the wiche that hated dedely a pore woman more than vii zere", says the man in the pulpit. When the former went to communicate on Easter Day, the priest insisted that she should first forgive the poor woman for her trespass, "or els he wold withdrawe fro hure here ryghtes". This she did verbally with reluctance, "and so for the shame of the world more than for awz of God.... For she wold not that worthy Estur day be withowte here ryghtyng".

Than, whan servis was do and all the pepull had eton, the neythbores com with this pore woman unto this worthy womans hous with presentes, to chere hure, and thanked god hizly that thei were acorded. But than this wreched woman seid, "Wene than that I forzave this woman hure trespasse with myn herte as I dud with my mouthe? Naye! Than I preye god that I never take up this rush at my fote". Than she stowped down to take it upp, and the dewell strangled hure even there. Wherefore, ze that make any lovedayes, loke that thei be made withowte anny feynynge, and latt the herte and the tonge acorde in hem.[2]

The anecdote then, in its way, as well as the moralization from nature, contributes, through the preacher's lips, to the growth of a literary Realism. Certain tales were obviously marked out by their contents as peculiarly appropriate for certain classes of the community. Thus the tale of "an hows of religiun", narrated in a sermon, is prefaced by the following comment, directed no doubt to such monks of the Worcester convent as were present on the occasion: "i pray the take hede, vor it is rith a notable tale, as me semz, and specialiche vor men o religiun".[3]

---

[1] *Jacob's Well*, p. 192. Again in *Handlyng Synne*, pp. 182–92.
[2] MS. Roy. 18. B. xxiii, fol. 71. Cf. a variant of the same story in MS. Harl. 2316, fol. 11 b.
[3] MS. Worc. Cath. Libr. F. 10, fol. 45.

Sometimes it is possible to recognize a predilection on the part of the preacher for incidents that can be localized in his own country, thereby to heighten the appeal of his particular narrative. The love-story of a "ʒong chanoun of a gret mynstre"—"in ingelond",[1] or the marvel that befell the corpse of some "clerke of ynglonde,...lered in parrysche in fraunce," that "lad evyll is liffe",[2] would naturally have special attraction for audiences of Englishmen. Thus Bromyard will refer to an incident in the Scottish wars,[3] and John Waldeby clinches his pulpit warning, that "he who abuses a privilege will be deprived of it", with the true story of what happened once in London. "Hoc enim verum ostensum fuit Londoniis...", he cries.[4] Tales of apparent English origin may often be detected in Latin sermons by some typical vernacular phrase which is there left recorded in the original language of delivery, or again by English names retained for the leading characters in the story, be they men and women or merely domestic pets.[5] But, on the whole, it is surprising to find how few of the anecdotes thus incorporated have any definite connection with the land where they were used.[6] The Church and the whole outlook of her ministry and instruction were still predominantly universal. Moreover, to medieval audiences in rural Shropshire, such as those privileged to enjoy the racy anecdotes of the Prior of Lilleshall, mention of towns like

[1] *Jacob's Well*, p. 177. Also in Odo of Cheriton (?), MS. Harl. 219, fol. 15 (unlocalized), and Caesarius of Heisterbach, *Dial. Mirac.* dist. ii, cap. 23.

[2] MS. Roy. 18. B. xxiii, fol. 114. Several examples are to be found in the *Spec. Laic.* for example.   [3] *S.P.* s.v. "Prelatio".

[4] MS. Caius Coll. Camb. 334, fol. 173 (a murderer punished); cf. another one by the same preacher—"de quadam villa Anglie"—a "Gotham" story—in MS. Roy. 7. E. ii, fol. 31.

[5] Cf. e.g. in Bromyard, *S.P.* The Three Executors (s.v. "Executor"): "Dixit Anglice—'And I take'"; another tale introducing: "quod vulgariter '*pillori*' nuncupatur" (s.v. "Juramentum"); the story of "Jankyn" (s.v. "Ipocrisis"); the tale of the dogs "Orri" and "Alriche" (s.v. "Exemplum"); and see further, under "Maria", etc. Similarly the names of the Devil's hunting dogs in Nic. Bozon (cap. xxii).

[6] For an example of a story variously localized (Cumpton, Oxon.; Hertfordshire; "Emmeton"; etc.), see J. A. Herbert, *Cat. of Romances in B.M.* vol. iii, p. 532.

"Glocesture", "Bristowe", "Norwych", or "Derbe" probably
meant little more than "Paryse" and "Coleyne",[1] or even
distant "Baldac".[2] Preachers, like Bishop Brunton of Rochester,
who display a definite national feeling in their sermons, occasionally reinforce their denunciation of the nation's sins with
a warning tale of some English monarch of the past. But this
selection from their country's annals is very limited as well as
crude, and exhibits little or no intelligent desire to use history
as an interpreter of morals beyond the scope of commonplace
"monkish" marvels, prophecies and monitory visions.[3] Even
in their more frequent use of the ancient historians of classical
times, indeed, the homilists like the schoolmen prefer the
wilder extravagances of myth and legend there offered to them.[4]
Crude and limited in the extreme as are these sermon references, however, to the records of English chroniclers, they
deserve our attention if only as an early attempt to provide
unlettered audiences with a first taste of the kind of knowledge
to be culled from history-books. One compiler of sermon
exempla appears to have had recourse to the *Chronica Majora*
of Matthew Paris, the *Gesta Regum* of William of Malmesbury
and the *Flores Historiarum* of Roger of Wendover for three
of his narratives.[5] But when we have to confess that they deal
merely with a vision of Pope Innocent IV,[6] the Witch of
Berkeley[7] and the Wandering Jew,[8] the word "history" seems

---

[1] Cf. in Myrc's *Festial*, passim; MS. Harl. 2250, fol. 87, etc. (also Myrc?).

[2] Baghdad. Cf. in *S.P.* s.v. "Avaritia"; *Gesta Rom.* Engl. version,
pp. 197–9; etc.

[3] Exceptions are the preacher of MS. Bodl. 649, as quoted above,
pp. 72–5, and Bromyard, *S.P.* s.v. "Bellum", where he gives illustrations from history of the destruction of armies through vice and dissension, notably from the Chronicles of the Crusades, mentioning King
Richard I, Godfrey of Bouillon, the duke of Brabant and the capture
of Jerusalem (*Historia Antiochena*), and Guy of Lusignan, King of
Jerusalem (*Historia Gallicorum*).

[4] Cf. Sir Jo. Sandys, *Hist. of Class. Scholarsh.* ed. 1903, p. 637.

[5] MS. Add. 6716 (15th cent.).

[6] fol. 25 b, col. 2 (see *Chron. Maj.* Rolls S. vol. v, p. 471).

[7] fol. 46 b, col. 2 (see *Gesta Reg.* Rolls S. vol. i, p. 253): also in *Spec.
Laic.* s.v. "De Sortilegiis", *Fasciculus Morum, Destr. Vic.*, etc.

[8] fol. 60 b (see *Flor. Hist.* Rolls S. pp. 352–5).

almost a misnomer. Bromyard's reference to the Saracen invasions of Spain and Burgundy, though historically true enough, is in little better case. For, his purpose in mentioning them is but to give an example of the kind of Divine punishment meted out to an unchaste people.[1] Bishop Brunton, in like fashion, gives the story of Anselm's vision of the death of King William Rufus, after the latter "had spoiled many churches of England and had extorted fifty thousand marks from the church of Lincoln".[2] He tells us that "Anselm saw in a night-vision how all the saints of England made bitter complaint of the said king. And the Lord said, 'Let Alban the Proto-martyr of the English come hither'; and he gave to him a fiery arrow, saying, 'Behold the death of that man of whom you have made so great complaint!'" St Alban promptly handed over the arrow to the spirit of Evil, avenger of sins, who sped it on its way "like a comet". "Shortly afterwards Anselm perceived in spirit that the king perished that very night, smitten by that self-same arrow. Early next morning, after celebrating mass, he got ready to return to his church; and when he had reached England, heard how King William had met his death pierced by an arrow, while hunting in the New Forest. No wonder! for divine castigation is 'a vigilant rod'...." In another *exemplum* furnished by the English Cistercian Odo of Cheriton,[3] and repeated by the author of the *Speculum Laicorum*,[4] King William Rufus himself has the warning vision in which he beholds himself devouring one of Christ's hands, "because he destroyed many towns and churches to give the wild beast peace", and seeking to devour the other "because he had imposed crushing taxation upon the whole of his realm". The latter injustice the king strives to justify thus—"I have to make great expenditure upon the

---

[1] *S.P.* s.v. "Adulterium".

[2] MS. Harl. 3760, fol. 191b, and again on fol. 203b.

[3] *Tractatus de Passione* (MSS. Bibl. Nat. Paris, 16506, fol. 282, col. 3, and Balliol Coll. Oxf. 38, etc.). See Hauréau, *Not. et Extr.* vol. v, pp. 168–9. For source, see Wm. of Malmesbury, *Gesta Reg.* Rolls S. vol. ii, p. 377.

[4] Ed. Welter, p. 48, no. 227.

knights, barons and sons of noblemen who are at my court, and therefore I cannot remit the taxation". Shortly after, however, he meets his fate. "Slain by an arrow in a grove, he fell into the well of hell." A Latin sermon of the early fourteenth century amongst the manuscripts of Gray's Inn Library introduces two other familiar anecdotes concerning English sovereigns.[1] One is the story of King John's dream of the lacerated Saviour. The other tells of a Norman knight who, when a royal hunt was in progress in Normandy, beat the English hunting dogs of the King of England and let the wolf escape.[2] The deathbed vision of another English monarch, the sainted Edward the Confessor, foretelling disaster to England as a punishment for the diabolic conduct of her prelates, appears in the fourteenth-century sermon-book of some unknown English homilist.[3] For a whole year and a day the terror-stricken realm was to be at the mercy of the enemy, and demons would haunt her soil.[4] No less gruesome is the story, frequently on the lips of English preachers, of the nun who, rather than meet King Richard I, who had fallen in love with her, tore out her eyes and sent them to him instead.[5] Medieval students, familiar with the merciless fashion in which the pulpit was wont to pillory the sins of the mighty, will not be surprised to learn that tales so derogatory of the blood royal could occa-

---

[1] MS. Gray's Inn Libr. 12, iii, fol. 13 (Jacques de Lausanne, c. 1307?).

[2] Also in Bromyard, *S.P.* s.v. "Ordo Clericalis" (the knight retorts to the king, by way of explanation, that he loves the wolves of Normandy more than the English hounds). The version of Jacques de Lausanne is in Hauréau, as above, vol. iii, p. 121.

[3] MS. Harl. 7322, fols. 51 b and 101.

[4] See Wm. of Malmesbury, *Gesta Reg.* Rolls S. vol. i, p. 277; and H. R. Luard's ed. of *Lives of Edw. the Confessor*, p. 430. Cf. the favourite prophecy of St Boniface in English sermon-literature, e.g. Bromyard, *S.P.* s.v. "Adulterium"; MS. Linc. Cath. Libr. A. 6. 2, fol. 59 b (15th cent.); etc.

[5] Cf. Odo of Cheriton, MS. Arund. 231, ii, fol. 107 b (mentioning Fontevrault); Bromyard, *S.P.* s.v. "Caro"; Waldeby, MS. Roy. 7. E. i, fol. 70 (attributing it to Peter Damian); etc.; and in many foreign collections. J. A. Herbert suggests (*Cat. of Romances in B.M.* vol. iii, p. 611) Herbert of Torre, *De Mirac.* vol. ii, p. 42, as the earliest authority.

sionally find their way into these homilies and treatises.[1] However, the inspiring example of the hero might be occasionally
as efficacious as the warnings of villany, from the preacher's
point of view; and there were heroes as well as villains amongst
the sovereigns of England's past. Says our homely vernacularist, proud to display to his congregation in a single sentence
a threefold mastery of historical literature, of theology, and
of Latin, all equally dubious:

> I rede in *Gestis Britoun, et recitat doctor Holcote, super librum Sapientie,*
> that Kyng Artour had in the inward parte of ys shelde ane ymage of our
> lady Mary, deprented beryng a child in her armes, the wiche ymage he
> wold behold when that he was werry in batell and feynte. And, for
> conforte and hope that he had in hur, he waxed fresche and herty aʒeyn
> and in als good poynte for to feyʒthe as he was at the begynnyng.[2]

Similarly the righteousness of King Henry III inspires two
familiar anecdotes given in the *Speculum Laicorum*.[3]

The element of humour in the sermon-tale might be expected
to loom large in our manuscripts from the place which it
occupies in the criticisms of pulpit degeneracy in the later

---

[1] Cf. further, e.g., a tale of King Henry II and a warning against Sunday
trading, quoted by Bp. Brunton, as before, fols. 110b and 211b—"in
cronicis", and by Bromyard, *S.P.* s.v. "Ferie seu Festa"—from Giraldus
Camb. ("in *Itinerario* suo *per* G[u]*alliam*, de rege Henrico secundo, qui
viz. cum de Ibernia rediens in castro esset de *Kaerdif*..."). See *Gir.
Camb. Opera*, Rolls S. vol. viii, pp. 180–1. On the subject of pulpit
invective against monarchs, cf. Hauréau, as before, vols. iv, p. 77 and iii,
pp. 105–6.

[2] MS. Roy. 18. B. xxiii, fol. 171b. Cf. another story, borrowed from
The Brut, in MS. Bodl. 649, fol. 113: "Lego in *Gestis Britonum* quod
quidam rex huius terre, rex Vortigerius..." (the story of the two sub-
terranean dragons that frustrated the building of a fort against the Saxons,
expounded to the king by Merlin). See *The Brut*, E.E.T.S. ed. F. Brie,
pt. i, pp. 55–8.

[3] Ed. Welter, p. 10. One of these stories is repeated by Bp. Brunton,
MS. Harl. 3760, fol. 189 (see below, p. 581). The reader might also compare the sermon reference to Thos., Duke of Clarence, in MS. Bodl. 649,
fol. 131 (A.D., c. 1421–2)—"Multum honorabatur et timebatur pro sua
humanitate. Salvo dumtaxat nostro principe dignissimo rege, reputabatur
tho dowtist werrour and the werthiest prince Cristyn. Omnes Christiani
reges, ut dicitur, non habuerunt meliorem militem..."—with the account
given of the Prince in *Henr. Vti. Angl. Reg. Gesta*, ed. B. Williams,
Engl. Hist. Soc. 1850, pp. 149–52 (from Thomas Elmham).

Middle Ages. However, sermon-manuscripts most likely to survive the rigours of the Reformation would be those of the more serious and Puritanical sort. Hence, for one reason, no doubt, the ribald *example*, while still to be met with pretty frequently in *exemplaria*, is none too common in the actual discourses themselves. A Latin sermon of Master Rypon of Durham, a preacher singularly free of anecdotal matter, presents us with what is termed in the margin of his manuscript a "narratio jocosa".[1] This we may take, then, to be a sample of the more restrained homiletic witticism beloved of the period. The narration deals with a certain bailiff, who was particularly oppressive in the way he collected rents from the poor. One day, riding out to a certain village in pursuit of his duties, he met with the Devil in human form. Said the Devil to him, "Whither are you going?" He replied, "To the next village, on my master's business". Mephistopheles then enquired if he was willing to take whatever was freely offered to him. The bailiff answered in the affirmative, and asked in his turn who the questioner might be, and what was his errand. The latter replied that he was the Devil, busy like him in quest of gain, willing however—"not to take *whatever* men would have given me; but whatsoever they would gladly bestow with their whole heart and soul, that will I accept". "You do most justly", said the relentless bailiff. Proceeding on their way together, as they approached the said village, they beheld a ploughman angrily commending to the Devil his half-tamed oxen that repeatedly strayed from the course. Says the bailiff to his companion, "Behold, they are yours!" "No," says the other, "they are in no wise given from the heart." Then as they entered the village, the strains of a weeping child greeted their ears. Its mother, powerless to correct its faults, was wishing it to the Devil.[2] Then says our bailiff, "This is yours indeed!" "Not at all," replies the Devil, "for she has no desire to lose her son." At length they reached the end of the village. A certain

[1] MS. Harl. 4894, fol. 103b. See further, Welter, *L'Exemplum*, p. 77.
[2] A similar incident—with disastrous results—forms the subject of other sermon-stories: cf. MS. Burn. 361, fols. 152–3; MS. Gray's Inn Libr. 15, fol. 31; *Handlyng Synne*, pp. 45–6; etc.

poverty-stricken widow, whose only cow the bailiff had seized the day before, espied him coming, and with knees bent and hands outstretched shrieked at him—"To all the devils of hell I commend thee!" Whereupon remarked the Devil—"To be sure, this *is* mine. Because thus cordially you have been bestowed upon me, therefore I am willing to have you". And snatching up the bailiff, he bore him away to hell.[1] "This narration, I say," adds the preacher, "although partly jocose, is none the less revocative of certain vices." Wherewith he proceeds to his more sombre moralizing again.[2]

From the general mass certain leading types of humorous story can be distinguished, which derive their subject-matter repeatedly from certain well-marked sources in the community. Prominent among these are the anecdotes dealing with the relations between man and wife in the sphere of the home. Tales which relate how the weaker partner manages to score off her unwitting spouse follow apparently an ancient Oriental tradition. But some, at all events, in our period, have a definite medieval and ecclesiastical flavour about them. An example of the kind occurs in a collection of pulpit stories made probably by a Dominican of the Cambridge House in the second half of the thirteenth century.[3] It concerns

a certain widow, who had all her husband's goods left to her by him in his Will, of which she was the executrix. Having cast all further thought of his exequies to oblivion, a week after his death, as she was coming from church, her servant with her, she espied a kite seizing one of her chickens in front of her eyes. Said she to her servant—"Run and rescue that chicken!" But when the latter replied—"I can't", she said to him—

[1] With the above cf. the version given by Rypon's contemporary, Chaucer, in the *Cant. Tales*, viz. the Frere's Tale. The same occurs in another roughly contemporary English homiletic collection, in MS. Cott. Cleop. D. viii, fol. 110. See also the important references given in Herbert, *Cat. of Romances in B.M.* vol. iii, p. 592.

[2] Cont.—"Primo, enim, docetur homo ne cum negligencia aut rancore diabolum nominet; 2°, ne sibi aliquid comendet, quia forsan talis commendacio potest sortiri effectum; 3[io], ne officiarii dominorum sint nimis cupidi; 4°, ne injuriam faciant pauperibus aut aliis, eorum personas ledendo aut illorum bona extorquendo, ne forsan eis finaliter contingat sicut ballivo contigit antedicto".

[3] See further in my *Preaching in Med. Engl.* pp. 60 et seq. Certain personal incidents are dated, 1243, 1247, 1250.

"All right, all right! Let the bird have the chicken for the benefit of my husband's soul!"[1]

A further story, that deals solely with the living—from the *Speculum Laicorum*—will show us the tables turned:

A certain man, who had a greedy wife, roasted a fowl for them both to eat. When the bird had been roasted, his wife said to him—"Give me the wing!" And taking it she ate it up, and likewise devoured alone every part of the fowl. Her husband, who watched her, said at length—"You have eaten up the whole thing yourself: there is nothing left but the spit.[2] It is only fair that you should have a taste of that!" And with that spit he beat her handsomely.[3]

A second class of anecdotes exhibits this grim sermon humour at the expense of fellow-clergy. Thus Bromyard relates how a certain man, clearly no friend to the begging Orders, was once asked "to say a good word" for certain Religious, on behalf of some special cause which they were pleading. His only response was to cry out—*magis ad derisionem quam ad utilitatem*—"A good word for the Brethren: a good word for the Brethren!"[4] As might be expected, the old spirit of rivalry and contempt between the Regular and the Secular clergy prompted a good deal of this type of comic story-telling. Such is well illustrated by a "merry jest", which savours of the age of Skelton, from the late thirteenth-century Dominican manuscript that we first alluded to. "When a certain very rich rustic, who was hard-hearted both to the poor and towards his own soul, had amassed so much wealth that he had a chest filled with money and other treasures, he had it set in front of him as he lay sickening on his deathbed." By the time that the priest could be summoned to make his Will, the sick man had

[1] MS. Roy. 7. D. 1, fols. 93 b–4. Cf. the interesting parallel to this tale in a sermon of Simon de Landiaco (13th cent.) in Hauréau, *Not. et Extr.* vol. iii, p. 278 (in like circumstances a son—"quadam die, cum veniret de foro, in equo suo portavit frustum carnis retro se. Venit canis et accepit frustum carnis. Et tunc dixit ille: 'Vade; pro anima patris mei sit! Diu est quod nihil dedi pro eo'."). For tales of wives scoring off their husbands when alive, cf. Bozon, *Metaphs.* cap. xliv, and MS. Roy. 7. D. 1, as quoted below, p. 428.   [2] "veru, id est, *spite*."

[3] *Spec. Laic.* cap. x, s.v. "Avaricia"; ed. Welter, p. 15. For another comical domestic tale at the husband's expense, see in my *Preaching in Med. Engl.* p. 194, conclusion of n. 4 from p. 193; and cf. poem in Chambers and Sidgwick, *E. E. Lyrics*, p. 208.   [4] *S.P.* s.v. "Oratio".

already lost power of speech. The priest, accordingly, suggested a plan to his wife and brother, whereby a "Ha!" from the patient might be taken to indicate approval of what was proposed to him, and silence as the mark of disapproval. Having won agreement for his plan, our priest said to the testator—

"Do you wish to bequeath your soul to God after your decease, and your body to Mother Church for burial?", and the latter replied—"Ha!" Then said the priest to him—"Do you wish to leave twenty shillings to the fabric of your church, where you have chosen to be buried?" But the other made no reply and kept a complete silence. Forthwith the priest pulled him violently by the ear, whereat the man cried—"Ha!" Then said the priest—"Write down twenty shillings for the church fabric: for see, he has granted it with his 'ha!'" After that the priest pondered how he could get for himself the chest with the aforesaid treasure. So he said to the sick man—"I have some books, but I have no chest to keep them in. That coffer over there would be most useful to me. Would you like me, therefore, to have that coffer to put my books in?" But the other said nothing whatever to these remarks. Then the priest pinched his ear so hard that those who were present declared afterwards that the pinch drew blood from the man's ear. Then the enfeebled rustic, in a loud voice, said to the priest before them all—"O you greedy priest, by Christ's death, never shall you have from me as much as a farthing of the money which is in that chest!" Having thus spoken, he turned to his devotions and expired. Accordingly, his wife and relatives divided the money between them. This happened in England, so it is said.[1]

One can picture the inward relish, the tumultuous laughter of soul with which the friar-preacher repeated that anecdote at the expense of his old rivals the parish *curati*. Perpetually they were the butt of Mendicant scorn and ridicule in the pulpits.[2] And no enemy of Pardoners, we may be sure, ever enjoyed himself better over a quip from mine host along the Canterbury Road than did our Dominican—"whan that he saugh that al the peple lough". A third type of sermon-anecdotes derives its humour from the stupidities and follies of rustics. Here the sermons of Odo of Cheriton offer numerous early examples,[3]

[1] MS. Roy. 7. D. 1, fol. 127.
[2] Cf. in my *Preaching in Med. Engl.* pp. 71–7. A significant class of sermon-stories, akin to the above though hardly humorous, tells of the immoral relations of the clergy with their mistresses and illegitimate offspring. See further below, pp. 247 and 276.
[3] See ed. L. Hervieux, *Les Fabul. Latins*, vol. iv, passim (cf. e.g. nos. iii, xxxiii, xxxiv, xl, xliia, xlvii, lxx, lxxiv, cviii, clxiv, etc.).

of which later homilists make free use, such as the tale of the
old woman who greased a bishop's hand,[1] or of the peasant
who drank ditch water on his way to a feast and had to be
excluded.[2] Even so solemn a preacher as Master John Waldeby
deigns to repeat the Gothamite story, from the same collection,
of the wise men of Wilby who sent the annual rent to their
lord tied round the neck of a hare, so that it might get to him
the faster.[3] Others tell, likewise, of the peasant who stubbornly
refused to give credence to a preacher discoursing upon hell,
because he had not been there first to see it for himself,[4] or of
yet another fellow-rustic who fell foul of his church crucifix,
and accordingly refused to go to church.[5]

This popularity of the comic tale in the preaching of the
thirteenth and fourteenth centuries has a significance for the
history of Renaissance literature which is not yet fully grasped
by all modern writers upon the subject. Thus, the editor of
a new selection of the *Facetiae* of Poggio Braccriolini and
Lodovico Domenichi for English readers has recently argued
that the "monkish" medieval tales of the period preceding
them are "impregnated with mysticism and seriousness", and
"have none of the irreverence and cynicism" of these later
collections. "The modern facetiae, that is the facetiae of the
fifteenth and sixteenth centuries, with their typically Italian or
rather Tuscan characteristics, may be said to have arisen somewhere about 1440 or 1450", and exhibit a new spirit, he says.
"The broader humour which is drawn from life rather than
literature, the humour of incongruousness and ridiculousness,

[1] Ed. Hervieux, vol. iv, p. 301. For Bromyard's repetition of this
story, see above, p. 42, n. 5.
[2] Ed. Hervieux, vol. iv, p. 266. Cf. *Spec. Laic.* s.v. "Amor Mundi";
Liber de Dono Timoris, MS. Sloane 3102, fol. 34b; *Gesta Rom.* E.E.T.S.
ed. p. 374; Felton, *Serm. Dom.* MS. Harl. 4, fol. 7; etc.
[3] MS. Roy. 7. E. ii, fol. 31 (see also Wright, *Lat. Stories*, Percy Soc.
no. 93; and, for the earlier history of the Gothamite legend, his *Early
Mysteries and other Lat. Poems of the 12th and 13th cents.* 1838, pp. 93–8).
[4] MSS. Add. 28682, fol. 210b, and Sloane 3102, fol. 19b; etc. (from
Et. de Bourbon).
[5] See above, p. 146. With these tales the reader may compare the
pathetic stories of the "holy simplicity" of lay-brothers in the monastery
(cf. the famous *Tombeur de Notre Dame*).

was the new note in fifteenth and sixteenth-century jocular tales."[1] Nothing, however, could be farther from the truth than this idea. When we turn the pages of Poggio and his fellows, what do we find? Precisely the same types of humour as those displayed by the pulpit two centuries earlier, the same favourite objects of ridicule and witty repartee, often the self-same anecdotes with some trivial variation, even when the raconteur is now some Italian scholar of the day and the scene has been transferred to Florence or Bologna.[2] The polished disciples of a Chrysoloras still continue to poke fun, though now less frequently with any pretence of a moral excuse, at the domestic follies of husbands and wives, the vices of the clergy, the simplicities of the rustic, the weaknesses of the female sex.[3] The little tricks that still amuse them, the riddles and play upon words, the outspoken witticisms of the humble at the expense of the great,[4] all are in keeping with those which formerly delighted the preachers' audiences alike in England as in Italy. Here at all events the new Graeco-Roman learning is responsible for no change in the current taste of educated persons. It serves merely to enhance a taste already acquired elsewhere from centuries of Goliardic verse and popular preaching. The humorous sermon-anecdote, then, we recognize as one more natural, typical product of that early pulpit realism

[1] Edw. Storer, *Facetiae of Poggio and other Med. Story-tellers* (Broadway Translations), pp. 6–8 and 28. For a ribald sermon-tale of the coarser sort in an English homily-book cf. Bozon, *Metaphs.* cap. cxlv (the Leicestershire juggler), and for sermon raillery and irreverent joking in general see my *Preaching in Med. Engl.* pp. 80–3 and 184–7, and J.-Th. Welter, *L'Exemplum*, p. 102.

[2] Storer's own selection furnishes at least two good examples. The story told of Dante and King Robert of Naples in Poggio (Storer, pp. 131–4, no. cix) is clearly only a form of Odo of Cheriton's (?) sermon-tale of the Philosopher shut out of the Palace (*see* MS. Arund. 231, ii, fol. 64b: not in Hervieux). Cf. again Domenichi's tale of the Numerous Doctors in Ferrara (Storer, pp. 121–3, no. xcix) with the sermon extract given above, p. 46.

[3] For typical sermon-stories at the expense of female vanity, see my *Preaching in Med. Engl.* pp. 170–1 and 217–18, and cf. further below, pp. 396 and 398.

[4] Two sermon examples will be found in my *Preaching in Med. Engl.* pp. 210 and 221, n. 1.

and feeling for raw humanity which was studied in our first chapter. Along with the Satire and the natural Simile it leads in the van of a new conquering Humanism, with weapons of Authority charged with the deadly explosive of laughter, that laughter which—to borrow a significant phrase of M. Bergson —in its very beginnings "indicates a slight revolt on the surface of human life".[1] For the rest, we can only add that the humorous sermon-tale is as clearly an important antecedent of the humorous episodes in our Renaissance drama.[2]

The predominating motive in the English choice of anecdotes for sermons is undoubtedly one which is common to all preaching of the time and has been noticed already in these pages in connection with stories of the saints and stories from the chroniclers. It is a characteristically childish affection for the marvellous in "store and cronicle, where that I rede a wondere thynge", as a simple preacher himself expresses it.[3] His medieval listeners, so straitened in their knowledge of the world about them, so narrowly confined for the most part to the common round and daily task "from dawn to evensong", would still gape spellbound at any "gret myracles" and "wondurfull thyng or dede"[4] presented in his narrative. To the pulpit, then, our literature owes at least something for an enterprise which thus opened a new world of legend and romance to those whose only source of popular fiction lay hitherto in the traditional folk-lore, all too imperfectly preserved. At the preacher's disposal there had accumulated a mass of stories of marvels wrought by relics, by the sacred Host itself,[5] or by some other means of divine intervention in the affairs of men; stories, likewise, of life and death, of mystery and adventure, many of which would have a vivid human interest for the ages of Chaucer and of Lydgate.[6] Examples in this category are far

---

[1] *Laughter: an Essay on the Meaning of the Comic*, Engl. ed. p. 200.
[2] See further below, in Chap. VIII.
[3] MS. Roy. 18. B. xxiii, fols. 95 b.   [4] Myrc, *Festial*, p. 257.
[5] Cf., e.g., the anecdotes, given in the *Spec. Laic.* under the heading— "De Eukaristia", and repeated in many other works; or the equally typical miracles of the sacrament given in a metrical sermon for the Corpus Christi Feast, in E.E.T.S. O.S. no. 98, pp. 168 et seq.
[6] Cf. *Miracles of oure lady*, ibid. pp. 138–67; etc.

too numerous and accessible already to require any fresh illustration at this stage.[1] We may note of them, in passing, that, unlike some classes of anecdotes we have considered, they were obviously intended to be taken very seriously. No one need doubt the truth of modern marvels of divine retribution, argues Bromyard, in view of the marvellous happenings recorded in the Old and New Testaments.[2] The inspired word of Scripture was adequate warrant.

The part played by anecdotes based on personal reminiscence, whether at first or second hand, was illustrated in an earlier chapter of the author's *Preaching in Medieval England*.[3] To the account there given of tales thus collected by preachers of the Mendicant Orders may be added several which lie scattered amongst the various *capitula* of John Bromyard's *Summa Predicantium*. Here, for example, the Dominican provides apparently out of his own stock of memories two typical devil-stories. One is of the usual deathbed vision of the demons, as seen by "a certain good man of Religion, when recently dying".[4] The other, "wont to be narrated by a trustworthy man who was accustomed to name both the place and the person" concerned, deals with a certain bailiff who threw up his post for conscience' sake, but later decided to return to it, when he and his wife felt the loss of their former gifts and perquisites too acutely. When on horseback one day, he rode into a fierce storm of lightning and thunder. In the midst of the tempest, the Devil in the form of an ape perched himself on his horse's neck, and, grinning derisively at him, exclaimed in English, "Welcome to wicke; welcome to wicke!", meaning "Welcome to your bailiwick!" or bailiff's office.[5] The panic-stricken man made a vow, then and there, that never would he perform that office again; and only thus was he liberated by God's grace from the monster.[6] The story, added to Master

[1] See esp. for Engl., J. A. Herbert, *Cat. of Romances in B.M.* vol. iii, passim: also the well-known studies of Mussafia, Horstmann, etc.

[2] *S.P.* s.v. "Exemplum". Cf. also above, pp. 125–6.

[3] See pp. 60–64.   [4] s.v. "Desperatio".

[5] Bromyard explains thus—"quod sonat in patria illa—'Bene veneris ad balliviam tuam', cum duplici replicatione".

[6] s.v. "Ministratio".

Rypon's jocose narration of the Devil and the Bailiff, throws a further interesting sidelight on the evil reputation of this class of manorial officials.[1] Amongst several death-bed incidents related is the story "of one whom I knew very well indeed",[2] says our friar. It reveals a situation much like that of the rich rustic and the grasping cleric which we found in another Dominican collection. Here the dying man again lies paralysed in speech, and the anxious Religious who stand around his bed are urging him to prepare his thoughts for death and receive the last rites of Holy Church.

They were shouting in his ears to the effect that if he were pleased to receive the sacraments, he should at least make some sign or motion with hand, tongue, or countenance. When they could get no sign whatever out of him, one of his friends said, "I will quickly get a sign out of him", and put his hand upon a chest at the dying man's feet in which was his money, his heart and his treasure too, as if wishing to open it and carry away the contents. As though suddenly aroused, the patient attempted to raise his head, and both with voice and expression quickly showed his dismay.... When a certain friend who loved him with special affection saw this, he blushed and withdrew.[3]

Two further reminiscences, dealing with recent events, are concerned with the fate of prisoners. Bromyard tells how he has actually set eyes himself on the type of unscrupulous manorial official whom he is about to describe:

I have seen one such [he says] who had been made gaoler in the aforesaid manner,[4] at a certain castle, where there were many rich men and nobles imprisoned in a bloody affray of the nobility. This man had exacted payments of money in a cruel and most excessive fashion from

[1] Cf. again below, pp. 323–7.
[2] "de illo quem peroptime novi."
[3] s.v. "Avaritia". A similar tale s.v. "Misericordia", § 40: the dying man cries out—"Adhuc vivo; adhuc vivo!" Other death-bed stories here are s.v. "Desperatio": the dying sportsman who could only talk of the merits of his hunting-dogs, when urged to final confession, and so died unshriven—"in canum confessione"; and s.v. "Executor": a tale of two clerics and a layman. See others below, p. 430: the dying drunkards.
[4] "Pro remuneratione et promotione dant [domini] vel—quod pejus est—quandoque vendunt eis aliquid officium in foresta vel terra vel castro vel dominio, ubi non est aliquid certum officio annexum de quo vivere possint, sed totum de mala questa. Vel si forte aliquid annexum sit, nimis tamen parum est pro ministri sustentatione."

their wives and friends who wished to enter and see them. When remonstrated with for this conduct, he replied that he had no conscience in the matter, because his lord had given him that office for his promotion and the reward of his services. And therefore it seemed to him that it was pleasing to his lord that he should collect his reward thus for his promotion, because in no other way could he get it, save by such extortions.[1]

A similar tale of oppression is told in the same work of "a certain city provost and castellan, who had many prisoners in gaol lately in a certain well-known city". He was convicted of putting the garment or tunic of an honest man among his prisoners upon a thief who was being detained in the same gaol, and of transferring the name of the former to that of the thief, for bribes given to him. Thus disguised, the thief was pardoned and set at liberty, while the honest man, in the felon's garb, was unscrupulously condemned.[2] Unlike the traditional narration of which the reader soon wearies, these stories of current life give valuable insight into the social conditions of the times. With two more such specimens, illustrative of contemporary business methods, our survey must close:

And this [truth] has been aptly set forth in an incident which concerns the affairs of a certain distinguished lord, but recently dead.[3] For, while alive, he had one evil practice, namely that, by whatever title or subterfuge he could put forward, he cheerfully confiscated the goods of his subjects at their death. He had also another practice which was good, namely that he gladly procured corn and suchlike for the poor when they were in need. It happened at his own death that all the goods found in his immediate possession or upon his manors were confiscated for the Crown, so that his executors could do nothing to help him [i.e. for the welfare of his soul] by means of them. By which circumstance God showed clearly that, as he had spoiled and oppressed others, so he himself should be spoiled.[4]

Finally, there is an *exemplum*

which I learnt from the lips of a certain very truthful and holy man, who

[1] s.v. "Dominatio" ("Sed quomodo potuit ei dominus dare quod nec ipse dominus juste accipere posset, si presens adesset?" retorts Bromyard. "Non solum sic in pecuniis miseros affligunt, sed—quod pejus est—in corporibus. Quia tales etiam incarceratos in profundissimis carceribus ponere solent, ut mercede liberiorem carcerem redimant").
[2] s.v. "Falsitas".
[3] Cf. another "narratio", s.v. "Humilitas": "sicut nuper accidit".
[4] s.v. "Dominatio".

asserted that he had himself witnessed the fact which he narrated,[1] concerning two merchants in a certain town who were partners in business. One night, one of them going to bed in health was suddenly carried off. The other, indeed, surviving for a short time, when he had communicated on Easter Day and for about a fortnight after had continually worn a sad countenance, in the end began to fall seriously ill. When advised to receive the Sacraments, he shook his head and said that the Host which he had received on Easter Day was still in his throat; and that, if he had a knife, he would slit his throat to remove that Host from it. And after being urged to bethink himself of the mercy of God, he asserted that he was damned, and testified that he had been in hell and had there seen his companion who had died before him, and the place next to him which was to be his own. Asked for the reason of this utter damnation, he replied—"Because we had grown rich at the expense of many whom we deceived, and especially in the sale of wool". His neighbours, however, thinking that he had gone mad, bore him to the church, and setting him before an image of the Crucified, exhorted him that he should deign to look at that image. But in no wise was he willing to lift his head to behold the crucifix. And even when they raised his head for the purpose, he would screen his eyes with his hand or hood; and thus the wretched man perished in desperation.[2]

One type of sermon *exemplum*, somewhat akin to the above, has not yet received that attention from students of our early

[1] Cf. other *narrationes* here, s.v. "Advocatus"—a story "which I learnt from a man worthy of confidence and of great authority and religious zeal"; s.v. "Mors"—"quod relatione audivi fide-digna de rege Sicilie"; and s.v. "Ornatus"—"quadam...evidentia quam valentis viri relatione didici, de quadam muliere in Italia...."

[2] s.v. "Mercatio". For a very late vernacular example of the use of stories thus gleaned, cf. Richard Whitford's *Werke for housholders* (ed. 1533, Wynkyn de Worde) on the sin of Swearing: "The story that followeth I herde at Stondon [i.e. Standon, in Herts.],...where for a tyme I dyd abyde in avoidynge the great plage;...where also this story was open in the knowlege of all the countree there aboute, a-done but small tyme before....And of her [the wife of the gentleman concerned] also I herd the same story, all though, as she sayde, she was not present..." (see further below, p. 423). "Another example...was shewed unto me by a bacheler of divinite called mayster George Werke, a felowe than, where I was also felowe, of the quenes college in Cambrydge; and after he was vycare of Harowe on the hyll. Whiche thynge he sayde, upon his conseyence, he sawe hym-selfe in a marchauntes house in London, whiche was his specyall frende...". Another—"of an honeste preest of my familier acqueyntaunce that was vicar of Halywell, where saynte Wenefredes well is, besyde the abbey of Basyngwerke in Flynteshyre.... Whiche thinge he sayde...he dyd se hymselfe".

literature which it deserves. This concerns what appear to be the records of impressions gleaned from foreign travel and personal observation of strange scenes and customs. Would, indeed, that some scholar might unearth for us the homilies of an English John of Pian da Carpine or William of Rubruck! That awakening desire to know more of the great world and its secrets beyond the limits of the local *patria*, to which even sermons bear witness in fourteenth and fifteenth-century England, is itself one of the early streaks of the coming Renaissance dawn. Few were better fitted to satisfy that craving than the much-travelled missionary friars, to whom then, we may be sure, the ancestors of our Elizabethan voyagers once listened open-mouthed and alert. Like the elusive author of Maundeville's *Voyages and Travels*, who had himself observed that "many men have great liking to hear of strange things of diverse countries", they would have no difficulty in recognizing the homiletic possibilities of such attractive information. As material for the pulpit it was palpably akin to those geographical descriptions and marvels which already served a similar purpose in recognized source-books of *exempla*. Thus, both Bishop Brunton of Rochester[1] and the Austin friar John Waldeby[2] continue to employ in their sermons the account given by Giraldus Cambrensis of the disappearing islands off the Irish coast. John Bromyard[3] repeats the irrefutable evidence provided by Mount Etna and other volcanoes for the existence of hell, as pointed out originally in Gregory's *Dialogues*;[4] while the *Gesta Romanorum* informs men, in its turn, that "Helle is in the middis of the Erthe, scil., in the centr[e] of the erthe, as seithe the Philesophir".[5] It is akin, also, in another direction, to the vivid sketches of current life and social types

[1] MS. Harl. 3760, fol. 41 b.   [2] MS. Roy. 7. E. ii, fol. 29.
[3] *S.P.* s.v. "Damnatio" ("...et quia poenas damnatorum non vident oculo corporali, ideo minus eas credunt. Propter tales ergo Deus aliquando poenas infernales visibiliter ostendit, sicut in partibus Ceciliæ patet, ubi ignem infernalem de lacis illis eructantem ostendit. Greg. *Dial.*").
[4] Bks. iii, ch. 38, and iv, 36.
[5] E.E.T.S. ed. p. 177. Sim. *Pricke of Consc.* ll. 6441–50. Cf. further, the story in MS. Roy. 8. B. xii, fol. 56, of the mountain "juxta civitatem Nepocianam" and the mysterious shouts (from the *Alphab. Narrat.*).

in the home country which were considered in an earlier chapter. To the *Summa Predicantium* we must turn again for samples of this fresh class of illustrations. Thus Italy provides our author with several interesting phenomena. He refers more than once to the unsettled state of the country. To travel there alone is to court disaster.[1] Merchant and pilgrim alike must engage an escort of armed soldiery to protect them from the brigands.[2] Even then the escort itself might prove treacherous, and act in collusion with the enemy.[3] It is a land of continuous warfare, where the city gate is invariably shut at night-time, and no dwelling is to be found outside its sheltering ramparts.[4] The swarm of mercenaries that infests it only tends to maintain disorder, ever increasing the destruction and spoliation of towns and castles alike. "For their own benefit they nourish wars and protract them as long as they can".[5] Such wars are utterly unjustifiable, declares the preacher. They spring up without the authority of prince or civic ruler. Their only cause is the hatred between the parties of Ghibelline and Guelf, fostered by greed and the lust for domination.[6] This rivalry "in Lombardy" is held up as a warning of what happens where a healthy feudal *dominatio* does not exist.[7] The servile and treacherous Italian nature is portrayed by several references to the applause of the Italian mob. "In that land of warfare", says Bromyard, frequent meetings are held by prominent members of the Ghibelline and Guelf parties, at which the popular "Vivat! Vivat!" is invariably raised in favour of the dominant party, however evil, unjust and hateful it may be. "Thus it often happens that they acclaim with their mouth the very man whom they desire in their heart to see hung."[8] Similarly, they have a custom of running to welcome Pope

[1] *S.P.* s.v. "Adulterium" ("...in Italia in terris guerrarum, ut vadant in numerosa multitudine...").

[2] s.v. "Angelus" ("...sicut patet in Lombardia, ubi mercatores et peregrini conducunt stipendiarios pro se tuendo contra spoliatores"). Similarly in the sermons of St Bernardino of Siena (cf. Ferrers Howell's *Life*, pp. 291, etc.).

[3] s.v. "Custodia".   [4]   s.v. "Misericordia".

[5] s.v. "Lex". Similarly, St Bernardino again, as above, pp. 297–8.

[6] s.v. "Bellum".   [7] s.v. "Dominatio".   [8] s.v. "Honor".

or Cardinal or Lord, when they enter their city or castle, with
cries of "Long live such an one!", in which acclamation the
enemy shares equally with the supporter. "Thus it comes about
that frequently, while they honour the entrant with their lips,
they are thinking how they can get rid of him; and sometimes
they carry their thought into practice."[1] A cynical tale is told
of the brigands "in some parts of Italy", who are said to turn
their sons out upon the roads to spoil the passers-by with the
following injunction: "Those who have gold or silver or other
things of use to us upon their person, you shall plunder. Those
who carry nothing, or those whom you cannot overwhelm,
you are to allow to pass on, for the benefit of your father's
soul!"[2] There is also a brief reference to the sentence "recently" passed by the Church upon the heretics of the Ferrarese
Marches, followed by the preaching of a Crusade against them.[3]
A comment, elsewhere, upon the statues and triumphal arches
erected by the ancient Romans—"as the evidence of these
things still shows"—suggests that Bromyard is speaking with
an eye to what he has himself gazed at with the curiosity of the
traveller. "For, to this day Rome displays many such statues
erected to the memory of those she desired to honour."[4] As
a judicial practice "in a certain praiseworthy city of Italy" has
caught the attention of our Dominican,[5] so from a neighbouring country he borrows the example of "a blessed custom
which the kings of France were wont to observe with regard
to the city-provosts of Paris; by means of which one of their
number was recently hung" for his misdeeds.[6] From him we

[1] s.v. "Adoratio".
[2] s.v. "Eleemosyna". Cf. MS. Bodl. 95, fol. 77 (the robbers and
murderers who trust in God to speed them).
[3] s.v. "Luxuria". [4] s.v. "Honor".
[5] s.v. "Judices" (appointment of a "judex extraneus"—"quem nec
consanguinei nec affines errare faciunt"). Another example of what
happened in an Italian city appears s.v. "Falsitas", § 18.
[6] s.v. "Judicium Divinum" ("quando enim ballivos et homines magni
officii de officiis suis amovere voluit, illos in custodia detinere solebat,
precone clamante ad illos quibus prefuit, et, si quem leserit, vel si cui
injuriam in officio suo fecerit, veniat qui lesum se sentit et querimoniam
suam libere deponat"). References to Welsh customs occur s.v. "Invidia"
and "Munus", § 16.

learn too that the fighting of duels was then apparently as notable a feature of the French as in later centuries.[1] Spain, where Christian and Saracen perpetually scheme against each other in turn, provides him with illustration of the unending strife which ensues between two neighbouring powers having a different code of laws and language.[2] Among more intimate matters of which the preacher has taken note is the "method of the vineyard-watcher in France, who climbs a tall tree, in the summit of which he has a tiny hut, which they call in French—*la garde*. And from there he calls out to those who want to break away from the proper route through the vineyard—'Va la voye; va la voye!' that is to say—'Keep to the road; keep to the road!'"[3] The same country, as we have already seen, has supplied him with a string of witty French proverbs, some with topical allusions.[4] Modern methods of publicity in advertising are evidently much older than many people would imagine. "For, in some countries," Bromyard tells us, "he who desires to advertise purchasable wine, that has been freshly exposed for sale in some tavern, carries a vessel of the wine through the city with a cup in his hand, crying out its price and the place where it can be obtained. To the passers-by who want to know the nature and worth of the wine, he offers a sample of it; so that they may know by that sample what it is like in the tavern, and so that, having tasted its relish in small quantity, those who are stimulated may desire a larger supply."[5] On another occasion we are introduced to the story of "the blind man who wanted to play at Kailes, a game which", as the preacher observes, "is commoner in parts beyond the sea; in which game a stick is hurled at some wooden pins, which are set up there".[6] It is as clearly the traveller who speaks here of his own observations, as when elsewhere the same homilist declares that in the virtue of hospitality England compares very unfavourably with other

[1] s.v. "Advocatus" and "Tentatio".   [2] s.v. "Bellum".
[3] s.v. "Crux".   [4] See above, Chap. 1, p. 42.   [5] s.v. "Gaudium".
[6] s.v. "Adulator". This game is the ancestor of the modern skittles or ninepins. For its later vogue in England (evidently scarce begun in Bromyard's day), cf. *Stat. of the Realm*, 17 Edw. IV, cap. 3: "and many *new imagined* games called Closh, Kailes...".

177

nations. The Englishman's house was clearly his castle in more senses than one. "Scarcely is there another land in which so few places of hospitality or 'God's Houses' can be found for the reception of the poor;...and even in those few, when a few enter with not a little pleading and sometimes payment too, those in charge devour all that they have."[1] The same fact receives even stronger emphasis in Bromyard's comments upon Jewish piety and the Jewish care for their own poor, which provide such formidable object-lessons for the Christians whom they put utterly to shame.[2]

There is another variety of the *exemplum* sometimes to be met with in contemporary sermons, which is really a development of the animated *figure*, and might be termed a hypothetical narration. The speaker puts forward for his illustration an imaginary but perfectly natural or possible situation in real life, as when Bromyard instances the likely case of a man setting out along the road to London and being robbed, or the remark of the callous wife or friend indifferent to the fate of husband or companion imprisoned in distant Scotland.[3] An early example of the kind can be seen in the sermons of Archbishop Stephen Langton.[4] When such a figure is carefully expanded, its contents may become as arresting and vivid as that of the ordinary anecdote. A picturesque case thus occurs in the anonymous fragment of a sermon which is probably the work of Richard Alkerton, a preacher at Paul's Cross in the early part of the fifteenth century.[5] Though recorded in the vernacular, it is obviously addressed to the clerical element in the congregation, as the following extract will show:

But that this be the more opyn [says the speaker], I put this ensaumple. I suppose that oure kyng hadde a certayn noumbre of kny3tes to be

---

[1] s.v. "Hospitalitas".
[2] Cf. s.v. "Fides", "Ferie seu Festa", etc., and in my letter in the *Jewish Guardian*, August 6, 1926.
[3] s.v. "Mors" . Cf. further, e.g., s.v. "Beatitudo" (the summons for promotion), etc.
[4] From MS. Magdal. Coll. Oxf. 168, fol. 54, in F. M. Powicke, *Steph. Langton*, Oxf. 1928, pp. 44–5.
[5] See *Preaching in Med. Engl.* pp. 23–4, and above, p. 104.

OLP   12 feried over the se to a certayn ile, and thou comest and seist thou art a shipman, and undertakyst to brynge these men saf to the yle up-on peyne of outlawerie of his lond and hongynge and drawynge, ȝif thou may be takyn; so that thei shul not perische be thi defaute or necgligence. And thou takist this ship with these knyȝtes, whos bodies the kyng chyargith more then al the temporal good of this reume. And when this ship is seylynge on the see in most pereiles, thou metyst with fischeris, and with hem thou dwellyst, and letist thi ship spille and hem that ben therinne. Whow darst thou evere se that kynges visage, whom thou hast so grevously despised and lost that he so tendirli lovyd?

This ship is Petres ship, that is, this cherche that saileth in the pereilous see of this world ful of wawis and tempestis, in the whiche ben knyȝtes; for every man is here a fiȝtere with the fend. And these knyȝtes the kyng of alle kynges more loveth thane alle the worldly goodes that ben in the worlde. (ffor I wot wel, thowȝ alle the temporal goodes of this worlde weryn drenchid in the see, Crist wolde not have put hymself so lowe to restore hem as he dede for man, whan that he was perisched.) This ship thou takest to governe, with hem that ben therinne, whan thou takist thi cherche with the parischynnes under thi cure. And but ȝif thou do thi devere, thou shalt ben outlawed fro the courte of hevene, and put in to the bitter presoun of helle ever with-outyn ende.[1]

Another homilist pictures, in similar fashion, the feelings of relations, if a sister or other female member of their family, in a state of great poverty, were to become the wife of the king of France or of his son and heir. So ought we to rejoice, says he, that the king of heaven deigned to wed our poor human nature at his Incarnation.[2]

A link between the more entertaining anecdote, the more instructive *exemplum* from natural history and the more weighty moral *dictum* of "the great clerk" is afforded us in the general contribution to medieval sermon-literature made by the classical writers of Greece and Rome. There is still discernible in our period an ancient difference of opinion as to how far the Christian preacher should make use of these pagan authorities in his oration. Master Ralph of Acton, in one of the sermons of his *Expositorium*, seems to echo the complaints of an earlier race of homilists upon the Continent directed against the

----

[1] MS. Add. 37677, fol. 99. Cf. here Latimer's 1st *Sermon on the Card*.
[2] MS. Add. 21253, fol. 23. Cf. Hauréau, *Not. et Extr.* vol. iii, p. 109. Another example in *Pricke of Consc.* ed. Philol. S. ll. 5780–5804 (the king's daughter handed over to his reeve).

"Sirens" of classical verse and the vain study of pagan philosophers.[1] Prior to a denunciation of those who cry out daily—"Jupiter omnipotens", "Divina Venus" and the like, thus trafficking in demons rather than deities[2] when they ought to be praising the Almighty, he calls to witness the words of St Peter: "Non enim ineptas fabulas secuti".[3] In these words the Apostle, he says, "contemns those who omit the Gospels and read and preach poetic fables, bucolic verses and comedies".[4] From the following introduction to a sermon probably delivered at Worcester, it appears that on another occasion certain members of a fifteenth-century English audience had themselves risen up to object—let us hope after the original discourse was ended—to a preacher who had ventured to refer to such trifles at the very opening of his address. "Crysten peple", begins our offended orator, "thie[s] wordes that I af take to speke of, at this tyem, thay er the wordis of seynt Powl, wryten in the pystell of this day....I rede in haly wryte: I sey noght as I rede in Ovidie, noyther in Oras. Vor the last tyme that I was her, ich was blamyd of som men[s] word, be-cause that I began my sermon with a poysy. And ther[fore] I say that I red in haly wryt, in the secund book of haly wryth, that [I] suppoise be sufficiant inowgh of autorite...."[5] The preacher's sarcasm at the expense of these typical forerunners of Victorian "Bibliolatry" would have been applauded, however, by the great majority of his educated fellow-divines. For, English Dominicans in particular had taken special pains to provide the pulpit with the most elaborate and often far-fetched moralizations of classical tales; while references to the ancient philosophers are common enough even in vernacular

---

[1] Cf. here Bourgain, *La Chaire franç.* pp. 251-2; Lecoy de la Marche, as below; etc.
[2] "et cetera magis demonia quam numina."
[3] 2 Peter i, 16.
[4] MS. Jo. Ryl. Libr. Manch. Lat. 367, fol. 137b.
[5] MS. Worc. Cath. Libr. F. 10, fol. 42. Wycliffe also attacks "poisies" in the monks' preaching (see *Engl. Works*, ed. F. D. Matthew, E.E.T.S. O.S. no. 74, p. 124), though here he may mean any kind of "rymes" (cf. ibid. p. 438).

homilies. To both Nicholas Trivet[1] and Thomas Walleys[2] has been attributed a Book of Moralizations of the Metamorphoses of Ovid, which owes something in its turn to the works of Alexander Neckham. Here the preacher is deliberately taught to "say this of Jupiter", or "say that of Juno", while a statement in the Second Epistle of St Paul to Timothy is unblushingly perverted to mean "that we must oftentimes make use of fables, enigmas and poems, that some moral sense may be extracted therefrom".[3] Robert Holcot's well-known *Moralitates*, compiled "in usum predicatorum", are stocked with classical *examples*; likewise his *Liber Sapientiae Salomonis*.[4] If we turn to John Bromyard, later in the fourteenth century, we shall find him discussing in the Prologue to his *Summa Predicantium* the actual propriety of employing for such a purpose the pagan myths and fables with which his volume teems. He begins by quoting presumably from Peter of Blois to the effect that, "in the case of herbs, no one seeks to find out in what land, or in the charge of what gardener, or by what culture they grew, provided that they possess healing power". So should it be with the health-giving *exemplum*. "For, from the moralization of Gentile fables a form of instruction is sometimes derived; and it is right, also, to be taught by the enemy, and to enrich the Hebrews with the spoils of the Egyptians."[5] "It is also to be noticed that, in this treatise, the Gentiles and

---

[1] Cf. MS. Bodl. 571 (first half of the 15th cent.), and MSS. Merton Coll. 85 and 299 and St Jo. Bapt. Coll. 137 at Oxford, as given by Hauréau, *Not. et Extr.* vol. iv, pp. 289–90.

[2] See *Hist. Litt. de la Fr.* vols. xxiv, p. 371 and xxix, pp. 505–6; Lecoy de la Marche, *La Chaire franç.* p. 478; etc. Hauréau (as above) and Coulton (*Five Cent. of Relig.* vol. i, p. 182) favour Peter Berchorius as author. See now, however, the correct history of this work and its anon. Franciscan author, in Welter, *L'Exemplum*, pp. 347–8, n. 35.

[3] See Coulton, ibid. App. xxv, pp. 543–5. Cf. further, a *Moralized Seneca*, by Nich. Trivet (Welter, *L'Exemplum*, p. 363).

[4] Used by Chaucer (*Cant. Tales*) for his Pardoner's and Nun-Priest's Tales (see Art. by Miss Petersen, in *Radcliffe Coll. Monographs*, no. 10, p. 98); Lydgate, *Aesop*, fable iii, 156 and 174 ("as writeth Holcot upon Sapience"); Hoccleve, *La Male Regle*, st. 32, l. 249 ("Holcote seithe upon the book, also, of Sapience, as it can testifie"); etc.

[5] Similarly in *Ovidius Moral.* as above (see Coulton, ibid. p. 544).

their works are frequently introduced as witness of the truth. And if anyone asks what these things, which are without, have to do with us in the doctrine of the Christian Faith, the blessed Gregory replies in his *Moralia*, bk. i, chap. vi—to confute our own shamelessness. . . . ." So it comes about that in the body of his work, Bromyard is prepared to mention in almost the same breath—"the fortitude of Samson, the beauty of Absalom, the wisdom of Solomon, the swiftness of Asahel, the riches of Croesus, the uprightness of Alexander, the power of Octavian, the longevity of Enoch".[1] "Not only Christ and other martyrs but also Socrates" thus figure together in his pages as joint witnesses to the truth.[2] Classical authors cited by him under the heading of "Bellum", for example, include Vegetius, whose *De re militari* is much in vogue with our preachers, Aristotle, Seneca, and Valerius Maximus. Under the heading "Consilium" further references will be found to Plutarch and Quintilian. Exhaustive analysis of these sources is unnecessary here owing to the learned work of M. Théodor Welter, recently published at Paris, which now provides us with systematic lists of all such authorities utilised in the greater sermon-books of Europe, including that of Bromyard.[3] To M. Welter we owe also an earlier list of the classical authors cited in the *Speculum Laicorum*, numbering no less than twenty-three.[4] If we turn from Latin sermon-encyclo-paedias to the separate discourses of other distinguished preachers, we shall find Archbishop Fitzralph[5] and Master

---

[1] *S.P.* s.v. "Bonitas".   [2] s.v. "Mors".

[3] *L'Exemplum*, passim (see esp. pp. 95–6; for Holcot, pp. 364–5; for Bromyard, p. 333). Cf. also the interesting collection of moral verses—"sans doute à l'usage des prédicateurs"—drawn from many of the above, indicated in Hauréau, *Not. et Extr.* vol. ii, p. 298.

[4] *Spec. Laic.* p. xx (Homer, Empedocles, Plato, Epicurus, Aristotle, Demosthenes, Dioscorides, Cicero, Jul. Caesar, Varro the Phil., Sallust, Quintus Curtius, Horace, Juvenal, Seneca, Pliny, Tholonius the Phil., Solinus, Marcion, Galen, Secundus the Phil., Valerius Maximus and Prosper). See also the lists of classical sources used in the *Fasciculus Morum*, as given by A. G. Little, in *Studies in Engl. Franc. Hist.* (Ford Lectures), p. 146; and, for the 12th cent., Bourgain, as above, p. 250.

[5] Cf. MS. Lansd. 393, fol. 81 (*Ethics*); etc.

Robert Rypon,[1] for example, frequently professing to quote from the works of Aristotle. Features of life in classical times help to enliven further the arguments of their discourses. Thus, Rypon presses home his attack upon those who indulge in gambling, by means of the story of an ancient Roman custom mentioned by Augustine:

> For the game of Dice or knuckle-bones was a theatre-game of the Ribalds in Rome, who believed in false gods, one of which gods or goddesses was the god or goddess of Fortune, to whose gift and grace they imputed any good piece of luck that befell them.[2]

At another time he borrows from Seneca a description of the three Graces.[3] John Waldeby, in his turn, essays in one of his sermons to answer that "difficult" question as to how a man may know whether he will be saved or not, by making use of an *example* from the poet Ovid.[4]

When the recorders of sermons in the vernacular proceed solemnly to quote from "Orace",[5] or "the wise man Tullius",[6] the reader by now will know what to expect. Where sometimes it becomes hard to stifle a laugh, their unconscious humour and delightful quaintness will often compensate him for any sense of outrage that their follies may inflict. Nor will it be necessary to warn him against that equally ridiculous habit on the part of some modern literary commentators, of assuming that the writer in question must have read the authors whom he quotes so glibly. Even the most learned had derived much of their knowledge of the literature of the golden age merely through the medium of a Solinus, an Orosius, an Isidore or a Rabanus Maurus,[7] and of its history from even later and less reliable

---

[1] Cf. MS. Harl. 4894, fol. 200b (*Metaph.*).

[2] fol. 23. Cf. *Ayenb. of Inwyt*, p. 169.   [3] fol. 59.

[4] MS. Caius Coll. Camb. 334 ("Dico quod difficile est; tamen verisimiliter potest homo conjecturare;...et hoc patet per exemplum...").

[5] Cf. MS. Roy. 18. B. xxiii, fol. 129b (*De Arte Poetica*).

[6] Cf. ibid. fol. 157b; *Ayenb. of Inwyt*, p. 147; etc.

[7] All these are quoted by Bromyard in *S.P.*; cf. s.v. "Matrimonia" (Solinus, on the women of India and "Suttee", etc.), s.v. "Consilium" (Orosius), s.v. "Judices" (Isidore, on the rock Scylla), etc. John Waldeby, e.g., in a sermon in MS. Caius Coll. Camb. 334, fol. 177, similarly quotes— "Solinus, *de Mirabilibus Mundi*", etc.

sources.[1] Those splendid misquotations of the preacher were drawn—like the poet Langland's own high-sounding references to "Porfirie and Plato, Aristotile, Ovidius,... Tullius, Tholomeus",[2]—from treatises but little more learned and accurate than his own.[3] More likely still they may have come direct from some crude collection of *Flores Doctorum* or "Proverbys of Phylosopherys",[4] where, perchance in the manuscript margin, the quaint little portrait of a red-haired, red-bearded "Tullius" in medieval Doctor's dress looked solemnly up at the clerical reader.[5] Little wonder that the "wise clerks" of olden time, pagan and patristic together, seemed to him of almost equal authority, although in the former case, of course, lacking the grace of a Christian heritage: "Thise were most resonable men that men shall rede of in olde tyme. And thes all tauȝthe to wurchippe and love vertewe, and he that doth othur weys doth aȝens reson."[6] In the great comprehensive system of Catholic Mother-Church, they still have their divinely appointed place.

In these foure vertues [Fortitude, Justice, Temperance and Prudence] studien these philosofres, and forsoken the worlde for to have these vertues and wisdom. And therfore thei were cleped philosofres. ffor philosophi is a word of gru [sic!], and is to seie—"love of wisdom".

[1] A good illustration occurs in Bromyard, *S.P.* s.v. "Bellum": "Hoc experimento patuit in Pompeio Magno Romanorum principe, de quo recitat Historia Scholastica [i.e. of Peter Comestor] quae continet Historiam Machabeorum cum Historia Evangelistarum, et accipitur a Josepho".

[2] *Piers Pl.* C Text, pass. xiii, ll. 173–5 (again called "poetes").

[3] Cf. two illuminating examples furnished by M. Hauréau, *Not. et Extr.* vol. i, pp. 100–1 (*Tract. Tullii*) and vol. ii, pp. 195–202 (Seneca).

[4] Cf. e.g. MS. Pembr. Coll. Cambr. 103, fols. 61, 63 et seq., *Proverbia et Dicta Philos.* (12th–13th cents.); MS. Linc. Cath. Libr. A. 2. 3, fols. 21b et seq. *Flores Aristotilis*, etc. (13th cent.); MS. Vernon, fols. 306 et seq. E.E.T.S. ed. O.S. no. 117, pp. 522–53 (c. 1370–80); MS. Harl. 4733 (by Master Benedict Burgh? c. 1450–75); and Caxton's *Dictes and Sayengis of the Philosophres* (1477, etc. from a Latin original through the French).

[5] Cf. MS. Linc. Cath. Libr. C. 4. 6, fol. 51: a series of *Flores Patrum* or *Sententiae ex Patribus* (fols. 47–62b), including further portraits of Augustine, Gregory, Jerome, Clement, Isidore, Bernard, and Anselm, etc.

[6] MS. Roy. 18. B. xxiii, fol. 142b (on the Stoics and Platonists). Cf. the citation of the pagans, Plato (*Timaeus*) and Julian the Apostate in a warning to priests to avoid lay society, shows, taverns, etc., in *Spec. Laic.* cap. xviii (ed. Welter, pp. 24–5).

And therfore philosofres beth as moche to seie as the lovers of wisdom. And whan they were paynyms and with-outen certeyn lawe, and knowe noght the feith 'and the grace of god ne of the 3iftes of the holy goost, but folowen her owne witte, 3it thorgh here owne witte thei come to so hye contemplacioun that thei tolde¹ noght of the world....And 3it we lye fouler, and walowe in sloes of synne than eny swyne doth in the sloes of this erthe. And therfore seith seint poule, that, [sith] the paynyms, that hath no lawe taght hem to do, do the lawe that thei knew noght, thei schal deme us false cristen men at the day of dome, that knoweth the lawe and kepith it noght.²

Their expositions of the world of Nature, its laws and constituents might well be read and repeated with respect. For it was through singular understanding of these that they had attained by close study to a knowledge of their Creator:

Many philosophres and hethen men couthe knowe God thorgh his creatures, as it were thorgh a myrour. But right savour of him had thei none. Thei seyh thorgh understondynge and resoun his fairnes, his goodnes, his myght, and his wisdom, thorgh sight of the creatures that he had made so faire, so good, so wel ordeyned bi skile to oure bihove....³

But, apart from the properties of natural things, the vernacular homilists will venture sometimes to refer their audiences to these same pagan philosophers for enlightenment in moral and spiritual affairs. Thus "Tullius, the wise clerke" is again referred to, this time on the subject of love.⁴ The same homilist, now preaching on the text—"Amice, quomodo huc intrasti?"⁵ opens with a quotation from the great pagan philosopher of medieval lore, concerning friendship: "Worshippfull men and wymen, the worthye clerke Aristotle, in the laste boke of is *Ethicus*, seyth that there is thre manere of frenshippes,—*Amicitia propter utile, Amicitia pro voluptate et Amicitia propter bonum morale....*"⁶ The rude author of *Jacob's Well* remarks how

it is rehersyd in the book of proverbys of phylosopherys that a leccherous persone seyde [to] a philysophre, Pyttagoras, that it was more solace

---

¹ = reckoned, accounted.

² MS. Harl. 45, fol. 20b (yet, he adds, because they lack the grace of the Holy Ghost, "her vertues beth to hem dede and withoute profite"). From *Ayenb. of Inwyt* (p. 126).

³ MS. Harl. 45, fol. 154 (*Ayenb. of Inwyt*, p. 245).

⁴ MS. Roy. 18. B. xxiii, fol. 122.   ⁵ Matthew xxii, 12.

⁶ MS. Roy. 18. B. xxiii, fol. 56. Cf. again the Three Companions of the Virtues, quoted from the *Ethics*, by Bromyard, *S.P.* s.v. "Cogitatio".

to hym to be conversaunt wyth foly wommen than wyth clerkys and
wyth phylosophrys. The philisophre sayde to him aȝen—"ther-of have
I no mervayle. for an hog or a sowe hath levere walewyn him in a foul
wose than in a clene ryvere.". . .[1]

Into the *Festial* sermons of John Myrc there comes even an echo
of the immortal "γνῶθι σεαυτόν", though sadly distorted,
from "*the Gestys of the Romayns*",[2] repeated again by another
English preacher, who quotes an *exemplum* from Seneca,[3] and
indeed by most vernacular homilists of the period, with some
considerable emphasis. So the great twin doctrine in Greek
ethics of "μηδὲν ἄγαν", so prominently set forth in a twelfth-
century homily,[4] finds its place in more than one argument of
Bromyard's learned encyclopaedia for preachers,[5] to be duly
re-echoed in verses by Lydgate and others upon the theme
that "mesour is tresour". It would be ludicrous, no doubt,
to speak of these scattered, garbled excerpts from classical
sources as though they were part of an officially recognized
scheme to hand on fragments of classical culture to the semi-
educated masses. No such generous attitude to popular education could ever have suggested itself to the majority of medieval
clergy, themselves often too illiterate, too contemptuous of
lay-folk, or else too jealous of their own privileged "cunning"
to welcome such a task. Of the Mendicants perhaps we may
say that their view of popular instruction was sometimes
wide enough to include these things as valuable for their own
sake to the ordinary man, not as mere appendages of the main
theme. This, however, must be a matter of doubt.[6] On the

[1] p. 159.   [2] p. 116.
[3] MS. Roy. 18. B. xxiii, fol. 171. Cf. also *Pricke of Consc.* pp. 5–7,
Jacob's Well, pp. 275–6; etc. The doctrine was popularized, of course,
through the medieval philosophers and mystics, in such works as the
Meditations of St Bernard (cf. also above, p. 78, n. 2).
[4] *Old Eng. Homs.* E.E.T.S. O.S. no. 34, pp. 101 et seq. (quoting—
"Omnia nimia nocent, et temperantia mater virtutum dicitur").
[5] Cf. *S.P.* s.v. "Ascensio"; "Conscientia" ("Conscientia bene ordinata
se habet inter nimis largam et nimis strictam, sicut virtus inter duo vicia,
sicut largitas inter avaritiam et prodigalitatem"); "Exemplum" ("Neutrum
extremorum sed medium eligendum est"); *Ayenb. of Inwyt*, pp. 168, 250–
60; and frequent denunciation of conduct "*out of mesure*". H. O. Taylor
errs here in his *Class. Heritage of the Midd. Ages*, pp. 16, 245, etc.
[6] See the accusation in B. Smalley, *Study of the Bible in the M.A.*, 2nd ed.,

other hand, it remains vitally true that by such means and such alone the common people in those early times did as a matter of fact receive their first lessons in general knowledge. To this extent then our pulpit may well claim to be the parent of popular adult education, before ever the tide of the Classical Revival or of the printing presses had set in.

Before passing to *exempla* of primitive natural history, the reader can take a last look at the sermon-anecdote in the shape of classical myths and marvels. For such will be found scattered throughout the *Summa Predicantium*,[1] and here and there in many manuscripts of homilies. A peculiar fondness is shown for the fantastic monsters of classical legend, as we might well expect in lovers of the medieval Bestiary. The Sirens and their part in the story of Ulysses appear alike in Holcot's *Moralitates*,[2] the *Gesta Romanorum*,[3] and Bromyard's *Summa*.[4] Argus with his hundred eyes and Polyphemus with but one furnish the latter with suitable *figures* of those who see only the faults of others and overlook their own.[5] The Austin friar John Waldeby, too, preaching upon the theme of "Carnal Delectation" as a special vice of prelates of the Church, moralizes the particular legend of Orpheus and Argus as follows:[6]

Matthew xxvi, 31: *I will smite the shepherd, and the sheep of the flock shall be scattered abroad.* As the poets relate, Argus the shepherd had a hundred eyes; and Orpheus, a most excellent player upon the lyre, wishing to steal his cattle, made all the eyes of Argus close in sleep, one by one, by playing upon his lyre; and thus having smitten off the head of the sleeping Argus, removed the cattle at his own will and pleasure. The moral of the story is that this Argus with the hundred eyes signifies each prelate, who ought to have eyes in every direction, seeking in advance to avert the perils of those committed to his charge. Whence prelates in Ezechiel and in the Apocalypse are called "beasts full of eyes, before and behind".[7] Orpheus singing sweetly to his lyre is the Flesh

p. 310, and Jacques de Vitry in Welter, *L'Exemplum . . .*, pp. 68-9 (*non solum ad edificacionem . . .*)

1 E.g. cf. the story of Daedalus and Icarus, s.v. "Ascensio", etc.
2 Cf. MS. Arund. 384, fol. 89b, etc.
3 Ed. Oesterley (Berlin), cap. 237.
4 s.v. "Audire" and "Crux". (Cf. also the "Sirenes" mentioned under "Adulator"). Other English sermons and *Exemplaria* which contain it are MSS. Harl. 7322, fol. 58, and Roy. 12. E. xxi, fol. 45.
5 *S.P.* s.v. "Correctio" (cf. "Timor").   6 MS. Roy. 7. E. ii, fol. 70.
7 See *Preaching in Med. Engl.* p. 252.

with its promptings to Lust, which sends to sleep all the eyes of discretion, and so, through the consent to sin, seizes and cuts off the reason which like a head should direct man, as the head directs and rules the members. Then it steals away the cattle committed to its charge, when it makes the whole strength of the body, subject to the reason of the mind, do service to the sin of Lust.

Other well-known classical marvels that make their appearance are the Chimaera, the Harpy, the Hydra, the Labyrinth, the warring Titans, and the deadly rock of Scylla.[1] Nor is the medieval appetite for the marvellous here limited to these. For that same element lies at the heart of such perennially charming stories as that of Daedalus and Icarus, of the painter "Zeusis" (Zeuxis) and his models,[2] or again of Virgil's magic mirror and brazen statue at Rome,[3] explaining their popularity with the English homilist and his audiences. Of a certain "brazen head" which bit off the hands of slanderers and liars, said to have been set up at Rome in classical times, one English preacher naïvely remarks: "I dowte not, and if that hedde were here and had that same law, then we scholde see many hondles men and women bothe in this towne and in other townys".[4] The same preacher regards the famous tale, which he gives from "Ovydius", of the infant "Herculesse" strangling the snakes in his "cradell", as a proof of his hero's gentle birth![5] Equally naïve and delightful is the use made by another of the classic tradition of Olympus:

Here-to I fynde likenes in poysye [says he]. The poyetys feynen and seyen that somtyme the grett Jubiter wold not dwell no where but on hie hilles. And thei sey that this was the skill—for he sawe well that on hie hilles growes floures and lilies; and so doth not in vales. Ryght so

[1] Cf. MSS. Arund. 384, fol. 86; Cotton Vitell. C. xiv, fol. 155; Roy. 7. C. 1, fol. 93 b (and S.P. s.v. "Munus"); Gesta Rom. E.E.T.S. ed. pp. 111 and 468; and S.P. s.v. "Ascensio" and "Judices", respectively.
[2] Thus spelt in a vernacular sermon in MS. Worc. Cath. Libr. F. 10, fol. 46 (from "Tullius"). Cf. again, MS. Roy. 12. E. xxi, fol. 44b.
[3] Cf. MSS. Roy. 7. C. 1, fol. 101b; Harl. 7322, fol. 97; Linc. Cath. Libr. A. 6. 2, fols. 117 and 128b; the Gesta Rom.; S.P. s.v. "Avaritia", etc. The Magic Mirror appears in Gower, Conf. Amant. bk. v, and Chaucer, Cant. Tales, Squieres Tale. On this and the Brazen Head and their Oriental origins, see Skeat (quoting Warton), The Prioresses Tale, etc. Clar. Press, pp. xxxiv–xlviii, and Herrtage, Gesta Rom. pp. 452–3.
[4] MS. Linc. Cath. Libr. A. 6. 2, fol. 117b.   [5] fol. 164.

godde of heven wold no where dwell but on the hie hill of heven, for
clennes and vertues that is therin amonge is aungels; and alwey the vales,
that is to seye the urthe, he founde full of synne. But ȝitt, as sone as is
modere was waxen here in this wale, he found in hure suche plente of
vertewes and goodnes that than hym thought was tyme for to com to us,
and rathur [= earlier], not.[1]

It has long been a recognized fact that the sermon-anecdote
of the Middle Ages, which in time tended to eclipse its moralization in importance, helped to kindle the popular passion for
Facetiae and the early forms of lighter fiction in the age of the
Renaissance. Apparently no one yet has done an equal justice
to the medieval preacher's contribution to the beginnings of
that demand for intellectual enlightenment on the part of the
people, which is another and yet more important mark of the
new era. For certain types of popular sermon might almost be
described as the forerunners of the modern University Exten-
sion Lecture. Whatever may have to be said about the Church's
prohibition of popular theological study and the veil cast over
"goddes privitees", it is certainly a different story where
popular natural science is concerned. Any close study of pre-
Reformation sermon-literature as a whole must convince the
student that many homilists did as much as they could with
the little worldly knowledge at their disposal, to press it into
the service of preaching. At a time when "the era of simple
credulity was giving place to the age of Reason", they, too,
as well as their audiences were obviously enjoying the search
after fresh information. The story of the pulpit will show us
again and again how often it is the Church herself that thus
helps to fashion the very instrument of her own future undoing.
Well might she boast that Catholic scholasticism took all
knowledge for its province, and that the kingdom over which
Theology reigned as Queen knew no bounds. But, in its
relation to the outer world, her official view of knowledge was
really as narrow and "departmental" as her current view of
Society, its separate duties and its component parts. Hence the
fatal error into which churchmen fell when they imagined that
a smattering of apparently harmless natural history and crude

[1] MS. Roy. 18. B. xxiii, fol. 118.

story-telling in the pulpits would satisfy all those—be they highly educated laymen or mere rustic boors—for whom initiation into theological mysteries was considered so palpably dangerous. It was the Church's spokesmen after all who first told men something of the mysteries of earth and heaven, who bade them consider the work of God's hands in sun, moon and stars, in cloud, rainbow and eclipse, who explained to them the wonders of the animal creation or the rare plants and minerals to be found in foreign parts. Could minds thus awakened and stirred be expected to stop further enquiry at the arbitrary bidding of the priesthood, where no natural barriers existed? Such an attitude is but one with that blind fear and invincible ignorance in which the official Catholic Church seems to stumble madly onward to the brink of the Reformation. When the University movement of the twelfth century first brought learning into the open from behind convent walls, she had launched the great Mendicant Orders to meet the new danger of this threatened secularization of knowledge. Now, however, the very Mendicant preaching originally designed to steer a safe middle course in the moral and mental instruction of lay-folk was itself helping unconsciously to create a fresh crisis, in which such secularization would become at last inevitable.[1] For good or ill, like the rising tide of democracy and education in modern times, this bursting of the barriers between knowledge secular and sacred, the free and the forbidden, the common concerns of the laity and the taboos of the priesthood was bound to come sooner or later in the very nature of things. Indeed, it was implicit in Christianity itself, so long at least as a Bible was allowed to exist anywhere. Wise, then, would be that institution that could foresee it in time, and boldly direct the flood into new and healthy channels. Instead, however, in our period we seem to hear only from the one side, the interdict of officialdom—"Thou shalt not melle the no farthur, but to beleve as holychurche techeth the

[1] The spirit of scepticism and enquiry on the one hand, and of contempt for the clergy and their doctrines on the other, among the people, is admirably illustrated in Bromyard. I intend to discuss this subject in a subsequent work on "Some Hidden Roots of the English Reformation".

pleynly";[1] from the other the plaintive cry of the future sectary—"Lord, giwe thou to me wysdoom that stondith about the setis!"[2]

How far then, we ask, did the English preacher of the later Middle Ages attempt to enlighten and interest his flock in the wonders of nature? There, visible to the rudest eye, blazed the noonday sun with its heat, and at night the stars, objects of mystery and wonder as soon as the rude mind pierces the veil of custom and begins to reflect upon them. "The philosophyrs seythe that, for the grete influens of hete, the sonne is callyd *Pater Omnium Methamathice* [*sic*!], 'ffader of all planettes'. Ensampyll by experiens. . . ."[3] Among its several marvels there is the phenomenon of the Eclipse, a striking topic even for sermon moralization in the age of Chaucer:

> With thre thynges the material sunne is maad derk fro men: that is, with ny3t, and with cloudes, and with the eclipce. . . . The thridde thyng that letteth the schynynge of the sunne is the eclipce. 3e schulleth understonde that the derknesse of the eclipse is of no defaute in the sunne, as it semeth in mennis si3t. But, as clerkys seyn, whan the moone is directli bi-twixe the erthe in whiche we dwellen and the sunne, than is causid the eclipse. Ri3t soo, whan men of holi cherche, that is, prelates and prestes, which principalli schulden take li3t of kunnynge of the sunne of cristis lawe, as the moone of the sunne, beth directli bitwixe it and the comen peple, with al hire power stoppynge and hidynge fro hem the verrei knowyng ther-of, than is causid a greet goostli eclipse of the sunne of cristes li3t and his lawe in cristen mennes soules.[4]

An interesting comment, indeed, upon a subject, quite remote from eclipses, which has just engaged our attention! Another

---

[1] MS. Roy. 18. B. xxiii, fol. 95.

[2] Wisd. ix, 4. From a Lollard Tract (by Wycliffe?), printed in Miss Deanesly's *Lollard Bible*, App. ii, p. 451.

[3] MS. Linc. Cath. Libr. A. 6. 2, fol. 25. In a sermon of MS. Camb. Univ. Libr. Gg. vi. 16, fol. 39, where the passage is repeated, "planetarum" is substituted for "mathematice".

[4] MS. Add. 41321, fols. 9b and 14b-15. (He goes on: "ffor manie of hem seyn that it is no3t lefful lewide men to knowe the blesside lawe of the goospel of oure lord jhesu crist, but oneli prestes and clerkes. But it sufficeth to hem to kunne her *pater noster*, and to bileeve wel. . .".) The Lunar Eclipse figures in Bromyard, *S.P.* s.v. "Invidia", and again in a sermon, with other astronomical matter, in MS. Bodl. 649, fol. 44.

homilist has yet more astronomical information to supply with regard to the planets:

> I rede in the sotell tretiȝe, *The Theorike of the Planetis*,[1]—and the same is had in dyvers bokes of the *Almageste* of Ptolome,—that the planetis have *epicicles*, all save oon; and when thei be in the nedir parties of the *Epicicles*, than ther mevyng is acordyng with the movyng of heven. But when that thei be in the over parte of thise *epicicles*, than thei move ever contrary to heven. Thise *epicicles* bethe rounde bodies of the wiche thise steres beth moved; for thei bere inmediatly the bodies of thise steres, the wiche *epicicles* beth ever in contynually movyng. And thei betokeneth the goodes of this world that be whirlyng aboute, withowten anny cesynge, and thei here uppe bodies of men here. . . .[2]

Similarly, John Bromyard refers to the nature of "falling" stars—"quae in Libro Metheorum[3] *assub* vocantur"[4]—as a simile for the hypocrite.[5] In another place he borrows from the same *Liber Metheorum* a figure of the moon's halo, "which when uniform and complete denotes fine weather; when broken in one place, wind; when broken in several, rain and storms".[6] From the Arabian astronomer "Albumasar", he quotes a passage concerning the moon in its relation to the tides of the sea.[7] The properties of the sun's rays and the nature of clouds, which again provide him with a lengthier simile,[8] become the subject of further observations on the part of a vernacularist. The latter distinguishes first the healthy clouds which give their rain and then depart, leaving the sun to shine.

> But ther been other cloudes as I seide, that ben clene withoute watir, and suche letten the liȝt of the sunne. For thei been lenger endurynge

---

[1] E.g. the *Theorica Planetarum* of Gerard of Cremona, the Younger, *de Sabloneta* (13th cent.): cf. MSS. Harl. 13, Roy. 12. C. ix, fol. 53, etc.

[2] MS. Roy. 18. B. xxiii, fol. 137b. See further, fols. 171 and 96b ("the planete Saturnus"); and the *Pricke of Consc.* pp. 204–8.

[3] I.e. Aristotle's *Liber Metheorologicorum* (or *Meteorologica*), in the Latin version made from the Arabic translation (as well shown here).

[4] Cf. *Engl.-Arabic Dict.* s.v. "Meteor"—(s.) شِهاب; (pl.) شُهب (shihāb; shuhub). [5] *S.P.* s.p. "Ipocrisis". [6] s.v. "Concordia".

[7] s.v. "Nativitas", § 9 (Abū Mashʿar: d. 885). Cf. again, s.v. "Electio" (the relative magnitude of Saturn and the Moon).

[8] s.v. "Gratitudo", § 5. Cf. *Old Engl. Homs.* (12th cent.), E.E.T.S. O.S. no. 53, p. 109.

and ever semeth to regne and regneth no3t. And suche, for defaute that the
sunne mai not come doun, gendreth corrupte eir; and so pestilence sueth,
as clerkis seyn. . . .[1]

Curious estimates of "astronomical" distance are sometimes
to be met with in sermon manuscripts, a crude attempt to
impress the lay mind with the vastness of the universe to which
it belongs. Thus Myrc informs his audience in a characteristically offhand manner:

> Thus sayde a gret phylosophur, Raby Moyses, that hit ys as ferre from
> erthe to Heven as an hole man my3t lyve a thowsand 3ere, and yche day
> goo a thowsand myle. But he that metythe this way, he can best telle
> the myles and the lengthe of hom.[2]

From contemplation of the earth itself in its relation to the
heavens, the medieval listener may be led on to consider its
varied products.

> A gret clerke, Albertus, in ys boke that he made *de Proprietatibus
> Elementorum*, telleth the skille why that erthe alon bryngeth forthe so
> many thinges of dyvers kyndes, as corne and gresse, floures and trees,
> metals and precious stones of sundre vertewes. And the skill is this: the
> firmament is rownde abowten the erthe, and the erthe stondeth but as a
> poynte in the midward; and therfore the bemes of the sonne and the
> steres gadere therto, and ther thei reste. . . .[3]

If "floures" or plants be next selected, then with Master Rypon
of Durham the homilist may tell how—

as Macer says in *de Virtutibus Herbarum*[4]—Rosemary grows, and is
warming and astringent; the root of which when chewed relieves the
toothache. The juice of it, when drunk, cures fevers. But if its root is
of such virtue, so much the more is its flower, which is the quintessence
of the root, of yet greater virtue, and is called *Anthos*.[5]

---

[1] MS. Add. 41321, fol. 13. Cf. in a Latin sermon in MS. Heref. Cath.
Libr. P. 5. 2, fol. 75b (evil monks of the day compared to the nature
of evil clouds).

[2] *Festial*, p. 152. Cf. similar estimates from "Raby Moyses" of the
distance between earth and heaven, given in a sermon-book—MS. Harl.
2250, fol. 83b, and the *Pricke of Consc.* p. 206. "Rabbi Moses" is,
of course, the Jew Maimonides: 1135–1204.

3 MS Roy. 18. B. xxiii, fol. 171b (Albertus Magnus: 1206-1280).

4 I.e. Macer Floridus: fl. 10th cent. (?) Cf. MSS. Harl. 3353 and 4346;
MS. Linc. Cath. Libr. C. 4. 8, fol. 62; etc.).

5 MS. Harl. 4894, fol. 119 (*Ros Marinus*).

From another we learn of

ane Erbe callyd *Agnus Castus*, off the whyche spekethe Albertus, *de Vegetabilibus, libro* 6º, *capitulo* 5º. Thys grete clerke seythe this erbe *Agnus Castus*, in somyr it bryngethe fforthe ffeyr ffresche fflowres, leves and ffrute. And off hys natur and kynde it desyrythe hote and drye. The leves, fflowres and ffrute be vertuous to kepe and cause continence and chastite, iff thei be caste in howses, or borne upon a man. Yff we speke off thys erbe gostly *Agnus Castus*, it mey be seyde [to be] the holy crosse, qwhos ffrute is *Agnus Immaculatus*, that chaste and immaculate lambe Criste Jhesu. . . . Bot as longe and qwhan the ffrute off thys herbe Criste Jhesu be sprynkytt and strewyd in the howses off owr sawles wyth continuall and besye devocion, than pur continence, chastite, and clennes shall not ffeyle.[1]

From Bozon we hear likewise of the properties of the mandrake, of hyssop, garlic and other herbs useful and dangerous to man.[2] If, on the other hand, the homilist shall choose to deal with precious stones "of sundre vertewe", he may follow Bromyard in describing their power to ward off the dangers of poisoning—"after the fashion of those lords, who, in fear of being poisoned, have, as it is said, upon their table a precious stone, which sweats in the presence of poison".[3] The virtue of Meekness, says another,

may well be likened to a cristall, of the wiche I rede *in Libro de Naturis Lapidum et Gemmarum*,[4] that every preciouse stone hath the more vertewe ȝiff he be ioyned to a cristall. For, and anny precious stonne have lost is vertewe, ioyne hym to a cristall and it shall rathur get ys vertewe aȝeyn.[5]

A popular series of outline sermons, probably the work of Robert Holcot, discusses the properties of the magnet (which appear again in the *Gesta Romanorum* and in the sermons of Bozon and Bromyard), the stone "Diacotos", the agate (called

[1] MS. Camb. Univ. Libr. Gg. vi. 16, fols. 37–37b. The *Agnus Castus* is called "Bishopswort" in the *Sinonyma Bartolomei* of John of Mirfield, the author of our homiletic *Florarium*. It is quoted again, from Albertus Magnus, *De Vegetab.* lib. vi. 1, cap. v, in a sermon by Robt. Holcot (cf. MS. Roy. 7. C. i, fol. 103b), of which there are several MS. copies extant.

[2] See *Metaphs.* cap. lvii, lviii, lxxxiii, lxxxiv, lxxxvi, xci, xcvi, xcvii, etc.

[3] *S.P.* s.v. "Detractio". See also s.v. "Crux".

[4] See P. Studer and J. Evans, *Anglo-Norman Prose Lapidaries*, pp. 88 and 134 (13th cent.). Not in Marbod.

[5] MS. Roy. 18. B. xxiii, fol. 170b.

Clades", or "Achates"), the sardonyx, the stones "Lepana" (or "Lippares"), and "Eptistos" (or "Epistites"), the amethyst and the jasper.[1] Bozon gives us, in addition, the Adamant, the ruby, the pearl, the chrysoprase, the Loadstone and the "Oyndre".[2] Occasionally the preacher may point to certain properties or features of well-known objects, to explain his argument as it were by simple experimental test. John Bromyard, we find, chooses "an example of the burning glass which, in receiving the rays of the sun, reflects them with intensified heat, so that that reflection will kindle inflammable matter that is very dry—as experiment teaches" (sicut experimentum docet).[3] Another optical phenomenon, which he says can be tested by experiment, is introduced to illumine a discussion on Humility. It is concerned with the fact that anyone at the bottom of a deep well can see the stars in clear daylight, or at least would see the heavens more vividly than another person who was not standing in so deep and dark a spot. The phenomenon itself is then duly explained.[4] John Waldeby sets out to give an even more naïve exposition, by natural experiment, of the purifying efficacy of Christ's blood: "Istud idem probo per artem".

Thus it is in practical life that, if, on account of long neglect, blood in a vessel becomes so dried and hardened that it cannot be easily cleaned off, if anyone should then take fresh blood and warm, such as proceeds from an animal, and put it upon the caked blood on the piece of cloth or vessel, that warm and fresh blood will thus loosen the caked blood,

[1] Cf. MSS. Roy. 7. C. i, fols. 93b, 102b, 105b, 108b, 111b, 114b, 116; Harl. 5369, fols. 266, 267. Cf. also the properties of "oyle", discussed on fol. 114b of the former, and in MS. Harl. 2398, fol. 26b; and Chaucer, *Cant. Tales*, Prol. 11, 498–500:

> "Out of the gospel he tho wordes caughte,
> And this figure he added eek ther-to,
> That if gold ruste, what shal iren do?" (The Persoun)

[2] *Metaphs.* cap. i, xvi, xxvii, xxxiii, xlvi, lvi, and lxxx. (The Loadstone and Adamant are probably the same.) The Onyx appears in Myrc, *Festial*, p. 107.

[3] *S.P.* s.v. "Gratitudo".

[4] *S.P.* s.v. "Humilitas" ("Cujus ratio est quia, cum circa oculos lumen non sit in quo virtus visiva sit dispersa, oportet quod ipsa in se fortior sit ad alta videndum...").

and, with the help of a little water, the vessel or cloth will be cleansed from that stain as clean as ever it was at the first.[1]

One *example* of this kind, at any rate, acquired a certain fame in England, in the theological controversies of the later Middle Ages. It was a favourite device of preachers and scholastics to explain the mystery of Transubstantiation by the figure of a broken glass mirror, in each fragment of which a separate face is reflected, whereas one face alone appeared in the mirror when whole:

> And that loke by skile. Lo! here:
> Bihold thi-self in a schewere.[2]
> Thou ne sest but onliche thi faas,
> The while al hol is the glaas.
> And brek the glas in two or thre,
> And so moni formes thou miht se.
> Beo the makyng of the oblee
> Wel and skilfoliche me may se
> Of wȝuche we make Godus fflesch,
> This is the saumple whose wol esch.[3]

It is this *figure* of the mirror which Wycliffe discusses in one of his most noteworthy pulpit attacks on the doctrine of the Eucharist, in a sermon based upon the text "Hoc est corpus meum".[4]

Most popular of all created things in pulpit moralization were the beasts, birds and fishes of the animal kingdom. Even to the medieval mind, their very nature like that of man himself proved them to be linked with the primitive substance of creation in a way that gave rise to the four humours that "reign in our body", precisely in accord with the ancient Greek ideas from which it was derived: "ffrendes, ȝe shall undirstond that philisophers seyth that every man and woman

[1] MS. Caius Coll. Camb. 334, fol. 173b. To this category of *exempla* may be added the popular cures for sickness which Bozon mentions (cf. *Metaphs.* cap. lxxxi, lxxxv, lxxxvi, etc.; also for the hair—xci and xcii).
[2] = mirror.
[3] Sermon on the Feast of Corpus Christi (E.E.T.S. O.S. no. 98, p. 177). Cf. further, Bromyard, *S.P.* s.v. "Eucharistia"; *Engl. Metr. Homs.*— MSS. Harl. 4196, fol. 102; Cotton Tib. E. vii, fol. 201b, etc.
[4] Matth. xxvi, 26 ("Wycliffe's Wyckett", §§ xiii and xiv, in many editions, cf. *Wycliffe Soc.* 1845, p. 281, etc.).

and beest is mad of foure elementes, that is to sey, feyr, eyer, watur and urthe; and the condicions of hem arne founden in hem".[1] At the same time here were beings with properties far outshining those of a more bulky inanimate nature, full of picturesque life and vigorous movement, blessed with a hundred little different tricks and varieties of mechanism, each one a fresh marvel calculated to delight the inquisitive sermon-hearer. Man himself, treated from the biological standpoint, gave the preacher almost unlimited scope for interesting discussion. Thus proceeds he who explains to the "wurchippfull frendes" of his congregation how "a gret clerke Aristotill, in a boke that he mad—*capitulo XV, de Animalibus*—telleth that the children here on urthe, for the most parte, folowen the properte and the condicions of her ffaders that thei com of".[2] Of the beasts of the field, others will dilate concerning their unique venous system,[3] their mode of rearing their young, their characteristic food and methods of chase, and numerous other peculiarities of their appearance and habits. The medieval Bestiaries have already been made the subject of specialized study on the part of modern antiquaries in several countries. But no one hitherto, apparently, has troubled to show what actual use was made of them by our English homilists in their work of popular religious instruction. The task is not idle, again, for the simple reason that it fills an unnecessary gap in the story of the education of the masses, and indeed proves further that there was no great gulf fixed in medieval times between the artistic symbolism of sculptor and wood-carver, the zoological literature of the "learned" and at least some popular understanding of the same. An earlier chapter of the present work revealed examples in the sermons of animal portraiture drawn from real life. Such, presumably, is a sermon account of three "propurtees" of "the boor of the wode", that

---

[1] MS. Roy. 18. B. xxiii, fol. 171b. Also in *Ormulum, Cursor Mundi, Gesta Rom.* (E.E.T.S. ed. p. 496), etc., and *Piers Pl.* C Text, pass. xi, ll. 128–31 (see Skeat's note thereto, referring to a Serm. of Augustine).

[2] fol. 166: (1) in shape of face and hands and quantity of growing; (2) in manner of bodily working; (3) in sounding of tongue and speech.

[3] Cf. Bromyard, *S.P.* s.v. "Conscientia" ("vene stricte, que animalia a veneni damno preservant").

"is more wylde than the boor of the feld.... ffirst a boor smyteth sore with his tusckis, that stonden in his mouthe; the seconde is that he wole gladli reeste him in foule slowis or mury places; the thirde is that he hath a foule stynkynge savur where he goth".[1] The characteristic feature of the descriptions now to engage our attention is that they are based upon the testimony of "philosophers" and "wise clerks", and therefore frequently give a certain rein to the imaginative powers of the narrator. Among natural "philosophers" often cited by name in the course of these sermons are such famous fathers of the medieval Bestiary as Aristotle, Pliny, Isidore of Seville, Vincent of Beauvais and Bartholomew Anglicus, whose De Proprietatibus Rerum has been spoken of as "Shakespeare's encyclopaedia". If we begin with the king of the beasts, we shall find that well-known legend of how the lion raises its still-born whelps to life with its cry and "keendly noyes", quoted in this fashion from the "notable clerk, Vincentius, in Speculo Historiali, libro X". So Christ, "by is noyse that he made on the crosse to is ffadur of heven on good ffridaye, he ʒave liff to mans soule, as doth the lion to is qwelpe."[2] Elsewhere, when the same homilist desires to show how "raveners" of the poor "ben likened to leons", he relates, as "Bartholomew telleth, that, when a leon commethe ther beestes ben, to fede hym, he goys in a circuite all abowte hem, and aftur that is non so bolde to pase that sercle".[3] So again, for example, he observes that "philisophers seyn that a bere of kynde loveth hony so gretly that, tho the bees stynge hym, he spareth not to ete itt".[4] Stories of the deadly struggles of the jungle must have brought to ancient sermon-audiences something of that childish excitement which the modern rustic still feels when the travelling menagerie enters his village, or, better still, when

[1] MS. Add. 41321, fol. 68b. Cf. further, Bozon, Metaphs. cap. v.
[2] MS. Roy. 18. B. xxiii, fol. 94b (Vincent of Beauvais: fl. 1244).
[3] fol. 134. He continues: "A sirs! On like wize thise raverners compasseth the pore peple uppon every side, castyng colors how thei myʒthe com to ther goodes. Thei feynen snares and grennes uppon hem, till that thei be in ther daungers; and then thei will redely compelle hem to sell hous and land..." (Bartholomew Anglicus: fl. c. 1240).
[4] fol. 133. Cf. MS. Roy. 12. E. xxi, fol. 56; Bozon, cap. vii; etc.

a thrill is evoked in the popular mind by vivid reminiscences
of big-game hunting.

Bartholomeus, *de Proprietatibus Rerum,* seys that ever betwix the
eddure and the Elephaunte, be keende, is grett strive. The neddur is fowle
and maliciouse, and the Elephaunte is stronge, fayre, and no-thinge
grevous. The neddyr, as this clerke seyth, will com and make hym for
to pleye with the elephaunte, and anon he pleys with the neddure; ffor
he thenketh non ewill. But at the last this malicious worme, the neddyr,
styngeth the elephaunte in the eye, as thei pley to-gethur, with is tayll.
And so sodenly the eddur distrowith the elephaunte.[1]

In the moralization which follows, the adder plays the part of
the Devil, and the elephant represents the human soul. Not
unnaturally the latter animal appears as a never ceasing source
of wonder to the medieval man of the West. Another English
homily of the period describes how these great beasts were supposed to be captured:

An Olyvawnte... hathe no joyntes in his lymmys, and therfore he may
never bowe; and when that he wyll reste hym he lenythe him to a tree. And
so, when that men ben in purpose for to take hym, then when he is absent,
they go and cutt this tree almoste a-two. And when this beste is dysposyd
for to go and reste hym, then he gothe to this tree and lenythe hym there
to; and then sodenly he fallythe downe, and so he is taken. And by no
menys he may not a-ryse, by cawse that he hathe no joyntes.[2]

As for "that old serpent", the adder, "cleped aspis", the device
by which it was said to stop one of its ears with its tail and the
other by pressing it to the ground, when "sche seeth a man
that can charme hir", became a favourite figure for the sinner's
refusal to listen to the preacher's exhortation.[3] "An neddur

[1] fol. 127b. See two interesting letters in *The Times* from a modern
zoologist on this subject, Aug. 7 and 14, 1929.

[2] MS. Glouc. Cath. Libr. Engl. Homs. (unpaginated), *Alius Sermo pro
XV Dom. post Trin.* Also, in Odo of Cheriton (see Hervieux, *Les
Fabulistes,* vol. iv, p. 316), and Bozon, *Metaphs.* cap. lxxiii. The de-
scription is really derived, by some curious confusion, from Caesar's
account of the German elks (*Comment.* lib. vi, 27). Cf. further,
"Aristotyll" quoted on the "Olyvawnte" in a sermon in MS. Linc.
Cath. Libr. A. 6. 2, fol. 187b; Holcot in MS. Roy. 7. C. 1, fols. 99b,
115b; and Bozon, cap. xiv, lxxi–iv, and cvi.

[3] MS. Harl. 45, fol. 163: cf. MS. Salisb. Cath. Libr. 103, fol. 112b
(unpubl. *Jacob's Well*); MS. Harl. 4894, fol. 17b (Rypon); etc.

glidynge uppon a stone" is an additional marvel of creation
to the observant who trouble to consider the matter:

> For, an eddur meves at ons is hed upward and the tail downeward;
> and ʒit at the same tyme som of the mydell parties of hym bethe meved
> unto the ryght side and som to the left side. This is a wondur, that anny
> best shuld so naturally at ons mewe tho parties to so many different
> posicions. Every clerke may merveill.[1]

Indeed, even the most familiar objects of the English countryside take on an atmosphere of mystery and of wonder, when
viewed through the spectacles of the natural philosopher. There
are the toads that swell up to immense proportions, and carry
in their systems poison with which to kill those who touch
them.[2] There is the tortoise, "of which it is said that for half
the year it will climb a certain tree, and in the end fall at a
slight puff of cold wind".[3] There is "the yrchon", that "goth
wyth hise scharpe pryckys to gaderyn hym a gret hurde of
applys, thynkynge in his kinde that his lyiflode schulde faylen
hym, but ʒif he gaderyd hym to-gedere a gret hepe of frute".[4]
He has a distant cousin in the "beeste of Inde that is clepyd
a portepyn. This beeste, whanne he is wroth, he casteth out
of his scharpe pynnes spytefully at hym that he is wroth
wyth".[5] Then, "thes backes [= bats] hath febull yʒen, as
philosofres seyn. And the cause is for the ...[6] is like cristall;
and that shuld be cause of ther siʒthe passeth into here wynges,
as it semeth well. For ther wynges be as thei were made of
leddir. And so, for ther flying thei have lost here siʒth".[7] Of
strange foreign beasts that attract attention there is, besides the

[1] MS. Roy. 18. B. xxiii, fol. 141 b (yet the "moving in this world of the
ghostly adder", i.e. the covetous man, is still more wonderful). The
Wolf and its "conditiones" appear on fol. 115: the Hyena, in Holcot,
MS. Roy. 7. C. i, fol. 98; Bozon, cap. cvii–ix; and *Ayenb. of Inwyt*,
p. 61: the Lynx, in the *Pricke of Consc.* p. 17, l. 576; etc. The above
reference to the adder is based on Prov. xxx, 19.
[2] MS. Add. 21253. [3] Bromyard, *S.P.* s.v. "Ascensio".
[4] *Jacob's Well*, p. 117 (also here, the Otter and the Fox). For the
Hedgehog and its hoard, etc., cf. further, Bozon, *Metaphs.* cap. lxvi–lxviii.
[5] Ibid. p. 154. See further below, p. 459 (from MS. Harl. 45, etc.).
[6] This illegible word seems to be *humour* (i.e. crystalline).
[7] MS. Roy. 18. B. xxiii, fol. 132 ("Trewly, on like wize, thise prowde
men, ever thei besy hem to flye uppward...."). Cf. Bozon, cap. cxii.

porcupine, the "foule that men clepeth a gamelyon".[1] "This
bryd lyveth be the eyre, and hath no-thyng in hym but wynde.
He wyl chaungyn hym to alle colourys that he seeth", as
Bromyard also observes.[2] Even the tiny bee and its manner
of birth, which reminds one of the legendary dragons born
of the slime, are not to be overlooked. "For the bee, that
maketh the wex, is as it were a clene maiden. For she groweth
of the hony with-out such maner gendrure that other bestes
kyndeli usen."[3] Finally, a yet stranger medley of purely
fabulous beasts is let loose in the sermons from the ancient
Bestiaries. Brunton[4] and Myrc[5] are only two recognizable
preachers of many who mention the unicorn, that "beryth a
horne yn his nose" like the rhinoceros of distant lands which
possibly gave rise to the original legend. The method of
capturing it, to which they invariably refer, is set forth in
English misericord carvings. The hunter "woll spye wher hys
walk ys, and ther he settythe a woman that ys clene mayden.
And when thys unycorn segh hyr, anon of kynd he falleth don,
and layth hys hed yn hur barme, myghtles wythoute strengthe,
and soo ys taken". The English version of the *Gesta Romanorum*
gives us the deadly Cockatrice: "As ofte tyme as she hathe
enye syght of...men, thei bethe dede thorowe the venyme
that passithe from hir syght".[6] Dan Michel of Northgate and
Bromyard refer to the cognate Basilisk;[7] while a Latin sermon

---

[1] = chameleon. MS. Harl. 45, fol. 147b. In *Jacob's Well*, p. 151, it is
called "gamaltan"; in *Ayenb. of Inwyt*, p. 62, "gamelos".

[2] *S.P.* s.v. "Adulator" ("de quo dicitur, quod videndo colorem
aliquem similis coloris efficitur"), and again, s.v. "Honor".

[3] MS. Harl. 2276, fol. 30 ("Wex bitokeneth the maydenhed of Marie,
Cristes modir....Now therfor gostli bere we Crist in wombe with
Marie maiden and modir"). Cf. Rolle's short Treatise on the Bee, described in Miss Allen's *Writings ascribed to R.R.*, pp. 269–71; and Bozon,
cap. cxli. Bromyard gives the Locust, *S.P.* s.v. "Dominatio" ("Locusta
enim pessimum est genus muscarum, que in terris calidis et orientalibus
in maxima volant multitudine..."); and Bozon, the "Eruca", here
identified with the glow-worm (*Metaphs.* cap. lxxv–vii), the Ant; etc.

[4] MS. Harl. 3760, fol. 95.   [5] *Festial*, p. 55.

[6] E.E.T.S. ed. no. 57, p. 240.

[7] See *Ayenb. of Inwyt*, p. 28, and *S.P.* s.v. "Acquisitio" and
"Invidia".

manuscript selects as a type of Lust the mythical panther (*pardus*) with its four heads and four wings.[1] Among mythical beasts must be reckoned also that "mermayde of the see" which Chaucer borrowed for a simile from the same source as the contemporary preacher:

For *Phisiologus* seith sikerly,
How that they singen wel and merily.[2]

In the preacher's case it is the flatterer who is "to be likened to a merveilous beste of the see that is cleped a mermayde,... that hath body as a woman, and a taile as a fisshe; and syngeth so mery that it makith schipmen, that hyreth it and taketh tent therto, falle in slepe and perisshe in the see".[3] Another terrifying half-human form, hardly less hideous than his classical namesake, bred of some wild travellers' tale and apparently known to Aristophanes, was

a maner of a beeste that is called "Ciclopes"; of which beest telleth a grett clerke—*et est Hillarius*,[4] *de Ymagine Mundi*. He telleth that ther is a beeste that hythes "*Cenopedes*" *vel* "*Cyclopes*". This beeste hath not but oon fote; never-the-lesse he is so swifte a beeste that, wondur is, he is of suche a keende that with is foote he kepeth hym fro the brennynge of the sonne, and fro alle othur tempestes, and in the shadowe of is fote he slepeth and resteth hym.[5]

In all such narrating we recognize vividly our Englishman's perennial love of "strange beasts" and "dead Indians" to which Shakespeare laughingly refers, a taste, then, duly fostered by an enterprising pulpit.

From the medieval wild-beasts' show, we pass now to the medieval aviary. Here the king of the birds is a regular sermon type of the wise and far-seeing prelate. "The eagle...among

[1] MS. Add. 21253, fol. 31b–32 ("propter varietates desideriorum"). The Mole appears on fol. 42, as type of the avaricious.
[2] *Cant. Tales*, "Nonne-Preestes Tale", ll. 4461–2.
[3] MS. Harl. 45, fol. 146b. *Jacob's Well*, p. 150, adds—"and clawys as an eryn". Cf. further, *Ayenb. of Inwyt*, p. 61; Bozon, *Metaphs.* cap. xxx; etc., and carvings on English medieval misericords and benches.
[4] An error for *Honorius* (of Autun): d. 1152 (see Migne, *Patr. Lat.* vol. clxxii, col. 115). *Cyclopes* is also here confused with *Monopes*.
[5] MS. Roy. 18. B. xxiii, fol. 77. The Sciapous: see M. R. James, art. "The Bestiary", in *History*, vol. xvi, no. 61, N.S., April, 1931, pp. 9–11.

other birds sees more acutely, and flies higher." He alone can
gaze into the sun with unflinching eye.[1] Yet even so lordly
a denizen of the air has one evil habit which allows him to
become a figure sometimes of evil pride. "The egle, as the
maister of bestiaris wryteth, ...he flieth hier than othur birdes.
He may also se farthur, ʒe, into dyvers reams. Nevertheles
he fedeth hym oft on stynkynge careyn."[2] The pelican, in its
turn, is more usually taken as a symbol of the redeeming
Christ, from the famous life-giving properties of "the bloode
of a pellycane, ...when it is droppid up on hyr byrdys, when
they ben dede".[3] Thus the beak that originally slew them in
righteous anger restores them to life again.[4] Master William
Lichfield, however, considers the pelican from another angle:

> Briddes that have litel fleshe fliʒen wele; so that they [that] have many
> federys, as is the pellicane, the ostryche and such maner foules that have
> myche fleshe, thay make sembland as they wold fliʒe, and betyn her
> wynges; bot her fete drawes ever up on the erthe. Thus many men makes
> countynance as thay wold do holy werkys, and maken myche dyn with
> her wynges, spekyng of holynes. But her lifyng is so full of fleshly lustes
> that they are no folowers of cristes passioun, but rather scorners....[5]

Another highly picturesque bird simile is that of the bittern,
whose weird cry is explained by the preacher in an equally
weird fashion:

> These glotenes moun wel be lickned to a foul that is clepid a bitore,[6]
> the whiche wol sitte bi the watir and putte his bile in a rude,[7] and ther-with
> maket an huge soun; so that men may here him afer cuntre. But whanne

---

[1] MS. Add. 21202, fol. 82b. Cf. Bozon, *Metaphs.* cap. xliv, and *Gesta Rom.* Engl. version, E.E.T.S. ed. p. 368; etc.

[2] MS. Roy. 18. B. xxiii, fol. 141.

[3] MS. Linc. Cath. Libr. A. 6. 2, fol. 166.

[4] Cf. Odo of Cheriton (Hervieux, *Les Fabulistes*, vol. iv, p. 269), and Bozon, *Metaphs.* cap. li.

[5] MS. Roy. 8. C. 1, fol. 132 (fol. 134b: "[the pellicane] is ever leene, and therfore he may fleʒe the better"). Cf. similarly Rolle's treatment of the storks, at the end of his Treatise on the Bee (Miss H. E. Allen, as before, p. 271). On the general subject of "disorderliness" in animal symbolism, see Coulton, *Art and the Reform.* pp. 268 et seq.

[6] This obviously suggests that the preacher is describing a bird unfamiliar to his audience.

[7] = reed.

he sitteth on drie grounde fer fro the watir, thenne he lifteth up his bile into heven and siteth stille, and no noyse maket.[1]

Master Robert Rypon remarks upon "aquatic birds", which, like the lustful, "delight to swim in troubled waters".[2] Of their number is the "Halcyon", described thus by another nameless homilist: "Seynt Ambrose telleth", he says, "of a birde whos name is Alchion, or Alcion. He seth...he maketh is neste be the see syde in an hard roche. And all the tyme that he bryngeth forthe is burthes, the floode with-drawith hym. Ther is nother no tempestes seyen".[3] Mention is made, by the same fifteenth-century preacher, of the parrot, enjoying a reputation for its talkativeness in days already ancient: "Clerkis, that tretis of keend, (thei) sey that the popinjey hath a properte for to gret and salute the grettest lorde of the world, that is the Emperour of Rome".[4] Of fabulous birds in sermon-literature, one example must suffice, which possesses at the least some curious foundation in fact. For Bromyard mentions the "Barnacle", or, as he puts it—"the bird called Bernac, which is nourished and born of timber, as they say, and finally adheres to the timber by its beak alone. When that has been removed, it plunges itself into the waters".[5] Last of all, the fishes of the sea are not forgotten, of which one of the greatest is the whale. For, "Balena est piscis, ut testatur Vincentius in *Speculo Naturali*".[6] Of the kindred "sea-pig" a homiletic tale relates how sailors, mistaking it for an island, settle upon its back and light a fire, only to perish beneath the waves when it suddenly dives.[7] Robert Holcot's sermons, already alluded to for their descriptions of gems, will be found to supply examples of several moralized fish—the carp, the sea-urchin,

[1] MS. Add. 41321, fol. 98.
[2] MS. Harl. 4894, fol. 19b. The partridge (see again Holcot, MS. Roy. 7. C. 1, fol. 105), the kite, and the crow, also appear here.
[3] MS. Roy. 18. B. xxiii, fol. 171b.
[4] fol. 173 (also "Ysodorus *in* [*Libro*] *Ethymologiarum*"). Numerous other birds appear in Bozon, cf. cap. vi, xiii, lv, lxi, cxxxiii, cxxxv–cxl, cxlii.
[5] *S.P.* s.v. "Exemplum". The Caladrius occurs in Bozon, cap. xlv.
[6] MS. Camb. Univ. Libr. Ii. iii. 8, fol. 156b. Cf. Bozon, cap. lxx.
[7] MS. Harl. 2316, fol. 54b (more properly, in Bestiary lore, the Aspido-chelone: see art. M. R. James, in *History*, as before, April, 1931, p. 6).

the dolphin, the "Roytarcius",[1] the "Fastex" or "Postex",[2] the cuttle-fish, and a fish called "Veneth".[3] To these we may add from Bozon, the crab [*sic*!], the conch, the "Affor", and the hippopotamus—"a great marvel of a fish,... which is now fish, now beast".[4]

When the wisdom and solemn fantasy of Bestiary-lore have been exhausted, there remains yet a further contribution to preaching from the animal world in the shape, not of instruction in natural history, but of entertainment once again by means of semi-humorous fiction, namely, the animal fable. Courthope, in his *History of English Poetry*,[5] has spoken of "the love of stories about beasts and birds, which the Teutonic races perhaps brought with them from their old homes in the East". The animal fable proper, however, so far as England is concerned seems to have been an importation from France along with the other Norman influences upon our language and literature, following the Conquest. Thomas Wright, who set himself to study the influence of the *Romans de Renart* in this country, has observed accordingly that the evidences of its popularity here appear at a later date than in France or Germany.[6] Whether or not the appetite for such fables was strong and indigenous, at all events the comparative rarity of this animal fiction in English sermons suggests that it remained, with few exceptions, as it had begun, the particular entertainment of the Anglo-Norman aristocracy. Nevertheless, England produced at least one leading moral fabulist of the Middle Ages in the person of Odo of Cheriton, and two subsequent preachers who made rich use of this same material. Like many of his English fellow-clergy of the early thirteenth century, Odo the Cistercian, it seems, had certainly studied in Paris; and there he had collected, no doubt, the Aesopic and romantic

---

[1] Called the "Coytar" in Bozon (*Metaphs.* cap. xxvi).

[2] Called "Fauste" in Bozon (ibid. cap. xlvii). See my *Preaching in Med. Engl.* p. 335 for other examples of its use in our sermons.

[3] Cf. MS. Roy. 7. C. 1, fols. 96, 102b, 103b–104, 109, 113b; MS. Harl. 5369, fols. 265, 265b.

[4] *Metaphs.* cap. x, xxvii, liv, and lii. The Beaver is similarly described in MS. Harl. 7322, fol. 106.   [5] See vol. i, p. 190 et seq.

[6] See *Latin Stories*, Percy Soc. pp. ix–xi.

fables which later graced his own sermons and collections of *exempla*.[1] Many of these fables, simple enough in their construction, present us with the natural humour and vivid imagination of those who watch animal and insect world with the eyes of lively, mischievous children. The animals themselves are regarded as little people, precisely as they appear in frequent representations upon the margins of illuminated manuscripts, engrossed in earnest conversation, fighting in miniature tourneys, playing on musical instruments, indulging in the various pastimes and mischiefs of men and women of the day. Behold, then, in Odo, the tortoise with her house on her back; the cockchafer, that for ever says "ferai bien; ferai bien" with his wings,[2] but does nothing but harm; the toad that thinks his son so handsome; the dung-beetles, yoked to the plough, that promptly halt when they come to the first cow-patch; the mouse that wants her daughter to marry the greatest lord in the world. Like impish children, or merry rustics, the beasts play tricks upon each other, wild practical jokes that not infrequently lead to disaster. Thus the fox pretends to be dead in order that he may catch the unwitting raven, or is admitted into the hen-roost on the plea of sickness, whereupon he straightway devours the hens. The hedgehog by inducing the wolf to kiss him is carried to safety, sticking to the wolf's chin. Teburg the cat from his point of vantage in the tree mocks Reynard, who, for all his bag of tricks and his boasting, cannot escape so easily from his pursuers. The ass, summoned to the lion's Parliament of Beasts by the fox, invites the latter to inspect the charter of his exemption written in his hoof! Who could fail to enjoy that delicious scene in which Isengrim the wolf, now turned monk and set to learn his *Paternoster*, is unable to resist saying "Agnus" or "Aries", with greedy eyes ever wandering in the direction of the sheep? This realistic humour is in perfect accord with the subsequent wit

---

[1] See for the texts and MSS. of these fables, Hervieux, *Les Fabulistes Latins*, vol. iv, and J. A. Herbert, *Cat. of Romances in B.M.* vol. iii, pp. 31–78.

[2] Cf. in Bromyard the Crow that sings—"Cras, cras!" (s.v. "Pœnitentia"), and the Cuckoo that cries—"Affer, affer!" (s.v. "Simonia"), etc.

of Chaucer and the broad satire of his successors, whose verse frequently deals with these same animal fables. Nicole Bozon, the Franciscan, is the English preacher upon whom the mantle of Odo of Cheriton seems to have fallen in the early years of the fourteenth century. His extant discourses in French are predominantly a *mélange* of Bestiary and Fable matter.[1] In the English version of the *Gesta Romanorum* about a dozen typical fables are to be found incorporated in the text. Thus, for example, the well-known scene, given by Odo, of the funeral of the Wolf reappears, at which urchins carry the tapers, a goat rings the bell, foxes bear the bier, and the bear says mass. In the moralization which follows, these beasts are held to represent evil types of monks.[2] Bromyard is the other chief preacher alluded to who makes frequent use of these droll stories in his *Summa Predicantium*. Here we have such fables as those which tell of the partridges calling in the hawk to assist them against the kites with disastrous results,[3] of the tortoise carried at his own request on the eagle's wing and getting dropped in mid-air for his presumption;[4] or, again, of Reynard and Tebert,[5] of the sick lion,[6] and the dispute between

---

[1] The reader can study the whole work with ease, either in the French edition (based on the Phillipps MS. at Thirlestaine House, Cheltenham) by Miss L. T. Smith and M. Paul Meyer (*Les Contes Moral. de N.B.*), or in the English translation of the Gray's Inn MS. by "J. R." (*Metaphs. of Brother Boʒon*, Constable). See also Herbert (as above) for an analysis of the extant Latin version (MS. Harl. 1288), pp. 100–5.

[2] E.E.T.S. ed. pp. 372–3 ("Right so ofte sithes it falleth when a riche man or an userere is dede, an abbot or a prelate makes come togedre a convente of bestes, that is bestiall levynge. It happenyth some tyme in a grete convente that there are many bestes...". See another quoted below, p. 342. Others in E.E.T.S. ed. on pp. 364, 367, 368, 369, 370, 371, 372, 373, 417.

[3] s.v. "Advocatus" ("Sic nonnulli forte in banco, sic in artibus, sic in aliis curiis, sic forestarii in forestis, sic curati in parochiis ponuntur ad custodiam et defensionem quemadmodum accipitres, ut predictum est...").

[4] s.v. "Ascensio" ("Sic ad literam omnes predicti loquuntur cum aliqua avi predali, qui precio dato modicum elevantur. Sed aliquis ex aliqua causa vel occasione pennis favoris et auxilii subtrahente, utpote quia munera non potest continuare, vel quia aliter offendit aquilam ... Et sic testudo dimissus, cadit"). Also in Odo of Cheriton.

[5] s.v. "Sapientia".   [6] s.v. "Accusatio".

the peacock and the eagle.[1] A mere passing allusion in the same
work to the story of the fox and the wolf in the well-buckets—
"sicut lupus et vulpes in situla"—shows clearly enough how
familiar these fables must have been to clerical readers of the
period.[2] The paucity of examples in other sermon-collections
may possibly be due to the severe criticism of "fablis" by
Wycliffe and other pulpit purists, whose gibes may have caused
a reaction even in orthodox circles.[3] Most of Bozon's and
Bromyard's moralizations, however, were strictly in the form
of relentless satire at the expense of the social pests of their day.
To those then who objected to such childish narratives, they
could at least retort in the words of Chaucer's *Nonne-Preeste*:

> But ye that holden this tale a folye,
> As of a fox, or of a cok and hen,
> Taketh the moralitee, good men.[4]

To sum up even in outline the influence of these multi-
tudinous *exempla* of the Middle Ages upon the world's literature of fiction and of popular instruction would be no easy
task. Preaching, and in especial the provision made for it in
the way of collecting and preserving illustrative matter of all
kinds, became the vehicle by which much of the lighter thought
and imagination of antiquity—classical, oriental and early
medieval—passed over into the thinking and writing of the
modern world. Through the sermon, "the short and farcical
stories of common life" were elevated from the status of mere
oral repetition to that of literature. If we take the case of but

[1] s.v. "Ascensio". *Esopus* is here frequently mentioned by name,
cf. s.v. "Advocatus", "Ministratio", etc.
[2] Ibid. The Fable is in Odo: cf. Wright, *Latin Stories*, no. lvii, p. 54.
Another similar allusion, s.v. "Confessio" (the Fox and the Hare). Cf.
also Bozon's remark: "*Here may be told* how the ape begged the fox to
give him the comfort of a share of his tail..." (*Metaphs.* cap. lxxiv).
[3] Cf. my *Preaching in Med. Engl.* pp. 239–40, and J.-Th. Welter,
L'Exemplum, pp. 102–7, esp. n. 70. Note also how the Parson of the *Cant.
Tales* refuses to tell a Fable (*Pars. Prol.* ll. 31–4):
> "Thou getest fable noon y-told for me;
> For Paul, that wryteth unto Timothee,
> Repreveth hem that weyven soothfastnesse
> And tellen fables and swich wrecchednesse."
[4] *Cant. Tales*, ll. 4628–30.

one great collection of homiletic tales probably made by Englishmen, namely, the *Gesta Romanorum*, we shall find their popularity extending far beyond the limits of English poetry in the fourteenth and fifteenth centuries. Yet even here, Chaucer in his *Canterbury Tales*, Gower in his *Confessio Amantis*, Lydgate, Hoccleve and others of the same school, are already in its debt.[1] Indeed the stories that they use are as often those of the contemporary pulpit as of secular minstrelsy, and frequently still have moralization of some kind or other attached to them. Turning to the Elizabethans, we find that dramatists like Shakespeare and Massinger construct some of their best-known plays from plots based upon these and similar sermon-tales—King Lear and his daughters, the "Bond" and the Three Caskets in the *Merchant of Venice*, the closing scene of *The Taming of the Shrew*, *Pericles* and Massinger's *Picture*, for example.[2] Spenser, likewise, has introduced a version of the first-named into his *Faerie Queene*. Even if they have passed into this greater literature by way of the *novelle* of a Boccaccio or a Bandello,[3] or some other intermediary, the original debt remains, as again in the case of Molière and Schiller in still later ages. The *Cento Novelle Antiche*, the *Decameron*[4] and *Heptameron* themselves, the *Facetiae* of a Poggio and the *Merie Tales* of a Skelton all remind us further of what Renaissance wit and raillery owed to the frivolities of the medieval pulpit. How, indeed, could the Church complain with any justice, when its own "materia dissolutionis" had already encouraged the *gentili donne* to become a little less genteel! If the literature of romantic fiction and jest has thus to pay its tribute to the ancient homilists, so also must the literature of the *Haus-Märchen*, the nursery fable and the cautionary tale for the young. The modern "Sunday-school" teacher, with her elaborate devices for the attraction of her

[1] Cf. eds. of the *Gesta Rom.* by Oesterley and Herrtage. Robt. Henryson's poem *The Bludy Serk* is another example (cf. above, p. 15).

[2] See also, in this connection, Douce's well-known *Illustrations of Shakespeare*, and Hazlitt's *Shakespeare's Library*.

[3] Cf. Dunlop, *History of Fiction*, vol. ii, pp. 14 et seq. 45; etc.

[4] See esp. A. C. Lee, *The Decameron, its Sources and Analogues*, pp. 274-7; etc.

charges, will learn with some astonishment, no doubt, that centuries earlier in Catholic England Brer Fox and his fellows had once provided a regular subject-matter for Sabbath-day discourses to adults. Here, indeed, Odo of Cheriton, Nicole Bozon and Dr John Bromyard, our medieval Lafontaines of the pulpit, stand side by side in the holy place with the Benedictine sub-prior of Durham who was not above alluding to the tale of Cinderella for one of his pulpit *moralities*.[1] Of equally early attempts to impart a more serious information upon the wonders of the Universe to sermon-audiences nothing further need be added. We have already marked in sufficient detail the smatterings of history, geography and "natural science", the lore of ancient "philosophy" and current travel with which our English sermons abound. Well, then, might the instructed listener declare that, although God was past finding out, yet he had himself perceived something of the breadth of the earth and the way where light dwelleth, that he was no longer wholly ignorant of the ordinances of heaven, the treasures of the snow and of the hail. If he could not bind the unicorn in the furrow, nor draw out leviathan with a hook, at least he had managed to learn a little of their curious habits. The lion and the wild ass, the ostrich and the eagle were but a few of the things too wonderful for him, which once he knew not, but now he knew. Like another Job, we behold him rapt and speechless with amazement at the new revelations, a prophetic symbol of his generation, staring wistfully out into the unknown but approaching future of discovery and emancipation: "I have heard of Thee by the hearing of the ear; but now mine eye seeth Thee".[2]

[1] MS. Harl. 4894, fol. 27. For a sermon-story as prototype of a well-known Hans Andersen fairy-tale, cf. MS. Add. 27336, fol. 76b (the Invisible Paintings = Robes). See also the numerous references to Grimm's *Haus-Märchen* in Herrtage, *Gesta Rom.*, as before.

[2] Job. xlii, 5.

CHAPTER V

The Preaching of Satire and Complaint

PART I

OF all the important types of composition in English literature, there is perhaps none which still presents a history so neglected, so disjointed and so little understood at its earliest stages as that of Satire and Complaint. The reason, indeed, is not far to seek. Since the nineteenth century, a genuine race of literary antiquaries, always far commoner on the continent[1] but boasting in its ranks at least three worthy sons of Cambridge,[2] seems almost to have died out, leaving few successors to continue the good work of investigation. Where they laboured with loving care to collect the scattered fragments of this ruder pre-

---

[1] Take for example the field of medieval homiletic literature which here especially concerns us. In France, we have the historic surveys of the many distinguished contributors to *Hist. Litt. de la Fr.*, and of other scholars referred to repeatedly in this present work. In Germany, we have the studies of Cruel, Linsenmayer, Schönbach, F. R. Albert, and others indicated, e.g., in Ficker and Hermelink, *Handb. der Kirchengesch.* Tl. ii, new ed. 1929, pp. 7, etc. In Italy, the surveys of Luigi Marenco and Francesco Zanotto. In Spain, Prof. Allison Peers, the authority on Ramón Lull, kindly informs me that to the best of his belief a great deal of work has been done by Spanish scholars on medieval Spanish preachers. In England, however, historians of the pulpit we have had none (J. M. Neale's *Med. Preachers and Preaching* is not a work devoted to English sermons and breaks no fresh ground). Apart from the editors Wright, Morris, T. W. Arnold, Herrtage, Miss L. T. Smith and Mr J. A. Herbert, who else has done work in any portion of this English field? Foreign scholars, such as Hervieux, Meyer, Petit-Dutaillis, Welter, Horstmann, Lechler, Loserth, Oesterley, Brandeis, and the Americans Crane, Gerould, Carleton Brown, Mosher, etc.

[2] Viz. Thos. Wright (of Trinity College), Fredk. J. Furnivall (of Trinity Hall), and Walter W. Skeat (of Christ's College). Dr Furnivall's clear grasp of the importance of sermon-literature is well indicated in his Preface to Andrew Boorde's *Introd. of Knowledge* and *Dyetary*, E.E.T.S. Ext. S. vol. x, pp. 24–5. Of Wright's inaccuracies I am aware.

Reformation literature and elicit its significance by patient and sympathetic study over a wide range, the modern literary historian of the Middle Ages in this country is inclined apparently to look with disdain upon all such pursuit of the trivial in letters as a pursuit of mere "curiosities".[1] With the late Professor W. P. Ker, he is far too prone to dismiss the mass of dreary-looking didactic works strewn about in the medieval library with the idle regret of Caxton's critics "that the things preserved are not always what we would have chosen",[2] stopping merely to glean from them such odd philological or prosodic information as they may have to offer him by the way. Now such an attitude of mind may be sound enough for the literary purist who seeks to educate our taste and quicken our powers of appreciation: for the literary historian, however, it is fatal. For, in literature as in politics, the historian must deal as lovingly and as faithfully with the small beginnings and the clumsy efforts as with the finer developments of his subject for any true appraisement of the latter; and it is just here that the evil effects of this neglect in the study of our literature are most apparent to-day. While the history of language and prosody has progressed apace, our corresponding knowledge of the growth of literary ideas and imagery in the period has lagged sadly behind. Thus, when these same literary historians come to deal with the more noteworthy authors whom they deem worthy of attention, they continue to attribute to them an originality here and there where no originality exists; or else they will glibly indicate a presumed indebtedness to earlier writers of the kind with whom they may happen to be familiar, repeatedly dragging in some remote analogue from continental literature to fill any gaps in their fanciful story. All the while they remain heedless of a mass of current writing, eloquence and ideas from which the early inspiration came, a rude mountain torrent rushing half-concealed in its rocky bed which ceaselessly feeds and links up the grander lakes of our medieval

[1] Cf. here, e.g., the late Prof. W. P. Ker, *Engl. Lit.: Mediev.* (Home Univ. Libr.), pp. 202-4.
[2] Ibid. p. 202. Cf. above, p. 9.

literature.[1] It is highly significant of this blindness that, in spite of the subsequent labours of the Early English Text Society and the many learned catalogues of manuscripts since made by Dr M. R. James and others, the work of a brilliant Dutchman, undertaken more than half a century ago in a spirit of true enthusiasm, should remain to this day by far the ablest exposition that we have of our early verse and prose.[2]

The study of early English satire, then, has suffered with other branches from this general neglect of the humbler literature of our own past.[3] Someone might urge, however, in defence of the literary historians, that in the present case the actual remnants of popular satiric verse in this country are so meagre and unimportant, when compared with their equivalent on the continent for example, that they are quite unworthy of serious attention. The excuse is invalid. Our historians here stand convicted out of their own mouths. While satire, it is true, may never have played so brilliant or profound a part in English life and letters prior to the eighteenth century as in the land of Rutebœuf, none the less they inform us that our earliest metrical examples represent for all time "the first recog-

---

[1] An admirable illustration is furnished by vol. ii of the *Camb. Hist. of Engl. Lit.* Here we have an authoritative history repeatedly vitiated by this weakness: cf. e.g. Prof. Manly on Langland, as discussed below. Prof. Whitney's chapter on "Religious Movements in the 14th cent." is a bold attempt to deal with Rolle and Wycliffe without previous mastery of contemporary English homiletic literature. Gower, Chaucer and their followers are brilliantly dealt with by other critics, but without any general introductory discourse upon that same literature which nourished them all. Finally, the Political and Religious Verse is relegated to a brief though attractive chapter of "Final Words" at the end of the volume, by Mr A. R. Waller. Needless to say no hint is here given of any links with pulpit tradition.

[2] I.e. Bernhard Ten Brink. It is a pleasure, however, to be able to record, where Englishmen have so grossly failed, the growing interest and activities of modern American scholars in these more neglected regions, such, for example, as the recent work of Profs. Carleton Brown and J. E. Wells, Miss H. E. Allen, Miss F. Foster, etc.

[3] An exception must be made in the case of the late Mr C. L. Kingsford's valuable little study of "political ballad-literature", in his *Engl. Hist. Lit. in the 15th cent.* Here, however, the writer is only concerned with one small corner of the field. An earlier poem like *Piers Plowman*, for example, naturally does not come within his purview.

nizable steps on the road of political and religious liberty".[1]
"Rude and imperfect as is the vehicle of expression, the popular
songs of England in the thirteenth and fourteenth centuries
reveal a consciousness of united purpose and corporate pride
in the nation, for which no contemporary parallel can be found
in any other country of Europe."[2] Thus far their importance
is set forth in unmistakable terms. What then has impeded
hitherto any coherent account of their origin and authorship?
The answer lies precisely in that disdain for the study of our
didactic and religious literature to which reference has just
been made. If, as we have seen, a knowledge of medieval
English preaching is essential to an understanding of the
growth of literary Realism; if, as we shall see shortly, it is
equally essential to an understanding of the miracle- and
morality-plays in this country, it is again equally essential in
the case of these other, lesser works. For, in its Satire and
Complaint we touch at once the profoundest and most abiding
influence of the English pulpit. The interpretative part which
it here plays is strictly analogous to that which will concern
us when we come to deal with the vernacular drama. Surviving
manuscripts of varying date supply us with a few scattered
examples of the rude poetry in question at various stages of
development. Their survival is clearly indicative of a much
larger output now irretrievably lost to us. It is only when
these odd remnants are set in their appropriate place against
the continuous background of the contemporary preaching
that their true interrelation and the common source of their
ideas can be recognized and understood. Then, and then only,
does their history become one intelligent, coherent narrative.

For a study of the origins of English vernacular satire, we
cannot do better than go back humbly to Thomas Wright and
reconsider with him the peculiar circumstances in which it
appears to have been born. In an illuminating preface to the
first of his several editions of *Political Songs of England*,[3]

[1] A. R. Waller, in *Camb. Hist. of Engl. Lit.* vol. i, p. 369.
[2] Courthope, *Hist. of Engl. Poetry*, vol. i, p. 198 (obviously taken
from Wright, *Hist. of Caricature and Grotesque*, p. 183).
[3] "from the reign of John to that of Edw. II", Camden Soc. 1839.

Wright has enumerated the several types of satirical verse existing at the time—roughly during the second half of the thirteenth century—when the vernacular species is first seen to emerge. One type is that of the well-known Goliardic Latin poetry, clearly the work of *clerici ribaldi*, wandering scholars from the Universities and the like, who in every civilized country of Christendom tilt with a gay irresponsibility at the corruptions of their age, particularly those of the various Orders and dignitaries of the Church whose own servants they are. As might well be expected, classical, scholastic and romantic elements all figure in their compositions.[1] But even here the influence of the contemporary pulpit is equally prominent. The reader who turns, for example, to Wright's collection of *Poems commonly attributed to Walter Mapes*[2] will find, apart from the fact that many of the pieces are actually termed *sermones* and are often little better than rude burlesques of current pulpit oratory, that many more betray alike in their subject-matter and characteristic treatment a homiletic ground-plan.[3] Alongside this Anglo-Latin verse, there is a further group of Anglo-Norman satirical songs which are correspondingly attributable to the wandering minstrels of the court. These in their turn have clearly arisen out of the feudal strife of the times. They display no general "political sentiment", but consist of personal attacks on particular opponents of the rival baron or party that employs the author. Naturally there is a very free interchange of subject-matter between the goliard and the minstrel, the clerical and the secular *jougleur*. The former may choose to sing in his Latin of the Court of Venus, of romantic love, or of the licentious delights of the wine cup and the gaming table. He may even exercise his art in fomenting the feudal antipathies of the neighbourhood, as when monks compose ruthless satirical poems against the people of a rival township or county, in open defiance of the first principles of their

[1] Cf. further, Wright, *Anglo-Latin Satir. Poets*, Rolls S. 1872, vol. i, Pref. and pp. 132–4.

[2] Camden Soc. 1841. See further his *Hist. of Caricature*, pp. 167 and 171–3.

[3] Cf. e.g. pp. 229–36, "De Diversis Ordinibus Hominum", exposing the typical vices of the various classes of society.

religion.[1] The Anglo-Norman verse-maker, on the other hand, may vie with the Latin *archi-poeta* in bitter caricature of the religious Orders, as in the poem *Le Ordre de Bel-Eyse*.[2] Further important elements common to both types of satirist are a genuine spirit of fun and roguery and the personal character of the abuse. Into this roguish world of French and Latin metrical caricature, then, there enters a third type of satiric poetry—"in ynglych tonge" and again of a different order. Wright observes that the age of Anglo-Norman verse-making seems to come to an end about the close of the reign of Edward II. But this new class of vernacular verse-satire, which had taken its rise in the previous century, now gathers force as both of the older varieties decline, and becomes steadily "more abundant". It "takes a permanent footing in English literature", and at length blossoms forth into "one of the most remarkable satires, as well as one of the most remarkable poems, in the English language", as we shall ourselves observe in due course.

Before proceeding to the question of authorship we must first decide wherein lies the novelty of these fresh "political" songs and poems, apart from a mere change of tongue. While the attacks of the older Latin versifiers upon the corruption of the Church still continue in them unabated, those equally characteristic features of the former which reflect the classical traditions and niceties of the Schools now disappear altogether. Furthermore, the sentiments of gay Romance and feudal pride to be found in the satirical lays of the Anglo-Norman *trouvère* are likewise missing from their English equivalent. Thus far we may note already that no feature now remains to suggest any exclusive concerns of the two great privileged classes of society. But we must go a step further. When "political songs began to be written in the English language", it was in itself "an acknowledgment that they concerned the whole English public". We need not be surprised to find, therefore, that they now give expression to "popular feelings", to the woes of a voiceless multitude of common men and women suffering from

[1] See further, *Hist. of Caricature*, pp. 181–2.
[2] See *Polit. Songs* as before, Camden Soc. pp. 137–48.

daily wrongs and injustice of all kinds. Hence, the old familiar note of undisguised fun, the impish delight in personal taunt and abuse akin to the careless school-boy spirit, has also vanished away. In its place are notes of solemn indignation, bitterness and pessimism. If the new satirist ever laughs at all, it is with a fierce, mocking laughter, that bursts out suddenly without warning here and there, filled often with the spirit of mad exasperation and a reckless despair. It seems to prophesy to the world at large some hideous future revenge, when the opportunity occurs to translate lurking thoughts and words into action. It is the poet's earnestness, then, his profoundly serious view of society underlying any little explosions of such mirth that will impress the reader. We shall understand him the more easily when we come to learn that this solemnity and pessimism are none other than the solemnity and pessimism of the contemporary pulpit. For, to that conclusion all the facts compel us. Even where the sentiment of patriotism has taken the place of the older feudal loyalties in the new type of song, in large measure a natural reaction against them, we deal —strange to say—with something already proved characteristic of the later style of English sermon propaganda.[1]

Who, then, were the original authors of this bitter stuff? Whence did it all come? We shall do well to reconsider these questions carefully; for their point is of some importance even for the historian. If this verse is really a popular product, then we have here the remarkable spectacle of a peasantry and a populace able to voice its own wrongs clearly and forcibly, able to criticize its own masters with real wit and understanding, alike deeply religious and widely national in outlook. Mr A. R. Waller, in the *Cambridge History of English Literature*,[2] is apparently unwilling to commit himself upon the subject, yet toys vaguely with the idea that it is "the speech of the land slave", "the poetry of the people" rising to the surface, and so forth. It is a view which betrays a singular lack of acquaintance with the contemporary intellectual level of peasant life. If we turn to Professor W. P. Ker, we get no better

[1] Cf. above, pp. 131–2, and see further below, p. 225, etc.
[2] Vol. i, p. 369.

enlightenment—even from a professed medievalist.[1] These anonymous songs and satires "express the heart of the people"; they "belong to the people". That is all that there is to be said about it. Further enquiry into their origins and authorship was apparently too trivial a task for this fastidious connoisseur, who so coolly disdains the current literature of religion because it is not to his liking, a literature, as we have said, crude but instinct with life and significance for the student who approaches it sympathetically. However, of the illiterate common people themselves, and of the tattered coarse-mouthed "jugglers" who entertained them, we know at least enough to know that not from such as these came verses sometimes constructed in the old Provençal manner, sometimes even "in highly elaborate form",[2] verses too which often express such accurate knowledge of the higher ranks in Church and State. "Patient beyond belief, the children of the soil do not, as a rule, make literature of their wrongs." Fortunately, no one, it appears, has ventured to attribute this verse to the old, dwindling race of courtly minstrels, the natural supporters of the privileged classes who are here most ruthlessly attacked. The "bourgeois satirist", whom Professor Courthope[3] mentions in connection with Jean de Meung, is obviously no nearer the mark. For the shrewd merchant and townsman would hardly patronize a literature so steeped in venom against their own persons and cherished pursuits. Whom then have we left? Continental scholarship, as is usual, and English scholarship where in the past it has worked in the same patient spirit of investigation, has already come near to the secret. For Thomas Wright,[4] and still more notably Bernhard Ten Brink realize that somehow "the clerical body" must be held responsible for much of this popular satirical verse-making. The latter, indeed, would divide responsibility for the English "political lyric" of this period "among two classes: the glee-men and the clergy in the broadest sense".[5] But he adds later—"Satire was, as a whole,

---

[1] *Engl. Lit. Med.* pp. 146, 149, etc.
[2] See here Chaytor, *The Troubadours and England*, p. 123.
[3] *Hist. of Engl. Poetry*, vol. i, p. 184.
[4] *Hist. of Caricature*, p. 184.
[5] *E. Engl. Lit. (Hist. of Engl. Lit.* vol. i), p. 314.

the province of the clergy, the learned. Neither rank nor
power shielded men from their attacks; all classes of society
had to submit to be pilloried by them. The abuses in State
and Church, especially the latter, bad measures of government,
social evils, moral rottenness in clergy and laity, all served as
material for satire".[1] Courthope, following this good example,
declares, even more decisively, that "many, perhaps most" of
these songs and poems "seem to have been composed by the
clergy". He even points to the signs of a "sympathy between
the clergy and the poor...in alliance against the extortions of
the rich and powerful", which some of them display.[2] With
the literature of English preaching as yet barely discovered, we
may well forgive all these scholars for having failed in their
day to recognize the poems as a direct product of this activity.
After all, two serious objections might seem to stand at first
sight in the way of such a belief, until the sermons themselves
dispel for us the illusion. Unrestrained attacks upon the follies
of churchmen could be reasonably expected of the gay, irre-
sponsible goliard, the impudent young clerk who strolled out
into a lawless world from the wanton turbulence of Parisian
streets and schools. But when once the threats and thunders
of ecclesiastical council and synod had begun to jeopardize his
very existence, was it in the nature of things likely that respectable and even highly placed preachers would continue regularly
in much the same strain? We shall see shortly that such was
the case even in this country. But again, it is clear, from remarks like that of Sir Adolphus Ward,[3] that older scholars
could hardly be aware that there was at the time a sufficient
volume of preaching in English, of any kind whatsoever, to
justify belief in a yet more vulgar use of the vulgar tongue
by clerical satirists of the pulpit. That circumstance, too, however, was definitely confirmed by the studies undertaken in
connection with the present author's first volume. For the

[1] E. Eng. Lit. (Hist. of Eng. Lit. vol. i), p. 316.
[2] Hist. of Engl. Poetry, vol. i, pp. 187–94. Courthope, however, is
apparently too much of a copyist to be perfectly sound and consistent
on such a subject. On p. 198, he speaks of the new Satire as "the result
of political as opposed to scholastic education", whatever that may mean.
[3] See below, p. 474.

THE PREACHING OF SATIRE AND COMPLAINT 219

rest, the preachers' efforts to compete with the lay minstrel on his own ground for the popular ear, already alluded to in these pages,[1] readily explain why they should have resorted to verse as a medium for fresh social propaganda. The sermons themselves, indeed, are witness to such metrical enterprise.[2] So, as the new evidence leads us on to the summit of the present argument, looking back we at length perceive in the panorama stretched beneath us a yawning gap, an ugly *lacuna*, now all too clearly visible in the historic landscape of our national literature. Much has been heard—and rightly so—in recent times of the wandering goliard[3] and the wandering minstrel, with their particular gifts to civilization. But where, alas!, is the writer who tells, with an equal intimacy, of the life and contribution of our wandering English preachers? When full justice has been done to their long-neglected "remains", we may look forward with confidence to the day when every textbook in the land will pay them their long-neglected due, hailing them as the fathers of vernacular satire, pioneers of the literature of popular freedom. Just a century after the appearance of what is probably the first political poem in English that we possess, there rises from the lines of the greatest poem of them all in medieval times a solemn, ghostly figure. It is the figure of a preacher, the angelic preacher of the *Vision of Piers Plowman*, who dares to speak out when all others in authority are keeping an unholy silence. "For", even then,

> lewed men ne coude
> Iangle ne iugge, that iustifie hem shulde;
> But suffren and serven.[4]

The reader must now be allowed to see how perfectly the theory just put forward, which would attribute to the pulpit these popular songs of Satire and Complaint, will bear minute examination in the light of the songs and satires themselves. The oldest group of all that we happen to possess date, not from the period of popular revolt, the period when English

---

[1] Cf. above, p. 16, etc.
[2] See my *Preaching in Med. Engl.* pp. 271–8, and below, p. 227.
[3] A notable example, of course, is Miss Helen Waddell's delightful *Wandering Scholars* (1927).   [4] See below, pp. 577–85.

had already asserted itself as the recognized national tongue in most departments of life, but from a much earlier age, when wellnigh every literary composition in the vernacular served the interests of religion and reflected homiletic influence, when, in particular, the distinctions between poetical reflection, religious song and the sermon itself are said to be imperceptible.[1] Accordingly, the oldest political songs may be hailed as the natural outcome of forty years or so of vernacular Mendicant preaching. Who, indeed, from the first, were more likely to give voice to the sufferings and wrongs of the common people than the early friars, those ardent champions of the poor and down-trodden, those natural enemies of misrule and luxury, vice and injustice in all ranks and classes of the community? Nowhere else, at all events, in contemporary literature but in their sermons and in those of other like-minded churchmen can we find these themes so consistently emphasized from the birthday of English satirical verse as we know it, onwards to the end of the Middle Ages. Méray, writing of the Mendicant preachers of France,[2] declares that men who had been villeins upon the manorial estate, by joining their ranks, thus became the respected critics and censors of the mightiest in the land. While the very strictures passed upon such upstart clergy by some of the most outspoken of their fellow friar-preachers, however, would prevent us from attributing too much of this denouncement to Méray's explanation, the fact remains that the preachers as a whole, high-born or low, took upon themselves this work of ventilating and satirizing public wrongs. In the earlier days of Mendicant activity, then, we picture the brethren moving about freely among the dregs of the population, often sharing the peasant's lot when actually out of the pulpit, stirred to indignation, eager to provide the voiceless multitude with voices of their own, so to ring in the era of redress from below as well as from above. Thus, while the more gentle friar Thomas of Hales will prefer to write an English *Luve Ron*, the merry Irish friar Michael of Kildare his "nonsensical poems", or friar Herebert his translations of

---

[1] Cf. Ten Brink, as above, vol. i, p. 211.
[2] *La Vie au temps des Libres Prêcheurs*, tome i, p. 15.

popular Latin hymns,[1] some other friar, no doubt, marching as field-chaplain with the men-at-arms,[2] will make a stirring patriotic refrain in the vernacular for their use, and others, yet more numerous, will fashion "political" songs for the people, each according to his special temperament or calling.[3] Later, as the Orders grew suspicious or disdainful of inflammatory writings in the vulgar tongue,[4] this work of versifying the social message of the pulpit would pass into other clerical hands, which had learnt from the former the art as well as the force of all such propaganda. For there is evidence to show that the perilous liberty of popular song-writing, like "the liberty of prophesying" in the open cemetery and market-place, was eagerly seized upon by the more "socialistic" priests, until, in the hands of wandering fanatics of the Church like John Balle, their rude verse became at length the song of actual revolution.[5] Are we not definitely informed that it was none other than a preacher, this same "mad priest of Kent", who composed the famous lines which inspired the insurgents of 1381?

> Johan the Muller heth ygrownde smal, smal, smal;
> The Kyngis sone of hevene shalle paye for alle.
> Beware or ye be wo.
> Knoweth зour frende from зoure foo.
> Haveth ynowe, and seythe "Hoo"!...

In the hands of Lollards like Jack Upland and the anonymous author of *The Ploughman's Complaint*, this same weapon was finally to be used against the very Orders who had done most to fashion it. Such is often the strange, precarious fortune of history. The fallen warrior is stabbed with his own sword.

Now it is no violation of our theory of authorship to find

---

[1] See my *Preaching in Med. Engl.* p. 273.

[2] Cf. A. Carpenter, *Destructorium Vicior.* pars. viii, cap. 10: "Unde Holkot in lectura *Lib. Sapientie*, lect. 115. Licet, inquit, clerici possint bello interesse ut suis exhortationibus, absolutionibus et spiritualibus suffragiis iuvent bellantes . . . "; and below p. 225.

[3] For similar evidences of clerical influence in the composition of contemporary German *Volkslieder*, cf., e.g., F. J. Snell, *The 14th Century*, pp. 72, 79, 81, 83, etc.

[4] Cf. my *Preaching in Med. Engl.* pp. 227-30, etc.

[5] See further in Chap. VI, here following.

that the earliest extant example of this kind of literature should happen to be, not a Satire or a Complaint upon the evils of the times, but a song of Victory from the supporters of Sir Simon de Montfort.[1] For, there is no need, even here, to speak with Ten Brink, of "the glee-man taking sides with the people in the civil wars of the reign of King Henry III".[2] Stubbs in his *Constitutional History*[3] has given us a far more likely hint, when he remarks of a kindred poem in Latin[4] dealing with the same historic episode—"It was clearly a manifesto, amongst themselves, of *the men* [i.e. the Franciscans] *whose preaching guided the people*". Let us now follow up Wright's original list of the earliest "Political Songs" in English, and glance at their subject-matter. We may notice in passing, apparently older than any in his collection, a typical "lament on the corruption and slavery of the church" expressed in a poem entitled *Hwon holy chirche is under fote*, which was first published by Morris, in his *Old English Miscellany*.[5] Further comment upon its themes of clerical Simony and Avarice and the like are for the moment unnecessary. For the period of the reign of King Edward I there appears first, a *Song of the Husbandman*,[6] describing the sufferings of the peasants, particularly at the hands of the various officials on the feudal manor. Next follows a piece *Against the Pride of the Ladies*,[7] denouncing explicitly their pride and extravagance in dress and other womanly vices, as in many later poems upon the sex.[8] From this topic we turn to a bitter *Satire on the Consistory Courts*,[9] on the endless vexation which these cause to the peasantry, the bribes that are necessary, the bullying character of the somnours, and other injuries of the system. Again, we are whirled away in a *Song on the Times*,[10] the first of several pieces now known by that title, to consider a contemporary world of sorrow and strife,

---

[1] *Song against the King of Almaigne*, or *Song of Lewis* (c. 1264). See Wright, *Pol. Songs*, Camden Soc. p. 69.   [2] Ten Brink, vol. i, p. 314.
[3] vol. ii, p. 313, n. 1. For further examples of themes of national politics in the sermons, see below, pp. 225, 580–8, etc.
[4] In Wright's *Pol. Songs*, Camden Soc. pp. 72–121.
[5] E.E.T.S. O.S. no. 49, see pp. 89 and 189.   [6] p. 149.
[7] p. 153. See also ed. Fairholt, Percy Soc. no. xxvii, p. 40.
[8] See below, pp. 401–3.   [9] p. 155.   [10] p. 195.

in which injustice, covetousness and pride reign, especially amongst those occupying the highest places. The Church, we read, which should exert all her energy to drive out the evil men in power is herself in evil state. The king's ministers are corrupt, and bribes are here also the order of the day. Penalties are inflicted on the innocent, while the guilty escape untouched. From the general we return to the particular with a *Song on the Venality of Judges*,[1] which, although set out in Latin, may be included in our list as typical of other vernacular complaints against the bribery and extortions of the law, from whom the poor can get no justice. Finally, there follows for the same period a highly significant vernacular *Song against the Retinues of Great People*,[2] and the expenses which they inflict upon the defenceless peasantry. For the reign of King Edward II, we have further *Songs on the Evil Times*,[3] dealing with the old abuses over again. One of exceptional length details with fearless precision the many iniquities in the Church, from the Roman Curia itself to the newly installed, youthful parish priest—the general simony and avarice, the corruption of the Church Courts, the vices of bishops, archdeacons, abbots and priors, monks and friars, officials and deans, and the rest. In the secular State there is a similar tale of corruption amongst knights, justices, mayors, bailiffs, beadles, merchants and others, all ruled by pride and fraud.[4] From the pages of Wright we can turn to yet other collections and behold the stream of Satire and Complaint gaining volume as it flows on to submerge wellnigh the whole of literature, sacred and profane alike, in the closing years of the Middle Ages.[5] Nor indeed will its force

---

[1] p. 224. [2] p. 237. [3] p. 251, etc. [4] p. 323.

[5] Cf., e.g., *The Land of Cokaygne* (looking back to older goliardic models) in Furnivall's *E. Engl. Poems*, 1862; *Narracio de Domino Denarii*, in Ritson's *Anc. Pop. Poetry*, 1833, p. 103, and *Sir Peny*, in Hazlitt's *E. Pop. Poetry*, 1864, p. 161; etc.; various other *Songs on the Times* (Edw. III, etc.), ed. Hardwick, Fairholt (Percy Soc.), etc.; others in Wright's 2 vols. of *Pol. Poems and Songs*, Rolls S.; in *Minor Poems of Vernon MS.*, ed. Furnivall, E.E.T.S. O.S. no. 117 (cf. "A Warning to be ware", p. 719; "Seldom seen is soon forgot", p. 715); *Twenty-six Polit. and other Poems* (15th cent.), ed. D. J. Kail, E.E.T.S. O.S. no. 124, 1904; etc., etc. Others will be found indicated in J. E. Wells, *Man. of Midd. Engl. Writings*, and below, pp. 227–35, etc.

be spent even then. For the moment, however, we must pause again to consider where the voice of the preacher is to be heard in this widely distributed criticism of abuses. Subsequent pages of the present chapter will show that these very complaints are sown broadcast over the whole field of medieval English sermon-literature. Not merely the general tone of condemnation in the poems, but the very phrases of satire or invective used are characteristic of the pulpit, which employs them with ceaseless reiteration. We have every reason to believe that the massive *Summa Predicantium* of the English Dominican John Bromyard presents us with the gathered fruits of Mendicant preaching in England throughout the fourteenth century and indeed even earlier. For the bulk of its material, as Mr J. A. Herbert rightly points out, has been drawn from thirteenth-century sources.[1] Here, then, we find, as in no other place, the detailed vituperation of the poets within the limits of a single compilation, work of half a lifetime of study and practical oratory. No offence or type of offender—high or low—seems to be omitted from its list. Of all things in the world, it is to this vituperation that the author loves to return, whatever may be the chosen theme of his discourse. Indeed, one is left wishing that we could have a fresh edition of the

---

[1] Dr Workman's suggested date (1410) for the completion of this huge work is certainly too late (*John Wyclif*, vol. ii, p. 219, n. 1). This reference, too, is drawn from and actually applies to a copy of his *Distinct. Theolog.* MS. Bodl. 859, fol. 225 b. Moreover the *Explicit* which supplies it refers more likely to the task of scribe than of author (it is certainly *not* the original autograph copy). We find Master Robt. Rypon, for example, quoting from the *Summa* (at least as far as the letter *S* [*Servire*]) in his sermons, one of which is internally dated A.D. 1401 (see my *Preaching in Med. Engl.* p. 69, n. 2), in a way that suggests that the work was already an established authority in his day (cf. above, p. 29). Again, the more expert opinion of Mr J. A. Herbert places the *Summa* at any rate "after 1323"; while the MS. Roy. 7. E. iv copy of the work is itself described as "late fourteenth century". Dr Coulton's suggested date is c. 1390 (see *Five Cent. of Relig.* vol. ii, p. 576). Now (1957), Dr. A. B. Emden, *Biogr. Reg. of the Univ. of Oxford*, vol. i, p. 278, shows that it is actually mentioned in a MS. sermon of 1354. The reader will hardly need to be reminded that the earliest version of Langland's *Vision of Piers Plowman* is generally dated c. 1370. Hence its special significance. For Welter's views, see *L'Exemplum*, Paris, pp. 329–30.

"political songs and poems", including *Piers Plowman* itself, provided with explanatory notes from at least this one encyclopaedia. But the testimony of Bromyard does not stand alone. Had we no other evidences, the same traditional language of complaint appearing regularly in vernacular sermons would still make it imperative to believe that here, in what after all has been its chosen task for centuries, the pulpit leads where poets merely follow and reiterate. The output of the former is like a vast, surging flood against the tiny trickle of the latter. One topic of some of these songs, however, might seem to lie wholly outside the scope of the homily. With patriotic ballad-themes, perhaps, we are hardly much concerned. Yet even here, although we tread ourselves on less certain ground, it is impossible not to observe what may well be further impressions of the preachers' footsteps. For, the more prominent among the latter have a curious knack of introducing into some of their sermons a note of strong national feeling against the particular enemies of England, be they Frenchmen, Scots, or Welsh who happen to have been troubling her peace.[1]

A final and a highly important point to be noticed about the early satirical poems is the evidence of homiletic origin which they show in the matter of style and construction. In almost every example a marked religious strain appears sooner or later in the verse, betraying the real character of the satirist. The

[1] Cf. Anon., MS. Hereford Cath. Libr. P. 5. 2, fols. 102b, 105, 80b, etc.—against the Scots, c. 1314?, and *Letters from Northern Regs.* (do. 1315), as quoted above, pp. 130–1: Thos. Bradwardine, MS. Merton Coll. Oxf. 180, fols. 183–8, *Sermo Epinicius*, 1346, celebrating the victory of Neville's Cross and also describing the Battle of Crécy, preached by a royal army field-chaplain at the siege of Calais (discovered by Dr J. F. Laun of the Univ. of Giessen, to whom I am indebted for this reference): Archbp. Fitzralph—against the French, c. 1345 (see my *Preaching in Med. Engl.* pp. 203–5): Bp. Brunton—French wars in Brittany and Battle of Poitiers, etc., 1376–9 (*Preaching in Med. Engl.* pp. 205 and 268): Robt. Rypon, MS. Harl. 4894, fols. 29, 188b, etc.—against French and Scots, c. 1400: Folsham, MS. Worc. Cath. Libr. F. 10, fol. 61—ref. to *Bellum de Cressy*, etc.: Anon., MS. Bodl. 649, fol. 1—ref. to Poitiers, and fols. 129 et seq.—French, Scottish and Welsh Wars (esp. Agincourt), 15th cent., as quoted above, pp. 72–5.

very title—"A Song of the Evil Times", by which some of them are described in modern reprint, would be better replaced by a favourite pulpit text—"Dies mali sunt".[1] In the poem *A Warning to be ware*,[2] for example, contemporary events such as the Peasants' Revolt of 1381, the Plague and the Earthquake of 1382 are characteristically explained to be warnings of God's vengeance for the national "synne and slouthe"—"as this Clerkes conne declare". In other poems there are passionate appeals to Heaven for a justice which earth denies.[3] Again, wherever each class of the community and its special vices are passed in systematic review, we have a feature of the poems which derives unquestionably from the traditional arrangement of the homilist's *Summa de Viciis et de Virtutibus*, and sermons proper which were expressly directed to the different ranks of medieval society. The vogue of this twofold tradition we can trace backward in an uninterrupted line, from the verse of Langland's *Piers Plowman* or the much later *Satyre of the Thrie Estaits* by Lyndesay to the homiletical works of a Guillaume Perault or a Jacques de Vitry in the thirteenth century.[4] Occasionally, an undisguised sermon-peroration makes its appearance in the poems concerned:

> Anurith God and holi chirch, [Honour]
> And ʒiveth the pouir that habbith nede;
> So godis wille ʒe ssul wirche,
> And joi of heven hab to mede.
> To whoch joi us bring
> Jhesus Crist, heven King.—Amen.[5]

Those unacquainted with medieval preaching in any land might well ask whether, from the side of the preacher, there are any indications that verse—and even vernacular verse—

---

[1] Ephes. v, 16. Cf. *Preaching in Med. Engl.* passim.
[2] E.E.T.S. O.S. no. 117, pp. 719–21. Cf. also pp. 206–8.
[3] On this point see especially below, pp. 294–304.
[4] See my *Preaching in Med. Engl.* pp. 264, 289–90, etc.
[5] *Song on the Times*, Wright's *Pol. Songs*, Camden Soc. p. 205. Cf. further, *On the King's breaking his confirmation of Magna Charta* (temp. Edw. II), Auchinlk. MS. Nat. Libr. of Scotl. Edinb. (in *Pol. Songs*, pp. 253–7):

> "Love we God, and he us alle
> That was born in an oxe stalle...".

played a prominent part in his usual exercises. Reference to his written remains will prove that to be the case. His solemn orations in Latin were sometimes punctuated with snatches of popular poetry. English verses decoraté the pages of his alphabetical note-book. But, above all, the whole sermon itself from quite early times was frequently metrical throughout. Some of the best-known Middle English poems in the language are nothing less than homilies of this kind. Readers familiar with one of these poems, from a manuscript in the library of Jesus College, Oxford,[1] will realize how slight is the gap between metrical homilies for pulpit recitation and metrical satires for popular use, without further introduction to the literature of preaching. The poem referred to is known as *A lutel soth sermun*, and opens with the preacher's invocation to silence and attention:

> Herkneth alle gode men
> And stylle sitteth a-dun,
> And ich on wile tellen
> A lutel soth sermun....

The body of the work, however, is taken up with matter typical, not merely of the denunciatory sermon, but of any of the "Songs on the Times" that have been already mentioned. The follies of the various classes reappear in all their variety. Here are the deceiving chapmen again, the bakers and brewers, the incontinent priest, along with the worldly maiden and her fond Jankin, Watkin and Wilkin. The homilist is already well on his way to become a maker of rhymes for the people. In the person of friar "Nicole" Bozon we have at least one recognizable preacher, specimens of whose prose homilies have actually come down to us together with specimens of his satiric verse.[2]

Thomas Wright, after describing a satirical *Poem on the Times of Edward III, from a Manuscript preserved in the Library of St Peter's College, Cambridge*,[3] with its now familiar

---

[1] MS. 29, lf. 258, printed in E.E.T.S. O.S. no. 49, p. 189. See also Miss B. D. Brown, *The Southern Passion*, E.E.T.S. ed. Introd. p. c.

[2] In this case, however, in Anglo-Norman French. See J. Vising, *Anglo-Norm. Lang. and Lit.* p. 65, etc. Wm. Lichfield is another English poet-preacher.   [3] Ed. Rev. C. Hardwick, Percy Soc. 1849.

criticism of the social orders, concludes his remarks with a
sentence which sets William Langland's famous satire in its
right perspective. "This poem", he says, speaking of the
former, "marks a period in our social history, and led the way
to that larger work of the same character, which came about
thirty years later, the well-known *Visions of Piers Ploughman*,
one of the most remarkable satires, as well as one of the most
remarkable poems, in the English language."[1] Too often, however, our modern literary historians have obscured this relationship by their failure to appreciate what Langland owed to
himself and what he really owed to others. Thus, through the
enthusiasm of Professor Skeat, for example, the *Vision* has
come to be regarded far too exclusively as an "extraordinary
manifestation of the religion, of the language, of the social and
political notions,...of the passions and feelings of rural and
provincial England",[2] and its author as a man of "remarkable"
political views, whose "originality is most surprising".[3] Yet,
with all his genius, it is equally important to remember
that the fourteenth-century poet is but one of a long line of
poetic homilists who had been harping for generations upon the
same general themes. Satirist and allegorist alike, they are
all disciples of the pulpit which had originally taught them
what to say. Their poems are but variations upon its own
familiar time-worn methods of speech. If Professor Courthope
had understood this fact, he would not have fallen into the
error of repeating of the particular poem in question that "the
manner in which the doctrine is conceived and applied is
Langland's own".[4] The "Faire Felde ful of folke", with which
the *Vision* opens, is itself, of course, only a highly developed
form of that same social vision which preacher and verse-
maker had been describing for generations, with criticism more
or less systematic of the vices of its several groups. The days

[1] *Hist. of Caricature*, p. 187.
[2] Clarendon Press Ser. ed. (of B text), 1886, p. xxiii, quoting from
Dean Milman's *Hist. of Lat. Christianity*, vol. vi, p. 356 (ed. 1855).
[3] See ibid. pp. xxvi and 147; and cf. Prof. Ker below, p. 548.
[4] *Hist. of Engl. Poetry*, vol. i, p. 349. Courthope is here again, I find,
merely copying from Marsh (*Origin and Hist. of the Engl. Lang.* 1862,
p. 296), who is quoted by Skeat, as above, p. xxii.

were still evil, and the preacher's message had never changed. As our examination progresses, we shall see how the other satires which follow in the poem conform again, like its allegories, to the pattern of the pulpit, when, as is natural, we miss their full development in the slender stock of more ancient English verse. Satire of the Rats and the Cat, satire of *Mede*, satire of the Courts at Westminster, satire of the Churchmen, satire of the Vices in tavern and fair, convent and parsonage, all and more will reappear in due course, their features but little altered, as we turn the sermon pages.

From the comparatively crude verse of Langland to the polished lines of Chaucer is a far cry in our literature indeed. Here, to be sure, is also a radical change of weather in the literary firmament. Chaucer, as has been said truly, is too genial a wit, "too little of a preacher and enthusiast", too much entertained with the world as he sees it, to be very much of a ruthless satirist. Yet even here in the new atmosphere of his satire, wherever it can be found, the atmosphere of the contemporary pulpit still pursues us.[1] Miss Grace Hadow, in her entertaining and suggestive little study of *Chaucer and his Times*, proceeds to examine in turn the various comic influences in English literature which could have influenced this "first great English humorist".[2] We have mention of the French *fabliaux*, the animal epic, rude popular rhymes and satirical poems in Latin, the miracle-plays, even the solemn romances— but no word of the humour of sermons. The old "lacuna" gapes before us again! Did Chaucer himself, indeed, never sit with laughter-loving "wives of Bath" who went regularly "to preaching" because it amused them,[3] and join in the uproarious merriment that greeted the preachers' witty caricatures in London, that city of many pulpits? The poet's own merry laughter seems to rise up before us from the page and mock his would-be interpreter, when we find Miss Hadow selecting

[1] Even Courthope, it appears, is prepared to state that Chaucer's "conceptions" were influenced by the miracle-plays (as above, vol. i, p. 298). How *near* we are to *sermon* influences again, already!
[2] See pp. 143–5.
[3] Cf. *Cant. Tales*, Wife of Bath's Prol. l. 557.

as the choicest sample of her hero's satire none other than a preacher and his sermon from the *Canterbury Tales*![1] It is quite impossible, of course, to conceive that he, who from his own confessions knew so much of "omelies",[2] should fail to draw inspiration from these past-masters in the art of vivid Realism and incisive portraiture. Nor are some of the poet's satires, which seem to have escaped Miss Hadow, half so genial as she would always have us believe. Those in which he attacks "Religious folk", for example, in the traditional manner, might well have dropped from the lips of his contemporary, John Bromyard himself.[3] Likewise, Professor Manly, we think, would hardly have ventured so rashly to suggest that Chaucer's Canterbury Pilgrims represent particular individuals of the poet's acquaintance,[4] had he realized how thoroughly representative and even commonplace many of them are in a contemporary literature which has been wholly neglected. The truth of the matter is that scholars for so long have been poking their noses into every conceivable foreign source-book and every kind of domestic record in their endeavour to throw fresh light upon the poet that they have entirely overlooked this modest field of the sermons which lies as it were at their very feet.[5]

Having once quitted the great master for his contemporaries and successors, we return immediately to a metrical literature which is steeped in the old familiar spirit and language of the preachers. The moral Gower himself is a warning of what is shortly to follow in this direction. In all the literature that has been published, it would be difficult to find a more perfect mirror of the social gospel as presented by the pulpit, its artistry as well as its doctrine, within a single frame, than his *Mirour de l'Omme*, or *Speculum Meditantis*. Mr G. C. Macaulay, although all too painfully silent again concerning the influence of con-

---

[1] Cf. pp. 157–65. See further, art. iv by C. O. Chapman, in *Publ. of the Mod. Lang. Assoc. of Amer.* March, 1929, pp. 178–85.
[2] See *Cant. Tales*, Epilogue, l. 1088.
[3] Cf. my *Preaching in Med. Engl.* p. 90, n. 3.
[4] See *Some New Light on Chaucer*, 1926, lects. iii–ix.
[5] I refer here particularly to *contemp.* English sermon-collections.

temporary English preaching upon the mind of his poet,[1] must be allowed to speak for what he calls—"as regards matter, the most valuable part of the *Mirour*".[2] It

is that which contains the review of the various classes of society. . . . He [Gower] describes for us meetings of city dames at the wine-shops, the various devices of shop-keepers to attract custom and to cheat their customers, and the scandalous adulteration of food and drink. The extravagance of merchants, the discontent and luxury of labourers, and the corruption of the law courts are all vigorously denounced; and the Church, in the opinion of our Author, is in need of reform from the top to the bottom. Gower's picture is not relieved by any such pleasing exception as the parish priest of the *Canterbury Tales*.

The significance of all these features for our main thesis will be apparent when we turn to the sermons and discover them there. However, our interpreter goes on—"The material which we find in the *Mirour de l'Omme* is, to a great extent, utilized again, and, in particular, the account given of the various classes of society is substantially repeated in Gower's next work, the Latin *Vox Clamantis*". Here the traditional homiletic view of the social organism, divided into clergy, knights, and labourers, is maintained; and the sins of each group are attacked in detail, those of the Orders, the secular clergy, and the lawyers receiving special attention. Finally, the Prologue to Gower's third great work, the *Confessio Amantis*, where the poet turns in despair to sing of Love, "is nothing but an abstract of the line of thought pursued in the *Vox Clamantis*".[3] Rehearsing the vices and corruption in Church and State once again, the poet decides not only that the days are evil, but that "the ends of the world are come". Clearly the preacher's message had weighed all too heavily upon his mind. So much, then, for John Gower. After him and after his friend Chaucer, apart from a few outworn romantic conceits of the feudal *trouvère*, there is strangely little left among the poets of Britain

[1] See *Works*, ed. Macaulay, vol. i, Introd. pp. xlvi–lxi. But note his recognition of the influence of earlier moral treatises, in *Camb. Hist. of Engl. Lit.* vol. ii, p. 139. His sole acquaintance with these leads him, however, to an exaggerated estimate of the literary and artistic achievement of the poet.

[2] *Camb. Hist. of Engl. Lit.* vol. ii, pp. 143 et seq.

[3] Cf. Courthope, as before, vol. i, p. 310, etc.

but these same pulpit themes of satire and unrelieved pessimism. It is common knowledge how that Lydgate, particularly in his minor verse, Hoccleve, in his *Regement of Princes*, and Henryson,[1] Dunbar,[2] Gavin Douglas[3] and Lyndesay,[4] north of the Border, all thus express the follies and empty vanity of Life, and cry as with one voice—"Dies mali sunt". In Alexander Barclay's[5] English version of the famous *Ship of Fools*, completed in 1508, we have a poem which, on the ground alone of the author's own prefatory argument, stands out as *The Satyre*. Modern historians, here again, have been all too ready to speak of its German prototype, the *Narrenschiff*, as though it were a work of daring originality and exaggerated pasquinade even amongst satires of the time. Likewise, Barclay's modern editor is driven to remark that few ecclesiastics of the poet's day would have dared to write in the same strain.[6] The pages that follow, however, will be sufficient to destroy any such notion. So completely is our *Ship of Fools*, from first to last, a compilation of the typical sermon-matter of a century and a half of preaching, that it would be almost true to say that, apart from its metrical form, there was nothing original about it but its woodcuts. In England, as in Germany or France, indeed, the pulpit had long prepared the way for its subsequent popularity. Barclay himself is no mere ribald, but a sincere moralist. The surrounding gloom, however, has continued to deepen, until the consciences of others have ceased to trouble them further, and they give up the struggle against evil in despair. By the time that "beastly" Skelton[7] is reached, the very

---

[1] Probably in Orders.
[2] First a friar Minor, later a secular priest. Cf. here his own lines:

> "In freiris weid full fairly have I fleichet.
> In it haif I in pulpet gone & preichet
> In Derntoun Kirk, & eik in Canterberry."

[3] A cleric: Bishop of Dunkeld, etc.
[4] His interest in preaching is patent in *The Monarche*, passim.
[5] Formerly a Benedictine monk; later a Franciscan friar; then vicar in Essex and Somerset, and finally rector of Allhallows, Lombard Street. See also Fr. A. Pompen, *The Engl. Versions of the S. of F.* 1925.
[6] See Introd. ed. Jamieson, Edinb. 1874 (in 2 vols.).
[7] In Orders, 1498; later, rector of Diss, Norfolk.

backbone of moral purpose in satire seems at last to be breaking. An age of coarse burlesque, of cheerful irreverence for sacred and romantic things, an age which begins to delight in fouling the nest which reared it has set in. For, without any spark of Idealism transcending what he sees, the Realist all too soon becomes a ribald and a cynic. The world of literature now seems at times wellnigh drowned in the peals of mocking, indecent laughter that betoken an inner bankruptcy and madness of soul. As the laughter dies down for a little, only Death and Destruction follow to ring the changes. English poetry thus has plunged into the full winter of its discontent. Abroad, the *Danse Macabre* and similar morbid satire had likewise succeeded to the cynical gaiety of Reynard and the medieval devils. We know now far better than we did how it all happened. Only the most superficial students of history will here attempt to argue that the forces chiefly responsible for this state of affairs lay outside the Church and the traditional sphere of her ministrations. Europe as yet was neither "enlightened" nor Protestant. Those intimately familiar with the current life, with the mind of her people and the products of her printing presses will not be deceived at this stage by any airy talk of a new Renaissance spirit from Italy, or by the literary affectations of the "educated" of that day. It was the harsh pulpit clamour of Satire and Complaint, echoing from generation to generation of preachers, that had sunk deep into men's minds and hearts, bringing forth corrupt thought. In a world of civil strife and simmering rebellion, for the moment that message seemed to find justification everywhere. Its mournful auguries appeared to the fevered brain to be coming true at last—until the mood changed to one of cheerful apathy or open defiance as courage returned. Such, then, was the bitter harvest reaped by those who had chosen to implant a gospel of denunciation and fear, in place of one of hope and present salvation in times of emergency. Such was the last great battle to be won by medieval Catholicism on English soil. For the Church it was a short-lived, inglorious victory, as well it deserved to be. For, the gospel which it had preached was, like its own system, itself a too thinly-disguised paganism, belonging, that is to say, to the Old Dispensation, not to the New; and man cannot live by Fear alone. Thus, as its smarting children reared mainly through repression, through taunts and threats of future punishment, grew to an independent manhood and a wisdom of their own, they turned to mock, to threaten, and then to eject their own short-sighted parent. Upon literature and religion in general, however, the struggle left its more enduring marks. While the old religious temper flourishes anew in Protestantism, even in letters, where the choicest Elizabethan verse spells the triumph of healthy nature over unhealthy dogma, it is a nature, nevertheless, that owes its moral instincts to a pulpit tradition of the past.

So we arrive, naturally and inevitably, at the last phase of this influence to which we need here give attention. After Barclay and Skelton, it is true, the traditional satire of the medieval homilists still lingers in the verses of Wyatt and of Gascoigne. But the fresh lyrical notes of the Renaissance grow ever clearer at its expense. The crude pulpit satires of the drunkard, the gossip, the swearer and the like, already embodied in medieval play and poem, may be said to be perpetuated in the scenes of low life in Elizabethan drama. Certainly, the traditional attacks on the female sex persist in much popular doggerel of that period.[1] Otherwise, that alone which concerns us yet a little is the part played by English medieval preaching as the precursor of Reformation satire. On the continent, the corresponding influence of "the forerunners of Luther and of Rabelais"—to quote M. Méray's sub-title[2]—has for some time past received from scholars the attention that it deserves. The famous author of *Gargantua* himself, for example, has been found to show acquaintance with such well-known satirists of the French pulpit as Olivier Maillard and Jean Bourgeois.[3] In England, on the other hand, where such Rabelaisian raillery is easily matched on the more earnest Protestant side by coarse and virulent poems of the type of *Doctour Doubble-Ale*, or *John Bon and Mast Parson*, medieval influences

[1] See below, pp. 401–2.
[2] *La Vie au temps des Libres Prêcheurs*, 2 vols. 1878.
[3] Cf. W. F. Smith, *Rabelais in his Writings*, Camb. 1918, p. 116.

have been most palpably neglected.[1] It is in the realm of
prose, however, that our English Reformation satirists achieved
their greatest popular triumphs, from the days of Bale and
Ponet to the author of the *Mar-Prelate Tracts* and indeed
beyond to a Prynne and a Bastwick. Here the case of S. R.
Maitland[2] will illustrate to perfection how elaborate researches
into a literary field of this kind may end in complete misjudg-
ment, from lack of knowing accurately what went before. That
well-intentioned person expended the greatest energy in exposing to the world what he considered to be the scandalous
ribaldries and excesses of the Reformation "Puritans" of
England. But from cover to cover of his most entertaining
book we are given no hint that, down to the eve of the Reformation, it was the Catholic clergy of every species in the Church
who for centuries had been accustomed, from their own pulpits,
to scold their fellow-clergy—and indeed the hierarchy as a
whole—in terms no less flagrant and sometimes no less indecent than the most scurrilous Reformer that Maitland could
produce. Indeed, we shall have occasion to see that even such
"Protestant" enormities as the "Pope-ass"[3] were nothing more
nor less than an orthodox Catholic creation popularized by
the preaching men. When that which was more often spoken
at the first in inner chambers had become at length noised
abroad—as sooner or later it was bound to be—what more
natural than that an irate people should adopt the language of
their former teachers? In a word, then, our medieval pulpit
satire adequately explains alike the coarseness and the acerbity
of both Humanist and Reformer. Even so gracious a man as
More was not above retorting from the opposite side with a
typical sermon *figure* of Luther himself in various stages of
drunkenness.[4]

Finally, that habit of ruthless satire and penetrating criticism

---

[1] See *Anc. Metr. Tales*, ed. Rev. C. H. Hartshorne, 1829, pp. 227–45,
and Hazlitt, *E. Pop. Poetry*, vols. iii, pp. 298–end, and iv, pp. 1–16.
Also, further, *Satiric Poems of the Time of the Reform.*, Scot. Text. Soc.
1889–93; *The Sempill Ballates*, ed. T. G. Stevenson, 1872; etc.
[2] *Essays on Subjects connected with the British Reformation*, 1849.
[3] See below, p. 284.
[4] See *The Supplication of Souls*, Engl. ed. 1557, pp. 331–2.

in sermons, which did so much to undermine the authority of the Church, worked in similar fashion against the strongholds of feudal privilege.[1] A continuous stream of scorn and reproof for all the current sources of pride and prestige in medieval society poured forth from the pulpits. The ears of the people must have grown quite familiar with homiletic phrases that often sounded to them like so many threats of destruction for the powerful and the rich. Hence, for better or for worse, we must acknowledge the sermons, however little so intended, as a primary literature of secular revolt, and their authors as the heralds of political strife and future social liberties. Such persistent ventilation of the sufferings and wrongs of the poor—not exceeded, probably, by the most outspoken champions of social revolution in any age—could only end at length in one result. If the evils remained, one fine day the oppressed would take matters into their own hands, and attempt what *prelatus* and *consiliarius* had been continually urged to do by the preachers, but all in vain. Speaking of the latter, M. Méray declares unreservedly: "Je continue à affirmer qu'ils ont plus fait pour battre en brèche le despotisme royal, la rapacité féodale, et la suprématie romaine, qu'aucune des classes de la société dans lesquelles ils prêchaient".[2] With this last word our preliminary sketch of the development of Satire and Complaint must end. Already it has carried us far beyond the limits of mere literature, into a realm where thoughts and actions are stirred and enlivened with equal force. As in the case of religious reformation we shall see likewise how in secular affairs the impact of the pulpit was perpetually making itself felt. By its ceaseless effort it had clearly helped to inaugurate for better or for worse yet another great movement in the national life.

From more directions than one in the formal pursuit of his art, there were influences calculated to inspire the English

---

[1] Cf. Courthope, as above, on the influence of "the bourgeois satirist", vol. i, p. 184.

[2] *La Vie au temps des Libres Prêcheurs*, vol. i, p. 2.

medieval preacher to satiric portraiture. Every preceding
chapter of the present study, indeed, may be said to have
afforded some illustration of the probable lines of his advance.
If we go back to the first, the reader is bound to see that the
everyday characters and scenes which the preachers sketched
with such vivid effect in exemplifying their arguments, sooner
or later would lead them on to behold the absurdities of
human life. Upon one who gazed so attentively at the contorted
beggars of the medieval gutter, the pranks of children and
animals, the very caricatures of the street juggler and acrobat,
thoughts of the weaknesses and follies of human society would
be continually breaking in. A sudden sense of the ridiculous
in our stern moralist's mind—and, in a flash, pulpit Realism
might be converted into pulpit Satire. This lighter vein of
rebuke was so well suited apparently to the taste of contemporary
sermon-audiences,[1] that the preacher would feel encouraged to
indulge his gift still further. For the sermons themselves tell
us how the people loved to hear their neighbours' vices lampooned from the pulpit. So solemn, however, are the speaker's
accompanying remarks as we read them to-day, unhappily
without the means of watching his face, that we cannot often
be sure whether he is giving us typical statements of facts or
picturesquely exaggerated satire. Bromyard describes,[2] for
example, how careless penitents "come suddenly to confession,
as though they were in a mood of cheerful levity, and say,
'Question me!' And marvellous it is how he who has not con-
fessed for a whole year before comes hurriedly to church, or
to Religious when he spies them crossing the road, quits his
travelling-carriage, and says, 'Hear me at once: I shall be very
quick: I have only one word to say!'" Is our Dominican
Doctor here describing a general practice in real life, or is he
merely caricaturing? One thing at least seems clear. Much
that has passed hitherto as the exaggeration of satire in the
current literature of verse, in view of the mass of new sermon

[1] See in my *Preaching in Med. Engl.* pp. 182–4; also Bromyard, *S.P.*
s.v. "Compassio"—"contra multos qui de consuetudine audiunt et
narrant, cum letitia et risu, ut dictum est, aliorum delicta."
[2] *S.P.* s.v. "Confessio".

evidence will certainly have to be taken as "gospel" truth. For, in the case just cited, for example, we have further confirmation in a sermon of Bishop Brunton, who appears himself to have overheard much the same kind of remarks.[1] The preacher who has an eye for the scenes of real life is likely also to be influenced by the satiric representations of current art. This fact, again, is emphasized in the sermons. Thus an English preacher, towards the end of the thirteenth century or the beginning of the fourteenth, who is probably one Robert of Basevorn, refers in his sermon satire upon human vanity to a grotesque carving of the times, in which "an ass was sculptured, and upon the ass an ape; and the ape had an owl upon its hand; the sculptor's description of which was—'Neyther more ne lesse then ape and oule and asse'".[2] Similarly, Bromyard, with characteristic wit, points to the grinning corbel-head or gargoyle that leers at us still from our ancient churches. For it has reminded him of the hypocrites. Says he:

> At times, on these great buildings, we see a stone displaying a grinning open mouth, and from other indications appearing as if it supported the whole edifice. But nevertheless a plain stone, sometimes hid in a corner, does far more of the work; for the other is rather for show than for support. Such may well be compared to those persons, who, when they hear the cry of poor beggars for alms, when even their friends show them their misfortunes and the losses which they have sustained by fire or water or from thieves, with open mouth bewail the ills and losses of the latter, saying—"I *am* sorry: may God help you!", but do not offer a helping hand by giving them anything, or by lending provisions and other necessaries.[3]

On another occasion, the same preacher makes use of the "gargoules" again.[4] With their distressed countenances declaring to the world that their work is too heavy for them, they are now satirical portraits of slothful clergy "who complain of the least task" that is not to their own liking. Of all

---

[1] MS. Harl. 3760, fol. 47: "Et hic contra multos, qui ita sunt negligentes circum mundationem conscientie, quod, quando veniunt ad confessionem, non plenam de peccatis faciunt deliberationem, sed dicunt confessori—'Domine, expedi me! Non habeo nisi unum verbum'...".

[2] MS. Add. 38819, fol. 229b (a Latin collection).

[3] s.v. "Compassio".

[4] s.v. "Bellum". Cf., again, s.v. "Obedientia" ("imaginibus assimilantur, que Gallice *garrule* vocantur...").

such graphic caricatures of the medieval artist none made greater appeal to the pulpit than that well-known pictorial device known as the Wheel of Fortune. It illustrated with a peculiar vividness the preachers' own favourite view of life, fundamentally harsh and pagan as it had remained, the inevitable round of existence for every mortal human being, the successive stages of man's tragic journey upon the earth from cradle to grave, the varying temporal fortunes of a world that offered him no abiding security.[1] So Bromyard, comparing Worldly Fortune to a contrary wife, reminds his hearers how "sometimes it is literally depicted thus upon walls in the form of a woman turning a wheel with her hands, who, as most often happens, shifts the wheel contrary to the wishes of him who is propelled on it or sits upon the top".[2] Bishop Brunton, who makes similar reference to the picture in one of his own sermons, may well have been inspired by the thirteenth-century example still surviving in modern times in the choir of his own cathedral church at Rochester.[3]

That great wheel [says another homilist, fifty years later] is *weele and honour* of the realm, which is now *up*, now *down*, now *hye*, now *low*, and revolves in the manner of a wheel. Upon that wheel very many both in Church and State ascend—*gape upward ful fast*.[4] Some *ar qwirlid up* suddenly upon it and become from *pore gentilmen grete astates and gret lordis*. Some *ar hurlid doun* from that wheel, from high honours and dignities to extreme poverty, *sorooful care* and misery. There is no trust nor worldly stability in mundane glory;...now it exists, now it is no more; to-day a man, to-morrow no man; to-day a lord, to-morrow *a lost man*; to-day *a dowti werrour*, to-morrow dead on the field of battle....[5]

[1] Cf. poems in Chambers and Sidgwick, *E. E. Lyrics*, pp. 166–8, 360; and E.E.T.S. O.S. no. 15, p. 266, etc.
[2] s.v. "Mundus". Cf. further, s.v. "Invidia", § 33; etc.
[3] MS. Harl. 3760, fol. 212. Cf. further MS. Harl. 7322, fol. 162b (a wheel with ten spokes); *Pricke of Consc.* Phil. Soc. ed. p. 36 (dam fortone); and *Ayenb. of Inwyt*, pp. 24, 76, 181. See also the *drawing* in MS. Linc. Cath. Libr. C. 4. 6, fol. 4b.   [4] Precisely as in the Rochester painting.
[5] MS. Bodl. 649, fol. 131 (again on fol. 122—*fortune rota*). Here the preacher goes on to give examples from the classics, and then bids his audience—"*go no ferthur* than to the lamentable history of the noble prince, the Duke of Clarence, on whose soul may God have mercy! Sublimely did he revolve upon the wheel of honour..."—"sed, salva Dei voluntate, sua rota nimis vertebat per ventum of wilfulnes; he war

A third source of inspiration for the development of satire, with which the homilist was in daily contact, was Holy Scripture. Emphasis was laid in our second chapter upon the preference shown by the orthodox for allegoric interpretations of the sacred page, and for the gloss as opposed to the naked text. In a work, then, that already itself abounded in symbolic figures, in animal imagery, in pithy descriptions of persons, there was ceaseless encouragement for those who were continually on the look-out for new types and representations of human vice and virtue. Indeed, if it were not for the strength of the Aesopic tradition and the influence of other early fabulists in the Middle Ages, it would be reasonable to attribute to Scripture this immense vogue of animal symbolism in the contemporary preaching. Of good and evil types of the kind there was here almost an unlimited supply. Thus, "the psalme seis thus—'*Factus sum sicut nicticorax in domicilio*'[1] that is to sey—'I am made as a niȝtraven in the evesynges of a howse'". Who, then, was indicated by the bird in question?—obviously, "thes peple of religion", continually "preyng on nightes", that "dwellen in houses ioyned to the chirch", "as munkes, chanones, nunnes, ankers, and hankeresses".[2] To be called a night-raven of this kind was distinctly a compliment. But what, indeed—when another species of "night-bird" is chosen as a figure of those that love the darkness rather than the light, because their deeds are evil![3] Here we get material for the

dreve fro wele in to woo;...periit et transivit e mundo" (i.e. 1421, Battle of Beaugé). For further examples of the influence of secular painting here, cf. Bromyard, *S.P.* s.v. "Correctio": "sicut janitor juxta hospitium depictus, qui gladium vel baculum super intrantes, quasi percutere et ab ingressu arcere volens, vibrat, neminem tamen ledit vel artat". Sim. s.v. "Timor" ("juxta portam"); and in Nic. de Biard (Hauréau, *Not. et Extr.* vol. iv, p. 102): cf. also ibid. p. 51, *processio Renardi* (as illustr. from Strasbourg Cath. in Wright, *Hist. of Caric.* p. 81) with the fable of our Engl. Odo of Cheriton and the Engl. *Gesta Rom.* as above, p. 206.

[1] Ps. cii, 6 (A.V. has—"an owl of the desert"). Cf. here, Rolle's *Psalter*, ed. Bramley, p. 353, v. 7.

[2] MS. Roy. 8. C. i, fol. 135. Cf. *Ancren Riwle*, pars iii, ed. Morton, King's Classics, p. 107.

[3] Cf. Bromyard, *S.P.* s.v. "Electio", etc.; Wimbledon, 1388 (owls and night-crows); Rypon, as quoted below, p. 444.

production of a satire. And right well did our preachers learn how to make use of it.[1] Animal similes, after all, formed only one type of pungent Scriptural imagery. The pulpit which adopted with a new force and fury the words of Ezekiel—"O Israel, thy prophets are like the foxes in the desert!",[2] adapted also the stinging phrases of a Greater than he. It was Holy Church that was now to be compared to "a den of thieves"; and the money-changers were her evil priests.[3] Prelates who won their way by craft and by deceit, by wisdom of this world, or by the help of powerful friends were now the "hirelings", who "entered not by the door into the sheepfold, but climbed up some other way".[4] Of the remaining sources of pulpit satire little further need be added. We have spoken already of the Fables[5] and of the Latin Goliardic verse that rivals the sermons in the ruthlessness of its own clerical assaults. There is also, as we shall see, a satiric tradition in the preaching of the Fathers and of the golden age of St Bernard upon the continent. Anecdotes and reminiscences, too, had frequently a like flavour. Such is the sermon-story of the priest who walked through a puddle, observing to his parishioners that they followed his example no better than his precepts,[6] or the tale of two preachers advised to preach particularly against slander in the town to which they were fast approaching, by the very man who turned out to be the greatest slanderer of the place.[7]

[1] Amongst numerous examples furnished below, cf. esp. the "four great beasts" of the Book of Daniel, etc. (p. 326, n. 2), and the sea monsters of Lamentations (p. 328). *S.P.* s.v. "Dominatio" is full of further examples.
[2] xiii, 4. See Bromyard, s.v. "Consilium".
[3] Cf. MS. Harl. 2276, fol. 119: ("But now we seen holi chirche set aboute with ful many money chaungeris, and also filled with many wickid marchaundises..." etc.); MS. Heref. Cath. Libr. P. 5. 2, fol. 68b ("spelunca latronum"...); etc.
[4] Cf. Brunton, quoted in my *Preaching in Med. Engl.* p. 253. Many other strange examples will be found in the pages following; cf. Philip, below, p. 269 (apes from Tharshish), etc.
[5] See above, in Chap. IV.　　　[6] MS. Add. 27336, fol. 28.
[7] MS. Harl. 1288, fol. 56. Cf. further above, pp. 163–5.

An attempt to illustrate, first, the Satire and Complaint of the English medieval pulpit against the Church and its various ministers may well begin with two sermon tales, which, although they originated on the continent, yet make their appearance in English homily-books from the thirteenth century onwards. They suffice to show us to what lengths on occasion the pulpit satirist was prepared to go, at a comparatively early date. A certain monk or friar, a master of the University of Paris, was once called upon to preach a Synodal sermon, according to some versions of the story, "in the presence of the King of France and many bishops". Upon entering the pulpit, the preacher "began his sermon thus, gazing around him on every side and repeating this phrase in French, several times— 'St Pere et St Paule, babimbaboo!', that is to say, 'St Peter and St Paul, it is meet to address you with that word of derision which people say to fools in expression of their folly!'" One narrative of the tale adds that the speaker accompanied his blasphemous text with the act of spitting,[1] a piece of crude dramatic realism which the medieval pulpit would hardly hesitate to display. When questioned by the august assembly as to the meaning of this insolence, he boldly explained as follows, to their utter humiliation: "The bishops with their caparisoned steeds and delicate dishes, with their costly garments and with their vices and delights believe that they will go to heaven. Therefore Peter and Paul, who suffered poverty and tribulation, hunger and thirst and cold, were the greatest fools!"[2] Outbursts of such daring and originality are rare in the corresponding sermon-literature of this country. None the less we shall generally find a similar spirit of vehemence, wherever monk or mendicant refers in his clerical orations to the sins of the *prelati*. The other story, equally popular in its day, tells of a certain bishop who was unable for some reason to compose his sermon for a forthcoming synod. He called

[1] Erasmus, *Colloq.* (see Méray, as before, ii, p. 130). Here the preacher is said to be the monk Robert de Lys. Cf. *Shakesp. Jest-Bks.* i, 134.

[2] Found in Odo of Cheriton (cf. MS. Arund. 231, fol. 63b, and ed. Hervieux, no. viii), Etienne de Bourbon (cf. *Anecd. Hist.* ed. Lecoy de la Marche), and the Engl. *Spec. Laic.* s.v. "Prelatorum Status"—all of the 13th cent. Cf. also, *Ayenb. of Inwyt*, p. 77.

upon a theologian at short notice to make one in his stead. On the way to the place of assembly, the latter was met by the Devil, who asked him whither he was going. "The priest replied—'To a synod, to preach there'. Said the demon, 'I will give you a good sermon which you shall deliver in synod', and handed it to him on a sheet of paper. The priest said, 'They will not believe'. The demon struck him in the face in token that they might believe", leaving a bruise for all to see, which disappeared later when the sermon was done.[1] His message was the famous "Devil's Letter", in which the Prince of Darkness greeted the Princes of the Church as his friends, in acknowledgment of the many souls which they were continually dispatching to him![2] From extant sermons of the fourteenth and fifteenth centuries, representative of all grades of the clergy in turn, we shall now give some examples to show what English preachers could do. Space forbids more.[3]

The sermons of an archbishop, Richard Fitzralph of Armagh, reveal to us some of the abuses which so often drove the fourteenth-century homilist to scathing satire and rebuke. In a synodal sermon, he declares that it is to be feared that many of his own order are compelled to confess that among the

[1] Version of MS. Harl. 268, fol. 10b.
[2] Also in Odo of Cheriton, in the *Alphabetum Narrationum*, in N. Bozon, and Bromyard s.v. "Ordo Clericalis" and "Prelatio". For further references, see my *Preaching in Med. Engl.* pp. 248–9, and Hauréau, *Not. et Extr.* vol. iii, p. 120, where the narrative is traced to the *Bonum Univ. de Apibus* of Thos. of Chantimpré (A.D. 1201–70).
[3] As I have already illustrated fully, from these sources, the preachers' attacks on (1) the ignorance of the clergy, and (2) the lack of faithful preaching, in my first volume, I shall not refer again to these subjects here. Students should refer back, therefore, especially to Chaps. I and VI of that work, to complete their survey of clerical condemnation, and also for details of the preachers quoted here, in the new text. However, more of the former is still continually coming to light, as fresh MSS. are examined. Cf. MS. Heref. Cath. Libr. P. 5. 2, fol. 77 ("Omnia destruuntur per ignoranciam prelati", etc.); Wm. of Rymyngton, MS. Bibl. Univ. Paris 790, fol. 107b ("O quam multi sacram scripturam despiciunt, studentes diligencius sciencias lucrativas *vel omnem literaturam penitus postponentes*. O quam negligenter et tepide divinum reddunt servicium, qui nec quod dicunt intelligunt nec advertunt...."), and further below. Among poets, cf. Jo. Audelay, *Poems*, E.E.T.S. ed. pp. 30–2.

prelates[1] are fornicators, gluttons, plunderers, thieves, robbers, and men of merchandize.[2]

For there are in the church of God those bearing the name of prelate—the greater and the lesser alike—who are fornicators. Not only are they not the husbands of one wife,...but they are the adulterers of many mistresses, to the manifest scandal of our status. There are others, by name prelates, not pastors but more truly gluttons, who once or more every day are inebriated with such drunkenness, and give vent to such filthy and scandalous scurrilities, that those sharing a common life with them abhor their society, on account of their vile mode of living. Alas! Alas! Alas! with what wicked temerity do such dare to handle the most spotless sacraments of the Church.... Others there are, plunderers in the Church of God, falsely called pastors, who from the goods of the churches —not only movable but immovable—provide for their own flesh and blood, namely their nephews and nieces—as they call the crowd of their own daughters and sons,[3] and so are unable to show that hospitality to which they are bound by their profession.... [4] Such prelates are plunderers, thieves, and robbers, and so are those who seize the fruits of churches and utterly despise the sacred service of them; who are always exercising the cry—"Shear! shear!, raise! raise!", and never fulfil the command— "Feed! feed!"; some of whom love the courts of princes, and neglect— nay, rather deceive—all their cures, nourishing themselves and ruining their subjects. Yet again, there are others, pastors in name but traffickers in deed, who sell to the laity not only the tithes of the Church but in addition the emoluments which spring from their spiritual jurisdiction for certain sums of money, against the Constitutions of the holy Fathers and the law of Nature.

So frequent is the sin of Simon Magus and Gehazi that "scarcely is there a single one amongst those promoted who is innocent of the crime of Simony".[5] Those who make entreaty on their

---

[1] With the following, compare the indictment of the bishops, etc. in the *Political Songs and Poems*, published by Wright (Camden Soc. as before), esp. pp. 32, 44, 48, 134, 234, 325, etc.

[2] MS. Lansd. 393, fol. 63b et seq.

[3] Cf. MS. Add. 21253, fol. 46b–47: "Prelati et clerici, qui bona, que habent de patrimonio Crucifixi, et que deberent pauperibus qui sunt filii ejus, tribuunt consanguineis suis, et de illis maritant filios suos et filias et nepotulos suos ac nepotes suas, cum non multum indigeant de talibus". Again, on fol. 76b. Cf. also a 12th-cent. (?) sermon in Hauréau, *Not. et Extr.* vol. iv, p. 109.

[4] Cf. Gascoigne (1450), *Loci e Libro Verit.* p. 43, etc.

[5] Cf. a vernacular preacher (early 15th cent.?), in MS. Roy. 18. B. xxiii, fol. 137b: "Symon also, and is felishippe Usury shuld be dryven oute of the churche, and also this inordinate lust sett in mans herte,...

behalf get paid likewise for their trouble. "For I hear from many quarters that there are a number of prelates who rarely confer a benefice on anyone, unless either they have received payment at their hands, or else have made sure of their reward when the deed is done—which is too disgraceful in the Church of God!" So the complaints multiply. In another sermon,[1] the same archbishop denounces in satirical vein the ecclesiastical "hirelings", with whom, he declares, the world is now filled:[2]

How many of all these princes of the Church observe such duties (after the pattern of Christ) in these days, do you think? Travel through the provinces and look at the cathedral churches, and you will find them replete with "flesh and blood", the nephews and grand-nephews of bishops, I perceive. Well do the princes of the Churches procure the services of their own flesh. The services of other men subject to them, approved by God in wisdom and holiness of life, they utterly neglect and despise. And thus, these latter languish in poverty....I have heard of a certain prelate who had bestowed a fat benefice upon one youth among his protégés,[3] that when someone asked him why he had not conferred it on a doctor, since he had very many suitable candidates in his diocese, he replied, "A heavy stone I cannot throw to a great distance; but I can raise it to my knees!"[4]

lechery". Also the elaborate account in MS. Harl. 45, fol. 69, of *Symony* and its types; *Ayenb. of Inwyt*, pp. 41–2; *Hand. Synne*, p. 180; etc.; and the equivalent passages in *Piers Plowman*, passim; also *Poems of Jo. Audelay*, p. 31. 　　　　　[1] MS. Lansd. 393, fol. 144 et seq.

　　[2] "Ecce quam grave periculum timoris et vecordie!—ita ut mundus jam mercenariis sit repletus". Cf. again, in MS. Harl. 2276, fol. 115 b–6: the "hirid" men, "that coveiten the mylke and wolle of her sheepe"; and above, p. 241.

　　[3] Cf. again, MS. Add. 21253, fol. 46b: "Homines hodie in multis locis, et maxime prelati ecclesie, qui nepotibus suis et consanguineis dant prebendas et ecclesias magnas, et eis aliquando committunt animarum milia ad curandum et ad custodiendum illas, quibus non committerent 5 pira et 5 poma ad custodiendum. Unde, bone Jhesu!, sicut dicitur in psalmo, 'posuerunt Jerusalem in pomorum custodiam': sicut dicitur quod quidam episcopus nepoti suo commisit curam 5 milia animarum, cui 10 pira noluit una vice committere ad custodiendum!" This latter tale is to be found further in Odo, in Etienne de Bourbon, in the *Spec. Laic.* and in other Engl. collections, e.g. MS. Roy. 7. D. 1, fol. 98b (see further, Herbert, *Cat. of Romances in B.M.* vol. iii, p. 75).

　　[4] The source of this remark will be found in the *Spec. Laic.* cap. vii (ed. Welter, p. 12) where the story is told of how St Edmund Rich was thus informed by Master Odo of Cheriton of the popular scandal caused by his promotion of his own brother Robert to a fat living: "Pater,

But what says this doughty champion of seculars concerning the rank and file of the priesthood? In a synodal sermon preached to a number of them gathered in Provincial Council at Drogheda, in the year 1354, he says:

> It seems to me that our priests are polluted with the vices about to be mentioned, from all of which they shall be cleansed by the medicine of this sacred Council. For there are among them men of carnal lust. There are others drunkards. There are some slothful. There are others who live too much like laymen. There are others too little given to hospitality. There are certain of them usurpers and plunderers, namely, the exempt Mendicants, who usurp the land-tithes.

All these, he goes on, must first be purged, if the vices of the common people are to be held in check.[1] Amongst bishops, we find Thomas Brunton of Rochester inveighing in his turn against the same kinds of offenders, particularly the men of his own rank. He likewise calls the latter hirelings, because, whereas they should be as columns bearing up the Church on their shoulders and ready to defend its liberties with their own lives, they allow

> Christ to be daily crucified afresh in his members, the innocent to be condemned, the poor ecclesiastics to be spoiled of their benefices, and the liberty of the church to be profaned to such a degree that in these days the holy church of God is in greater servitude than it was under Pharaoh, who had no knowledge of the Divine Law....And the reason for this is, according to report, either because they covet great offices, or aspire to be translated to richer bishoprics.[2]

Elsewhere he speaks of them as "Dumb dogs", of their evil life which prevents them from daring to correct the lives of their subjects, preferring rather to live thus "in ease and delicacies", and of their fawning upon the great and influential for such ends.[3] "Assuredly, if there were not notable defects

vulgariter dicitur quod nemo potest ponderosum lapidem remocius projicere, sic nec vos talem ecclesiam; sed eam in gremium fratris vestri projecistis...".

[1] MS. Lansd. 393, fol. 86. For sermon attacks on the Friars, cf. refs. in my *Preaching in Med. Engl.* p. 13, and cap. ii, passim; MS. Bodl. 95, fol. 14 (against their child-stealing); and below, p. 502, n. 1; etc. With these cf. the well-known criticisms in *Piers Plowman, The Complaint of the Plowman*, etc.　　　　　[2] MS. Harl. 3760, fol. 187.

[3] Ibid. fol. 217b. Cf. *Poem on the Evil Times*, in Wright (as before, Camden Soc.), p. 343.

among incumbents, prelates and especially confessors, so many abominable crimes and errors would not reign in England".[1] Like Master Rypon, as we shall see, he arraigns the promoted clerics, "who, when exalted to fat livings and busy with great ceremonies, leave their benefices and cause them to be served by hirelings".[2] Like Bromyard, he lampoons the insatiable greed of the churchmen of his day:

> In the matter of title and honours, so ambitious are the ecclesiastics that, if they possess a fat living, it is not enough for them unless they have a prebend. If they have a prebend, they are not satisfied unless they have several. If they have several, they affect to be a bishop; and then a bishop at court.[3]

Like all preachers of his day, he speaks openly of clergy "in life and example worse than the people", telling the story—"in cronicis"—of how once "when many nobles had gathered at a certain church to make a peace treaty, they asked the priest kindly to celebrate mass for them. But that priest was afraid to proceed to the Office of the Mass, because he had been sleeping that same night with his concubine".[4]

To do adequate justice to that great monument of Dominican preaching, the *Summa* of John Bromyard, in respect of its Complaint and Satire against the clergy, would require the space of a volume. From the papacy itself down to the newly fledged incumbent he indicts the whole hierarchical edifice from its topmost pinnacle to its humblest supports, as in the "political poem" that was mentioned.[5] As he beholds it, the Church has now fallen on evil days, and her glory is departed. In his own quaint phraseology, the word "Tunees" may well be written over her. For, as in Africa there is a city which is

---

[1] Ibid. fol. 143. [2] fol. 125b.
[3] fol. 128. Himself a Royal Confessor, Brunton is naturally loud in his complaints against the false confessors of his day—"pro magna parte veritatis oppressores, adulationis artifices, fabri laudis", etc. Cf. fols. 36, 141b, 239, etc. See also other denunciations quoted in my *Preaching in Med. Engl.* and Gasquet, *Old Engl. Bible*, chap. iii, passim.
[4] fol. 50b ("incontinentes", etc.). See again, on clerical immorality, fol. 310b, etc.; and cf. *Piers Plowman*, A text, pass. iii, ll. 145–7, etc. For further references to such tales, cf. below, p. 276.
[5] Cf. above, p. 223, *Poem on the Evil Times*, in Wright, Camden Soc. pp. 323, et seq.

called in the vulgar tongue "Tunees", that is to say—"Tu non es", "Thou art not" (as once thou wast wont to be), because it occupies the site of the once fairer, richer, and more powerful city of Carthage destroyed by the Romans, "so those who have beheld the primitive state of the Church, of Christianity and of religion, and compared it to the modern state of the same, can say—'Thou art not, namely, as once thou wast wont to be',—when 'righteousness lodged in it' (Isaiah i, 21)". Only the youths and light persons who have never seen the first glory of the temple will rejoice over it in its ruined state. The mature will be provoked rather to weeping with Christ, "when he beheld the city": "Aha! Aha! upon my sanctuary, because it is profaned; and upon the land of Israel, because it is desolate". "Of the modern state of the Church that saying of 4 Kings, ii [19] may be quoted: 'Behold the situation of this City is very good; but the waters are bad', that is, the clergy, by whom others ought to be cleansed."[1] Elsewhere, in still more scathing terms, Bromyard compares it to the night vision of a certain most fair lady, whom, according to the story the beholder took to be the Blessed Virgin Mary, until the apparition turned its back on him, to display a most foul posterior.[2] Of all the contemporary vices which profaned its leaders, none was more prominent to the eye of our Dominican than the vice of avarice and the scramble of clerics after worldly wealth. Again and again he returns to the same theme with increasing grief and anger:

As among the Clergy so among Religious, Money or Meed is lord of the sciences and of the churches. Moreover, everywhere it opens the gates of lands and palaces, and the doors of inner chambers.... And in all lands it slays and makes alive, it leads forth to the infernal regions and brings back, it opens and shuts the prisons, it slays the souls that are not dead, and gives life to those that are not living, "it raiseth up the needy out of the dust, and lifteth up the poor man from the dung-hill, to set them among princes, and make them to inherit the throne of glory" (1 Sam. ii, 8). "It shutteth, and no man openeth; it openeth, and no man shutteth!"[3]

[1] s.v. "Civitas". See Ezek. xxv, 3.
[2] s.v. "Ordo Clericalis" and "Mundus".
[3] s.v. "Munus". Cf. further below, pp. 252-5, etc.

It is a truly terrible picture that Bromyard paints in the most ruthless detail. Dealing with the summit of authority,[1] he dares to state that, if only "those who preside in the highest Court of the Church" would care more for souls than for "collecting florins and moneys, there would not be so many adulterers, usurers, fornicators, perjurers, lechers and the like, amongst clergy and people". "So many pecuniary Bulls and excommunications of those stealing temporalities show them to be lovers of moneys; and so many dissimulations of the sins committed against God's Commandments show them to be neglecters of souls." If church taxes and tithes are not paid to time, the unfortunate offenders are visited with the most rigorous punishments of the Church.[2] Where it is a case of clergy living immoral lives and other serious breaches of God's law, a money fine is deemed sufficient by those in authority— "in which case it seems that they are more intent on filling their purse than correcting the fault". Bromyard, like Langland,[3] is clearly nervous and hesitating at the first, as he approaches criticism of the deeds of cardinals and Papal Curia.[4] It is a perilous path to tread: "I am much afraid (*expavesco*) to speak very vehemently; nevertheless I dare not be silent, lest I incur the 'Woe!' of Isaiah, who says (vi, 5)—'Woe is me, because I kept silence!'" Later on, as he completes his unpleasant duty, he tactfully softens the sting of his rebukes thus:

I defame not the gods but the vices; neither do I set my face against the heavens but against the earthly scene, after the manner in which Paul rebuked Peter (Gal. ii). Nor do I touch the mountain but the mortification (*nec tango montem sed mortem*); nor, again, do I intend to reveal the shamefulness of the Father, fearing the offence of Cain,—but rather, when coming upon the nakedness of my Father, to cover it as a thing to be ashamed of, following in their footsteps and rendering that which is due, fear to whom fear is due, honour to whom honour, etc. (Rom. xiii, 7).

[1] s.v. "Honor". Cf. Gascoigne, *Loci e Libro Verit.* pp. 152-3, etc.
[2] See further below, pp. 260-1.
[3] See *Piers Plowman*, B text, *Prol.* ll. 107-11 ("Ac of the cardinales atte Courte....Forthi I can and can nauȝte of courte speke more"). Cf. also, *Poem on the Times*, c. 1388, in Fairholt, *Satir. Songs and Poems on Cost.* Percy Soc. p. 48 ("Here myght I more sey/Tamen ordo vetat seriarum..."), Wright, *Pol. Poems*, Rolls S. vol. i, p. 277.
[4] Also, s.v. "Honor".

Yet, like Langland, he has spoken vehemently enough in these
pages of the Papal Bulls which reveal a love for the moneys
of the penalized and a neglect of the proper correction of souls,
of the hideous, exorbitant system of tithes, annates, first-fruits,
crushing exactions at episcopal consecrations and during va-
cancies, or for the execution of any other business at the Papal
Curia, all of which, he declares, work the ruin of people and
prelates alike.[1] From occasions such as these, the preacher
argues, the newly consecrated themselves are driven to sin,
"those who lend them money on interest incur new ruin, the
guarantors are excommunicated, pauperized, and when they
run to Rome vexed and shamefully treated in many ways, their
subjects are weighed down and taxed by the ruthless methods
by which the money is raised, and wellnigh the whole world
complains". If Christ Himself was so careful not to cause
offence to the weak or the ignorant, "so much the more should
they be, who hold the place of Christ". If He pronounced
such stern judgment upon whosoever should offend one of
those little ones that believe on Him, "what shall be the punishment of those who offend many little ones and great ones,
too?" What, then, is the speaker's view of the root cause of
all this trouble, and what is the true remedy?

Once the burdensome multitude of cardinals[2] is got rid of [he replies],
the excessive swarm of their horses and retinues, their inordinate love of
kindred and the haughty vanity of all their trappings, then the necessity
for such large contributions will cease.[3] Therefore they should give up
all these things, lest they offend the little flock which believes in Christ

[1] Cf. Langland again, later in the *Vision*, A text, pass. ii, l. 18; B text,
pass. ii, l. 23, etc.: "In the popis paleis, she [i.e. *Mede*] is pryve as myself",
and *Poem* in Wright, Camden Soc. p. 324; and with these, Bromyard,
further quoting the remark of a great cleric to the Papal janitor (s.v.
"Munus"): "Magnus canis custodiens ostium, cui, si aliquid in os
projecissem, me intrare permisisses!"; etc.

[2] "Servorum" is cunningly substituted for "Cardinalium" in the
Venice ed. of the *S.P.* 1588, published under the patronage of a Roman
Cardinal! It is a quaint little example of the craven duplicity of Roman
methods in the post-Tridentine era. The trick is repeated again here, a
little later ("praelatos" for "cardinales").

[3] Cf. *Piers Plowman*, C text, pass. xxii, ll. 415 et seq. (the Cardinals
with "here pelure and palfrayes" and extortions, and "the pope that
pileth holichurche...", etc.).

and has been redeemed by His blood. Although it may be possible for them to receive without great sin the year's income of the church from those consecrated at the Curia, the first-fruits of vacant churches, and even—when it pleases them—the tithe of the church, yet they ought to refrain from such things to avoid scandal, lest the source of life become a source of poison.[1] For if only those who preside at that most Holy See knew how not only infidels, Saracens, Jews, schismatics and heretics, but even the faithful—I do not say are offended by—but actually curse their pomp, which they judge to be haughty and a deviation from the path of Christ,... they would cease from such things, for the sake of example.

"If Constantine, the Saracen Emperor was unwilling to shed the blood of youths for the sake of his life and bodily health, wherefore are these Christians willing to destroy souls for the sake of their own proud and worldly maintenance, they who ought the rather to be their salvation?"[2] To the sins of the papacy Bromyard would apply the excuse of Chrysostom for the earlier lapses of Rome's first bishop as narrated to us in the Gospels. In another part of his *Summa*, he makes the strange suggestion that "God, the highest corrector of men, has permitted Peter, his vicar of Correction on the earth to sin, so that, from the state of his own frailty he might learn to sympathize with the weaknesses of others".[3]

Turning to the diocesan Church Courts and the administration of the law by bishops, archdeacons and officials, Bromyard,

[1] Cf. here the orthodox vernacular preacher of MS. Roy. 18. B. xxiii, fol. 69: "Wold God that ther longed not so meche riches as ther dose to that office [the pope]; but that itt were pore as Crist lefte it with Petur! And than ther wold no man make no debate ne striff ther fore. And than shuld all othur clerkes lese meche of here covetize, and ȝeve hem to prechynge and to teche the pepull goddes lawe aftur tho gospell; and than shuld muche flaterynge in sermons be lefte...". (This—in a sermon delivered before the bishop, for whom the speaker was deputizing.)

[2] Bromyard's practical proposals here are interesting: "Sanctius ergo, et pro se ipsis et pro aliis, esset pauciores et de toto mundo electos habere cardinales, utpote qui totum mundum sunt recturi, in quibus ecclesie potius quam persone vel parentele esset provisum, qui de terris Templariorum vel de aliqua certa et eis assignata portione sine scandalo viverent, muneribus et exactionibus in sempiternum exclusis—quam semper quasi de incerto et de male acquisito, et cum multorum vivere maledictionibus" (s.v. "Honor").

[3] s.v. "Correctio". Cf. Migne, *Patr. Gr.* vol. l, col. 728.

like the authors of vernacular *Songs on the Times*, discovers another hotbed of corruption, where money rules.[1] More than once he tells how bishops and their ministers receive money or gifts—"especially from their Religious and ecclesiastics, who ought not to spend the goods of the Church on things of this sort"—as virtual payment for the privilege of committing certain infamous sins. "By means of a little money given to the sumners or the ecclesiastical judges, who ought to be punished along with them with an equal punishment, adulterers and fornicators are always able to persist."[2] The prelates, in their turn, "strive with this and other moneys acquired to aid and enrich their own nephews, who quickly spend it in the tavern or on a life of lust. Thus, concerning these goods, the prophecy of Micah (i, 7) is fulfilled, which says—'For they have been gathered of the hire of an harlot, and they shall return to the hire of an harlot'".[3] It is a vicious circle in which those who originally paid the money, and those who eventually spend it, seek to pursue the same vice unchecked. For the rest, through the "avarice and negligence of those who rule" in the Church, "almost every law, decree, decretal and constitution is annulled, unless it be lucrative of moneys".[4] If corporal punishment were given, as it should be, to those who break the commandments of God, then there might be some hope of reform. But as this brings no enrichment to the bishop's or archdeacon's purse, it is neglected.[5] The prelate who is

[1] Cf. here, *Poems* in Wright, Camden Soc. pp. 157, 326–7, 332, etc.

[2] s.v. "Adulterium". Cf. similarly, s.v. "Ministratio" (..."pro muneribus peccare permittunt..."), etc.; and with these the *Song on the Evil Times*, in Wright as above, p. 326: "And thise erchedekenes,... he wole take mede of that on and that other, And let the parson have a wyf and the prest another, at wille"; and Rolls S. vol. i, pp. 313, 324; etc. Also *Piers Plowman*, A text, pass. ii, ll. 154–5; B text, pass. ii, ll. 172–80; C text, pass. iii, ll. 187—91; *Poems of Jo. Audelay*, E.E.T.S. pp. 35–6; etc.

[3] s.v. "Munus".

[4] s.v. "Mandata". Cf. again: "de pena que est pecuniaria, magnam habent diligentiam...", etc. See also, s.v. "Correctio", passim (e.g.— "circa leges et decretales lucrativas pecuniarum non dormiunt;...circa leges vero et statuta, ubi nihil lucrari possunt, negligentes sunt...", etc.); "Lex", and "Ordo Clericalis". Similarly Rypon, MS. Harl. 4894, fol. 24b: "Sic, prothdolor!, quasi totum corpus ecclesie per avaritiam est infectum...".   [5] s.v. "Mundus", "Luxuria", etc.

slothful in all such correction, Bromyard declares to be a friend of the sinner, in consent with the sin, and therefore himself guilty of death.[1] "He who does not correct crimes is not to be called a bishop but a 'dirty dog' (*canis impudicus*)!" An actual instance is given of such episcopal connivance—"as was recently disclosed in the case of a certain man, who is reported to have given twenty pounds annually to a certain great prelate; so that, for the whole year, he remained with his concubine without fear of his fellows and secure from interference".[2] Finally, that particular severity shown towards the poor which forms the chief complaint of a metrical *Satire on the Consistory Courts*,[3] figures likewise in the Dominican's pages. Bromyard uses the fable of the innocent ass sentenced to beating and death by the lion in court to illustrate the fate which awaited those of humble rank. Therein he follows the example of the Franciscan Bozon in the early part of the same century,[4] and a homiletic tradition which has inspired the author of yet another *Song on the Times*[5].

But, alas! those who at the present time should rule the people rightly, on the contrary spare the haughty lion and beat the whelp, fight with the sword against the flies, and caress the wolves, which fact is manifest, as in every court where the ass is beaten. For the poor and the simple are harshly punished and oppressed, and the powerful escape. Concerning such Bernard speaks, dealing with that saying of Matthew xxiii [24]— "Ye blind guides, which strain at a gnat, and swallow a camel". "Our prelates", he says, "strain the gnat and swallow the camel".[6]

[1] s.v. "Correctio" (quoting Ambrose). Cf. Wm. of Rymyngton, MS. Bibl. Univ. Paris 790, fol. 109: "prelati tot mortibus digni sunt quot ad suos subditos perdicionis exempla transmittunt".
[2] s.v. "Munus". Cf. s.v. "Divitie", the story of the archdeacon pocketing the fines which should go to his bishop; also the Commons' Petition, 1372 (*Rot. Parl.* vol. ii, p. 314), to deprive any beneficed priest who lives openly with a concubine, if the Ordinary fails to do this after six months, and Chaucer's *Freres Tale.*
[3] Cf. Wright, Camden Soc. pp. 155, 157, 332, etc.
[4] See *Contes Moral.* cap. iv.   [5] Wright, ibid. pp. 195–202.
[6] s.v. "Correctio". Similarly in N. Bozon, cap. xxii. Cf. again the preacher of MS. Add. 41321, fol. 86: "In this blyndnesse ben prelates and curates of the chirche, that demeth a gretter synne and more scharpeli chastiseth hire peple for failynge of hire tithes, thanne for levynge of grevousere thynges of the lawe, that is, meercy, feith and doom. And

Even when the guilty have been sentenced to bodily punishment, "they come a little later to their judges, and offering money to them"[1] thus avoid the penalty. The "simple" on the other hand may be seen doing their penance naked in church and market-place, with other humiliations. In his righteous indignation, the preacher compares the ecclesiastical judges to "a rotten and feeble column", which, under the weight imposed on it, falls and crushes those beneath, "because it is either of bad marble or else 'crooked' and not 'straight'".[2] But even apart from courts and lawyers, whose easy facilities for divorce are also described in the *Summa*[3] as in the above-mentioned poem, "alas! all things are obedient to money", even where such a matter as church burials is concerned. As in the fable of the ass which secured burial in the churchyard for a gift of three marks bequeathed by it to the Ordinary, so, says our homilist, "many, less worthy than asses, for moneys accepted or hoped for, are buried in the holy place"— plunderers, usurers, and tyrants, in the very church itself— "thus making it, to the letter, a 'den of thieves'".[4] Evil

suche, seith Crist, techeth the peple bi hire ensaumple to size the gnatte and swolewe the camele". Cf. further, the thirteenth-century preacher quoted in Hauréau, *Not. et Extr.* vol. iv, p. 231.

[1] Cf. Wright, as above, for references, in the *Poems*, on the need for bribes here.

[2] s.v. "Justitia". Cf. the thirteenth-century Friar Minor, in Hauréau, *Not. et Extr.* vol. iv, p. 249.

[3] s.v. "Adulterium" ("Quando uxor displicet vel·alia concupiscitur propter pulchritudinem vel huiusmodi, divorcium procuratur. Primo clam per conspiratores vie excogitantur, falsi testes inducuntur et subornantur. Deinde ad capitula curritur ordinariorum, partes citantur, munera advocatis et judici offeruntur. Judici vero prima facie se reddenti difficilem minantur, parentela falsificata adducitur. Sic ergo quid muneribus, quid minis, quid falsitatibus separantur, et alia more ducitur ribaldorum: et sic precedente mendacio adulteria inundaverunt"), and "Juramentum". Cf. Bp. Brunton, MS. Harl. 3760, fol. 188 ("falsa divortia"), and Wimbledon (?) as below, p. 281: also with these *Piers Plowman*, B text, pass. ii, l. 175 ("devorses"), pass. xv, ll. 236–8, C text, pass. xxiii, ll. 138–9; *Poems of Jo. Audelay*, E.E.T.S. pp. 35–6; etc.

[4] s.v. "Dedicatio". The story appears also in MS. Roy. 7. D. 1, fol. 98, and MS. Add. 6716, fol. 21b, col. 2 (here of a bishop and a vicar). With it cf. the 15th-cent. *facetia* of Poggio, *Of the Curate who buried a Little Dog* (ed. Storer, p. 41).

priests could likewise rejoice at the funerals of their parishioners, "like parchment-makers rejoicing over the death of the sheep".[1] Where, asks Bromyard further, is a bishop ever found to neglect that law of the Church which grants him the procurations at the Dedication of Churches? Yet to other laws and decretals concerning piety, charity and the care of souls bishops give little heed.[2] "Through their cupidity they have now become the Devil's Procurators and the promoters of vice."[3] "There is no difference between them and the merchants, save that the bargains and sales of horses and other things, which merchants conduct openly, they do secretly in corners."[4]

The scramble for fat livings, that favourite theme alike of preachers and verse-makers, furnishes our Dominican Doctor with ample scope for his satire. Brunton's sketch of the insatiable cleric reappears here, again and again[5]—those, as he puts it, "who pile prebend upon prebend, when scarcely they can bear the weight of one",[6] and those who hope to end their days as "a bishop or a courtier at the court of prelates and princes".[7] Likewise, with the equally graphic and frequent description of "the young scholars, poor and often innocent in everything at the first, who before they grow rich are devout in their attendance at the churches, in their prayers and the many things they promise to God; but who, as soon as they have increased, and waxed fat and wealthy, repudiate God, their maker". Such Bromyard compares to the dog that sits diligently watching those who are eating at meal-time until he receives his morsel, then promptly turns his back on the company to enjoy it.[8] More vivid and entertaining still are the

---

[1] s.v. "Invidia".   [2] s.v. "Luxuria".   [3] s.v. "Mundus".
[4] s.v. "Prelatio" (prelates permitting markets in churches, and bargaining over benefices, etc.). For their extravagant vanities, e.g. in tournaments, jousts, clothing, adornment, worldly honours and lusts, cf. further, s.v. "Divitiae", etc.
[5] See s.v. "Dominatio", "Acquisitio mala", etc.
[6] s.v. "Avaritia". Cf. in Hauréau, *Not. et Extr.* vol. iii, p. 228 (12th cent.).
[7] s.v. "Dominatio".
[8] s.v. "Amor Carnalis". Similarly, s.v. "Operatio" and "Ordo Clericalis". Cf. *Poem* in Wright, Camden Soc. p. 230, and *Twenty-six Pol. and other Poems*, E.E.T.S. p. 61 (c. 1418).

snatches of current conversation that allow us to listen to the very phrases of these worldlings. Thus

the greedy think to extinguish their greed, when they say—"If only I had...one church or prebend, I should never want any more". But when they have got it, they start complaining that the place is in a bad atmosphere, or too near the high-road which brings them too many guests, or too far away from a good town, or else because there is no pasture or wood or fish there. Therefore they must have another place where they can have pastures for the summer, and fire-wood for the winter, and a third, where they can spend Lent and have fish. In addition they must have another prebend in their own district.

So the fire grows with each fresh log; so the ill-greased cart squeaks the more, the more it carries; so the dog waits for his bone "with great longing", and then looks for another as soon as he has swallowed the first! He who has a horse must then have a bit and saddle for it. He who has land needs many servants to work it.[1] "They litigate, they plead, they go to diverse courts—even to Rome itself—with many toils and expenses, for benefices, prebends and earthly gain." But where are they seen to do such things for the good of souls?[2] We listen again and hear the sycophants actually pleading for their particular protégé: "'So-and-so, our young relative, is so charming and well-read' (although, as a matter of fact, he may be the worst kind of lecher and illiterate). 'Do give him such-and-such a benefice, or write for him to such-and-such an one for a vacant church!'"[3] With ruthless satire Bromyard exposes all such monsters. He compares prelates who secure benefices for their young relatives or subservient clerks to the thieves who employ a boy to clamber through narrow apertures and let them in where they cannot find entry themselves. Just as the fool in the story set a cat to guard his cheese from the ravages of the mice, "so the same can be said of fatuous patrons and prelates, who hand over souls to be guarded from the

---

[1] s.v. "Avaritia". Cf. in MS. Add. 21253, fol. 6: "isti clerici, isti ypocrite et papelardi, qui non sompniant nisi in prebendis habendis et honoribus et dignitatibus ecclesiasticis"; and abroad, Nic. de Biard (13th cent.), in Hauréau, *Not. et Extr.* vol. vi, p. 2.

[2] s.v. "Ordo Clericalis".

[3] s.v. "Adulator", and much more in a similar vein, s.v. "Electio". Cf. *The Complaint of the Ploughman* in Wright, Rolls S. vol. i, p. 315.

demons into the care of wicked incumbents, who make worse destruction of them than the demons themselves: for the latter would not commit so many acts of fornication, nor give so many bad examples as they do".[1] Hear him again, for example, upon the methods of those whom he calls the "foxy" type of scheming hypocrites—"to be found first and foremost amongst unpromoted clerics, or those who desire higher promotion...."

Foxy they may be called, because, as it is told of the fox in the fable that he lay down in the road and pretended to be dead, so that he might be put into the cart and eat the poultry which it was carrying,...so the hypocrites pretend to be modest, humble, compliant and dead, as it were, to all vices and sins, especially in the eyes of those who can assist them further to the thing they are panting after, in order that they may be set in offices and promoted.

The very words they use with which to cloak their guile are at once true and false, as when they declare themselves unworthy, or even unwilling at the first, to forward their own ends. Nevertheless, "after they have got what they wanted... they show their real quality". But if anyone else tells them the real truth about themselves, they get angry at once, in spite of all their "humble" speech.[2] Others, who "have been already detected from some past action as 'foxy', pretend that they have wholly put away that manner of life", and are now reformed.[3] Such prove to be as the Priests of Baal, ruthless to those under them; "and such come to the holy war of the Church as a horse to the stable, for the sake of their 'stall', to eat and grow fat".[4] The ambitious and worthless who thus climb to high office in the Church, through influence of some powerful prelate or patron whom they have bribed or served, Bromyard compares to the ivy clinging to the wall and climbing thus to the church roof, only to damage the cement and ruin the building.[5] There is no manner of lying and deceit to which they will not condescend, to get their own way:

[1] s.v. "Prelatio". The story is in Jacq. de Vitry, and *Spec. Laic.* cap. xi.
[2] s.v. "Humilitas"; cf. also, s.v. "Ministratio"; *Jacob's Well*, E.E.T.S. ed. p. 74, and MS. Harl. 45, fol. 39.
[3] s.v. "Ipocrisis".   [4] s.v. "Bellum" and "Ministratio".
[5] s.v. "Ascensio". Cf. further, on this vice, *Ayenb. of Inwyt*, p. 42.

One will obtain an ecclesiastical benefice or Order before he is of lawful age, because it is stated on oath that he is of lawful age.[1] Another will obtain his benefice in simoniacal fashion, as happens when someone suspected of Simony—because he has given something for the benefice to which he is being presented, and has been summoned before the bishop to clear the aspersion on oath—swears with his compurgators that he never gave anything, nor knew of anyone who had given on his behalf.[2]

Of beneficed clergy *as a whole* our Dominican declares—"If they could receive without order or priesthood or celebration of masses that benefice which the promoted or that stipend which priests get with order and priesthood, scarce a hundredth part of them would be ordained".[3] Wellnigh all of them are merely after what they can get.

Did space permit, we should have to follow Bromyard further as he censures with equal force and minuteness the other characteristic vices of his fellow-clergy. Now it is "the swine, that is, those leading a swinish life in the Church", that he is attacking.[4] We recognize them as the oft-depicted evil "prelates and clergy who consume the goods of the Church that are owed to the poor upon illicit uses, namely on prostitutes, actors and relations, to enrich them out of the patrimony of Christ",[5] while they themselves "celebrate scarce once a year, or never at all".[6]

---

[1] Cf. here, again, Bp. Brunton, MS. Harl. 3760, fol. 143b: "Alius ante legitimam etatem lucratur beneficium curatum, quia juravit eum etatis legitime extitisse. Alius optinet beneficium per fictum titulum sic juratum, cum tamen in veritate nullum titulum habet".

[2] s.v. "Juramentum". Cf. s.v. "Electio"; and MS. Add. 41321, fols. 68–68b: "If a prelatie or a personage be voide of a pastour, or any other cure that nedithe of a hed,...with symonie of selver, or with lordis ceelis,...in stede of a good man, [they] sette a schrewe on benche". Also MS. Add. 21253, fol. 14: "Omnes illi qui emunt spiritualia pro temporalibus, ut sunt illi qui dant militibus et aliis pecuniam muneratam ut conferant eis aliquam ecclesiam".   [3] s.v. "Ordo Clericalis".

[4] s.v. "Electio". Similarly s.v. "Ordo Clericalis" ("sicut porcus in luto vilitatis et carnalitatis").

[5] s.v. "Munus". Cf. s.v. "Arma", and "Ordo Clericalis"; also *Old Engl. Homs.* (12th cent.), E.E.T.S. O.S. no. 53, pp. 31 and 163; *Jacob's Well*, p. 211; MS. Harl. 2398, fol. 104, etc.; and other excerpts in my *Preaching in Med. Engl.* pp. 42, 43, 125, and here below. With these cf. *Piers Plowman*, C Text, pass. xviii, ll. 66–71.

[6] s.v. "Missa" and "Ordo Clericalis".

The priests of Bel[1] and Judas[2] fed their own wives and legitimate sons out of the patrimony of the Temple. But these from the patrimony of Christ nourish the wives and clothe the adulteresses of others and harlots also, and maintain illegitimate sons—future robbers and imitators of their fathers' crime. For, if they remained in secular society, they would not be able to support legitimate wives of their own on account of their poverty. Therefore they get ordained, so that they may support strange women and themselves out of the goods of Christ....

Wherefore, in very truth, it is to be feared that, when one takes into account the number of the clergy in proportion to that of the people, in no profession or so large a multitude of the people is there to be found so putrid a section, so many damned of any status as there are of damnable clergy. The evidence of this damnation lies in the fact that not only does their own sin involve themselves, but it is also a cause of damnation to others. For, if now any reprove the people for lechery, usury, drunkenness or any vice whatever, immediately they hold up some one of the clergy as a shield of excuse for their conduct. Wherefore, it would seem to follow that the infamy of the clergy is more harmful than their sin: because by the sin he alone perishes who sins; but by the infamy thereof, many....

In modern times, our homilist continues, the image of Christ in the person of pure and virtuous rector, vicar and priest has now in some parts been replaced by the idol and image of Venus, with the result that popular devotion and the giving of tithes and offerings cease, and loss, detraction and damnation increase.

Sometimes, indeed, this is openly shown by the people's words.... They reply—"Why should I give tithe to a rector who keeps a concubine; and why should I help a church in which all the ministers are polluted?", or "How should I lead a clean life, when I have so many foul examples before me?"...It would be better [adds Bromyard] that the church should have no minister at all, than such an one who defiles his flock and the Church's status, violates Christianity and leaves the community desolate with sin and vengeance...."Woe, woe upon my sanctuary, because it is profaned!"[3]

On the other hand, we read that "when the bishop or someone else in office strives to correct the infernal hog, the latter complains, as it were, of the injury done to him; and all his accomplices and supporters rise up against the corrector, and persecute him with words and sometimes with blows".[4] Some ecclesiastics, we are told, were actually in the habit of arguing from

---

[1] See Dan. xiv, 9–20: Vulg. version.   [2] Cf. Jo. xii, 6.
[3] s.v. "Ordo Clericalis" (Ezek. xxv, 3). Cf. Rymyngton, as below, pp. 274–5.   [4] s.v. "Correctio".

the *Decretum* that "for those who have no wife it is lawful
to have a concubine!"[1] Small wonder, then, that Bromyard
is forced to declare, like the poet Gower after him, that the
inchastity of the priesthood is a scandal and a cause of ruin
to the whole country.[2]

An astounding picture is drawn for us in this sermon-encyclopaedia of some of "the homes of ecclesiastical men, which
not merely women, but those who by a truer as by a more
special name are called prostitutes not only enter but dwell in
for days and nights". "When these things are seen and considered," comments our author here pertinently, "it is no
wonder if the ruin of the Temple of the Church and of all
spiritual Christianity follows."[3] He does not even hesitate to
repeat in another place the story "which a most famous master
in Theology told, when preaching to the University" of a
certain woman who wrought a rector's downfall by sending
her daughter to the rectory, dressed up for the occasion,
ostensibly to fetch the washing.[4] Some of these so-called
pastors, we are informed,

more readily lead hounds and falcons to the chace than Christians to
devotion: and, what is worse, lead more flocks to the Devil by their wicked
conduct and example than to God by preaching or holiness of life....
More do they abound in eatings and drinkings[5] than do lay-people as
a rule, and they are more given up to idleness: for neither in bodily nor
in spiritual things do they know how to occupy themselves usefully.
Whence follow the aforesaid vices.... Daily one hears how the *curatus*
diligently examines his servants when they come to him, enquiring what
sheep, lambs, sheaves they have, and whether they have as many that
year as they had last, and how many Marks he owns, and how many
he can levy, and how they can sell everything at a better price.

Rarely or never, however, are they heard to enquire about the
souls of their subjects and their spiritual condition. When
tithes of milk, calves and the like are not rightly paid, they

---

[1] See s.v. "Luxuria".   [2] s.v. ibid.

[3] s.v. "Ordo Clericalis". For a concrete example of this license, cf.
the 13th-cent. Evesham case described in Coulton, *Five Cent. of Relig.*
vol. ii, pp. 372–3 (cf. also, p. 357, etc.).

[4] s.v. "Luxuria".

[5] Elsewhere in the same chapter, Bromyard observes—"Those who
drink a bottle or a flagon in a day do not give a quart or a pint to God in
a fortnight".

are frequently heard and seen to make complaint to bishops
and their officials, demanding letters of citation and excommunication against the offenders. When the Commandments
of God are broken, with no chance of temporal gain for themselves, rarely or never are they known to interfere.[1] Scarcely
is there an illiterate priest who cannot cite the *De Canonica
Portione*. But the laws which prohibit sacrilege and concubinage
he cheerfully neglects.[2] "Among forty who know the *Canones
Pecuniales* so well, there is not one who knows the *Canones
Poenitentiales*, which they are obliged to know".[3]

They look after their church as men look after an orchard or its produce.
While there is fruit in it, it is diligently guarded, and that on account of
its fruit. So, while there are sheaves in the field at autumn time, custodians
of the church are multiplied in their houses, and look after the sheaves
as well they know how, giving orders to their servants, as Pilate gave
orders to the Jews—"Go, guard it as you know!"—Matth. xxvii [65]....
In which matter, because frequently they have no confidence in them,
they themselves take care to be present personally if they can, by every
possible means, so that the fruit may be the better collected and guarded.
But in Lent and at other times when it is the autumn of souls, such an
one is in no wise to be found there. But he is at the courts or the schools,
or is residing elsewhere to save expense....
Daily experience shows that if at any time a poor man or a pilgrim
come to such a man's house, begging alms, the farmer or bailiff will
make reply—"My master is not at home". (Lo, there is no man in his
house![4]) To whom the poor man answers—"And where is your master?"
Says the other to him—"At the king's court or at the court of some other
prelate or prince, or at Oxford, or Paris, or Bologna". (Lo, he has gone
a long journey![4]) Says the poor man—"Is there no one who could help
us with alms for love of God?" The other answers—"He has sold up
everything, and taken the money with him". (Behold how he took with
him a bag of money![5]) Says the poor man again—"When will he come
home?" The other replies—"In the autumn we hope for his return".
(Lo, how he will return on the day of the full moon![5])[6]

"When once ordained", says our pulpit satirist elsewhere,
"they try to be absent from their flock as much as possible....
So much so, that they appear to have made a compact and

[1] s.v. "Ordo Clericalis".   [2] s.v. "Luxuria".
[3] s.v. "Correctio" (mentioning specifically, under the heading of
Canon. Pecun., the *Constitutio Bonifaciana de Canonica Portione*).
[4] See Prov. vii, 19.   [5] See Prov. vii, 20.
[6] s.v. "Ordo Clericalis". With this whole passage, cf. *Piers Plowman*,
C text, pass. xvii, ll. 363–4.

indenture between them and the demons, to the effect that they
themselves should have the wool and milk of their sheep, that
is, the temporal benefits, and that the devils should have the
souls of them."[1] In the same vivid passage and in others like
it we are afforded further glimpses of the unbecoming appearance of these sons of Satan. "They are ashamed of the tonsure.
Therefore they cultivate a fashionable head of hair, or have a
small tonsure, so as not to be recognized as priests." They
"put on a garment which in colour or form is too secular";
and go "resplendent in wondrously-wrought clothing, with
long beard and hair after the manner of a comet".[2]

Of monks and monasteries, the *Summa Predicantium* tells an
equally sinister tale.

If two men come to a monastery gate, one of whom has a devil with
him—because, that is to say, he is a plunderer, a usurer and a most evil
fornicator—but nevertheless is in a position of authority to be able to
do temporal harm to the convent, the great gate is at once opened to
him. All will go forth to wait upon him with beaming countenance and
fair speeches (although, none the less, he is really being received with the
most unwilling heart and private execrations), and will procure for him
dainty meats and drinks and beds and everything else in superfluity, along
with his horses and dogs and his huge retinue of servants. But indeed
if the other comes on foot, without horses and dogs and with the appearance of poverty, even to the very gate of those who have been
founded for the express purpose of giving hospitality on behalf of the
souls of their founders—for which reason they have received broad
estates and copious revenues—and asks in the name of Christ,[3] yea, even
although, as a man of good life, he bring Christ with him, yet he will
find the gate shut, and the porter hostile, who will either completely
shut him out, or, after long discussions, excuses and murmurings may
reluctantly let him in. Once inside he will find everyone with a sour
face and slanderous speech, the food poor, the guest-house and dorter
cold, and the bed hard....[4]

[1] s.v. "Custodia".
[2] s.v. "Custodia", "Gratitudo", "Inconstantia", "Ordo Clericalis",
etc. Cf. Absalon of St Victor (12th cent.), in Hauréau, *Not. et Extr.*
vol. iv, p. 30, and further below, p. 277, etc.: in Engl. verse, e.g., a ballad
against Clerical Attire, in MS. Harl. 372, fol. 113; Wright, *Pol. Songs*,
Rolls S. vol. i, pp. 307, 331-2, etc., and Camden Soc. pp. 328-9; Fairholt,
Percy Soc. pp. 56-7.   [3] Cf. Rule of St Benedict, cap. liii.
[4] s.v. "Hospitalitas". With this cf. the exactly similar account in the
Poem on the Evil Times, in Wright, Camden Soc. pp. 329-30; also the
worldly abbots here and in the sermon quoted below, p. 263, note 3.

When Religious houses had suffered at the hands of extortionate nobles, we read, they were in the habit of stopping their almsgiving to the poor. "It is wonderful!"—exclaims Bromyard; "The Devil harms them, and they revenge themselves upon God, by expelling him from their gate!"[1] Our Dominican, as he notices in his travels the half-ruined state of some of these convents, house falling upon house, the tumbled-down barns, the impoverished lands and manors, the roofless buildings at the mercy of the rain and in utter disorder, is driven to see in it all the signs of God's departure.

For, as the ruined manor of a temporal lord is the sign that he is generally absent from that place, and as a paleness of the members is the sign of a frigidity and indisposition of the stomach, so ruin in ecclesiastical houses signifies the absence of God, and adversity in external goods signifies the extinction of interior warmth and charity.

Little wonder that monasticism had fallen on such evil days, when we read further in these same pages of indolent monks, drawn mainly from the dregs of high society,[2] living in luxury and wantonness and the neglect of true worship.[3] The hypocrite clad "in the garments of Religion" is here cleverly satirized by means of a vivid little English anecdote:

[1] s.v. "Eleemosyna".

[2] Cf., e.g., s.v. "Adventus" ("The worst is given to God. If they have a son who is weak or deaf or crooked, he will become a Religious..."), and see further below, p. 382.

[3] s.v. "Paupertas" et "Religio". I have refrained from giving quotations from these, as they will be found in Dr Coulton's second vol. of *Five Cent. of Relig.* pp. 400–1, and 576–81. Cf. further MS. Heref. Cath. Libr. P. 5. 2 (unpubl., early 14th-cent. sermon), fol. 75: "Sic abbates qui nunquam in conventu jacent vel comedunt vel divinum officium audiunt. Onus quod conventus sustinet temperare nesciunt. Sed certe seculares sunt hodie omnes abbates, prout ex eorum conversacione apparet, secularibus actibus totaliter et eciam hominibus adherentes, per vias transeuntes non ut patres monasteriorum set domini castellorum, nec rectores ecclesiarum set domini provinciarum..."; (fol. 75 b): "Set timendum est quod multi monachi hiis diebus sequuntur aliam naturam nubis" (falling as rain, to be turned to mud, etc.). This is from a *Sermo inter Religiosos,* c. 1320 (?). Cf. also Gascoigne, *Loci e Libro Verit.* p. 143, etc. For the *Poems,* cf. Wright, Camden Soc. p. 329; Rolls S. vol. i, pp. 334–6; *Piers Plowman,* B text, pass. x, ll. 306 et seq., C text, pass. vi, ll. 157 et seq., etc.; and Chaucer's "Monk" (abbot?), *Cant. Tales, Prol.* ll. 165-207: see D. Knowles, *Relig. Orders in Engl.,* vol. ii, p. 366.

A certain man as he entered the hall of a nobleman, seeing an ape in front of him dressed up in the silken garments of one of the children, thought it was actually his lord's own son, because it had its back to him at the time. When he was addressing it with due reverence, he discovered that it was an ape that was grinning at him. "Curse you!", said he to it, "I thought that you were Jankyn, my lord's son!"[1]

Truly, as others remark, "the habyte makyth noȝt the relygyous".[2]

It would not be fair to quit this great storehouse of Dominican preaching without giving one or two further examples of the more developed satire of which its author is capable. Undoubtedly one of the most brilliant examples occurs in a long indictment of the sins of the greater clergy.

They knew [says the writer] that those substitutes [whom they had placed in their parishes] were too slothful and insufficient to guard the souls [committed to their care] and to rescue the prey from the Devil's mouth. They knew, too, on the other hand, that the Devil carries off souls by earth and by air, by water and by fire. Therefore they have provided themselves with the swiftest hounds that run upon the earth, so that the Devil should not make away with the souls of parishioners by that route. Likewise, with falcons and birds that travel by air and by the waters, lest they should escape in those regions....So, men of this kind protect those who bring them dogs and falcons, rich gifts and fruits; but the poor, who bring only their own souls, they love not.[3]

On another occasion we listen to an amusing caricature of the self-important prelates and clerics who think themselves indispensable in the particular office which they hold, and imagine that no one else could do the work which they have to do, or at least do it so well. Such are like the lunatic (Atlas), of whom the story-books tell, who imagined that he was holding up the heavens with his hands, and that if he put them down for an hour, even to eat, the heavens would fall and the earth be destroyed. Yet, if they were removed by death or other circumstances, "and another column, that is, a useful person set in their place, the house would no more fall than before; nay rather the work might be better done than it was formerly".[4]

---

[1] s.v. "Ipocrisis".
[2] *Jacob's Well* (unpubl.), MS. Salisb. Cath. Libr. 103, fol. 122b; cf. similarly MS. Harl. 45, fol. 135b, and *Ayenbite of Inwyt*, pp. 165, 243; etc. ("Habitus non facit monachum").
[3] s.v. "Custodia".   [4] s.v. "Ministratio".

Equally amusing is the description of the hypocritical clergy who win their way

after the manner of kites, which, as they ascend, cry with a charming and spiritual voice, saying, "Fi! fi! fi!", as if they cared nothing for the whole world, and as if they were so spiritual and intent on the things of God that they neither cared for nor contemplated temporal affairs, and in no way sought their own. But as soon as they have spied a corpse, they descend with all haste upon it; and then once more hungry ascend on high, so that they may sight their prey from a distance the more easily.[1]

The servile flatterers in the Church are compared to the little lap-dogs that follow their masters and mistresses about, fawning with their tails, as great dogs, reared to protect the sheepfolds, rarely do. They are like the chameleon, which is said to adapt its colour to what it sees, or "the weathercock on the belfry that turns its beak at every wind".[2] If the reader has any doubts as to the force of this grand indictment, he cannot do better than turn himself to our orthodox Dominican's chapter on *Ordo Clericalis*, from which not a few of the previous quotations have been taken. Here, in a work remarkable for its own length, is the longest chapter of all, composed of no less than eighty sections. From beginning to end, with little respite, it is one long-drawn cry of anguish and bitter complaint over the state of the clergy, amplified by all the powers of similitude and satire of which our pulpit was then capable. In a single section, for example, negligent and evil clerics are compared to wicked physicians, blind leaders, a sick stomach, a diseased root, blind blood-letters, a sun eclipsed, the smoke of an extinguished candle. The antiquity of much of this traditional pulpit language will be gauged from a study of the sources quoted. These include Eusebius of Caesarea, Ambrose, Chrysostom, Augustine, Jerome, and above all Gregory the Great and Bernard of Clairvaux, as well as Canon Law and Scripture itself. A final question remains to be answered: Bromyard speaks openly of evidence that the very infidels are now scandalized by the Church's corruption, whilst "other

[1] s.v. "Ascensio". Cf. the 13th-cent. Domin. Amand de St-Quentin, in Hauréau, *Not. et Extr.* vol. iv, p. 202.
[2] s.v. "Adulatio". See also the example cited below, p. 317. Cf. the servile councillors in *Rich. the Redeles*, ll. 111-2, E.E.T.S. ed. p. 528.

Christian princes and lords of ecclesiastical rank seeing her
miserable dissolution and most open ruin and infamy" pour
scorn on her ministry and strive to spoil her. But was there
yet a ray of hope? The present state of the clergy moves our
Dominican to declare—"Truly, it is to be feared that in this
disaster the disease of the Church is rendered incurable".[1]
Already the night was come.

In the sermons of a learned Austin friar, contemporary of
John Bromyard, one Doctor John Waldeby, we find the same
fierce spirit of denunciation, the same outspoken discussion
of clerical vices. In a discourse on the text—"The Days are
Evil",[2] for example, he bewails the prevalence of gluttony[3]
and lust amongst those who quit the school of the true philosophy of Christ for "the Devil's school, in this our University".[4] Alas! they pass into the ranks of both secular and
regular clergy. Officials of archdeacons and deans to-day "cite,
excommunicate, and spoil the poor and simple, who are not
strong enough to resist"; but give license to those fornicators
who give them money to fornicate as they please. Hypocrisy
and a "feigned holiness", he says, "if I mistake not, are in-
toxicating the English Church". Lying has become an "art",
in which the most proficient now ranks as the great man of
the day. "This duplicity knows how to subvert kings and
kingdoms, make schisms in the Church, pervert peace and stir up
war, and—what is worst—transform good into evil, and truth
into falsehood....Never, as it seems, did this pernicious duplicity reign as it does to-day among the people of our nation".[5]

<hr/>

[1] s.v. "Ordo Clericalis", §68. Cf. Bernard, *Sermo in Cantic.* 33.

[2] MS. Caius Coll. Camb. 334, fols. 196 et seq.

[3] "Sed prohdolor! diebus hiis hec gula censetur jocunditas; et plerisque
clericis et etiam religiosis videtur deesse bona societas, si non ad crapulam
vel ebrietatem pertrahatur ipsa gulositas."

[4] I.e. Oxford ("Adeo namque convaluit hec scola diabolica in univer-
sitate nostra,...quod quis non estimatur in sua facultate proficere ac
nomen laudis cum aliis merite possidere, nisi cum talibus Epycuri
discipulis valeat, sciat, et velit carni ac sanguini complacere. Et ob hanc
causam, ut timeo, inter alias decrevit nostra Universitas..."). Cf. also,
in my *Preaching in Med. Engl.* pp. 34-5.

[5] Similarly in MS. Camb. Univ. Libr. Ii. iii. 8, fol. 148 (Wimbledon).
Cf. here, *Piers Plowman*, C text, pass xxii, l. 457.

So the unending stream of complaint rolls on its way, from sermon to sermon. "The strong men of Israel, that is, all his subjects, are slain by the wicked example of their own prelate"; and "evil and lascivious priests" squander the alms of the faithful on foul pursuits.[1] If we turn to the Franciscans, and take as typical representative preachers of our period friars Staunton[2] and 'Nicole' Bozon, in the first half of the fourteenth century, and friar Nicholas Philip, a hundred years later, we shall find the same tradition maintained in much the same language. Staunton, inveighing against the lechery of the clergy, declares—

But, alas! it is to be feared that what Paul says to the Corinthians [x, 8] is now generally applicable to the priests.... For those priests who should be most spotless upon the breast of God have now become most foul in the Devil's service. For with those hands with which at night they handle the prostitute's flesh, with those same hands, I say, in the daytime they handle the Flesh of Salvation[3]....But, alas! it must be bewailed of many priests, that those who should be an example of good conversation in good works now have become an example of perdition in their own evil examples and evil works, of whom it may be said in the words of Jude in his epistle [v. 18]—"There shall come mockers in the last time, walking after their own ungodly lusts"[4]....

In the solemn language of Staunton, who has also some bitter things to say against prelate and bishop,[5] we miss that vein of satiric humour which characterizes a good deal of the

[1] Cf. MS. Roy. 7. E. ii, fol. 31; and MS. Caius Coll. Camb. 334, fol. 155, etc. (what they spend thus on their prostitutes should be given to the poor).

[2] For the approximate date of this author of the *Tractate on the Ten Commandments* here quoted, see my art. on "Some Franciscan Memorials at Gray's Inn", in the *Dublin Review*, vol. 176, April 1925, p. 280, n. 2. Dr A. G. Little suggests that he is Wm Staunton, 51st Master of the Friars Minor at Cambridge (see *Engl. Hist. Rev.* April 1927, p. 277).

[3] Similarly Nich. Philip, as quoted in my *Preaching in Med. Engl.* p. 250, n. 1; Bozon, *Metaphs.* cap. xxii (5th hound); Anon. MS. Heref. Cath. Libr. P. 5. 2, fol. 77; Wm of Rymyngton, MS. Bibl. Univ. Paris 790, fol. 114 ("qui eisdem manibus et eodem ore de die pertractat et recipit gloriosum corpus et sanguinem Jhu. Christi quibus nocte precedente membra meretricis et eius spurcitias pertractavit") and again fol. 106b; Jo. Myrc, *Man. Sacerd.* lib. i, cap. xvi; etc., etc.

[4] MS. Gray's Inn Libr. 15, fols. 52b–53b.

[5] Cf. *Preaching in Med. Engl.* p. 67.

Mendicant preaching. For this we must turn to the sermon-outlines of his contemporary Nicholas Bozon. Bozon, indeed, is not so much concerned with the sins of the clergy as with those of the oppressive layman. None the less, as one who "spares the powerful and strong, and strips the simple folk", the rich prelate is now and again the butt of his typical scorn and complaint. Such he compares to "the tree that bears large nuts, also has large and very bitter leaves and is of evil smell and worse taste, whose shade is so dangerous that it causes divers diseases in those who rest under it". As for their pride and partiality for the great, the prelates at their ease, he says, are bold like the snail that pushes out its horns when in safe company, only to withdraw them hurriedly when threatened by opposition. While they fawn on the mighty, they bully the poor: "Wherefore said the sheep to the crow that sat on her back and tore her wool—'You would not do so to the mastiff that is called Griffin!'"[1] No more terrible example of satire and rebuke is to be found, perhaps, in the whole literature of the English pulpit, than in one of the synodal sermons preached by the Franciscan Nicholas Philip. Parts of this sermon have already been quoted in the present author's first volume. But, in addition, we find Philip declaring[2] that

now most priests indulge more in sensual pleasure than do the burgesses, more in harshness than soldiers, more in finery and vanity than women, and more in levity and wit than actors....For already that prophecy of Isaiah [xxiv, 2] has been fulfilled—"As with the people, so with the priest". "But would that he were no worse!", adds Bernard[3]....This, chiefest of all, destroys the Church, namely, that we see the laity are better than the clergy. For the layman would be horrified to spend his goods and his time as do the ecclesiastics on the lusts of the flesh and the vanities of the world.

[1] See *Metaphs.* cap. iv, xxii, xxiii, xciii, cxix, cxxii, cxxxiv, cxliv.
[2] MS. Bodl. Lat. Th. d. i, fol. 87b.
[3] Repeated again and again in our sermons: cf. Anon. *Old Engl. Homs.* (12th cent.), E.E.T.S. O.S. no. 53, p. 163, Mannyng (*Hand. Synne*), John of Mirfield, Bromyard, William of Rymyngton, Rypon, Wimbledon, Myrc, Folsham, Philip, etc., also Anon. MS. Roy. 18. B. xxiii, fol. 91: "And therefore seis seynte Bernard of suche prestes, ... 'A! lorde, ... howe, even as the werst of the peple is, so is the preeste now adaies' ". Rymyngton adds (MS. Bibl. Univ. Paris 790, fol. 113b)—"Set quod dolendum est—'sicut *peior* de populo, sic sacerdos'".

Such are priests of Baal in their pride: "For so greedily do priests labour to heap together more benefices, offices, pensions and the like, that some of them would seem to desire to be as another god". Moreover, they are the priests of Dagon, he says, in their lust for temporalities:

For whom do they collect them, I ask? Certainly not to feed their parishioners, the poor and the weak, but to promote their own nephews, their sons and prostitutes; not to expend them upon study or on books, but to buy birds and palfreys; not upon the apparel of their altars, but upon the clothing of their mistresses,[1] whom many of them keep—not, however, in hiding, but all too openly, as do other public fornicators, to the blaspheming of God, the scandal of the world, the contempt of their order, and their own infamy.

So ignorant are they, that they are quite unable to correct popular errors in belief.[2] The friar's fury reaches its climax in a satirical comparison bordering on the indecent. As climbing monkeys display the "turpitudinem posteriorum", so do these worldly priests—"to the derision of men". "The church has brought many apes from Tarsis",[3] he comments. "So is it with such priests unworthily promoted to prelacy!"[4]

Exchanging now the word of the friar for that of the monk, we pass to the sermons of Master Robert Rypon, sub-prior of Durham, once the Benedictine prior of Finchale, and another enemy of Lollards. Fortunately, however, there is no further need to repeat at length the old accusations which here cluster, as thickly as ever, about his synodal orations. Rypon is a more ponderous and unoriginal orator, but little given to satire, or sermon embroidery of any kind other than endless quotations from the ancient Fathers and homilists. In the earlier part of his series he deals with the prelates: "For a surety, I dare to say in all fear that Lucifer sits among many of them, 'for their works do follow them'[5] (Apoc. xiv, 13). And in truth it seems

---

[1] Cf. here the detailed account given in *Old Engl. Homs.* (12th cent.), 2nd Ser. E.E.T.S. O.S. no. 53, p. 163.

[2] fol. 88. Cf. here a 13th-cent. Mendicant, in Hauréau, vol. iv, p. 243.

[3] See 1 Kings x, 22, and 2 Chron. ix, 21.

[4] fol. 88b. See further in my *Preaching in Med. Engl.* pp. 249–50.

[5] Cf. the monastic homilist of MS. Add. 21253, fol. 54: Evil prelates as "the Devil's hunting nets"—"per quorum malum exemplum diabolus venatur multos laicos cum illis".

to some that Anti-Christ draws near". Very naturally the latter
will subvert the higher ecclesiastics first, so that the lesser will
be an easier prey for him later on. Further signs of his coming
are to be seen in the Papal Schism—"a division in the Church
which has indeed now persisted for a long time",[1] and the
appearance of the Lollards and other false schismatics.[2] As for
the anti-pope—"whoever he shall have been—he may rightly
be called 'the servant of the servants of the Devil', along with
the rest of his subjects, whether patriarchs or cardinals, who
cling to him in schism". Some even believe, says Rypon, that
he is Anti-Christ himself.[3] A stray shaft of satirical wit pierces
the Benedictine's account of the higher ecclesiastics aforesaid.
"After a little while, the horns of pride begin to grow on them",
he says, "upon the countenance, in gesture, and with subtle
adornment. They give themselves up to banquetings, fowlings,
huntings and other frivolities.[4] Rarely do they celebrate masses;
for their own 'cures' they care not, copying that rule of the
law—'He who does anything through another, evidently does
it himself'." Others hoard up the money given them "in a
napkin", like the servant in the parable, and do nothing. These,
says Master Rypon, are "like a certain demon—in English
Thrus [?]—whom Bromyard[5] calls Gerard, who was wont to
grind corn. But when some householder gave him a new tunic,
and he put it on, from that time onwards he refused to grind,
saying in English—'Suld syche a proude grome grynd corne?',
that is to say, 'No!' Thus, too, such men, when clothed in a
priestly vestment, refuse to serve God or man, save with the

[1] On fol. 55 of this MS. (Harl. 4894) Rypon says: "quod scisma
duravit jam per 32 annos...", i.e. 1410, if this reckoning is not
that of the later scribe of the MS. "A.D. 1401" is the date actually
mentioned in one of these sermons. See my *Preaching in Med. Engl.*
p. 208.

[2] MS. Harl. 4894, fol. 40.

[3] fol. 55.

[4] Cf. again, fol. 194 ("amplam habent familiam, nobiles apparatus
equorum, faleras, accipitres, venationes, aleas, negociationes", etc.—
from Bernard); similarly, in fol. 207b, adding significantly—"novit
mundus!".

[5] See *S.P.* s.v. "Servire", § 8 ("qui Gerardum se nominavit");
repeated s.v. "Divitiae".

greatest sloth".[1] There is lurking humour also in the familiar little sketch of the tireless clerical aspirant who celebrates "almost daily", sweats at his Biblical studies, and preaches to help the neighbouring "curates"—all to win a benefice and a perpetual holiday for the rest of his days.[2] In the actual vehemence of his complaints, Rypon certainly gives place to none. "Sicut populus, sic sacerdos: populus insolens, insolentior est sacerdos." "In truth", he declares, "there is no type of sin among the people that is not current among the clergy—and even worse."[3] The sloth, insolence, and pride of the priesthood are the undoing of the laity. Some, who rarely or never go near their livings, "the more greedily exact" the fruits of them, "so that they may live the more luxuriously in courts, universities, or cities". Others "decorate and adorn their own halls, chambers and beds more sumptuously than the altars of their church". Others again, throw their devotions to oblivion and immerse themselves in various worldly occupations. "Are not the goods of the Church, through the insolence and pride of the priests, notably consumed amongst the great men of the world, nay rather amongst their own relatives and nephews, not to mention their sons and daughters, their concubines and harlots?"[4] A famous satirical passage from St Bernard[5] is quoted, which depends for much of its force and point upon a favourite medieval form of Latin punning. It tells of the clergy, how you may see them daily glittering like the prostitute, arrayed like actors (or minstrels), with the trappings of a king. More brightly gleam their spurs than their altars; their tables are resplendent with cups and dishes, they indulge in feastings and drinkings, in the harp and the lyre, their presses are over-

[1] fol. 55. This tale is clearly a variant of the story of Philip the Fool, in the *Spec. Laic.* cap. vi (ed. Welter, p. 11). When he gets a new tunic from his master, he "does not know himself".

[2] fol. 203b. (For the Latin, see my *Preaching in Med. Engl.* p. 31, n. 4.)

[3] fol. 194. Cf. other monastic preachers, likewise, e.g. Folsham, in MS. Worc. Cath. Libr. F. 10, fol. 55; Anon. MS. Add. 21253, fol. 87 ("Immo multotiens sunt sacerdotes pejores laicis"); and Wm. of Rymyngton, as above, p. 268, n. 3.

[4] fol. 95. Cf. again fols. 57b, 203b, 216, etc. See similarly, above, pp. 258 et seq.; and abroad, in Hauréau, *Not. et Extr.* vol. iv, p. 243, etc.

[5] *Super Canticum*, Sermo xxxiii (Migne, *Patr. Lat.* vol. clxxxiii, col. 959).

flowing, and their cupboards full. By means of such things do they desire to be, and are in fact made provosts, archbishops, bishops, archdeacons and deans of churches. When once promoted, some of them are to be found more readily in the stable than in the choir; others run swifter to the cookhouse than to mass; they care more for a roast pasty than for Christ's Passion; more for boiled lamb than for Christ crucified; they study more in salmon than in Solomon; and so forth.[1] As for the worst vice of all, Rypon returns to expose it again and again.[2] For, "evil priests make the people to sleep in their sins". Finally, each Order of Society, he tells us, in this welter of wickedness, falls to blaming the other, crying—"Ah! Thou that destroyest the temple!" Skelton's picture, in *Colin Clout*, of a kingdom divided against itself is no exaggeration of a profane and anti-clerical poet of the world. For it is to be found here, word for word, in the sombre Latin of Rypon,[3] as again in Bromyard and in the works of other homilists:

> For, as farre as I can se,
> It is wronge with eche degree.
> For the temporalte
> Accuseth the spiritualte;
> The spiritual agayne,
> Doth grudge and complayne
> Upon the temporal men.

[1] fol. 196b, and again on fol. 203b; cf. fol. 207b. Also in Bromyard, s.v. "Ordo Clericalis". Cf. further Folsham, in MS. Worc. Cath. Libr. F. 10, fol. 55 ("in gestu namque sunt histriones, in convictu nebulones, in affectu citherones, in templis simulacra, in curiis dedali, in cubilibus sardanapalli..."); MS. Heref. Cath. Libr. P. 5. 2, fol. 78 ("non apparent clerici, set ribaldi..."); Bp. Repingdon?, MS. Jo. Ryl. Libr. Manch. Lat. 367, fol. 256 ("...non decet clericum vestiri ut militem vel histrionem..."); Wm. of Rymyngton as below, p. 274 n. 3; etc.

[2] E.g. fol. 213 ("Revera hujusmodi sacerdotes sunt magis carnales pessimis sacerdotibus qui fuerunt in veteri testamento", etc.).

[3] fol. 198, quoted in my *Preaching in Med. Engl.* p. 130, n. 3. Similarly in MS. Bodl. 649, fol. 133, as quoted above, p. 74. Cf. also, MS. Roy. 18. B. xxiii, fol. 167: "Also the lay man seth that the covetize of men of holy churche is cause of this [myschef]. And thei sey that the wrathe and envy that reyneth amonge the comon pepull wil be cause of the confucion and destruction of the world. So that lordes accuseth commoners, and thei accuse holy churche, and thus ich on accuseth other".

In two synodal sermons preached at York in the years 1372 and 1373,[1] we have perhaps the darkest account of the Church and some of the fiercest denunciation of fellow-clergy to be found in all English sermon-literature. They fall from the lips of another monk, the distinguished Master William de Rymyngton, S.T.P. and Chancellor of Oxford University, sometime prior of the Cistercian Abbey of Sawley and author of several treatises confuting the errors of Wycliffe, against whom he is said to have worked "night and day to uncover his crafty designs".[2] Well-nigh every clerical crime thus far mentioned he mentions again, sometimes with added vehemence. In the kind of dress many of them favour, the priests, he says, look like devils or torturers, and behave accordingly. "In truth, not without cause can the laity say with Isaiah (lix, 9), when they see such set before them—'We looked for light, and behold darkness; brightness, and we have walked in darkness'". Already lay-folk defend their own crimes by arguing that, if the *curati* who know the law and its penalties can follow their own lusts, they themselves can live as they please with far less danger. "This palpable darkness obfuscates already the whole face of the earth's sphere."[3] Instead of giving the light of good doctrine and example to their subjects,[4] these *curati* aforesaid

[1] I am here greatly indebted to the kindness of Fr. Joseph McNulty, B.A., of the Collegio Beda, Rome, who has not only furnished me with his transcripts of these sermons, from the MS. in the library of the Univ. of Paris, but also allows me to give quotations therefrom. See his art. on W. of R. in *Yorks. Arch. Soc. Jrnl.* vol. xxx, 1931, pp. 231–47. It is to be hoped that these sermons will be published in full.

[2] See here, Workman, *Jo. Wyclif*, vol. ii, pp. 122–3 and H. E. Allen, *Writings ascribed to R. Rolle*, pp. 347–8.

[3] MS. Bibl. Univ. Paris 790, fols. 107–7b. Cf. again, fol. 109: "Nam ex perversa vita curatorum et nimium voluptuosa presumunt laici singula que placent eis esse licita seu venalia, nec a Deo inperpetuum punienda; vel desperant simpliciter de vita beata...".

[4] Cf. fol. 108: "Set prohdolor hiis diebus huius modi lux multociens extinguitur in curatis, qui nec verbo doctrine nec exemplo bone vite lucent suis subditis, quin pocius quasi per Egipti tenebras eos obnubilant et involvunt...". Fol. 108b: "Multi similiter docere subditos suos parvipendunt, dicentes ad hoc se nullatenus obligari, dum religiosi predicant tam frequenter. O periculosa sentencia! O infelix opinio! O voluntas mortifera!...".

actually lead them on to worse crimes, while those in higher authority, blinded by simony and avarice, allow the latter to wallow in their filthiness uncorrected.[1]

Do priests serve the Lord, think you, who frequent taverns and public places more freely than the churches, delight more in wanton ditties provoking to lechery than songs of devotion and angelic hymns redolent of the praise of God, care more for archery competitions, wrestlings and public shows than for the Church's sacraments...?[2] Ceaselessly do they concentrate upon worldly tricks to collect wealth, rarely or never upon sacred literature for the instruction of their parishioners. While they ought frequently to be praying to God for the remission of the people's sins, they are miserably toiling to get prostitutes[3]....O wretched modern condition of the clergy! O marvellous perversion of the priest-hood! O abominable confusion of the *curati*, whom from the obscenities of lechery, the embraces of the prostitute and the public keeping of harlots Reason does not restrain, Sacred Authority does not withdraw, the Love of God does not attract, nor Fear of the Almighty repel, and Shame of public scandal wholly fails to prevent....Rightly, as I think, it would please God better and be more profitable to His Holy Church not to have any priest save one only for a distance of ten leagues, rather than this disreputable modern crowd of presbyters....[4]

O poisonous pride of the priest! O contagious cupidity in the *curate*! O scandalous lechery of the priest, which, with regard to their subjects, is a fomentation of crime, an obstacle to correction, an example of iniquity, a principle of rebellion, á source of presumption, a radical occasion of impenitence and the greatest cause of eternal damnation! How, I ask, shall that priest or *curate* correct delinquent lay-folk, who is pompous of speech and impatient, too dainty in his appearance, the slave

---

[1] Cf. fol. 109b: "Lux iusticie in iurisdiccionem habentibus errores debet corrigere, precipue clericorum, ne quasi laici ad animarum regimen assumantur,...ne sacerdotes in spurciciis viventes publice retineant con-cubinas...". Fol. 110: "Quis iam suis utitur flagellis ad expellandum simoniacos et illiteratos ab ecclesia? Quis iam persequitur atque fugat fures et latrones, mercenarios et lupos rapaces ab ovili dominico? O causa radicalis omnium malorum...!"

[2] Cf. the warning to priests in Jo. of Mirfield's *Flor. Barthol.*—"non est licitum ire ad spectacula diebus festivis, vel intendere turpibus salta-tionibus vel cantilenis..."; *Gesta Rom.* p. 158; etc.; and with these *The Complaint of the Ploughman*, in Wright, Rolls S. vol. i, p. 330.

[3] fol. 113b. He goes on—"et partem patrimonii Crucifixi pauperibus debitam consumunt in ornatu meretricio, canibus, adulatoribus et aliis voluptuosis ac excessivis usibus apparatus....Tales sunt sacerdotes qui lascivioribus militibus, armigeris et aliis insolenter viventibus se ipsos assimulant et conformant in victu, vestitu, gestu, verbis et opere...".

[4] fols. 113b-4.

alike of gluttony and lechery, given over to filthy lucre and frequently slothful or at any rate engrossed in vain or illicit pursuits? If such an one, with the blessed Paul, rebuke a wanton youth for the flowing locks about his neck that resemble a woman's, at once the reproved layman could make this reply—"To be sure, far more ought you, as a priest, to cut your tonsure and beard and be shaved in proper fashion, after the manner of those who set a perfect example!"[1]...[If rebuked for other sins], quickly will a man of the kind fling back at him the retort—"*You* are far more bound to observe the stainlessness of chastity than I am, many times over, you who daily consecrate and consume the body and blood of Jesus Christ!"....[2]

O damnable, negligent life of the priesthood! O too lukewarm devotion of the clergy! O insolent manners of the *curati*! You who spurn the lesser things of the Law, in spurning the less you neglect the greater, in neglecting the greater you trifle with the greatest, and in trifling with the greatest you mortally despise the Commandments. So, neither by word of doctrine, nor by example of good living do you nourish or instruct your people. What will you answer at the Last Judgment, what will you say, what will you do, how will you explain away your iniquities, how will you avoid eternal damnation, where everything will have been arrayed against you?...No appeal from the Judge will avail you there; but, whether you like it or not, you shall appear judged effectually....[3]

John Myrc, Prior of Austin Canons of Lilleshall in Shropshire, as the one English representative of his Order whose actual sermons have yet come to light, shall be our next spokesman for the canons-regular. His still unprinted *Manuale Sacerdotum*, written expressly to help a clerical brother in the performance of his parish duties, is a further "Song of Complaint" against the vicious habits of contemporary clergy. The latter here stand revealed in the glaring colours of such chapter-headings as "The Priest who loves the tavern more than the church", "The Priest as gambler", "The Priest as fornicator", "The Priest as business-man". "What shall we say", cries Myrc, for example, in the second case, "of the priest who, while flinging the dice upon the gaming-table, at the same time flings his soul to the Devil! He makes of the gaming-table an altar for himself, upon which he offers up the goods of the

[1] Cf. here the earlier sermon-story, in MS. Burn. 361, fol. 151, of the Northamptonshire youth too fond of his "crocked" hair; and *Ayenb. of Inwyt*, p. 177.
[2] fol. 115. Cf. here the early 14th-cent. Domin. John of Naples, in Hauréau, *Not. et Extr.* vol. iii, p. 97, and a 12th-cent. example, in *Not. et Extr.* vol. ii, pp. 220–1. [3] fol. 117.

Church to the Devil and even the goods of others too. With false oaths and other crafts of deception he toils to win profit."[1] In this same connection, the Austin Canon relates a grimly satiric tale here attributed to Peter Cantor.[2] "Cantor tells of a certain cleric, who, when he had lost at dice all he had but five shillings, began to reproach himself and blaspheme God, promising those five shillings to the man who should tell him how best to offend God. This was the advice he received: 'If you wish to offend God above every other sinner, become an official and a questor *at a bishop's palace*'!" Another significant tale of the kind runs as follows: "I have heard of a certain rector", says Myrc, "who chose rather to lose his church than dismiss his concubine. Dismissed from the church, he came to his concubine, telling her how he had elected to lose his church rather than put her away. Her reply was, 'And I elect rather to reject you than to dismiss the church. For he who is rector of that church, without any doubt will be my paramour'".[3] With some lines from Myrc's satire of the promoted cleric, the reader must be content and pass on:

In modern times, far more priests have gained promotion by adulation and simony than by uprightness of conduct and learning, in the Church. For scarcely anyone at all is promoted without bribe of hand or tongue or sycophancy. For, either he gives bribes with his hand or flattering words with his tongue, or else fawns by performing some toilsome

[1] Lib. i, cap. xv, MSS. Harl. 5306, fol. 18, York Cath. Libr. xvi. O. 11, fols. 44b–5b, "De Sacerd. Aleatore". He goes on: "Ludit enim ut illudat, quia ludus ipsius illusio est.... Vix autem reperies aliquem sacerdotem qui ludum istum frequenter exerceat, qui non invigilet clamdestine alienarum rerum surrepcioni, immo et libidini collum submittit. Denique, dum que sua sunt perdiderit tunc in altum erigit et loquitur adversus Deum iniquitatem...". Cf. Hauréau, *Not. et Extr.* vol. iii, pp. 287–8. [2] d. 1197.

[3] Cf. the *narratio* of a prostitute who made it her chief business to bring about the downfall of "holy men", given in a 15th-cent. vernacular sermon in MS. Roy. 18. B. xxiii, fol. 108b. For earlier stories of the kind, see *Spec. Laic.* ed. Welter, pp. 71–2; MS. Roy. 7. D. I, fols. 132b–5b; MS. Add. 33956, fols. 82b, 85–5b; *Hand. Synne*, pp. 252–6; Bozon, *Metaphs.* cap. cxxxix; Bromyard, *S.P.* s.v. "Luxuria", §§ 48–9, etc.; etc. One is of a priest "in marchia Wallie": cf. with this the Welsh scandal described by Gascoigne, 1423 (*Loci e Libro Verit.* pp. 35–6). See also a poem in Chambers and Sidgwick, *E. E. Lyrics*, p. 220.

office. Therefore, he who enters his benefice with sin, must of necessity live henceforth in sins. Thus promoted, indeed, because he is not wise in the things of God, he conforms himself to the way of the world. And because he is dead in soul, he thinks of nothing but his present life. He adorns not his soul with good habits, but his body with delicate clothing. He buys a long sword for himself, so that he may be thought bold and austere. With this he girds himself under his thigh, in most threatening fashion. Upon his other thigh he hangs a dagger, ornamented here and there with gold or silver. His head he covers with a cap, more often than not hung around with a broad liripipe. If you were to see him thus loaded with weapons, a knight rather than a priest, you would find practically no difference between him and a knight in his bearing, in his movements, or in the clothing of his body.[1] A knight is addressed as "Sir"; a priest is also called "Sir". A knight makes use of gold; and so does that priest. A knight is dressed according to the form and fashion of the world. But neither here is there any difference between the two. Thus he (the priest) conforms to the world in such a way that in nothing does he differ from the people, save possibly in the tonsure which is reserved for him. So the prophecy is in truth fulfilled which says—"And as the people shall be, so also shall be the priest".[2]

[1] Bp. Repingdon?, in a sermon, MS. Jo. Ryl. Libr. Manch. Lat. 367, fol. 256, quotes St Bernard thus: "nempe habitu milites, questu clericos, actu neutros se exhibent: nam neque pugnant ut milites, neque ut clerici evangelizant...".

[2] Lib. i, cap. xiii, MS. York Minster Libr. xvi. O. 11, fols. 39 b–40; etc. Cf. the inmate of another Austin priory, John of Mirfield (c. 1370), in his *Flor. Barthol.* MS. Camb. Univ. Libr. Mm. ii. 10, fol. 85 b, etc. "De Indumentis": "Nec vestes rubeas an virides, nec fissas superiores, nec annulos, nec aurum, neque argentum in fibulis vel ornatu zonarum vel calcarium vel sellarum querant. Omnem enim ornatum in vestibus curiosum vel superfluum, et in calciamentis, equitura, superlectili, mensa et prandio clerici deponere debent....Clerici saltem beneficiati uti non debent caligis rubeis aut viridibus. Similiter etiam arma clericis portare prohibetur....Sed de his constitutionibus et observationibus modicum curant clerici moderni. Immo in habitu et in gestu sicut se habet populus sic etiam sacerdos. Et inde Deus irridetur, decus ecclesie offuscatur, clericalis ordinis celsitudo deprimitur, Christus a suis militibus insignia ferentibus aliena deseritur, et decor honestatis ecclesie maculatur; dum clericum a laico respiciens oculus non discernit, fitque vero omnibus fidelibus scandalum et despectum non modicum". Similarly, Wm. of Rymyngton at York, 1373, MS. Bibl. Univ. Paris 790, fol. 107: "Set heu modernis temporibus quis multociens discernere sufficit inter lucem et tenebras, inter sacerdotem et armigerum, militem et rectorem? Nam de multis sacerdotibus corona nulla est vel minima, capillatura notabiliter inordinata, barba non rasa set vix superficialiter tonsa, corpus tunica vestitur strictissima usque ad nates turpissima decurtata, argentea zona vel

278 THE PREACHING OF SATIRE AND COMPLAINT

The secular clergy, rectors, vicars, distinguished preachers
at the city crosses and others, whose sermons and manuals
remain to us, are themselves no more eulogistic about their
own order, no more hopeful about the state of the Church
and the world in general, than those who loved to criticize them
from opposite camps. Thus William de Pagula (or Paull), a
Berkshire vicar, in his *Oculus Sacerdotis*, written in the first
half of the fourteenth century, quotes from "Hugo" (of
Fouilloy) a bitter censure familiar to generations of English
preachers and sermon-audiences.[1] Its particular interest lies in
the fact that it points us to the origin in sermon-literature of
Langland's famous portrait of Parson *Sleuthe*, here already in
embryo in one of the most popular clerical manuals written
by an Englishman, before ever the *Vision of Piers Plowman*
had taken shape:

> I have be prest and persoun passynge thretti wynter,
> ʒete can I neither solfe, ne synge, ne seyntes lyves rede.
> But I can fynde in a felde, or in a fourlonge an hare,
> Better than in *beatus vir*, or in *beati omnes*
> Construe oon clause wel, and kenne it to my parochienes.[2]

It is interesting to see how once again in these lines the clerical
poet has created a picturesque living personality out of the

aurea cingitur, cui, ut vulgariter loquar, baslardus appenditur paris forme,
et tandem in pedibus longa nimium calciamentorum liripipia sive rostra
. . ."; etc. Cf. *Piers Plowman*, B text, pass. xv, l. 120; xx, 218 and C text,
pass. xxiii, 219; *Poems of Jo. Audelay*, E.E.T.S. p. 15; etc.

[1] MS. Roy. 6. E. i, fol. 24b. Again, in Bromyard, *S.P.*; Rymyngton,
MS. Bibl. Univ. Paris 790, fol. 113b; Rypon, twice—MS. Harl. 4894, fols.
196b and 198; Myrc, *Man. Sacerd.* Lib. 1, cap. xiii, MS. York Minster Libr.
xvi. O. 11, fol. 40b; etc.; Philip, MS. Bodl. Lat. Th. d. i, fol. 89; etc.
Cf. abroad, friar Baldwin of Maclix (13th cent.), in Hauréau, *Not. et
Extr.* vol. iv, p. 40. See further below, p. 595.

[2] B text, pass. v, ll. 422–6. Cf. further the simple vernacular writer
of MS. Harl. 2398, fol. 27: "Sleuthe maketh a man of holy churche yvel
seye his servyce and here hourys,...in the morwetyde syncopyth here
wordes, and lytel contemplacioun and devocioun in here servyce-seyenge,
more entendynge to haukynge and to huntyng and wrastlynge and to
daunsynge and to waste so here tyme amys. They ʒeve hem more to
chaffarynge and to swerynge than to her ordynal or to her canon, other
fullynge [= baptizing], other burynge, other to eny other sacrament of
holy churche". See also, MS. Roy. 18. B. xxiii, fol. 67b; *Gesta Rom.*
Engl. version, E.E.T.S. ed. p. 158; and MS. Add. 21253, fol. 169 (Latin).

appropriate statements of a sermon commonplace. Says the homilist—

> And many are the priests, in these days who neither know the law of God, nor teach others. But giving themselves up to sloth, they spend their time upon banquetings and carousals, they covet earthly things, they grow wise in earthly things, constantly in the streets, rarely in the church, slow to investigate the faults of their parishioners, *ready to track the footprints of hares* or some other wild beast, swifter to collect dogs than to summon the poor. More freely do they offer food to a dog than to a poor man; more wait upon them at table than at mass; they wish to have men servants and maid servants with them, but not clerics. These are they whose chamber is more ornate than their church, their table better prepared than their altar, their drinking-cup more costly than their chalice, their tabard nobler than their chasuble, their shirt more delicate than their alb, (their horse dearer than their missal[1]).

William of Rymyngton, the monk of Sawley, makes typical play out of the phrase which concerns the hare, thus: "Curiosius venantur leporem in silva quam lepram in anima".[2] In his sermon of the year 1388, Thomas Wimbledon adduces as a sign that the end of the world draws near the corruption of the higher clergy, by way of what Foxe calls "a proper similitude".[3] This we shall find again, in a similar context, in the sermon of another London preacher, Richard Alkerton, delivered eighteen years later.[4] It tells how that, when the "tops of the hills" become enveloped in darkness, we may know that the night of the world's end "is niȝ". Wimbledon has more to say here of the great palaces which prelates build for themselves—"like churches", of their chambers painted with divers colours, and the statuary adorned with sumptuous clothing and paintings, of fat palfreys, hounds, hawks, and worse, which they feed out of the proceeds of the Church. A Cambridge manuscript of Latin sermons, which are probably Wimbledon's also, is full of the more lively, sarcastic kind of censure that we found typical of Bromyard. The clergy are now "fallen

---

[1] Not in Pagula's version here.

[2] As above. He adds also: "et cultellus sive baslardus gloriosior est vexillo crucis, quantum ad argentum et aurum operis curiosi".

[3] I have used here, following, for convenience, Foxe's text of the sermon, amending where necessary, *Acts and Mons.* Ch. Hist. ed. 1855, vol. iii, pt. i.

[4] MS. Add. 37677, fol. 58 b. Again in MS. Add. 41321, fol. 18 (Anon.).

stars"[1] "already more dark than the laity, and in every variety of vice more dissolute", themselves "laymen in their accumulation of temporalities, merchants in their trading of all kinds, knights in luxury of clothing, women in their inconstancy of soul".[2] Ecclesiastical judges, who vex the poor and needy, and afflict the stranger wrongfully,[3] are wicked physicians, taking no steps to heal their patients.

> For every vice and for every sin they prescribe only a single medicine —that which is called by the popular name of "pecuniary penalty". This certainly appears to be well called "a penalty", because it is very "penal" to many; nevertheless, whether it ought to be called a "medicine" I do not know. Yet, in truth I think that if it is a medicine, it deserves rather to be called "a laxative medicine for purses", rather than "a medicine for souls!"

Again, "To-day, our 'Moses', that is, the priests of modern time, can veil their faces in confusion. For already the sons of Israel and the faithful common folk are ashamed to regard them, nay rather blush, sometimes shaking their heads over the fact that they can see nothing commendable in them". "They deserve to be called, not priests of God, but the priests of Dagon in their avarice,...priests of Baal in their pride,... priests of Baalfegor[4] in their lechery,...and priests of Nanea[5] in their ignorance." The ship of the Church in the hands of these incompetent seamen is now in danger of complete destruction from the billows of a tempestuous sea of misery and disaster.[6] Ecclesiastics who ought to preach Christ, preach

---

[1] MS. Camb. Univ. Libr. Ii. iii. 8, fols. 129, et seq.

[2] Cf. in another sermon here, ibid. fol. 149: "in confabulationibus cum mulieribus, in aliis diversis lasciviis, in emptionibus, in venditionibus", etc. Also, Alkerton? in MS. Add. 37677, fol. 99: "Conteckoures, tayerne goeris, lecchoures, that gon with long harneised baslardus and other develis aray; and tho that hav takyn this gret charge, gon they not and dwelyn with lordis, and ben hawkeris, stywardis of housholdis, clerkys of kychyn, and other suche officeres, that many a soule is spillid that sholde have ben wol heiȝ in hevene, hadde thei ben wel governyd of here curat?"

[3] See Ezek. xxii, 29.

[4] See Num. xxv, 3 (A.V.—Baal-peor).

[5] See 1 Macc. i, 13.

[6] See my *Preaching in Med. Engl.* p. 37.

"themselves" and the doctrine of their Father the Devil, namely lies and slander. Faithful, modest priests who do their duty they abuse with the names of "heretic, wretch and lollard".[1] As for clerical avarice, "neither greater nor less, for the most part, are content with their possessions, their status or their rank. They are like a man with the dropsy", says our preacher; "the more he drinks, the worse he grows". They rival the laity "in the magnificence of their steeds and cellars,[2] in the pompous throng of their servants, each according to his ability, some like squires, others like knights, others like barons, others like earls and dukes. Nay, rather do they strive to appear more stately than kings in secular pomp and worldly vanities, heedless that they have been constituted dispensers of goods and the bailiffs of Christ. But tithes, oblations and the other revenues of their livings they call 'their own incomes'; so that if one of their churches is worth forty pounds, its incumbent says that he has an annual income of forty pounds".[3] "In the court Christian, false marriages are contracted time after time (*multotiens*), false divorces,[4] and many other injurious arrangements, which cannot easily be enumerated, and all these by legal process. . . . In the Church court, two persons are joined in matrimony, to-day, and to-morrow by the same law they will be separated, and likewise in diverse other cases." Finally, the Papal Schism is considered another "sign in the heavens" of the impending doom of the world.[5] And who shall wonder?

Sermons and pulpit-manuals left to us in the vernacular very naturally are wont to approach even nearer at times to the letter

[1] fol. 147b. Cf. *Poems of Jo. Audelay*, p. 15.

[2] ? "sellarum"= saddlery.

[3] Cf. Gascoigne on Bp. Pecock, *Loci e Libro Verit.* p. 100, and the warning of the *Poem*, in *Twenty-six Pol. and other Poems*, E.E.T.S. p. 32.

[4] Cf. above, p. 254, espec. n. 3.

[5] fol. 149 (mentioning Urban VI). Cf. also, MS. Roy. 18. B. xxiii, fol. 138b: "Haa! good god, now mercy! For our synnes beth not unpunyshed. Lo, sirs! I sey itt with sorefull hert, scismes and divisions have now reyned in our daies amonge men of holy churche, that welny3 holy churche stondes in desolacion". Again, fol. 69: "Wold god that all bisshoppes shuld be choson in this maner nowadaies, and namely the pape; ffor than we my3th be secur that he were very pope, and than ther shulde be none suche striffe as ther is nowe for that office!...".

as well as the spirit of the so-called "political" songs and poems.
Although, in actual age, they may appear to be mere echoes
of the latter, yet from the complete concurrence of their subject-
matter with that of the older homilies preserved in Latin, we
know that they must represent a prior tradition of vernacular
preaching. Here, then, we read again, for example, of
"coveitous prelates of holy chirche"—

that setteth imposiciouns upon her sugettes, and chargeth hem wrong-
fulliche in her visitaciouns, and maketh hem to paye hem that hem lust,
or what thei wole aske; or elles *travailleth hem by sumpnynge* to appere
in fer stedes,[1] and in other maner processe, til they have what thei wole....
Officiales and denes,[2] that sitteth and holdeth her chapitles and concistories
more for to wynne silver than for to destroye synne; but, by reddour of
the lawe of holy chirche—as doynge out of chirche, cursynge and otherwise—maketh poure folk that may overdoo bodiliche penaunce for her
synne, or 3eve hem what thei wole aske. And grete men, that thei dore
noght dele with, thei suffreth hem [to] slepe and deye in her owne synne,
in sclaunder of holy chirche. And that thei thus taketh, thei clepeth hit
"redempcioun", that is, "forbiggynge". But it is open extorcioun,
or robbynge.[3] *Sompnoures and bedelles*, that beth mynistres to this
lawe, that procureth to do men be accused, and in other wyses greveth
men by colour of her offices, to have of her good,[4] and so robbeth the
peple....[5]

With one further vernacular specimen, however, our survey
must end. It forms part of a brilliant, though clumsily phrased
description of the pompous ecclesiastics aforementioned:

Pride thanne schal be ful hi3 in prelatis. For hir pride schal passe alle
temporalle lordes in alle thynges that longet to lordes astaat, as in stronge
castellis and ryalle maneris, proudeli aparaylit withinne in halles, chaumbres

---

[1] = in distant places.

[2] I.e. rural deans. This passage suggests that even in the late 14th
(or early 15th?) cent. their authority had not yet been taken over completely by the archdeacons. However, their mention here coupled with
the officials may mean that, like the latter, they were now merely delegates
of the archdeacon, presiding for him in his own court. For their oppression in the 13th cent., see a sermon of Jacques de Vitry, in Hauréau,
Not. et Extr. vol. ii, p. 12. Cf. *Poems of Jo. Audelay*, p. 36.

[3] With this compare *Poems*, in Wright, Rolls S. vols. i, p. 332 and ii,
p. 236, and *Piers Plowman*, as above, p. 252, n. 2.

[4] = goods.

[5] MS. Harl. 45, fols. 66b–67. Cf. in *Jacob's Well*, p. 129, etc. and
Piers Plowman, as above. (The italics in the quotation are mine.)

and alle othure houses of office. Also in proude araye of here owne per-
sonnes, bothe in costlew cloth and pelure as fyn as emperour, kyng, or
quene. Also in gret multitudo of fatte horses and proude, with gai gult
sadeles and schynyng brideles, with miche wast and proude meynye more
niseli disgysid thanne any temporal lordes meynye; sittynge atte mete
eche day schynyngeli, with precious vessel and rial cuppebord bothe of
selver and of gold, and her meynye fallynge doun as to a god at every
drauȝte that they schul drynke. And manye othure poyntes of pride
schulle folowe hem whiche were to longe to reherce here.... Than they
schullen drawe in to kynges services, as into chauncerie or in to cheker,
or in to kynges houses, for to gedere to-gedere gold and leye it upon an
heep, to marchaunde ther-whit aftur dignitees or prelacies or benefices
of the cherche....

Prelatis now-adaies ben as hie above semple curates and preestis as
kynges above the comen peple, and taketh of hem grete taliages and
subsidies, and traveileth hem to gret cost, whider hem liketh and whanne
hem liketh, for thynge that ofte litil availeth to any helpe of soule; as
theuȝ thei hadde non other kyng, but oneli hem alone. There, also, as
Crist hadde never hous of his owne bi title of worldeli lor[d]schipe, to
hile[1] in his heved, ne greet multitude of proude araied meyne, but 12 seli[2]
pore men, withoute ȝemen[3] oɾ pagis, to whom we reden he servede ofter
than ever we rede thei servede him, whiche also never rood at greet
araie, nether he, nether his meyne, but ones sempeli on an asse sadelid
with his disciplis clothes,—prelates, that ben now-a-daies, hav many
dyverse castellis and maners, as rial as the kynge him selfe, to chaunge
whanne so evere hem likith for to take diverse eiris, withynne araied as
realli[4] with costli clothes of gold and selk and in multitude of other iewellis
bothe of selver and of gold; in al maner housis office as thouȝ it were in
Salamons temple, and so greet multitude of meyne of knyȝtes, squyers,
ȝemen and gromes, myche more nyseli disgisid than any seculer lordis
meyne. Whan he schal on[i]wer ride oute, ȝea, thouh it be to visite his pore
scheep, he mut ride with foure or fyve score hors proudeli apareilid at
alle poyntes[5], his owne palfrai for his bodi worth a 20 or 30 pound, al
bihangid with gliterynge gold as thouȝ it were an hooli hors[!], himself
above in fyne scarlet or other cloth as good as that, and withynne with
as good pelure as the quene hath any in hire gowne; hir persones and
hir clerkis rydynge aboute hem, al in gult harneise, with bastard swerdis
overgild bi hire sides hangynge, as thou it were Centurio and his knyȝtes

---

[1] = cover.   [2] = simple.
[3] = yeomen.   [4] = royally.
[5] Cf. again, here, fol. 1: "sadeles with gingelinge brideles and v score
or vi score hors of prout arayed men, as thouȝ hit were a kynge rydinge
toward a revel. And her chariottis with her jeweles goynge to fore, ful
of grete fatte hors, fed for the nones". These processions of greater
ecclesiastics would be about all that the ordinary priest would see with
his own eyes of their activities, apart from the random Visitation itself.

ridynge toward Cristes deth.[1] . . . God, for his endeles merci, make of hem sone an ende![2]

Let the reader now turn to the poem known as *The Complaint of the Ploughman*, and compare the preacher's phrases with the Lollard poet's indignant verse.[3]

Thomas Wright, in his *History of Caricature and Grotesque in Literature and Art*, describes a curious phenomenon known as the Pope-Ass, popularized by Lutheran satirists of the sixteenth century.[4] It was supposed to have been found dead in the Tiber, in the year 1496, a symbol of all the notorious vices of the Holy See. Wright himself, however, does not seem for once to have recognized its historical ancestry. For, a medieval sermon-story, derived apparently from Peter Damian, and made familiar to medieval homilists by the thirteenth-century *Speculum Historiale* of Vincent of Beauvais, tells how Pope Benedict IX appeared after death in the form of a monster with the head of an ass and the body of a bear, explaining that he had been made to take this shape because of his bestial life. The tale, which re-appears in several English collections,[5] may be taken as the crowning expression of all that our preachers have dared to say of the Church to which they belonged. None but those, indeed, like the present writer, who have wandered from manuscript to manuscript and library to library, only to be surfeited with such matter as our chapter has disclosed, can realize the force of their indictment. Orators, undoubtedly, have always exaggerated, and hyperbole is of the stuff and essence of satire. But when all the vesture of possible exaggeration has been stripped from off these sermons, the stark body of their naked charges stands out only the more

[1] Clearly an interesting reminiscence of the contemporary miracle-plays.
[2] MS. Add. 41321, fols. 17–17b and 100–1 (probably a Lollard collection).
[3] Wright, Rolls S. vol. i, pp. 307–8 ("That high on horse willeth ride / In glitterande gold of great array /" etc.).   [4] p. 254.
[5] MS. Add. 6716, fol. 41b, *Fascic. Morum, Destruct. Vicior.* (and Migne, *Patr. Lat.* cxlv, col. 428). For another surprising story of the fate of an evil Pope, in Engl. sermon-literature, cf. *Spec. Laic.* cap. lxix (ed. Welter, p. 94, no. 478).

grimly. Neither the fundamental truth nor the far-reaching influence of this clerical exposure will escape the historian's eye. He will understand, as never before, the depth of feeling which lies behind the denunciatory and satiric verse of the later Middle Ages in England. At all events he can no longer mistake it merely for the ravings of a few disgruntled heretics, or of a company of mischievous, ill-informed bards of the pavement. With the actual truth or falsity of the charges, we are here happily not concerned.[1] What does concern us is the fact that no society on earth could withstand for ever the continuous shock of such Complaint, from within as well as from without its borders. Spreading from the pulpits into the streets, it threatened the very foundations of Holy Church, and helped to sweep away the waning respect of many for her ministers and her sacraments. There was now no secrecy even for the more intimate reproaches of the synodal sermon within chapter-house walls. They leak out anon either through the indiscreet zeal of the orthodox or the deliberate malice of Lollards. As this exaggerated impassioned speech of responsible persons in the Church's midst passed thus into the current coin of popular rhyme and song, it was as surely the prelude to a revolt as in any other of the great revolutions of history. It is interesting to note how sometimes even the very chronicler who supplies us with concrete cases of infamy will himself drop suddenly into a picturesque phrase of this same pulpit satire. Thus, forty years before the *Vision of Piers Plowman* was given to the world, a monkish chronicler of Malmesbury, recording the papal appointment of a time-server to the vacant see of Canterbury, whose chief claim to distinction lay "in ludis theatralibus", in place of the learned and virtuous nominee of the monks, adds—"But the lady *Pecunia* decides every matter in that Court!"[2] Such and such, then, were the impressions of the faithful. The modern reader may well be left

---

[1] The reader who wishes to consider this question is here referred to the remarks on pp. 567–8, below.

[2] *Chron. Edw. I et Edw. II*, Rolls S. vol. ii, p. 196. This chronicle abounds in typical pulpit sayings (cf. again, e.g., p. 207—"Nam armiger militem, miles baronem, baro comitem, comes regem in omni fere cultu antecedere nititur et laborat..."—with p. 313, below). Our sermons,

wondering at the end wherein lies the peculiar crime of those old Protestant Reformers, who saw in the Woman of Babylon, "Mother of harlots and abominations of the Earth", an unerring prophecy of the medieval Romish *Ecclesia*. Something not so far removed even from this language, indeed, actually finds expression in the orthodox homiletic literature of our period.[1] As historians, then, we must at least admit that no other body in the whole history of Christendom has ever argued so eloquently for the title, by the mouths of its own most zealous sons.

indeed, give a fresh significance to the comments of Bp. Stubbs upon the character and denunciatory language of its unknown author. Says Stubbs in his Introduction here: "The passages are curious both in themselves and in the illustrations they furnish that the zealous rebukes of a friend may in time of peace be clothed in language not very different from that which the enemy takes up in open warfare" (pp. xlvi–vii).

[1] Cf. the Oxford Chancellor Thos. Gascoigne's repetition of a remark made by Alphonso, King of Aragon, to Pope Eugenius IV, in the year 1440: "The Roman Church is already a very harlot!" (*Loci e Libro Verit.* p. 125).

CHAPTER VI

The Preaching of Satire and Complaint

PART II

THE English pulpit of the Middle Ages which lavished its censure and its satire so profusely upon the clerical orders was equally ready to rebuke the sins of secular society, those other offenders of the realm who likewise find their place with the former in the bitter indictment of satirical poem and song. Although it is highly important to note that all classes of the community shared the fury of the preachers' attacks, as in Langland's great poem, yet it is very naturally the rich and the powerful who are singled out for the worst degree of criticism. Just as we are bound to see, therefore, the effects of age-long pulpit invective against the Church in the subsequent violence and raillery of the Reformation, so we may expect to find the fruits of these parallel attacks on feudal power and privilege in the future struggles for popular liberty, from the Peasants' Revolt of 1381, onwards. This fact alone, apart from questions of literary influence, endows our next survey with an importance which English historians would be expected not to overlook. Nevertheless—such is the case—save for certain investigations of a few English sermon-manuscripts at Oxford and Cambridge made by Professors André Réville and Petit-Dutaillis nearly forty years ago,[1] no serious work has yet been done by historians, English or foreign, in this particular field. In breaking new ground, then, in the few pages which follow, we purpose to give some rough indication of the kind of material that waits to be explored. For, without that material, our social as well as our literary history must remain unnecessarily incomplete.

[1] See *Études d'Histoire du moyen âge, dediées à Gabriel Monod*, ed. Lavisse, 1896, Paris, pp. 373–88 (cf. also *Studies and Notes supplm. to Stubbs' Const. Hist.* vol. ii, pp. 276–8).

M. Petit-Dutaillis, in the essay referred to, was enquiring into the possible influence of clerical preaching upon the insurgents of 1381. In his verdict he has already gone some way towards determining the correct limits of this regular homiletic indictment of wealth and privilege in fourteenth-century England. The extant sermons of Mendicant and Secular give no evidence whatever of communistic doctrine, such as Froissart imputed to the chaplain John Balle,[1] and Langland to the friars.[2] On the other hand—to quote the words of M. Petit-Dutaillis himself—in all of them there is "souvent un ton très agressif pour parler de la haute société et des pouvoirs établis". There is the fiercest denunciation of all those who oppress the poor, be they lords, knights, lawyers, merchants or ecclesiastics. Such is the case even where preachers like Bishop Brunton—whom our French Professor does not mention—or friar Waldeby, in discussing the general problem of rich and poor, produce nothing but theological banalities upon the Divine purpose in their creation and the religious duties incumbent upon them both.[3] The names of these two eminent persons remind us further that violent language of this kind was by no means confined to the poorer and more obscure clergy, whom Dr Workman · rightly emphasizes as prime agitators in the revolt.[4] Brunton was a great prelate at court. Waldeby was a learned doctor of Oxford; and a third preacher mentioned by M. Petit-Dutaillis is an archbishop with whom we are already acquainted. We shall have occasion in due course to add other names, no less distinguished, to the list. For, a wider survey of the literature of English preaching than any which the learned French scholar was able to make during his visit, will carry us yet further along the road of exasperation and rebuke, even in the company of those loudest in their support of the existing social order as the express work and will of Heaven. The conservative and "loyal" aspect of this

[1] See Lord Berners' ed. of the *Chronicles*, cap. ccclxxxi.
[2] *Piers Plowman*, B text, pass. xx, ll. 273–5.
[3] See esp. Brunton, in MS. Harl. 3760, fol. 111 b et seq., and later below in Chap. IX, p. 560 (Waldeby, in MSS. Caius Coll. Camb. 334 and Roy. 7. E. ii; etc.).
[4] See *Jo. Wyclif*, vol. ii, pp. 224–5, and 238–9.

social gospel of the preachers will have to be dealt with in a concluding chapter. But we may remark here, in passing, that our final judgment upon that gospel, while confirming M. Petit-Dutaillis for the most part, will be one which contradicts directly the assertion of Professor G. M. Trevelyan, that "Wycliffe was one of the very few men who could see both the rights of the lords and the wrongs of the peasants".[1] Indeed, no better summary could be given than this of the attitude of the whole orthodox pulpit of Wycliffe's own day.[2] The preachers all "see" thus far. They all declare fearlessly what they see. But there, for most of them, direct responsibility in the matter ends. Indirectly, none the less, the mere unceasing ventilation of the crimes of nobleman and prelate in this fashion had a profound twofold effect upon our subsequent history. In the first place, it proved to be an incitement to the discontented masses, leading them to agitate and rebel for a time. In the second, it played at length into the hands of the monarchy, enabling it to assert itself triumphantly as the sole champion of law and order in the State over a truculent nobility and a decadent church. The story of the young King Richard setting himself at the head of the angry rebels at Smithfield, with the cry— "I am your leader!", seems like a direct response to the preachers' appeals, and a pathetic prophecy of future achievement. At all events it is reasonable to believe that, without

---

[1] See *Engl. in the Age of Wycliffe*, p. 202; and cf. a similar false claim made on behalf of Langland by Prof. W. P. Ker, mentioned below in Chap. IX. Here, then, is another typical case where the study of the sermons not only corrects such misjudgments, but also explains the similarity of views held by very different thinkers and writers of the period. It is amazing to reckon up the number of minor doctrines and ideas supposed to be characteristic of Wycliffe—even by living scholars such as Loserth (cf., e.g., his Introduction to the Latin *Sermones*) and Workman—which are nothing more nor less than pulpit commonplaces of the orthodox. The reason is, of course, that hitherto there has been no substantial *corpus* of medieval Engl. homiletic literature with which to compare the Reformer's own well-known homilies. The latter have stood out for years as almost solitary and unchallenged examples of the art in England.

[2] Dr Workman seems to have missed this point in his recent study of Wycliffe.

this age-long exposure and scorn from the pulpits, fomenting a general spirit of hatred and distrust, accustoming men's ears to unrestrained criticism of the privileged orders, the Tudor monarchs would never have accomplished so easily what they did in both Church and State.

The immediate task of the present chapter is to show how the contemporary preaching inspired the writing of popular verse directed against the vices of the laity. But, before we begin to examine the homilists' complaints and satire in detail, we may well stop to enquire more fully in what way and to what degree the latter were calculated to promote a spirit of revolution. Sir Charles Oman has pointed out the significant fact that in "the Great Revolt of 1381", although there were no attacks on the clergy as clergy, there were many assaults upon them in their capacity of landlords. Professor Trevelyan reminds us too that the disendowment of the Church and the abolition of the hierarchy were said to be amongst the demands of the London rebels.[1] Finally, there is the murder of Archbishop Sudbury to recall in the same connection. All this, on the face of it, suggests that the pulpit attacks that we have witnessed on the misspent patrimony of the Church, the avarice, negligence, and worldly pomp of ecclesiastics and monks took deadly effect. Similarly, in the rebellion of Jack Cade, when the insurgents "entended", as the irate More put it, "to kyll up the clergie, and sel priestes heddes as good chepe as shepes heddes, thre for a peni, bie who would",[2] we are bound to feel that the same influence was at work with equally devastating results. At all events we have the assurance of Thomas Gascoigne that religious discontent loomed large.[3] What now of secular enemies? Neither MM. André Réville[4] and Petit-Dutaillis, nor the other historians of the revolt appear to have traced back the famous argument of John Balle concerning Adam and Eve to its immediate ancestry. Yet

[1] *Engl. in the Age of Wycliffe*, p. 234.
[2] *Supplic. of Souls*, Engl. ed. 1557, p. 302.
[3] See *Loci e Libro Verit.* p. 43, etc.
[4] See esp. his valuable *Les Paysans au moyen âge*, Paris, 1896, p. 60, and *Le Soulèvement des Travailleurs d'Angleterre en 1381*, 1898.

herein lies perhaps the most significant illustration that we possess of the way in which an apparently innocuous pulpit theme of the times became the popular watchword of revolution.

> When Adam delved and Eve span
> Who was then a gentleman?

—this, in the first instance, was nothing more nor less than a popular rhyming couplet based directly—like other poems of our survey—on a favourite homiletic argument, in this case one which English preachers of the fourteenth century were wont to use in support of their innocent diatribes upon the Pride of Life and emptiness of human boasting. Early in that same century we actually find it, still in its pure homiletic form but now translated into verse, in a vernacular poem "made up of commonplaces of ascetic theology" once attributed to Richard Rolle:

> When Adam delf and Eve span,
> Spir, if thou wil spede,
> Whare was than the pride of man
> That now merres his mede?
> Of erth and slame, als was Adam,
> Maked to noyes and nede,
> Ar we, als he, maked to be
> Whil we this lyf sal lede....[1]

We find typical pulpit references to the same theme in Bromyard, and also in a sermon by Bishop Brunton of Rochester,[2] preaching, as Gasquet has reminded us, in the same county and about the very same time as the "mad priest of Kent" himself. "All Christians," Brunton declares, in the opening sentence of his *Exordium*, "rich and poor alike, without

[1] MS. Camb. Univ. Libr. Dd. v. 64, and MS. Thornton, Linc. Cath. Libr. A. i. 17. See Horstmann, *Yorksh. Writers*, vol. i, pp. 73 and 367, who refers the ideas of the poem to the *Spec.* of St Edmund Rich; and Miss H. E. Allen, *Writings ascribed to R.R.* p. 296, who gets near to the connecting link between Balle and the poet, but misses it through not knowing the pulpit currency of this theme. Cf. further, *Poems of the Vernon MS.* pt. i, E.E.T.S. O.S. no. 98, pp. 227, ll. 243–4 (a transln. of St Edmund's *Speculum*, pt. i).

[2] MS. Harl. 3760, fol. 111b, et seq. "*Simul in unum dives et pauper.* Ps. 48. [49, 2] ... quia, cum vanga quandam tellurem foderat Adam, etc. Ita etiam in morte sunt similes divites et pauperes ... "

distinction of persons, are from one father, Adam . . . ". When, after citing their common religious privileges, he goes on— "In these and many other things the rich and the poor are *alike and equal*", it is easy to see, with the change of a mere word or two, how the preacher's spiritual message could be expanded and perverted into an argument for communism. Misunderstanding or mischief running rife in the ranks of the more ignorant clergy and their discontented people would readily explain how just such a false impression of the bishop's remarks might get about in his diocese.[1] It is in the impassioned language of John Bromyard, however, *celeberrimus ac moralissimus sacrarum literarum professor eximius*, that we behold the theme actually catching fire, shooting out its menacing sparks upon those sitting around, as the preacher kindles it with the flame of his bitter satire. His motif is still nothing more than a powerful spiritual and moral corrective, wholly innocent of any revolutionary intent. But no one can fail to see what effect his words must have had, if they happened to fall upon "the inflammable material" then lying about "at the mercy of a spark".[2] "All are descended", he says,[3] "from the same first parents, and all come of the same mud. For, if God had fashioned nobles from gold, and the ignoble from mud, then the former would have cause for pride. But whereas all are of one material, in that fact 'thy boasting is excluded'."[4] "True glory does not depend upon the origin or beginning from which anything proceeds, but upon its own condition. For thus, if it were not so, lice and other worms which derive their origin from man, would be noble. Thus, too, the putrid apple which comes from the best tree, the Devil who is sprung from the most righteous God, Cain also who was from

[1] It is interesting to notice that this very preacher shows himself nervous of such misrepresentation. See in my *Preaching in Med. Engl.* pp. 218–9.
[2] Ch. Petit-Dutaillis, *Stud. supplm. to Stubbs*, vol. ii, p. 278.
[3] *S.P.* s.v. "Gloria". Cf. here, Chaucer, *Cant. Tales*, Parson's Tale, § 66; and Gower, *Mirour de l'Omme*, ll. 23389 et seq. (as cited by Coulton, *Mediev. Village*, p. 236, who has not identified his doctrine, however, with the current English preaching: see also, p. 248). Cf. sim. *Ayenb. of Inwyt*, pp. 87 and 89 (A.D. 1340).   [4] See Rom. iii, 27.

righteous Adam, and chaff which is from the best grain, all would be in themselves of the noblest quality." Thus does our friar ridicule the feudal pride in noble birth and parentage.[1] In the realm of the spirit, then, at all events, all were equal in endowment and in opportunity. A man's worth depended solely upon his character, upon the way in which he lived in his particular calling and environment. This doctrine brings us already to what Acton has called "the secret essence of the Rights of Man" and "the significant and central feature" of Modern History—"the indestructible soul of Revolution" hidden in Religion.[2] Not content to stop here with the conditions of birth, in the very same part of his great book for preachers Bromyard goes on to pour fresh scorn upon the mighty in their death:[3]

Where are the evil lovers of the world [he asks] who a little while ago were with us? Where are the evil princes of the world, the kings, earls and other lords of estates, who lived with pride and with great circumstance and equipage, who used to keep many hounds and a numerous and evil retinue, who possessed great palaces, many manors and broad lands with large rents, who nourished their own bodies in delicacies and the pleasures of gluttony and lust, who ruled their subjects harshly and cruelly to obtain the aforesaid luxuries, and fleeced them? Where, moreover, are the false wise men of the world, the judges, assessors, advocates, swearers and perjurers...who for bribes were wont to sell God and the kingdom of heaven, and purchase hell? Where, again are the usurers, who used to make a penny out of a farthing, and from eleven pence make twelve, and out of a peck of wheat or its value make two or three pecks; the false merchants, who knew how to deceive a man to his face,...and the cruel executors who increased the sorrows of widows? Where are the wicked ecclesiastics, who showed the worst example to the people; where are the haughty, where the envious, the lustful, the gluttonous and the other criminals?...You will find that, of all their riches, their delicacies and the rest, they have nothing; and the worms, as you will see, have their bodies. ...Their soul shall have, instead of palace and hall and chamber, the deep lake of hell, with those that go down into the depth thereof. In place of scented baths, their body shall have a narrow pit in the earth;

[1] Cf. similarly Nic. de Biard and Jacq. de Vitry, as quoted in Hauréau, *Not. et Extr.* vols. ii, p. 289 and iv, p. 77. See also *Old Engl. Homs.* (12th cent.), E.E.T.S. O.S. no. 53, p. 219.

[2] *A Lecture on the Study of History*, pp. 26–7.

[3] s.v. "Gloria", as before. Cf. further below, pp. 527–30, and in *Preaching in Med. Engl.* p. 344 (from § "Mors").

and there they shall have a bath more black and foul than any bath of pitch and sulphur. In place of a soft couch, they shall have a bed more grievous and hard than all the nails and spikes in the world; in place of inordinate embraces, they will be able to have there the embraces of the fiery brands of hell....Instead of wives they shall have toads; instead of a great retinue and throng of followers, their body shall have a throng of worms and their soul a throng of demons. Instead of large domain, it shall be an eternal prison-house, cramped for both. Instead of riches, poverty; instead of delights, punishment; instead of honour, misery and contempt; instead of laughter, weeping; instead of gluttony and drunkenness, hunger and thirst without end; instead of excessive gaming with dice and the like, grief; and *in place of the torment which for a time they inflicted on others, they shall have eternal torment.*

With such intensified horrors, and yet more, the fate of those who oppressed the poor was thus regularly depicted by the preachers, in the very presence of folk who had most reason to know the truth and justice of that indictment. For, from the lips of Bromyard himself and others, we learn that such was the case.[1] Who can be surprised, then, that an irate and impatient peasantry, fired afresh by the preacher's taunts, eagerly misconstruing or twisting his words, decided at length to wait no longer for the distant revenge of another world, but to strike here and now for themselves? Would not so just and understanding a God march with their hosts and bless their banners? The evil lords, lawyers, ecclesiastics and the rest, whom they sought out for vengeance, could hardly be allowed to triumph by One who knew their iniquities so well, and in fact had already prepared for them a still more terrible fate. Had not the Dominican himself declared that the rich, like the pig, are of profit only in their death?[2]

To us, acquainted, alas! in modern politics with the effects of heated platform oratory, it seems nothing short of a deliberate courting of disaster, when we hear the same preachers actually picturing to their audiences that far-off day of Divine vengeance. Through missing this curious climax to the social gospel of the times, which revealed the oppressors before the Judgment-seat, forced "in the presence of the whole world,

---

[1] Cf. s.v. "Acquisitio (mala)": "Quando pauperes seu simplices audiunt predicare contra divitum injusta acquisita, inaniter gloriantur...". Cf. further above, p. 237, n. 1.   [2] s.v. "Avaritia".

to display all their misdeeds upon their foreheads, and carry the sack of their evil gains", historians of the "Great Revolt" hitherto have been led astray in their search for immediate causes. It is not, as Sir Charles Oman imagines,[1] "the friars' old doctrine of evangelical poverty, rather than Wycliffe's theories of Dominion" that "is at the bottom of the preaching of John Ball and his allies, and of Wat Tyler's Smithfield demands", but something quite distinct from both sets of ideas. Even M. Petit-Dutaillis, in his rebuke for the socialist orator who "said recently that the Church had for long known how to soothe human misery with promises of the Beyond", has failed to bring out the real significance of that message.[2] In the great contemporary Judgment-theme, however, as expounded from the pulpits, we shall find sufficient to explain the whole conflagration that ensued. Its supreme importance for our enquiry lies in the fact that it deliberately set forth a doctrine of vengeance, which, with human nature as it is, could only end in one result. Sacred orators of the Church, as hostile to class war, to earthly revenge and social revolution as any Luther, were here themselves unconsciously formulating a revolutionary charter of grievances. With the one hand they were really instructing the rebels of to-morrow how to present their case and prepare for the struggle, while, with the other, they sought to restrain them from taking any action in the matter. Everyone can guess which hand was likely to prevail. At a crisis, the Church, with its confused Judeo-Christian theology,[3] could naturally do little better than excite and

---

[1] *The Great Revolt of 1381*, as before, p. 20. Dr Workman falls into the same error (*Jo. Wyclif*, vol. ii, p. 239).

[2] *Études Hist.* as before, p. 388.

[3] I have already alluded casually in my first volume (cf. pp. 129 and 340, n. 1) to the prevalence in our sermons of this characteristically pagan and primitive vindictiveness. It is only typical, of course, of the more learned medieval Catholic theology, as well set forth, for example, at the fountain-head, in the hideous doctrine of Aquinas—recently re-pilloried by Dean Inge—which declares that the bliss of the redeemed in Paradise will be enhanced by sight of the agonies of the tortured in Hell. We cannot therefore attribute it here entirely to the hot passions of the pulpit or of excitable public men. I postpone full discussion of the subject to my future study of Theology in the sermons.

repress by turns like an ill-balanced, disconcerted ship's captain upon the bridge who loses both head and temper in the oncoming storm. Two points, however, must be remembered in the medieval preachers' favour, reckless though their policy appears on the surface. In the first place, the very Judgment scene itself was certainly designed not to excite but to pacify and console the sufferers, while it warned the offender. The righteous poor were by means of it to know that "Vengeance is mine, saith the Lord; I will repay". This latter was a doctrine enforced by the pulpit with equal care: "All tho that all-wey be redi to avenge hem-selfe by dethe othur betynge, thise men taketh the office on hem that longeth to allmy3thy God: for God shuld only take veniaunce. For Scripture seith—'*Mihi vindicta; et ego retribuam*'. Thise men have playne cause to drede and leve here foly".[1] It was not for them to struggle and rebel. God himself had appointed their lot in this life; and their revenge and reward in the next were secure in heaven, if they remained patient a little longer.[2] "Nam multum merentur patientes pauperes apud Deum", declares Brunton.[3] Bromyard, for his part, bids the honest simple peasantry, when they behold the sinners and the wealthy winning and boasting of their ill-gotten wealth, their food and clothing, their dainties and the splendour of their homes and horses, "say in their own hearts with the country mouse (of the fable)—'I prefer my rustic poverty, with security and happiness, to those splendid banquets and robes with remorse of conscience, so many snares of men and demons and the fear of punishments in hell'".[4] God, he says, like a good house-

---

[1] MS. Roy. 18. B. xxiii, fol. 132b. Cf. similarly, *Old Engl. Homs.* (12th cent.), 2nd Ser. E.E.T.S. O.S. no. 53, p. 179, where the same text from Rom. xii, 19 is also quoted: also Bromyard, *S.P.* s.v. "Advocatus": "Ita simplices damnificati talibus [i.e. their manorial oppressors] maledicunt, rogantes quam de eis vindictam accipiant. In quo tunc eos non laudo, quia peccant..."; etc. See further below on Medieval Revenge, p. 459.

[2] For more detailed illustration of this subject, see below, pp. 569–74.

[3] MS. Harl. 3760, fol. 111b. Cf. metr. hom. in *O.E. Misc.* E.E.T.S. p. 75.

[4] *S.P.* s.v. "Ministratio". This well-known fable becomes the subject of a 15th-cent. poem by Robt. Henryson (*The Uponlandis Mous and the Burges Mous*). Cf. further, Bozon, *Metaphs.* cap. l.

holder will not fail to reckon up the faults of his household
at the year's end, and see to it that proper amends are made.
"Therefore, let the simple who suffer many wrongs from the
powerful fear not. . . . Although God now seems to connive
at such things, nevertheless in the end the harmful shall perish."[1]
At death, like the falcon and the fowl respectively, the rich,
after an easy life, will go to the midden, the poor to the king's
table.[2] "Sir, thoʒ god sende the litill, thou art never the lesse
beholden unto hym for too skilles. On ys, thou haste the lesse
to ʒeve hym acountes of at the daye of dome; and anothur,
the lesse ioye that thou haste in this worlde, the more thou
shalte have in heven."[3] Such, then, is God's good will and
purpose for the "pouere man", his hope and consolation upon
earth. "When he comyth to the deth with pacience, then shall
he be a kyng in heven with the kyng of pore men. But if
he grucche ayenst his neighbour of his stat, and be a thef and
ravissh that wher he may, then he is ytake and put in the preson
of helle."[4] We must forgive the psychological blindness which
failed to see that injured and impatient folk, confronted with
such a picture, would not be for ever content to exchange the
practical opportunities of the moment for the somewhat un-
certain sublimities of a future existence in the unknown. For,
in the second place, Holy Scripture itself seemed here to set
the preacher an example. He was not slow to grasp the
significance of the parable of Dives and Lazarus, with its terrible
account of the rich man's end. Thus, John Waldeby, the Austin
Friar, for example, chooses to describe Domesday in actual
Biblical phrases:

For "the Father hath committed all judgment unto the Son".[5] And,
in truth, "the Lord hath heard the desire of the poor", etc.[6] And elsewhere—"He shall spare the poor and needy", etc.[7] But to the rich miser
what shall he say? Surely Luke gives the answer (xvi, 25)—"Son,
remember that thou in thy lifetime receivedst thy good things, and like-

---

[1] s.v. "Nocumentum".
[2] s.v. "Divitiae". Sim. MS. Roy. 18. B. xxiii, fol. 134.
[3] MS. Roy. 18. B. xxiii, fol. 61.
[4] *Gesta Rom.* Engl. version, E.E.T.S. p. 71. Cf. also below, pp. 361–9.
[5] See John v, 22.   [6] See Pss. x, 17 and lxix, 33.
[7] Ps. lxxii, 13.

wise Lazarus evil things. But now he is comforted, and thou art tormented . . . ".¹

Bromyard himself declares likewise that Christ at the Doom will say to the rich—"Woe to you that are rich! for you have received your consolation . . . ",² and to the poor—"Come unto me all ye that labour . . . ".³ Even more threatening and relentless are the words of St James in his Epistle,⁴ as quoted by the Franciscan Nicholas Bozon in a sermonette "against the rich":

> Go to now, ye rich men, weep and howl for your miseries that shall come upon you. Your riches are corrupted, and your garments are moth-eaten. Your gold and silver is cankered; and the rust of them shall be a witness against you, and shall eat your flesh as it were fire. Ye have heaped treasure together for the last days. Behold, the hire of the labourers who have reaped down your fields, which is of you kept back by fraud, crieth: and the cries of them which have reaped are entered into the ears of the Lord of sabaoth. Ye have lived in pleasure on the earth, and have been wanton; ye have nourished your hearts, as in a day of slaughter. Ye have condemned and killed the just; and he doth not resist you. Be patient therefore, brethren, unto the coming of the Lord.⁵

We can see the great Judgment-theme of revenge taking shape, as it were, in England, as far back as the thirteenth century, in such warning tales as that of the *Speculum Laicorum* which describes the fate of the steward of a certain English earl, who "was so harsh to his lord's poor tenants that he utterly destroyed them by false accusations and extortions". The preachers tell in vivid detail how, after death, he appeared to one of the tenants, straight from hell, "clad in a black cloak,

---

¹ MS. Caius Coll. Camb. 334, fol. 155. He goes on, later: "Audiant [divites] pauperem refrigerantem, divitem gravioribus penis estuantem. Pensantur pro divitiis pene, pro paupertate refrigerium, pro purpura flamma, . . . ut, salva sit equitas statere . . . ". Cf. also typical sermons against the rich, based on this parable, in MS. Add. 21253, fol. 104b; Brunton, MS. Harl. 3760, fol. 111b; and Bromyard, *S.P.* s.v. "Divitiae": also *Poems of Jo. Audelay*, E.E.T.S. pp. 20–1.

² See Luke vi, 24–5.   ³ s.v. "Divitiae".

⁴ Jas. v, 1–7. Also quoted in *Jacob's Well*, p. 121; etc.

⁵ *Metaphs.* cap. cxix. Cf. the further use made by this preacher of *Scriptural* denunciation of the rich and great (e.g. caps. iv, vi, xi, xii, xx, xxii, xxiii, etc.); and of Baruch iii, 16–9 in *Gesta Rom.* p. 57.

shooting out his tongue and with his own hand cutting it with a razor into little pieces, then throwing the bits back into his mouth, and ever again shooting out the same member whole once more, to be cut up again: thus he continued to do...". Eventually, "when he lifted up his cloak, his body appeared like blazing iron". This, he explains, is the awful penalty for his earthly crimes.[1] In the sermon-metaphors of Bozon, early in the century following, the Judgment scene is already pictured to us with the special offenders in the foreground. As a warning to the rich, "fattened from the toil of the poor", the Friar Minor bids them refrain from molesting simple working folk at the thought of that last day of reckoning.

The righteous poor will stand up against the cruel rich at the day of Judgment, and will accuse them of their works and severity on earth. "Ha! ha!", will say the others, horribly frightened, "these are the folk formerly in contempt. See now how honoured they are among the sons of God! What are riches and pomp worth to us now who are abased!"... At the day of Judgment the simple folk will be exalted for their good deeds, and the haughty abased for their pride. Then God will do as the mender of old clothes, who turns the lappet to the front, and what was uppermost, downwards....

Here then, at last, "the rich and poor meet together".[2] The former,

when they shall come before the Lord of Heaven to render account of all their deeds and all their words, will be then as false, stinking hounds cast out of God's feast, through the stench of the money for which they trotted and galloped, spurred and ran in this world; and the others will make themselves very much at ease.... For which the former will only have mockery in heaven and in earth, as saith the Psalmist—"The righteous also shall see and fear, and laugh at him: Lo! this is the man that made not God his strength, but trusted in the abundance of his riches, and strengthened himself in his wickedness!"[3]

Such language, however, pales into insignificance before the grand indictment of the Dominican John Bromyard. Behold then the introductory setting of this preacher's scene. On the

---

[1] Cap. xi ("De ballivis et eorum periculis"), ed. Welter, p. 18.

[2] (Prov. xxii, 2) cap. xxiv. Note further how Bozon actually advises the poor to shun the rich, in this life, "to eschew evils that may turn to their hurt" (cap. l), and so *definitely encourages* the attitude of suspicion and estrangement.

[3] (Ps. lii, 6-7) cap. cxlv. Cf. further Wisdom v.

left, before the supreme Judge's throne, he tells us, stand "the harsh lords, who plundered the people of God with grievous fines, amercements and exactions,...the wicked ecclesiastics, who failed to nourish the poor with the goods of Christ and His poor as they should have done, the usurers and false merchants...who deceived Christ's members", along with the scoundrels of lower society, thieves, and the like ("although all these others, in diverse ways, committed theft, too—the lords by their confiscations, the prelates by their withholding, the usurers, merchants and other false men by their deceits...". Among the righteous, on the right hand, are many who have been "afflicted, spoiled and overwhelmed by the aforesaid evil-doers". Then will the oppressed bring a fearful indictment against their oppressors, in the Divine presence.

And with boldness will they be able to put their plaint before God and seek justice, speaking with Christ the judge, and reciting each in turn the injury from which they specially suffered. Some of them are able to say, as the subjects of evil lords—"We have hungered. But those our lords standing over there were the cause of this, because they took from us our labours and our goods". Others—"We have hungered and died of famine, and those yonder did detain our goods that were owing to us". Others—"We have thirsted and been naked, because those standing opposite, each in his own way, so impoverished us that we were unable to buy drink and clothing". Others—"We were made infirm. Those yonder did it, who beat us and afflicted us with blows". Others—"We were without shelter. But those men were the cause of it, by driving us from our home and from our land;...or because they did not receive us into their own guest-houses". Others—"We were in prison. But those yonder were the cause, indicting us on false charges, and setting us in the stocks". Others—"Our bodies have not been buried in consecrated ground. Those yonder are responsible for this, by slaying us in numerous ways and in various places. Avenge, O Lord, our blood that has been shed!"..."Our labours and goods...they took away, to satiate their greed. They afflicted us with hunger and labours, that they might live delicately upon our labours and our goods. We have laboured and lived so hard a life that scarce for half the year had we a good sufficiency, scarce nothing save bread and bran and water.[1] Nay rather, what

[1] Similarly s.v. "Munus" (poor tenants—"who perchance for many days lack a sufficiency of barley bread or bean bread"). Cf. here *Piers Plowman*, A text, pass. vii, l. 270 and B text, pass. vi, ll. 282 et seq.; also John Balle's Sermon (in Froissart, as before)—"They have their wines, spices and good bread, and we have rye, bran and straw, and drink water".

is worse, we died of hunger. And they were served with three or four courses out of our goods, which they took from us, that is to say, after their manner and denied to us in our necessity. We hungered and thirsted and were afflicted with cold and nakedness. And those robbers yonder gave not our own goods to us when we were in want, neither did they feed or clothe us out of them. But their hounds and horses and apes, the rich, the powerful, the abounding, the gluttons, the drunkards and their prostitutes they fed and clothed with them, and allowed us to languish in want.. . . .

O just God, mighty judge, the game was not fairly divided between them and us. Their satiety was our famine; their merriment was our wretchedness;[1] their jousts and tournaments were our torments, because with our oats and at our expense they did these things. Their plenty was our scarcity. Their feasts, delectations, pomps, vanities, excesses and superfluities were our fastings, penalties, wants, calamities and spoliation. The love-ditties and laughter of their dances were our mockery, our groanings and remonstrations. They used to sing—"Well enough! Well enough!"—and we groaned, saying—"Woe to us! Woe to us!" O just Lord, the minstrels and the rich and shameful persons who received from them food and robes, cried "For largess! for largess!"; and we, the poor, their subjects and creditors, cried "Flee away! flee away!";[2] for such help themselves freely as often as they like, that is, they borrow and pay back unwillingly.[3]

"Without a doubt", adds Bromyard, "the just Judge will do justice to those clamouring thus." Terrible as is the indictment of the wronged, terrible likewise will be the fate of the oppressors:

Many who here on earth are called nobles shall blush in deepest shame at that Judgment-seat, when around their necks they shall carry, before all the world, all the sheep and oxen and the beasts of the field that they confiscated or seized and did not pay for. God himself, perchance, shall

[1] Cf. *Poem on the Times* (temp. Rich. II), in Wright, Rolls S. vol. i, p. 272 ("The ryche make mery/*Sed vulgus collachrimatur*").

[2] MS. Roy. 7. E. iv, fol. 199 b has—"A lachesȝe, a failande (punning upon the "A largeeȝ, a vayland!" of the former), a maveiȝ robbeour, a deleuȝ payour!"

[3] *S.P.* s.v. "Furtum" (Bromyard goes on to elaborate, point by point, the attempts of the rich to justify themselves, annihilating their excuses one by one). Cf. similarly Myrc, *Festial,* E.E.T.S. ed. pp. 4–5; MS. Harl. 45, fol. 114b, based on the *Ayenb. of Inwyt* ("ȝoure hondes beth ful of blode. . ."); MS. Add. 41321, fol. 19; *Pricke of Consc.* ll. 5560–77; *Jacob's Well*, p. 121 ("pore men schul aske vengeaunce on the, afore the ryȝtfull iuge. . ."); *Gesta Rom.* p. 57; *Hand. Synne*, pp. 218–9; etc.

place the latter upon them, He who shall bring to judgment all things whatsoever that have been done.[1]

It is difficult to write with restraint of this superb masterpiece of homiletic art as it appears at full length in its original Latin, enriched with all the power of Satire and Complaint, all the dramatic force of which the pulpit is capable. No Judgment scene in any miracle-play can approach its atmosphere of passion and suspense, and the majestic terror of its appeal. For sheer intensity of feeling it rivals even the masterpieces of later Revolutionary oratory. Nor is it surpassed in grandeur by anything in the *Vision of Piers Plowman,* which has itself been rightly described, by those unaware of its true source of inspiration, as "the cry of an injured man who appeals to Heaven for vengeance". In the preaching of Bromyard there is much else to be found of a hardly less inflammatory character. Thus, under the heading of "Divitiae", he declares that the rich "are deceived in thinking that they are the masters of their own riches, since only for a short space are they the guardians thereof". He rebukes their folly in imagining that the whole world was created for them, or at all events in making use of it as though it had been created for their benefit alone.[2]

Many of them, if they restored what did not belong to them, would have less than a beggar, because they would have no clothing at all to cover them; because, although they ride great horses and live splendidly and nobly in the world's eyes, yet this is not of their own goods, but of

[1] *S.P.* s.v. "Judicium Divinum". With this might well be put Master Wm. of Rymyngton's sentence upon the evil clergy (MS. Bibl. Univ. Paris, 790, fol. 109b): "O quot de Christi patrimonio voluptuose viventes tantum vel plus quam laici divicias querunt inextinguibili cupiditate, eciam cum iniuriis proximorum! Quot suorum pauperum parochianorum indigencias relevare contempnunt, communiter pascentes canes venaticos et non pauperes, armigeros atque nobiles et non claudos ac debiles, adulatores et ministrallos et non viduas vel pupillos! Quid coloris, quid racionis, quid excusacionis habebunt tales in extremo examine iudicis omnipotentis, qui illis proprium commisit patrimonium fideliter dispensandum?... O dura captivitas peccatoris in carcere Gehennali! O irremediabilis afliccio! O pena interminabilis, quam nullius argenti vel auri preciositas redimit, nulla potestas eripit creature, nec eidem ullius prudencie cogitata cautela succurit. Set in quantum quis temporalibus rebus abutens delectabatur in terris illicite, in tantum punietur per ignem inextinguibilem sine fine". [2] Sim. *Handlyng Synne,* p. 196.

the goods of others, either borrowed for the period that ends at General Judgment or wrongfully seized in some other way.[1] It would be far better, therefore, for their soul *that they should be drawn by horses to the gallows of the world*, than that they should ride thus to the gallows of Hell....

The poor for their good works are not rewarded, but are so oppressed by the rich and powerful that however true a cause a poor man may have against a rich man in this world, it will none-the-less happen to him as it did to the lamb at the hands of the wolf, and as the earthen pot against the brass pot by which it is always broken.... The poor man, indeed, if he steal the rich man's goods, is hung. The rich man is not punished at all for seizing the goods of the poor, even when he is worthy of the gallows. Wherefore says Chrysostom, *super Epistolam ad Hebreos, Sermo ii*—"If it were possible to give the rich their deserts, you would see the world's prisons everywhere full of them".

Other preachers too, as we shall see, besides our Franciscan and Dominican, voice the sufferings of the poor, "where they are in great necessity, as is the case in years of dearth",[2] sometimes in tones of passion that seem to well from the very sufferer's own heart. Frantic peasants would thus learn to set over against their own pitiable state—wont, as the preacher expresses it—"with gret traweill, wo and sorowe to till here lyvelod, in cold, frostes and snowes, reynes and stormes"[3] —a new and terrible revelation of "avaritious laymen and clerks", who "possess so much wealth that it rots in their coffers; and, when they see Christ's poor dying of hunger, are unwilling to disburse anything to them from their riches. Likewise, they have so many pairs of clothing hanging on their perches, that often the latter are devoured by moths. And yet they will not give one old pair of clothes to Christ's poor, when they behold them dying of cold in the winter".[4] Their

---

[1] See further below, pp. 337, 406, etc.
[2] *S.P.* s.v. "Misericordia". [3] MS. Roy. 18. B. xxiii, fol. 168b.
[4] MS. Add. 21253, fol. 105 (the whole idea is clearly inspired by James v, 1–3). Similarly in Bromyard, *S.P.* s.v. "Divitiae"; *Jacob's Well*, p. 121 ("...in kepyng vytayle so longe tyl it han perysched and lost in stynkyng and rotyng, in sowryng, in mowlyng, or lost wyth mathys; in clothys lost wyth motthys and wyth myʒs; and in kepyng monye in exces, tyl it be ruste-fretyn, where-wyth manye pore folk myʒte a be relevyd and holpyn. Thi rust-fretyn monye, thi vitayles perysched, thi mothe-fretyn clothys schal accusyn the a-fore God at the dreedfull dome and schal askyn vengaunce on the..."); MS. Jo. Ryl. Libr. Manch. Lat. 367, fol. 256; *Pricke of Consc.* ll. 5560–77; *Ayenb. of Inwyt*, pp. 258–9 (women's robes); etc. Cf. also Bozon, *Metaphs.* cap. ci; and below, p. 398.

worst suspicions, then, were true! In the blazing words of
St Bernard, already more than two centuries old, the pulpit
takes up their bitter reply: "The naked cry out; the starving
cry out. 'What good to *us*, toiling miserably in hunger and
cold', they say, 'are all your many changes of raiment spread
abroad on your perches, or folded in your portmanteaus? It
is our stuff that you are squandering; it is from us that you
have cruelly stolen what you expend so inanely!'"[1] Says
another in milder tones—

> Certes it semeth that it may not be with-oute grete outrage and synne
> that oon persone schal have for his owne body so many robes and
> clothinges in a ӡere of dyverse coloures, and riches, thorgh whiche many
> pore men and nedy persones myght be sufficiantly susteyned and clothed
> as charite asketh. And ӡit, ӡif suche robes and clothes, after that thei
> have wered hem as longe as hem lust, were afterward ӡeven to the pore
> nedy, and for love of God, ӡit schulde it somwhat helpe to the soule.
> But thei beth ӡeven comounliche to harlottes, mynstralles, flaterers,
> glosers and other suche; and that is grete synne.[2]

The reader who has followed thus far, should now turn back
to Froissart's short summary of John Balle's sermon-message.
He will find, probably to his amazement, that, apart from its
opening and closing passages, it is virtually a brief restatement,
word for word, of what he has just been reading. Further
comment is hardly necessary. We have at last a measure of the
extent to which the preaching not merely of friars but of other
orthodox churchmen of the day was ultimately responsible for
the outbreak of the Peasants' Revolt. Strangest thing of all,

---

[1] Repingdon?, MS. Jo. Ryl. Libr. Manch. Lat. 367, fol. 256 ("et
Bernardus..."). Similarly *Jacob's Well*, p. 306 ("Seynt bernard seyth...".
N.B. mention of "the gold in ӡoure brydellys and in ӡoure aray, and the
gold in ӡoure chystes", "the rust-fretyn monye in ӡoure cofferys", and
the many "garnementys foldyn in ӡoure pyles, in ӡoure malys, in ӡoure
cloth-sacchys, in ӡoure fardellys, in ӡoure summerys, or spred abrode in
ӡoure perchys"). Cf. Menot, in Lenient, *La Satire en France au moyen
âge*, p. 311; and poem in E.E.T.S. O.S. no. 15, p. 212.
[2] MS. Harl. 45, fol. 164. Similarly MS. Salisb. Cath. Libr. 103 (unpubl. *Jacob's Well*), fol. 113. All this side of the preachers' sympathies
does not seem to me to be brought out sufficiently in Dr Coulton's
Mediev. Village (cf. cap. xviii)—at all events so far as England is concerned. Indeed, it will be seen that my evidence as given above definitely
supports Guérard against him (p. 231). See further below, pp. 565–74.

as some of our most recent footnotes testify, this violent up-
rising of the lower orders, in defiance of the Church, of Society,
of all law and order and the revealed Will of Heaven, apparently
makes not the slightest difference to the preachers' future tone.
No political storm, no civil earthquake, so it seems, could ever
shake that citadel of unchanging tradition, the medieval pulpit.
Within seven years after the revolt had been stamped out with
prison, sword and gibbet, from Paul's Cross, the most famous
pulpit in England, we catch the following impassioned phrases
from the lips of Master Wimbledon:

And covetise maketh, also, that rich men eat the poore, as beastes done
their lesous,[1] holding them lowe. This may we see all day in deed, I
dread. For if a ritch man have a field, and a poore man have in the middest,
or in the side thereof, one acre; and a rich man have all a streete saveth
o house that some poore brother of his owneth, he ceaseth never till hee
get it out of the poore mans hand, either by praier, or by bying, or by
pursuing of disceit.[2] Thus fared it by king Achab, that, through his false
queenes ginne, slow the poor man Naboth,[3] for that he woulde not sell
him his vineyarde that was nye to the kinges palace. Uppon which
proces, thus saith Saint Ambrose: "How farre will ye ritch men stretch
your covetise? Will ye dwell alone upon the earth, and have no poore
man with you? Why put ye out your fellowe by kind, and challenge to
your selfe the possession comen by kinde? *In commune to all, rich and
poore*, the earth was made. Why will ye ritch chalenge proper right herein?
Kinde knoweth no riches, that bringeth forth al men poore. For we be
not got with rich clothes, ne borne with gold ne with silver. Naked hee
bringeth them to this world, needie of meat, and of drink, and clothing.
Naked the earth taketh us, as she naked brought us hither. Shee cannot
close with us our possession in the sepulchre; for kind maketh no difference betweene poore and rich in comming hither, ne in going hence.
All in o maner he bringeth forth; all in o maner he closeth in the grave.
Who so will make difference of poore and ritch, abyde till they have a
little while leyne in the grave. Than open, and looke among dead bones,
who was ritch, and who was poore; but if it be thus—that mo clothes
rotteth with the ritch then with the poore. And that harmeth to them
that beth on live, and profitte not to them that beene dead. Thus saith
the doctour, of such extortion, as it is writ: "Other mens fields they
repeth; and, fro the vine of him that the harme oppressed, they plucke

---

[1] (lessows) = pastures. Ed. 1563 reads—"Even so as beastes eate
grasse, keping it under".
[2] Cf. the story of the *Gesta Rom.* (Juror of York), as below, p. 343,
n. 3; *Handlyng Synne*, p. 194; etc.
[3] Cf. similarly Bromyard, *S.P.* s.v. "Falsitas", and above, p. 115.

OLP   20

away the grapes". They leveth men naked, and taketh away her clothis that hath nought wherewith to helle them in cold. . . .[1]

It is no longer difficult to understand precisely why, when the revolt had subsided, both friar and Lollard received a share of the blame, and why both could repudiate the charge with equal warmth.[2] All preachers of rebuke and complaint, in fact, high and low,[3] orthodox and unorthodox together were guilty in greater or less degree of the same kind of inflammatory language, however easily they might refute the charge of communistic sympathies. In the light of our knowledge of what they said, the most recent account of the rising, by John Wycliffe's latest biographer,[4] appears, therefore, to be no nearer to the truth than any of those which have preceded it. Indeed, a large part of the second section of Dr Workman's chapter[5] will need to be rewritten with an entirely different emphasis. For, it is as idle to say, for example, that "the attacks of town-mobs on the foreign[6] merchants were the results of forces almost wholly secular", as it is to speak at all of any distinctive "Wycliffite" view of the situation. Attacks on the merchant class, as we shall soon see, were as profoundly typical of the current orthodox preaching as any other single feature of the Reformer's tract on *Servants and Lords* to which Workman adverts—duties of servants, duties of lords, waste and oppression of prelates and lords, abuses of tally-sticks and retainers, of lawyers and the rest.[7] This very tract, indeed, furnishes us with an excellent summary of the contents of our new chapter. Finally, inasmuch as that type of preaching was

[1] See Job xxiv, 6–7. *Acts and Mons. of Jo. Foxe*, Ch. Hist. ed. vol. iii, pt. i, p. 299.

[2] Cf. *Chron. Angl.* Rolls S. p. 312; *Fascic. Ziẑ.* Rolls S. pp. 272, 292–5, etc. Officialdom, as usual, is pretty wide of the mark.

[3] Cf. further, Stat. by Roy. Ord., to discover and arrest unlicensed wandering preachers, preaching temporal and spiritual sedition: *Rot. Parl.* vol. iii, pp. 124–5; *Stat. of the Realm*, vol. ii, pp. 25–6.

[4] H. B. Workman, *Jo. Wyclif*, vol. ii, cap. vii.

[5] I.e. pp. 236–45.

[6] Cf. e.g. above, Myrc's typical remarks on the Flemings, p. 134, n. 3; and the *Ayenb. of Inwyt*, p. 35: "the Caorsins thet leneth and destruith the contraye".

[7] See pp. 243–4.

not limited to England, but was spread abroad throughout Christendom, it goes far to explain also why "a wave of democratic agitation was sweeping over Europe" at the same period. In the Peasants' Revolt, as in that later Civil War between Puritan and Cavalier, it is still equally impossible to say, therefore, where the religious influences end and political influences begin. In both upheavals, the pulpits of the land were often no better than war-drums, stirring the blood of the insurgents, roaring men on to rebellion and to carnage. In both they were propagating—in Lord Acton's fine phrase—"a doctrine laden with storm and havoc".[1]

> And yet not long agoo
> Was preachers on or twoo,
> That spake yt playne inowe
> To you, to you, and to you—
> Hygh tyme for to repent
> This dyvelishe entent
> Of covitis convente.
> From Scotland into Kent
> This preaching was bysprent;
> And from the Easte frount
> Unto Saynct Myghelles Mount
> This sayeng dyd surmount
> Abrode to all mens eares
> And to your graces peeres,—
> That from piller unto post
> The powr man he was tost;
> I meane the labouring man,
> I meane the husbandman,
> I meane the ploughman,
> I meane the playne true man.[2]

Pride and avarice, or the rush for wealth, were amongst the most prominent vices of the churchmen, with which we found the preachers so concerned in our previous chapter upon their complaints. These two vices appear again, closely interrelated,

[1] *The Study of Hist.* as before, p. 27.
[2] From the early 16th-cent. poem, *Vox Populi, Vox Dei*, formerly ascribed to Skelton; see W. C. Hazlitt, *E. Pop. Poetry of Engl.* vol. iii, pp. 267 et seq.

as the besetting sins of secular society, alike in sermon and song. We cannot do better, therefore, before proceeding to a more systematic examination of the separate classes of that society, than to take some note of what were for the contemporary moralist two burning problems of the hour. First, then, of pride. Courthope, in discussing the satirical aspect of the French *Roman de la Rose*, has spoken picturesquely of Nature and Reason, "like bulls in the china shop of Chivalry", crashing about among all the delicate ideals of the feudal system.[1] Among the latter he mentions "Pride of Ancestry". No simile better describes the ruthless scorn which English preachers poured out unceasingly upon this and every other ideal, which medieval men of the world sought after or held most dear, everything of which they would be most naturally proud as successful members of feudal society. The sermons themselves give interesting insight here into the psychology of the times.

The ʒiftis of kynde are theis,—noblei of kynrede, gentilnes of blood, plente o childrin, avauncement bi eritage, strengthe, beuʒte, comelines of person. The ʒiftis of fortune arn theis,—londis or rentis, gold or silvyr, tresour, catel, clothing, hors, harneis, juellis, lordschipe, worchep and frenschip. ʒiftis of grace arn divers that God ʒif a man, as—eloquense in speking, coriouste in craft, in reding, or such othir. Theis thre maner of ʒiftis ben oonli cause whi a man waxith proud.[2]

Human nature, the English nature in particular, has here remained fundamentally the same. For each victim, intoxicated thus one way or another by "the develes wyn"[3] of pride, the homilist had a ready and often a witty retort. Those, "prowde that they come of noble kynne, and sayne they are gentilmen", may well beware.

But forsothe, and we be-holde wele here stock that they came of, and we shall se a falle. For it is tolde of oon that was an evyll doere and so prowde that his neghbores myght not lyve in pease for him: there come to him a riche man and a good man of that same contre, and asked hym

[1] *Hist. of Engl. Poetry*, vol. i, p. 184.
[2] MS. Bodl. 95, fol. 24. Cf. MS. Camb. Univ. Libr. Gg. vi. 16, fol. 48b; MS. Linc. Cath. Libr. A. 6. 2, fols. 76–76b; MS. Harl. 2398, fol. 6; MS. Roy. 18. B. xxiii, fol. 66; MS. Harl. 45, fol. 38; *Jacob's Well*, pp. 69–70; *Ayenb. of Inwyt*, pp. 16–24; *Pricke of Consc.* ll. 5896–911; *Spec. Laic.* cap. lxxxii (ed. Welter, p. 105); *Hand. Synne*, pp. 107–9; etc.
[3] MS. Harl. 45, fol. 36.

why he was so prowde. The tothere answerid and seide—"for he was a gentillman". "It is sothe," seide the tothere; "thou arte a Gentillman on thy fadres syde. But thy modre was a strumpet! Wherefore, and thou loke wele aboute, thou hast no matter to be prowde." Se, frendes, here is a falle![1]

Equally culpable are those "proude of here witt", when God might easily have made them fools, says another; so, too, of those proud of their "bodely stren3ght or bewte": "And 3itt the fayrest man that leveth and also the strongest, God may make hym ryght fowle and ryght febull, lesse than in an houre!"[2] Even nature offered her sharp reproof to such as these. For, "of erbis and treis spryngithe bawme and oyle and wynne un-to mans sustynaunce". "And thu, prowde man, bryngythe forthe nyttis, lyce, fleen and other dyverse vermyns", and yet worse.[3] Still more typical of their age, perhaps, were those proud of their office, proud of lordship and maintenance, of might and of a great reputation, "desyring worschyp aforn othere", and "lokyng after reverence, to sytten above, to spekyn first, to have the woordys out of anothere mannys mowth, to takyn worschip of the world, passing alle othere"[4]—in short, the great feudal nobility in all its glory. From the vernacular homilies, in particular, it is possible to piece together a very remarkable mosaic of the intimate behaviour of these much-hated enemies of the people, and their imitators. We behold them at close range, the grandees of the modern popular story-books—"prowde in lokyng, prowd in spekyng, prowde in hey3 crying abovyn othere,... prowd in goinge, standyng and syttyng",[5] "grym in spekynge, heynes[6] in berynge,...sory in blamynge, loth to be under-nome".[7] Their characteristic talk is "with braggynge" and "with bostynge"[8]—"to reherse that thei have don, to be holdyn dowty, and that men schulde knowe it, to have a gret

---

[1] *Gesta Rom.* Engl. version, E.E.T.S. ed. p. 416. Cf. Bromyard, *S.P.* s.v. "Dominatio" ("...licet apud mundum nobiles reputentur et curiales,... tamen apud Deum et totam curiam celestem sunt vilissimi rustici").

[2] MS. Roy. 18. B. xxiii, fol. 66. Cf. *Hand. Synne*, p. 115.

[3] MS. Linc. Cath. Libr. A. 6. 2, fol. 100. Cf. further, in my *Preaching in Med. Engl.* p. 341.

[4] *Jacob's Well*, p. 69.   [5] Ibid.   [6] = heinous.
[7] MS. Harl. 2398, fol. 9.   [8] Cf. ibid. fol. 11.

name".¹ Such an one "telleth by his owne mouth, for to be holde the more worthi, his nobles, his riches, his witte,...or elles of his folies or his myght,...or ʒeveth to losengers of his good, to preyse him so, to grete loos and preysinge".² When the story of past achievement is exhausted, they will boast of the future, and "seyn thei schal makyn this and that, as castellys or cherche, howse, or suche an-other werk". The preacher's satirical comment, as they pass, is as admirable as his descriptions: "Thei fare as the cuccuke, that syngyth but of him-self!"³ But, woe to those who must meet them in the way. The Devil has whispered in their ear—

Thou arte a lord of gret powere, othur thou arte strenger than anothur Considere this in thi soule. Othur thou arte comliere, feyrere, wysere in werkyng, more sotell in undirstondynge, more aboundant in ryches than othur ben. Qwy maketh thou, than, thiself egall with othur; and why arte thou so famuliere with powre men? Make of thi selfe to the peple as thou arte worthy; and than othur men woll holde the in reputacion and wurchippe. ("Lo, sirs! lo, sirs! This is the drynke the wiche the dewell maketh many on dronkon!").⁴

On their servants they will vent their spleen: "wen lordes or ladyes are wroth and gretly angrid, then thay sayn to her servantys, or to her maydynes—'Go fro me: go out of my syght: go out of my house!'"⁵ As for their attitude to the poor in general—especially those distinguished for their "low-nesse of blod, or foulnesse of body, other of evel schap of body other of lymes,...dulnesse of wyt,...unkunnynge of craft,... foule clothes",⁶ and so forth—some rich men, "for pryde, deyneth noght to speke with a pore man, ne unnethes to loke on him. And if thei speketh with him, hit schal be overthwerte

¹ *Jacob's Well*, p. 149.
² MS. Harl. 45, fol. 38. Cf. fol. 145, *Jacob's Well*, p. 70, and *Ayenb. of Inwyt*, p. 25.
³ *Jacob's Well*, p. 149, and *Ayenb. of Inwyt*, p. 22.
⁴ MS. Roy. 18. B. xxiii, fol. 131b ("For it maketh men blynde", he goes on, like the bats).
⁵ MS. Roy. 8. C. i, fol. 127b. Cf. MS. Roy. 18. B. xxiii, fol. 114b; "ffor, and thou serve an erthly lorde and displeyse hym, anon he will cast the in prisone, and wil not forʒeve the thi trespass".
⁶ MS. Harl. 2398, fol. 8. Similarly Bromyard, *S.P.* s.v. "Eleem." ("quos fortuna et non natura tam fecit deformes, macilentos, nudos, et decoloratos per famem et frigorem").

and despitousliche".[1] "Thei have of hem grete disdeyn for her poverte", and will even poke fun at their simplicities.[2] Furthermore, this "vaynglorie" of theirs "makes theym to cost more then they may geve, to make grete festes, and parties to holde. And thus they oversett the pore, and putt be-nethe and robben hem that lytill have, to maynten wyth theyr astate".[3] In the struggle to outshine his fellows, "everi lord bi-holdeth othur, how he is arayed, how he is horsid, how he is manned; and so envyeth other. And for to parforme this, her owne lyflodes wolen not suffice; and therfore thei bersten over and drynchen the cuntree".[4] They grow "desirous unto worldly worshippes; not only content to loke unto on cites and lord-shippes, but in to dyvers kyngedoms (they) desireth besely to be proferred".[5] One description of the lordly "householder" is worth reproducing at greater length:

ffor it is so now-a-dayes, thowȝe a man be indewyd with grete riches of the worlde, or with wisdome, connyng or eny other soche ȝyftes of grace or of fortune, al these or eny other that ben lyke to the same may not plese astate with-owte thei be mengyd with pride. Wherefore these grete lordes and other astates, the whiche ben indewyd with grete abun-daunce of riches, ȝit thei wold have moche more then thei have; and peraventure it is full evyll spent, owte of reson or owte of mesure. And thowȝe thei have never so moche, ȝit thei wyll be in dett and come more be-hynde in one ȝere then he may com before in v ȝere aftyr. And the speciall cawse is for to mayntayne theyre pride. For he wolde be callid manly and worchypfull; and also in holdyng of grete festes, feding riche men.[6] And the pore man stondythe at the gate with an empti wombe. He may rather have a knoc then a crust of brede. And so these riche men will feede them that hathe no nede; and he that hathe nede schall go with-owte. Then commythe mynstrells and cowrtyers, and thei schall have grete ȝyftes. And there gothe ther expences a-wey, be-cawse thei wolde be magnyfyed, and to bere theire name a-bowte of grete worchype.

¹ MS. Harl. 45, fol. 92. Cf. Bromyard, as above; *Jacob's Well*, p. 76, and unpubl. MS. Salisb. Cath. Libr. 103, fol. 107 (treating the poor—"as thouȝ he were of another kynde", etc.); *Ayenb. of Inwyt*, p. 196. Also the poem, E.E.T.S. O.S. no. 98, p. 333; and *Piers Plowman*, B text, pass. xv, l. 197.　　　　　² *Jacob's Well*, p. 76.

³ MS. Roy. 18. B. xxiii, fol. 152. Cf. MS. Harl. 45, fol. 38 ("foole largesse"); *Ayenb. of Inwyt*, p. 21; and below, pp. 321–2, etc.

⁴ MS. Add. 41321, fol. 19.　　　　⁵ MS. Roy. 18. B. xxiii, fol. 141 b.

⁶ Cf. here an anon. preacher's praise for his former master—"the noble knight, Sir John D." (early 15th cent.)—"a manful man *erat* de mete-ȝevyng" (MS. Bodl. 649, fol. 120b); and Chaucer's *Frankeleyn*.

Soche a man so dysposyd, when he sittithe at home in his cheyre among his prevy meny, then hathe he his communycacioun withe them. And then ther schall be grete preysyng of hym—how worchypfull an howseholder he is, in grete commending of him. But ther is none that rehersithe to hym of his grete wronges and oppressyng the pore pepyll by the menys of extorcioun; or how he hathe agrevyd his pore ney3bors wrongfully, ther-of is no communicacioun. And then puttythe he this question to them that ben abowte him, saying as Criste seythe in the gospel,... —"What seyth the pepill of me, that I am?" Se now this prowde wretcche, how he exaltithe him-selffe; and so feyne wolde be commendyd in worchyp of the worlde. ... And 3it thei that stonde a-bowte him will flater hym and preyse him an hundrythe tymes more then he is worthi; and so berithe him on honde that he is the beste man in al a cuntre. And peraventure thei lye on him every worde. For the moste parte of hys neybors cursythe him grewsly.[1]

This disease of pride runs through all classes of the community. Thus "bayles and auditores", for example, are specially prone to the infection, and scheme for "a grete name in the contrey in the which they dwelle".[2] The lowly raised to high position "will not deign to look upon their inferiors or the poor, save from a distance and from the tips of their eyes".[3] "When he lokythe a-pon hymselve and a-pon his grete aray, his wif and his meyny, his rychesse, and all-so his place, his worschipp and his honour, mervell he may that he, that was so pore and so nedy, thus hy3 now is brou3t. He is blynd as a bere. For with bry3tnes of a bason thu my3t make a bere dede."[4] The Latin sermons, many of which are older in date than their vernacular counterpart, only serve to show us afresh how unchanged and hoary are these traditional satires of the pulpit. Thus Bromyard exposes the same cherished ambitions and boasts of the mighty, the desire to excel one's

[1] MS. Linc. Cath. Libr. A. 6. 2, fol. 21 b. Cf. 122 b-3, and Bromyard, S.P. s.v. "Falsitas" (however evil and tyrannous the knight, or harmful the lord, or simoniacal and unchaste the rector, if he keeps a good table, has a great household, clothes many squires and gives presents lavishly, such an one is reckoned courtly); and *Ayenb. of Inwyt*, p. 25.

[2] *Gesta Rom.* p. 416 (Engl. version).

[3] MS. Add. 21253, fol. 32 b. Cf. Bozon, *Metaphs.* cap. c.

[4] MS. Bodl. 95, fol. 41. This latter refers to the brutal contemporary practice of blinding bears with red-hot pans, as mentioned in other sermons: cf. again Bozon, cap. cx; Bromyard, S.P. s.v. "Invidia"; etc.

neighbours whether in dress, or pride of ancestry, or titles for
one's children, or retinue, or hospitality, or worldly honour
and worship, even in the building of great castles and "curious
works" of art, and the reputation "for having so fair a concubine, for playing well at chess, or for being skilful with the
lance or the dice-box".[1] "The squire is not satisfied unless he
lives like a knight; the knight wants to be a baron; the baron,
an earl; the earl, a king....He who perchance can only spend
twenty marks justifiably, spends thirty or forty."[2] Similarly,
with the pride of lesser men, the ministers of lords and ladies,
who boast of their success, their riches, their intimacy and
special favour with their masters, and the gifts they win.[3] Many
of the latter, Bromyard says, are like the bad dog in the story,
which was only "belled" because it was a nuisance. "As the
ape, which is afraid when it occupies a low position, but when
on high grins upon all around and mocks them, so are many
when placed in positions of power."[4] Nor are we allowed to
forget that pride of the lordly exhibited even in their death,
in sumptuous funerals and rich marble tombs, polished and
carved and painted, "really ornyd with precious clothinge of
silke and of palle",[5] agreeing ill with the rotting, worm-eaten
corpses within them. Those who erect church windows and
other memorials to their own honour and glory (like Langland's
Lady Mede), says the Dominican, ought strictly to give more
prominence in the inscription to the names of the poor and
simple whom they have spoiled on their road to riches, than
to their own proud names. They merely rob Peter to give to
Paul or to God an unacceptable offering.[6] Bishop Brunton,
in his turn, bewails the strife and murders that ensue, when

[1] See s.v. "Ascensio", "Beatitudo", "Bona Fama", "Discretio",
"Filiatio", "Gaudium", "Laus", etc. Cf. Old Engl. Homs. (12th and
13th cents.), E.E.T.S. O.S. no. 29, p. 49.
[2] s.v. "Dominatio". [3] s.v. "Ministratio". [4] s.v. "Superbia".
[5] Gesta Rom. Engl. version, p. 305. See refs. given in my Preaching
in Med. Engl. p. 158, n. 3; and Hand. Synne, p. 276.
[6] See ibid. pp. 162–3; similarly Bromyard, S.P. s.v. "Eleemosyna".
Cf. Barclay, in his Eclogues:
"They robbe Saint Peter therwith to clothe Saint Powle,
And like as dayly we both may see and here,
Some pill the churche, therewith to leade the quere...".

outraged pride seeks to avenge the insult offered by another. Like Bromyard, and again like Master Rypon of Durham, he denounces the excessive expenditure of haughty nobles that leads to an empty purse and the spoliation of "neighbours and poor tenants with exactions and extortions", to maintain their proud estate.[1] Rypon, and the anonymous preacher who is probably Wimbledon, together witness to the new growth of a more general social pride and ambition among the lower orders of society, prophesying the demise of feudal civilization. Jack is now as good as his master. "Now is the knave clothed as was formerly the knight, and the servant-girl as her mistress. It is a grave mistake!", says the one.[2] Says the other— "Scarcely is there any man to-day content with his status. Inferiors are always eager to be equal with—or perchance to outshine—their betters, by any means that they can".[3] "This pest, namely of pride, is mother and source of all the vices." The very standards of right and wrong are confused and perverted thereby. "A prowde man is callyd an honest man. ffor now a dayes, thowȝe a man be never so prowde of hert or of speche, of cowntenaunce, thynkyng in hys hert that ther is none so feyre ne so fressche, so lustye ne so iocunde, so goodly, so manly, so bewtyfull as he is, and women in theyre degre on the same wyse,...what is that pride? Nay, forthe, he seythe it is clenlynes and honestye...".[4] The Benedictine subprior of Durham would attribute even the Papal Schism to its ravages. For "it seems to some discreet persons, that the pride and vainglory of the ambitious are the outstanding causes of it".[5] Little wonder, then, that the very heavens rained down indignation, to the eye of the simpler homilist: "So it semeth that for pride commeth often tymes grett vengeaunce ryghtfully".[6]

[1] MS. Harl. 3760, fol. 128b ("superbi domini"). Bromyard and Rypon, as below. Cf. *Piers Plowman*, B Text, pass. xiv, ll. 204 et seq.
[2] MS. Harl. 4894, fol. 27 (see also fol. 67b, etc., and below, p. 369). Cf. in *Poem on the Times* (Rich. II), in Wright, Rolls S. vol. i, p. 272 ("Gentyls, gromys and boyys / Socii sunt atque gulosi"); etc.
[3] MS. Camb. Univ. Libr. Ii. iii. 8, fol. 145b.
[4] MS. Glouc. Cath. Libr., *Sermo V post Trin.* (unpaginated).
[5] MS. Harl. 4894, fol. 27.
[6] MS. Roy. 18.B. xxiii, fol. 124b.

Avarice, twin sister of Pride, or better, perhaps, the favourite daughter of her womb, figures under many names and disguises in the two literatures of our study. "Thet is the maystresse thet heth zuo greate scole thet alle guoth thrin vor to lyerni, ase zayth the wrytinge. Vor alle manere of volk studieth ine avarice, and greate and smale, kinges, prelates, clerkes, an lewede and religious."[1] It is hard to say whether she and her many-sided activities give more scope to the preachers or to the poets of satire. The latter, for example, have told of her enterprise, in our period, in the rôle of "Sir Peny" and of the Lady Mede.[2] The former delight to picture the power which she exerts as that of a deity, working miracles and commanding everywhere the worship of men.[3] "To such a degree are the people of to-day given up to avarice", says one of the preachers just quoted, "that they would sooner do things for gold than for God. They expose themselves to every peril on land and on sea, peril of thirst, peril of hunger, peril of cold, peril of rivers, peril of robbers" for gold, but not for God.[4] "Indeed, I fear that there are few now in the world, who would not grieve more over the loss of a little gold, than if they had lost God, through mortal sin. · And over the discovery of gold they would boast more than if they had found God by grace, whom they had lost. . . . *Now nys no god but gold alone.*"[5] If a poor man, the speaker goes on, were to come asking help of some rich neighbours, "for the love of his father and mother and all those dear to him", they would

---

[1] *Ayenb. of Inwyt*, E.E.T.S. ed. p. 34.
[2] See in J. E. Wells, *Man. of Writings in Mid. Engl.* p. 239, etc. (as publ. in *Reliq. Antiq.* Ritson, Hazlitt, etc.): cf. abroad, the vogue of *Dom Argent*, e.g., as discussed in Lenient, *La Satire en France au moyen âge*, pp. 179–91.
[3] Cf. *Hand. Synne*, p. 199, and Bromyard, s.v. "Avaritia", etc.
[4] See again below, p. 352 (the merchants), and cf. MS. Roy. 18. B. xxiii, fol. 84: "Thei love so moche the rychesse of this worlde, that thei traveyleyn hem-selfe almoste to the dethe. Aldaye we mowe see that for good and catell men put here bodies in grett aventure on the see and on the londe, and wakon nyght and day, and suffres many grett deseses for temporall good. . .", etc. (but not for "goostely good").
[5] Later, the preacher inserts in this Latin sermon the phrase—"God schal be god, wan gold nys none".

deign neither to hear nor see him. If, redoubling his entreaties, he were to beg,

"My Lord, for the love of Christ crucified and all the saints of God, help me, lest I be destroyed unjustly by my adversaries", still there would be "neither voice, nor hearing";[1] although three or four words from that lord would probably expedite the whole business. But if that same poor man were to sell the few things he has and needs, or borrow gold for the purpose and offer it along with his request, then "the blind and deaf" would straightway both hear him and smile upon him. Lo! what great miracles gold works in days such as these![2]

Bromyard speaks frequently in a like satirical vein: "To money all hearts and deeds alike of evil men are obedient. Thus a certain one was wont to say that if he wanted a god other than the God of heaven, he would have money for his god; for having money, he would have all things", in earth and in heaven too—to wit, the power of redemption from his sins![3] Again, although the crosses of the penitent, the Crusader and others, he declares, can do much for body and soul, yet some people prefer to put their trust in the cross of wealth on which their god, silver, was crucified. For this god actually works more miracles than the true God with his cross of wood.[4] The latter rectifies *some* that are lame and bent, but not all. "The former, however, rectifies all cases in the courts of the false, however 'tortuous' and 'curved' they may be. And if it be had in plenty and in due reverence, it makes the lame walk and the captives go free. Deaf judges and lords and those in power, who—however unjust be your case—offer a deaf ear,

---

[1] See 2 Kings iv, 31 (the MS. here has "spiritus", in place of the Vulgate—"sensus").

[2] MS. Camb. Univ. Libr. Ii. iii. 8, fol. 145. Cf. again, MS. Roy. 18. B. xxiii, fol. 122: "What shall I then seye of thise ryche men that, be lawe and connynge rewle, governe all other? ȝiff thei plete for a man, and is quarell be trewe, anone thei wene that thei have getton heven for here mede. But for gode that is, after that ther love is sett. ffor, and thei do itt principally to resceyve grett ȝeftes, ther trewly, than, thei have resceyved hire mede, and no rewarde in heven . . .".

[3] *S.P.* s.v. "Avaritia" (cf. Eccles. x. 19: Vulgate version).

[4] This is precisely the imagery of *Piers Plowman*, C text, pass. xviii, ll. 200–9 (the Noble and the Cross). The idea occurs much earlier in the *De Cruce Denarii*, a satiric poem attributed to Walter Map (ed. Thos. Wright, *Lat. Poems attrib. to W. M.*, Camden Soc. 1841, pp. 223–6: see also App. pp. 355–62).

it makes to hear. Thus 'the deaf hear'. Dumb advocates, also, it makes to speak. Thus 'the deaf speak and the blind see'".[1] Page after page in the same bitter satirical strain will be found in the *Summa Predicantium*. "Money conquers: money rules."[2] Money bribes or gifts, we are told, will free the robber, the murderer, the deceiver in the law courts, and even in the prison, where God Himself would never shield the culprit from his just retribution.[3] Juries, judges, advocates, are all amenable to the same influence. Like weathercocks, says the preacher, they will turn automatically at every wind of silver.[4] Laws will be stretched to meet the briber's case. Legal proceedings will be dragged out unnecessarily for the sake of greater fees.[5] As Wimbledon puts it again—"Sheriffs and bailiffs will return poor men's writs with a *Tarde venit*, except they feel money in their hands. And yet, I hear say of men that have proved both courts, that the court which is called more spiritually Christian is more cursed".[6] A fragment of verse inscribed in friar John of Grimston's sermon note-book sums up the situation:

Pecunia
- maket wrong rith.
- maket day nith.
- maket frend fo.
- maket wele wo.[7]

Space forbids us to follow the wellnigh endless ramifications of avarice, as it pushes its way up and spreads through the whole atmosphere of medieval Society. Langland's description of "the route that ran aboute Mede" in *Piers Plowman* is

---

[1] s.v. "Crux". Cf. further Bozon, *Metaphs.* cap. iii ("a purse of silver can do more on earth than Truth..."); *Jacob's Well*, p. 137: "the coveytouse lovyth bettyr a *d.* and *ob.* than God..."; MS. Harl. 2398, fol. 79 (men putting their whole trust and soul in "londes, rentes, gold and selver", etc.); and Coulton, *Life in the Midd. Ages*, vol. i, p. 112.
[2] s.v. "Munus".
[3] Cf. s.v. "Divitiae", "Falsitas", etc.
[4] s.v. "Acquisitio mala". Cf. *Gesta Rom.* Engl. version, pp. 58–9.
[5] s.v "Advocatus", "Judices", etc.
[6] Cf. further, below (the lawyers), pp. 341–8, etc.
[7] MS. Advoc. Libr. Edinb. 18. 7. 21, fol. 14.

merely the metrical paraphrase of typical sentences in Brom-yard—

> As of kni3tes and of clerkis, and other comune peple,
> As sisours and sompnours, shireves and here clerkes,
> Bedelles and baillives, and brokoures of chaffare,
> Forgers and vitaillers, and vokates of the arches.[1]

Every grade of society and every type of person, says the Dominican, is smitten with this vice—clergy, laity, craftsmen, merchants, the advocate, the bailiff, etc.: their sole concern is how to acquire worldly wealth. "It makes the dishonest labourers work badly; it makes the poor into robbers; it makes the middle class become usurers and concealers of corn, when the poor perish with hunger; it makes the lords tyrants; it makes false meddlers cite their neighbours before kings' courts to engage in lawsuits with them for the evil enrichment of their lands. This is therefore a general famine and disease, contaminating the whole body in wish, or word, or deed."[2] Here, and elsewhere, we read how the greedy layman, like the greedy ecclesiastic, seeks to pile land upon land, lordship upon lordship, bailiwick on bailiwick.[3] "If he have a house, he wants a village; if he have a village, he desires a whole city. If he has got the latter, he desires a county, and then a kingdom. To be sure, even if he have a whole kingdom, he will not be content, not even if he alone should have all the kingdoms of the world."[4] Like Alexander, he will sigh for fresh worlds to conquer. Bromyard compares the struggle to that of the Titans warring against the gods, with mountain piled on mountain.[5] "Ever the more thei have, the more thei nedeth. ffor the more a man hath, the more meyne he mote have. And the more meyne that he hath, the more sustenaunce hym nedeth. And he that hath moste hors hath moste nede of stables and knaves...."[6] Vivid, thumb-nail sketches of the avaricious man in various walks of life are no more hard to find in these sermons than are those concerning the proud:

[1] B text, pass. ii, ll. 57–60.
[2] s.v. "Avaritia".   [3] s.v. "Ascensio". Cf. above, p. 255.
[4] MS. Camb. Univ. Libr. Ii. iii. 8, fol. 149b.
[5] s.v. "Ascensio".
[6] MS. Harl. 45, fol. 107b. Sim. *Ayenb. of Inwyt*, p. 210.

Thou may see also what the covetouse man is, and what likynge that he hath in is wikkednes. ffor he is ever besie to gadere to thethure myche good[s] and to ley up; and bethenketh hym full narrowly how that he may begyle is evencristen, and to oppresse is poure ney3bors; and will be an entremettoure in every mans cause; and therby he hopes, with-in processe, to lede and rewell all the countrey. 3itt itt is now3the inowgh to hym but 3iff he be a grett purchesoure; and 3iff a poure man have a crofte beside hym, that must nedis be is, or els he will make hym to lese as muche as it is worthe.[1] Suche a man among grett men and lordes is a grett ffelowe. But be is poure ney3bour he settis no price. And 3iff a man tell hym of is grett exstorcioun that he hath don, he lifteth up is shuldur and law3heth hem to skorne, and seyth—"What grewith it me thoo thei curse me!" (Poure men...arn worthe a thousaund of hym, ffor al is riches.)[2]

Like Dives, however, such an one, after all, doth but "make hym fat to the fendis lardre".[3] Further, avarice makes men fight one with another, like dogs over a bone, neighbour with neighbour, brother with brother, son with father, brother with sister; "and wellnigh all strifes, discords and law-suits are caused by Avarice".[4] He, to whom we first listened on this topic, shall close the discussion for us:

This vice is the reason why there is so much falsity, so much trickery, and so much ingratitude amongst men.... This vice is the cause of that Schism and discord, which now are and for long have been in the Church. Through this vice our realm [of England] has been so impoverished that the people have scarcely the where-withal to live, because the proud and the worldlings expend the treasure of the realm in evil and useless fashion.[5]

The task of illustrating fully and adequately the preachers' Satire and Complaint, as they concern each separate class of the community, will have to wait for other hands. Here a few more or less typical examples must suffice to whet the reader's appetite. Students of the future will be able to trace at their leisure the gradual elaboration of these pulpit criticisms in England, where they may be found at least as early as the twelfth century. In the *Speculum Laicorum*, in the century fol-

[1] Cf. Wimbledon, above, p. 305.
[2] MS. Roy. 18. B. xxiii, fol. 122b.
[3] MS. Harl. 2276, fol. 3b.   [4] *S.P.* s.v. "Avaritia".
[5] MS. Camb. Univ. Libr. Ii. iii. 8, fols. 149b–150.

lowing, knights, merchants, usurers, lawyers, bailiffs, peasants and thieves are amongst the victims subjected to this kind of treatment. Likewise, the "class attacks" of Nicholas Bozon and the various English exponents of Peraldus and Lorens, early in the fourteenth century,[1] offer us a further salutary reminder of the antiquity of many of the sermon complaints as set forth in later homilies. These, and the many older surviving examples in continental manuscripts, are of the first importance when we come to consider the debt of earlier poets and song-writers to this pulpit tradition. To the clamour raised against the greater nobility of England, the present chapter has already borne its witness upon almost every page. Every fresh sermon-book that we handle seems to tell a similar tale. An exceeding great and bitter cry goes up from the pulpits of the land against those who are here pictured as monsters of cruelty and extortion. It is but the clear and more enduring expression of another and a far deeper cry, hoarse and inarticulate:

> This wickede pride amonge lordes and knyttes, that causeth this oppressinge of the pore peple, maketh now so gret a noyse and soun, that it is a gret clamour in al this rewme, in everi schire therof, of the extorcioneris that dwellen therinne, whiche beth as tiraunte kynges, over-ledynge the peple, as Pharao ladde the childern of Israel. . . . The tirauntie and wrongful overledynge on the pore peple...of this tirauntes is so gret and peineful to bere, that the noyse and the cri of here preyeris is herd in to the heres of god in hevene, as it was of the cheldern of Israel, for the wrongful oppressinge of Kyng Pharao in Egipte.[2]

Bromyard can imagine yet another sort of clamour, rising in accusation against the same race of tyrants: "If now the sheep and oxen, the fowls and capons and all the beasts which the

---

[1] E.g. Robert Manning of Brunne, Michel of Northgate, etc. (cf. my *Preaching in Med. Engl.* pp. 289–90).

[2] MS. Add. 41321, fol. 19. Cf. further *Old Engl. Homs.* (12th cent.), E.E.T.S. O.S. no. 53, pp. 177–9, 211; etc.; Bozon and Bromyard, as here quoted, passim; Brunton, as below, pp. 581–4; Rypon, MS. Harl. 4894, fol. 27 ("talliantur, spoliantur et crudelius tractantur", etc.); *Gesta Rom.* Engl. version, pp. 42, 57, 59, 129, etc. (taxes, tallages, extortions, spoilings and robbings, etc. of the poor, bondmen and tenants, etc.); MS. Harl. 45, fol. 66b ("byreveth and bynemeth here poure tenantes;...taxith and pileth here bonde tenauntes and othre..."); etc. For the *Poems*, see Wright's collections aforementioned, and Kail's Introd. to *Twenty-six Pol. and other Poems*, p. viii; etc.

rich eat and do not pay for...were to cry out in their bellies [as in St Patrick's case], there would be a greater noise, perchance, in their bellies than in Noah's Ark where all the animals were together".[1] Nothing that the powerful enjoy or delight to do, apparently, is without its accompaniment of anguish for the peasantry. "What sort of persons, for the great part, are the rich and mighty men of the world?" asks Master Rypon, in his sermon. "Assuredly", he replies, "they are proud and greedy, exactors and oppressors of the poor; the fairer among them are the more lustful; the stronger are violent smiters, not defenders of their country; the eloquent and worldly-wise are the greatest deceivers of their neighbours with falsities, lies and subtleties; the well-born are now frequenters of the greatest ribaldry, for they are gamblers, perjurers, and filthy talkers."[2] To a similar question, raised in one of his own discourses, Bishop Brunton makes similar reply, calling the "*magnati*"—"extortioners, destroyers of their tenants, detainers of tithes and oblations, violators of church rights, and always the most unpleasant schemers against the Church".[3] As a class, none it appears had a good word to say for them, save their own heralds, retainers and flatterers, who cry fawningly—"I am wholly at your service, always ready to do your will and favour".[4] In a borrowed fable of the wolf and the shepherd, Bromyard reveals in a single sentence the fundamental cause of most of their characteristic vices. The wolf had killed more sheep than he needed for his own personal sustenance, simply because he had other people in mind. There was the dignity and pomp of his lady to be maintained;[5] there were sons to be promoted; there were daughters to be given in marriage with suitable dowries; there was a retinue of servants to be nourished. For these and like reasons, he had

---

[1] *S.P.* s.v. "Furtum" (cf. the Miracle of St Serf, as recorded in Andrew of Wyntoun's *Orig. Chron.* ed. Scot. Text Soc. vol. iv, bk. v, cap. xiii, pp. 82–5).

[2] MS. Harl. 4894, fol. 173b.   [3] MS. Harl. 3760, fol. 142b.

[4] *S.P.* s.v. "Amor Carnalis". Cf. again, s.v. "Adulatio".

[5] Cf. here the sermon-story of the English knight who fleeced the poor to secure the money to provide his wife with new elaborate headgear, in MS. Add. 27336, fol. 70 (Ital. prov.).

so inordinately "eaten and drunk and clothed himself out of the labours of the poor".[1] Six further sources of extravagance are specified of the nobility in another part of the *Summa*: their dress, the beauty of their steeds, the splendour of their houses, and gold and silver plate, the size of their households and the variety of their food.[2] A further vignette by the same master hand will show us how the evil end was often accomplished, when lords were hard put to it to keep up their estate. He says that the nobles

in their youth are attracted to hunting, to jousts and the like, and all forms of sports and amusements which delight the body. Because they cannot indulge in these without great expense, frequently they become out-of-pocket. To have this state of deficiency made clear to them, fawning counsellors are called, who say, "Your land is rich, your men—God be blessed!—are well off. Therefore you can impose a levy on them, without causing hardship".[3] And if that lord himself is not yet accustomed to the cruelty of his advisers, and, wishing to act more mildly, would say—"It is better to do thus...", they resist him, saying—"My lord, you pay attention to your pleasures and amusements, and let those who have greater experience meddle with the control of your estate".[4]

So the evil is done. Bromyard compares the nobleman thus provoked into a policy of oppression by his own ministers to the lion that is said to lash himself with his own tail to excite the passion of cruelty towards his prey.[5] A vernacular homilist here utters a significant warning:

Grete lordes and men of grete estate schuld busiliche take hede what thei schulde hyre, and what they schulde leve. But ofte in her contrees is lesynges, flaterynges and losengries grete chepe; and no thing so dere

---

[1] s.v. "Acquisitio Mala". Cf. s.v. "Avaritia".

[2] s.v. "Nobilitas". Cf. further, e.g. MS. Salisb. Cath. Libr. 174 (*Liber Sermonum* of Thos. Cyrcetyr), fol. 286; etc.

[3] Cf. again, s.v. "Adulator": "Dicent, 'Habes rusticos divites tales et tales. Potes accipere ab eis xx marcas, et non gravabis eos. Habent enim boves et oves multas'..."; and s.v. "Consilium": "Respondit, dicens, 'Oportet vos habere taxam populi vestri, vel decimum denarium ecclesie; quia ad illos subditos vestros oportet vos habere in necessitatibus vestris recursum'. Postea petitur a secundo et tertio, et omnes dicunt quod primus bene dixit, quia nullus vult offendere".

[4] s.v. "Dominatio". On the subject of evil counsellors, see further, s.v. "Consilium", "Mundus" (The Weathercocks, as in *Rich. the Redeles*; etc.); *Handlyng Synne*, p. 277; etc.

[5] Ibid.

there as is treuthe and sothfastnes. And therfore thei beth comounliche deceyved. ffor thei hyreth to lightliche, and leveth to sone that men seith, if hit be to her likynge.[1]

At this point we can follow the preachers afield, as they introduce us to scene after scene in the lives of these oppressive noblemen, pointing with angry finger at the source of each new oppression. Like the brutal ass in Æsop's fable, we are told, terrifying the little birds and ruthlessly trampling on their nests as he strays into the undergrowth, they bring terror to the poor and simple, with their threats and their pomp.[2] "Sometimes, they speak in person, saying—'Sell me such and such land, or such and such a business, because it would be pleasant to me!' or 'Give me so much money for my daughter's marriage, or for some other reason. Otherwise it will go ill with you; because you did such and such a thing to me',— attributing to them what they never did at all." At other times they will send an intermediary to perform the ruthless task, with guile and caution. "This messenger of Satan, despatched to the simple man, says to him—'Do this, because so-and-so is your friend. Otherwise his case will go ill!'" Like the ape, sociable and placid in youth, but vicious and hateful in old age, seneschal, bailiff, or attorney, says Bromyard, once amiable and charming enough in student days, but now primed by their own lords and masters to be otherwise, become "cruel, hellish, diabolical lions". "It behoves them to enrich their lord. Otherwise they will not be reputed discreet; nor will they be able to hope for greater things for themselves. Therefore such an one says to himself—'Unless I produce from my office as much as my predecessors, or more, I shall lose my tips and my office as well'."[3] Well do they know how to extort

[1] MS. Harl. 45, fol. 162b. Cf. *Rich. the Redeles*, E.E.T.S. ed. pass. iii, ll. 117–8.

[2] Cf. here Bozon's shrewd advice—"By this we learn how we ought to play with people who are in power in a bailiwick or lordship, who thro' being provoked by big words will not be overcome, nor be stirred by threats, but will be overcome by water—soft speech and prayers" (cap. lxviii).

[3] s.v. "Advocatus". See further s.v. "Dominatio" ("dominos ad crudelitatem exasperant, intantum quod si forte vellent [domini] in aliquo mitius agere, et causas et inopias pauperum audire, et de gravi exactione

a fine of five shillings for an offence involving sixpence. As for their evil masters, they indict, tax, cruelly illtreat and imprison their subjects who refuse to sell them land at their bidding or otherwise refuse to fulfil their requests, thinking that, because they allow them to live on their estates and defend them against other lords, they have a right to fleece them at pleasure. Others will even allege "acts of piety" as their excuse for such conduct.[1] Page after page of the fiercest denunciation will be found in the sermons against these "officers of gret men that wereth her lyverethes; the wiche, by colour of lawe and aȝens lawe, robbeth and dispoyleth the poure peple, now betynge, now sleyinge, now puttynge hem from hous and landes. Like as thei here there lordis saile blowe, so thei be meved".[2] "Prevey robbers ther buthe mony, and menteynyd by ther maisters, as fals bedels and baylyes, fals heywardes and iaylers, ...fals assisers and okerers, fals auditars and recevers."[3] They themselves are "day theves" lurking in the woods; and their "seculer lordes beth trees of this wode, under whos power they lorketh and spoyleth the peple".[4] Like "infernal millstones", between them they grind the poor, "one lying stationary in peace, while the other travels round".[5] The poor, indeed, lay almost wholly at their mercy. Bromyard tells us how their masters have only one reply for the tenant who seeks an interview: "You may go to my seneschal or my bailiff!" "Thus the lords neither know nor care to know the miseries of their subjects."[6] Sometimes it happens, however, that those who thus encourage or connive at acts of cruelty on the part of their officials are themselves bitten by them. For, the wicked

seu a mercatione vel redditu quem propter paupertatem vel infortunium solvere non possent eos in aliquo alleviare,...dominum verbis provocant", etc.). Cf. further, Bozon, *Metaphs.* cap. v (many stewards would rather go with their lords to hell than speak up against their will in defence of the poor); etc.

[1] s.v. "Acquisitio Mala". See further, s.v. "Justitia".
[2] MS. Roy. 18. B. xxiii, fol. 142.   [3] MS. Bodl. 95, fols. 5 b–6.
[4] MS. Harl. 2398, fol. 100.   [5] *S.P.* s.v. "Nocumentum".
[6] s.v. "Dominatio". Cf. further, s.v. "Divitiae" (the cruelty of the rich is largely due to the fact that they have no experience of the miseries of the poor, and therefore are quite unaware of what the naked, the hungry, the homeless and the imprisoned suffer).

bailiff or reeve, who does not hesitate to bully and fleece his
lord's tenants, urging him on with a "so-and-so did thus
against your estate—or despised you thus—or said this about
you...",[1] will not hesitate, when the time comes, to cheat his
own master.[2] Alas! as Bromyard admits, it all comes back
upon the unfortunate peasantry, they who, in the end, alone
have to bear the brunt of every adversity on the baronial
domain. As for the swarm of unruly retainers—"no hounds
were ever readier for the chace, no hungry falcon for the bird
it has spied than are these to do whatever their great lord bids
them, if he should want to beat or spoil or kill anyone".[3]
Their livery may be safely trusted to shield them from any
just penalty in the courts for their misdeeds.[4] For the rest,
they are as the whelps of the lioness that, the more they are
multiplied, the more increase the hunger and rapacity of their
parent, and as "the locust that hath eaten that which the
palmer-worm hath left".[5] They follow their lords about
greedily collecting the spoil that has escaped the latter; and,
when their masters' hosts or visitors have been already burdened
enough with the costs of entertainment, they will not go away
without receiving their own share of gifts. "When they get
outside the gate, they immediately hold conference among
themselves, saying—'What have you got?' If, to be sure,
nothing has come their way, they grow angry, slanderous and
abusive." Once off duty, "they think and say the foulest
things, and act after the manner of hogs that are always ready
to wallow in filth: like hogs, too, they are always eating. What
is left over or what they can lay hands on—that properly

---

[1] *S.P.* s.v. "Ministratio". Cf. MS. Harl. 45, fol. 71; etc.
[2] Cf. *Ayenb. of Inwyt*, E.E.T.S. ed. p. 37 ("ontrewe reven, provos,
and bedeles, and seriions that steleth the amendes and withdraȝeth the
rentes of hire lhordes..."); Rypon, MS. Harl. 4894, fol. 36b (con-
cealing rents); MS. Harl. 45, fol. 65; *Jacob's Well*, pp. 128–9 ("baly,
sergeaunt or reve" falsifying their lord's accounts, slily reckoning receipts
less than expenditure, etc., for their own profit: "also a baly that may
areste a theef and letyth hym scape, for mede"; etc.).
[3] *S.P.* s.v. "Falsitas".   [4] s.v. "Correctio".
[5] See Joel i, 4. The passage is used similarly in the *Epistolae* of Peter
of Blois, xcv (Migne, *Patr. Lat.* vol. ccvii, col. 293), from whom Bromyard doubtless derived the idea (cf. further below, pp. 331 and 336).

should be set aside as alms—they carry off for their concubines and other dishonest persons. . . . Are they not admirably portrayed by the hog?"[1] In an equally brilliant little satire our friar-preacher pictures the whole tribe of insatiate feudal monsters as beasts of prey attacking a corpse. First come, says he, the larger beasts to pluck the larger morsels, such as the lion and the bear. These are "the great prelates and lords, who devise and levy great and excessive exactions and dues for the marriage of their daughters, for the knighting of their sons, for superfluous expenses at tournaments and the like, for mishaps and for horses lost in the wars, for the ransom of those imprisoned in enemy territory, and much else". When these have had their fill and gone away, then come the lesser beasts, who did not dare to touch the corpse earlier when the greater beasts were at it. These are "seneschals and bailiffs: and they vex the people with grievous and unjust amercements and fines for the lord's work, and gifts and gratuities for their own". Finally come the kites, crows and other birds to take their share—the lesser retainers, for their perquisites. By the time these finish, "they leave neither flesh nor sinews on the bones".[2]

[1] s.v. "Dominatio". Cf. further MSS. Harl. 45, fol. 77b–8 and Salisb. Cath. Libr. 103 (unpubl. *Jacob's Well*), fol. 102b (against the lord's "yvel meyne"); Bozon, *Metaphs.* cap. lvi; etc. For prelates' retinues, see *S.P.* s.v. "Correctio".

[2] s.v. "Ministratio". See here the yet more elaborate satire of the feudal oppressors, s.v. "Dominatio", compared to the "great image" and the "four great beasts" of the Book of Daniel (chaps. ii, 31–3, and vii, 3–7), and the four pests of Joel (i, 4): (1) the great tyrant-princes, as the head of gold, the lion and the palmer-worm; (2) their great counsellors, judges and chamberlains, as the breast and arms of silver, as the bear "with three rows in the mouth and teeth", and as the locust; (3) the lesser ministers, e.g. constables, bailiffs, provosts, castellans, seneschals, etc., as the belly and thighs of brass, as the leopard, and as the locust-grub (bruchus); (4) lesser "ministers", e.g. grooms, squires, footmen, etc., in hall and stables, as the legs of iron, as the "fourth beast" (like a wild boar), and as the mildew (Vulgate version). "De predictis quatuor simul copulatis potest dici illud (Prov. xxx, 21)—'Per tria movetur terra, et quartum non potest sustinere.'" etc. Another detailed figure of the diabolic feudal state appears s.v. "Servire". Animal imagery is freely used elsewhere for such social pests: cf. further, e.g., *Spec. Laic.* cap. xi (ed. Welter, pp. 17–8): evil bailiffs compared to the crab preparing to devour the oyster, to the bear, etc.; Bozon, *Metaphs.* cap. v (stewards

Even so, the tale of woe is not ended. For there thrives within castle and manor-house walls another unholy throng of heralds, minstrels, jesters and other idle flatterers, who, as we have seen, receive the robes and food denied to the honest beggar.¹ These are a further source of mischief. For "they spread false tales among the great, saying 'He said such things as this', or 'He did so-and-so against you', and thus stir up quarrels and wars".² In a figure of the "ecclesia malignantium", Bromyard compares the hall or court of an evil prince to the Human Belly, "wherein much filth is collected". Its sevenfold iniquity includes false adulation, a greedy lust for offices, the taking of bribes and the sale of justice, envy and false pretences of friend- ship with the lord, with sham salutations, honours, gestures, evil confederacy, banquetings, vain sports, unnatural night revelry and daytime repose.³ Finally, we descend to the lordly retainers of the animal world, the lap-dogs, palfreys, apes, falcons, hounds and other pets so delicately nourished and tended at the hands of their fond masters and mistresses. With glowing sarcasm our Dominican tells how the wealthy

provide for their dogs more readily than for the poor, more abundantly and more delicately too; so that, where the poor are so famished that they would greedily devour bran-bread, dogs are squeamish at the sight of wafer-bread, and spurn what is offered them, trampling it under their feet. They must be offered the daintiest flesh, the firstling and choicest produce of every dish. If, glutted, they refuse it, then, as though they were infirm, there is a wailing over them on the part of those whose bowels yearn with pity for the afflicted....⁴

as the wild boar), lxviii (bailiffs as the hedgehog), xcix (bailiffs and stewards as the ant-lion); etc. See also, Odo of Cheriton (Herbert, *Cat. of Romances in B.M.* vol. iii, p. 71); MSS. Add. 21253, fol. 31; Harl. 2398 (*Memor. Cred.*), fol. 20b; Harl. 45, fols. 67, 71; *Jacob's Well*, p. 129; *Ayenb. of Inwyt*, pp. 39, 43; etc. Abroad, cf. Nic. de Biard, on "the wolf" (Hauréau, *Not. et Extr.* vol. ii, p. 285).

¹ See above, p. 11; and cf. *Piers Plowman*, C text, pass. viii, ll. 102 et seq.
² s.v. "Bellum". ³ s.v. "Servire".
⁴ Cf. here, Chaucer's *Prioresse*, who feeds her hounds on "rosted flesh", "wastel-breed", etc., and weeps over them (*Cant. Tales*, Prol. ll. 146–50). Bromyard continues—"Et quia delicatus catellus panem vel carnem non recipit nisi minutatim fractam et manu porrectam, eodem ore non loto quo posteriora socii tangit digitos tangit porrigentis, quos

After luncheon, for the larger hounds whole bread is brought in, and these folk break it and offer it to them with their own hands, where they permit the fragments left over to be given to the poor—and that by the hands of others, contrary to that injunction in the last Chapter of the Book of the Proverbs[20]...and in the 58th Chapter of Isaiah[7]—"Deal thy bread to the hungry". The latter does not say—"to the dog", as is plain from what follows, but—to the poor man. None-the-less, alas! where they daintily cherish the dog, they despise their own flesh. For, their acts prove this. For, where many deaths of men have been seen or heard to occur from starvation, who has seen dogs dead from starvation in any number,—or even a very few of them? The Prophet continues—"Bring the needy and harbourless into thy house": he does not say—"dogs". And yet where the poor are not even received in barn or granary, dogs in the house are welcomed to chamber and to couch!...He continues—"When thou shalt see the naked, cover him": he does not say the ape or the palfrey which they cover, turning away naked God's son....

Therefore the aforesaid are not to be called "men" but cruel "sea-monsters, that have given suck to their young"[1] (Lament. iv, 3).

Space alone forbids us to reproduce more of this homiletical indictment of the medieval aristocracy. For much more yet remains. Our preachers do not forget to denounce many of those feudal wrongs which play so large a part in the historic attacks made subsequently upon that great privileged class. When existing manorial rights and customs are deemed in-sufficient, then, we are told, "wyckede lordes...rereth yvele lawes and yvele customes, the whiche beth selde undo other relesede, after that they beth bygynne".[2] They encourage their bailiffs to establish yearly precedents in their favour, and struggle to maintain their ancient rights by taking matters into court and hunting up the law-books.[3] They have another evil practice of fixing by statute "a certain price for things offered

non lotos ori proprio immediate dirigit, sciens quod 'non lotis manibus mandicare non coinquinat hominem' (Matth. xv, 20 and Mark vii, 2). Sed prohdolor! tarde ita delicate nutrirent vel familiariter, exemplo Sancti Lodovici, os tangerent leprosi vel mendici!" The occurrence of the above passage of Scripture adjacent to mention of the *catelli* eating of the crumbs that fall from their masters' table in the same chapter (q.v.) would seem to have suggested this association of ideas.

[1] s.v. "Eleemosyna". Cf. further on the decay of almsgiving by the rich, MS. Bodl. 649, fol. 44 (an "eclipse"); Bozon, *Metaphs.* cap. lxxii; etc.

[2] MS. Harl. 2398, fol. 21 b.

[3] s.v. "Consuetudo" and "Feriae seu Festa".

for sale on the domain, as in the case of animals, wine and the like; which statute they commonly call by the name of 'Assise'".[1] Then "the rich man goes hunting with his dogs and falcons, and catches the hare or the bird, and tramples down the poor man's corn, while the latter gets no share in the booty".[2] Well do they merit the curses of the rustics for their callous conduct, declares the indignant preacher.[3] "Again, the poor and middle-class folk are taxed, and the aristocracy are exempted".[4] In this fact alone Bromyard sees imminent danger to the State. "Such a community", he declares, "will be neither peaceful nor durable." Wages are frequently left unpaid; and then "servants are robbers, carrying off their lord's goods at their own pleasure".[5] To whom, indeed, might the poor man turn for redress? As we have seen, he "is helpelissh in this cause. For, and he compleyn to anny othur gret man, ther is no rekener; for he is of the same condicions hymselfe, and commonly the gret holdeth togethur. . . . And ʒiff he goth to the lawe, ther is non helpe; for trewly lawe goys as lordshipp biddeth hym".[6] The *Summa Predicantium* speaks ominously of the "hatreds and cursings engendered" by such violation of justice in the courts.[7] Brunton, in one of his sermons, pictures the typical result when "discord arises between two temporal lords, or between a prelate and a temporal lord" on neighbouring estates. "At once the temporal lord provoked to malice gives orders to his servants, as follows: 'Such-and-such a prelate has proceeded against me unjustly. I give orders that

[1] s.v. "Lex".
[2] s.v. "Ludus". Cf. further the humanitarian objection to hunting, from the animals' point of view, in John of Mirfield, *Flor. Barthol.*, MS. Camb. Univ. Libr. Mm. ii. 10, fol. 258; and Thos. Gascoigne, *Loci e Libro Verit.* p. 224.
[3] s.v. "Nobilitas".   [4] s.v. "Civitas".
[5] Brunton, MS. Harl. 3760, fol. 124b. Cf. also, Bromyard, *S.P.* s.v. "Dominatio"; MS. Harl. 2398, fol. 21b; MS. St Albans Cath. fol. 36b; *Hand. Synne*, p. 83; etc.; and see further below, p. 365.
[6] MS. Roy. 18. B. xxiii, fol. 134. Similarly Bozon, *Metaphs.* cap. lv. Cf. further the vivid passage in *Jacob's Well*, p. 41 (the peasant discovered by his lord's steward to be behind with his rent "in the old court-rollys and rentallys, and in the newe, bothe"); etc.
[7] s.v. "Civitas".

if any of his servants or tenants or his animals stray on to my domain, they are to be dealt with severely, and the animals seized'. And thus frequently servants and tenants who have done no wrong are outrageously beaten, and their beasts impounded, until they die." After a while, peace is proposed by a mediator, and the hostile lords make peace and proceed to discuss compensation for the damage done. But alas, the outraged tenants and dependents get no compensation: "The lords have all".[1] Those who sail the sea of this world, says Bromyard, are always in danger of the rocks and tempests of great men, tyrants, false princes or local magnates who through pride or avarice are at enmity. Unable to please both of the contending parties the unhappy "mariner" is sure to be shipwrecked by one of them.[2] Finally, as they fleeced their enemies and their subjects, so the nobility fleeced church and monastery, when it suited them.[3] "Those who were wont to be founders are nowadays confounders."[4] The one duty which would have justified their existence, and for which they were originally constituted, they now neglect: "Non patrie defensores!"[5] Little wonder that the homilist attributes to them and their misdeeds a yet more ominous disaster:

For batels beth reysed welny3 in every lond [of] Christendom, shedyng of Cristen blode continually, gret and huge. And to sey shortely, welny3 in every coost of the marches, Cristens mens lordeshippes decresses and goys downeward, and the lordshippes of hethen men groweth upward

[1] MS. Harl. 3760, fol. 122b et seq. Similarly in Bromyard, *S.P.* s.v. "Dominatio" and "Justitia". Cf. the final remark in Bozon, *Metaphs.* cap. xii ("So the rich take all").

[2] *S.P.* s.v. "Judices".

[3] Cf. Brunton, MS. Harl. 3760, fol. 113b ("...valde habent timere divites et domini temporales, qui, licet sui predecessores sancte et iuste regulati monasteriorum pauperum Christi fuerant fundatores, isti tamen consilio malo ducti student quomodo huiusmodi locorum deo dedicatorum esse poterunt confusores..."); Bromyard, s.v. "Avaritia", "Bellum", "Dominatio", etc.

[4] MS. Heref. Cath. Libr. P. 5. 2, fol. 68 ("Hodie [ecclesia] violatur et opprimitur per maiores et magnatos terre, et ipsorum spelunca est. Nam ipsi qui solebant dotare et fundare, ipsorum successores nituntur destruere et eradicare....Illi qui solebant esse fundatores sunt hodie confundatores..."); etc., etc.

[5] Rypon, MS. Harl. 4894, fol. 173b (as before).

and increseth. For seuerly oure Cristen prynces, with-in this XL ʒere and lasse, hath lost more than the thirde parte of Cristendom. Lo! ther peyn answeres to ther synnes. For, lik as oure princes and lordes spoyleth and robbeth ther sugettes and doth daily, even so God suffreth the ethen princes to robb and spoile oure lordes and princes, even as thei do to othur. . . .

Sith than every charite begynneth of hymselfe, and I see so gret perils and, by synne, vertews distruccioun, ther-fore I pray as the prophete dud—"Lord, make me sauf; for the seyntes ben gon!"[1] [*Vulg.* Ps. xi, 1]

The lesser nobility, the knights and their attendants receive comparatively little notice in English sermons of the four-teenth and fifteenth centuries. But the verdict of the preachers is summed up in that familiar appellation—"carpet-knights". The very satirical phrase used of them in a *Poem on the Evil Times of King Edward II*[2] occurs in the *Summa Predicantium*—"liouns in halle, and hares in the feld".[3] It was derived in the first place, apparently, from some version of the twelfth-century *Epistolae* of Peter of Blois, Archdeacon of Bath and later of London, a favourite homiletic source for subsequent generations.[4] Early in the thirteenth century, the English homilist, Odo of Cheriton, passes a similar judgment upon the decadence of some of them in one of his sermons.[5] "Is not the hand of the English knighthood, once strong and gracious,

---

[1] MS. Roy. 18. B. xxiii, fol. 139. Cf. again, fol. 168 ("ther-as sumtyme amonge lordes was fortune and grace reynynge, that aʒeyns hem myght no reme stonde, but ther enmyes were full fayne to take pese and treuse with hem, now is grace and fortune with-drawe, and we be not only sett aboute with enmyes with-oute forthe, but also with-in. . . . Thus the world is transposed up-so-downe. . .").

[2] See Wright, *Pol. Songs*, Camden Soc., as before, p. 334.

[3] s.v. "Militia" ("Hi sunt in pretoriis leones, in preliis lepores").

[4] The paragraph of Bromyard, *in the middle of which* the phrase occurs, is clearly taken from *Epist.* xciv. The phrase itself, however, is missing in the version given in Migne, *Patr. Lat.* vol. ccvii, col. 293 (Bromyard quotes—"sicut ait Petrus Blesensis in quadam Epistola"). Peter was born c. 1135, and died c. 1204.

[5] See Herbert, *Cat. of Romances in B.M.* vol. iii, p. 37, quoting MS. Arund. 292, fol. 23 b, and Hervieux's ed. (*Fabul. Lat.*); etc.

now feeble?" asks Bishop Thomas Brunton, a century later.[1] Rypon, our representative monastic orator, about twenty years after Brunton, echoes the same sentiment: "Assuredly, what Valerius says (lib. iv) is true to-day. To-day many knights are given up to wantonness and ease, to dicing and fowling. Many of them spend more time upon the ornamentation of their clothing than upon exercises of arms, the business of wars and the endurance of labours".[2] All, with one accord, look back from their own day and generation to some golden age of chivalry in the past, more imaginary than real, doubtless, when "there were many strenuous knights in this land, alike of the Round Table as of the *gartir*".[3] But now—"the days are evil". It is to Bromyard, however, that we must turn again for the more detailed and vivid analysis of their condition. The waning of the Crusades and the Crusading spirit had already spelt a decline in their manners and morale, as it had closed a healthy field for their activities away from the temptations of life at court or upon the manor.[4] The unsuppressable Dominican bewails that, alas! few in his day take the Cross and go to the Land of Promise, either in the letter or in the spirit, electing rather to remain "in Egypt and Babylon, that is, the land of Confusion—in delights and sins". Amongst reasons here given for the unpopularity of Crusading are the fear of imprisonment and slavery as captives in the Land of the Infidel, the fear of

[1] MS. Harl. 3760, fol. 152. Cf. Folsham, referring in his sermon to the older knighthood (MS. Worc. Cath. Libr. F. 10, fol. 61) under 'King Edward", at the Battle of Crécy,—"quia nullus fugeret, nec haberet fossales milites secum...".

[2] MS. Harl. 4894, fols. 188b–189. Similarly poems in Wright, Camden Soc. p. 335, ll. 253–7, and Rolls S. vol. ii, p. 252; etc. (Cf. later here— "rapientes aut destruentes bona proximorum suorum:...debent milites honorare sanctam ecclesiam, non spoliare...", etc.) Judging from the number of stories in the *Gesta Rom.* (Engl. version) in which knights commit acts of fornication and adultery with the daughters of their friends and hosts, one would gather that their moral reputation was very low, to say the least. This seems borne out by Brunton, MS. Harl. 3760, fol. 142b, etc. ("eo quod non est natio sub celo ita de adulterio diffamata sicut natio Anglicana").

[3] Anon. (c. 1420), MS. Bodl. 649, fol. 119b.

[4] Cf. here the literary historian, Courthope, *Hist. of Engl. Poetry*, vol. i, p. 203.

expense and of a lack of provisions for the expedition, a carnal devotion to one's family, home and estates, and finally the insignificance of the forces on the Christian side.[1] Bromyard's satire of the "carpet-knights" is as deliciously amusing as it is evidently true to life. Like retired commanders or half-pay colonels, sitting at their ease with their fellow-clubmen amid the luxuries of Pall Mall, they love to rattle off armchair reminiscences by the hour, boasting of the deeds they never did, or could do. "Some do go, indeed, to the Holy Land", says Bromyard, "out of a certain curiosity or spirit of amusement, with the intention of returning, so that they can narrate what they have seen and heard, in boastful fashion among their neighbours, *with additions (cum additamentis)*!"[2] As for those who do not go, "many, sitting and bragging in their own land, boast how they would like to kill many Saracens, and do wonderful deeds, saying—'They are dogs! One Christian against twenty of those dogs!' But when it comes to the point, they are afraid of a petty insult". They are like the little bird in the fable, says the preacher, which in some countries is known as St Martin's bird. He boasted that he could prop up heaven on his own legs, if it were to fall down. Just then the branch of a tree fell. In terror, he cried out—"in French" —"God and St Martin, help your bird!"[3] When they go in all their pride and splendour to the tournament and the joust, it

[1] s.v. "Crux". Cf. poem in Wright, Camden Soc. p. 334, ll. 248–50.

[2] s.v. "Bellum". Cf. here the Lollard(?) preacher on the contemporary pilgrimage-making in MS. Add. 24202, fol. 27b: "for men that may not haunt her leccherie at home as they wolden for drede of lordis, of maystris and for clamour of neȝeboris, thei casten many dayes byfore and gederen what thei may...to go out of the cuntrey in pilgrimage..., and lyven in the goinge in leccherye, in gloutenie, in drunkennesse, and mayntenen falsnesse of osteleris, of kokis, of taverners, and veynly spenden hore good...; bostyng of her glotenie whan thei comen home that thei never drank but wyn in al the iourney....And summe men don it of her owne grett wille, rather to see faire cuntreys than for ony swete devocioun in her soule to God, or to the seynt that thei seken". With Bromyard's mention of their "tall stories", cf. *Piers Plowman*, A text, Prol. ll. 48–9, B text, Prol. ll. 48–52, etc.; and Chaucer, *Hous of Fame*, bk. iii, ll. 2122–4.

[3] s.v. "Crux". The *exemplum* of St Martin's bird is taken from Odo of Cheriton, where it is similarly applied. See above, p. 205. (Here the bird is said to be Spanish.) It occurs also in MS. Harl. 7322, fol. 26 b.

is largely with a view to making topics for future conversation of a similar kind.

Who has been heard to praise, or could praise any of them for strenuous battling with the enemy, or for their defence of country and Church, as Charlemagne, Roland, Oliver and the other knights of antiquity are commended and praised? But rather for this—that they have a helmet of gold worth forty pounds, *ailettes* and other external insignia of the same style and even greater price; that so-and-so carried into the lists a huge square lance such as no one else carried, or could carry, and that he flung horse and rider to the ground; and that he rode so well and wielded that lance of his so nimbly, as if it were of the lightest: or again, that so-and-so came to Parliament or to the tournament with so many horse. And what, after all, is praise of that kind, but praise of the impious, of wretches and of the timid?...For they expose themselves in places and times of peace and not of war; and to their friends, not to their enemies. Of what value are arms adorned with gold, then, that only make the enemy bolder (as is shown under *Arma*...),[1] which, too, when in flight from their foes, they fling away, so that they may flee the faster—as happened of late? What praise is it to bear a most mighty lance against a man of peace, and to fling horse and rider to the ground; and not touch the enemy with any lance whatever, because one does not want to approach him near enough to let him touch one with the longest kind of weapon? Or what praise is it that such a man rode so well and wielded his lance with such ease, that he conducted himself so nimbly against his friend and neighbour and fled so nimbly from the enemy of the realm? What praise is it that such are glorious and seek praise in prohibited deeds of arms, as in tournaments and the like, while in deeds of virtue, such as in just wars and in defence of their own country, they are timorous, cowardly and fugitive, allowing the enemy to devastate the land, to plunder and to pillage, to burn the towns, destroy the castles, and carry off captives?[2]

Upon the tournament and the joust our medieval preacher looks with angry countenance. No outward show of brilliance in the lists, no glittering finery in the stalls, no brave pageantry of knights and men-at-arms, bright eyes of ladies[3] or gay laughter and excitement of holiday throng can ever deceive him. For him it is no romantic spectacle such as the minstrel praises. Beneath the surface and behind the scenes his eye

---

[1] q.v. ("que tamen vanitas hostes potius provocat quam terreat...").
[2] s.v. "Nobilitas". Cf. further, s.v. "Labor": "sicut ergo miles equum suum morti exponit pro vana acquirenda gloria"; etc. For the knights' love of tournaments, see further s.v. "Arma" ("milites et generosi moderni").   [3] On women's evil influence here, cf. *Hand. Synne*, p. 154.

travels to the needless suffering inflicted upon the innocent, discerning only the waste and extravagance that spell some fresh impoverishment of the needy. "Greed, lust of pleasure, vanity and hurt on either side", these are the influences which he sees here at work. Tournaments, he reminds his audience, in the first place, are forbidden by the Church "because of the deaths of men and perils to their souls which often arise therefrom".[1] But, were there no ecclesiastical prohibitions, natural law and man's commonsense should be enough to prevent such irrational games—"in which one is injured while the other is made glad; in which one is tortured in soul and suffers loss, while the other gains nothing". Above all—

the tournament of the rich is the torment of the poor: for, while the former are spending lavishly upon such amusements, they either torture their subjects with tallies and exactions, or else, where they pass by, pay nothing to them save "wooden money".[2] At the same time, along with this, they bring with them a host of malefactors, all of whom must have hay and oats, food and drink on account, like their lords, while they are on the road. . . . Little wonder, therefore, that they indulge freely in such amusements, for the purposes of which they seem to have so much without paying for it. If they stayed in one place, they would have to pay, or else borrow upon interest.

Thus "with the most lavish expenditure, with grievous blows, hard suffering and wounds, they purchase the garments of vanity in their sports of arms; with the greatest expenditure, I say, both of horses and of the gifts which they bestow so plenteously on heralds and minstrels, for the praise of men and the brief reward of vain men's applause". "Where have tournament-players ever been seen or heard to give as many

[1] "Secundum Hostiensem" (i.e. Henricus de Segusia (Susa), the famous Canonist; Cardinal Bishop of Ostia, 1263–71; ambassador of Henry III to the Pope in 1244). Cf. again s.v. "Arma".

[2] I.e. the abuse of the tally-sticks: see further s.v. "Eleem."; above, p. 82, and below, p. 338. With this cf. *Poems* in Wright, Camden Soc. pp. 377–8 and Hartshorne, *Anc. Metr. Tales*, pp. 36 et seq. (*Tale of King Edward and the Shepherd*): "and payen but a stick of tre"; *Piers Plowman*, A text, pass. iv, l. 45; B text, pass. iv, l. 58; C text, pass. v, l. 61; *God spede the Plough*, E.E.T.S. ed. l. 30; etc. For Wycliffe see Workman, vol. ii, p. 244. (For the purveyors themselves, cf. in our sermons, again, MS. Salisb. Cath. Libr. 103, fol. 106b: "A lord sendyth hys purveyourys aforn there he wyll come".)

horses to the Church or the poor as they lose in the lists?"
asks our homilist indignantly. For the dishonest knight, indeed, the tournament might actually provide the means of
enriching his own stables.[1] To the preacher's rebukes, however, he and his kind offer a ready excuse—"How shall we
know how to defend Church and Realm from enemies, unless
we learn to have the use of arms?" "They add, moreover,
that they hold tournaments and jousts for such purposes!"[2]
Such, then, are the medieval heroes of the turf, as our pulpit
sees them. Such are they, who, in the sarcastic words of Peter
of Blois,[3] repeated by Bromyard,

bear shields richly gilded, and cause the plunder of their enemies rather
than the strife, the campaigns and the conflicts to be depicted and read,
so that they may delight with a kind of imaginary sense of heroism in
battles which actually they would not dare to enter or witness. They
return from the expedition, without wound or scar, with arms whole by the
grace of God. Everyone runs to see them. They sing of battles long
drawn out. . . .

However, "In peace, plunder; in war, flight" is their true
motto. As the preacher proceeds, we observe that even the
courtesies of Chivalry are waning. "Forsooth, the order of
Knighthood now is to observe no Order. For, his mouth is
polluted with great foulness of words who swears the more
detestably and fears God the less, who vilifies God's ministers
and has no respect for the Church."[4] These are the things
which are reputed braver and more distinguished in knightly
circles, to-day, says our preacher. Those who do them would
seem to belong to the Order of the Knights who crucified Christ,
he adds, mocking Him and spoiling Him of His garments,
slaying and losing Him afresh.[5]

The knights in their own homes, like every other class of

---

[1] See s.v. "Acquisitio Mala".

[2] *S.P.* s.v. "Ludus". See, s.v. "Audire verb. Dei", Bromyard's reference
to a sermon preached against tournaments which touched the heart of a
certain great man. Cf. further, MS. Bodl. 95, fol. 15; *Hand. Synne*,
pp. 153–4; etc.   [3] *Epist.* xciv, as before.

[4] Cf. further: "juramentis suis et aliis peccatis Christum, quantum in
eis est, iterum crucifigunt et occidunt". Similarly, poem in Wright,
Camden Soc. p. 335, ll. 260–4; *Piers Plowman*, A text, pass. iv, l. 105; etc.

[5] s.v. "Militia". Cf. the miracle-plays, as quoted below, p. 495.

society, now aimed apparently at copying the vices of their superiors.[1] At least, such is the testimony of the contemporary pulpit. A vernacular homilist, probably at the end of Richard II's reign, complains thus:[2]

Also thei that ben in the estaat of kny3thode, thoru this foule synne of pride, stieth faste and passeth hili hir estaat in al maner aparaile that longeth unto hem above hire auncetres[3] that weren bifore hem, whiche hadden myche more lifelode than thei have now. ffirst, in proude araie of houshold. There-as hir auncetres weren wond to be servid in hir houses at mete in pewtre vessel, but if there weren any peeris of the reem, now it is no3t worthe but if a mene bacheler, 3ea, and dyverse squyers also whiche ben come up of non olde auncetrie, but bi extorcions crepen so hi3e, musten be served with sylveren vessel; and the leste page in his house, hire clothynge also axeth so hie cost, bothe in cloth, peerlis and pelure, that oo garnemente passeth in coste half moneie of hire lifelodes in a 3eer. There also, as sum tyme a worthi bacheler of gret estaat hilde him apaied to ride with 5 or 6 hors, now a pore squyer wole ride with 9 or 10 3emen, alle of sute of as gret araie as sumtyme weren ful worthi squyers.
But what wole falle of this pride? I am sikir... that other thei mut be stronge thefes to robbe here neiboris in the cuntre, or wrongful extorcioneris, to meyntene with hire proude estaat; or falle in to so gret dette, for borwynge to that proude araie, that nether thei ne hire executours moun never quyte halven del, and hire eiris haven levere hire faderis soulis li3e in helle thanne selle any percol of hire heritage to quyte with hir faderis dettes.... [So it comes about that, in addition to the greater nobles] smallere men, as kny3tes and squyers of the cuntre overledeth hire pore tenauntes and hie semple nei3heboris a-boute with wronge amerciamentes and hie proude thretynge wordis, that thei ben ful fayn, for to lyve in pees, to fyne at hire wille; and if he mai have any color to his nei3hboris lond, he my3te as wel atte firste goo ther-fro and seie it is not his, as forto with-stonde suche a man bi plee.[4]

"The kny3t", says another, moralizing from the game of chess, "betokenyth gentilmen that rennyth aboute and ravisshith and ioyeth for her kynrede, and for habundance of richesse."[5] Whether in time of war or so-called peace, it is all the same with them. The monkey does but copy his master. Sometimes,

[1] Cf. here, above, p. 313.
[2] MS. Add. 41321, fols. 101–101b, 103b.   [3] = ancestors.
[4] Similarly Bromyard, S.P. s.v. "Militia": "sicut faciunt quidam qui occasiones querunt ut aliorum possessiones vel pecunias extorqueant".
[5] Gesta Rom. Engl. version, p. 71.

indeed, he would manage to score off him as well, when the chance came to get a better mount.[1]

To-day [continues Bromyard] they receive their blades from off the altar, that they may make profession that they are the sons of the Church, and that they have taken the sword for the honour of the priesthood, the protection of the poor, the avenging of evil-doers and the freedom of their country. But, forsooth, the whole matter is turned the other way. For to-day, as soon as they are decorated with the belt of knighthood, they rise up against their fellow Christians, rage violently against the Patrimony of Christ, plunder and spoil the poor subject to them, afflict the wretched pitiably and pitilessly,[2] and fulfil their extravagant wills and lusts.[3]

Like the barons, they are accused of inflicting unjust tallages, exactions and abusive customs upon their subjects, and extorting excessive fines from them.[4] In wartime proper, they go with the armies, not with the prayers of the people behind them,

but with the curses of many. For they march, not at the king's expense or their own, but at the expense of the churches and the poor, whom they spoil in their path. And if they do happen to buy anything, they give nothing but tallies in payment. Christ fed five thousand on five loaves. These men do a greater miracle; for they feed ten thousand on little tallies,...not once or twice, like Christ, but frequently. And not men only, like Christ, but dogs and horses too; not with bread and fishes like Christ, but with delicate meats (and rich armour)....Thus, while the English army was recently marching by against the enemy, in proud array of this kind, a certain worthy person remarked that they seemed to be going to a feast rather than to war![5]

Such, then, are the vices that Chaucer's Knight eschewed.

It would be idle to attempt here any kind of systematic survey of the preachers' revelations on the subject of lawyers

---

[1] Cf. *S.P.* s.v. "Labor" ("sicut ergo miles in casu lucri vel vanae gloriae equo non parcit, sed eum cum calcaribus urget et perditioni exponit, et specialiter quando sub largo domino militat, a quo sperat equum habere meliorem").

[2] "miserabiliter atque immisericorditer affligunt miseros."

[3] s.v. "Militia". Cf. MS. Add. 21253, fol. 105 ("raptores, bedalli, *et milites*"), and above, pp. 320 and 321, n. 5.

[4] s.v. "Mundus" (Chess moralization, § Miles).

[5] s.v. "Bellum". On the pillaging of the people in wartime, see further s.v. "Ministratio".

and the law. Specialists who work on the early history of English legal practice will in future turn to these long-neglected sources and give us the relevant detail in its proper setting. For, in some points, apparently, the revelations are invaluable.[1] Our present concern, however, is merely to make their existence known, and, in particular, to connect them with the current popular literature of complaint. Of all classes in the kingdom, destined to benefit from the new gospel of Piers Plowman in Langland's *Vision*, we read:

> Men of lawe lest pardoun hadde, that pleteden for Mede.
> For the sauter saveth hem nou3te, such as taketh 3iftes
> And namelich of innocentz, that non yvel ne kunneth.
> *Super innocentem munera non accipies.*[2]

Probably about the very period when the poet was cogitating these lines of his new version,[3] Bishop Brunton of Rochester delivered a sermon, in which he dealt with the subject of English justice in those times. After quoting a passage from the Book of Proverbs[4]—"The vows of the just are acceptable with God", he proceeds thus:

> But these things notwithstanding, to speak solid truths, it is the same with the Justice of the English as it was with the Justice of the Jews at the time of Christ's Passion. For, just as Christ had manifold testimony of his own justice from his opponents, namely from Pilate, Pilate's wife, Judas the Betrayer, the thief and the centurion, yet contrary to all justice was betrayed to death, and Barabbas, the famous thief and murderer, was freed from the death which he deserved, the Jews unanimously striving for the death of Christ, in these words—"Come, let us oppress the just man, who is contrary to our doings",[5] so also is it with the powerful men of the world to-day and the leaders of our realm.[6] If one just man

---

[1] The late Mr Herman Cohen, barrister-at-law and author of *A History of the Engl. Bar and "Attornatus" to 1450* (1929), kindly wrote to me as follows (Oct. 1927): "Your *Preaching in Med. Engl.* has been very useful to me in revealing Bromyard's chapters on 'Advocati' and 'Judices' for some research work on the Early English Bar;—indeed in some points invaluable...". "The criticisms of Bromyard re-echo John of Salisbury and William of Drogheda; but he is the earliest I know to suggest that sometimes petty jurors were bribed, etc."

[2] B text, pass. vii, ll. 39–41.

[3] Cf. below, p. 579.   [4] xv, 8.

[5] Apparently a combination of Wisdom ii, verses 10 and 12.

[6] Cf. similarly a 13th-cent. Secular, in Hauréau, *Not. et Extr.* vol. iv, p. 231.

is found who will not consent expressly, for the fear of God, to their own evil plans, or who secretly speaks against them or publicly rebukes or interferes with them in some way or other, immediately, as though he were their enemy, they strive to oppress him, by slandering him in private, by reproving him verbally, or by actually persecuting him. And so, "the just perisheth, and no man layeth it to heart" (Isa. lvii, 1). If a voluntary murderer or most notorious thief, who according to every law ought to pay the just penalty of his wickedness (2 Machab. vii), is captured in order that justice may be done upon his person, as though in compassion, they strive to free him from danger, some saying—"He is young: if the youth has done wrong, the old man will be able to amend". Others declare—"He is of our blood: if the Law proceeds against him, the whole of our clan will be shamefully disgraced". But, in the case of such men, to spare on grounds of relationship would be to offend both God and the Law. . . .[1]

And in the realm of England so many laws abound, and yet there is no utterance or observance of the laws.[2] It seems likely that unless these injuries, injustices and wrongs are very quickly reformed by execution of the laws, it will be, in short, the destruction or at least the transference of this realm, according to that saying of Ecclesiasticus x, [8]—"A kingdom is translated from one people to another, because of injuries, injustices and wrongs, etc."[3]

With this general verdict the English pulpit would appear to be in entire agreement—exactly, indeed, as we should now expect. The stern condemnation of the poet, the actions of the insurgent peasantry, the anger of the homilist who affirms that "the myȝty juges of this worlde...shall not yn the day of doome ben mor worth than wormys, or ellis worse",[4] all express in their own way a common woe, from which the poor and innocent suffered daily. Bromyard declares that England now enjoys an evil name among foreign nations for her lack of justice, for the reign of perjury and false-witness, for the crimes that flourish unchecked and unpunished—robbery, murders, mutilations, woundings and cruel beatings.[5] The reasons are not far to seek. In a brief catalogue of the prevalent vices of each social class, this eminent preacher and canonist

[1] Similarly Bromyard, s.v. "Falsitas" and "Divitiae".

[2] Cf. *Poem on the Times* (15th cent.), in Wright, Rolls S. vol. ii, p. 252 ("Many lawes and lytylle ryghte / Many actes of parlament / And few kept wyth tru entent"); and further, below, p. 583.

[3] MS. Harl. 3760, fol. 236.　　　[4] *Gesta Rom.* Engl. version, p. 305.

[5] s.v. "Falsitas". See also s.v. "Civitas" and cf. Brunton, MS. Harl. 3760, fols. 142b–143b, etc.

attributes four to the judges, the first of which is the significant word "*Munera*".[1] Here, then, is the equivalent of Langland's well-known phrase—"Ac symonye and cyvile and sisours of courtes were moste pryve with Mede of any men, me thou3te."[2] Equally significant are the remaining words of the homilist— "*Amor, Favor, et Odium*". All the satires and complaints of English medieval preaching against the law do little else than ring the changes on these unhappy themes. In respect of them, as we have seen already in more than one sermon-collection, the ecclesiastical lawyer was held as guilty as, if not guiltier than his brother of the civil court.[3] "For bothe Cristen courte and seculere courte...goon for golde and 3eftes, and trewthe is forsakon."[4] We may well begin our brief survey on this occasion, not with the more elaborate and better-informed Latin sermon-manuals, but with those penned in the vernacular, and therefore alike in their brevity and simplicity more in a line with the popular metrical songs. These give us in the main a threefold impression: first, that the lower orders of society are entirely at the mercy of a class of trained and educated specialists who take full advantage of their superior equipment in a highly technical field. "The wytty men of this worlde, as justycis, vocates and men of lawe, these men have power in length and brede and depnes upon gentylmen of myddel degre and upon pore men, theym to deme and to juge as they lyst."[5]

[1] s.v. "Equitas" ("munera, amor, favor et odium").

[2] B text, pass. ii, ll. 62–3. For the particular meaning of "Symonye" here, cf. Skeat's note, Clarendon Press ed. 1886, p. 115, n. 62.

[3] Cf. above, pp. 251–5, 266, 280–2, etc.

[4] MS. Roy. 18. B. xxiii, fol. 93. Cf. MS. Camb. Univ. Libr. Ii. iii. 8, fol. 149: "Attendamus, queso, ad jurisperitos tam ecclesie quam regni, et videbimus quod tota die false et nequiter coguntur homines perdere bona sua, false et etiam injuste compelluntur emendas facere, ubi non deliquerunt..."; MS. Add. 37677, fol. 100; *Ayenb. of Inwyt*, p. 39; etc.

[5] *Gesta Rom.* Engl. version, p. 434. Cf. also Bozon, *Metaphs.* cap. xxii (Baudewyn: boldness of mind; thro' wiles and knowledge proceeding against right); and Brunton, MS. Harl. 3760, fol. 190: "Nam ubi mediocres et subditi penas sustinent in presenti, per quas purgantur, domini tamen et consiliarii, quantascunque injurias irrogant ecclesie et publice utilitati, evadunt communiter impuniti...". Cf. the warning to Judges not to oppress the poor in the Poem in *Twenty-six Pol. and other Poems*, E.E.T.S. p. 36.

The unknown author of this remark, in another part of his
expanded English version of the *Gesta Romanorum*, moralizes
the fable of Reynard the Fox and Tebert the Cat, to much the
same effect. "Bi the foxe", he says, "are undirstondyn vokettes,
prelates of causes temporall, courteers, jurrours and wily men,
that hav xviii sleightes and wiles passyng tho a pokefull."[1] In
the second place, we are impressed with the prevalence of the
contemporary belief that he who has no money with him, will
never have the ear of justice. "A man that shuld ʒe[ve] jugement
in the peple shuld be like a balaunce ʒeldyng to every man
right. But trewly, ʒeftes blyndeth so the jugges yʒen, that thei
may not see the ewen ryght wey in the balaunce."[2] A favourite
satirical story which may be found in the Latin *Alphabetum
Narrationum*[3] and the *Summa Predicantium*, as well as in English
vernacular sermons, tells of a certain judge, who, prior to the
commencement of a trial, received the present of an ox from
one of the litigants. His wife, however, about the same time,
was the recipient of a cow from the opposing party, and
straightway made earnest appeal to her husband on behalf of
her benefactor. When the day of trial came, the judge gave
free rein to the latter, as he pleaded in court. Up rose his
enemy and whispered to the judge—"Thou oxe, speke for me
as thou hyʒtest me!" But back came the reply—"The oxe
may noʒt speke, for the cowe wyl noʒt sufferyn hym!"[4] The
moral for us of the story lies in the fact that, as other records
show, judges were wont to "take mede on bothe sydes", and
favour "him that ʒevyth him most";[5] also that the pulpit was
thus repeatedly denouncing such actions. Not only judges,

[1] *Gesta Rom.* p. 371. Again in Bozon, cap. cxvi, and Bromyard, s.v.
"Sapientia".
[2] MS. Roy. 18. B. xxiii, fol. 135. Similarly, *Gesta Rom.* as above,
p. 321; Bromyard, *S.P.* s.v. "Dominatio", "Munus", etc.; *Piers Plowman*, passim; *Song on the venality of Judges*, in Wright, Camden Soc. pp. 224
et seq., and Poem in *Twenty-six Pol. and other Poems*, E.E.T.S. p. 6; etc.
[3] s.v. "Ballivus".
[4] *Jacob's Well*, p. 213. Cf. the variant of this story in the *Spec. Laic.*
cap. iii (ed. Welter, p. 7),concerning the widow's cart *v.* her opponent's
ox (the ox "draws" the cart).
[5] Ibid. p. 131. Cf. Bromyard's story of the old woman greasing the
eccles. judge's (or bishop's) hands, as above, p. 42, n. 5 (from Odo).

but "many pledours and advocatis...settith alle her hertes on wynnynge so fer forth, that some of hem taketh other-while of both sides".[1] The homilist's complaint is but an echo of earlier plaints against "valse plaiteres" as well as "demeres"[2] in a similar strain. So, "this false queste-mongeres...for a litill money, or els for a good dyner will save a theffe, and dampne a trewe man. And 3itt, and he be wrouthe with is ney3bore and com to asyse, he will for a peyre of gloves of vi pens put hym from is londe."[3] "How mony cursed falsnes and how mony vyces buthe menteynyd in this world by the lawe,...and yn speciell now a daies by fals quarelles for to gete mannus goodes! Amonge the comen pepell they call hit lawe to wynne ther by; but sothely lawe is hit non. For gold or sylver or som other 3efte wol turne the lawe a-non, and make the wronge as hit were very ry3t, and of the ry3t the wronge."[4] So, further, with "bailyes and othre mynistres of lawe, that myghte take theves and doo [to] be chastised by the lawe, and wil not;...the jorroures also, that beth swore to trye whether thei be theves or trewe men, and falsliche and wityngliche acquyteth hem".[5] Lies, indeed, are the order of the day. With some men "it is a crafte", we are told, "to knowe the virtue of lyenge". Many lie too much, and many

---

[1] MS. Harl. 45, fol. 76. Similarly, the *serjeants-at-law*, in Bromyard, s.v. "Advocatus"; advocates, lawyers, and pleaders in Bozon, *Metaphs.* caps. ii and xxii (Baudewyn); and do. in Odo of Cheriton (cf. Herbert, *Cat. of Romances in B.M.* vol. iii, p. 70, etc.): abroad, cf. in Hauréau, *Not. et Extr.* vol. iv, pp. 32-4, 227-8, etc., and Lenient, *La Satire en France au moyen âge*, p. 309 (Menot).

[2] Cf. *Ayenb. of Inwyt*, p. 40 ("hi nymeth ari3thalf and alefthalf").

[3] MS. Roy. 18. B. xxiii, fol. 113b. (Such, says the preacher, shall be hanged by their false tongues, in hell!) Cf. here the vivid tale of the Juror of York, who got possession of a poor man's "close" by ruse and false quest, as told in the Engl. *Gesta Rom.* pp. 386-7. Brunton, MS. Harl. 3760, fol. 143b, says: "Quando, producti et pro utraque parte in judicio constituti, jurant dicere solidam veritatem, illam celant pretextu odii vel favoris, muneris vel timoris, amicitie vel dominationis, pro quorum perjuria unus terra hereditatis vel jure patronatus privatur, et alius injuste lucratur".

[4] MS. Bodl. 95, fol. 80.

[5] MS. Harl. 45, fols. 65-6. Cf. further for bribing of jurors, Bromyard, s.v. "Falsitas", and below, p. 346.

too little, they say. The virtue of the craft exists in adhering to "the mene".[1] Meanwhile, the unfortunate peasant at court, with no money in his purse, is "tarried" by the justice "from day to day". His only hope is "to folowe hym from place to place, till at the last he [the judge] spedeth hym for pure anger and tene, for that he crieth so all day uppon hym".[2] "Lawe", as Langland complains, "is so lordlich, and loth to maken eende withouten presentes or pons."[3] To all such evil conduct Master Ralph of Acton makes solemn reply: "Whoever speaks the truth for a price or does justice for reward sells God, who is himself both Truth and Justice".[4] Finally, we have to note the evil influence exerted by the powerful, in whose hand lies not merely the power to bribe, but the power to threaten and coerce the hand of justice.

By unjuste dred, on word acombers the jugges, whan an erthly man is more drad than God, othur the right. Such a jugge was Pilate, demyng Crist to dethe, dredynge, 3iff that he had saved hym, that the Jewes wold have peched hym to the Emperour. And so he preferred mans drede, afore the drede of God. ... And trewly, so many men, as I wene, verely in arbitrement, in juggement and on questes, thei preferre the drede of othur grett men in the world byfore the drede of almyghty God; nothur thei drede not to be wittyngly forsworne. ... Sewerly, thise pepull seweth ther maister Pilate here; and so shall thei in hell eternally.[5]

Catalogues of typical legal offenders, occurring in manuals framed on the pattern of the *Ayenbite of Inwyt*[6] and earlier *Summae* of vices, again demonstrate the way in which the

[1] MS. Bodl. 95, fol. 10b. Cf. above, p. 266. For false oaths in law-courts (lay and eccles.) see Bromyard, s.v. "Juramentum".

[2] MS. Roy. 18. B. xxiii, fol. 122. (He goes on—"Troweth thou that he is grettely to be preysed for a ryghtwis domysman or a ryght justice? I sey, nay. ffor and he loved the vertewe of ryghtwisnes, where that he myght aspie that anny wronge were do, 3iff no man procured hym therto, he shuld be besie hymselfe to redresse that wronge...".) Similarly Bromyard, s.v. "Falsitas" ("usque ad raucedinem"); *Gesta Rom.* p. 58; and abroad, Menot's sermon-story, in Lenient, as before, p. 310.

[3] *Piers Plowman*, A text, pass. iii, ll. 156–7; etc.

[4] MS. Jo. Ryl. Libr. Manch. Lat. 367, fol. 123.

[5] MS. Roy. 18. B. xxiii, fol. 135. Cf. Bromyard, s.v. "Judices"; Brunton, as quoted in Gasquet, *Old Engl. Bible*, p. 83 et seq.; Wimbledon in Paul's Cross Sermon of 1388; and Bozon, *Metaphs.* cap. lv.

[6] Cf. here, pp. 39–40, 44, etc.

homilist influenced the song-writer in the construction of his verse.[1] Thus we pass in brief review the crimes of the false plaintiff, the false defendant, witness, juror, advocate, pleader, procurator, attorney, notary, clerk, doomsmen civil and ecclesiastical, and "assessoures and counsailloures to domesmen".[2] At the end of one such list, the preacher relaxes for a moment from the prolonged note of complaint, to remind us of the happier fact that, "of alle these degrees and astates, by the grace of God, there beth ful good men and trewe, and wel and truliche ruleth wel the lawe, bothe in spiritual lawe and temporal lawe, after her conscience". Though the complaints are here our concern, it is well to note that there is another side to the picture, of which the homilist is fully aware. That very fact, indeed, gives the greater weight to his censures.

John Bromyard, as the reader will now guess, is as ready as ever with the fiercest satires, to mock and to denounce the corrupters of justice. Justice, he tells us, in symbolic representation stands with her belt "mid-way" in its proper place. But just as a belt which carries a purse sags with the weight of it, so the "justice" dispensed by advocates, judges, jurors and the like commonly "sags towards the heavier purse".[3] Money, again, is the only key that admits to the courts of false men of law. There, instead of the psalm formerly sung in the courts of ecclesiastical prelates—"Blessed is he that cometh in the name of the Lord", there is another psalm in use—"Blessed is he that cometh in the name of Money!" As for those who preside in them, "never or rarely do they study, save when they see gain or have hopes of earthly enrichment. But when they see great gains and but little justice ahead, they pass sleepless nights, as it were; they open books; they turn many pages; they ponder the laws; they confer with their colleagues;—

[1] Cf. above, pp. 226 and 320.

[2] MS. Harl. 45, fols. 67 et seq.; *Jacob's Well*, pp. 130–1. Cf. MS. Bodl. 95, fols. 5 b–6 ("fals advocates and pleders, fals somners and notaryes..."); *Handlyng Synne*, p. 48; etc.

[3] Cf. here, in Hauréau, *Not. et Extr.* vol. iv, pp. 33 and 174, and Bozon, *Metaphs.* cap. xxii (Baudewyn).

and all, so that they may prepare their sickles for the harvest".[1]
"We have the law!" they cry. "Nevertheless, they only have
it to collect meed, as reapers the sickle for gathering the sheaves.
Wherefore, in their hands the law is as they wish, stringent
or liberal. To him who gives them nothing it will be stringent:
...he who gives liberally will find it liberal in his case."[2] The
"oil and wine", which should be used to heal the oppressed,
is poured on the heads of the mighty who are vicious.[3] Judges
ought, says Bromyard, to be strictly impartial, not influenced
by "faces", like certain of their number once, "who did not
expedite the suit of an abbess who came repeatedly to their
court, until one day she brought with her the more good-
looking nuns of her House!"[4] The bench, we are here informed, is so quick a route to wealth, because of the gifts
that come its way, that in a short while after promotion, its
occupants will be found buying lands, building mansions, and
laying up a fortune.[5] However, Bromyard notes that the unjust judge sometimes gets his deserts in this world, when he
becomes the object of "popular hatred and infamy". But the
unfortunate person who was driven to law had yet other perils
to encounter. Our Dominican warns him that he may have
to steer clear of the Charybdis of a corrupt jury, as well as the
Scylla of an unjust judge. When a certain justice "enquired
of his jury, according to custom, whether they were all agreed,
one of them made answer—'No! because each of my fellow-
jurymen has received forty pounds, and I have only received
twenty!'"[6] Just and honourable men, knowing well that the
accused may revenge himself upon them with injury or murder
or the burning down of their houses, if they justly convict him,
will bribe the judges to avoid being placed on the panel. "The
false men, who see in such jury-service the opportunity of enrichment, give bribes to the aforesaid justices, to be set thereon",
in their place. So it comes about that "in every direction truth

[1] s.v. "Justitia". See further in Chap. II, p. 63, above, for Bromyard's
development of this figure, here.
[2] s.v. "Acquisitio Mala".
[3] See Luke x, 34.   [4] s.v. "Judices".
[5] Similarly, Poem in Wright, Camden Soc. p. 338, ll. 325–7.
[6] s.v. "Judices".

and justice perish, and injustice reigns. For, not he who shall do more justly, but he who gives and takes more, is set in offices and juries. He, who can bring in his train more thieves and murderers, is master of all".[1] An honest justice who finds himself faced by such a gang, is naturally helpless "to break the line, arrive at the truth or correct any of the others". They are "the twelve Apostles of the Devil", cries the irate preacher, for ever on the look-out for what they can gain, fearless in diabolic scheming, because of their secret influence, and often actually in league with the criminal himself.[2] So, likewise is it with those other "twelve Apostles of falsity and Anti-Christ", the compurgators, who "should go to London, or some other place, to witness for the truth concerning some matter which has hitherto been pleaded in the local court".[3] Have we not actually here, in Bromyard's vivid narrative, the fundamental idea which inspired Langland's incident in *Piers Plowman's Vision*, when the supporters of the Lady *Mede* "wenden...to Westmynster", to witness to her disputed deed of marriage?[4] The reader must be left to discover for himself the many similar wiles of contemporary counsel which figure in the section devoted by Bromyard to the *Advocatus*. All craftsmen, says he, would at once refuse a job for which unsuitable materials were provided. If a carpenter were offered wages for the building of a house with planks that were too short or otherwise unsuitable, he would at once say—"I will not take the wage or have anything to do with it, because that timber is of no use". Similarly, the physician who can see no hope of saving his patient. So, in every craft but that of the advocate and the lawyer. No case is too palpably unjust for them. Indeed, some prefer to under-

---

[1] s.v. "Dominatio". Cf. legislation concerning Corruption of Jurors, *Rot. Parl.* vol. iii, p. 140.

[2] s.v. "Falsitas". See also Bozon, *Metaphs.* cap. lii.

[3] s.v. "Munus" ("primo die nituntur accipere ab una parte, jurantes et fingentes quod pro illa parte dicent. ... Alio die accipiunt ab alia parte; et que pars plus dederit duodecim illos perjuros pro parte sua habebit...."). Cf. further, s.v. "Judices".

[4] B text, pass. ii, ll. 157–60; A text, pass. ii, ll. 128–31; etc. Also, Poem in Wright, Rolls S. vol. i, p. 273.

take false cases rather than the true, because they can make
more money out of them. If warned of the dangers of such
action, they cry like the chief priests and elders of the Jews
to Judas—"What is that to us?" (as though one should say—
"the guilt is yours, not ours!"). "Let the risk be the client's!"
Such advocates prove to be like the hawks of the fable, called
in by the partridges to defend them against the kites. They
do worse harm to their own side than the original assailants.
Their fees are often scandalous, and without any relation to
what their clients can really afford to pay. Like highway-
robbers, they threaten those who refuse to give them what
they want, "displaying a turbulent face, and calling them hard
men and wretches", until the victim submits—"redeeming the
time, because the days are evil". They suppress the truth, like
false merchants. They exaggerate their risks and labours, and
prolong cases unnecessarily.[1] Like dogs rending a garment,
they snatch each for his own fragment of the law, leaving the
poor litigant naked. Finally, like the wicked jurymen, they
are often no better than demons linked together in an unholy
conspiracy to advance each other's interests. "To their client
they say—'I tell you seriously, I will do nothing without a
colleague!'"[2] When they have secured by the usual means a
judge and a jury to their liking, they dance with their client,
like turn-spits around the fire, while each one tries to push the
other into it, boasting and saying, "The verdict will be for
us. For we have a judge on our side, who is favourable to us,
and such and such a man of local influence".[3] Woe to him,
then, who unwitting puts his hand into such a thorny hedge
swarming with vipers. He will be bitten, indeed![4] In the long
history of Christian oratory, it is not often that we can point
to specific achievements in the field of practical politics, and

[1] Cf. again in Hauréau, *Not. et Extr.* vol. iv, p. 32, and Menot, in
Lenient, as before, p. 309. With Bromyard, here cf. *Piers Plowman*,
A text, pass. iii, l. 136; etc.
[2] s.v. "Amor Carnalis".
[3] s.v. "Advocatus". Cf. here the merry behaviour of the Judges and
Counsel with the Lady *Mede*, *Piers Plowman*, A text, pass. iii, ll. 26–9; etc.
[4] s.v. "Falsitas" (see Eccles. x, 8). Cf. Poem in Wright, Camden Soc.
p. 339.

hail them as the fruit of faithful pulpit denunciation. The harvest of such efforts is usually reaped by other men, in spheres far beyond the preacher's direct reach. But may we not attribute to all this unrelenting exposure by our medieval homilists a share in the launching of a certain remarkable *Avisamentum* by the Convocation held at London in the year 1439? It is a direct attempt to call attention to false indictments at law, perjury and other abuses which bore down upon the poor, and to secure their suppression.[1]

So little is said in either sermon or poem by way of complaint against the medieval physicians that we are perhaps hardly justified in giving them a place of their own in our treatment of the classes. However, that little which we may glean from the surviving literature agrees sufficiently well to indicate a common attitude of suspicion and reproof in poet as in preacher. In a so-called *Poem on the Evil Times of the reign of Edward II*,[2] we read of false physicians sending men to the grave through false treatment, or else swearing that the patient "is sekere than evere 3it he was", in order to extract yet more money from his pocket. While their own medicines often make men worse instead of better, they are careful to feed well off the housewife's store and enjoy themselves generally at her expense. If we turn now to the London clerk John of Mirfield,[3] writing his *Preacher's Dictionary* after the middle of the same century, we may find an added reason for the poet's scorn of their incompetence, apart altogether from the primitive state of medical knowledge. The former complains that

at the present time, not only ignorant men—but what is much worse and must be judged yet more horrible—vile and presumptuous women usurp that office to themselves and abuse it, since they have neither

[1] Wilkins, *Conc. Mag. Brit.* vol. iii, p. 534.
[2] See Wright, Camden Soc. pp. 333–4.
[3] *Flor. Barthol.* MS. Camb. Univ. Libr. Mm. ii. 10, fols. 119b et seq. (concerning Physicians and their Medicines). Much of this is in the language of Eccles. Constitutions, etc.

learning nor skill. Whence, because of their stupidity, the worst kinds
of mistakes are made, oftentimes involving the death of the patient; since
they operate neither wisely nor with proper diagnosis, but casually, and
are wholly ignorant of the causes and names of the diseases which they
declare that they know how to heal and can heal.

Here, then, in addition, we have anticipated another typical
passage in the *Vision of Piers Plowman*:[1]

> I cacche the crompe, the cardiacle some tyme,
> Or an ague in suche an angre, and some tyme a fevre,
> That taketh me al a twelf-moneth, tyl that I despyse
> Lecchecrafte of Owre Lorde, and leve on a wicche,
> And segge that no clerke ne can, ne Cryste, as I leve,
> To the souter of Southwerke, or of Shordyche dame Emme.

These old and familiar complaints against the incompetent[2]
quack and the woman doctor linger on in other literatures until
Tudor times—and indeed far beyond. In John of Mirfield's
careful warnings that the physician should not have secret conversation with any woman of the house, save where essential
for the patient's treatment, neither talking improperly, nor
throwing rash glances in their direction, "especially in the
patient's presence", and the like, we have further hints of the
kind of behaviour which our poet denounces. "Nor let him
sow discord amongst the patient's domestics," he goes on,
"nor offer advice unsought, nor brawl with those of the house,
nor commit any other improper acts or anything that could
reasonably displease folk. For all these things destroy a good
opinion, and give the physician an evil name." "For lay-folk",
adds the homilist very significantly, "are always wont to speak
ill of physicians." Alluding once more, this time in real satiric
vein, to the doctors of his own day (*moderni medici*), he specifies
as their three most coveted qualifications—"subtle lying,[3] dis-

[1] B text, pass. xiii, ll. 335–42. Similarly C text, pass. vii, ll. 78–83.
(It is interesting to recall that Jo. of Mirfield is himself writing in London,
at St Bartholomew's Priory, Smithfield.) Cf. further below, p. 595.

[2] Cf. here esp. Alex. Barclay on Physicians, in the *Ship of Fools*. (In
the woodcut accompanying, the doctor still "wags his patient's urine in
a vessel of glass", in the characteristic attitude singled out by the satirist
alike of the poem above and of the carved misericords at Beverley
St Mary and elsewhere which portray the physician as an ape.)

[3] Cf. here, again, the *Poem* above-mentioned ("and make many a
lesing…").

honourable procedure,[1] and a boldness in killing". Rarely is
a doctor a good Christian, he says. "Their deeds prove them
to be disciples, not of Christ, but of Avicenna and Galen."
And therewith he reminds them that if the patient is a poor
man, it is their Christian duty to cure him for nothing.[2]
"'O wretched physician,' says Lanfranc, 'who, for the money
that thou mayest not hope to get, dost desert the human body
travailing in peril of death; and dost allow him, whom, according to the Law of God, thou shouldest love and have most
concern for, of all creatures under heaven, to be in jeopardy
of life and limbs, when thou canst and knowest how to apply
a suitable remedy!'"[3] Alike to the preacher's and to the poet's
eye, the physician's chief ambition in life, and therein his chief
vice in an age of general cupidity, was "the silver for to
winne". As Chaucer slily puts it, of his pilgrim Doctour:

> For gold in phisik is a cordial;
> Therfore he lovede gold in special.[4]

"Leches, physicyons, taverners and tollers" are the four examples singled out by a fifteenth-century English preacher in
his sermon, of "all suche that by fals soteltees takyn falsely
mennus goodes". "All suche", he adds, "byn prevey thevys
and wyckud in her lyvynge. Though all suche ȝeve almys-dede
and offere in the churche of suche fals goodes-geten, God is
not plesed ther-wyth."[5]

---

[1] The scribe has here (fol. 120b) "honeste" for "inhoneste".
[2] On the other hand, he has already remarked earlier: "et scias quod
bona remuneracio de labore et salarium bonum artificem reddit auctori-
zabilem, et confortatur inde fides infirmi super eum. . . . Ideo veridicus
versificator ait—
> 'Empta solet care multum medicina iuvare;
> Si detur gratis, nihil affert utilitatis'".
[3] fol. 120b. Cf. a similar warning in Bromyard, S.P. s.v. "Advocatus",
§7. Lanfranc = Lanfranc of Milan: d. 1315.
[4] *Cant. Tales*, Prol. ll. 443–4. Cf. further, *Piers Plowman*, A text,
pass. ii, ll. 199–200, and B and C texts corresp.; also C text, pass. iv,
ll. 302–3.
[5] MS. Bodl. 95, fol. 6. Bromyard alludes in passing, s.v. "Invidia",
to evil physicians rejoicing when there is much sickness about.

We come now to that sturdy middle class of English society, represented by the merchant. In days when, according to one of our homilists, quoting the words of a "grete clerke"— "the world precheth to man-keend that thei shuld gadere goold and sylver and draw to all maner of riches",[1] it is easy to guess what the peculiar vices of his class will be. In the race for new wealth, none runs faster or more doggedly. He "ne suffreth him nouȝt to have slepe, ne reste, by niȝte ne by day; bot maketh him travayle in water and in londe, in chele and in hete, in feyntyse and in werynesse. Ryȝt as a spythur destroyeth here-self in makynge a webbe for to take a flye, ryȝt so the coveytous man destroyeth his owene body for to gete thys worldes goed".[2] "These young men", says another, "expose themselves *in aventure* of their life, *suffer mani mischeves*, many perils on sea and land. In the daytime they are so tormented *in tene and labore* that at nights they have no rest; they have *dremes* in plenty *and mony brok slep.*"[3] "And it is not in one tyme of the ȝere, but in all tymes of the ȝere",[4] adds a third. Their gains, indeed, and the dangers that they have escaped are their favourite topic of conversation.[5] We get interesting insight into the social ambitions of this rising middle class in a passage of Bromyard denouncing false pity. "Merchants and moneyed men", he relates, "reckon themselves 'ennobled' and on the road to enrichment, when they are seen to have friendship with the nobility, when they can wear their robes and are summoned to their banquets, and when they can go a-hunting with them. But the end of all those things is that, when they ask for...the money back which (after it has been acquired with great labour) they bring and lend to them, they will be friends no longer."[6] Needless to say, no respectable English

---

[1] MS. Roy. 18. B. xxiii, fol. 125. Cf. MS. Add. 21253, fol. 73b.

[2] MS. Harl. 2398, fol. 22b. Cf. MS. Roy. 18. B. xxiii, fols. 84, 142, etc.; *Gesta Rom.* Engl. version, p. 71; and the Poem *Dispute* (Vernon MS.), E.E.T.S. O.S. no. 98, p. 344 (the chapmen).

[3] MS. Bodl. 649, fol. 44. (The phrase—"thes ȝonge chapmen" occurs again in MS. Harl. 2398, fol. 21b.)

[4] MS. Linc. Cath. Libr. A. 6. 2, fol. 60b (the risks and travail of the merchants). See further *S.P.* s.v. "Mundus". [5] *S.P.* s.v. "Locutio".

[6] Cf. here, *Piers Plowman*, B text, pass. v, ll. 254-5.

preacher of the times, least of all our strait-laced Dominican doctor, would approve of any such mixing of the classes.[1] The "middle-class creditors" just mentioned, he compares here, indeed, to the beasts in the fable who thought themselves so superior when they went a-hunting with the lion, until the time came for sharing out the booty.[2] But mere social vanity of that kind is not the besetting ṣin of the merchant, against which preacher and song-writer[3] are united in their complaint. Bishop Brunton will give us a summary of the more general indictment: "False merchants, in these days, infringe the Rule of Justice. In every craft so much trickery is employed—in measures, in usury, in weight, in the balance, in mendacious mixtures and false oaths—that each man strives to deceive his neighbour.... Therefore let merchants beware!...".[4] Trick by trick, we are enabled, with the strange help of the pulpit, to study afresh the familiar "wilis and falsede" of these medieval business men "for to gete good".[5] They remind us once again that the swindlers of the modern world of business would not be able to teach very much to their brethren of the hard, matter-of-fact fourteenth century. The commonest deception condemned in sermon-literature is the use of false weights and measures, for the sale of both solids and liquids.[6] One form of this consists "in bying þe þe more, and sellyng þe þe lesse; and, thowȝ thi mesure or weyȝte be trewe, ȝit thou takyst it large inward and ȝevyst it scarse owtward, aȝens

[1] Cf. in Chap. IX, below, pp. 557–9.
[2] s.v. "Misericordia". Cf. also Bozon, *Metaphs.* cap. lxxv.
[3] Cf. the false chapmen of the poem *On the Evil Times of Kg. Edw. II*, Wright, Camden Soc. p. 339; *Piers Plowman*, passim, esp. *Avarice*, in B text, pass. v, C text, pass. vii; and Gower, as above, pp. 230–1.
[4] MS. Harl. 3760, fol. 124.
[5] MS. Add. 41321, fol. 103b (mentions also—"artificeres").
[6] Cf. *Old Engl. Homs.* (12th cent.), E.E.T.S. O.S. no. 53, p. 213; *Ayenb. of Inwyt*, pp. 44–5; Bromyard, s.v. "Falsitas", "Mercatio", etc.; Rypon, MS. Harl. 4894, fol. 68b, etc.; Waldeby, MS. Caius Coll. Camb. 334, fol. 178b; MS. Roy. 18. B. xxiii, fols. 94, 137, etc.; MS. Harl. 2398, fols. 21b, 100b, etc.; MS. St Albans Cath. fol. 35b; *Jacob's Well*, p. 133; etc. These and other general statements following should be compared with the contemporary concrete cases recorded in such works as Riley's *Illustrations of London Life*, or L. F. Salzman's *Engl. Industries of the Middle Ages*, pp. 309–10.

trewthe".[1] Such diminution of the real quantity of the article sold can be—and was—accomplished in a variety of ways, we are told. Either the balance itself may be false, or "with a certain trick they manipulate the balance and thus put weight on it, to press it down without good and true weight"....[2] Again, "they mingle bad and extraneous matter with the stuff that is to be weighed in sly fashion, like those who mix sand with wool, or wet the wool to make it weigh heavier, or else blend old and bad stuff with new and good samples, showing a sufficient weight by means of good and bad together".[3] Similarly, too, with measures, liquid as well as dry. Here the "false breweres and tappesteres" and taverners of the day were particularly notorious, in their sale of drinks: "The iust weiȝtis and mesures ben yvel weied and fillid, as tapsteris don, that fillen the mesure with frothe. As myche as thei withdrawen of the mesure, so myche thei drawen to hem of the wrathe of God!"[4] Some, says Bromyard, keep two measures of the same nominal content, a larger one for buying and a smaller one for selling. "When their friends want to borrow, they are wont to say to them—'Are you buying or selling?'", and lend them accordingly. From these petty deceits, we may pass on to study the gentle art of "false schewynge; as when a marchant can sotelliche adresse his ware to make hit seme better than it is, and scheweth it in derke place, to hyde the defaute therof, or to make seme the better, as doth drapers, mercers, and many

---

[1] *Jacob's Well*, p. 133. Similarly, *Ayenb. of Inwyt*, p. 44: see also Hauréau, *Not. et Extr.* vol. iv, p. 136; etc.

[2] *S.P.* s.v. "Mercatio". Cf. in Lenient, *La Satire en France au moyen âge*, p. 309 (15th-cent. preachers: "le joli tour de la balance").

[3] s.v. "Mercatio". Cf. again, here—"lolium vel vilia cum frumento vel alio blade componunt, dicentes illud (Amos viii, 6)—'*Quisquilias frumenti vendabimus*'". Also MS. St Albans Cath. fol. 36—"Whan a man makith a thinge hevyer, bifore that it be weied", etc. Also, Lenient, as above, p. 309.

[4] MS. St Albans Cath. fol. 35b. Cf. *Ayenb. of Inwyt*, p. 44, and Bromyard, s.v. "Falsitas" ("Vix venditur mensura bladis vel *potus* vel panni, quin ista herba [falsitatis] in mensura crescat"), etc.; MS. Harl. 2398, fol. 21b; MS. Roy. 18. B. xxiii, fol. 94 (tapsters and taverners); etc.: abroad, Lenient, as above, p. 309, and Hauréau, as below, p. 355, n. 5. With these, cf. e.g. the Satirical Poem of friar Michael of Kildare (c. 1308), in *Reliq. Antiq.* vol. ii, p. 176.

other suche".¹ Cloth, Bromyard adds, was treated in this way, "so that the stuff might appear more beautiful and better than it was, the real colour being in some way or other concealed, and some other displayed by means carefully thought out, even by some transparency of light passing through another colour". Thus, he goes on, "they get for that cloth more than it is worth, and by that fact show themselves to be 'the sons of darkness', and of the number of those of whom the Saviour saith (John iii, 20–21)—'For he that doeth evil hateth the light; and he that doeth truth cometh to the light, that his deeds may be made manifest'" (!). Another curious practice of the kind mentioned concerns "the false displaying of corn, with regard to its quantity". This was done by cunningly making a large heap in the barn with a gap in the middle, and thus disposing of it for more than its true value.² Indeed, there was no end to their cunning. Defective or adulterated goods would be sold as good and whole. Thus, sellers of corrupt mutton are said to smear and colour the sheep's eyes with blood, in order to make the carcasses appear fresh.³ Likewise, the skin-dressers sell old and rotten skins as new, skilfully concealed by cleansing and by the superficial adornment—not only of linings but of words!⁴ Further examples given by our preachers include "a crokyd hors for a clene", scabby sheep sold for healthy, copper for gold, "wyne medlyd wyth watyr for wyn", "a ruynous hows for trusti hows, mete and drynk corrupte for heyl mete".⁵ "Corsoures that have false hors", says one, "thei wyll, wyth false othys, swere that it hath no

¹ MS. Harl. 45, fol. 71 b. Cf. *Jacob's Well*, p. 134 and *Ayenb. of Inwyt*, p. 45; also MS. Harl. 2398, fol. 100b (with "sleythe or cautele"), and MS. Roy. 18. B. xxiii, fol. 94 (do.).
² *S.P.* s.v. "Mercatio". Cf. the well-known case of the London dough-seller, in Riley, *Memor. of London*, p. 163.
³ *S.P.* s.v. "Ornatus".
⁴ *S.P.* s.v. "Luxuria". Cf. here, *Piers Plowman*, C text, pass. vii, ll. 258–61 ("with false wordes and wittes,...with gyle and glosynge...").
⁵ Bromyard, s.v. "Mercatio", and *Jacob's Well*, p. 212. Cf. also, MS. Harl. 2398, fol. 3b ("syllyng a badde thyng for a goede"). See further tricks mentioned by Jacques de Vitry in a sermon, Hauréau, *Not. et Extr.* vol. iv, pp. 56–7, and by Berthold von Regensburg (13th cent.), as quoted by Coulton, *Life in the Middle Ages*, vol. iii, pp. 57–62.

defawte."¹ Others again would play dishonest tricks with the money, "making a jump" when counting out change, or giving false coin mixed up with good—"a badde peny, other a nobul, for a goed".² Alas! the long list of frauds is by no means ended yet. For we have elaborate accounts of the methods of medieval profiteers, who manipulate prices and take advantage of famines and fluctuations in the market.

The methods of withholding are manifold [says Master Rypon]. Some hold back for a time, that they may acquire more later on;...as, for example, those, having a quantity of corn or other goods for sale, who suspect that things will be very dear in the future, and, in hope of future gain, withhold corn from the market, which nevertheless if sold would be a timely benefit to the whole country. Without doubt such men harm not one person only, but the whole country-side, doing contrary to that injunction in [1] Thessalonians, iv [6]—"that no man over-reach and circumvent his brother in business".

Sometimes, however, the selfish monsters got their deserts, as this same preacher testifies: "In the meantime, mice devour the corn, and, when the wind blows, there will come good weather and perchance ships into the bargain, with plenty of grain. Then, frustrated in their scheme, they lose a great part of their corn—but not the curse thereof!"³ Bromyard describes how in such seasons of dearth, sometimes deliberately and artificially produced by the action of the forestaller, a man in the stress of hunger "would give a kingdom or an inheritance of a thousand pounds for a single loaf", if he could.⁴

Once again, then, that most solemn and tragic censure of all pulpit censures falls justly on the head of the merchant, as it fell upon the heads of noble, knight and lawyer: "He hath oppressed the poor and needy, and hath spoiled by violence". Who was it, indeed, that his "false othys and auncerys and false weyȝtes and mesurys" were most calculated to deceive and injure, but the "symple folk, that arn his neyghbourys and

¹ Jacob's Well, p. 134. In Ayenb. of Inwyt, p. 44, called "romongors of hors". Cf. Bromyard, as above, p. 25.
² MS. Harl. 2398, fol. 3b, and Bromyard, s.v. "Mercatio".
³ MS. Harl. 4894, fol. 36. Cf. Handlyng Synne, p. 176.
⁴ s.v. "Mercatio". Cf. further, on this subject, s.v. "Avaritia", also Jacob's Well, pp. 123, 212, etc.; Sermo in festo Corp. Christi, as below, p. 358; Ayenb. of Inwyt, p. 36; and Hauréau, Not. et Extr. vol. iv, pp. 97-8.

kan no wyles than he doth straungerys that arn slye and als wyly as he"? The homilist calls him a fox. For "a fox is a dysseyvable beeste, and rathere he devowryth and sleth tame bestys than wylde".[1] "ffor they bigylen simple men", says another, "as foxes deseyven briddes that are simple, as hennes, geese and suche other, and lyven by falshed and ravyn, as foxes done."[2] All such false dealing, Rypon and others stoutly declare to be theft.[3] The *Summa Predicantium*, which, in its invaluable way, gives us the stock excuse of those who "deceive the simple, in selling to them more dearly than they would do to other people who know how to deal with them"—"The buyers have their own senses and intellect, even as we have; . . . they can buy the things or leave them!"—gives also the excuses that are made for selling defective goods. How wonderfully modern they are! "You may buy it for so much, exactly as it is. I am not willing to guarantee it, or to be held responsible for its defects. You see what it is like. If you want to buy, you can buy!" When the homilist argues with them that such excuses are invalid, that it is their duty to help and not deceive their neighbours, that horses, for example, have many defects not apparent to the senses of simple folk, they will reply—"We bought that horse as a good one; or we took that false money as good; and so of the other things. Why, then, can we not expose them for sale to others as they came to us?"[4] "I muste nedys weyin falsly chese and wolle, spyserye and othere thinges, and selle be false mesurys as othere don; ellys schulde I loose ther-on. . . . I muste nedys be wyles, defraude and falsnesse dysseyven my neyȝboure. For ȝif I dede truthe, I schulde nevere thryve, but ben a beggere. And nedys I and

---

[1] *Jacob's Well*, p. 118. Cf. Bromyard, s.v. "Civitas".

[2] MS. Roy. 8. C. 1, fol. 130b. Cf. Bozon, *Metaphs.* cap. iii.

[3] MS. Harl. 4894, fol. 68b. Similarly, MS. St Albans Cath. fol. 36 ("If thou sillist to thi neiȝbore a thinge for xl pens, and knowist wel that it is dere ynouȝ of sixe, as myche as thou takist of him more than resonable wynnynge thou stelist and art a veri thefe"); MS. Roy. 18. B. xxiii, fol. 94 ("privey theves").

[4] s.v. "Mercatio". Cf. another excuse, s.v. "Eleemosyna": "Alii dicunt—'Bonum forum est. Pauperes non indigent". (Bromyard retorts —"Si pauper satis posset habere ad victum et vestitum pro quadrante et illo careret, quid valeret sibi bonum forum?")

my wyif and my chylderyn and my meyne muste lyve!"[1] As with the deceiver, so with the profiteer. Upon whom should the iniquity of those who "makyn a derthe" in "corn or vytayles", or take advantage of one, crush heavier, than upon "the poore people", that "schulde nedys bygge of the at thi prise"?[2]

> He bieth corn aȝen the ȝere
> And kepit it til it be dere.
> But ther-of doth he wiseliche,
> If he departe it skilfulliche?
> Nay for sothe; thenkith he nouht
> To pore men departen ouht.
> Bouhte he nevere so good chepe,
> He ne rewith not the pore to wepe.
> He ne rouhte how al the world ȝode,
> So that his owne geting were gode.
> For this is the mokereris answere:
> "Go ȝoure wey; corn is ful dere!"
> Also for sothe, with-outen gabbe,
> The same answere he schall habbe,
> Whan alle the aungelis in hevene beth,
> And alle on erthe that suffrid deth
> Schul ben at on parlement....[3]

God's answer then shall be short and to the point—"Go to hell; for heaven is dear!"[4] In some places there was another kind of middleman whom the market had to support, apparently, at the expense of the unfortunate consumer. Such was the case

in all maritime cities, where foreign merchants, who come with their ships, cannot sell freely to the people and to all-comers, but are compelled, by cursed statutes, to sell to some great men of the city, who sell therefrom to the others, as they please. And that impoverishes the city for two reasons. First, because fewer merchants and those only who are invited, as it were, come to such cities; with the result that where once twenty ships were wont to arrive, now scarcely five come. Secondly, because the arrival of the merchants will not be an advantage to the whole city, as would be the case if they could sell freely and in a good market, but only for those first buying from them; since they sell to the people more dearly than the original merchants would do.... Woe to them who frame iniquitous laws![5]

---

[1] *Jacob's Well*, p. 261.   [2] Ibid. p. 212.
[3] *Sermo in festo Corporis Christi* (metrical), E.E.T.S. O.S. no. 98, p. 171 (MS. Camb. Univ. Libr. Dd. i. i. version).
[4] Ibid. p. 173.   [5] *S.P.* s.v. "Civitas".

We must pass hurriedly over the "false sleythes in byynge"[1] practised by that same merchant class whose "syllynge" we have just considered. Here full advantage was taken of the ignorance of the seller, as well as of the urgency that might drive him to part with his treasure at a price far below its proper value in the market.[2] Again, it was the overdriven poor who were destined to suffer most. "A certain layman, let us say, for example, finds, amongst the goods left to him by his father, a book, which he is compelled to sell by urgent necessity; but he is ignorant of its price and value. If, therefore, a cleric is able to get this book for half a mark in English money, when it is worth twenty pounds of the same money, he will not be an honest purchaser. Nor would a trustworthy man do this." We watch now, not the cleric, but the merchant, urging on "some simple and less shrewd man to sell his inheritance for less than it is worth, with fallacious blandishments, false promises or deceptive little gifts and invitations to dinner". If this fails, he may try "threats, terrors or the entreaties of men of influence—which are the equivalent of threats—or again many tricks with cruel circumvention. For, sometimes they persecute a man of this kind, indict him, fling him into prison, attack him, promote diverse lawsuits against him in the courts, or cause them to be promoted. Then, at the last, by these means, bound and impoverished, he is compelled to give or sell what they want, to escape at the very least with his life".[3] We shall not fail to find those twin faults of Sabbath-breaking[4] and false swearing, which are attributed to this class by the faithful *Piers*,[5] duly elaborated in the same sermon-literature. "I muste nedys swere and forswere me in chaffarynge and in other wyse", they say, "ellys no man wyll belevyn

[1] MS. Harl. 2398, fol. 100b.
[2] Called "lyther bergaynyng" (i.e. "*wicked* bargaining") in *Jacob's Well*, p. 133. See also p. 123.
[3] *S.P.* s.v. "Mercatio". Cf. *Hand. Synne*, p. 193 (making the seller drunk, etc.); and *Avarice* in *Piers Plowman*, C text, pass. vii, ll. 260–6.
[4] I.e. by Sunday trading. See *S.P.* s.v. "Feriae seu Festa"; Brunton, MS. Harl. 3760, fol. 110b; etc.: and cf. Lipson, *Introd. to Engl. Econ. Hist.* p. 206.
[5] *Piers Plowman*, B text, pass. vii, ll. 18–22.

me."[1] Finally, there is a rich mass of homiletic material, to which both Odo of Cheriton and Bishop Grossetête contribute in the early part of the thirteenth century, dealing with the ethics of usury and the usurer himself, who is sometimes appropriately bracketed with the "mercator infidelis".[2] The English usurer was clearly as skilful an evader of the law at his business of "selling time"—to use Bromyard's phrase[3]—as his brother of the shop and the stall, with his faked merchandise. One ruse was to pretend that the loan was payment for an animal bought and then hired out to the borrower. But this and much else besides, with not a few highly amusing anecdotes about usurers, must be left to the reader to discover for himself.[4] "The tyme", as preachers say, "suffreth not now."[5] We ended our previous section on the law with what appeared to be an illustration of some practical outcome of the preachers' faithful reproofs. Here, then, is another example, equally appropriate to the occasion. It is a Provincial Constitution of the year 1429, published by the Archbishop of Canterbury, Henry Chichele, for the abolition of "lyggyng wyghtys". "For there are," it declares, "as the voice of the public proclaims and authoritative experience of these things manifests, in some cities, boroughs and other places of our province of Canterbury, numerous ruthless purchasers, who, unmindful of their salvation, are wont to buy fraudulently from the simple

[1] *Jacob's Well*, p. 261. Cf. further, p. 133 ("lesyng and forsweryng in thi sellyng, sparyng none othys..."); Bromyard, *S.P.* s.v. "Equitas" and "Mercatio"; Waldeby, MS. Caius Coll. Camb. 334, fol. 173 ("in foro"); MS. Harl. 2398, fol. 21 ("false assisours and merchauntz, that forswereth hem by alle the lymes of Gode, forto wynne the worldes catell..."), fol. 100b ("othes swerynge" in "by3nge and syllyng").

[2] For Odo, see Herbert, *Cat. of Romances in B.M.* pp. 71–2 and 77; Grossetête, in MS. Bodl. 830, fols. 67b–8: also *Spec. Laic.* cap. lxxxvii (ed. Welter, pp. 110–11); Bozon, *Metaphs.* cap. xxii (Trebelyn); Bromyard, *S.P.* s.v. "Usura"; *Ayenb. of Inwyt*, pp. 35–6; MS. Harl. 45, fols. 63b–4b (12 "Manners" of Usury); MS. Add. 37677, fol. 100b; *Jacob's Well*, pp. 122–4, etc.; *Hand. Synne*, pp. 86–93, 181–92; MS. Add. 21253, fol. 105; MS. Harl. 2398, fols. 3b, 21b; etc.: abroad, Hauréau, *Not. et Extr.* vols. i, pp. 170–4; iii, pp. 73, 129; iv, p. 136; etc.

[3] Similarly, *Piers Plowman*, C text, pass. vii, l. 247.

[4] s.v. "Usura".

[5] (MS. Roy. 18. B. xxiii, fol. 134b).

common folk and others, wool, honey, wax, and other things required for human uses...."[1] Was it not the pulpit that had helped to make vocal that popular indignation?

A page or two will enable us to dismiss the one remaining class of society which still concerns us. Although there may be comparatively less complaint in the sermons against "alle lybbyng laboreres, that lyven with her hondes",[2] as a class, and but little in the poems, with the exception of *Piers Plowman*, that little is important. For it establishes once and for all the strict impartiality of the pulpit—which is identical, of course, with the impartiality of Langland—the fact that it spared no rank or order, high or low, from its searching scrutiny and correction. The stinging blows of its satire or its warnings were dealt out to each in turn, wherever they were needed, without any of that petty truckling to democracy which mars now and again some of our modern preaching. In no case, perhaps, is this fact better illustrated than in the sermons of Nicholas Bozon. He who spoke, as we saw, almost with venom of the rich, bidding the poor man beware of his company, does not hesitate to liken the bad servant (or serf) to an ass, whenever he discusses him. "The bad servant", he says, "is likened to the ass in Holy Scripture, because he is by nature a very forgetful beast, and wants often to be kept up with the rod and oft loaded with work: *Ecclesiasticus* xxxiii [25]—'Fodder and a rod and a burden are for an ass: bread and correction and work for a serf'."[3] Of satire, apart from Bozon, however, it is significant to note that there is practically none where the working classes are being chastised. The word of warning, too, apart from general indictment of the grosser sins, seems on the whole less violent.[4] God knows!—and the medieval preacher knew, as we have seen—the peasant had smitings,

[1] Wilkins, *Concil. Mag. Brit.* vol. iii, p. 516.
[2] *Piers Plowman*, B text, pass. vii, l. 62.
[3] *Metaphs.* cap. xv: cf. further caps. cxxi and cxxxi, and below, p. 364.
[4] Abroad, apparently, this is not so much the case. See important examples in Coulton, *Mediev. Village*, pp. 242–7, which in many of their details should be compared with the following.

scornings, and suffering enough already, at less honourable hands. Yet, while the pulpit did not overlook the extenuating circumstances, it was never blind to the fact that his sins were many. "Muche peple of this world, as experience proveth, ben dronkenlewe and unclenly. I can not see that Crist dwelleth in hem", says one of our homilists quite frankly.[1] And in the long familiar catalogues of other sins which the pulpit exposed, it was only natural that the lowest orders would stand pre-eminently convicted, with their animal instincts and their ignorance:

brekynge of holy dayes, takynge of the sacrament of housell unworthiliche, unreverence doo to goddes body in that sacrament, failynge in goddes service, in sclaunder to hali chirche, gilery, wicchecraft, ydel pleyes and japes, carolinges, makynge of fool contynaunces, to ȝeve ȝiftes to iogeloures...ffor her ydel tales and japes, smytyng, snarlynge, ffyndyng and usynge of novelryes, sturdynes aȝenst men of hyer estate, in kussynge with mouth, in clippynge, in tokenes makynge, in bekenynge, in wrastlynge, in other dedes of strength doynge.[2]

Still more, perhaps, in—"fals labour, takyng more than thou hast deservyd in fals servyse, in falsnese of thi craft,...in raveyn, thefte and mycherye, in false tythynges and wyth-holdyng thi dettys fro dede, qwyke, and fro holy cherche".[3] In the more specific denunciation of working-class vice, it is possible to distinguish two separate types of offender—the skilled workman of the towns[4] and the rustic serf and labourer on the manor. Against the former, Rypon appears to be com-plaining, when he expresses the wish that "all those learning a craft would make it their sole aim to seek the means of providing food and clothing for themselves". His words are a further testimony to new ambitions and self-assertion in the humbler ranks of the nation.

[1] MS. Roy. 18. B. xxiii, fol. 131 b.
[2] MS. Harl. 45, fol. 58. Cf. similarly, *Jacob's Well*, pp. 294–6.
[3] *Jacob's Well*, p. 196; and see here below, following.
[4] Cf. the list of "men of craft" in ibid., pp. 40–1: "wryȝtes, smythes, weverys, brewsterys, baxterys, thaccherys, cordewanerys, tay-lourys, sowsterys [= seamstresses], tylerys, masouns, plomerys, tannerys, peyntourys", carefully distinguished from "the comoun labourerys and alle servauntys" (in Articles of the Great Curse). The former are naturally more on a level with the merchant in the preacher's eyes.

But assuredly [he goes on] the habits of certain craftsmen prove that some of them learn, not merely in order to find food and clothing, but to heap together riches. In token of this, they practise so many falsities and tricks to deceive people, as I could disclose singly in case after case, concerning each type of workman, if time permitted. Whence we experience generally that false craftsmen of this kind, nay rather, very many others too, who have worldly knowledge, reckon long periods all too short, provided that they are making direct gain, and reciprocally judge short periods to be too long, while they are busy with jobs which retard them from the search for profits and enrichment.

So, in making goods for sale, Rypon continues, or in shooting at the butts, in drinkings, in useless and unnecessary occupations such as chess and dice-playing, gossiping and coarse jesting, they are tireless, day and night; but negligent and slothful about spiritual things.[1] Elsewhere, the monk of Durham warns them, further, that "they ought to receive a strictly legal and just *quid pro quo*" for their labours. "Otherwise, if workmen are knowingly and negligently lukewarm, and artificers false in their tasks, they are the servants of the Devil."[2] In the words of another, similarly—"A servant or a werkman that taketh his ful hyre and deservith hit noght as he shulde do, he stelith it".[3] Bromyard devotes a whole section of his *Summa* to "Operatio" and the "Operarius",[4] where, after his usual fashion, he elaborates spiritual duties and shortcomings with numerous illustrations from the current work-a-day world, in which ordinary workmen and their failings play so large if so humble a part. Here he refers, for example, to slothful workmen who scarce do in two days what they could do in one, actually doing as little as possible without any sense of duty, thinking only of their wages, their food and their drink. Under other headings, he speaks of those "who are negligent in their work, because too much pay is put into their hands before the termination of their job. And so they

[1] MS. Harl. 4894, fol. 183b. Cf. here *Norwich Records*, vol. ii, p. 104; *Little Red Bk. of Bristol*, vol. ii, p. 106; *Coventry Leet Bk.* p. 656; etc.
[2] MS. ibid. fol. 55.
[3] MS. Harl. 45, fol. 65b. Cf. MS. Roy. 18. B. xxiii, fol. 94 ("fals servauntes in ther werkes, that take trew hire and do not trewly ther werkes"); MS. St Albans Cath. fol. 36 (servants and workmen similarly defrauding); MS. Bodl. 95, fol. 6 (false servants); *Hand. Synne*, p. 85; etc.
[4] "Operatio, seu Operarius."

give themselves up to games and drinking".[1] The tavern, then as now, was a sore temptation. "At least once a week, that is on the holyday," we read, "workmen and craftsmen get drunk, whereby their goods are diminished."[2] As for Sabbath-breaking, "they excuse themselves, saying—'If I do not work, the jobs will go to another who will do them; so I shall lose continuous employment and my wages'".[3]

Master Rypon's message to the "Agricultores" is that "they should labour with regular diligence, unspotted by the sins of theft, fraud, lying and lust", rather than live lazily or beg.[4] To the manorial servant, working on the land or within his master's own mansion, there were natural temptations at times, common to all flesh, to slacken and to defraud. "Sir, thou seest well every day at eye", says a simple preacher, "that many men in this worlde serven grett men and lordes, som withe here goodwill, and som aʒeyne here will. But thei that serve with here goodwill are worthy to be rewarded for hure traveyll; and thei that serveth aʒeyns hur will are worthy to have ryght nowthe."[5] The latter, says friar Bozon, are like the ass as described by Pliny, that "much dislikes to wet his feet". Just as he deliberately shakes some of his master's goods from off his back into the stream that he is forced to cross, so the un-willing servant does his task in such a way that it would have been better left undone. He foolishly tries to excuse himself by accusing his lord of harshness and hostility to him.[6] Such plain speaking from the pulpit was as necessary then as now, particularly "as it farith ofte of servantes that, at hir ferste comynge in to service, thei beth buxom, besy and preste, but afterward thei slaketh and wexeth froward".[7] Human nature has not changed in that respect. Another contemporary

---

[1] s.v. "Gaudium".

[2] s.v. "Labor". Cf. *Coventry Leet Bk.* as above, p. 786; and Riley, *Memor. of London*, p. 538, and see further below, pp. 427–41.

[3] s.v. "Feriae seu Festa". Cf. further, on false workmen, s.v. "Falsitas" ("vix servit quis vel operatur artifex sine ista mala herba falsitatis"); s.v. "Furtum" (as above, p. 300—where the false "operarii" stand with the usurers and false merchants at the Doom).

[4] MS. Harl. 4894, fol. 189.   [5] MS. Roy. 18. B. xxiii, fol. 114.
[6] *Metaphs.* cap. cxxxi.   [7] MS. Harl. 45, fol. 52b.

preacher furnishes us with a vivid illustration of their "fro-wardness":

> Thi servaunt or thi bonde-man is fals and unkynde to the, that wyl no3t serve the; but rennyth awey to thi most enemye and servyth him, tyl thou puttyst hym in prisoun or in stokkys; and thanne he turneth to the, and servyth the awhyle. This is for no love, but for dreed. For, whenne he is lowse, sone after he rennyth away a3en. Thou kunnyst hym no thank, for he servyth the no3t for love.[1]

Says Bozon again, speaking of a like situation, "as the goat does not know how to stay in one place at peace, so many servants do not know how to stay in good service, but always seek to hide their bad qualities by often changing. And the more often they change, the better they become known for foolish people".[2] Verily, is not this our modern housewife's cry? Apart from wasting his lord's goods,[3] with so much luxury and abundance around him, there was, for the servant, a still more serious temptation to what the homilist calls "litel thefte", or "mychery". Such "is whan menis servantes or other steleth mete, drinke, polayle,[4] scheves in hervest, or othre smale thinges, and thinketh it is noght to charge, ffor it is a custome".[5] Bromyard, again, gives us the typical excuses made: "They assert that their lords are hard on them; also that they cannot live on the proceeds of their post; that, more-over, he pays their wages badly, and that their lords are them-selves rich. Therefore it is no sin to take from them".[6] The Dominican's ready retort is that they are breaking their oath of fealty, and are therefore at any rate no less wicked than their masters. But not only had the preacher to warn and protest repeatedly against the defrauding of secular masters. There was a further duty common to all lay-folk, high and low, rich and poor alike, towards Holy Mother Church, which many were all too ready to shirk in those days, if and when they could. The warning to pay tithes faithfully, indeed, was

---

[1] *Jacob's Well*, p. 186.
[2] *Metaphs.* cap. xv.
[3] Cf. MS. Harl. 2398, fol. 100.   [4] = poultry.
[5] MS. Harl. 45, fol. 65 b. Similarly, *Jacob's Well*, p. 128. Also, MS. Bodl. 95, fol. 5 b (mychers), etc.; *Spec. Laic.* ed. Welter, p. 9 (petty thefts).
[6] *S.P.* s.v. "Furtum". Cf. *Gesta Rom.* Engl. version, p. 71.

itself a duty as it was a commonplace of the medieval pulpits.[1] Bishop Brunton in his sermons is particularly concerned with the negligence of the rich in this direction.[2] But an anonymous preacher, earlier in the same century, having dealt with "the greater folk and the magnates of the earth", turns to make special complaint "of the lesser folk and the common people". "For the churches and ecclesiastics", he asserts, "they care little or nothing: nay, rather do they scorn and despise their rights, and take from the churches their liberties. They pay tithes badly, and reckon churches and churchmen of no account."[3] Again, "the common masses also assault the Church: they tithe falsely and against their will; they make but small offerings; they conspire against the rectors of the churches, and in their wrath actually arrange that little shall be given to them, thus to hinder devotion".[4] The author of Jacob's Well, who specifies with care that "the comoun labourerys and alle servauntys owyn to payin the tythe of here hyre, after that thei have takyn up here resonable expense", according to the Extravagants and other Constitutions of Canon Law,[5] devotes a whole homily to the subject. With the reinforcement of Scripture and two warning anecdotes from the great clerks, he denounces the false tither, who grumbles at "the trewe tythyng" of his honest neighbour and will even steal back the tithe that "dreed of schame and sclaundere" has compelled him to offer. Such men, he declares, slay Christ like Judas, and break the Decalogue three times over.[6] Finally,

---

[1] Cf. Archbp. Fitzralph, 1351-4, MS. Lansd. 393, Sermons xxxix–xli ("de male decimantibus"); Jo. of Mirfield, *Flor. Barthol.* s.v. "De decimis et oblationibus"; Bromyard, *S.P.* s.v. "Decimae" (with interesting arguments, anecdotes, and popular excuses, etc.); Rypon, MS. Harl. 4894, fols. 21 and 68b (cf. "falsificant Deum qui dedit ecclesiasticis decimas quas ipsi subtrahunt contra donum et promissum Dei"); *Spec. Laic.* cap. xxiv; etc. See also my *Preaching in Med. Engl.* pp. 46, 251, 270, 297, etc.   [2] MS. Harl. 3760, fol. 78.

[3] MS. Heref. Cath. Libr. P. 5. 2, fol. 68. Similarly abroad, see Hauréau, *Not. et Extr.* vol. iv, p. 136 (Sacrilegium).

[4] Ibid. fol. 67. Cf. *Old Engl. Homs.* (12th cent.), E.E.T.S. O.S. no. 53, pp. 215-7.   [5] p. 41.

[6] Cap. vii (De Exhortacione Decimandi), pp. 43-7. Cf. further, *Ayenb. of Inwyt*, p. 41; and Poem in *Old Engl. Misc.* E.E.T.S. p. 77.

there were other temptations to defraud one's own neighbour, leading "housbands...to erie into his neihboris lond and ripe into his corn, to mowen into his medewe and tiȝe into his lesewe,¹ to destrie hit with his beestis and make nevere amendes";² or again to steal a neighbour's capons, his hens, or the fruit of his garden.³ Borrowers of other men's horses and beasts—"to ryden ther-on or to werkyn ther-with", are likewise cautioned by the preacher to make good any loss or damage incurred, and "to restore that thyng aȝen to the owenere".⁴

All these little hints and warnings in the sermons serve to remind us intimately that, whatever differences of wealth and occupation might exist between man and master on the feudal domain, there was often no fundamental difference between them in the matter of vice and virtue. Indeed, it is to the lasting credit and honour of the preachers that they recognized this fact, and never failed to probe beneath outward deed and appearance to the hidden thoughts and motives of the mind. Thus, the poor man, they declare, may be as guilty in his heart of those twin vices of pride and avarice as any nobleman of the land. For "pryde is also ofte tymes in pore men yvel yclothed, as wel as in ryche men. ffor ofte tymes pore men gruccheth aȝenst god and holdeth hemself more worthy, and to have more mede byfore god than thylke that be at more ese. And some beth so deceyved".⁵ "For", adds another, "sum beggere desyreth in wyl to have more rychesse, ȝif he myȝte have it, and wolde have more worschypp, and makyth more of hymself, and heyere in herte beryth him than sum ryche man. This man, be he nevere so poure in catel and in nede, he is noȝt poure in spiryte."⁶ As for avarice, Bromyard warns the poor and simple when they begin to give themselves airs, as the sermon turns on the subject of riches, that "if they held

<hr/>

¹ = pasture (cf. above, p. 305, n. 1). Tiȝe = tether.
² MS. Add. 41321, fol. 103b. Cf. here, *Piers Plowman*, C text, pass. vii, ll. 267–71; etc.
³ *Ayenb. of Inwyt*, p. 38.   ⁴ *Jacob's Well*, pp. 204–5.
⁵ MS. Harl. 2398, fol. 9b. Cf. above, p. 294, n. 1.
⁶ *Jacob's Well*, p. 308. Cf. similarly, *Old Engl. Homs.* (12th cent.), E.E.T.S. O.S. no. 34, pp. 113–15.

the place and power of the wealthy, they would do even worse; for they show this in smaller matters", as, for example, in passing on false coin to their neighbours.[1] None can be more offensive than "the poore man...avauncyd heer to worldly richesses and possessions".[2] This was straight hitting from the shoulder, indeed. So, John Myrc even ventures to assert that the poor man's complaint against the rich is only a case of "the Mote and the Beam" over again.[3] Others speak of envy,[4] and false flattery to win favour and promotion in the service of lords.[5] We catch, in the sermons, too, the husband-man's proverbial note of anxiety and grumbling: "Thus thei grucche, ʒif god sende hem angyr of herte or sykenes, or poverte, or outerage wedyr, or fayling of frute, or dere ʒerys, or ʒif God sende a man werldly good and take fro another his good. Thanne thei seyn that god is noʒt ryʒtwyse, and blamyn hym for his dede....Also thei grucche aʒens man, as ser-vauntys aʒens here mayster or maystresse,...or as pore men aʒens ryche, or as bondemen aʒens here lordys, or as lay-men aʒens preestys".[6] The *Speculum Laicorum* gives two anecdotes upon this subject, contrasting the fate of a certain complaining

[1] s.v. "Acquisitio mala". Cf. the sound remark of MS. St Albans Cath. fol. 40b: "Manye wolde fayne stele if thei dursten, [but] for the galous".

[2] *Gesta Rom.* Engl. version, p. 291 (similarly in Bozon and Bromyard). The homilist goes on—"And thenne thei neythir knowe God ne hem-selfe. They make diverse and depe diches, scil., malice and wickidnesse aʒenst the poore, in the which the devel ofte tyme makith hem-selfe to fall".

[3] See *Festial*, E.E.T.S. ed. pp. 86–7.

[4] Cf. MS. Roy. 18. B. xxiii, fol. 154.

[5] Cf. *Jacob's Well*, pp. 120–1; MS. Harl. 45, fols. 38b, 57b ("ʒiftes, procurynges and flateringes", etc.); etc.

[6] *Jacob's Well*, p. 155. Cf. again, *Jacob's Well*, p. 100, and MS. Harl. 45, fol. 151b ("Sotheliche, suche men beth noght wise that woleth that God schulde telle hem whi he sendeth hem anger, siknes, poverte, or eny other unese as stormes, wedres, failynge of fruytes, scarcenes of sustenaunce, losse of goodes, or other suche....Thei seie in her hertes, or with her mouthes, that God is not rightful, and gruccheth aʒeyn him, and blameth hym..."). Similarly, *Ayenb. of Inwyt*, p. 68. With these cf. now *Piers Plowman*, C text, pass. vii, ll. 110–4; also the peasant's anxiety—"thouʒt and drede and sorinesse"—lest he lose what he has won by his toil, in a poem of the Vernon MS., E.E.T.S. O.S. no. 98, p. 344.

husbandman in Kent, whose barley-field escaped God's rain after the drought, with that of the jolly farmer who says: "I never want any other weather than God wants: so all weathers are to my liking!"[1] Last of all, in the matter of dress, there was open evidence before the eyes of all men that the spirit of social pride and ambition had infected even the lowest ranks:

Nouȝ also the comyn peple is hie stied into the synne of pride. For now a wrecchid cnave, that goth to the plouȝ and to carte, that hath no more good but serveth fro ȝer to ȝer for his liflode, there-as sumtyme a white curtel and a russet gowne wolde have served suchon ful wel, now he muste have a fresch doublet of fyve schillynges or more the price; and above, a costli gowne with bagges hangynge to his kne, and iridelid[2] undir his girdil as a newe ryven roket,[3] and an hood on his heved, with a thousande ragges on his tipet; and gaili hosid an schood as thouȝ it were a squyer of cuntre; a dagger harneisid with selver bi his gurdel, or ellis it were not worth a pese. This pride schulle ther maistirs a-buye, whanne that thei schul paie hir wages. For, there-as thei weren wont to serve for x or xii schillingis in a ȝer, now thei musten have xx oor thritti and his lyverei also therto; not for he wol do more werk, but for to meynten with that pride.[4]

Their women-folk were already no better. John Waldeby bemoans characteristically, in one of his sermons, that "whatever vanity or finery can now be found amongst lords and ladies in clothing and adornment, their servants and maids usurp for themselves. And this is a great sign of the ruin of this world....As the servant, so also is his lord!"[5] Rypon links up this particular folly, likewise, with the general unrest and insecurity of the times: "The garments, I say, of the proud and those who were once noble are now divided as spoil, along with their bed-quilt, amongst grooms and maid-servants and

[1] Ed. Welter, pp. 79–80, nos. 409 and 410: the latter is also in MS. Add. 18364, fol. 60b.

[2] = pleated.

[3] = rochet (surplice or episcopal vest of·linen).

[4] MS. Add. 41321, fols. 101b–2. The reference to "bag-sleeves" indicates a date from c. 1380–c. 1440: cf. further below, p. 409.

[5] MS. Roy. 7. E. ii. fol. 17b. Similarly, *Pricke of Consc.* pp. 42–5; and the *Bk. of the Kni. of La Tour-Landry*, p. 31. See also above, p. 314, and below, pp. 408–11.

prostitutes, and others still worse and prouder than formerly.
...Hardly anyone now is satisfied with his status, but pants
after a higher, and inanely affects to be reputed better than
he is by other people".[1] Here the preachers' verdict seems to
have coincided for once with that of the upper classes. For a
vernacular homilist tells us that "on the other side, the lordes
and the grette men seyn that the pride and the nyse aray that
reyneth among commeners is cause of this myschef (that is
fallen in this reme)".[2] Looking back at all these denunciations
of the unfaithful husbandmen, the reader is now in a position
to understand the real source and significance of Chaucer's
account of the faithful *Plowman*. Dressed in his simple frock,
the latter is but a man after the preachers' own heart. He is
a good and honest worker, contented with his lot, who loves
God, whether his fortune be good or bad, tithes fairly, and
lives to help his neighbours in the spirit of peace and charity.[3]

Seven important groups of the community have mono-
polized our attention in the two chapters of the present study
that have dealt thus far with the preaching of Satire and Complaint. The scope of that preaching, however, has been by no
means exhausted. For, if we were to turn and consider the
various minor social groups of those who pursue lawless
and perverted vocations, we should find our medieval pulpit

[1] MS. Harl. 4894, fol. 27b. Cf. a similar point in the song *Against the
Pride of the Ladies*, in Wright, Camden Soc. p. 153; and Hoccleve, *Reg. of
Princes*, E.E.T.S. ed. p. 17; etc. There is an echo in the sermons of
attempts to keep the ambitious poor in their place. Cf. *Gesta Rom.*
Engl. version, pp. 310–11: "Justicis, sherrevis and bailifs", etc., "when
that thei se a man gadery or purchesse, thenne thei sey—'Loo, he is a
carle, and wolde be moore than his syr was! Late us take fro him the
richesse". It is a sidelight on the ruthless surveillance of the medieval
peasant and his actions, from which he was rarely free.
[2] MS. Roy. 18. B. xxiii, fol. 167 ("the comon peple", for their part,
blame "the exstorcion and the misgovernaunce of the lordes").
[3] *Cant. Tales*, Prol. ll. 529–41. See further below, pp. 571–4. Note
also how this evidence weakens the argument of Manly (*Some New Light
on Chaucer*), as above, p. 230.

quite as adequate for the new enquiry as for the old. One final illustration of the former must now suffice. Its interest and significance for us lie particularly in the fact that it proves once again the direct dependence of the satirical poet upon these homiletic models. No one yet, apparently, has detected the literary history of that pathetic little group of social outcasts—pathetic, for all their idle rascality and foul misconduct—with whom Piers the Plowman declares that he will have nothing to do:

> And alkyn crafty men that konne lyven in treuthe
> I shal fynden hem fode, that feithfulliche libbeth.
> Save Iakke the iogeloure, and Ianet of the stues,
> And Danyel the dys-playere and Denote the baude,
> And Frere the faytoure, and folke of his ordre,
> And Robyn the rybaudoure, for his rusty wordes.[1]

Although the faithful Ploughman is fully aware that truth bade him not to deal with these, while "holicherche is hote of hem no tythe to take", yet even he cannot dismiss them from his sight without a compassionate sigh for the evil fortune which has driven them to such degradation: "They ben ascaped good aventure", he says. "Now God hem amende!" They are indeed beyond the help of man, as the modern social worker knows who mixes with the dregs of our human civilization to-day. We saw, but a little while ago, how Langland fashioned a lively Dickens-like character in *Parson Sloth*, out of the bare line or two of a famous pulpit commonplace.[2] Here, he gives similar vitality to an equally familiar homiletic list of disreputable and discredited "Crafts of Folly".[3] "Jakke the iogeloure", then, is only one of the nameless band of jugglers condemned thus by the preacher because "thei getyn here good wyth false iapys and lesynges, and getyn here lyvyng wyth wrong". Janet of the stews, who follows next in the poem, is none other than the poor "common woman", the

---

[1] B text, pass. vi, ll. 70–9. Cf. A text, pass. vii, ll. 63–6, and C text, pass. ix, ll. 69–75.

[2] See above, Chap. v, p. 278.

[3] See MS. Harl. 45, fol. 71 b et seq., and *Jacob's Well*, pp. 134–5; all based on the *Ayenb. of Inwyt*, p. 45 (discourse on Avarice); etc.

prostitute, who is briefly described along with the juggler in the same homiletic indictment. Daniel the dice-player is the evil gamester, whose various activities "at the tabelys and at the dyse" are there set forth in even greater detail than those of his fellows under the heading of "Foly Pley".[1] "Denote the baude" is apparently the "latch-drawer" of the series, a dirty tramp who pesters the good housewife at the door, when her husband is away from home, with a long story of his misfortunes. Nor will he go until he has won something for his importunity: "And ȝif the wyif be alone, thei folwyn here in-to the spense, that for dreed sche is fayn to ȝyven hem what sche may".[2] "Frere the faytour" is there too, with his brethren, amongst the "faytours that getyn mete and monye of pyteous folk wyth wyles, as to makyn hem seme crokyd, blynde, syke, or mysellys, and are noȝt so". Nor finally is Robin "the rybaudoure", the teller of coarse tales and jokes, missing from the preacher's comprehensive list. For it is he who is held guilty of "harlotrie", that is, "makyng iapys a-forn folk" and "other unthryft", for a precarious livelihood. The faithful are warned to avoid their company, and give them no charity to maintain their evil pursuits, precisely as Piers states. If time and space permitted, one could go on to indicate further suggestive parallels of this kind between the poem and the sermons. The value of the latter, indeed, is again well brought out a little later in the same *Passus*, where a somewhat obscure reference to the Pardoner, under the guise of "Robert Renneaboute", which appears to have eluded Skeat, is at once made clear by means of them.[3] However, it is now high time to

---

[1] This subject is common in our sermons. Besides *Jacob's Well*, etc., as above, cf. Bromyard, *S.P.* s.v. "Ludus", etc.; Jo. of Mirfield, *Flor. Barthol.* ibid.; Rypon, in MS. Harl. 4894, fol. 23; Myrc, *Man. Sacerd.* cap. xv, MS. Harl. 5306, fol. 18; etc., etc.

[2] This is the only character which does not fit easily into the homiletic scheme. Elsewhere in the poem the type is clearly referred to under the name of "Roberdes knaves". (See Skeat's excellent note, A, B and C texts, Prol., ll. 44 and 45, E.E.T.S. ed. pt. iv, § 1 (Notes), p. 8.)

[3] B text, pass. vi, l. 150. Prof. Skeat here actually gives no note whatever upon the phrase, leaving it to be inferred that Langland is alluding to the "Robertes men" again—which would be absurd, however, in the

middle of a passage devoted to Religious. Let us now turn to the sermons. Cf. first, the preacher of MS. Worc. Cath. Libr. F. 10, fol. 49: "Mor-over, whan the schriveste te, go to him that hath cure o thi sowle, as to thi propre prest, thi person or thi pentauncer, and to no *ronners over contreys*. For, trest wel therto, thei ha no powr for the most part to asoyle the; and terfor, the mor harm is, thei bygyle fowle hemsilf and te bothe. For these it be that seynt Peter speke of.... 'Ther schal come', seit seint Peter, 'e the laste dayes, glosers and deseyvors of the peple, goyng abowte onliche for hir owne profit and hir owne coveytise.' For we se now alday, thei a man had slawe his fader or his modir, ʒe, or do the greityste synne in al this world, we[l] for a peny or tweyn a schuld be bothe schreyve and soyled". Again, MS. Add. 41321, fols. 84b–5: "Also in this blyndenesse beth alle thoo that bileven that, for a bulle purchasid of a fals pardener thoru a fals suggestion and symonye of selver, and thei paie him thanne a peny and leie hit on hire hevedes, thei beth asoiled of alle hire synnes, as thei witterli wene. But the hooli goost seith in the Book of Priveites— 'Quantum glorificavit...', that is, 'how myche a man hath ioied in delitis of synne, so myche ʒeve him tormente, sorwe, or weilynge': that is, the riʒtwisnesse of God wole that, as myche lust and likynge as a man hath had in synne, so myche peyne evene weied therwith him behoveth to have therfore, other in this world of sorwe of herte, other of penaunce wilfulli taken or enioyned of here sovereyne and schrifte, or of meke suffrynge of tribulacioun, or ellis at the laste in the peyne of purgatorie.... Alle such ben maad blynde or blyndefeld for a tyme, as men pleyen a-bobbid [i.e. Blindman's Buff]; for thei beth bobbid in hire bileve and in hire catel bothe, bi suche *lepers over londe*, that libbeth bi hire lesyngis".

On the subject of the Pardoner (in *Piers Plowman* as in the sermons) see further in my *Preaching in Med. Engl.* pp. 99–110. I find now, however, that I was mistaken in speaking there (p. 109) of an almost complete silence about him in the sermons. In addition to the two new and unpublished excerpts just given, cf. further MS. Bodl. 95, fol. 14: "Perdoners and fals prechours, wyth othyr suche, that, ʒyf a man have but on peny, they wol have hyt, thouʒ he schuld [lack] bred and watur, and al hys howsehold. Or yf a man had but a buschel of corne, ʒyt wol they have halffe; and ryʒt have they non there-to, but ʒyf they...be-hote men muche mede to gete here good from hem. For ʒyf thu wol ʒeve hem nowʒt, they wol not come at the, to preche ne to bryng perdon.... ʒyf they may gete here dowter or here mayde, he wol lyʒtely stele hem a-wey and defowle hem wyth synne. And there-fore men schuld besyly be ware of al suche...". Also Bp. Repingdon (?), MS. Jo. Ryl. Libr. Manch. Lat. 367, fol. 299b (the Devil's Doctors): "Nunc videndum est qui sunt isti medici sub quorum custodia anima fluxum sanguinis paciens deterius se habet: dicendum quod adulatores sunt, qui veniunt ad vos in vestimentis ovium, intrinsecus sunt lupi rapaces; qui dicunt opere vel sermone —'Date nobis, et orabimus pro vobis; et pro annuali redditu concedemus vobis participationem omnium orationum, vigiliarum et abstinenciarum

proceed to some consideration of a yet more intimate type of satire which concerns the individual rather than the class, and the home and the leisure-hour as often as the place of business.

que fuerint inter nos';...vel alii adulatores qui pro denario promittunt indifferenter omnibus indulgenciam et remissionem peccatorum, non attendentes ad contricionem, ad confessionem, vel alia que necessaria sunt ad peccatorum remissionem...".

In view of poems against the Lollards, another lawless group, further sermons dealing with them, in addition to those quoted above, p. 84, and in the author's *Preaching in Med. Engl.* pp. 135–40, may here be indicated—in MS. Worc. Cath. Libr. F. 10. Cf. fol. 45 b ("...fals techers as lollardes and swich other that be now-a-daies, that be takyn vor cristen men, make anon orrible noise and a grews e this eris o gode men, whan thei stond up and preche thinges [that] be the contrarie to hir feith..."); fols. 49 b–50 ("...this lollardes and tis fals ypocrites that be now-a-day.... For we se now so miche folk, and specialiche thes lollardes, thay go barfot, thei go openhed, ȝe, thei wassche sothylike hir clothes withowtyn with teres of hir eȝen, that miche of the peple is fowle blynded and deseyvyd bi hem. For thei wene that tei have plente inow with-in hem of the water of holi levyng; and truliche, it is nothyng so. For ther was a lollard at Oxenfort but awhile agon, that forsuk al his errours and al his mislevyng, and turnyd aȝen to the levyng of other good cristenmen, and tan a told certeyn rytes and doyng of hem, ȝe, so cursed and so oreble to her that, e good feyth, ich am grevyse for to telle hem.... Therfor, ȝif any swich come to ȝow to preche or to teche, ȝe, for Cristes sake, her him nawth, but put him away fro ȝe....I blesse God, it is seide in other cuntreys that ȝit ȝe ha wel holde swich maner of men owt o this toun; and terfor, i dowt nat troffe, ȝe spede te beter in al ȝour doyng, ȝe, and ha miche the mor worschipe a this world and also gret thonk o God almithte.... Thei the go to ragged and to rent and schewe out-ward, it is nothyng in her herte; for mor prowder men, mor envyus men, than thei be with-inne, bethe none in this world...").

CHAPTER VII

The Preaching of Satire and Complaint

PART III

IN a poem known as *The Hye Way to the Spyttel House*, a metrical dialogue of early Tudor date,[1] its author Robert Copland tells how he took shelter from wind and shower, one chill November night, in the porch of St Bartholomew's Hospital, in London. Finding himself alone in the company of the porter, he begins to talk, the conversation turning at length upon the crowd of wretched, ill-clad beggars and outcasts that soon cluster about them at the gate. Copland is anxious to learn who finds lodging at such a place; and the porter, with a loquacity characteristic of his calling, is ready to satisfy his questioner's curiosity to the full. Among the many types thus described to us, in the course of the poem, are the idle vagabonds, tramps with their tale of an old soldier's evil lot, the self-maimed, whining rogues of the pavement, the "nyghtyngales of Newgate"—false deceivers all, priests and clerks of vicious life and drunken, slothful habit, negligent bailiffs, stewards, farmers, servants and the like, merchants, craftsmen, innkeepers fallen on evil times, sometimes even the very spoilers of the poor now poor themselves, in short, most if not all of the very folk who have been engaging our attention in the two previous chapters. Neither the poet's curiosity, however, nor the porter's tale of woe is sated yet. Copland's own guess, alas! proves to be all too correct. There are yet others that sink to a last lodging within these same poor-house walls, victims of the "shrewd wyfe" that gave them no peace at home with her continual babbling, quarrelling and complaint, masters that failed to be master in their own house, parents who spoilt and pampered their children—"in ydle wantonnes

[1] Printed (as well as written) by R. Copland, Lond. c. 1531; reprinted in W. C. Hazlitt, *Early Pop. Poetry of Engl.* vol. iv, pp. 17–72, etc.

suffryng them to be", horrible swearers and blasphemers, "grete dronkardes, that suppe all of by pottes and tankardes, tyll they be so dronke that they cannot stande", men of strife and ill-temper, disturbers of the peace, women who once loved extravagance and finery—and "a M. mo than I can tell". It is these latter, then, common prey of the follies of domestic life, that the present chapter will present to us from the sermon page. The actual source of Copland's poem may well be a tract by Robert de Balzac; but the matter and message of it belong to a hoary tradition already familiar enough. Therein, the *Hye Way to the Spyttel House*, with all its limitations, serves us as a useful literary signpost. For, while, in common with other satirical poems and ballads of the times, it points forward to some famous characters and scenes of the Elizabethan drama, it points us backward to the same road stretching without a break to *Piers Plowman's Vision*[1] and other verse satires of the Middle Ages, and behind them to the real home of all these graphic word-pictures of social types—the medieval sermons themselves. Line upon line we shall rediscover them there, often with scarce a phrase or a feature changed. "Sethen than, som men nedeth to be tauȝthe to consceyve qwhat ther is necessary to hem goostly,...som nedeth to be undirnyme that ben enclyned to fleshly lustes,... som nedeth to be chastized for ther dedly offence, and som nedeth by ensampull be lerned and by experience"[2]—in this very fashion, let us begin with the preachers' chastisement of the Fair Sex, and see whither it will lead us.

In a brilliant little essay on "The Position of Women in the Middle Ages",[3] Miss Eileen Power has recently re-emphasized the immense influence exerted by the Church's well-known attitude toward the sex upon the literary world of the day. At the same time she well argues that this doctrine of subjection and criticism can have borne little relation to the facts where the medieval housewife frequently played so active

[1] It is worth noting that Robt. Crowley, the famous first printer of this poem, was a contemporary of our author and printer Robt. Copland.
[2] MS. Roy. 18. B. xxiii, fol. 135 b.
[3] *The Legacy of the Middle Ages*, Oxford, 1926, pp. 401–33.

and dignified a part in the society of her age. There is no need for us, then, to labour the point that here we are concerned with another literary conceit that springs direct from the preachers. To the vast mass of the middle and lower orders, for whom no romantic minstrelsy had provided a chivalrous ideal, the pulpit, their one oracle of learning and refinement, presented a picture of womanhood, ill-balanced, indeed, but sufficiently realistic and lively to appeal to the lay mind. Thus early there grew up in popular verse a traditional satire, half-comic, half-tragic, from which neither the greatest of medieval English poets nor the greatest of all our dramatists could escape in their day, and one that stubbornly persists through the literature of following centuries to that of modern times.

Hitherto sermons and treatises of continental homilists have furnished wellnigh all the known examples of this repressive ecclesiastical treatment of the sex. An American contributor to the *Cambridge History of English Literature* who reminds us further of the secular contributions of France to what he calls "Buranic" verse in this country, discerns also "a native English contribution", of some considerable antiquity. But there his enquiry ends.[1] The voices of our English preachers have remained as usual unheard. Nevertheless, he who listens to them now will soon learn that their outlook is no brighter, no more in accord with the tender voices of passion and of poetry stirring within the lover's breast, than that of their brethren abroad. Where healthy human nature seems to demand some positive doctrine of sexual happiness, they speak only, as in the realm of public affairs, of sin and temptation, of forbidden pleasures and lusts, of needful fears and repressions, haunted by the same old shadow of Original Sin, the same primitive ascetical ideals as their ancestors. Woman's chief glory—not merely her little foibles and excesses—is by them accounted a snare and a delusion, her greatest field of activity little better than a wilderness of briars and pitfalls. "Woman,"

[1] Prof. F. M. Padelford, in vol. ii, p. 385. Strangely enough, the very sample of verse which he here quotes contains a phrase that is referred to in one of our sermons. However, he is not even apparently familiar with the complete context in its primitive proverbial form. Cf. above, p. 44.

says our thirteenth-century author of the *Speculum Laicorum*, quoting Vincent of Beauvais, "as saith Secundus the Philosopher, is the confusion of Man, an insatiable beast, a continuous anxiety, an incessant warfare, a daily ruin, a house of tempest, a hindrance to devotion."[1] We have already heard a part of Master Rypon's equally pessimistic denunciation of womanly beauty, a century later. "Truly, vain it is", he continues, "because it has no stability: for it wanes either through old age or else through infirmity.... If only such folk would call to mind how vile they were at their beginning, and how much viler they will be at their end, they would not boast so inanely of their... beauty."[2] In no sphere, perhaps, does the sheer, overwhelming pessimism of the pulpit show itself more clearly than in its treatment of the theme of matrimony. Bromyard's discussion of the subject is as usual a fair sample. In his chapter on *Matrimonium*, the dignity and worth of marriage occupy no more than one-seventh of the total discourse. Nor is the reason for this far to seek. For, as he tells us elsewhere, while the Old Testament ideal of womanhood was Fecundity, its New Testament and therefore modern equivalent is the state of Virginity.[3] Marriage at the best, as in Langland's vision of *Do-bet*[4] and in sermon-literature generally, figures but as a poor third in the list of three permissible conditions for human life, with a mere "thirtyfold" as its reward.[5] For the rest, it is to be pictured as a life-long curbing of desire, interrupted at certain intervals by solemn dedication to the equally burdensome task of

[1] cap. liii (ed. Welter, p. 77).
[2] MS. Harl. 4894, fol. 180. See further above, p. 48.
[3] s.v. "Maria", and again s.v. "Munditia".
[4] *Piers Plowman*, C text, pass. xix, ll. 84 et seq.; B text, pass. xvi, 71, etc.
[5] (See Matth. xiii, 23; etc.) s.v. "Matrimonium". Cf. further, e.g., MS. Add. 21253: "Aliud faciunt centesimum ut virgines, aliud sexagesimum ut vidue, aliud tricesimum ut conjugati..."; MS. Salisb. Cath. Libr. 103, fols. 115b–19b: "...Thretty comyth of thre and ten: therfore ȝif thou kepe in thi wedlok thre and ten, thou schalt have thryes ten medys—ȝif thou kepe thre in thi wedlok, that is, *ffidem, prolem et sacramentum....* Thanne, for thise iii that thou kepyst in thi wedlok and for thise ten comaundmentys that thou kepyst, thou schalt have in heven iii and x medys, that is, thryes ten corouns, that is, xxx specyall ioyes...". *Ayenb. of Inwyt*, here, pp. 221–2, is unusually laudatory.

replenishing the race upon earth[1] and repairing the ruin of Lucifer in Heaven. The Dominican points sorrowfully to its discomforts, its anxieties, its worries, its perils. Husbands may lose wealth, strength or comeliness and become displeasing to their spouse. Her safety, on the other hand, may be a continual source of anxiety to them during their absence. She, again, by her very fecundity or sterility, her beauty or her ugliness may "render the marriage tie irksome or dangerous". If her husband be rich, due provision for a large family leads to endless worry and the risk of many vices: if he be poor, then is the old proverb all too true which says—"a large family and little food is a nuisance". If the wife be sterile, then is the husband sad that he has no heir. "If she be fair, then, as happens frequently, she is vain and extravagant in adornment, clamorous and wearisome unless she have the money for the adornment that she desires; and sometimes she is lascivious...." "If indeed she be uncomely, her company will be disagreeable", and so forth. Alas! the tale of likely woes is by no means ended thus. "Daily experience suffices to show that those who wed for beauty, for sensual pleasure or for riches swiftly lose peace of heart and rest of body, and are changed into states of the greatest hatreds, discords, blows and adulteries." Wise, then, was that "certain noble widow", mentioned by Bromyard, who, "for the aforesaid causes, is said to have repulsed all the suitors who begged her to marry them, with the words—'I want no more husbands: for, if I had a good one, as the other was, I should be afraid of losing him as I lost the other; and if he were bad, it would be an annoyance for me to live with him'".[2] One more typical story from an English sermon will illustrate the woman's point of view again, before we pass on: A certain king, says the preacher, desired a rich

[1] Yet Bromyard observes elsewhere, be it noted, that the world of his day is already over-populated: e.g., s.v. "Mors" ("Moderno vero tempore, cum sicut terrarum termini et possessiones artantur, quia possessores et habitatores multiplicantur quibus terra vix sufficit..."), "Munditia"; etc.

[2] S.P. s.v. "Matrimonium". Cf. similarly, Bozon, *Metaphs.* cap. cxxxvi; *Gesta Rom.* p. 173; and further, e.g., Jo. of Mirfield, *Flor. Barthol.* MS. Camb. Univ. Libr. Mm. ii. 10, fols. 114 et seq. (De Matrimonio et sponsalibus), and fols. 141 et seq., on Women.

marriage for his fair daughter, but found her obdurate. She would be spouse to none other than Jesus Christ himself. When wrath, threats and bribes all failed to move her, the disappointed parent fell sick. On her going to console him, he explains the cause of his sickness, and she, apparently relenting, now declares—"Fadere, be no thinge discomforde; for I am redie to fulfill youre will, so that ȝe may fynde in all youre londe suche on in whom that I may fynde mater for to love, and to suche on will I gladely be wedded to".

Than this kynge wexed glade and joyfull and kevered[1] owte of is sekenes, and hastely sende is messangeres in to alle the londe and bade that all that weren rycheste, fayreste and strengeste shuld com to the weddynge of is dowȝtur. And when the daye was sett of hure weddyng and alle the lordes were comon, than seid the kynge to is dowȝtur that she shuld chese hure an husbond on of alle thoo lordes that ther were gadered. Than this mayde answered and seid—"ȝe lordes that be gadered here, understond ȝe me: Covenand was made betweyne my lord my fadur and me that, ȝiff it so were that in all is londe that he myȝthe fynde suche oon in whom were matur and cause of love and whom that I myght fynde in my herte for to love, that I shuld take hym to my husbond; and that is the encheson[2] that my lorde my fadur sende after you that I shuld chese on of you to my husbond. Neverthelesse, I fynde noon suche: for why? ȝiff I chese me a ryche man, sethen that rychesse sone commes and lithely goth a-veye, and also it suffreth mans soule to have no reste ne quyete of herte, als longe as we were ryche we shuld have no reste ne murthe, and lythely thorowe an anguysche that we myght be put in shuld leson oure rychesse, and than shulde oure love departe. And ȝiff that I chese me a fayre man to my husbond, he may thorowe sekenes waxe foule and discolourd, and so lese I my love. And ȝiff that I chese me a stronge man, he may in batell be slayne or els be wounded and beton that he waxe lame and croked, and on this maner I shuld lese my love. And therfore, lordes, I latt you witt that I will not on this maner besett my love. A-fore as muche as ȝe be commen fro fare countres to my weddynge, here-to fore you all I shall be wedded". [Whereupon, she knelt down and, raising her eyes to heaven, commended her soul to Christ her spouse before them all.] And, with thise wordes, the rofe of the house opened, and with a grett liȝthe hure soule in the lykenesse of a fayre colver,[3] seying all that ther were gadered, was lifte up in to the blisse of heven. On this maner shuld we goye in the love of almyghte god, aftur the ensampull of this holy maydeyne....[4]

---

[1] = recovered.   [2] = reason.   [3] = dove.

[4] MS. Roy. 18. B. xxiii, fols. 78 et seq. A similar story appears in Bromyard, S.P. s.v. "Amor". Cf. further, e.g., Master Ralph of Acton's praise of Virginity, in MS. Jo. Ryl. Libr. Manch. Lat. 367, fol. 118

There is another complaint of the contemporary pulpit, however, to which we must give ear, while upon this subject. We have already had occasion to observe the "commercial" and ambitious spirit of the age in all ranks of the community. Even marriage did not escape its contagion in a world of ordinary folk well hedged about by class distinctions, and still innocent of any industrial system or the prospect of rich heiresses upon the other side of the Atlantic. In view of man's frailty, says the preacher, God has permitted marriage, "to lyve in Goddes law"—

But mony wedd hem wyvys for her worldly goodes, for her grete kynne, other for ther fleschely lust: as, be a woman a pore wenche, and ther-wyth well condiciond, abell of person, and have no worldly goodes and be come of sympell kynne the whiche may not avaunce here, full fewe men covetyn suche on. Som had lever to take an olde wedow, though sche be ful lothelyche and never schall have cheldren. And, fro the tyme that he hathe the mocke that he wedded her for, and felethe her breth foule stynkynge and her eyen blered, scabbed and febyll, as old wommen buthe, then they spend a-pon strompettes that evyli-getyn goodes. And sche shall sytt at home wyth sorowe, hungry and thrusty. And thus levythe they in a-vowtry, peraventure all her lif tyme.[1] If a mayde be to wedde, the furste thynge that a man woll aske—what her frendes woll ӡeve to mary here wyth: and but they acorde ther in,...they kepe not of here. It semeth, then, they wedden the goodes more than the womman.[2] For, had not the goodes be, sche schuld goo un-wedded, as all day is seyne.

And thus hit farethe in this worlde bothe by man and womman. Suche maner of maryage, y drede, is full dampneabill for ryche men. For her ryches they schulde take pore dameselles to her wyves, principally for the love of God, to kepe hem frome synne; and then were hyt medefull to fore almyӡti God. But, and a ryche man have mony dowters the whiche schuld be maried, if eny of hem be unsemelyche the whiche schuld have

(compared to a harp); and for important foreign references, Coulton, *Five Cents. of Relig.* vol. i, p. 445: also the story above, p. 11.

[1] Cf. here *Piers Plowman*, A text, pass. x, ll. 182-3 ("to wedden an old widewe, for weolthe of hire goodes..."), and C text, pass. xi, ll. 254-69 (remarking further—"A mayde wel ymanered, of good men yspronge, bote hue have eny other good, have hure wol no ryche..."); also Alex. Barclay, *Ship of Fools*, ed. Edinb. 1874, vol. i, p. 247 et seq. ("Of yonge folys that take olde wymen to theyr wyves for theyr ryches").

[2] Cf. similarly, *Piers Plowman* (marriage "for covetise of catel", etc.).

the heritage, her frendes schull a-non aȝenst her wyll mak her a womman of relygyon,[1] and put her from her herytage when sche is yeonge, and ȝeve hyt to a nother douȝter the whiche is more semely, thouȝ that sche be not disposed to have an husbond. Thus men fallen in grete perell a-ȝenst God almyȝty.[2]

If the preachers' regular view of matrimony was as gross and materialistic as many of their sermons imply, we can hardly be surprised that some men looked upon marriage with the cold, calculating eye of the business man. Not only the bonds of natural affection between husband and wife, but also those gentle arts of love-making which had done so much in the romantic sphere to soften relations between the sexes left the homilist not merely cold but critical. "In kyssynge and grypynge and beholdyng" of the apparently harmless sort, he sees as much poison as "in spekynge and in takynge hede to wyckede and unclene speches, and in other unlawesom touchynges onlyche by schrewede delectacioun, and in other lecherous fykelynges and ragynges".[3] For they are all accounted one and "lecherous" together. "Speche of women and kyssynges and nyce contenance-makynge draweth ofte tymes men and women to lecherye, as seyth seynt Poule."[4] Hence the need for sweeping prohibitions. A passage in another of these sermons puts the matter beyond doubt:

Som seyen, peraventur, that such clippyng and kyssynge may be had with-owten synne. I say, nay! Loo! a notabull story, 2 Reg. 11ᵐᵒ of Davit, that noble kynge and prophete.... Take hede now! ȝiff David, the wiche is cheff of prophetes and so enspired with the holy goost... was

[1] Cf. Bromyard, s.v. "Eleemosyna" ("Si etiam habeant filium vel filiam gibbosam vel corpore deformem, dicunt—'Ista debet poni in religione'"); similarly, s.v. "Adventus" (If they have a one-eyed daughter, she will become a nun; if fair, she will remain in the world; etc.).

[2] MS. Bodl. 95, fol. 12 et seq. For the antiquity of these same complaints, see a sermon by Nic. Biard (first half of 13th cent.), in Hauréau, *Not. et Extr.* vol. vi, p. 4; Bromyard, in *S.P.* s.v. "Matrimonium"; etc.

[3] MS. Harl. 2398, fol. 98b. Cf. again MS. St Albans Cath. fol. 34 ("aȝenstonde styfli al the temptaciouns of lecherie, and fle wisely alle the spicis ther-of, as nyce lokingis, unclene ragyngis, touchingis, hondlyngis, lecherous lokyngis, ribaudrie, harlotrie..."); *Jacob's Well*, p. 219 and MS. Salisb. Cath. Libr. 103, fol. 114b, etc.; *Ayenb. of Inwyt*, pp. 46–7; *Hand. Synne*, pp. 244–5; *Ancren Riwle*, ed. King's Classics, p. 154; etc.

[4] Ibid. fol. 36b. See 1 Cor. vii, 1.

thus overcome,...how darst thou than, that art nothur holy ne so wisse as David was, seth that thou art [not] stered to lechery by clippyng and kyssynges? I beleve the not, that seys thus; for the sentence of scripture, me semeth, is aȝeyns the!¹

This same speaker goes on to develop an interesting, half-satirical simile upon this very theme. Love-making he compares to the "thre condicions that tavernars useth". "First, a taverner settes owt a wyne garlond to draw men to is taveron. On like wize mans flessh and wommans settes owte nyse and degyse aray....The secounde condicion of the taverner is to ȝeve men a tast of is wyne, to stere hem to by ther of." This corresponds to what the speaker is pleased to call—"unclene kyssynges, clippynges and other unhonest handelynges", to which the display of finery leads. "The third condicion of a taverner, aftur that he hath ȝeve men a tast, he bryngeth hem to a place where thei may drynke aftur here plesaunce, and make ther cownaundes [and] trete ther maters aftur hem liketh. And enon so dothe the flesshe: for aftur clippynge and kissyng and unclene towchynge, he [the Devil] bryngeth thise unclene pepull to som plase that pleases hem, wher that thei may make here cownauntes of sensuall love."² To the ears of John Bromyard, the love-ditties of the dancers sound no better than pig-squealing.³ It was certainly a rude age, in which the preacher's indiscriminate prohibitions might seem justified by the low level on which men's minds and manners still dwelt. Nevertheless, the tragedy remains that, over against the follies of the Venusberg, there was set no other fair castle of Earthly Love to which men and women might be bidden to repair. Those tempted to be filthy were thus often in reality left only

¹ MS. Roy. 18. B. xxiii, fol. 133. See, for the other side, the *Forma Confessionis* for a female penitent, in MS. Bristol City Libr. 6, fol. 135. Cf. also, the argument of Bozon, *Metaphs.* cap. xxi: "St Paul does not say '*Fight* fornication', but '*flee*' [1 Cor. vi, 18]; for it is hard by any other way to escape their hands..."; and Bromyard, *S.P.*s.v. "Tentatio".
² Ibid. fols. 132b–3.
³ Cf. s.v. "Chorea": "...ad modum porcarii qui, volens omnes porcos similiter congregare, facit unum clamare: sic dyabolus facit unam cantilenam incipere quam ipsemet dictavit....Ita spiritus malignus dictat cantilenas ad fatuos amores...". Cf. again, MS. Add. 21253, fol. 81b–2 ("contra cantilenas"), and the *Spec. Laic.* (ed. Welter, pp. 32–3).

to be filthy still. "Fugiamus Helenam!"[1] There blares forth
through the land the blast of a thousand homiletic trumpets
against the monstrous regiment of women in "wowynges",
"kyssynges", "derne[2] syngynges, gay aray, nyce chere", even
"songys of love paramour and letterys of love",[3] and all such
"thynges that beth forbode as dawnsynge of wommen and
other opene syʒtes that draweth men to synne".[4] Where alas!
is our merry medieval England? "So, yf thou wolt be Cristes
clene childe, flee as Cristes coward the companye of folyes
women, ne be thou nouʒt to famylyer with non maner women."[5]
Here the voice of the typical Puritan speaks out already, even
as of him who sternly requires "stilnesse in berynge, honeste
in clothynge, abstinence in mete and drynke, schame in seme-
launt and chiere"[6] in his ideal medieval woman. It is an interesting commentary upon the survival of this Augustinian
Dualism and what Dr Coulton has rightly called "the High
Ancestry of Puritanism" to recall in this connection the
brilliant rebukes of Sir Edmund Gosse for the extreme Evan-
gelicalism of his own upbringing:

> It divides heart from heart. It sets up a vain, chimerical ideal, in the
> barren pursuit of which all the tender, indulgent affections, all the genial
> play of life, all the exquisite pleasures and soft resignations of the body,
> all that enlarges and calms the soul are exchanged for what is harsh and
> void and negative. It encourages a stern and ignorant spirit of con-
> demnation; it throws altogether out of gear the healthy movement of the
> conscience; it invents virtues which are sterile and cruel; it invents sins

---

[1] Thus actually quoted in a French sermon, along with the injunction—
"Flee all women!". See *Hist. Litt. de la Fr.* vol. xxvi, 457.

[2] = secret (used especially of love).

[3] See *Jacob's Well*, p. 164.

[4] MS. Burney, 356, fol. 50b. For other English denouncers of the
dance, in addition to those published by Coulton, cf. Jo. of Mirfield, *Flor.
Barthol.* MS. Camb. Univ. Libr. Mm. ii, 10, fol. 258b, quoting Chrysost.
("Ubi saltacio, ibi dyabolus..."); Bp. Repingdon (?), MS. Jo. Ryl.
Libr. Manch. Lat. 367, fol. 210 ("Corea est quasi exercitus diaboli..."); etc.

[5] MS. Harl. 2398, fol. 99. Cf. the Engl. *Spec. Laic.* cap. liii (as before):
The society of woman to be avoided—(1) "quia hominem illaqueat",
(2) "commaculat", and (3) "rebus et virtutibus spoliat": Bozon, *Metaphs.*
cap. xxi, quoting Prov. v, 8 ("Keep ye far from her company", etc.);
Bromyard, *S.P.* s.v. "Luxuria" (flee women as lepers), "Ornatus"; etc.

[6] Ibid. fol. 37b. Cf. also above, p. 119.

which are no sins at all, but which darken the heaven of innocent joy with futile clouds of remorse.[1]

There is one favourite saying of our homilists which, like their scorn of women's kisses, has passed into some other literature of their own day: "Who was strenger than Sampson, wyser than Salamon, holyer than David? And ȝit thei were al over-comen by the queyntise and whiles of women".[2]

With this general background established, we must pass on to examine in detail those particular onslaughts of the pulpit against feminine vice which left their mark even more indelibly in popular verse and prose. For, although now and then a kindlier, fairer attitude is expressed, as for example in the typical marriage sermon of the day,[3] yet it is with the complaint and the satire that we are here concerned. "But what am I to say of modern women?" asks Robert Rypon: "Assuredly, not 'a woman that was in the city, a sinner', but 'a woman that *is* in the city, a sinner'".[4] A passage in the Book of Proverbs describing a type of evil womanhood seems, in the first instance, to have supplied the leading spokesmen of the Church, so well versed in recondite Scripture, with an answer to Master Rypon's time-honoured question. At all events it becomes the authoritative ground and substance of their attacks. As one of them reminds us, for example, it speaks "of a foolish woman, garrulous and vagrant, impatient of quiet, not able to keep her feet within the house, now is she without, now in the

---

[1] *Father and Son*, ed. 1907, p. 367.
[2] MS. Harl. 45, fol. 101b. Similarly, MS. Add. 21253, fol. 119; MS. Harl. 2398, fol. 99; Wm. of Rymyngton, in MS. Bibl. Univ. de Paris, 790, fol. 106b; Bozon, *Metaphs.* cap. xxi; Bromyard, *S.P.* s.v. "Ornatus"; *Ayenb. of Inwyt*, p. 204; etc. Cf. a poem attributed to Lydgate (see below, p. 403); a poem of the Vernon MS., in E.E.T.S. O.S. no. 117, p. 705, st. 3 (where the saying is controverted); etc.; also Chaucer, *Cant. Tales*, Wife of Bath's Prol. ll. 682–96 and ll. 713 et seq.
[3] Cf. MS. Camb. Univ. Libr. Gg. vi, 16, fol. 29b (man should not set woman in his conceit in vile subjection or evil dignity of worship and reverence beneath him; but woman to be equal and fellow unto man...); *Hand. Synne*, pp. 68–9; etc. See also above, p. 20; and abroad, Robt. de Sorbon, in Hauréau, *Not. et Extr.* vol. i, pp. 188–202.
[4] MS. Harl. 4894, fol. 181 (see Luke vii, 37).

streets"—inconstant as the swallow.[1] The curious Scriptural
context of this passage and the fact that the Vulgate version of
it differs somewhat from that of our Authorized English text
together may explain why scholars have failed to recognize it as
the ultimate source of at least two well-known characters in our
medieval literature, one in the miracle-plays, the other in the
Canterbury Tales. For, strange though it may seem, "Noah's
wife"[2] and the Wife of Bath[3] are both typical descendants of
this ancient parent. "Foolish" is perhaps the commonest of
all epithets to be hurled at the sex, when the pulpit turns to
denounce it. Our preacher finds in the words of Jeremiah a
further hint of the *mulieres fatuae* which reveals at once the
true cause and effect of their folly: this, in spite of the fact
that the prophet has here made use of the masculine gender!
"Those that lay wait as fowlers and hunters", says the former,
"are the demons; their snares, decoys and traps are wicked and
foolish women, who in their pomps and wiles catch men and
deceive them."[4] And again—"This is manifest among those
foolish women: for, women while they are chaste and virgin
are marvellously modest; but, after they have begun to sin
and are foolish, they fear no shame or derision".[5] The second
curse of womankind, as mentioned in our original passage of
Scripture, is her garrulity and love of gossip. "There are two
kinds of dogs", observes the English author of the thirteenth-
century *Speculum Laicorum*: "for, some are well-bred, others
low-bred. The well-bred, indeed, are silent and free from guile;
the low-bred are ill-tempered and fond of barking. So is it

---

[1] MS. Add. 21253, fol. 45b (see Prov. vii, 10–12, *Vulgate* vers.:
"praeparata ad capiendas animas; garrula et vaga, quietis impatiens, nec
valens in domo consistere pedibus suis, nunc foris, nunc in plateis...").

[2] See further below, p. 492.

[3] The whole of the *Wife of Bath's Prol.* is nothing but a series of
brilliant literary variations upon these pulpit themes. See further below,
pp. 388–9. This kind of evidence again goes far to destroy Prof. Manly's
main contention in his recent book, *Some New Light on Chaucer* (New
York, 1926).

[4] MS. Add. 21253, fol. 54b (see Jerem. v, 26, here quoted by the
preacher). Cf. similarly, Bromyard, *S.P.* s.v. "Confessio" (the Devil
as a fowler, with his *domestica avis* as decoy); and Jean d'Aunay (13th
cent.) in Hauréau, *Not. et Extr.* vol. iv, p. 154.   [5] Ibid. fol. 57.

with women: the daughters of nobles are artless, silent, and lovers of solitude; the ignoble to be sure are loud and roamers in the streets."[1] It is generally the "woymen" again who, according to our preachers, were wont to "rowne togedyr" in church during sermon-time, while "the fende sate on hor schuldyrs, wrytyng on a long roll als fast as he myght".[2] And it is of such that Bromyard speaks, when referring to the quarrelsome habits of the scold, "who wrangles with her neighbour and recites all his faults—*cum additamentis*".[3] Even when the gossip may be less definitely spiteful, a rebuke from the pulpit is none the less needed: thus Dr William Lichfield, the eloquent divine of All Hallows the Great in London:

Eve, oure oldest moder in paradise, held long tale with the eddre, and told hym qwhat god had seyd to hire and to hire husband of etyng of the apple; and bi hire talkyng the fend understod hire febylnes and hire unstabilnes, and fond therby a way to bryng hir to confusioun. Our lady seynt Mary did on an othere wyse. Sche tolde the aungel no tale, bot asked hym discretly thing that she knew not hir-self. ffolow therfore our lady in discret spekyng and heryng, and not cakelinge Eve that both spake and herd unwisely. Have 3e not the kynde of an henne. An hen, qwen sche hath laid an ege, sche can but cakyl—and qwat cometh therof? Cometh on and taketh hir herne away and oft etith hem, of wich sche my3t have bro3t forth qwyke byrdes and gode. Thus the fend liges in wait wen men and wemen doun wele or seyn wele; wyche wordes or dedes, if thay wer wisely contynewede, shold be os bryddes styynge up to hevene. And wat tym thay bosten of hire gode dedys or fallen into vayn talkynge with veyn cumpany, thay lese oftyme by myche speche and unprophetable talkyng gode wordes and dedis byfore done.... Oure lady seyn Mary...was of so litel speche that nowere in the gospel we fynden of hir speche but iiii tymes, and tho were wordes of gret discrecion and grete myghte.[4]

[1] Cap. xxi (ed. Welter, p. 33).
[2] See my *Preaching in Med. Engl.* pp. 176–7. Cf. also the satirical poem, *The Proude Wyves Pater-Noster* (Hazlitt, *E. Pop. Poetry of Engl.* vol. iv, pp. 147–78). [3] *S.P.* s.v. "Desperatio".
[4] MS. Roy. 8. C. i, fol. 124 (largely derived from the *Ancren Riwle*, cf. ed. Morton, King's Classics, pp. 59 and 121). See also above, p. 44 (ever jangling as a pie or a jay). The passage referring to the B.V.M. seems to have been derived from St Bernard (cf. Myrc, *Festial*, p. 230, top: "for seynt Barnard seythe..."). The four occasions mentioned were (1) to Gabriel at the Annunciation, (2) to Elizabeth, mother of St John the Baptist, (3) to her Son at the Disputation in the Temple and (4) at the Wedding-Feast in Cana.

So much, then, for this fatal inclination to "over muche spekynge" and "curiouse and bold tellynge of talis". Woman's third vice, according to our text in *Proverbs*, is that of the erring monk—"instabilitas loci", an equally fatal attraction to the outside world, its freedom, its publicity and its scope for yet more pleasant gossip. Having been permitted, for her frailty, to escape the strait and narrow way of Virginity, she now finds herself no better satisfied with the enforced seclusion of married life. When her proper place is in the home, she will wander abroad, like the Wife of Bath, "walkinge out by nighte" as well as by day—"and for to see and eek for to be seye of lusty folk":

> And if the cattes skin be slyk and gay,
> She wol nat dwelle in house half a day,
> But forth she wole er any day be dawed
> To shewe hir skin, and goon a-caterwawed.
>
> .   .   .   .
>
> And so bifel that ones in a Lente,
> (So often tymes I to my gossib wente,
> For ever yet I lovede to be gay,
> And for to walke in March, Averille, and May
> Fro hous to hous, to here sondry talis),
> That Jankin clerk and my gossib dame Alis
> And I my-self, in to the feldes wente....[1]

With these lines of Chaucer the reader will now be able to connect certain rebukes for "nyce maydenes that walketh aboute in medes and in fayre places", which were quoted in an earlier chapter.[2] When we come to deal shortly with the female love of finery, there will be yet more in the same strain to prove how faithfully our poet's words here reflect the typical maxims of the pulpit. It is Nicholas Bozon, however, who points us in a homily on Widowhood to the actual source in Scripture which gave rise to at least a part of this whole homiletic idea. Says he—"Of this St Paul complains,[3] saying—'They go wandering about from house to house, and are not only idle

---

[1] *Wife of Bath's Prol. (Cant. Tales)*, ll. 351-4, and 543-9.
[2] See above, p. 119. Cf. further, e.g., Bp. Brunton on the "Sunday excursionists" of his day, in MS. Harl. 3760, fol. 110b ("Sed quomodo dies festi hodie venerantur? Certe hiis diebus...peregrinaciones faciunt, ut liberius peccent et mala desideria compleantur").   [3] 1 Tim. v, 13.

but tattlers also and busy-bodies, speaking things which they ought not'".[1] As for the straying cat and its "senged skin" to which Dame Alice refers,[2] this also is a hoary commonplace of our pulpit. Bozon himself tells, for example, of "a man that complained to his neighbour that his cat would not stay at home. 'No?', said the other: 'Shorten her tail, cut her ears and singe her fur; then she will stay at home.' So I say to you of women: should they be foolish, shorten their tails,[3] or disarray their heads and discolour their clothes. They will not then be so much desired of folk".[4]

Before treating of womanly fashions we must consider a kindred vice of married dames, which, although not specifically mentioned in the passage quoted from the Book of Proverbs, is one against which our pulpit does not cease to complain, namely, that of disobedience to the wishes of their rightful lords and masters. The first womanly virtue, we are told, is to obey.[5] But alas! ther. is common amongst the sex, as Bromyard observes,[6] a certain unnatural condition of contrariety, or wilfulness, which is one of the risks which every intending husband must be prepared to face. For example, the latter may well take warning of "the bitter wife who always quarrels with her spouse on his return", as noted in our *Summa*.[7] A lively story is here repeated of the husband who hit upon a desperate plan by which to cure a wife whose spirit of contrariety invariably drove her to do the reverse of what he commanded. On his departure for town, one day, he left

[1] *Metaphs.* cap. cxxxvii. Cf. *Hand. Synne*, p. 119; *Ayenb. of Inwyt*, p. 226.

[2] *Wife of Bath's Prol. (Cant. Tales)*, as before, ll. 349–54. No section of the poem illustrates better the debt of contemporary thought and literature to the pulpit than does the whole of this Prologue. Even the personal life-history of the narrator is thus clearly built up from it, quite apart from the many stories recapitulated from "clerk Jankin's" book.

[3] For explanation, see below, pp. 397–8.

[4] *Metaphs.* cap. liii (Fable): derived from Odo of Cheriton, see Sermons, MS. Arund. 231, fol. 208b and Fables, ed. Hervieux, iv, p. 287. Also in Jacques de Vitry (*Exempla*, ed. T. F. Crane, p. 209); *Spec. Laic.* s.v. "Luxuria" ("Refert Odo de C."); Bromyard, *S.P.* s.v. "Chorea", "Ornatus"; etc.   [5] Cf. MS. Add. 21253, fol. 89.

[6] *S.P.* s.v. "Matrimonium". Cf. above, pp. 163–4; and poems in Chambers and Sidgwick, *E. E. Lyrics*, pp. 207–11.   [7] s.v. "Conscientia".

but a single injunction behind him, namely, that she should
on no account climb a certain rotten ladder in one of the
rooms, "because he knew that she would do the very reverse
of what he said". So, true enough, "as she was climbing that
ladder, while her husband was away, she fell 'with Simon
Magus', and broke both her legs".[1] Another homilist calmly
tells us of a certain knight who in desperation went even further
to rid himself of a faithless wife by presenting her with two
boxes of sweetmeats, one containing good and the other
poisonous sweets. He had merely to bid her eat the good and
avoid the bad to bring about her death at her own stubborn
hands.[2] This reproof for the disobedient shrew, strange as it
sounds coming from emissaries of the Christian gospel, has
further a noteworthy little history of its own in the annals of
our literature. For, by way of "a merry Jeste of a shrewde
and curste Wyfe lapped in Morelles skin, for her good be-
havyour",[3] this traditional pulpit theme passes into various
ballads and plays, until the great master of Elizabethan drama,
Shakespeare himself, immortalizes it in his own version of
The Taming of the Shrew. As though once more to remind us
indisputably of its medieval homiletic origin, the master-poet
has here chosen as the basis of his closing scene none other
than a typical *exemplum*, which can still be found in its fifteenth-
century English dress in English versions of the *Book of the
Knight of La Tour-Landry*.[4]

It is woman *par excellence* as a lover of finery, the mirror
of fashion, the decked and painted idol of May-tide, that calls
down the full fury of the English preachers in satire and complaint. This feminine weakness, if not the source, is at any rate

[1] Cf. the equally ruthless story of a defiant wife in the *Book of the
Knight of La Tour-Landry*, Engl. version, cap. xviii (E.E.T.S. ed. pp. 25–
6): also *Piers Plowman*, B text, pass. xvii, ll. 316 et seq. (C text, pass. xx,
l. 299). [2] MS. Add. 18364, fol. 62.
[3] Publ. in W. C. Hazlitt, *E. Pop. Poetry of Engl.* vol. iv, pp. 179–
226; etc.
[4] The Story of the three Merchants and their wives: cap. xix (E.E.T.S.
ed. pp. 26–8). See *The Taming of the Shrew*, Act v, Sc. ii.

a mirror of some of the other evils which have just been mentioned. Why after all does the maiden thus deck herself, but to wander abroad and display herself in public? Moreover, wives that have fine clothes "should adorn and prepare themselves to please their husbands",[1] say the homilists. Yet, in spite of all her protestations to the contrary, the latter have observed that it is not for her own husband's eyes that the proud hussy as a rule will take such pains with her appearance.[2] And therein lies further at least one proof of womanly inconstancy. This last complaint, like others to follow, serves to remind us again of the antiquity and close continuity of the whole pulpit tradition. For it is to be found alike in the thirteenth-century *Tractatus* of the Dominican preacher Etienne de Bourbon[3] and the sermons of his contemporary, the Franciscan Berthold von Regensburg.[4] Putting aside all such well-known preachers of France and Germany, however, as superfluous for our present argument, we may discover half a century earlier in the sermons of our own English Odo of Cheriton[5] that denunciation of women's finery, their love of cosmetics and other evil fashions, which persists unabated to the days of Chaucer and the satiric poets that succeeded him. Let us now take some examples from these neglected English preachers, whose word and testimony have lain hid for so many generations.[6] Bishop Brunton of Rochester,[7] the Austin

[1] MS. Add. 21253, fol. 89; *Hand. Synne*, p. 116; etc.

[2] Cf. John of Mirfield, *Flor. Barthol.* cap. "De Indum." (MS. Camb. Univ. Libr. Mm. ii. 10, fols. 85 et seq.) as quoted in my *Preaching in Med. Engl.* p. 218. Similarly in the *Tractatus* of Etienne de Bourbon, and Jean d'Aunay, in Hauréau, *Not. et Extr.* vol. iv, p. 177.

[3] See ed. Lecoy de la Marche, *Anecdotes Hist.*, where the preacher gives further a personal reminiscence, pp. 228-42.

[4] See Coulton, *Med. Studies*, 1st ser. 2nd rev. ed. p. 25, and *Life in the Midd. Ages*, vol. iii, pp. 63-5.

[5] Cf. refs. in Herbert, *Cat. of Romances in B.M.* vol. iii, pp. 36, 54 and 65. Another early example from the Engl. *Spec. Laic.* is given in my *Preaching in Med. Engl.* p. 170. See also below, p. 396 n. 3, etc.

[6] The instructed reader, of course, will compare these fresh examples with those already known in the sermons of Bernardino of Siena and other continental preachers such as the two mentioned above. Others will be found, again, in Coulton, *Five Cent. of Religion*, vols. i and ii (see under "Dancing", etc.).   [7] MS. Harl. 3760, fol. 149b.

friar of Yorkshire, John Waldeby,[1] the Dominican John Bromyard[2] and the London clerk, John of Mirfield, at St Bartholomew's, Smithfield, all denounce those who with gross presumption tamper with the handiwork of God—

as do those women who put upon their head hair that is not their own, or an unnatural colour on their face. For, to put hair on the head or give a new complexion is the special concern of God. They, therefore, who do this kind of thing desire along with Lucifer to be equal with the All-highest; and for this reason the unnatural colour on their face makes them grow old before the proper time, and in the future they will be punished for it as well.

Says the Austin friar, in taking up the same strain:

If a noble painter, in his execution of some figure, sculptures it well and artistically and also puts suitable colours upon it, would not the pupil or the owner of the figure do insult to such an artist, if he altered the form and colour of that same figure? So, when women set about adorning their own persons, by constricting themselves in tight clothing they wish to appear slender, and with artificial colours they desire to seem beautiful, thereby expressly insulting their Creator.[3]

Friar Waldeby goes on to declare that such victims of fashion "display and present their bodies as weapons of the Devil, with which the souls of men are slain". Eventually he uses a yet more picturesque and pungent simile:

In the chambers of lords, chimneys of stone or of plaster are sometimes erected[4] and whitened and ornamented at the top with battlements, turrets and windows: yet there comes out thence a smoke that is filthy and very blinding to the eyes of those who are near. Thus do these wanton women set themselves up in public like graceful columns, but within they are as empty as a chimney, because they lack virtues. They ornament their head like the chimney-top with garlands, crowns and gems set therein: nevertheless nothing comes forth thence but foul smoke and temptation to lechery.

"Everyone knows", echoes the monk Robert Rypon in his turn, "how a sow rolls its nostrils in the foulest dirt. Thus do such foolish women roll their beauty in the foulest dirt of lust.... With them it is as with the worms that glow resplendent at night, but in the daytime appear most vile." Like leaves,

---

[1] MS. Roy. 8. C. 1, fol. 13.   [2] *S.P.* s.v. "Ornatus".

[3] *Flor. Barthol.* as before. Cf. further, *Hand. Synne*, p. 112; *Book of the Knight of La Tour-Landry*, p. 68; and *Hamlet*, Act iii, Sc. i, ll. 150–2.

[4] Cf. *Piers Plowman* as below, p. 412.

he adds, they will flourish at the first, but then wither and fall into the mud, at length to be trampled upon.[1]

It is to the Dominican John Bromyard, however, that we must go for the full blast of such contemporary indictment in this country. The rains and snow of late winter are now over: the soft breezes, the balmy air, "the tendre croppes and the yonge sonne", bursting leaf and singing bird proclaim the coming of spring. The rigours of Lent now give place to the rejoicing of Eastertide; and the thoughts of men and women turn to the open, the merry greensward, May-games and revelry, whither they will go with heads rose-garlanded for the feasts and shows.[2] But for the preacher it is a season of gloom. All the good work of Lenten shrift and sermon threatens to be undone. For, the Devil, like a king seeing his subjects rebel in Lent, collects his army to recapture them at Easter—*cum augmento*.[3] "To the contrite sinner he displays the pageants, games, dances and the like which, by the Devil's own instigation, begin everywhere about Eastertime, to annul the contrition which they had in Lent";[4] and everywhere the centre of evil attraction is woman.

Because the servants of the Devil have rebelled stoutly against his dominion and have denied his rule, at that season he makes ready his army against them in mightiest array in the dances and pageants, leading forth his knights and amazons armed with every sin, having, for their helmet, horns and head-dresses and frontlets, and likewise with the rest of their armour, so that from the sole of their foot to the crown of their head you will find nothing save the Devil's sharpest arrows in them... to wound the heart of the beholder.[5] Neither do they lack for their war-horn the drum, nor the trumpet to call them to battle. Alas! these are arrayed against God and his followers much more mightily and diligently and with greater and more fervent zeal and sign of rejoicing than I perceive in the case of many of Christ's knights fighting against the Devil and his ministers; and many more folk join their ranks. For, if all the knights of Christ and his whole army, namely, the apostles, martyrs and

[1] MS. Harl. 4894, fol. 177.

[2] Cf. Bromyard, *S.P.* s.v. "Munditia" ("Rosarum decor...in capitibus et sertis, et festis et spectaculis portatus").

[3] *S.P.* s.v. "Chorea".   [4] s.v. "Contritio".

[5] Cf. here Waldeby, MS. Roy. 8. C. 1, fol. 13: "Sic mulieres sic se perornantes exhibent et offerunt corpora sua tanquam arma diaboli, quibus anime hominum occiduntur". Similarly, Nic. de Biard (13th cent.), in Hauréau, *Not. et Extr.* vol. vi, pp. 3–4.

all holy men in the state in which they were in the Church were to march through the city of God, ready to fight for Him by teaching or preaching His Commandments, and in another procession were to march the women in their wanton array, frolicking, dancing, or stepping out with their signs of levity, I do believe for certain that these latter would attract after them far more hearts and ears and eyes more readily and more intently than the former....[1]

Elsewhere, the Dominican employs yet another scathing satire for these scenes of gaiety and springtime fashions:

For, here the church of the malignants, namely, the congregation of the Devil's parishioners, is conducted after the manner of the Church of God. In place of the clerk who rings the bell to call the people to worship, they have a flute-player: for the Devil's and Hell's altar and for their altar-stone they have a fashionably attired body and head.[2] Because, just as the sacristan makes more adornment of the altar at the greater feasts when more people come to church, thinking that there will be more folk to look at it that day, so does the sacristan of Hell, Pokerellus, with regard to these women, saying to them—"To-day is a great feast:[3] many folk will see you. Adorn yourself, therefore, that you may be reputed beautiful and that those who behold you may delight in your loveliness!" Lo! then, the Devil's altar, which is more gladly seen than God's altar: the altar of the Devil, I say, because, according to Augustine in his Rule, it is a crime to seek or wish to be sought after in this fashion. With the altar thus prepared for celebration, the Devil's service proceeds, at which he who starts the love-ditty takes the place of the priest. The place of the clerks is occupied by those who take up the songs and carry them on; and that of the parishioners by those standing or sitting around, who look on and listen with more delight and for a longer time than they would have heard mass or preaching before luncheon.[4]

Another English preacher of the period, who may be Bishop Repingdon, likewise speaks of those who are in this respect— "apes of the clergy".[5] "For as the clergy go in procession on feast days, singing around the church in honour of God, so

---

[1] s.v. "Bellum" (similarly, s.v. "Ornatus": the Devil's boxers or knights, armed for battle). Cf. further in the sermons of Bp. Repingdon (?), MS. Jo. Ryl. Libr. Manch. Lat. 367, fol. 210: "Item, quod corea est quasi exercitus diaboli patet Parisiensis in tractatu de Viciis, ubi probat quod coreas ducentes contra omnia sacramenta ecclesie quoddammodo faciunt; primo, contra Baptismum ..." (Parisiensis = Guillaume Perault).

[2] Dr Coulton has missed the significance of the two-fold comparison here in his translation of the passage, in *Five Cent. of Relig.* vol. i, p. 535.

[3] Cf. s.v. "Confessio": "Sicut enim divites renovant frequenter vestes corporis... et hoc specialiter in magnis festis".

[4] s.v. "Chorea".   [5] "quasi simee clericorum."

these women go in procession upon the left foot towards Hell, for their wantonness and lechery; and those who ought to be at Vespers are to be found at the dances."[1] The "Continental Sunday" is clearly no modern invention of the Devil. Bromyard further compares these overdressed "city madams" and damosels of the market-place to beasts of burden:

For, just as horses and pack-animals for sale are decorated, and some kind of notice is put on their head, so the Devil's pack-horses wear garlands on their heads that they may be the better and sooner sold.[2]

Again they take the place and do the office of masks. For two kinds of men use masks, to wit, those who play and those who rob. For players in the play which is commonly called a *Miracle* use masks, beneath which the persons of the actors are concealed. Thus do the demons, whose game is to destroy souls and lure them by sin: in which game they make use of masks, that is, the fashionably attired and those who dance, "whose feet run to evil" (Prov. i).[3] ... Thus it is written in Ecclesiasticus:[4] "Use not much the company of her that is a dancer, and hearken not to her, lest thou perish by the force of her charms".

And again—

In the woman wantonly adorned to capture souls, the garland upon her head is as a single coal or firebrand of Hell to kindle men with that fire; so too the horns of another, so the bare neck, so the brooch upon the breast, so with all the curious finery of the whole of their body. What else does it seem or could be said of it save that each is a spark breathing out hell-fire, which this wretched incendiary of the Devil breathes so effectually...that, in a single day, by her dancing or her perambulation through the town, she inflames with the fire of lust—it may be—twenty of those who behold her, damning the souls whom God has created and redeemed at such a cost for their salvation. For this very purpose the Devil thus adorns these females, sending them forth through the town as his apostles, replete with every iniquity, malice, fornication and the like....Secondly, they are the Devil's nets, with which he fishes in God's fish-pond, seeking to transfer His fish to the lake of Hell.... The Devil draws one such person through the town, or sends her to a house where he knows there are fish to be caught, and catches more folk by suggestion of her lips or the stimulus of her adornment than the fisher of souls for

[1] MS. Jo. Ryl. Libr. Manch. Lat. 367, fol. 210.
[2] Cf. the French satirical poem, *Des Cornetes*, in Fairholt, *Satir. Songs and Poems on Costume*, Percy Soc. p. 39.
[3] Similarly the masked robbers are moralized as soul-stealing demons. Étienne de Bourbon, it will be remembered, uses jugglers' masks—"quae dicuntur *artificia*, i.e. *masques* Gallice"—as a figure of the elderly women who paint their faces, for the same ends.
[4] ix, 4.

God.[1] ... By a single round of the town or one foolish appearance at the window she converts many to the Devil.[2]

Thirdly, they are the Devil's decoys, snaring the heedless bird into the gins of the fowler;[3] while their very cauls may be compared to the decoy-nets.[4] "Foul and ancient hags who strive to paint and deck themselves as fair young maidens" the Dominican compares to "reforberes" of old garments and to the false mutton-sellers and skin-dressers mentioned in our previous chapter, who make old and worthless goods seem new by superficial decoration.[5] Those who cover their heads with glistening headgear and their faces with paint—"so that nothing of their own appears save their eyes, which they consider beautiful"—he likens further to the painted tombstone that covers a rotting corpse within.[6] "Such as paint and adorn themselves proudly to appear fairer than they are should reflect how in place of their crisping hair there will one day be but a skull, and so forth."[7] To that same fate shall come all those whose "pomp is nurtured in tunics and 'horns' and 'tails'".[8] Even in this life these devotees of the great god Fashion have allowed themselves to suffer needlessly in his service: "Where, again, shall be found those", asks Bromyard, with cynical

[1] Cf. here the poem of the Vernon MS.—Friar Henry's "luytel Sarmoun", which describes the Devil as fishing with the hook of Hell-pain baited with Woman as the worm to catch men, E.E.T.S. O.S. no. 117, pp. 477–8.

[2] s.v. "Luxuria". Sim. "Tentatio" (at house-doors, in church, etc.).

[3] s.v. "Confessio". Cf. "the Devil's Mouse-trap", in Old Engl. Homs. (12th cent.), 1st ser. pt. i, E.E.T.S. O.S. no. 29, p. 53.

[4] s.v. "Ornatus".   [5] Ibid. etc. See above, p. 355.   [6] Ibid.

[7] s.v. "Mors": similarly, s.v. "Ornatus" ("pro suavi odore, fetor; et pro zona, funiculus; et pro crispanti crine, calvicium; et pro fascia pectorali, cilicium"). See further in my Preaching in Med. Engl. p. 344, and Isa. iii, 24. Cf. Robt. Henryson's (or Patrick Johnstone's?) poem, The Three Died Powis, and the French poem Des Cornetes, in Fairholt, Satir. Songs and Poems on Cost. as mentioned below (Percy Soc.), p. 37; etc.

[8] s.v. "Acquisitio Mala". For typical examples of warning sermon-tales on this subject, cf. MS. Burn. 361, fol. 151b (a woman slanders Bro. Hugh of Gloucester while he is preaching against women's finery, and goes mad the same day); MS. Harl. 1022, fol. 1b (a countess drawn to hell by devils for her excessive love of "sere atyre"); Jacob's Well, p. 80; MS. Roy. 8. F. vi, fol. 6; MS. Add. 11284, fol. 64 (see my Preaching in Med. Engl. p. 170); Hand. Synne, pp. 113–5; etc.

scorn, "who would lay bare their breast and compress their feet in the tightest shoes and thus diligently adorn their body for love of God, as do the proud, to destroy their own souls and those of others?"[1] So vain is the sex, indeed, that even the gift of a new pair of gloves might be enough to seduce the damsel.[2]

These latter comments serve to remind us of the way in which specific offences in current costume were singled out for attack. Thus, the low-necked dresses aforesaid move Thomas Gascoigne to special wrath, who suggests that they became generally popular in the early years of King Henry VI's reign. This fashion, he says, is not according to the requirements of nature, office or rank, but is a great allurement to sin and offers poison to those beholding it, although no one by the grace of God would drink of such poison.[3] Another female enormity of the kind was the "sideless gown",[4] in full vogue by the second half of the fourteenth century. Accordingly, we are not surprised to find that Master Bromyard has something pretty scathing to say of it: "Christ opened his side for the redemption and salvation of many", says he. "And these others open their side for lascivious and carnal provocation, and for the perdition of those who behold them."[5] The case of what are scornfully derided as "tails" supplies us with one of several instructive parallels to the remarks of Chaucer's *Persoun* about

[1] s.v. "Labor", and again "Ornatus" (mentioning foot-wear again). Similarly, Etienne de Bourbon ("Pedes affligunt arctis solutaribus, capita et facies ablutionibus et aliis vanis cultibus, et sic de aliis membris. Vidi ergo aliquos de multa vanitate conversos ad statum penitentiae..."). Cf. also the story, repeated from the *Dialog. Mirac.* (dist. iv, cap. 12) of Caesarius of Heisterbach, in the *Spec. Laic.*, of King Philip of France rebuking a young *monk* for wearing tight shoes. On the subject of Woman and her mirror, cf. further, *Old Engl. Homs.* 2nd ser. E.E.T.S. O.S. no. 53, p. 29; and *Ayenb. of Inwyt*, p. 176.

[2] See *Gesta Rom.* Engl. version, E.E.T.S. p. 71.

[3] *Liber Veritatum*, s.v. "Ornatus" (*Loci e Libro Verit.* pp. 144–5). Cf. further, *Poem on the Times of Rich. II*, in Wright, Rolls S. vol. i, p. 276, and below, p. 403.   [4] Or *sideless cote-hardie* (Druitt).

[5] s.v. "Passio Christi" ("Qua vanitate multum utuntur modo qui aperturas habent, et super tunicalibus suis fere ab humero usque ad crura, ut interiores ostendant curiositates circa cingulum et corporis facturam..."). Cf. *Poem*, as before, in Wright, Rolls S. vol. i, p. 276.

current "superfluitee of clothinge, which that maketh it so dere to harm of the peple"—here notably "in lengthe of the forseide gounes".[1] For, the long trains of ladies' dresses frequently call down the ire of the pulpit upon "these papelards,[2] when they draw their gowns through the mud, and seem good and holy", or, in haughty indifference to the welfare of priests and people, make them drink of the dust in the ill-swept churches.[3] "Such ladies", says the same anonymous preacher, "often sin in the matter of length, who drag long tails after them, 'clothing' the earth with precious raiment and caring nothing for the nakedness of Christ in his poor folk.[4]...They ought to be very afraid lest a devil may be sitting at rest on their tails: because the story is told of a certain saint that he once saw a devil laughing, and asked him why he laughed. The latter replied—'I saw a friend of mine having a ride on a certain lady's tail, and, as she drew it to her, my friend fell off into the mud. And therefore I laughed'."[5] Gascoigne is under the impression that this iniquitous fashion began during the reign of King Richard II and his Queen Anne of Bohemia, at least—"secundum relacionem antiquorum".[6] But pulpit condemnation of it in

[1] *Cant. Tales*, Persones Tale, § 27, "De Superbia".

[2] = hypocrites (*paplardi*).

[3] MS. Add. 21253, fol. 106 (see further in my *Preaching in Med. Engl.* p. 171). Cf. also, MS. Bodl. 649, fols. 156b–7 (*mulieres caudate*); Bromyard, as above; *Jacob's Well*, p. 80; Gascoigne and Lyndesay, as below: also in Hauréau, *Not. et Extr.* vol. iv, p. 136.

[4] Cf. Chaucer, as above: "trailinge in the dong and in the myre, on horse and eek on fote,...that al thilke trailinge is verraily as in effect wasted, consumed, thredbare, and roten with donge, rather than it is yeven to the pore..."; and the poems, *The Schole-House of Women*, in Hazlitt, *E. Pop. Poetry of Engl.* vol. iv, p. 120, ll. 394–5 ("a tail come raking after"), and Lyndesay's *Supplicatioun againis Syde Taillis*, etc.

[5] MS. Add. 21253, fol. 106. Also in *Spec. Laic.* cap. lx (ed. Welter, p. 84, no. 435: "Refert mag. J. de Vitriaco"); Bromyard, *S.P.* s.v. "Ornatus" (from Caesarius of Heisterbach); MSS. Roy. 7. D. 1, fol. 121; Harl. 2316, fols. 58 and 463, fol. 19b; Add. 6716, fol. 1b, col. 2; etc. A variant of the same tale appears in MS. Harl. 1022, fol. 1b (see Horstmann, *Yorksh. Writers*, vol. i, p. 157).

[6] s.v. "Contra caudas dominarum" (*Loci e Libro Verit.* pp. 11–12). Note his delightful explanation—"Ista cauda que Anglice *trayn* vocatur, quia trahitur, et ad malum trahit!"

England goes back at all events to the thirteenth century, and on the continent to the preaching of Jacques de Vitry in France and Caesarius of Heisterbach in Germany, which suggests that it was widely popular in the early years thereof.[1] Etienne de Bourbon when repeating the warning, presumably for the benefit of thirteenth-century Parisian ladies, adds a significant remark concerning tailed and horned dames who thus insult God's special creation by degrading themselves to the level of brute beasts: "It is amazing that they do not blush with shame to be tailed, since Englishmen blush to be called 'tailed'!"[2] Mention of "horns" here serves to remind us that, corresponding to the iniquity of long trains trailing at the feet of these *belles*, at the other end of their person appeared a second fruitless excrescence, that of "grete heedys in aray".[3] The author of the *Ploughman's Crede*, borrowing the preachers' phrase, speaks of their wearers as "grete-hedede quenes, with gold by the eiȝen".[4] "Along with their middle", says the author of the *Speculum Laicorum*, "they are wont to adorn the two extremities of their body, namely their heads and their feet."[5] It is interesting to learn how these monstrous headdresses provoked mockery in their own day, precisely as they would do now. Bozon devotes to them a delightful little satiric fable. Says he, the birds in parliament once sent to ask the owl to be queen and help-mate to their king. When she enquired of them the reason for this signal honour, the messengers replied—"for your large head". "Indeed!", said she, "so help me God! If my head were plucked, it would be as small as yours!"[6] Wherefore Bromyard is led to speak sarcastically in his turn of "the Devil's owls, that have big heads and little

---

[1] See T. F. Crane's ed. of the *Exempla of J. de V.* p. 101; the *Dial. Mirac.* of C. of H. dist. v, cap. vii; Guil. Perault, *Summa de Viciis, de Sup.*; *Man. des Pechieȝ* (= *Hand. Synne*, p. 119); *Spec. Laic.* as above.

[2] For the history of this strange legend, see Dr G. Neilson, *Caudatus Anglicus*, Edinb. 1896, where it is said to be common from the 12th cent. onwards. The above example is not given.

[3] MS. Salisb. Cath. Libr. 103 (unpublished *Jacob's Well*), fol. 113.

[4] E.E.T.S. ed. l. 84. Cf. also *Piers Plowman*, B text, pass. v, l. 31.

[5] cap. lx (ed. Welter, p. 84).

[6] *Metaphs.* cap. liii (of the shunning of younger adorned women).

sense".[1] As for those who adopt the "horned" variety, they resemble not only beasts but devils.[2]

True to the unchanging conventions of the pulpit, English sermons preserved in the vernacular introduce us to the same scenes and the same language of complaint as their older prototypes in Latin. "With there gay heddes sett up on hyȝe and horned as an unresonabyl best, withe theyre bedys and lytill devocion, and there rynges full gay, and hyr kyrtyll sleveles to make hem to seme praty for to synne, and many other sympil tokens moo",[3] the mischief-makers reappear in all the familiar finery. Thus, on the subject of May-tide temptations, a quaint vernacularist begins his discourse with the following:

Good men and wymmen, now is passed the holy tyme of Ester, and iche man and wyman is shryven and houseled,[4] so that thei have forsaken the devell and all is werkes and been turned to God and to is servyce. Wherefore be reson it owȝt to be no nede to preche you, ne for to teche you for to kepe you from the dewell and is engenes...for the feend hase lost is preye, and therfore he is full sorye. But he goyth aboute to restore hym aȝeyn that he hathe lost, that is mans soule, to restore itt aȝeyn to hym by synne. ffor nowe he seis that the tyme is fayre and warme, and metes and drynkes amenden and been more delicious than thei were, and many beth now fayre clothed, and wymmen nycely arayed: all this hym thenketh that is conabull[5] to hym, and thus with many othur colours he disseyvith the pepull.[6]

Another witnesses again to the fact that

in a day, thorgh nyce lokynge or thenkynge on women that beth gayliche atyred and fayre to schewe hem as foles to the sight of other foles,[7]... when thei atyren hem so, to that ilke entente that men schulde the more byholde hem,...may many a mannes soule be lorne.[8]...And suche women that so attyreth hem for suche cause may be cleped the develis grenes or snares. ffor many a man by suche grennes beth take and broght to the develis hond.[9]

[1] s.v. "Ornatus". Cf. in Hauréau, *Not. et Extr.* vol. iv, pp. 175–6.
[2] *S.P.* ibid. [3] MS. Glouc. Cath. Libr. *Sermo Dom. V post Trin.*
[4] = admitted to Communion. [5] = convenient.
[6] MS. Roy. 18. B. xxiii, fol. 97. Cf. here the poem, "Lenten is come with love to toune", esp. l. 32 (Chambers and Sidgwick, *E. E. Lyrics*, pp. 8–9).
[7] Cf. again, MS. Harl. 1197, fol. 1b ("women that arayin hem nycely to be seen of foolis..."); *Jacob's Well*, p. 159 ("nyce wommen"); MS. Roy. 8. C. i, fol. 123 ("strumpetes aray to gret boldenes"—Dr Lichfield); *Ayenb. of Inwyt*, p. 47; *Old Engl. Homs.* as above, pp. 396–7; etc.
[8] = destroyed, lost. [9] MS. Harl. 45, fol. 95b–96.

At the Judgment they shall answer for their misdeeds and for the souls they have thus damned, adds the homilist.[1] St Bernard, he says, calls "women that busieth hem aboute gay apparaile to schewe hem with to menis sight"—"the doughtres of Babiloyne, that is to seie *schenship*, or *confusioun*". "Thogh thei schyne withoute as gold and silver, thei mote nede at the laste leve alle that and beth foule in soule, thorgh synne."[2] Other preachers, who prefer to specify each several detail of the proud woman's "outrageous array", thereby serve to remind us further of the homiletic tradition that inspired Langland's lovelier description of the Lady Mede and Chaucer's vivid picture of the Wife of Bath:

Wommen with here hedes y-horned, schort clokes unnethe to the hupes,[3] with bendels,[4] chapellettes and frontelles y-set above the heued y-lyche to a wylde beste that hath none resoun. Sche hath also fyletes, skleyres,[5] crymyles,[6] kyrcheves, y-colored garlondys of perreye[7] to have upon the top—though that the heved be al calwe[8] on the cronne, they chargeth it nou3t[9]—and chapellettes y-poudryd wyth perry, and of many nyce dysgysynges of atyre: so that y can nou3t wryte ne discryve suche dyvers thynges as men and wommen use now a day.[10]

At this point the reader must be left to discover for himself the way in which, not merely the preachers' detailed objections, but the very imagery with which they clothed them passed into the popular satirical verse of their own and of subsequent ages. For it is all there for the seeking. Indeed, in Elizabethan times a kind of continuous literary warfare ensues over this theme, in which the party maintaining the old critical view

[1] Similarly, also Rypon, MS. Harl. 4894, fol. 177.
[2] MS. Harl. 45, fol. 123b ("for her lyfe nys but as a blaste of wynde, that schal passe and turne to grete schame and schenschip.."); *Ayenb. of Inwyt*, pp. 228–9. [3] = scarcely to the hips.
[4] = bands or scarves. [5] = veils. [6] = plaits or fringes (?).
[7] = jewelry. [8] = bald. [9] = they care not.
[10] MS. Harl. 2398, fol. 9. Cf. further, e.g., MS. Bodl. 95, fols. 54–54b ("rynges...on owre fyngerys and owre gay glovys to kepe owre hendys whyte,...ful streyte schone and ful thycke y-lasyd, and whyte scho and a redde,...garlondys and perles on owre hed,...bedys and broches, and...precyous stonys and gloryous gordellys of gold and of sylver, and streyte-lasyd sydys..."); *Jacob's Well*, p. 80 ("longe traynes", "brode hornys", etc.); *Hand. Synne*, p. 279 (the "develys sayle"); *Ayenb. of Inwyt*, p. 176 ("great hornes"); etc.

seems on the whole to have come off triumphant.[1] Besides certain poems in the Wright and Early English Text Society collections which deal with the subject, there is the illuminating series of *Satirical Songs and Poems on Costume*, edited by F. W. Fairholt for the Percy Society,[2] and another series amongst the *Remains of Early Popular Poetry* published by W. C. Hazlitt.[3] In a fourteenth-century poem of the Vernon MS.,[4] for example, will be found scornful mention of the "hornes" again, the "selk scleyres" and the tight-laced gowns: while even so late a composition as Gosson's *Quippes for Upstart Newfangled Gentlewomen*, issued towards the end of the Tudor régime,[5] presents us with wellnigh all the typical satires of our pulpit within the limits of a single piece. Here are the "sadled" beasts of burden, the Devil's "ginnes" and fowling-nets, his "baytes wherewith to hell he draweth huge heaps" of fish when he chooses to go a-fishing, the masks of the maskers, the armoured "Amazones", the proud peacocks[6]—"whome preachers still in vaine beseech". Three poems of the Fairholt collection deserve special notice. One, an early fourteenth-century French poem, *Des Cornetes*,[7] gives us the correct interpretation of an English satirical misericord carving in the Parish Church of Ludlow, which the late Francis Bond completely misunderstood.[8] The poet tells how, if the men-folk do

[1] Cf. here Hazlitt, *E. Pop. Poetry of Engl.* vol. iv, p. 100.

[2] 1849: no. lxxxi.   [3] 1866: vols. i and iv.

[4] See E.E.T.S. O.S. no. 98, p. 336.

[5] Eds. 1595, 1596: reprinted in Hazlitt (as above), vol. iv, pp. 247–62.

[6] Cf. for the Sermons, below, p. 411 (MSS. Harl. 45 and Salisb. Cath. Libr. 103), and Etienne de Bourbon (expressly of the women); etc.

[7] pp. 31–2 (MS. Bibl. Nat., Paris).

[8] See *Wood Carvings in Engl. Churches, Misericords*, Oxf. 1910, p. 180. There is no sign of gag or bridle in the figure, as Bond thinks. An earlier reproduction of the same in Wright's *Hist. of Caricature* (fig. no. 67, p. 102), shows a sword in the hand of the right-hand male figure (since broken off), with which he seeks to defend himself, while his companion on the opposite side holds up a shield.

not protect themselves from the women, they will be slain. For the women have horns with which to kill them. The men may well be afraid of such a beast. For, when she fumes and pricks and strikes and pushes, she frightens the poet more than thunder or tempest. The wisest man living does not see at all how he is to defend himself against them. Later, we hear how a bishop preached against their enormities, with promise of special pardon to those who mock them in public.[1] A passage of Bromyard now reveals this quaint conceit in its true homiletic setting. The Dominican quotes from Scripture—

Exodus xxi [28]—"If an ox gore a man or a woman with his horn and they die"—and shortly after [v. 29]—"If the ox was wont to push with his horn yesterday and the day before, and they warned his master and he did not shut him up, and he shall have killed a man or a woman, then the ox shall be stoned and his master put to death". So the soul which has the mastery in a horned woman, as of a butting ox, after reason or conscience or the preacher shall have warned it that those horns are a cause of damnation to others, is spiritually slain and doomed to everlasting death for whoever's death it has caused: for, "that horn made war against the Saints"—Dan. vii [21]. In which death, as God testifies —Isaiah iii [17]—"The Lord will make bald the crown of the head of the daughters of Sion, and will strip their hair"....[2]

Another poem of the series, a typical macaronic complaint, in Latin and English, upon the evil times of the reign of Richard II, speaks explicitly again of such efforts of the pulpit, and in this case of their palpable failure:

> Wantounly brestes *procedunt arte prophana*;
> Prechour ne prestes *possunt hec pellere vana*.[3]

The third more noteworthy effusion is *A Dyte of Womenhis Hornys* by the poet dan Lydgate.[4] When all this cruder sort of literature has been examined, there yet remains to be taken into account all that poets like Spenser and the Elizabethan dramatists owed to a tradition ingrafted by centuries of relent-

---

[1] p. 34. Cf. also pp. 36–7.
[2] *S.P.* s.v. "Ornatus".
[3] p. 47 (MSS. Harl. 536 and 941).
[4] p. 51. See also *Minor Poems*, ed. Halliwell, Percy Soc. p. 46, and *Reliq. Antiq.* vol. i, pp. 79–80.

less preaching into their whole view and treatment of the
weaker sex.

So much, then, for the part played by woman in our sermons.
In illustrating the English preachers' attitude to the question
of fashions and finery in dress, however, it would be wrong
to leave the impression that she alone was singled out to suffer
at their hands in this respect. Indeed, pulpit discussion of the
subject proceeds generally on a much wider plane, and, like
the satire of the poets, includes both male and female in its
indictment. Master Rypon, in the course of one of his sermons
on the Magdalene, actually introduces his remarks with a brief
historical sketch of the evolution of costume.[1] Says he:

Where before sin the naked body was without natural shame, immediately after sin was committed, the whole naked body was encompassed
with the shame of its nakedness: wherefore, because it lacked clothing,
there was thus fashioned for it a tunic of skins at the first, in token that
through his sin man was become like the beasts which by nature are clad
in raiment of skins alone. But later, as their pride grew, men used garments made of wool. Thirdly, through the more ample nourishing of
carnal delight, they used garments made from plants of the earth, namely,
of linen, and fourthly silken garments which are fashioned from the entrails
of worms; all of which kinds of raiment are now rather for vain-glory
and worldly pomp than for the necessity of nature, diversely decorated
as it were in an infinite variety of ways, and assuredly most of all to excite
lust alike in men as in women. In proof of which some men wear garments
so short that they scarcely hide their private parts (*et certe ut apparet
ad ostendendum mulieribus membra sua ut sic ad luxuriam provocentur*).
Likewise also, certain women give artificial decoration to themselves by
painting their faces to please the eyes of men. In truth, whosoever do
so have the true likeness of harlots. For they rejoice more in artificial
beauty than in natural beauty; and be they men or women, such as adorn
themselves in their garments or by means of some other artificial decoration, to give wanton pleasure to each other, are well compared to a

[1] Similarly Repingdon (?) in a sermon, MS. Jo. Ryl. Libr. Manch.
Lat. 367, fol. 256: "Nostra vestis prima multum fuit vilis, scil., pellis
cum lana, *Gen.* 3: '*Fecit Deus Ade et uxori sue tunicas pellicias*', i.e. de
pellibus animalium mortuorum. Deinde processum est ad lanam: deinde
ad stercora vermium, i.e. ad sericum: deinde ad pannum deauratum:
demum ad lapides preciosos...".

painted sepulchre in which lies a foul corpse, or to a dung-heap covered with a vine. So, for a surety, beneath such adornment of the body, whether artificial or even natural, there lurks the vilest filth, yea rather, a soul befouled with the vilest sins.... Wherefore, men and women adorning themselves to excite lust, without a doubt, in the eyes of God are more shameful and foul than the foulest corpses or dung-hills.[1]

Students of the *Canterbury Tales* will not need to be told why a certain unsavoury passage has been allowed to stand in the above quotation. They will recognize it at once as a significant parallel to certain statements in the *Persones Tale*,[2] all the more significant, indeed, as it falls from the lips of an English homilist who was actually preaching in this country while Chaucer was alive. With regard to Rypon's main argument, however, Bromyard here takes the view that God was giving us a good example in clothing our first parents in tunics of the skins of dead animals—without silks or finery, gold or silver or precious stones. So Christ himself, he adds, hung almost naked on the Cross.[3] Preachers and verse-makers alike in these later Middle Ages at all events agree unhesitatingly that extravagance in dress has now reached its craziest limits. "So myche disgisynge of araie was ther never, I trowe, fro the bigynnynge of the world."[4] As examples of extreme foppishness in his own day, Bromyard cites the case "of a certain fool who, when recently condemned to be hung, while the priest was speaking to him of Confession, was actually lamenting the loss of a cap on his way from the prison": likewise "of another fellow of the kind, who, when invited to a feast, made out that he had come naked, when his horse was clad with the

[1] MS. Harl. 4894, fol. 176b. Similarly, MS. Jo. Ryl. Libr. Manch. Lat. 367, fol. 256 (Repingdon?): "3[io] peccatur in indecencia que respicit ...vestem, ut si sit nimis curta"; and Gascoigne, s.v. "Ornatus" (*Loci e Libro Verit.* p. 144): "per aperturam togae". MS. Add. 21253, fol. 106b (marginal schema) describes the sin of men's and women's costume as consisting in its *preciositas, mollicies, superfluitas, magnitudo, longitudo, multiplicitas.* Cf. Et. de Bourbon, *Anecd. Hist.,* p. 235.

[2] § 27, 421. Cf. also a poem of the Vernon MS. in E.E.T.S. O.S. no. 98, p. 336, l. 275.

[3] *S.P.* s.v. "Ornatus". Cf. further, *Ayenb. of Inwyt,* p. 258.

[4] MS. Add. 41321, fol. 108. Cf. again, e.g., *Pricke of Consc.* ed. Philog. Soc. pp. 42–5, ll. 1516 et seq. (the world now turned upside down: cf. above, pp. 314 and 369).

finest scarlet".[1] In view of some of the fashions in vogue towards the end of the fourteenth century, there seems ample ground for many of these complaints. Bishop Brunton in the south and Rypon in the north discuss the whole question in their sermons in strikingly similar language. Says Brunton:

> As for pride of dress, so foppish are folk of the present day that it is impossible to distinguish between knight and squire, between cleric and layman, between the wife of an earl and the wife of a burgess....Once upon a time in the realm of England, there was such an abundance of riches and treasure that all had plenty and lived of their own. The reason was that the greater lords were content with a few necessaries, as was the knight with one robe a year and one course at luncheon, etc. But to-day they are so dandyfied, so pompous and luxurious that, although they appear great and rich without, yet in actual fact, if they had to render account of what was theirs alone, they would be reduced as it were to nothing. Thus is fulfilled that which is written concerning the kingdom in *Ecclesiasticus*: "The house that is very rich shall be brought to nothing by pride".[2]

Rypon, whose lament in the same strain over the finery and impudent airs of grooms and maid-servants in the present "iron age" was cited in a previous chapter,[3] attempts to give us further both date and explanation of his own for this radical change in manners. It is, as usual, the Frenchmen's fault. He tells how, according to the account of elderly persons, at the beginning of the Pestilence and for a long while before, men were simple and clad in homely fashion. But, after the Pestilence, when the war with France began, then began also the pride of the French to infect the English,[4] and now the present age is surfeited with it—especially in pride of raiment, in baselards, in horns, and in the various adornment of colours; all of which amongst not a few are occasion of the thefts, plunderings and other extortions that now disgrace the realm.[5] Another preacher, however, in the earlier part of the fourteenth century, has already ventured to behold in the victories of Scotland over

---

[1] *S.P.* s.v. "Superbia".
[2] MS. Harl. 3760, fols. 128–128b (see Eccles. xxi, 5: also quoted by Rypon).
[3] See above, p. 369.
[4] Cf. also Bromyard, below, p. 408.
[5] MS. Harl. 4894, fol. 27b.

a decadent English knighthood the fulfilment of a certain prophecy concerning the sin of "varietas vestium" which would inevitably bring national disaster in its train.[1] Here there would seem to be some connection of ideas with that curious record of the English Chronicle which tells how the Scots at York, about this same time, pinned upon the church doors of St Peter in Stangate an insolent little verse mocking the current foppishness of Englishmen in beards and attire,[2] a variation of which is actually to be found in one of our later sermon-books.[3] Since of this *varietas vestium*, argues the preacher aforementioned, "we see more among us now than our fathers saw—even to the third and fourth generation", these prophetic sayings "suffice to explain the ignominy of the pursuers which has befallen us for this action". Finally, Gascoigne, who reminds us further that ornamentation of clothing was originally designed for the practical purpose of distinguishing easily one office or rank from another, discerns a third outbreak of extravagance about the year 1429.[4] The truth is, we fear, that the fops have always been with us.

In the ranks of fashionable society the rage to be smartly dressed developed at length into a rage for novelty and a passion for change. Fashions came and fashions went with startling rapidity. Bromyard describes with his usual vividness how

from day to day the desire and appetite for elegance, singularity and vanity in all outward adornment, whether of hair or clothing, meets the

[1] MS. Heref. Cath. Libr. P. 5. 2, fol. 105 (see above, p. 130). Cf. Poem in Wright, Rolls S. vol. i, p. 275 ("Ware ʒe the prophecye").
[2] See *The Brut*, ed. F. W. D. Brie, 1906, E.E.T.S. O.S. no. 131, vol. i, p. 249 (cap. ccxiii).
[3] MS. Worc. Cath. Libr. F. 10, fol. 238:

> "Longe berdes hertles
> Streyte cotes graceles
> Peyntet hodes wytles
> Longe tepetes redles   [helpless]
> Partie hosen thryftles
> Makeyt this world laweles".

A still later variation (temp. Henry VI) is printed from MS. Harl. 372 in Wright, *Pol. Poems*, Rolls S. vol. ii, p. 251.
[4] *Loci e Libro Verit.* pp. 144–5.

eye. So it befalls that amongst such folk no fashion pleases them for long; because, inasmuch as that piece of singularity or elegance which originally was but rarely seen begins to be used and seen by many, it begins to displease them when the cause of its singularity and vanity ceases along with the admiration of men.... Whence it comes about that they devise some new piece of foppery to make men gaze at them in wonderment anew.[1]

Thus the nobility, beholding their cherished inventions in common use amongst "ribalds and vile persons", promptly "scorn them as too common and therefore unworthy of admiration, as is evident in the case of garters and the like".[2] After the manner of pet monkeys, says Bromyard wittily, that love to copy the little tricks and habits of their owners, struggling ostentatiously to put on their spurs and gloves, if they can get hold of them, amid the general laughter and joking, imitating their walk and manner as well as they can, so do the fops. "If they chance to have seen some new vogue or eccentricity among any people, in any city or land, in the cutting of cloth, the wearing of large beards, or in oaths and so forth",[3] they must at once adopt it for themselves: this, too, in spite of any personal discomfort which it may involve for the wearer.[4] The excuses offered by these slaves of the fiat of fashion are old and familiar enough. Thus, they seek to "hide" their proud array "under the cloak of custom, saying that they *must* be conformed to others in their district".[5] After all, "*they* are not the inventors or inventresses of such novelties and eccentricities; and therefore not they but the inventors of them sin. For they merely follow suit, lest they should be laughed at for their singularity and boorishness". But our Dominican proves unrelenting: "I do not see any great difference between those who invent and those who use, save that it is with the

---

[1] *S.P.* s.v. "Inconstantia".   [2] s.v. "Juramentum".

[3] s.v. "Exemplum" (similarly s.v. "Inconstantia").

[4] Cf. s.v. "Anima": "In corpore longam barbam portant, quae, si pro remissione peccatorum injunctum fuerit, non facerent. (Sed in hoc sicut Saracenis assimilant....) Secundo, hoc ostendunt in vestibus ex transverso scissis, quae mores signant Deo et ecclesiae contrarios". For the fashion in beards, cf. the contemporary satirical verse (as quoted above, p. 407, n. 3): "Longe berdes hertles...".

[5] s.v. "Falsitas".

inventors as with those wishing to catch apes: the users, to be sure, are just the apes that are caught".[1]

Sometimes they excuse themselves by saying—"Can I not do what I like with my own?" The answer for them is "No!" Because, just as a man is not allowed to use the poison that he keeps in his house to the injury of others, nor his fire in such a way as to consume them, so neither may he make use of garments or other ornaments of the head at the cost of poisoning or consuming others spiritually.[2]

Finally, as Bromyard further indicates, much of this finery was only acquired "with blood", through wealth ill-gotten at a dire cost to the poor and those who had been defrauded.[3] Through the whole of society, from the top wellnigh to the bottom, this particular poison threatened to run. In the burning words of the prophet Zephaniah, the preacher cries: "I will visit upon the princes and the king's children and all such as are clothed with strange apparel".[4]

And this word can be understood not only of clergy who wear raiment of too secular a colour or pattern, to whom their bishop ought to say: "I will visit...etc.", but also of seculars, who frequently change the form of their garments to conform themselves vainly to the habits of vain men and other nations, whom God visits with violent slaughter in their own land and with ignominious capture and imprisonment in the lands of others.[5]

Of the clergy something has already been said elsewhere.[6] Of the laity little now need be added concerning detailed censure of the enormities of the male sex. A preacher who may be Repingdon, for example, attacks in one of his discourses the popular bag-sleeves or "pokys",[7] which were sometimes

---

[1] s.v. "Ornatus" (the ape-catchers are here said to sit under the trees where the apes are leaping and put on spurs and gloves in full view. They then move away, leaving this attire, which snares the prey to imitate them and be caught in its struggles).

[2] s.v. "Exemplum."

[3] s.v. "Ornatus". Cf. further above, pp. 301–4, 311, 321 n. 5, etc.

[4] Zeph. i, 8. Quoted again in a sermon of Repingdon (?), MS. Jo. Ryl. Libr. Manch. Lat. 367, fol. 256. Cf. here especially his comment: "*Vestis peregrina* est que statui persone sic indute non concordat".

[5] s.v. "Inconstantia". Similarly Repingdon (?), as above.

[6] See above, pp. 262, 271, 275, 277, 279, 283, etc.

[7] "[vestis] nimis longa, cum duabus manicis ad modum sacculi mendicantis pendentibus."

lampooned as "devils' receptacles",[1] "along with an infinity
of other most evil inventions, in which men provoke God to
vengeance upon them".[2] Artless vernacular sermon-writers
also witness to the spread "of dyvers atyre, as of strayt clothes
and schorte, and daggede[3] hodes other typpes,[4] chausures[5]
dysgysed and y-tyed up streyt in thre stedes,[6] baudrykes[7] and
baselardes[8] and crakowes[9] of half a fote longe, harlotes[9] and
laddes[10] and other dysgysynges",[11] of "myche wast in iaggid
and dagging"[12] and the rest; while satirists in verse likewise
pour out their ridicule now upon the excesses of gallants and
courtiers,[13] now upon the finery of grooms and serving-men.[14]
No wonder that, apart even from questions of pride, the wearing
of fine clothes came to have so fatal an attraction for the masses.
"For we may se now al day", says a homilist, "that, be it
never so pouer a man, and a have on a gay gowne of selk or
ell[s] a pair o curel bedes hongyng abowte his nekk, eny man
is fain to make him cher and also for to be mek and lowliche
to him."[15] Against the general worldliness and self-interest of
the times the pulpit was at a disadvantage, even with Scripture

[1] Cf. Anon. monast. biog. of Rich. II, in J. R. Planché, *Cyclop. of
Costume*, 1876, vol. i, p. 466 (s.v. *Sleeve*); Hoccleve, as below; etc.
[2] MS. Jo. Ryl. Libr. Manch. Lat. 367, fol. 256.
[3] I.e. with foliated or scolloped edges (cf. Chaucer, *Persones Tale*, § 27,
ll. 415–20): a fashion said to have been introduced c. 1346.
[4] = either tippets, or edgings (or else ornamental girdle-ends?).
[5] = boots, shoes.   [6] = places.
[7] = belts.   [8] = daggers.
[9] = long pointed shoes of the period.
[10] = shoe-thongs or shoe-latchets.
[11] MS. Harl. 2398, fol. 9. For hair-curling, see above, p. 275, n. 1.
[12] MS. St Albans Cath. fol. 19 (as in Chaucer).
[13] Cf. *Richard the Redeles*, pass. iii; poems by Gower, Hoccleve, etc.,
and others on the Evil Times (e.g. in Wright, *Pol. Poems*, Rolls S.
vols. i, 251, 275; ii, 254, etc.). Also, late examples, such as *The Treatyse
of a Galaunt*, and *Jack Puffe, Gent.* (in Hazlitt, *E. Pop. Poetry of Engl.*
vols. iii, 147 and iv, 311).
[14] See a short satirical poem *of the Finery of Serving Men*, in Fairholt
(as above), p. 58; Hoccleve, *Reg. of Pr.* E.E.T.S. ed. Ext. S. vol. lxxii,
pp. 17, 20; poem in E.E.T.S. O.S. no. 98, pp. 335–6; etc.: and cf. above,
pp. 314 and 369.
[15] MS. Worc. Cath. Libr. F. 10, fol. 49b. Cf. Hoccleve, *Reg. of Pr.*
pp. 20–1.

and with satire as its privileged weapons, along with the very evidences of nature:

ffor if such coste and outrage in clothis were noght synne, God wolde noght so scharpliche i-spoke there aȝenst, as he ded in the gospel, of the riche man that was clothed in purpur and bys. He is a grete fole and more witles than a child that hath wit and pryde of his clothinge or apparaile of his body, that schulde be nothinge but a tokene and a knowynge of our forme fadres schame and of oure owne. ffor the use of clothinge and coverynge of body was firste founde for the synne of oure forme fader, thorgh whiche he and alle his ofspringe were dampned for to hyde his schame and oure. Whi schulde than a man have likynge to see a bere[1] heled with riche clothes, seth it is a token that a dede body lieth ther under? Hit is no wonder thogh a pocok be proude of his fayre taile, ne a cok of his combe; for kynde maketh him so, and he hath no witte ne resoun to the contrarie. But man that hath witte, skill and free wille, and wote wele that kynde ȝeve him noght his riche ne gay apparaile, schulde not pryde him therof; ne women of the queynte ne riche atyre of her bodies and of her hedes.[2]

Apart altogether from the iniquities of current dress, there were other fashions of the day which sometimes raised the homilist's ire when he looked out upon the contemporary scene, "remembering the former things of old". Now, in fourteenth and fifteenth-century England, there was a reprehensible "tendirnes" abroad, a perilous effeminacy amongst the prosperous, we are told, as "whan a man delitith him in softe clothing, in nesche bedding; he moste ofte be waische, ofte bathid, ofte kempt and kerchevid and cherschid so tendirli".[3] "Lyvyng be harde metis and drynkis, liggyng on harde liters out of lyȝnen clothis"[4] and the like were not for these degenerate sons of hardy grandsires. The Fiend had a

---

[1] I.e. bier. (Cf. MS. Salisb. Cath. vers.—"ffor, whan a hers is dyȝt wyth fayre clothys, it is a tokne that ther is a deed cors wythinne. So man and woman gayly dyȝt in aray out of mesure it is a sygne that a deede soule is withynne.")

[2] MS. Harl. 45, fol. 163 b. Similarly in MS. Salisb. Cath. Libr. 103, *Jacob's Well* (unpubl.), fols. 112–3; and *Ayenb. of Inwyt*, p. 258.

[3] MS. Bodl. Laud Misc. 23, fols. 33–4. Similarly in MS. Harl. 45, fol. 51, and *Jacob's Well*, p. 104.

[4] Ibid.: cf. Langland, *Piers Plowman*, B text, pass. xiv, l. 233.

habit of reminding them that they were tenderly nourished, that any undue strain upon the body might be their death. With so tender a complexion, "it were a foul happe to for-do" oneself. "This branche of slowthe", adds the speaker, "is myche noryssched in lordys courtys."[1] We get an interesting echo here from the contemporary pulpits in Langland's complaint that lords and ladies now forsake the hall for the cosy delights of "a pryve parloure" or "a chambre with a chymneye".[2] It was not mere privacy, apparently, but their chief article of furniture that made the latter so attractive.[3] For Bromyard freely denounces those who have suffered no "imprisonment" in God's cause against the Saracens, but only one for their own delight in "that prison-house of the Devil, that is to say, their own dark chamber, in which they shut themselves up in bed until nine o'clock in the morning or until noon", indulging their carnal appetites.[4] "God", cries the indignant friar, "made the night for rest and the day for waking, and these infernal owls turn night into day and *vice versa*. Such are of the household of 'Draw-sheet', who is the chief Chamberlain of Hell and is said to have told someone that his job was to make men lie for a long while under the sheets."[5] "And suche one", say the preachers in chorus, be their language Latin or vernacular, "is the develes bolster, or his couche that he resteth him on."[6]

[1] *Jacob's Well*, p. 104.   [2] *Piers Plowman*, B text, pass. x, l. 94.
[3] For beds in *parlours*, cf. Miss Abram, *Engl. Life and Manners in the later Midd. Ages*, p. 175.
[4] *S.P.* s.v. "Furtum" ("Nec dicere possunt 'in carcere fuimus' [cf. Matth. xxv, 36] nisi pro delictis suis, non pro Deo inter Saracenos; nisi forte carcerem dicere velint illum diaboli carcerem, i.e. obscuram cameram suam..."). Cf. again, similarly, s.v. "Labor" ("Vel ubi sunt qui tamdiu seipsos in locis obscuris pro amore Dei incarcerarent, sicut faciunt ociosi in lectis suis omni die pro carne sua male nutrienda?"). "Judicium Divinum", § 22, etc. Also, in my *Preaching in Med. Engl.* p. 170.
[5] s.v. "Anima" (Bromyard also gives the demon's name in French— "Tyrelincel"). Similarly, *Man. des Pechiez* (= *Hand. Synne*, p. 144).
[6] MS. Harl. 45, fol. 51. Similarly, *Jacob's Well*, p. 104 ("his softe fedyrbed"), p. 114 ("the feendys pylwe"); Bromyard, *S.P.* s.v. "Otium" ("Ociositas") ("quasi mollis culcitra in qua diabolus quiescit, et diaboli sedile super quo sedet in lecto calido"). Cf. here the misericord carving at Christchurch Priory, Hants., sketched by T. Wildridge, *The Grotesque in Ch. Art*, p. 34.

Even Scripture lent its testimony against this form of extravagance:

Of the beds of the proud there is mention in the Book of Hester, ii,[1] where it is said that "the beds were of gold and silver, placed in order upon a floor paved with porphyry and white marble, which was embellished with painting of wonderful variety". Assuredly, in the beds of the proud three things are reprehensible—the softness of the quilts, the costliness of the coverlets and the great size of the beds: for some folk are so proud that they want to have beds so large that the Devil too can lie comfortably with them. But in the small bed of the poor there is no room for the Devil to rest.... Verily, these proud persons who lie in beds of pride should greatly fear that which is spoken in the Book of Amos, vi— "Woe to you that sleep upon beds of ivory, and are wanton upon your couches!"[2]

In this connection the old sermon-story is worth recalling that tells how once a luxurious student at Bologna was converted by the Dominican who bade him reflect how hard would be the beds in Hell.[3] Bromyard himself repeats the tale of a certain Bishop of Toulouse rescued from a life of ease by similar thoughts of future torments, while at rest in his comfortable bed.[4] Along with the iniquities of "softe and delycat beddyng" there are sometimes linked those of "swete bathys",[5] another weakness of the well-to-do which stirred the pulpit to wrath. Bromyard, who declares that the evil rich at their death shall have in place of a soft couch, a couch harder and more bitter than all nails and spikes, declares also that, "instead of their odoriferous baths, they shall have a bath in hell blacker and fouler than a whole bath of pitch and sulphur".[6] Such, indeed, was the fate of the wicked clerk Odo as revealed in another

---

[1] Esther, i, 6.

[2] (Amos vi, 4) MS. Add. 21253, fol. 162. Cf. love of rich bedding denounced in Hand. Synne, p. 119; and of "zofte bed clothes" in Ayenb. of Inwyt, p. 47. Cf. Perault, Summa de Viciis, de Superb.

[3] Spec. Laic. cap. lxxxv (cf. MS. Add. 11284, fol. 89b); etc. Probably derived from the 13th-cent. Dominican, Etienne de Bourbon (see Lecoy de la Marche, Anecd. Hist. p. 29). Also in the Tract. of Humbertus de Romanis (see Hist. Litt. de la Fr. vol. xxix, p. 548, and Welter, L'Exemplum, p. 224), and other sermons (cf. Hauréau, Not. et Extr. vol. iii, p. 285). The torment of a wicked clerk in hell, who had similarly indulged himself in life, was "to be put upon a bed of blazing coals and the hottest iron". (See S.P. s.v. "Poena"; etc.)

[4] S.P. s.v. "Cogitatio".

[5] Jacob's Well, p. 9.

[6] S.P. s.v. "Gloria".

favourite sermon-tale, he who in his lifetime "was wont to be bathed delicately and lasciviously".[1] Others denounce the lovers of sweet-smelling herbs and spices that only stir likewise to lechery.[2] Let those prone to such temptation follow the example of Christ who communed with the sick. "Qwy shold not a man, that sum tym delites hym to mych in swet smellynges, suffer to hevy smell, specially in confortynge of seke folke sum tyme?"[3]

A current fashion, and another supposed hall-mark of the *élite*, which drew far more of the attention of both preachers and versifiers was the use of oaths in conversation. These latter too had their changing vogue, precisely as in the case of costume. What to-day was hailed as *le dernier cri* to-morrow would be considered vulgar and trite by "these inventors of new oaths, who inanely glory in such things, and count themselves the more noble for swearing thus", the author of the *Summa Predicantium* informs us. "This is to be seen", he says, "among those who consider themselves of high breeding, or are proud. Just as they invent and delight in everything of the nature of outward apparel, so do they also in the case of vows and oaths.... Strange vows and swear-words invented by them are already so common that they may be found daily in the mouth of any ribald or rascal you please." By this time, therefore, he adds sarcastically, it ought to be fashionable to use no oaths at all in speaking, and to follow therein the vogue of Christ, for a change![4] The prevalence of this habit in the Middle Ages is, of course, a matter with which not merely the proverbial schoolboy but every ordinary theatre-goer or novel-reader of to-day is familiar. In the contemporary literature of Complaint we read of it in Langland, in Gower, Chaucer,

---

[1] *S.P.* s.v. "Poena". Cf. *Jacob's Well*, as before ("bathyd and boyled and sodyn in pycche and oyle all sethyng over the fyir"); etc.
[2] MS. Worc. Cath. Libr. F. 10, fol. 46 ("hote spiceri, hote erbis"); *Jacob's Well*, p. 218; etc.   [3] MS. Harl. 45, fol. 130.
[4] s.v. "Juramentum". Cf. s.v. "Exemplum", as above, p. 408.

Hoccleve, Barclay, Hawes and other pre-Reformation poets, not to mention the writers of anonymous verse.[1] But, as usual, the direct source of this complaining and satire has remained undisclosed, even where it has been rightly conjectured. Such censure, indeed, was no original whim of the poets, nor does it mark any independent puritanical reaction amongst the masses. It is merely one more typical little tribute to that amazing influence which the pulpit once wielded over the thoughts and aspirations of men. Subject and treatment alike are conspicuous pulpit commonplaces. In whatever sermon-collection the reader chooses to look, there he will find the preacher's expatiation upon the wrongs of "false swearing", which usually includes in its purview the various forms of perjury, as well as these "vayne and orrible othes" that "draw Crist lyme by lyme",[2] so "foul in the ears of the faithful". Similarly, in tractates upon the Decalogue popular at this later period, discussion of the Second Commandment leads inevitably to the same theme:

In this heste ys forbode alle maner of heresy, that ys for to mayntene eny poyntes aʒenst the byleve of holy churche, and al maner sclandere and unreverence to God and to holy seyntes; and specialyche ys forbode al maner forsweryng upon the boke wytynglyche, as in enquestes, other assyses....

Also thou schalt nouʒt swere by diverse lymes of Criste an-ydel, as by herte and soule, by bones, woundes and his feet, ne by other lymes: for who so doth he despyseth and offendeth more Crist of hevene than dude the jewes that dyde Crist on the rode. Also, thou ne schalt nouʒt swere by none creatures, as by sonne, by mone, by wynde, ne by none other creature that God ordeynede. Bot thou schalt seye "it ys so" or "it ys nouʒt so": for thou schalt swere non other wyse, but yf nede it

---

[1] Cf. *Poem on the Times*, c. 1388, in Wright, *Pol. Poems*, Rolls S. vol. i, p. 277, and Fairholt, p. 48 ("armys, sydus and bonus *horum quidam recitabit.*"); *The Complaint of the Plowman*, in Wright, ibid. p. 311 ("And Cristes membres all to tere on rood, as he were new y-rent"); etc.

[2] E.g. *Spec. Laic.* cap. lxvii (ed. Welter, pp. 90–2); Bromyard's capit. "Juramentum", in *S.P.*; Rypon, MS. Harl. 4894, fols. 99b–100; Waldeby, MS. Caius Coll. Camb. 334, fol. 173; *Ayenb. of Inwyt*, pp. 63–5; *Jacob's Well*, pp. 152–3; etc. For Wycliffe, Purvey, etc., see Workman, *Jo. Wyclif*, vol. ii, pp. 27–8. Cf. also, the *Merchants*, as above, p. 359, and *Knights*, p. 336, etc.

make for to certyfye the sothe by-twene ney3ebores, yf eny stryf falle bytwene hem.[1]

There is nothing peculiarly Lollard in such sentiments, as Dr Workman would have us think, in spite of a remark by Chaucer's Host in the *Canterbury Tales* which, if taken alone and taken seriously, might appear to support him.[2] Upon the iniquities of swearing and the need for its denunciation the preachers, orthodox and unorthodox alike, are in perfect accord. What, then, do they tell us of the Englishman's fondness for the habit? The Third Commandment, says one, "is all wey brokyn a-monge lered and lewde, a-monge yeonge and old, a-monge ryche and pore, frome a litill yeonge chyld that can unnethe[3] speke, to an olde berded man that age hathe ny3 be-nome[4] his ry3t speche".[5] Clearly, from the threats and prohibitions of the pulpit, the priest and his subordinates, in this as in most other respects, were often no better than their parishioners. "For the lawe of holi chirche seith that a clerke that swerith bi creatures schal be rebukid moost scharpli. If he contynue in the synne he schal be acursid. If ony man swerith bi the heer or bi the heed of God, or usith blasfemye a3ens God in ony maner, if he be in ordre of the chirche, he schal be degratid...."[6] "And thenne, nother clerkes, ne kny3tes, nother laboreres scholde take thus this holy name an-ydel and withoute cause, as false cristene men now doth

---

[1] MS. Harl. 2398, fol. 2b. Similarly MS. St Albans Cath. fols. 13b–18, as quoted below; etc.

[2] See *Jo. Wyclif*, vol. ii, pp. 27–8, and *Cant. Tales, Shipman's Prol.* l. 1173. The whole of the above denunciation occurs, e.g., in the definitely anti-Lollard *Jacob's Well*, p. 153 (cf. here, Chaucer, *Pardoners Tale*, ll. 629–59, and *Persones Tale*, § 35).

[3] = scarcely.   [4] = deprived of.

[5] MS. Bodl. 95, fol. 1b. Cf. MS. Roy. 18. B. xxiii, fol. 86b: "horible swerynge, as the most parte of the pepull dose now-adaies". For the use of oaths by Women, cf. the sermon-story in Wright, *Lat. Stories*, Percy Soc. p. 61, reprinted in Coulton, *Engl. Life in the Midd. Ages*, vol. iii, pp. 86–7.

[6] MS. St Albans Cath. fol. 14. Cf. also Myrc, *Man. Sacerd.* cap. xv, *De Sacerdote Aleatore*, MS. Harl. 5306, fol. 18 ("effundunt juramenta") and *Instructions for Par. Priests*, l. 28 ("And grete othes thow moste eschewe").

many tyme."¹ In customary graphic style, the preachers sketch
for us the various types of swearers whose habits have remained unaltered through all the intervening centuries. Who,
for example, does not recognize those that can "scarce speak
a few words without adding a vow or an oath",² the men that
"sweryn customabely at iche woord and recke nevere how",
careless of the way in which they call God to witness at each
idle oath that escapes them, the mad-cap swearers—"as whan
a man sweryth to don a thyng that may noȝt be don wythoutyn
synne", the excitable fellow that "sweryth oversone for
wretthe, and whanne he hath don, he repentyth hym;...or
whan men sweryn in certeyn for a thyng that is in dowte; or
whan a man behotyth³ an-other a thyng that he may noȝt
perfourme"?⁴ Certain places were naturally marked out as the
special haunt of such blasphemers. "Christ's blood, these days,
is reckoned of little price amongst the greater part of the
people", mourns the friar John Waldeby, in a sermon. "For,
if one comes into the market-place or the tavern where these
infernal dogs, that is to say, the swearers are, one will find
Christ's blood held at so small a price and in such little reverence
among them that scarcely a single word will escape their lips—
be it true or false—without mention by name of the blood of
Christ in an oath along with it....And not only Christ's
blood, but all the members of Christ."⁵ From the open ale-
house door, the passing preachers, like the poets Langland,⁶
Chaucer⁷ and Hoccleve,⁸ heard issuing forth in their day the
"gret othus and sweringes" from within, and remarked

¹ MS. Harl. 2398, fol. 89b.
² *S.P.* s.v. "Juramentum".   3 = promises.
⁴ *Jacob's Well*, p. 153. Cf. sim. *Ayenb. of Inwyt*, p. 64.
⁵ MS. Caius Coll. Camb. 334, fol. 173. (For the market-place, cf.
above, p. 359.)
⁶ See the confession of Glotoun, following the Tavern Scene, in
Piers Plowman, B text, pass. v, ll. 375–7 and preceding it l. 314 ("Thanne
goth glotone in and grete othes after"), and A text, pass. v, l. 178 ("othes
an hep").
⁷ *Cant. Tales, Pardoners Tale*, ll. 465 et seq.
⁸ *Reg. of Princes*, E.E.T.S. ed. p. 23 ("To the taverne quykly I me
spedde..."). Cf. further, *Poem on the Times*, c. 1388, in Wright,
Rolls S. vol. i, p. 277; etc.

accordingly.[1] At another time, as they would come by a group
intent upon their "fole pley"—"at the tabelys and at the dyse",
there again greeted their ears the "multeplienge of ydel wordes,
othes and lesynges: as whan many pleyeth to-gidre on this
game, eche of hem maynteneth his parte with grete othes and
lesynges and many ydel wordes". So too, finally, "whan some
foles lesith at his game, thei chideth and curseth God and his
halowes, and despiseth hem and setth many sclaundres wordes
of hem".[2] Chaucer's hypocritical Pardoner, therefore, follows
the recognized homiletic plan when he condemns in his *Tale*,
at some length, "this fruyt" that "cometh of the bicched
bones two".[3] A homilist of the more genuine sort repeats a
story from Caesarius of Heisterbach of a blaspheming dice-
player struck dead at the game before his companion's eyes,
while a voice from heaven declares—"My dyspy3t that thou
dost to me in thin horrible othys and in thin wrecheful and
malycyous cursyng wyl I no lenger suffere!"[4] Turning to
Bromyard again, we find him commenting upon the laughter
which this evil habit provokes amongst bystanders, as the shrill
expletives of the swearer come hurtling through the air.[5]
Therein, says he, the Christians are worse than the race that
originally crucified Christ. For Jews, who themselves are
scarcely ever heard to swear save by their law, prefer to withdraw from the society of Christians who swear profanely in
their presence. Whereas, the latter "laugh to hear such things,

---

[1] In addition to Waldeby, as above, cf. such sermons as are referred
to below on pp. 427–41, e.g. Bromyard, s.v. "Ebrietas" and "Gula";
MS. Roy. 18. B. xxiii, fol. 85 ("blasfemynge God with many grett othes");
MS. Add. 41321, fol. 98b ("swerynge and slaunderynge"); John Lacy's
Treatise on the Decal. ed. Royster, pp. 21–3 (as quoted below, p. 441);
Jacob's Well, p. 148; *Ayenb. of Inwyt*, p. 56; *Hand. Synne*, p. 29; etc.

[2] MS. Harl. 45, fols. 72b–3. Similarly *Jacob's Well*, p. 135; *Ayenb.
of Inwyt*, pp. 69–70; and cf. Myrc. *Man. Sacerd.* "De Sac. Aleatore", as
above, p. 276.

[3] *Pardoners Tale*, ll. 591–3 and 629–59. Cf. Hoccleve, as above ("and
pleide at dyce...").

[4] *Jacob's Well*, p. 100 ("Cesarius tellyth..."). See *Dialog. Mirac.*
dist. vii, cap. xliii. Cf. the chess-playing knight, *Ayenb. of Inwyt*, p. 45.

[5] "[jurantes] alte et clamorose ad risum vel scandalum aliorum." Cf.
MS. St Albans Cath. as follows below.

who, nevertheless, if insulting remarks were made in front of them about their father or their earthly lord, would either defend the outraged by fighting, or at least be offended and withdraw".[1] "Even for the sake of a penny" they will take God's name in vain.[2] Now and again English homilists sum up for us the regular excuses with which these blasphemers seek to defend their evil conduct. The arguments of the latter are feeble enough; but they serve to illustrate admirably both the common mentality of the times and the faithfulness with which our sermons have conserved it:

> But now-a-daies men hav iiii lewede excusacions to menteyne with her idil sweringe. The frist...is this: "It is good", thei seien, "to have God in mynde, and nempne his name oft".[3] These men ben as madde and as woode to have mynde on a iust kinge to be-traie him and slee him, and to reherce ofte his name in dispite to teche other men to dispice him. In this same maner doon men that taken thus ofte Goddis name in idil bi her customable sweringe....
>
> The ii[e] excusacioun...is this: "Thouȝ y swere ofte and nedeles, it cometh of a custom", thei seien, "and y do it not for dispite of God, but for liȝtnes of my tunge[4] and for myrthe of othere men aboute". Certis this is a woodnes unsuffrable to al cristen men! It is as oon to excuse thus these ydil swerers and to excuse a theef areyned at the barre for felony, that seith thus to the iustice—"I have hade so long a custom of thefte that I can not cese"....
>
> The iii lewid excusacioun is this: "God is merciful and iust", thei seien, "and therefore he wole not dampne men for a litil ooth that schapith him with unavisement"....[The reply is—] sithen God is so greet a lord and comaundith his legeman up on peyne of hanginge and drawinge in helle withoute eende to kepe so esy commaundement,...he [the swearer] is worthi to be dampned the depper therefore....[5]

[1] S.P. s.v. "Juramentum". Cf. MS. Roy. 18. B. xxiii, fol. 88, and the further picturesque elaboration of this last argument s.v. "Gloria".

[2] s.v. "Avaritia".

[3] Similarly in MS. Roy. 18. B. xxiii, fol. 88 ("Is itt not good to have God in mynd?").

[4] Cf. the similar excuse given in Bromyard (s.v. "Juramentum") and the following interesting observation: "Alii se excusant passione vel tedio, sicut quidam, quorum mala est consuetudo in aliquibus mundi partibus quod, quasi pro omni tedio quod sentiunt, Deum vel matrem suam vel sanctos blasphemant vel eis abrenunciant, dicentes Gallice—'Je reney Dieu, etc.'"

[5] The speaker adds: "It was litil to Adam to ete an appil in paradice outaken the forbedinge of God. But for he ete ther-of, he and al mankinde was iustli dampned".

The iiii lewid excusacioun is this: thise ydil swereris seyn that men wolen no leeven[1] but thei sweren, and therfor thei sweren thus....[2] [The answer is—] these comoun swerers sweren oft fals and bi triflis, that no wise man wole leve hem, swere thei never so fast....[3]

Another homilist gives us a fifth excuse—"And som seyne, 'Y may swere, for God swere hym-selve'". "Butt God owȝt before the to have som privelege", is his quaint retort, "sethe that he is lorde, and thu his servant to do that he byddethe the. Or if thow be knowynge evyn with all-miȝty God in witt, powere and wisdome, then thu myȝt swere as God ded. Butt, and thu swere otherwise, thu faylyst of thy crafte...."[4] The way of the rebuker, however, remained hard and thorny:

Alas that no man now-a-daies unnethis canne speke ony word but if an ooth be at the other eende. More and alas, than, if outher man wolde mekeli warne hem of her oothis, a-noon thei wole be wrooth with him and dispise him smerteli. But moost alas that prelatis and lordis, that ben ordeyned to teche Goddis lawe and to constreyne othere men to kepe it, thei suffren suche idil swereris to dispise God in her owne heringe and chastice not hem therfore, sithen thei myȝte do this with a litil worde or bi puttinge hem a-wei fro her service. Certis it is wonder, outtaken[5] the eendelis merci of God, that the erthe openeth not and swolowith hem quyk to helle for this treson, and many mo.[6]

It is this homilist, be it noted, who uses, in common with others, the very phrases which Chaucer puts into the mouths of his Pardoner and his Parson, concerning—"greet swereris that dismembre Crist, sweringe bi his yȝen, armys, naylis, boonys, herte, blode and soule. Hem thinkith that the cursid iewis deden him not turment y-nouȝ, but if thei with her grisli

[1] = believe.
[2] Cf. similarly MS. Roy. 18. B. xxiii, fol. 88, and MS. Harl. 2398, fol. 87: "And these grete swereres...sey that no man wolde trowe hem, bot yf they swere so. And thus by here lesynge they greggeth here synne; for the worlde wole wytnesse that suche grete swereres beth more false of here tunge than men that swereth lytel". Cf. also p. 359 above.
[3] MS. St Albans Cath. fols. 14b–17.
[4] MS. Bodl. 95, fols. 2–2b (MS. Harl. 2398, as above, however, considers that the fact that it is recorded in Scripture that God himself swore shows that not *all* forms of swearing are evil).
[5] = apart from.
[6] MS. St Albans Cath. fol. 17.

oothis al to drouჳ Cristis lymys fro lymys (as crowis plucken a careyne)".[1]

Faced with the problem of this malignant cancer spreading rapidly through the whole social system, the pulpit was naturally driven to do more than merely to complain. Bromyard suggests that special penalties should be inflicted upon swearers, like those decreed by St Louis of France, "who ordered such to be branded upon the face with a hot iron for a perpetual memorial of their crime, and later on, indeed, ordained that they should be set in a public place in the high stocks, which in their tongue are called *escale*,[2] similar in form and in mode of punishment to that inflicted upon cutpurses in the realm of England". In the kingdom of Sicily, he observes further, the tongues of such blasphemers are ordered to be cut. Like the homilist whom we last quoted, he looks anxiously to the secular powers for the only measures likely to prove a sound corrective: "If princes and lords of the present day would now decree such penalties in every country against those giving vent to foul oaths, they would amend them quicker than the preachers. For the offenders would quit their evil habits more speedily for fear of punishments to be felt than for fear of those eternal punishments with which the preachers threaten them". What folly it is, he points out, to train one's family and retainers to be respectful and courteous towards all men, and not to insist upon the same reverence where God and his saints are concerned.[3] The more normal line of action for the pulpit, however, was to emphasize those very threats

---

[1] Ibid. fol. 18. Similarly MS. Harl. 2398, fol. 87b ("... dismembreth Crist, swerynge by his heorte and his soule and blod and bones.... And so dyde never the cursede Jewes..."); *Ayenb. of Inwyt*, p. 64; Bromyard, *S.P.* s.v. "Juramentum": "Isti membratim et per pecias gladio dyaboli, i.e. lingua sua [corpus Xti] dividunt...": elsewhere they are likened to archers shooting at Christ bound to the Cross. For Chaucer, see *Cant. Tales, Pardoners Tale*, ll. 472–5, and *Persones Tale*, ll. 590 and 599. His remark about "the devel" in the latter is also to be found in Bromyard ("sicut in aliquis sanctorum gestis legitur"). Cf. further Stephen Hawes' *Conversion of Swearers*; Barclay, *Ship of Fools*; etc.

[2] (Mod. *échelle*) here in the text *scala*. Cf. earlier in this same *capit.* § 11, an *exemplum* mentioning—"quod vulgariter *pillori* nuncupatur".

[3] *S.P.* s.v. "Juramentum".

which our Dominican is here driven to disparage. God himself would take vengeance upon the sinner. Thus Bromyard, along with the rest, assails those whom he likens "to beasts,[1] yea, to Jews, or Saracens, or robbers, or to Judas, or even the very devils themselves, or whatever else is of worse condition and of greater ingratitude": "As little choughs chatter at the eagle or the falcon, so do these little hell-choughs at God and the saints", he says. "But just as that noble bird, if he can touch the chatterers, will give them what they deserve, so God and the saints, who can touch them, do give them their deserts, alike smiting them with diverse diseases here on earth and elsewhere committing them to eternal damnation."[2] In yet more vivid language, our homely vernacularist pictures the swearer's fate and the indignation of an outraged Deity:

Almyghty God compleyneth hym of thise grett swerers be the holy profhete, seying on this wyse—"*Circumdederunt me canes multi, et consilium malignantium obsedit me*".[3]—"Many houndes", seyth Crist, "hase goyn abowte me, and the counsell of wicked men hath blynded [sic!] me. Thei have reysed[4] and thridlyd[5] my hondes and my fete, and thei have nowmbred all my bones. For som caches my hede, som my bonys in is mowthe, like as he wold burste hem all to morcels." Anothur caches all the blessed bodye in is mowthe, like as he wold swalowe it up and make an ende there-of: som "be the blode", som "be the herte", som "be the sides", som "be the fote", som "be the nayles". And he that can reken up moste grett othes holdes hymselfe moste wurthye amonge these grett swerers.

But what rewarde shall these grett swerers have for ther traveyll? Trewly the Wise Man seyth that thei shall fall in many myscheves; and therfore he charched is sonne that he shuld not use is mowthe to swerynge: "*Jurationi non assuescas os tuum, multi enim casus in illo*".[6] Thorow swerynge me[n] falleth to many myscheveth thinges, and namely in thre: for than thei breke Goddes commandement, and so thei be in the wey of dampnacion; for God biddeth man uppon peyn therof that no cristen man take the name of is lord God in veyn. The seconde myscheffe is this, that comes of customable swerynge: he that customable swereth is often forsworne, and so the common lawe berethe wittenesse. Se[7] that be the weye of keende every man is a-shamed to be ofte overtaken ffalsely forswore, so every man shuld be ashamed to swere customable. The thryde

[1] s.v. "Locutio", he likens them to "the Devil's hunting-dogs" barking at God and his servants.

[2] s.v. "Juramentum".   [3] Psalm xxii, 16.
[4] = scratched.   [5] = pierced.
[6] Ecclesiasticus xxiii, 9.   [7] (Sen?) = since.

myscheffe is this, that the veniaunce of God shall not departe aweye fro
the hows of a grett swerere: "*Quia vir multum jurans replebitur iniquitate,
et non discedat plaga de domo eius*".[1] ffor that man that mekell swereth
shall be fulfilled wyt grett sekenes. ffor ofte tymes he is falsely forsworne; and therefore the vengeaunce of God shall fall on hym, or els
on som of is. ffor as seynt Poule bereth wittenes[2] that the ryghtwis
vengeaunce of God at the daye of dome shall be shewed uppon ilke
rebelte[3] and dispite that is done azeyns God, and uppon ilke wronge that
is done azeyns man. And than these grett swerers shall departe from the
hows of God and be commytte to the bitter peyns of hell. There[fore]
every man shuld fully ransake up all is liff and take good hede to is
wordes, ziff he have forfett[4] God in orable othes....[5]

Another anonymous preacher, crying to his congregation—
"O how evil it is to swear by the members of Christ and to
blaspheme Him!", adds the warning note that "ofttimes men
given to oaths and blasphemies perish by sudden death".[6] So
the pulpit is led on to furnish from its ample store those lurid
tales and reminiscences that depict the sinner's tragic end. The
fashion is already set in the *Speculum Laicorum*.[7] Two hundred
years later, Brother Whitford of Sion, looking back over a
long and interesting life in the world, as he sits to write his
Werke for Housholders in the quiet Isleworth cloister, is able
to recall two such incidents of his own, which had often been
used before, doubtless, to heighten the effect of his oratorical
appeals. One of them, described to him by the victim's widow,
while, like Milton, in retreat from the plague he tarried in a
Hertfordshire village to escape the contagion of the city,[8] tells
how God "dyd openly punysshe" a "usuall swerer" of those
parts who went a-hunting on the Holyday. This "gentylman,
that was called Mayster Baryngton", foiled of his prey and
fortified with drink at a neighbouring ale-house,

began to swere after this unhappy custome, sayeng—"By goddes blode,
this daye is unhappy!" And in a whyle after, in swerynge so, he bledde

[1] Ecclesiasticus xxiii, 12.
[2] A reference, perhaps, to 2 Thess. i, 6–9 (a passage curiously vindictive
and "medieval" in tone).   [3] = rebellion.   [4] = offended.
[5] MS. Roy. 18. B. xxiii, fols. 84b–5.
[6] MS. Add. 21253, fol. 18.
[7] Cap. lxvii, ed. Welter, p. 92, no. 470b: a rich man's fate in hell ("qui
per passionem, corpus, sanguinem seu plagas Jesu Christi solito non
formidat jurare"). Cf. above, p. 418.   [8] See above, p. 172.

at the nose and, therewith more vexed, he began to rayle and rayne God (as they saye), in swerynge "goddes passyon", "goddes woundes", "goddes flesshe", "goddes nayles", and ever his holy and blessede blode; tyll at the last he fell ferther to blede at the eares, at the eyes, at his wrestes and all the ioyntes of his handes, and of all his body, at his navyll and foundement and at other places of his body in mervaylous great quantyte and stremes of blode, and shotynge out his tonge in a mervaylous horryble, ugsome and ferefull maner, as black as pytche, so that no persone durst come nere hym, but stode aferre of and cast holy water towarde hym. And so he contynued ever swerynge, blasphemynge and bledynge tyll he expired and was deed. . . .

The other incident concerns the fate of a young apprentice in London who for a similar vice was stricken "with a greate mervaylous sekenes, so that no physyke ne medycyne myghte helpe ne ease hym, but that he laye styll in bedde so longe that the flesshe and the skynne of his armes and fyngers and of his legges, thyes, shynnes, fete and toes dyd devyde in sondre, as thoughe they hadde ben slytte with a knyfe that the bare bones myght openly be sene and feled".[1] Thus he died. An earlier sermon-tale, which comes from Worcestershire, tells us of one who, with equally disastrous result, was in the habit of calling upon the Devil for his favourite expletive. "He was wont to swear lightheartedly but none the less frequently—'The devel me adrenche!'" Consequently, one day he fell into a ditch and was swiftly drowned, while his companions all managed to make their escape.[2] However, for less-favoured homilists there was always the classical *example* available which they, like the author of our St Albans Tract on the Decalogue, could "rede in the gestis of romaynes"[3]—of how a certain profane justice was granted a vision of the havoc which his oaths were causing. There appeared to him, one day, the infant Christ in His Mother's arms, "with his hede all to-broke, and his eyen drawen oute of his body and layde on his breste, his armes broken a-twoo, his legges and his fete also". "Then anoon,

[1] As usual the Divine punishment fits the crime. This "yong man dyd use to swere for his commune othe—'by the bones of god', or 'by godes bones'".

[2] MS. Add. 33956, fol. 82b ("inter Evesham et Wylecestre [?] in Anglia").

[3] MS. St Albans Cath. fol. 45. Cf. *Gesta Rom.* Engl. version, E.E.T.S. p. 410; Myrc, *Festial*, pp. 113–4; and *Hand. Synne*, pp. 25–8.

in the siȝt of al the peple, the erthe openyd, and the iustice fel doun in to helle. . . . " "Where-fore, syres," adds our homiletical *raconteur*, "do ȝe as cristen men schulde do, leven ȝoure oothis and doith reverens to Cristis pasciouns and to his woundis, and teche ȝe alle othere men to do the same. Amen."[1]

Discussion of the swearers has already brought us close to the tavern door, if no further towards this ancient lair of the drunkard. It is now time to pass in and consider its typical occupant—typical, that is to say, from the medieval satirist's and moralist's point of view, a figure half-tragic, half-ludicrous, by no means yet banished from our modern life. Professor Manly has reminded us in a well-known chapter how the portrait of Glotoun in Langland's immortal poem "has often been cited as one of the most remarkable pieces of *genre* painting in our early literature".[2] Neither he, however, nor Professor Ten Brink, who is probably responsible for the phrase,[3] nor indeed any other of the many interpreters of *Piers Plowman's Vision* has been able as yet to set that picture in its proper place in the National Portrait Gallery of our more primitive literature. Its relation to what has followed may have been perceived clearly enough. Its direct relations to the past and the current have been disregarded. Nevertheless, it is true—and a fact of some importance—that Langland's *Glotoun*, like Chaucer's "dronke man" in the *Pardoners Tale*[4] and, for the matter of that, all the "drunk men" in English literature and upon the English stage, the Falstaffs and other tavern-goers of Elizabethan comedy, the popular burlesques of more modern time have their real prototype as literature in the satires of the pulpit. No doubt, for centuries, the drunkard's antics had found a place in the ruder mimicry of such street

[1] MS. St Albans Cath. ibid. (= Myrc, *Festial*, p. 114).
[2] *Camb. Hist. of Engl. Lit.* vol. ii, p. 16.
[3] See *E. Engl. Lit.* (*Hist. of Engl. Lit.* vol. i), p. 359. Cf. Skeat, *Piers Plowman*, Clarendon Press Ser. 1886, p. xxxiii.
[4] *Cant. Tales, Pardoners Tale*, ll. 549–72.

entertainers as the "jugoulour" and the "harlote". The caricatures of the latter may well have influenced the minds of thoughtful and observant friars like Bromyard;[1] but where have we any trace of their own "literary remains"? Certainly not in the rude scenes of the miracle-plays, as a subsequent chapter will testify, in spite of the suggestions of modern scholars to the contrary. In sermons, on the other hand, we have ample evidence that, from the beginnings of Mendicant oratory, as in patristic literature, the follies of the inebriate both ludicrous and tragical, were held up to audiences in all their grim reality—to audiences, moreover, that we happen to know were often all too ready, like Chaucer's Friar, to laugh and "gale" at the wrong moment. Here, then, at least is one well-established tradition of the kind. Miss Abram, who as a rule is remarkably accurate in such matters, declares in her *English Life and Manners in the Later Middle Ages* that "drunkenness,...which to us seems to call for far more blame than wearing gold and silver collars and bells, aroused very little indignation" in moralists of those times.[2] For once she may have been misled by the actual paucity of moral literature in print. But, in any case, in the *Old English Homilies of the Twelfth Century*, edited by Dr Morris in 1873, there is ample denunciation of this vice,[3] while the published portion of *Jacob's Well* states explicitly, three centuries later, that unnecessary drinking is venial sin, immoderate drinking in oneself or making others drunk a deadly sin.[4] Moreover, reference to Mr J. A. Herbert's masterly catalogue of *Exempla*,[5] which has not yet received that attention which it deserves from students of social history, would have revealed the further fact that the *Speculum Laicorum* contains a whole section "De Ebrietate et ejus malis",[6] embellished with no less than ten warning anec-

---

[1] Similarly, the satires of Latin goliardic verse, which without such mediation could never have reached the masses.

[2] p. 267. However, in her excellent App. of Authorities, she finds an exception in the *Kni. of La Tour-Landry* (p. 333).

[3] Cf. E.E.T.S. ed., 2nd ser. O.S. no. 53, pp. 11, 13, 31, 37, 210–13.

[4] E.E.T.S. 1900, p. 146.

[5] *Cat. of Romances in B.M.* vol. iii, pp. 385–6.

[6] cap. xxix (ed. Welter, pp. 44 et seq.).

dotes. Of these, one at least, as Mr Herbert points out, is frequently to be found in other medieval collections.[1] Earlier still in the same thirteenth century, the Cistercian Odo of Cheriton attacks the drunkard in a sermon.[2]

Inebriety must be shunned, says the *Speculum Laicorum*, because it befools, enfeebles and impoverishes man, and hastens his death. Likewise, Master Ralph of Acton, in one of his discourses, specifies three evil effects of drunkenness: "First, it deranges man's senses: secondly, it alienates the mind: thirdly, it excites to shameful and improper things".[3] For illustration of the first point, we have only to turn to John Bromyard's amusing little sketch of "the topers who imagine that they see two candles, where there is only one". Thinking that one will be sufficient for them, they blow out what they fancy to be the other, only to find themselves plunged in darkness. Then, filled with astonishment, they say—"Where is the other candle?"[4] A sermon, probably delivered at Worcester, gives us a similar scene in vigorous English—*cum additamentis*:

Also glotenie maketh a man or a womman nat onliche blynd bodiliche but also gostliche. Vor it bryngeth him, as we se wel, anon rith in to drunkunhode, and t[h]anne i sei he is blynd. Thow a now se thre candeles, ȝe, thre mones ther a nother man seth but on, ȝit i seye he is blynd. How truliche a may nat se what is good and what is evel!...I pray the, is nat t[h]is a grete blendnes, thynkis te, whan a man hath sete ate nale hows or ate taverne alday,—ȝe, nat onliche alday, but also meche of the nith t[h]erto,—and ate laste cumth hom as drunke as a dosel,[5] and chit his wyf, reprevith his children, bet his meyne, ȝe, unnethe a kan go to bedde but as a his browth t[h]erto with his servauntes hondis![6]

[1] *Cat.* pp. 131–2. Cf. also in print, *Hand. Synne*, pp. 37, 210–3.
[2] Cf. MS. Arund. 231, vol. ii, fol. 52b. For preachers abroad, cf. Hauréau, *Not. et Extr.* vol. iv, p. 217 (fr. Hugh, Domin. 13th cent.).
[3] MS. Jo. Ryl. Libr. Manch. Lat. 367, fol. 104b. Cf. also *Ayenb. of Inwyt*, p. 248. [4] *S.P.* s.v. "Misericordia".
[5] Apparently, the spigot or faucet of a barrel. I have not met with the expression elsewhere.
[6] MS. Worc. Cath. Libr. F. 10, fol. 43b. At the request of the Cath. Librarian (Rev. Canon J. E. H. Blake), this passage, with some of its context, was supplied in modern spelling for the *Worc. Dioc. Gazette*, vol. xxxiii, Nov. 1926, pp. 207–9. With the last sentence, cf. *Piers Plowman*, A text, pass. v, ll. 208–9 ("With al the wo of this world, his wyf and his wenche/beerin him hom to his bed, and brouhten him ther-inne"). See also *Man. des Pechiez*, E.E.T.S. O.S. 119, p. 210.

Sometimes this optical delusion, bred of the ale-house and the wine-cup, apparently could take an even more disastrous turn. Sermon-stories are not wanting which tell how the drunkard returns home late from the tavern to his wife and two children who are sitting around the hearth awaiting him. Seeing what appear to him to be no less than four children in front of him, he angrily asks his wife who the other two may be. When she affirms that there is none but his own two present, he straightway accuses her of lying and adultery. Having done her to death, and the two sons also in a fit of rage, he recovers later from the effects of intoxication only to hang himself in despair, when the truth has dawned upon his mind.[1] In another tale of the kind, the sequel is pleasanter. The raging husband in this case insists on the alternatives of death or purging by ordeal for the unfortunate woman. Picking up a plough-share he puts it on the fire, and, when it is red-hot, says to his wife: "Hold this iron in your hand immediately; or else you shall die by torture!" She, with exquisite presence of mind, replies: "Sir, since it must be so, hand me the glowing iron to hold". He, out of his rustic wits with drink, takes grip of the fiery metal with bare hand, to give it to her—"and lo! his hand was so burnt thereby that for a long while after he could do nothing with it, while his spouse remained uninjured".[2] Thus the monster had his deserts, and the preacher's audiences, doubtless, their subsequent laughter: and for ourselves—what clearer anticipation of the future scenes of Tudor low-comedy? Certainly no temperance orator of Protestant times ever painted in more lurid, realistic colours the drunkard's homecoming than did our medieval homilists. In the few but well-chosen phrases of sermon after sermon we watch this "rake's progress" as in some pictorial series of Hogarth. Among the more entertaining caricatures is one which actually gives us the medieval equivalent of the street lamp-post, to wit, the village cross:

And assuredly, gluttons and drunkards are sometimes so blinded and befogged with the wine which they have imbibed to excess that they fail

[1] See *Spec. Laic.* ed. Welter, p. 44.
[2] MS. Roy. 7. D. 1, fol. 131 (13th-cent. Engl. Domin. collection): also in *Spec. Laic.* as before, p. 45.

to recognize their own wives and children; and, when they leave the tavern to go to their own homes close by, so benighted are they on this account, that the broad highway where three waggons could pass and meet them seems to them like a narrow foot-path. Moreover, they are blinded, because, whenever they catch sight of any tree or cross in their road, they believe that they see a man or a robber.[1]

Says another, in much the same strain:

And ofte as thei goth homward toward hire beddes, thei drencheth hemself in dichis bi the weie. And thou3 thei comen hoom into hire chambre, thei leteth the candel falle and brenne hire bed, hemself and hir wyfe, hire children and alle hire godes....Ne unnethe knoweth [the drunkard] any of his dedis whiche he dide to-dai, so clene is his mynde waschen aweie with a litil drynke.[2]

And a third:

ffor, thu1gh glotenye, haveth y-be ofte men y-perysched. For what is fouler than a dronken man? For evere he is redy for to fy3te, to chyde and to other sickenesse for to do. ffor glotenye is y-cleped maister of synne; for a man that is ytake with glotenye may withstonde no man that wolde do him yvel.[3]

Behold him, then, as he stumbles out of the tavern door—"smerte to yvel weyes goynge, the hondes redy to blood-schedynge, the wombe in lecherye brennynge, the ey3en to vanytees and ydelnesse lokynge, and the herte to wyckede thynkynge".[4] Well might the penitent confess on the morrow:

> Whil 3at i was sobre
> Sinne ne dede i nowht;
> But in drunkeschipe i dede
> 3e werste 3at mihten ben thowht.[5]

But what, on the other hand, if the morrow found our toper of yesterday in no repentant mood? A further homiletic

---

[1] MS. Add. 21253, fol. 8. Cf. in Hauréau, *Not. et Extr.* vol. iii, p. 342 ("Ebrii,...quando descendunt in tabernam faciliter descendunt; sed, quando exeunt via eis stricta est"—and they get bumped about like well-buckets).

[2] MS. Add. 41321, fol. 97b. (This homilist here quotes "Doctour Lync." (i.e. Grossetête) on the same subject.) Similarly in MS. Harl. 2398, fol. 33: "And ofte men seeth dronken men a-drenche hemself in water, and ofte sleeth hemself in other maners. Some brenne hemselfe and here childrene and here owene house".

[3] MS. Harl. 2398, fol. 32.   [4] Ibid. fol. 33.

[5] MS. Harl. 2316, fol. 15. Cf. MS. Bodl. 95, fol. 80 (Drunkenness leads to lechery, and "unclennes in beddes"); etc.

passage based on the *Somme le Roi* enables us to follow up his career, when, like Langland's *Glotoun*, at length he "wakes from his winking and wipes his eyes", asking as his first question—"Wher is the cuppe?"[1]

God biddeth hym aryse erliche out of his bed and goo to chirche to the servise of God. The wombe seith "Nay: that may not be doo! ffor I am so foul of mete and drinke undefied[2] that I mote abide til I have swet and bettir slept; ffor the chirche wole abide in to that I come".[3] And whan suche oon...gynneth to ryse of his bed, he bygynneth not to seie his matynes or other prayers. But anone he asketh what he schal ete and what he schal drynke, and whether eny suche mete may be founde, or drinke....After matyns he gynneth laudes thus—"Lorde", he seith, "that we hadde ʒister day [was] good mete and good drinke!" And after ward he wexith sory[4] and seith thus—"The wyn that we drank to-nyght was so stronge that it hath made myne heed ake alle this nyght, that I was nyghe dede, and am ʒit as hevy as leed; and myn heed is so dasy that I am noght of myght to goo ne ryde none weies, till I have dronke ones or twyes"....

This synne schameth moche a man and bynemeth[5] him his good name. ffor ofte suche bycometh taverne-goers and afterward dys-pleyers, and sithen they beth-comen wrecches and harlottes and useth many vilenyes. And ʒit thei beth-come ofte leccherous, and after that theves and rob-boures, and at the laste beth taken for thefte and an-honged. And this is the ende that this synne ledeth a man to.[6]

So, finally, the sermons bring us to the drunkard's deathbed, with that wealth of anecdote which those concerned so inti-mately with the last hours of the dying were well able to amass. Bromyard can speak at second hand from the testimony of a friend:[7]

---

1 *Piers Plowman*, A text, pass. v, ll. 212–33; etc.   2 = undigested.
3 Cf. above, p. 44.   4 = sorrowful.   5 = takes away.
6 MS. Harl. 45, fol. 138. Similarly, *Ayenb. of Inwyt*, p. 51, and *Jacob's Well*, p. 141. Cf. the similar list of resultant evils in *Old Engl. Homs. of the Twelfth Century*, E.E.T.S. O.S. no. 53, pp. 11 and 212–13; and in a poem in Chambers and Sidgwick, *E.E. Lyrics*, p. 224.
7 Cf. further two similar tales in the *Spec. Laic.* as before, p. 46, etc. One, printed from a Thoms MS. in Haupt and Hoffmann, *Altdeutsche Blätter*, vol. ii (1840), p. 79, is of a dying Kentish drunkard—"in tempore dom. regis Henrici III"—who can only mumble "couppe, couppe!" to the priest. "Et sic sacerdos tedio affectus recessit, et ille miser pre nimia sumpcione potus crepuit medius et mortuus est." The other, also in MS. Roy. 7. D. i, fol. 131, tells of the dying toper only roused by a crony's offer to drink his health (" *Wesseyl*, vicine, *wesseyl!* ").

When a certain man of the kind was enfeebled unto death, in a town well enough known, and was visited by the good vicar who related the story to me, the latter admonished him to confession and communion, but could get no other response from him than this—"Good ale! good ale!" And when those present made mention of the priest to him, in the hope that he might alter his remarks, he said—"Has the priest brought me some good ale or a good drink?"

A peep into Hell, no doubt, would reveal him now amongst those "who drink of another cup, of which fire and sulphur are part".[1]

"Drunkenesse", then "is modir of vices." Upon this point the verdict of the pulpit is clear and emphatic. "For whan man is overcomen with drynk, where ben his wittis thanne? He farith as it were a queynt[2] candle, and as he were deed in donge. His wit and resoun is drenchid in draftis.... Bi the mevyng[3] of the feend thei hav difformed Goddis ymage, that graciousli is ʒoven to man, bi walewyng in the foule, thicke plud of drunkenesse, as unwitti and drunken swyn."[4] Not only is it "a wilfulle woodnesse, of the whiche cometh man-slawter, spousebreche, and many other mescheves",[5] "bot more wrecchednesse ʒut comyth therof. ffor it maketh the peple that is riche pore. It discovereth a mannys consaile: ffor, ther that dronkenesse regneth, ther may no thyng be pryvy ne derne".[6] Bromyard reminds men significantly of the common proverb— "Wine and Confession reveal all things", and sermon-stories seek to illustrate it by telling how the thief in a state of

---

[1] S.P. s.v. "Ebrietas."

[2] = quenched (as in Lydgate).   [3] = moving.

[4] MS. Harl. 2276, fol. 36 b. Cf. similarly Old Engl. Homs. (12th cent.), E.E.T.S. O.S. no. 53, p. 37; and MS. Add. 41321, fol. 69, where they are likened to the wild boar (see above, p. 197).

[5] Cf. here the story of the priest (or hermit), who, bidden to choose one of three sins, chooses drunkenness as the least heinous and finds that it leads to the other two (rape and murder), in Spec. Laic. p. 45; also Holcot in MS. Roy. 7. C. I, fol. 117; MS. Harl. 2316, fol. 15; MS. Add. 6716, fol. 49 b, col. 2; MS. Add. 27909 b, fol. 5 b (13th cent.): printed in Wright, Lat. Stories, pp. 83 and 235 (no. 97). A series of pictures illustrating the tale occurs in MS. Roy. 10. E. iv, fols. 113 b–8 b (lower margins). Another warning tale against drinking and tavern-haunting is told in MS. Burn. 361, fol. 155 b (= Spec. Laic. p. 46, no. 210).

[6] MS. Harl. 2398, fols. 32 b and 33 (derne = secret).

intoxication betrays himself, or how the drunken wife of a murderer once betrayed her own husband.[1] Nor is the full tale of woe yet told. For, "of dronkenesse cometh warre, pestilence and hunger. For, ther-as dronkenesse and glotenye regnyth, ther falleth most suche dyverse pereles".[2] In short, like the other vices with which we have dealt, it has a wider social bearing beyond the mere limits of the individual, his family, or his own home. It, too, helps to disturb the realm and impoverish the nation both materially and spiritually. As we might well expect in the case of a learned University theologian and a canonist, a man of travel and affairs, the author of the *Summa Predicantium* gives particular heed to these larger implications of the vice. With praiseworthy courage and insight, he enlarges upon "the manifold frauds, plots and conspiracies for thefts, false witness and the like hatched" in the taverns, "the many things which the Devil makes a man promise under the influence of drink, which he revokes when sober", upon the foolish judgments and sentences passed, the inordinate counsels given, "as in the case of those who hold their parliaments, their councils and trials, after they have been heated with wine". He complains that, in contrast to Seneca's story[3] of the woman who appealed successfully from Philip drunk to Philip sober, if the modern tipplers make any ruthless ordinance, while in that state, for the devastation of their subjects, it is in no wise revoked. Whereas, any solace thus decreed is subsequently ignored. He tells how others are induced by the same curse to make unjust apportionment of the goods of God, so that "while one goes hungry, another is drunk".[4] Who, indeed, can wonder at it! For, "intrat potus, exit sensus". "And not only does it lead to sins, but it also damages the reputation.[5] Because, just as it gives a man a foul breath in the morning, so it gives him a foul reputation with God and all good men. For every good man loves such per-

---

[1] Cf. *Spec. Laic.* p. 46, no. 211; etc. [2] MS. Harl. 2398, fol. 33.
[3] Also in MS. Harl. 7322, fol. 91 (narrat Valerius).
[4] 1 Cor. xi, 21. Bromyard adds here—"sic de pannis, sic de pecuniis, sic de omnibus aliis bonis".
[5] Cf. above, p. 430, MS. Harl. 45, fol. 138.

sons the less for it,...and they are laughed at by everybody."
Finally, that which can play such havoc in the State is likewise
a menace to the Church: "The priest and the prophet have
been ignorant through drunkenness; they are swallowed up
with wine; they have gone astray in drunkenness".[1] Did time
permit, we might well listen further to this astute preacher as
he deals one by one with the idle excuses of the intemperate.
Some, who have committed a crime in a drunken fit, can only
cry piteously to the one who later reprimands them—"Spare
me, my lord; drunkenness made me do that!" There are those
who seek to defend the habit by arguing that the occasional
folly of the drunkard is as nothing when compared for example
with that of the perpetually fatuous serfs.[2] Others put forward
as their excuse that they have bought the drink and therefore
must consume it, or that their imbibing never does any hurt
to their neighbours. "He does not drink to excess who damages
no one", they say. Others, again, protest that their orgies are
rare and exceptional occurrences, or that the instigation of
society and of their friends invariably proves too strong for
them. The last-named Bromyard declares to be worse than the
irrational animals, that at no man's urge will take more drink
than is good for them. His reproof is repeated by one whose
homely words suggest an audience of simple country-folk:

We mown lerne sobrenesse aftir ensaumple of dyverse beestis out of
resoun. For, take good heede to an oxe or to an asse, and thou shal not
fynde hem drunke. For these beestis eten not but whan thei hungren;
nor thei drynken not but whan thei ben athriste. But we mai se many
men ofte tymes foule drunke and gluttid with dyverse lusti metis out of
resoun.[3]

[1] Isaiah xxviii, 7 (as quoted here by Bromyard). On this subject, see
further in my *Preaching in Med. Engl.* pp. 31, 32, 33, 39, 40, 108, 125,
250; etc.

[2] Bromyard's reply is—"Non: quia isti frequenter et gratis sensus
amittunt; illi semel et inviti".

[3] MS. Harl. 2276, fol. 36b. Cf. the sermon-story of Master Walter,
in MS. Roy. 7. D. 1, fol. 131b, given in my *Preaching in Med. Engl.*
p. 193. It illustrates both the "instantia amicorum" and the good example
of animals. Similarly in Hauréau, *Not. et Extr.* vol. iii, p. 341, quoting
the French proverb: "Menez le buef à l'iaue, ja ne buvera si n'a soif"
(repeated again, vol. iv, p. 174). This well-known saying occurs also,
in another context, in *Old Engl. Homs.* E.E.T.S. O.S. no. 29, p. 9.

The Dominican has hopes of correcting some at least of the guilty by reminding them of the well-known fate of fellow-drunkards, whom death met by the way with despair and damnation. However, for those "so blinded by that sin that they fear neither infamy, nor hell-pains", he will furnish another kind of warning.[1] Let them beware of the impoverishment of worldly goods that so often follows from it in this life,[2] of "the paralysis, blindness, headaches and many inconveniences", the bad taste in the mouth, the trembling of the body, derangement of the mind, transformation of the face, quivering of the tongue, and all the other physical ills that intemperance produces![3]

Let us return now from these moral digressions to our original study of the hero of Langland's tavern scene as revealed to us in the sermons. Thus far we have been concerned almost entirely with his unfortunate career from the moment when he set out homeward from the tavern door. But what of the scene in the tavern itself? To say that Langland here "presents the veritable interior of an English ale-house in the fourteenth century, with all its basenesses and its gross hilarity",[4] may suffice for one who is capable of telling us later that the author of this part of the *Vision* "exhibits no special theological knowledge or interests" and "may have been a layman".[5] Those, however, who have adequate acquaintance with the rich

[1] "Ideo istam penam post precedentes posui, quia plus apud mundiales timetur", he explains. Cf. again, above, p. 421.
[2] "Saltem timeant rerum et bonorum diminutionem quam ex ebrietate consequi optime vident." The *Spec. Laic.* mentions similarly, as the fourth good product of *Abstinentia*—"diviciarum accumulacio".
[3] *S.P.* s.v. "Ebrietas".
[4] Prof. J. M. Manly, in *Camb. Hist. of Engl. Lit.* vol. ii, p. 16, as before.
[5] Ibid. p. 35 (a definition of "*A*" is on p. 31). Manly's argument here, as in his handling of Chaucer, is vitiated throughout by this kind of naïve error. Obviously, unless one knows intimately the "social, theological and various" other ideas of the time and comes to the poem soaked in the contemporary language of expression, the characteristic phrases, imagery and arguments of the popular literature of religion, such misunderstanding is bound to occur. However, this is no place in which to discuss the Professor's main thesis in detail, although I propose to do so on a future occasion.

homiletic background of the poem are not likely to rest content with so facile an interpretation. In the literature of the medieval English pulpit, the tavern and the ale-house, apart from the acknowledged fact that they are the occasion of much gluttony and drunkenness in the ordinary way,[1] stand for a very definite menace to the common weal. They have established themselves as deadly rivals to the ordinances of the Church, to the keeping of holydays and fast days, above all to attendance at divine service. Thus, leaving aside for the moment all satirical treatment of the theme, we read in straightforward fashion in the sermons of Master Rypon, for example, how that "in this time of Lent, when by the law and custom of the Church men fast, very few people abstain from excessive drinking: on the contrary, they go to the taverns, and some imbibe and get drunk more than they do out of Lent, thinking and saying—'Fishes *must* swim!'"[2] And again:

> Most of all on feast days, also for the nights following, they go off to the taverns, and more often than not seek food such as salt beef or a salted herring to excite a thirst for drink.[3] At length they get so intoxicated that they fall to ribaldries, obscenities and idle talk, and sometimes to brawls, by reason of which they fight amongst themselves, sometimes mutilating and killing each other. Such ill deeds, in truth, follow from drunkenness and gluttony.[4]

Thereafter, on the morrow when he has come to, "suche a man seith he may not faste, ne do penaunce, ne be at chirche to praye and worschip God; ffor he seith that he hath an yvel heed. (And ther-fore he seith soth: for he hath made it yvel!)"[5] It is a vicious circle, giving little chance of escape to its victims; and earlier preachers of Langland's own day denounce the habit in no less vehement terms. Bishop Brunton of Rochester for example makes the same complaint of Feast-day drunken-

[1] Cf. MS. Camb. Univ. Libr. Gg. vi. 16, fol. 57 ("occasion off glotonye and drunkunschep is offten goynge to the taverne or to the alehows and offte drynkynge"), and *Old Engl. Homs.* E.E.T.S. O.S. no. 53, p. 11.

[2] MS. Harl. 4894, fol. 43b. Similarly in MS. Harl. 45, fol. 139, the "drynkeres and ryatoures"—"seie that men may noght faste (and there thei lyen falseliche)...".

[3] Bromyard also refers to this habit, s.v. "Trinitas," § 17.

[4] fol. 28.

[5] MS. Harl. 45, fol. 139 (similarly *Ayenb. of Inwyt*, p. 51; etc.).

ness.[1] Waldeby[2] and Bromyard[3] tell again how the tavern
hinders God's service and cuts short the very sermon; while,
earlier still, Archbishop Fitzralph reminds us in one of his
pulpit discourses that, even when once safely inside the holy
place, our toper, like brother *Sleuthe*,[4] may yet "have his
tongue in the church, and his soul in the tavern".[5] Here Sloth
and Gluttony, indeed, go hand in hand to the same spot, even
if they happen that day to have been to church in the morning
—"soone aftir [mete], at the ale, bollyng[6] and synginge, with
many idil wordis, as lesinggis, bacbitingis and scornyngis,
sclaundris, yvel castingis with al the countenaunce of leccherie,
chidingis and fiȝtingis, with many other synnes, makinge the
holi daye a synful daye".[7] Whereas, the proper duty "aftir
mete", on such occasions, we are told, is to "visite them that
ben sike and in myschef, and speciali tho that God hath mad
nedi, other bi age or bi syknes, as pore feble, pore crokid and
poor lame",[8] or else "go afterwardes to the sermon, if ther
eny be".[9] "Thurgh that synne" of "Slewthe", says another—

it fallyth that a man forsakyth his gostlyche goedys and desireth fleschlyche
lustes, and with-oute devocioun and with lite[10] redynge other syngynge
other biddynge his bedys, nouȝt recchynge in what manere he passyth
forth the day; and delyteth him more in ydelnesse and in syngyng at
the nale[11] for to be ypreysed of men, more than for to go to churche and
worschipe God.... And it makyth him dredful eny thyng to suffre for

1 MS. Harl. 3760, fol. 110b.
2 Cf. MS. Caius Coll. Camb. 334, as quoted in my *Preaching in Med.
Engl.* p. 178.
3 Cf. *S.P.* s.v. "Feriae seu Festa", as quoted in my *Preaching in Med.
Engl.* p. 179; and s.v. "Gula" ("...in cibis vel potationibus *et tabernis*
sedentes, ad cibum anime ire nolunt..."), "Audire verba Dei"; etc.
4 *Piers Plowman*, as quoted here, below. Cf. further "Glotonye",
B text, ll. 92–6, etc.
5 MS. Lansd. 393, fol. 27b (*Sermo in processione...in vulgari*, A.D.
1345). Cf. further, e.g., a story of tavern-haunting on Fast-days, in the
13th-cent. *Spec. Laic.* cap. i, ed. Welter, pp. 5–6 (St Edmund Rich).
6 = drinking (cf. boller = a drunkard, *Town. Myst.*).
7 MS. St Albans Cath. fol. 19. Cf. the warning in *Hand. Synne*, p. 37.
8 Ibid. fol. 22.
9 MS. Bodl. 95, fol. 106b: similarly in the poem of the Vernon MS.
quoted in my *Preaching in Med. Engl.* p. 145.
10 = little.   11 = ale-house.

Godes love, as fastynge or wolwarde[1] goynge, other goynge in pilgrymage, or eny goede werkes.

...Men and women synnyth in sleuthe when they ne kepyth nouȝt come atte churche upon holy dayes, and when they ne attendeth nat to here bedys-byddynge, in hurynge of masse and matyns, and when they ne entendeth nat to here prechynge and techynge. (Also sleuthe maketh a man to make noyse and ianglenge in holy churche.)[2]

It will now be clear enough that no mere poet's idle fancy decreed that *Glotoun* should set forth in the *Vision* on a "Fastyng daye", upon that fatal outing which landed him in the tavern, with "holi chirche" as his original goal—"for to here Masse". The very situation, as a pulpit commonplace, is actually provided by John Bromyard in his *Summa*: "Volentes ire ad verbum Dei [diaboli] ducunt ad tabernam".[3] Nor shall we fail to understand likewise why his ready yielding to temptation cost him not only his Friday Evensong but all his Sunday devotions. As for *Sleuthe*, let the poet himself repeat in his own verses what the homilists have just told us:

And ȝif I bidde any bedes, but if it be in wrath,
That I telle with my tonge is two myle fro myne herte.
I am occupied eche day, haliday and other,
With ydel tales atte ale,[4] and otherwhile in cherches:
Goddes peyne and his passioun ful selde thynke I there-on.
I visited nevere fieble men, ne fettered folke in puttes,
I have levere here an harlotrie, or a somer-game of souteres,
Or lesynges to laughe at and belye my neighbore,
Than al that evere Marke made, Mathew, John and Lucas:
And vigilies and fastyng-dayes, alle thise late I pass.[5]

To the voice of Complaint thus raised against the taverns, the pulpit added the voice of Satire. Without having recourse to earlier models in continental preaching of the thirteenth

---

[1] I.e. "without any lynnen nexte ones body, *sans chemyse*" (as a penance).

[2] MS. Harl. 2398, fols. 27–27b. I am fully prepared to believe that the original text of this and the previously quoted MS. may be later than the two earlier versions of the *Vision*. But their arguments can be traced back at least a century, in the ways I have already indicated elsewhere, in homiletic literature.

[3] *S.P.* s.v. "Audire (verb. Dei)". Under "Gula", he mentions also the tempting in of passers-by.   [4] =ale-house.

[5] *Piers Plowman*, B text, pass. v, ll. 407–16. Cf. further, in his confession, ll. 456–62 ("Shal none ale after mete holde me thennes").

century,[1] the reader may find in dan Michel's *Ayenbite of Inwyt*, completed at Canterbury in the year 1340, a typical example which must have enjoyed considerable popularity in this country.[2] It pictures the tavern as the Devil's School, where his disciples study, also as the Devil's Chapel, where his services are held and his special miracles wrought. Says our monkish homilist, God works miracles in the church, making the blind to see, the crooked to walk, the mad to be sane, the dumb to speak, the deaf to hear, and so forth. So likewise, in the tavern the Devil performs his marvels. The glutton, who goes in upright, comes out unable to stand. He who goes in in full possession of his wits leaves like one lost and demented, unable to speak or comprehend anything. As for the lessons which he is taught in that "school-house", they are gluttony, lechery, swearing and forsweaing, lying, slandering, the denial of God, evil tales, quarrelling and many other sins of the kind. Strifes, debates, murders spring up there. There, too, men learn to steal and to hang. "The taverne is a dich to thieves, and the dyeules castel vor to werri God and his halȝen;[3] and tho thet the tavernes sustyeneth byeth velaȝes[4] of alle the zennen[5] that byeth ydo ine hare tavernes." Often where later homilists make use of these figures—generally that of the Diabolic Church—they follow the regular practice of their art by filling in for themselves further details of the scene, such as the rude pot-house songs, snatches of lewd conversation from the bench of cronies, the low tricks played amongst this fellowship of Satan. Thus, for example—

when that good men ben at ther servyce on the halydaye, than the [glotons] sitt faste in the devels servyce, with many rybald wordes and songes of lecherie, blasfemynge God with many grett othes,...and ilk besy to begyle othur with many qweynte sleyȝthes.[6] So thei forȝett God

---

[1] E.g. the *Somme le Roi* (see Ch.-V. Langlois, *La Vie en France au moy. âge*, vol. iv, p. 166.

[2] See edit. R. Morris, E.E.T.S. pp. 56–7 (Mätzner, *Altengl. Sprachpr.* p. 107). Similarly, in MS. Harl. 45, fol. 143, MS. Bodl. 95, fol. 80, and *Jacob's Well*, pp. 147–8 (beginning of a sermon *de gula*); etc. Cf. abroad, Meffret, as given in Coulton, *Five Cent. of Relig.* vol. i, p. 531, n. 2.

[3] = saints.   [4] = fellows, companions.

[5] = sins.   [6] = cunning tricks.

and all goodenes, and becomes the devells children for to dwell with hym with-owten ende.[1]

And 3it more sorowe is, these costomable lechours, when age suffreth hem no lenger to the dedus of unclennes, 3it woll thei than synge and make bost at ther owne lewdnes in lechery; 3e, and tell more therof at the taverne than ever he tolde othur thenketh to telle to is confessour [all the] dayes of is liff. And by this evell ensampull of old men, 3onge men spare not for no drede of God, nothur thei leve not for no shame of the worlde to renne to here lechery with a like desire, as a bere renneth to ete hony.[2]

Another quaint vernacularist, preaching in the same strain, has a more uncommon comparison of his own to offer us in place of the Devil's Church. After rehearsing the habits of the bittern,[3] he likens that bird to the

glotons sittynge in the taverne, puttynge hire mouthes into the bolle, til thei ben drunke. Thenne thei crien with grete voice, boostynge, swerynge, lyynge and slaunderynge, and al hire evele dedes which thei have doun of many 3eres afore freschli rehercynge and reioisynge. But suche men sittynge in the drie cherche bi hire confessour, fer fro the taverne, for to schryve her synnes, sitten as dombe and wolen speke no word.[4]

Bromyard, for his part, chooses the simile of the fowler.

For, as the fowler strives to gather the birds together into one place to ensnare and catch them there, so the Devil gathers many to the tavern, where out of twenty scarce one or two escape who could say—"The snare is broken, and we are delivered" (Psalm cxxiii); because all are ensnared, some by excessive drinking, some by foul speech and ditties, immodest looks, illicit oaths, lusts, and impure and vain narratives, some by lechery and incest,...some by murder,...some by tumult, debate and the revealing of secrets,...some by falsity,

and so forth.[5] All this, indeed, brings us very near to the atmosphere of Langland's immortal den of rogues. But there is extant a homiletic tract in English on the Ten Command-

[1] MS. Roy. 18. B. xxiii, fol. 85.
[2] Ibid. fol. 133. On their evil influence over others, cf. again, MS. Harl. 45, fol. 139: "These glotonous, leccherous drynkeres and ryatoures, amonge alle other synnes, thei doth oo synne that is cleped the develes maistres, that is, with-drawynge of other men from alle manere goodnes..." (viz. from fasting); and *Hand. Synne*, pp. 262–3.
[3] See above, p. 202.   [4] MS. Add. 41321, fol. 98b.
[5] *S.P.* s.v. "Ebrietas". Cf. also the ale-house "realism" in *The Southern Passion*, E.E.T.S. O.S. no. 169, p. 71, with the editor's comment (p. xv). Ps. cxxiii, 7, above, is the *Vulgate* reference (= A.V. cxxiv).

ments, bearing the name of a Dominican recluse of the fifteenth century as its author or scribe,[1] which brings us nearer to it still, in substance as well as spirit. Although here preserved in a manuscript of much later date than Langland's *Vision*, the tavern scene which this tract presents is none the less sufficient to establish a definite link with the early thirteenth-century tavern scene in the *Songe d'Enfer* of Raoul de Houdenc, a didactic poet already mentioned in our discussion of the *Pilgrim's Progress*.[2] For, in both cases the characters infesting the tavern are the vices personified and still bear their names. In view of the examples already given, then, this late survival in English homiletic literature—of what indeed has already been recognized in its French dress as a possible prototype of the equivalent scene in *Piers Plowman*[3]—we may safely take to be itself merely another survival of numerous earlier pulpit efforts of the kind in this country. Its author, who has his own faculty for picturesque language, begins by upbraiding those, whom he addresses later as—"ʒe devilles portures!", with the usual admixture of satire and rebuke:

Bot ʒe salle undurstande, ʒe wyn and ale sitteris, and ʒe displeers and hasardurus, that spenden the halyday in gloteny and in waste,—and woon of ʒow destrith that wolde susteyne mony mesurable men, in the luste of glotene,—and alleso wastith ʒoure good and other mennes to, and maketh ʒowre baly ʒowre go(o)d and ʒowre chirche the taverne....

Unlike the other homilists that we have quoted, however, he goes on to depict the entry—not of *Glotoun* alone, but all the Seven Deadly Sins, one by one, into that Devil's Conventicle:

Lo, ʒe glotonus and wastures of mannes sustinans, heer[4] ʒe mowe here[5] that Go(o)d warieth[6] ʒow, and ʒowre maystur the wicked spirit gladeth ʒow and biddith ʒow alle be mery and glad. "For this wol make ʒow men", he saith, "and I wol rewarde ʒow in tyme to comynge for ʒowre ocupacion."
Therwith cometh in Pride and settith him in the middel of alle; and

---

[1] MS. St John's Coll. Oxf. 94, edited, as *A Middle-Engl. Treatise on the Ten Commandments*, by J. F. Royster, Studies in Philol. No. vi, Univ. of North Carolina, and written by a Domin. friar, "Jon Lacy, anchor", at Newcastle-upon-Tyne, A.D. 1434.   [2] See above, p. 104.
[3] See Miss D. L. Owen, *Piers Plowman*, 1912, pp. 51 and 139.
[4] = here.   [5] = hear.   [6] = curseth.

than he beginneth to boste and ruson[1] him self of many thinges that he hath not, ne kowde, and alle saien it is sooth. Then Covetise herith that, and than cometh he in boldely and he cherith tham alle; and anoon he biginneth for to bargen, and then lacketh not gret othes and sweringes, and than is ich of tham abowte to begyle other. Then cometh in Lechere, and he lokuth al abowthe the hows, and then he settith him downe on the benche; and then beginneth he to speke and bringe in oolde storius of wemen and of lustus and ribaldry, and faste he rusith himself of olde synnes, and alle lauȝen and been glad to here his prechinge. Than cometh in Glotone, the stuard of that howsolde, and he cherith tham alle, and bidithe tham sitte stille and be mery and glad, so that noon of ȝow [sic!] go hoom bot it be so he be sad, or a staf in his hoonde for fallynge. Than Slowthe herith this mawndement, that is the marchel of that halle, and then he overloketh tham alle; and then he chargeth Idulnes to cheren tham alle and to sitte stille, and that the cuppe be not empte ne tume.[2] Than, at the laste ende, comith in Wrath, and he bringeth with him Envye, and rekunneth ther acunthes,[3] for that he is tresureer of that howsoolde. He chargeth that noon of hem parte from other in charite. "And loke", he saith, "wen that ȝever ȝe com togedur, that noon speke good of other, ne of ȝowre neiȝbures." And then saide thai alle "Amen".[4]

So we return once more to the moment when, with the homilists' aid, we beheld the medieval ale-house give up its prey, a hell of earth from whose leering jaws the victims escape for a little into the night. In a solemn *Monitio* of the year 1401,[5] the historian may discern further some signs that preacher and poet had not failed wholly to re-awaken the national Church to a sense of this evil in her midst. At all events, with the medieval preachers' cry still ringing in our ears—"Lef thi sittyng atte a nale hous; lef thi goyng to the taverne!"[6]—it becomes a little easier to understand the subsequent zeal of Reformation Puritanism in this direction.

Our study of medieval intemperance will have already

---

[1] = extol, boast.   [2] = light, empty.   [3] = accounts.
[4] fol. 123 et seq.; ed. Royster, pp. 21–3.
[5] (ex reg. Arund.) See Wilkins, *Concilia*, vol. iii, p. 266 ("in diebus dominicis colitur taberna potius quam ecclesia, comessationes, ebrietates et negotiationes abundant et frequentantur"). The words of this enactment have been copied into the bottom margin of Jo. of Mirfield's *Flor. Barthol.* in MS. Camb. Univ. Libr. Mm. ii. 10, fol. 50b ("Sed hodie in quadam Constit. Provinc. aliter provisum est et statutum in hiis verbis...").
[6] MS. Worc. Cath. Libr. F. 10, fol. 44.

revealed the fact that this vice is closely linked in homiletic lore with that of gluttony in the more modern and restricted sense of the term. Indeed, it is under the heading of *Gula* that many of the preceding quotations are to be found. The same is true also of the tavern: "for, this synne is ofte i-do in tavernes; ffor that is cleped the welle of glotonye".[1] Even the same kind of imagery is used for both vices in common, as when Bromyard speaks further of "those gluttonous priests of Bel", who serve the god of their belly[2] in the temple of the cookhouse or the tavern "at the altar of the table spread for them with the odour of incense, that is, with the savour of meats".[3] In considering this subject of gluttony, then, the student may well use for his poetic parallel that opening section of the *Pardoners Tale* which has already furnished him with a representation of the drunkard, so obviously modelled, for all its added humour and roguery, on current homiletic lines. Not only has the poet here made use of Bromyard's simile of "the develes temple",[4] but his Pardoner's complaints concerning extravagance in food likewise follow the preachers' example. This latter is well illustrated in the case of one whose complaint carries us back to the denunciations of changing fashion in dress, with its story of primitive simplicity and subsequent excess, and the ill effects of all this modern luxury upon the character of the race. Says he:

ffor, at the begynnynge of the worlde mannys fode was bot brede and water, and now sufficeth nouȝt to glotenye alle the fruytes of treene, of alle rotes, of alle herbes, of alle bestes, of alle foules, of alle fysches of the see. Now mote men ordeyne pyemente, clarye, vernage, creet[5] and other dyvers confecciouns. The metys schul be y-sode with grete busynes and with craft of cokys, more for lykynge of mannys body than for susteynaunce of mannys kynde: ffor the kynde of man is lytel ther-with amendyd....[6]

[1] MS. Harl. 45, fol. 142. Cf. *Ayenb. of Inwyt*, p. 56, and *Jacob's Well*, p. 147.

[2] Cf. *Jacob's Well*, p. 141; *Ayenb. of Inwyt*, pp. 50, 248; etc. (Philipp. iii, 19).　　　　　　　　　　　　　　　　　[3] *S.P.* s.v. "Gula".

[4] *Cant. Tales*, Pardoners Tale, ll. 468–70.

[5] All these are the names of wines, some of them honeyed and spiced. (Cf. Warner, *Antiq. Culin.* etc.) The three first are all mentioned by Chaucer in his *Cant. Tales*.

[6] MS. Harl. 2398, fol. 31 b. Cf. here Chaucer, *Cant. Tales*, Pardoners Tale, ll. 537–48.

The reign of this latest epicureanism spelt not merely an elaboration of dishes and viands but also an elaboration of the meals themselves. "Merry Andrew's" prescription of two meals a day for the non-manual worker had clearly become insufficient long before the Tudor régime under which he lived; and the pulpit apparently would be inclined to disagree with Mr Salzman that "breakfast as a regular meal is little heard of" in the medieval period.[1] In the opening years of the fifteenth century, for example, Dr Lichfield, who attacks dainty and costly "metes"—"qwer homly met ar sufficient and holsom ynogh", has something quite definite to impart upon the matter. For, amongst the temptations of the voice of gluttony is one to eat "to sone or to erly". Thus "many men", we are told, "son after they are out of bed, thay eten and drynken with-oute nede but for lust. *Eccles.* x,[2] seys Salomon—' *Ve tibi terra, etc.*', 'Wo to the erthe of wom the king is a childe, and qwos princes eten erly'". "Wat tyme that a man demys as a childe, that is, to ete erly, and wilfully cheses to ete or drynke to erly", he executes his foul lust against reason. "Wo to siche a man! ffor, as the servauntes of God bygynen at morne to serve God after her connynge, so such glotons...begynen first at morne to thinke on hir wombe,...an[d] hastily they hyen hem qwat mete or drynke thay may come by: thay snacchen theron as hogges."[3] It was the "rere sopers and unmesurable late drynkyngs",[4] however, at the other end of the day, that raised the homilists' ire in a way that certainly puts the early morning breakfast of the Middle Ages into the background. These well-known extravagances may serve to remind our anxious generation that the modern "night-club" and "cabaret" are but a recrudescence of the habits of yesterday:

Also, right as a man may synne in over erliche etinge and drinkynge, right so he may synne in over-late soupers. Wherfore thilke men and women that useth to soupe late and longe, to wake on the nyght and waste the tyme in ydelnes and vanitee, wast and nicete, late goth to bedde

[1] See *Engl. Life in the Midd. Ages*, Oxford, 1926, p. 95.
[2] v. 16.
[3] MS. Roy. 8. C. 1, fol. 128b. Cf. further above, p. 430 (MS. Harl. 45, *Ayenb. of Inwyt* and *Jacob's Well*), and below, Bromyard, p. 446.
[4] MS. Harl. 2276, fol. 114b.

and late aryseth, thei synneth in many maneres. ffirste, for thei wasteth the tyme in grete ryot and foly, and turneth the tyme aȝenst kynde, that is to seie, the nyght in to the day and the day in to the nyght....But men schulde spende the day in good werkes and the nyȝt in the reste of the body, as nede asketh, and the remenant in prayer, worschippynge and thonkynge of God...Also, in suche wakynges, men useth many vanytees, as playenge at the chesse and at the tables, and in tellynge of many yvel tales, also lesynges and bakbitynges; and thus thei leseth her tyme and deserveth maugre,[1] and noght onliche greeveth God but also her owne soules.[2]

Rypon, who discerns another class of men, equally reprehensible, who turn day into night, taking their ease from morn till evening "in feastings and drinkings and other delights", then falling to work at nightfall—"as thieves commonly do", has a comment upon the former[3] which makes one think that, monk though he was, the looks of these gay night-revellers and diners-out were not unknown to him. Perhaps he had met them on the road returning from their revels, or later at the table, during one of his preaching expeditions around Durham or Finchale.[4] Seneca compares them, he says, to birds that fly around in the night; and well may he do so. For birds eat to grow fat, and when caught alive they are kept in dark cages and fed for the table. So likewise with the feeding of these "night-strollers and light-fleers":[5] the very fear of their fate imprints itself on their fat bodies; for "assuredly, as is often the case, such have a complexion paler than that

[1] = misfortune.
[2] MS. Harl. 45, fol. 139b. Similarly *Jacob's Well*, p. 142 ("rere soperys", etc.); *Ayenb. of Inwyt*, p. 52; *Hand. Synne*, p. 232; MS. Bodl. 95, fol. 37 ("reot" and "reer sopers"); etc.; and in verse, e.g. *Poem on the times*, c. 1388, in Wright, Rolls S. vol. i, p. 277; Fairholt, p. 48; etc. Cf. abroad a 12th-cent. sermon, in Hauréau, *Not. et Extr.* vol. ii, p. 305 (Geoffrey of Troyes).
[3] "Alii sunt qui vertunt noctem in diem...[see Job xvii, 12], illi qui totam noctem insompnes deducunt in suis excessibus, et in diebus dormiunt...." Cf. similarly Bromyard, *S.P.* s.v. "Dominatio", "Servire" ("in innaturalibus vigiliis de nocte et dormitationibus de die noxia et infelix *vacatio*. Noctem, inquit, vertunt in diem..."), etc.
[4] See in my *Preaching in Med. Engl.* p. 54, n. 3.
[5] Earlier he has remarked, following John iii, 20: "odiunt enim lucem, quia male agunt".

of the infirm, so that amongst the living their flesh is as the flesh of the dead".[1]

The medieval "rake's progress" in gluttony, indeed, is sketched for us in the sermons with a vividness not far behind that which told of the drunkard. In the realm of animal imagery he "is liknid to a bere, ffor two skilis. On is this: the bere hath alwei a talent in his tunge to serteyn metis, the whiche he lovith; and that makith him ofte licke his tunge, as experience schewith wel at the iȝe. Riȝt so a glotoun[2]. . . . And an other skile is this: the bere hath so gret talent to hony and deliȝt therto that, whan he comith to a place where he gessith to fynde a swarm of bees, he lickith awe[y] her hony that thei have so long traveilid aboute". So the glutton wastes the fruit of other men's labours.[3] This latter point proves that the vice had its important bearing on the whole social problem of rich and poor, a bearing, indeed, which those who expressly viewed society as a delicately adjusted system of mutually dependent parts could never afford to overlook. Hence the special enormity of those who "recken not what thei spende, so that her mouth be feed deliciousli. . . . Where is the reuthe of such men that thei shulden have upon the pore? For bi the lawe of charite such superfluyte of goodis shuld refresshe pore men, and not be spendid in this wickid use",[4] whilst others lack. The modern economic historian is apt to see the growth of all these new luxuries for the table as part of the natural development of civilization, along with the other amenities of life and the gradual enrichment of progressive peoples. Not so the preachers. To them it was only a natural development of the wickedness in human hearts. Thus Bromyard, who is a fair spokesman, explicitly attributes the extravagant ways of dressing, varying, and enriching dishes in vogue in his day to the ever-growing desire of the glutton to indulge

[1] MS. Harl. 4894, fol. 94b. Perhaps cf. Chaucer, *Pard. Tale*, ll. 547–8.
[2] Who loves delicacies so much that he is always talking of them.
[3] MS. Bodl. 95, fol. 35b (following Barthol. *de Propr. Rer.* lib. xviii). Similarly *Jacob's Well*, p. 142.
[4] MS. Harl. 2276, fol. 36. Cf. here the confession of *Glotoun* in *Piers Plowman*, B text, pass. v, l. 380 ("And y spilte that myȝte be spared and spended on somme hungrie"), and below, pp. 447 and 565.

his appetite, even beyond the bounds of natural capacity. "Therefore do they seek diligently for ways and modes in things to eat and drink, for diverse colours, flavours and varieties of dishes, so that the flavour and odour, the colour and variety seen may provoke their appetite." So "with new and unusual condiments their palate is tickled".[1]

Before lunch-time the glutton hungers and thirsts for food and drink, or rather has an appetite for them. Immediately after breakfast in the morning, he desires an appetite for his lunch at noon. After lunch, for-sooth, he is anxious to have hunger and room enough to take his supper. But if he has filled his "cod"[2] so full at luncheon that no space remains for supper—especially where he hopes that a good table is to be provided, he grieves.

When he and his kind resort to wine for an appetite, it only sends them to sleep, as St Bernard points out, from which they awaken later with fresh regrets. As the meal draws to an end, "if, in truth, they have not been gorged, they will murmur: if they have more than they can devour, they are sad.... Some groan, saying—'What good food that is, if only someone could eat it!'"[3] Rypon actually mentions in a sermon the disgusting practices to which the greedy resort in order to enjoy further dishes;[4] while his Dominican brother declares that some folk spend more over physicians and electuaries than they do upon the actual purchasing and preparation of banquets. One day they stuff; on the next they send for the doctor to relieve them.[5] "These glotones beth never glad bot that they mowe waste muche mete and drynke, and studye in what maner the[y] mowe adrawe here fulnesse to be aȝen hungry ofte for to ete and drynke."[6] So at length folly brings its own richly merited reward. For,

surfet bredith syknesse; and as muche harm as hunger doth to a man, ȝit muche more harme doth superfluyte of mete and drynke....For,...

[1] Cf. here Chaucer, *Pardoners Tale*, ll. 544–6, and MS. Harl. 45, fol. 142 ("a curiouste or busynesse to seche and ordeyne delicious metes and drinkes"); *Jacob's Well*; etc.

[2] *saccum* (cf. Chaucer, *Pardoners Tale*, l. 534).

[3] *S.P.* s.v. "Gula". Cf. further *Jacob's Well*, p. 144: "stodying at o meel how thou mayst fare wele at the next meel...".

[4] MS. Harl. 4894, fol. 24b (*vomitus, eructationes*, etc.).

[5] *S.P.* ibid.   [6] MS. Harl. 2398, fol. 32.

excesse of mete and of drynke wastyth a mannys body and maketh him rote, and megryth[1] him with longe sykness, and bryngeth him in to wickednesse. . . . Of all synnes that ther be, glotenye is most perilous. For ther-with he leseth his reson, . . . his wyt and his minde.[2]. . . The man that is usaunt to glotenye is alle mannys fole.[3]

By means of this same literature, we are enabled to catch a glimpse of the banquet table itself, with those that have a share in it, as seen by the critical eyes of faithful churchmen. Then as now the lavish hospitality of friends or rivals, and the jealous regard for a social reputation, such as Chaucer's *Frankeleyn* enjoyed, often led men on to an extravagance which seemed to brook no limits:

ffirst [the devel] scheweth a man, for to begile him, good wyn and delicious metes, as he dede the appel to Eve. And if that may noght availe, he biddeth and counsailleth a man to ete and drynke as other men doth, so that he may be felawliche and noght singuler, and that men clepe him not "ypocrite" or a "paplard", or "that he is an averous[4] man and a scars of herte so that he may not spende".[5]

Thus it comes about that, under pressure of mere social necessity, ambitious householders, faced with the task of giving a dinner-party, were driven to "spende more peraventure in deyntee in a day than myghte of comoun mete, as profitable for the sustenaunce, be i-now for an hondred pore men". Apart altogether from the sin of "outrageous costes and dispensis nedeles", there was further risk of sin "in veynglorie which thei have in suche doynge. ffor it is ofte i-doo, noght onliche for the lust of the body, but also for pompe and pryde, and for to gete loos[6] of a grete mete-zever for deyntees and many cours". We watch the excited hosts and hostesses, anxious to outdo their neighbours

first, in busynesse of getynge and dightynge of mete, afterward in the lust and delite in etynge, and the thridde, whan thei recorde how wele

---

[1] = emaciates.   [2] And therefore cannot repent.
[3] MS. Harl. 2398, fols. 32b–33b. Cf. *Jacob's Well*, p. 145 ("Crisostomus seyth, et recitatur in canone de consecracione, dist. v [c. 28] . . . ").
[4] = avaricious.
[5] MS. Harl. 45, fol. 141b. Cf. *Jacob's Well*, p. 143, and Bromyard, *S.P.* s.v. "Falsitas" (Those who wish to live of their means are called misers; etc.).
[6] = honour, praise.

thei beth fed, the whiche is veyn glorie, and also how busy thei were aboute the dightinge therof in dyvers maneres. And when the likerous[1] mete cometh eche after other in sondry cours, after the manere of service, than mote thei have bourdes,[2] tryfles and janglynges of vanitees for an entremes,[3] and so wasteth the tyme and forʒeteth hemself,[4] and resoun slepeth.[5]

It is to the *Summa Predicantium* that the reader must turn, if he would learn more of the fashionable conversation of these lordly dinner tables. Its privileged author describes how the feasters love to

narrate with loud laughter and merriment their loss of God, of their heavenly country and their own soul through gluttony, lechery and the like; boasting of how much they have drunk, of how they have tricked someone or beaten him, of the number of women with whom they have fulfilled their lusts, or of some evil deed that they have perpetrated.[6] And yet frequently do they make their jokes and boasts about such things!—and far more commonly of them than of good works. No wonder! for such deeds are commoner.

They glory in the fact that no one dares to correct them, and laugh with their equals and inferiors at the vaunting and filthy talk that quickly goes the round of the guests.[7] Such banqueters, with their oaths and scurrilities that provoke God, are worse, says Bromyard, than the very dogs, that at least "do

---

[1] = dainty.   [2] = jokes.

[3] A dish served in between the courses. (*Jacob's Well* version adds here (p. 144): "to letyn here mete synken".)

[4] Cf. here *Piers Plowman*, B text, pass. v, l. 378 ("over-seye me at my sopere"), doubtless following the oldest version of the above as in *Ayenb. of Inwyt*, p. 56 ("the wreche him voryet").

[5] MS. Harl. 45, fol. 142 b–3. Similarly *Ayenb. of Inwyt*, pp. 55–6, and *Jacob's Well*, p. 144. Cf. again MS. Bodl. 95, fol. 80 b; Ch.-V. Langlois, *La Vie en France au moy. âge*, vol. iv, p. 165; etc.

[6] Cf. here s.v. "Servire": "Alii per modum joci trufantes et deridentes —'Tu es ineptus inter mulieres!', et his similia dicentes...". A story follows—"sicut patuit nuper de quodam domino, qui noviter ad dominium suum veniens cum servis suis ludendo dicere solebat quod mulieres vocabant eos 'capones': quorum unus postmodum propter huiusmodi peccatum de curia licentiatus dixit in aula, coram domino et familia publice, quod nunquam illud fecisset nisi talia verba fuissent".

[7] s.v. "Gloria". Similarly s.v. "Consuetudo", and Anon., MS. Add. 21253, fol. 103 b ("unde lingua specialiter cruciabatur propter inutilia et inhonesta que in mensa loquebatur"); fol. 107 ("in hoc peccant multi loquando inutilia verba in conviviis in mensa sua,...et inhonesta...").

not bark at you while they are eating in your presence".[1] As
for the love of dinner-table scandal, our Dominican again
speaks out with the vehemence and certainty of one who knows:
"But alas! 'all tables are full of vomit' (*Isaiah* xxviii);[2] for
commonly everyone is more willing to believe abominable and
defamatory statements made at their tables than things edifying
to hear, and the worst slanderers rather than the best preachers".
As an example, he puts forward the case of the worst lecher
of one of the Orders, who, having quitted it to escape correction, now regales his companions with a scandalous account
of his former status, "not because the status was itself bad,
but because he misbehaved himself in that status". At once
he receives more credence, more favour, more sympathy than
those who remain in Religion. For, the evil-minded ever
rejoice to hear the worst of their fellows. "We are all like
that!" they cry gleefully.[3] So, as Bromyard points out again, the
superabundance of food leads on to detractions, to vile oaths,
jesting and forbidden amusements—"according to the French
proverb which says—'*Je ne puys jouer ne rire, si le ventre ne
me tire*'".[4] "And then may the stomake seie and crye—'Throte,
thou sleest me! ffor I breste nyhe for full'. But the likerous
throte answereth and seith—'Theigh thou breste, I schal ete
of this cours or messe that now is come'. And after suche
likerous etynge cometh veynglorie."[5] "So thi bely hath
nevere ynow, but evere cryeth—'ȝeve me more!', til it endyth
wyth deth."[6]

Within the limits of a single chapter such as the present, it

[1] s.v. "Gratitudo".   [2] v. 8.
[3] s.v. "Detractio".
[4] s.v. "Gula". Cf. again, MS. Add. 21253, fol. 107 (*detractoria*).
[5] MS. Harl. 45, fol. 142b: also *Ayenb. of Inwyt* and *Jacob's Well*,
as before; *Somme le Roi* (Ch.-V. Langlois, *La Vie en Fr.* vol. iv,
p. 166); etc.
[6] *Jacob's Well*, p. 146. (Cf. further here: "glotonye sleyth glotouns in
iiii. manere of deth: in deth of kynde, in deth of synne, in deth of evyll
name, and in deth of helle...".)

is obviously quite impossible to deal with more than a select few of the preachers' many satires of the pests of society, much less to do even a bare justice to their often brilliant characteriza-, tion. Each well-known type, indeed, requires a single chapter to itself. Nevertheless, one of them must be included which serves to illustrate most admirably the power of the pulpit to reveal a world now separated from us by many centuries, yet still strangely akin to our own in its human vices and follies. The portrait of *Envye* in that masterpiece of satirical literature, the *Vision of Piers Plowman*, is a portrait of the medieval back-biter. No product of the poet's genius bears more clearly upon it the marks of its homiletic origin. If we begin with his first metaphor of "an addres tonge",[1] we find that it is at least as old in English homiletic literature as a twelfth-century sermon which compares back-biters to "spotted adders that bear poison under their tongues".[2] "These spotted adders", says the preacher, "betoken the deceitful folk that dwell in this world, that speak as fair before their fellow-Christians as if they would embrace them; and as soon as they have turned away from them, they slander and detract them with evil words.... These men that thus pull to pieces their fellow Christians behind their backs have the name of Christians, but nevertheless they are Christ's enemies, and are man-slayers...."[3] The same fact is true of Langland's subsequent analogue of the "luther dogge".[4] This likening of "envye to an hound" is part of a pulpit commonplace in which the Seven Deadly Sins "arn likind to seven divers beestis", as "an holi man wriȝtith in his book—*et est sanctus Thomas*...

[1] *Piers Plowman*, B text, pass. v, l. 87. (N.B. that Skeat has already indicated Ovid, *Metam.* lib. ii, 775, as a source for the earlier description, and also parallels to Langland's treatment in poems by Dunbar, Skelton and Spenser.)

[2] *Old Engl. Homs.* ed. Morris, 1st Ser. pt. i, O.S. 29, p. 51. Similarly Bromyard, *S.P.* s.v. "Detractio"; *Ayenb. of Inwyt*, p. 26; *Hand. Synne*, p. 141; and the *Ancren Riwle* (cf. ed. King's Classics, p. 63). The whole concept, of course, is derived from Scripture (cf. Ps. cxl, 3; etc.).

[3] p. 53.

[4] *Piers Plowman*, as before, l. 118.

vel Albertus...in componendo theologye...".[1] In the same
century as Albertus Magnus and Thomas Aquinas aforesaid,
the English author of our *Speculum Laicorum* likewise compares the detractor to "the treacherous dog that pursues a
man silently behind his back, and then first barks when he bites
him".[2] In the century following, Bromyard observes of his kind
that "at the Devil's court they occupy the place and office of dogs:
therefore they are appropriately called in French—*le brachet
au diable*, for the many features which they have in common
with dogs".[3] A contemporary adds yet more sarcastically in his
sermon: "Thus truly do they bark and bite, by taking from
a neighbour the good name which he had. These folk in their
condition are much worse than dogs, because at the first they
lick and caress a man and his status, afterwards they bite him—
which dogs do not do unless they happen to be rabid".[4] It
is not so much in the commonplace analogue, however, as in
the picturesque, homely detail of their rebukes that the preachers
here reveal a spirit of close kinship with the author of the
Vision. The confessions of the poet's *Envye*, indeed, prove
once again upon inspection to be nothing more nor less than
the preachers' general report cast into the first person singular
and enriched with a few added personal touches. Here, too,

---

[1] MS. Bodl. 110, fol. 23b. (Cf. Bozon, as indicated in Herbert,
Cat. of Romances in B.M. vol. iii, p. 104, no. 25; MS. Glouc. Cath.
Libr. Hom. Dom. iv post Oct. Epiph.; MS. Linc. Cath. Libr. A. 6. 2,
fol. 58b; etc.)

[2] cap. xxv, "De Detractoribus et eorum Periculo" (ed. Welter, pp. 39–
41). Also here compared to the Bear (*Physiol.*), the Beast with three
rows of teeth mentioned in the Book of Daniel (vii, 5: Vulg. version):
similarly in MS. Add. 21253, fol. 31b ("...i.e. tres modos detrahendi, qui
sunt mala augmentando, bona diminuendo et indifferentia pervertendo"),
and Bromyard, *S.P.* as below. See also *Ayenb. of Inwyt*, p. 66.

[3] *S.P.* s.v. "Detractio": later the mad dog spreading rabies among
the sheep, vividly described (§ 10). Cf. again *Jacob's Well*, pp. 86–7;
and below, p. 456.

[4] MS. Camb. Univ. Libr. Ii. iii. 8, fol. 146. In Bromyard, and MS.
Add. 21253, fol. 33, the detractor is further compared to a privy ("orificium
private per quod omnis fetor egreditur, totam domum inficiens..."—MS.
Add. version). The idea is derived from the *Ancren Riwle* (cf. ed. King's
Classics, p. 64).

in sermon writ, is the immortal argument of Shakespeare's Iago upon the subject:

> Who steals my purse steals trash; 'tis something, nothing.
>
> .   .   .   .
>
> But he that filches from me my good name
> Robs me of that which not enriches him
> And makes me poor indeed.[1]

The sermons mirror to us, as perhaps we find mirrored no-where else so clearly, a feudal society still split up into a number of tiny, half-isolated communities, in which evil gossip and the breath of slander will run riot and play havoc with reputations wholly at their mercy. (Let the modern historian of the Middle Ages, therefore, be ever upon his guard!)[2] Across the dinner table of the mighty, along with Bromyard, we have already caught the accents of the back-biter who loves there to belittle his absent foes.[3] The same indefatigable homilist tells how "detractors and defamers" will "strive to ruin or diminish the reputation of their neighbours by means of signs, nods, words plain or artificial, in ballads or defamatory libels (*scriptis quae appellantur libelli famosi*)". Heavy sighs, a grave and distressed countenance, a casting down of the eyebrows and a wailing voice all play their part in the hypocrites' scheme of dissimulation.[4] If a friend of the slandered happens to cross their path at the wrong moment and overhear their remarks, they protest—"We did not speak in a spirit of detraction, nor with ill will, but in fun—or in sympathy or condolence with him". But alas! their behaviour is no joke. For, as the Dominican here states, two realms or two countries, two com-munities or two towns are thus sometimes inflamed and heated

---

[1] (*Othello*, Act iii, Sc. 3.) Cf. Bromyard, *S.P.* as above: "Quarto, detractor crudelior et periculosioris conditionis est latrone et homicida, quia fur aufert exteriora bona..."; *Jacob's Well*, p. 84; MS. Worc. Cath. Libr. F. 10, fol. 44b, and MS. Roy. 18. B. xxiii, fol. 84, as quoted below, pp. 454 and 460. The whole idea is derived from Prov. xxii, 1 and Ecclesiasticus xli, 15, and to be found in its expanded form in Canon Law (see *Corp. Jur. Canon.*, C. vi, qu. i, cap. xv; ed. Richter and Friedberg, 1879, i, 557). In MS. Worc. above, it is attributed to Aquinas.

[2] Cf. the chronicler, in my *Preaching in Med. Engl.* p. 125.

[3] See above, p. 449.   [4] Cf. *Ancren Riwle*, as before, p. 66.

with the fire of mutual wrath and hatred; and from a disturbance thus raised between two great men, the disturbance of a whole district or township may easily follow. Similarly, some ruthless calumny whispered in a lord's ear by an envious rival will set master against man and friend against friend on the feudal estate, with disastrous results for the innocent and defenceless; while the evil rumour grows each time that it is repeated.[1] "To-day", complains another, "men more readily speak ill of their neighbours than good. And these detractors never speak good of anyone, but rather invent wicked lies about them, increasing the evil and diminishing the good."[2] Bishop Brunton asserts, in his turn, by way of illustration, that "if detractors see a man and woman talking together perchance for edification, immediately they cry out in the hearing of each of them that they have sinned together; and by pretext of that outcry, when the whole neighbourhood is alive to the scandal, those two, although innocent, are summoned before the Ordinary and compelled to purge themselves, just as if they were guilty of that misdeed".[3] Such is the power of the scandal-monger in the land. Detraction, says the unknown author of our "Hereford" homilies wittily, is the Englishman's characteristic: "Assuredly, in these days there is no such joy in the world [as the Apostle Paul mentions]. For, each man rejoices in evil

---

[1] *S.P.* s.v. "Discordia": "Primo, discordiae seminatio patet frequenti aliquorum consuetudine qui, invidentes de alicujus familiaritate vel amicitia quam habet cum aliquo domino, vel de hoc quod officium aliquid occupat quod ab ipsis vel ab amicis suis occupari vellent, per aliquem de eorum foederatione loquentur illi domino, dicentes— 'Domine',—dicet ille per quem loquentur—'vellem vos de una re prae- munire, sed nollem hoc alios audire'. Detractionis vero curiosus auditor jurabit ei, sicut est fidelis miles vel fidelis homo, quod nunquam pro eo audiatur. Qua promissione habita, narrabit quod—'talis sic de vobis loquebatur, vel sic, vel sic contra vos fecit. Sed bene scio quod si esset ad rationem positus, negaret; nec possem istud probare, quia testes deficiunt'. Dominus ille cor habebit grave contra illum, nec aliquid de cordis gravamine exprimere poterit propter jus jurandum. Et sic ille miser discordias provocat. Nec modo faciunt tamen inter dominum et subditum, sed etiam inter socium et socium, vicinum et vicinum. Audientes enim aliquod verbum de ore unius quod posset esse contra alium, illud ei narrant forte cum augmento".

[2] MS. Add. 21253, fol. 65.   [3] MS. Harl. 3760, fol. 124.

conversation about another: each defames the other—*et illud est proprium Anglicorum!*"[1]

We cannot dismiss this subject without adding three typical samples of vernacular preaching upon it, which the reader shall be allowed to enjoy without further comment. The first is taken from a sermon at Worcester, where the preacher is again discussing those "develis children", the envious back-biters:

> Lord God, vor ther be ani swich maner o man now-a-day, ȝe truliche, i drede me al to manie. Vor ye schalt se now, ȝif a man be ani thyng vertuus towird for to thryve or to cum to ani other estat, a-non other kurside schrewes have envye therto, a-non they be abowte with al the crafte thei can to lette his good name, ȝe, thei go to his frendes priviliche and, undur[?] a vals colour, a vals confessiun, al-to rendelyth, al-to terres[?] hym in as miche as in hem is, akursid helle-howndes as t[h]ei ben....
>
> ȝe, it is wirse, as seynt Tomas previth wel,...for to ben a bakbïter thane to ben a thef. Vor a thif doth nawth ell[s] to a man but taketh awey his riches; but a bakbiter taketh awey mannes good name that is beter to the than al the tresur of the world, as wittnesseth wel the wisman Salamon,...wher a seith o this wyse: "Take hede", a seith, "of thi good name; vor that proffit the more than al the tresur and al the riches that [ben] e this world". Whi so? "Vor thi riches", a seith, "schal abide but a whil; but thi good name schal lest *in eternum*...".[2]
>
> [Following a comparison of the back-biters to the great winds that assault the fair fruit-tree[3]—] An[4] t[h]ey [i.e. the back-biters] se a man that is but a wretche, that is but unthrifti, hath noyther fruit nor leves up-on hym, is nat able to come to non estat no[r] degre of wirschepe her-afterward, hym thei pas over, hym thei speke never a word of—and why? Thei wot wel inow a may nat be miche wors than a (h)is. But, an t[h]ey se another that bigynnyth to floressche with the flowres o vertu, bigynnyth to bryng vorth fruit of good doctryne, ȝe, bigynnyth for to take the bowes of estat and of wirsthepe, at hym they puf and blowe with al the myth in hir bodi, vor to bryng hym downe, and[4] t[h]ey mythte; thei fantesie vals lesyngis, vals talis up-on him....[5]

[1] MS. Heref. Cath. Libr. P. 5. 2, fol. 45 (the preacher's reference is to Paul's Epistle to the Philipp. iv, 1). Cf. *Hand. Synne* on Envy, p. 140.

[2] Ecclesiasticus xli, 15–16. See above, p. 451, n. 4.

[3] See above, p. 38.   [4] = if.

[5] The fifteenth-century English version of the *Gesta Rom.* gives us further details of their procedure here (ed. Herrtage, E.E.T.S. p. 311): "For ther woll shrewis arise ayenst [a man sette in hye dignite, whiche usithe to correcte ivel men and women], and sey that he is to boistous to many, and to warme, and knowith not him-selfe, to woode by his power, and to coveitous. And ther-fore such a man thei accuse, and makith him be deprivid of his office". Cf. also *Ayenb. of Inwyt*, p. 28.

Vor Cristes sake leve it [i.e. back-biting]; stond nat in halkis nor in hyrnes, bi day nor bi nith, demyng thi neȝebours and demyng thi brethrin, niggyng thi soverein;[1] but go and ocupi the abowte sum other good ocupaciun. ȝif the be a man of the world, ocupi the a-bowte bodiliche travaile or ell[s] abowte sum other thyng that longeth to the: ȝif the be a man of holi chirche, go bid thi bedis, say thi sawter, or el[s] ocupi the abowte sum other holi contemplaciun. But peraventur, the seist to me— "Sir, me tunge is for the most part so drie and so weri whan i sei anithyng, that i mai nat bidde me bedis, i make no prayours, no[r] i mai nat dur ani while e seyng of my sawter". A vundir[2] thyng abowte cawtil[3] of the devels! Whan the schalt serve God, anon rith the tunge is drie; but it is nat weri vor to stonde al day, ȝe, vrom morn til eue, vrom midday to midnyth, niggyng thi neȝebours, demyng thi brethrin and t[h]i sovereyne that is abowte the. I speke noyther of Richarde, nor of Robert, nor of William, nor of dan Ion; and t[h]ervorin no man ha me su[s]pect that i speke of hym, but ȝif it be swich an unthrifti man that be gilti e this same synne that i speke of: vor wite he wel, of him i speke and of no other....[4]

Our second passage occurs in a homiletic discussion of the several types of "manslaughter", among which back-biting finds its due place:

ffor men and women also now-on-dayes, if they heren a sclaundre of a man, be it soth, be it les, thei wil iangle therof largeli al aboute behynde his bak, and make it more and wel wers than it was bifore. And whanne they comen before hym that is ther sclaundryd, to hym wolen they say nevere a word therof to warn hym of his harm and of hys schame; but flateren hym and glosyn hym, and as to the syȝt schewyth hym gret

[1] halkis, hyrnes = nooks, corners: niggyng = despising. Cf. here, MS. Roy. 18. B. xxiii, fol. 85: "Than, thou ronker and rownere, that arte the dewels ste, scheff stewarde, chaumberleyn and keper of is courte in resceyvynge of cursed tales and bacbytynges and slaunders that are putt up to the, thou hast grett list to heed hem and to tell hem forthe to other suche here as thu arte: sitt thu never so prively rownynge in an hyrne with thi compere, trust trewly iche worde that ȝe speke God hereth hem...".

[2] = wonderful.   [3] = cunning trick.

[4] MS. Worc. Cath. Libr. F. 10, fols. 44b–5. This last section of the preacher's remarks is interesting apart from its peculiar naïveté and directness. In the first place it reminds us that his audience is a mixture of layfolk and monks, assembled probably in the Cathedral church for a Sunday sermon. Layman and Religious alike are accordingly warned and exhorted together in the usual somewhat impolitic style (cf. my *Preaching in Med. Engl.* pp. 94, 141, 182–4, etc.). Finally, in his concluding statement, he shows himself anxious to avoid a suspicion of pursuing the evil practice of which Chaucer's Pardoner boasted (see ibid. p. 187).

frendchipe and love. And somme gon abou3t here ney3eboris fro hous
to hous and tellen sleveles[1] talis and apposyn[2] her ney3boris sutely[3] and
undirgropyn[4] hem slili, and comyn in with a flateryng and seyn—"I aske
not this for hindring of ony man, and that that thu tellist me schal be
conseile"; and al this is to seche out sum yvel tale of hem that thei haten.[5]
And whanne that thei drawen out of hem a yvel tale, a-noon be the backe
turned, thei sclatren[6] out to alle that wolen here hem so fer forth that,
if thei my3tten do her nei3boris to hange and to drawen with oo fals
lesing,[7] it schulde be blowen out a-noon. And here-of comyn mony
debatis and stryvyngis, foule chiding, eche man to wrangle with othere
as were houndis and cattis. Suche men, in as myche as in hem is, sleen
al tho of the whiche thei tellen suche bacbitingis.[8]

With the final excerpt we return again to the subject of the
"luther dogge", as vivid a piece of description as any we have
encountered in sermons redolent of the English countryside:

But now trewly, the more harme is, many men now-adayes will speke
or[9] that thei lerne to speke, and will deme or thei have ordeynt aryght-
wisnes: but for to deme falsely thei ordeyn them falsenes inow3the.[10]
Swiche maner of men ben these liers, fflaterers and jangelers that sowys
discorde amonge ney3bors. They may well be lykened to a wode[11]
hownde: for as thu seest well, a wode hownde he goys evermore with
an opon mowthe, and is tounge waverynge owte of is mowthe; and the
cause ther of is wodenes is a venemous worme that lieth undur is tounge.
He bargeys[12] oftentymes ageyns reson, somtyme a3eyns men in the
strete, and sometyme at is owen shadowe. Ryght so doys a fals bacbyter
and a false demere. He hathe is mouthe evermore opyn and is tounge
is waverynge in ys hede to speke of every-thinge of man to shewe here
defawtes over all....Anothur condicion hath the wode hounde: when
he cometh into the strete, he wyndeth and turneth hym all aboute, and,
3iff he mete with anny man, he stondith and barketh a3eyns hym. Ryght
so the false demere and the bakbyter, whether that he com in fayre or
merkett, he turneth hym all abowte to aspie every man and womman
where that he fynde som defaute, in-someche that, and[13] he here anny
man seyinge is bedis, he demeth hym ane ypocrite and wold ben holden

---

[1] = unprofitable.
[2] = raise objections to.
[3] = subtly.
[4] = grope under, i.e. to find out things about them.
[5] Cf. here the female gossips, as above, pp. 387–9.
[6] For "clatter"= talk idly.   [7] = lie.
[8] MS. Laud Misc. 23, fol. 14b et seq. (= MS. St Albans Cath. fol. 27,
the greater part missing in this copy). For an account of this work, see
my article in the *Trans. of the Herts Archaeol. Soc.* for 1924, pp. 43–59.
[9] = ere, before.   [10] = enough.   [11] = mad.
[12] = barks.   [13] = if.

holy; and iff that he see hym not so, than he demeth hym undevoute and worldely; and ʒiff that he see hym a pacient man when that he is anhanggred, than he demeth [hym] herteles and dredefull; and ʒiff he answere ageyn shortely, he demeth hym prowde and unskilfull; and ʒiff that he see a man speke trewly, he demeth hym a pynchere;[1] and ʒiff that he speke nowʒthe, than he demeth hym a feynere; and ʒiff that [he] be of sympull berynge and havynge, than he demeth hym a gaderere; and ʒiff he be of grett berynge, than he demeth hym a waster; ʒiff he speke fayre, than he demeth hym a flaterer; and ʒiff that he speke not, than he demeth hym a thynkere. So that what thinge a man doth, he demeth hym amysse.[2] Thus it farethe nyʒ in all states[3]—that God do bote,[4] when that is will is!...For now everyman will deme, be he never so lewde. He will not let nother of kynge, pope, ne of clerke, ne of craft, ne connynge, thoo that he be as lewde therof as is an asse. And therfore the lewde man demeth amysse, and speketh amysse and al-day falsely. Whi is this?—ffor thei ben prowde men; and se this ben ensampull, as thou seest well that ʒiff a man have a bade stomoke he hath than an ewill-saverede mowthe, and the mete that commeth therin, be it never so good, he demeth it bitter; also ʒiff a man loke in a ʒalowe[5] glas, he demeth all other thinges ʒalowe. So it fareth by this false demers, that arne bad them-selfe and therfore the[i] deme al-other badde. This is a gret myscheff in this world....

. . . .

The second drynke of this wynus braunche is the drynke of Envy. And this drynke is perlous, for he setteth a man anon in to a fewere.[6] For, like as a man in the accesse is now hote and now cold, ryght so the Envious man hath ioy of the adverste of goodmen, and now he sorowith of ther prosperite....This fewere putrifieth the innere parties of the sowle....Such maner of Envious men ben wers than dewels. Loo I rede—Luc. 8[7]—that Crist cast owte a legion of dewels owte of oo man. A legion is the nowmbur of six thowsand, six hundred, sixti and six: all thise dewelles had dwelled in this man many ʒeres—and ʒitt none of hem labored to put owte other. But trewly, and[8] twenti men dwell

---

[1] = a haggler.
[2] Cf. here Bozon, *Metaphs.* cap. cxxxiii (with fable): "For no one can please all; if he is quiet and natural in hall, then is he held particular or haughty; if he is affable and amusing, braggart or boaster; if he eats little and drinks little, then is he fastidious or dainty; if he eats well and drinks well, then he is a glutton or extravagant; if he is liberal or generous, then he is foolish or too lavish;...Wherefore one knows not how to live, so perverse is the age...". From this typical pulpit theme, the poet William Dunbar fashions his poem "How sall I governe me?" (*Poems of W. D.* ed. H. B. Baildon, Camb. 1907, pp. 156–8; etc.).
[3] = estates [4] = amend. [5] = yellow.
[6] = fever. [7] Luke viii, 27–31. [8] = if.

now in a parishe, thre other foure of hem can not leve in rest and pes, but rather besieth hem in that thei may ether of hem to distroye other. A good God! ʒiff anny man list to knowe this[e] envious men, I sey thei may be knawen by ther language.... The langage of hell useth thise envious men, the wiche speken ever slaundre and detraccion of ther neyʒbore owt of charite....[1]

. . . . . .

Thise fals ypocrites and bacbytors, thei will com to the churche and knokke hem selfe on the breste and turne the eyen owteward, as thei wold goth to heven all hote; but ʒitt thei will bacbite here even-cristen and make wreuth and debate wher-as love was afore. ʒitt thisse maner of pepull ben holden goddes children now-a-daies.[2]

Just as envy leads on to wrath in the sermon-narrative, so *Wratthe* appropriately follows *Envye* in the procession of Deadly Sins in the *Vision of Piers Plowman*. In one of our homily-books we have a vivid little outline of the progress of a quarrel, expanded from the *Ayenbite of Inwyt*,[3] which could be matched with ease in other works of the kind, wherever the discourse turns upon the hot-tempered "fole" unable—"to suffre a litil wynde of thi neiʒboris tunge that is blowen aʒens thi luste, that nye thou waxist woode for

[1] The preacher continues (fol. 132b): "Loo a figure to our purpose...". Just as Jael, Heber's wife (Judges iv, 17-21), slew the sleeping Sisera "with a nall thorowe is brayn", after offering him milk, so these "envious bacbiters...ʒeves first mylke to drynke, commendynge a man other a womman; but son after sewethe the nayll of bacbityng, the wiche slayth the man slepyng, for he heres it not, but it sleyth is good name for ever in this world".

[2] MS. Roy. 18. B. xxiii, fols. 120, 132-132b, 166-166b. Other warnings against false judgment of one's neighbour, and the like, are given on fols. 92b ("alle evill demyng cometh of envie", etc.), 99b ("...Now sirs,... every man loke to hymselfe, and bere a good tonge, and speke well of every persone, not to sey thus—'Ill did he, and he'...", etc.), 119, etc. An early vivid description of the back-biter and his habits will be found in the *Ancren Riwle* (ed. King's Classics, p. 66), repeated in Lichfield's Tract, MS. Roy. 8. C. 1, fol. 126b. Cf. also *Hand. Synne*, pp. 54-5, 122-5, 140-1; and the poem "Kepe thy tunge", in Chambers and Sidgwick, *E. E. Lyrics*, p. 191. See, too, Ecclesiasticus xxviii, 13-30.

[3] E.E.T.S. ed. pp. 65-6.

wraythe and leesist pacience, pees and charite and God hiṁ-silf":[1]

When the fend seeth love and pees amonge good men, he hath therto moche envye and doth all that he can or may, and with the fuyre of ire he stureth hir hertes to discord and stryf.... After stryf cometh chidynge with grete noyse and cry. And right as fuyre caste first up smoke and afterward bresteth up the leie,[2] right so after ire and yvel will cometh stryf and debate; and whan oon seith to an other—"It is thus", the tother seith—"Nay!": the ton seith—"It was thus!", that other seith—"It was noght so!" Thus bygynneth stryf; and after that cometh chidynge, with "Thou lixte" and "Thou lixt".[3] And after these two cometh the thridde that is disdeyne, as whan that oon stureth that other with felownes[4] and venymous wordes, and then her tunges biteth more scharpliche than eny rasoure, and more swifte and wors smytinge than eny arowe, and more perisshynge than eny allis[5] poynte. And suche men beth likned to a beste that men clepeth a porke-despyne [sic!], that is bred in Ynde and is covered with scharpe pynnes of horne. That beest is felle[6] and sone wole be wroth; and whan he is wroth, anone he scheteth out some of his scharpe pynnes of horne and hurteth that that is beside him.... [Following further mention of "cursynge or myssaienge"[7] and "reprovynge", occurs] maanas, or thretynges, whiche stereth menis hertes to yre so that mellees[8] and werres bigynneth amonge hem and seseth noght til the ton of hem be vengyd of that other.[9]

So, once again, the evil brood of sin grows and multiplies, as each new vice is hatched. Wrath, in its turn, may express itself

[1] MS. St Albans Cath. fol. 42b. Bromyard (s.v. "Discordia") attributes human discord to men's alienation from God and their refusal to live—"*secundum rationem intra*" (i.e. Conscience).   [2] = bursteth up the flame.

[3] Cf. here, *Piers Plowman*, B text, pass. v, ll. 161–4 (and the equivalent in C text, pass. vii). The C text version clearly owes much to the *Ayenbite* and its derivative homily-books. For the poet's references to *Wratthe* amongst the clergy, cf. in my *Preaching in Med. Engl.* pp. 71–2.   [4] Felonous = wicked, mischievous.

[5] Awl's. (The scribe here has written—"all his" in the MS. which suggests that he was writing by dictation; hence perhaps his error.)   [6] = ruthless, cruel.

[7] "As whan that ton mysseieth and curseth that other.... And Salamon seith that the mouthes of suche men beth as pottes boylinge ful of licoure, of whiche some dropes fleeth out and scaldeth men that thei may reche."   [8] = fightings (*mélées*).

[9] MS. Harl. 45, fols. 150–1. Cf. again, Bromyard, *S.P.* s.v. "Discordia": "Ex discordia oriuntur animositates, lites, guerrae, et huiusmodi, quae corporibus nocent et animabus, et terram quamcunque maxime destruit". For source, see *Somme le Roi* (Ch.-V. Langlois, *La Vie en France au moyen âge*, vol. iv, p. 155): also *Ayenb. of Inwyt*, pp. 65–7.

in the home "whan thou in thi fervent ire, wyth-outyn ony abyding or with-outyn any avysement, hastely takest vengeauns in stertyng therto as a wood man to bete or to chastyse or to don ony other dede of vengauns, or in smytynge thi chylderyn, thi servauntes or othere dyspytously and oute of mesure",— "and recchyst nevere what vessell thou brekyst".[1] Or, in the outer world, it may show itself in the "dedes that [men] do agaynest theyre even-crysten[2] wyth malice, to pursue theym wyth many a false cause. Yf he may no nother vengeaunce on hym take, he forbarres hym wynnynge in bargayne or in eny other thynge, wyth betynge or bostynge of him and his men, and gladly wold harme hym-self to hynder that other".[3] Such is human spite: and even worse, for murder is rife as a weapon of revenge.[4] It is a sorry world, then, that our preachers behold with their somewhat jaundiced eyes—

Thoo thinges that God loveth, as charite, mekenes, chastite, soburnes and all these other, men nowe-adaies moste dispises and hateth: and all that the dewell principally loveth, as hate, envie, pride, drunkennes, glotenye, lecherie and other synnes, men love moste, full-fillynge the dewelles will. Experience here-of we have, for ther was never more enmyte, hate, envie and chidynge and all other in the worlde than is nowe every day more and more. Ther is never oon welny3 that loveth is ney3bore; but many on, in all that thei may, greveth and distroweth him, and not oonly is goodes but is good name and is good fame.[5]

For the sake of our opening poem and also of what follows in the chapter ensuing, one further domestic weakness must be

[1] *Jacob's Well*, pp. 92–3. See *Ayenb. of Inwyt*, p. 30.
[2] = fellow Christians.
[3] MS. Roy. 18. B. xxiii, fol. 154b. For other examples of medieval vengeance in this literature, cf. MS. Camb. Univ. Libr. Gg. vi. 16, fol. 54 (vengeance by Common Law, slandering, despising, beating, indicting, outlawing, banning, cursing, etc.); *Jacob's Well*, p. 92 (biding the time for revenge by law, lordship, or help of wicked company, etc.); etc.
[4] Cf. Brunton and Bromyard, as above, pp. 340, etc., and again, s.v. "Discordia" ("turbati ira et discordia,...ad multa homicidia et injustas tracti vindictas, a diabolo capiuntur..."); etc.
[5] MS. Roy. 18. B. xxiii, fol. 83b–4.

allowed to detain us for a moment, ere we close. Again, it is a subject of complaint old yet ever new on the lips of the world's moralists. In the sermon of Reason (or Conscience) in Langland's *Vision*, the preacher, it will be remembered,

Chargede chapmen to chasten heore children.
Let hem wonte non ei3e, while that thei ben 3onge.[1]   [awe

The dearer the child, he goes on in the B-text version of the poem, the stricter should be its upbringing, as witnesses Scripture: "Qui parcit virge, odit filium".[2] Of the charms of young children we have already heard something in contemporary pulpit literature.[3] The same source makes it clear that medieval youth in the early years of puberty was as difficult to handle, as tiresome to control as any of the modern species in a world of psychology and godless revolt. However simple the prescribed remedy might be, to the religious mind and conscience of that day youth, in actual fact, remained a social problem of the first magnitude—"so rebelle and unbuxom as hy al day beth bycome".[4] The complaints of our homilists are deliciously naïve at times upon this theme. Says one of them:

The fourte [thing] that Salomon cud not undirstond is the vey of an lusty man in is 3onge age: and trewly this semeth a wondir in that Salomon cud not conceyve the veye of this lusty man. And 3itt Salomon knewe the nature of every thinge fro the hi3e cedre tre to the smale erbe in the gardeyn; and in moralte, how cunnynge that he was his proverbes declareth, the boke of Ecclesiastes *et Cantica Canticorum*. How ever was it, than, that he conceyved not the weye of a lusty man in is 3onge age? Sirs, Salomon conceyved not the cause of synfull lyvynge of a 3onge man, I mene—why a 3onge man is prompt unto vicious lyvynge. For here-of there is no cause but the evell will of this lusty man; and that may not be conceyved for ys unstabulnes and fre choys of ys soule.[5]

Says another, with equal naïveté—

Ther is another "lepre" of 3onge folk that thei ben moche smyttid with now-a-daies, and this is veyn lau3tre and idul wordis, and many other vayn iapis, that seelden or never thei kunnen stynte from hem.[6]

[1] A text, pass. v, ll. 32–3.
[2] B text, pass. v, ll. 33–41 (cf. C text, pass. vi, ll. 137–40). The Scriptural quotation is from Prov. xiii, 24 (cf.—"and Salamon seide...").
[3] See above, pp. 34–5.   [4] MS. Harl. 2398, fol. 75.
[5] MS. Roy. 18. B. xxiii, fol. 142 (see Prov. xxx, 18–19, Vulg. version ("et viam viri in adolescentia")).
[6] MS. Harl. 2276, fol. 37.

Plays and dances they prefer, he says, to the hearing of God's Word, and the street jester to His ministers in the Church. In a loftier sphere, Bishop Brunton of Rochester utters his complaint from the pulpit "against the many sons of most noble lineage who, when they are children and under a master, serve God at Vespers and Masses, recite litanies and have a conscience to put away all such vices [as the speaker has just referred to]. Nevertheless, when they have attained lordship of the highest eminence, they sleep until Terce and scorn divine worship".[1] Likewise Robert Rypon points to the mass of young men in his day who serve the world and commit adultery with her, quitting their true spouse, the Faith of Christ's Church, in deed if not in word, for an unbroken intimacy with worldly wealth and pomp, and a vicious household.[2] Nor was mere worldliness their only typical vice:

> This was the maner and the custom [of the] philosophure Pitagoras, the wiche was hasked in is scole, that is disciples shuld sitt vii ȝere and no thinge do in scole but here hure maisters techynge and leven is seynge, and att the vii ȝeres ende thei shuld begynne to appose and to answer of that that thei had herde beforne: ffor he wold that non of is techynge shuld ȝeve sentence, nother dome of no thinge till that thei knewe well that thei cowde. Wold God that the custom here-of were well kepte among us! For than shuld ther be not so many lesynges as be nowe. ffor now-a-dayes assone as a man comes to mans state, anon he will ȝeve sentence and dome of every crafte and connynge, thoo he knowe no more ther-of than can the howle of musik.[3]

It was the first years of manhood and freedom, then, that often revealed to our grieved homilists the radical failure of youth's upbringing. According to most of them, the system was not rigorous enough, and the environment was poisonous. At the same time it is not true to say that they had all failed to realise that stern discipline, if too stern, might prove the very parent of future reaction. For Bromyard observes that "the boy beaten too frequently or for a trivial cause is hardened and

[1] MS. Harl. 3760, fol. 125 b. Sim. Bromyard, *S.P.* s.v. "Servire".
[2] MS. Harl. 4894, fol. 185.
[3] MS. Roy. 18. B. xxiii, fol. 119 b. Cf. the rebukes for disobedient and disrespectful young men in *Old Engl. Homs.* (12th cent.), E.E.T.S. O.S. no. 34, p. 109; and for idle youths, *Hand. Synne*, p. 166.

cares little about the blows".[1] Scripture itself, however, had prescribed a generous use of the rod: man, therefore, had merely to obey.[2] Whatever educational theorists may think nowadays of the doctrine of *Qui parcit virgae*, honoured by Catholic and Puritan alike, few, we imagine, will quarrel with the preachers' further advice to parents. Children, for example, must learn early to honour God, and their earthly father and mother also:

Thus shuld faders teche ther children in there ʒougeth, and not to shrewe[3] ther moders and to be froward, proude and unbuxom, to swere and curse and lie, and to smyte and to sey that he is to ʒonge to lerne anny good.[4] But to lerne shrewdenes he is old inowthe: and ther is the cause, when that thei com to age, that thei worshippe not ther faders and ther moders, but as Caymes children to serve Goddes curse. And therfore bereve youre children suche vices, whilst that thei be ʒonge, and suche ydell condiciouns, and teche hem to kepe Goddes commaunde-mentes and to torne here tongues; for be oure speche men may knowe what that we be—whether of heven or of hell.[5]

This veneration or "worshipping" of parents is a subject of sufficient importance with the pulpit to warrant a section to itself, apart even from "Filial Correction", in our thirteenth-century *Speculum Laicorum*.[6] We gain a more precise definition of its scope from a Treatise on the Commandments written approximately a century later. "Worschiping of fadir and

---

[1] *S.P.* s.v. "Excommunicatio".

[2] The sermons of Bozon illustrate admirably the influence of Scriptural injunctions with regard to the chastisement of children. In addition to Prov. xiii, 24, he quotes Prov. xxii, 15 and xxix, 15; Ecclesiasticus vii, 23 and xxx, 12; Hebr. xii, 6 and 8. (See *Metaphs.* cap. xix, xl and xliv.) Cf. further, MS. Harl. 45, fol. 77 ("chastise hem withoute sparynge..."); MS. Harl. 2398, fol. 93b ("Yf they trespasse aʒenst Godes hestes, [parents] owene to blame hem ther-fore scharplyche and chasty hem a thousand-folde more than for trespasse, [etc.]...aʒenst here owene persone. And this techynge and chastyng scholde in fewe ʒeres make goede cristene men and women"); etc. There is, perhaps, further evidence of reaction against the strict Catholic practices of youth in later life, in a sermon passage of MS. Roy. 18. B. xxiii, fol. 108: "It is a comone proverbe bothe of clerkes and of lay men—'ʒonge seynt, old dewell'".

[3] = curse.

[4] For parents' excuses, cf. *Hand. Synne*, p. 163.

[5] MS. Roy. 18. B. xxiii, fol. 92–2b.

[6] cap. lxii (ed. Welter, pp. 86–7), with three warning tales.

modir", says the homilist, "stondith not oonli in bodili reverence, as doynge of[f] of hodis and knelinge,[1] thouȝ this be good, but also in dede", such as the succouring of them in want and old age.

And thouȝ thei be angeri,[2] ovyr-thwart,[3] pore, witles, feble, cold and unclene, thu schalt not have scorne of hem, thou schalt not be squoymes ne schamed of hem, but suffre hem mekeli and loweli and bi esi speche, and mekeli conforte hem in her grete nede, as thei holpen thee and serveden whanne thu were ful litil childe and haddist greete nede in thi swathinge cloutis[4].... There-fore think not hevely to dwelle with thi modir in hir widowe-hous, thu that laiste in the streit chambre of hir wombe....

But now what drede, what perel it is to the child that wole not worschipe dewli fadir and modir. He schal have no ioie of his owne sones; his lyf schal be schort; the groundis of his hous schal be drawen up bi the roote. ffor cursinge of his modir he schal be sclaunderid with [ill] fame; he schal be cursid of God.[5]

Alas, the preacher has further to mourn the disastrous consequences to society as a whole of the current lack of parental respect:

And yf this lessoun hadde be tauȝt and ykept in Engelonde, I trowe the londe hadde ystonde in more prosperite than it hath ystonde many day; and it may be that [for] vengeaunce of this synne of unworschepynge and despysynge of fadres and modres, God sleeth children by pestylence, as ȝe seeth al day. ffor in the olde lawe children that were rebelle and unbuxom to here fadres and modres were ypunysched by deth, as the fyfthe boke of holy wryt wytnesseth.[6]

But apart from the need for due reverence, parents had further to be reminded of their primary task in the direct inculcation of virtues in the growing child:

Also fadyr and modyr schuldyn techyn here chylderyn gode thewys[7] and to kepyn hem fro evyll cumpanye and fro sweryng and fro lesynges,

---

[1] This is charmingly illustrated in a French treatise on the Decalogue in MS. Fitzwm. Mus. Camb. 22, fol. 179.
[2] = afflicted, and so ill-tempered.
[3] = perverse.   [4] = swaddling bands.
[5] MS. St Albans Cath. fols. 23–4 and 26. Cf. *Hand. Synne*, pp. 38–40.
[6] MS. Harl. 2398, fol. 93b (see Deut. xxi, 18–21). Cf. a similar explanation of infant mortality "bi pestelence" offered in MS. St Albans Cath. fol. 25.
[7] = habits.

and when thei trespasyn chastyse hem, and noȝt for-beryn hem to longe. For as a ȝung thyng kepyth the schap that it takyth whil it is lytell, so wyll a chyld kepe badde thewys that it takyth in ȝouthe.[1]

Again, alas, the voice of complaint has to be raised against those who, so far from teaching good habits to their offspring, are themselves bad company, prime sources of corruption to the coming generation by reason of their evil example. Of the poisoned atmosphere of many homes in which the medieval child was reared, the previous pages of this very chapter have told already a vivid enough tale. Nor, indeed, was the pulpit slow to point out the effects of all this adult misbehaviour. The rush after wealth, high position and worldly success in its influence upon the early training and outlook of the young has already caught our attention in some of the older Latin sermon-books.[2] Thus Bromyard tells us further how, like the *nouveaux riches* of our own day, so eager are many in his own to rank as men of high birth and social standing that, when they cannot attain these things for themselves, they will spare no expense to procure for their sons and daughters some marriage alliance with the mighty, so that their grandsons may enjoy the coveted honours of nobility. Sometimes, however, death or ingratitude robs them of the reflected glory that they sought for themselves at so costly a price, and with so little regard for the real welfare of their children or of their own souls. The ambition of modern parents, he declares, is the flat contrary to that of Job. He strove in thought and deed to bring up his sons for God, to restrain them from sin and make them rich in the things of the spirit. Nowadays parents nourish children for the world, to be boastful, prolific and rich. "If they should see them poor, they are saddened and sigh. If they see them sinning, nobody is sad."[3] Some take the trouble

[1] MS. Salisb. Cath. Libr. 103, fol. 102b (unpubl. *Jacob's Well*). Cf. Bozon, *Metaphs.* cap. xl, cxxviii, cxxix, cxl; Bromyard, *S.P.* s.v. "Feriae seu Festa"; *Ayenb. of Inwyt*, p. 220; etc.

[2] See my *Preaching in Med. Engl.* p. 33, and above, p. 255. Cf. further Bozon, *Metaphs.* cap. cxxv.

[3] The more vivid expansion of this complaint in MS. St Albans Cath. fol. 24 is interesting: "And thouȝ thei seen and heeren her children breke the commaundementis of God fro morowe til even, thei chargen not a

to send their sons in youth to the courts of nobles and the like for their education: but not so for the art or education of the soul. "What is worse, they recall them from such things as the latter with all the means in their power, rejoicing to see them led to the gallows of hell with oaths, fopperies, bad manners and dissolute company, grieving and weeping when they see them learning the art of a good life."[1] Instead of keeping them at home, as they should do, to prevent their copying the evil fashions and finery of their elders,[2] by dressing them up extravagantly, by taking them to shows, by loading them with ill-gotten gain, or sacred orders and benefices of which they are quite unworthy, they seek to win them for the world.[3] Thus Bromyard: the cry of the vernacularists is much the same:

Bot som men setteth here chyldren to lerne Jestes of batailles and of cronycles and novelleryes, oft of songes that stereth hem to iolyte and to harlatrye, and some setteth hem to nedeles craftes for pryde and coveytyse that harmeth here soules, and some setteth hem to lawe for wynnyng of worldlyche worschepe, and herto costeth hugelyche in many weyes. Bot in al this Godes lawe is put be-hynde.... Some techeth here children to swere and stare and fyȝte, and to bescherewe alle men aboute; and of this they have gret joye in here herte. Bot certes they beth Sathanas-ys techers and procuratours to lede hem to helle by here cursede ensample and techynge and noryschynge and meynteynynge in synne, and beth cruel sleers of here children: ȝe, more cruel than though they hackede here children as smal as mosselles to here pot.[4]...

þese, but lauȝen and iapen and ioien there-inne, and conforten hem there-to. But if thei seen her children have a worldeli schame or velany, thanne thei wepen and maken sorowe ynouȝ, and cher[i]se hem and glosen hem, and suffren [hem] to be as nyce and as wantowne in halle and in chambre, in chirche and in chepinge as hem lust hem silf".

[1] Here clearly speaks the friar, recalling the parental bullying sometimes meted out to sons who joined the Orders at Oxford and elsewhere against their parents' wishes. (Bromyard adds further—"quomodo, viz., mundum fugiant et cum vita sancta et religiosa ad coeli palatium perveniant".) Cf. the case of friar Robert of Ware, as related by him in the Prol. to his sermons on the B.V.M. (13th cent.), in MS. Gray's Inn Libr. 7, fol. 62 (see my art. in the *Dublin Rev.* April, 1925, vol. 176, pp. 282–4); and above, p. 246, n. 1.   [2] S.P. s.v. "Ornatus".
[3] s.v. "Filiatio", "Ab Infantia" and "Exemplum".
[4] Similarly MS. St Albans Cath. as before. On children learning to swear, cf. MS. Bodl. 95, fol. 2 ("And mony faders and moders techen her cheldren thorowe her cursed othis to dispise God;...and thus her

And suche fadres and modres that menteyneth wytynglyche here children in synne and techeth hem schrewednesse beth worse than the cursede fadres that culleth[1] here children and offreth hem up to stockes, worschepynge fals mamettrye.[2] For they children were dede in here 30uthe and dyde no more synne. Bot thes children of cursede fadres and moders, that techeth hem pryde, thefte and lecherye, wraththe, coveytyse and slouthe and glotenye and menteyne hem ther-ynne, beth holde on longe lyf and in encresyng of synne to more dampnacioun of eche partye. And no wondere though God take vengeaunce on the peple, both olde and 30nge: for alle communelyche despysede God in this, that they haveth ioye and merthe and despyseth correcciouns and re- prevynges. And ther-fore God mote punysche this synne for his ry3tful mageste.[3]

One source of infection in the home, and all may be corrupted:

We schulde fynde modyr and wyif now-on-dayes that, 3if the sone or husbonde speke or do evyll, thei schull speke or do wel werse. 3if the man sey—"Go we to evyll", they wyll seyne—"Renne we". The modyr and wyif, chyld and dow3ter, servaunt and alle, 3if the mayster be rédy to wyckydnes, all the mene[4] schal helpyn forth to makyn it wel worse. Thise householdys wyll fare evyll in the ende.[5]

As usual the pulpit is ready with its solemn warnings of the fate in store for the parent who fails to rear his son in good habits.[6] Sooner or later the latter will turn and curse him. Master Ralph of Acton thus retorts to the indignant *pater- familias*: "O wretched father, accusing your son for this! He does it, because you taught him so. If you wanted him to

faders techythe hem the crafte that they schuld use ever to blaspheme God", thus preparing them "to be brondis in hell fyre"); MS. Roy. 18. B. xxiii, fol. 88; and abroad, an early 13th-cent. sermon in Hauréau, *Not. et Extr.* vol. ii, p. 107.
    [1] = killeth.
    [2] = idols (cf. Ezek. xxiii, 39; etc.).
    [3] MS. Harl. 2398, fol. 94b. Similarly in MS. Roy. 18. B. xxiii, the vices of "men of age" are a disastrous influence ("But now-adaies olde men ben ful of vices, and so thei be but children. And therfore—'cursed is the child of an hundreth 3ere olde'" [see Isa. lxv, 20]).
    [4] = household.
    [5] MS. Salisb. Cath. Libr. 103, fol. 136.
    [6] The *Spec. Laic.* cap. xxxviii (ed. Welter, pp. 60–1) mentions as hindrances to proper correction—(a) in the *corrector*: (i) nimia simplicitas, (ii) carnalis affectionis immensitas, (iii) nimia mundani dampni meticu- lositas; (b) in the *corrected*: (i) cordis elacio, (ii) cordis infatuacio, (iii) peccatorum inveteracio.

prove dutiful, why did you not teach him to be just yourself?"[1]
A favourite *exemplum terribile* on the subject is the story drawn
from the *Liber de Disciplina Scholarium* of pseudo-Boethius[2]
—of the son who, when condemned to death for crimes learnt
in youth, bit off his father's nose as the latter approached to
give him a farewell kiss at the foot of the gallows.[3] If no such
disaster should befall the negligent parent in his lifetime, Master
Thomas Wimbledon would yet remind him of the solemn
question of God Almighty which he must answer at the Doom:
"How haste thou governed thy wife, thy children and servants?
Haste thou brought them up after the laues of God and continued them there in, as much as lyeth in thy pouer?"[4] Apart
from stray references in the *Vision of Piers Plowman* and other
poems of Complaint, we have now to note as the fruit of all
this earnest exhortation a contemporary literature, in verse[5] as
well as prose, setting forth the right and proper upbringing of
children, ancestor, therefore, of a didactic poetry for the young
to which some well-known English poets have contributed in
more recent times.

---

[1] MS. Jo. Ryl. Libr. Manch. Lat. 367, fol. 57 b.

[2] cap. ii (Migne, *Patr. Lat.* vol. lxiv, col. 1227).

[3] *Spec. Laic.* as above (ed. Welter, p. 61, no. 296). Also in Jacques
de Vitry; MS. Harl. 7322, fol. 35; and MS. St Albans Cath. fol. 26 ("so a
greet clerk tellith of a childe that was not tauȝt of his fadir and modir,
but he was suffrid to do what he wolde.... Whanne he stood at the ladder,
...he preiede his fadir to kisse him,..[and] he bote of his nose...").
Another story of the kind, in MS. Roy. 7. D. 1, fol. 85, and the *Spec.
Laic.* (no. 297) tells of a youth led to the gallows who exclaims to his
father—"Pater, tu me suspendio tradidisti; quia, dum potuisses, me
corripuisse neglexisti". No. 298 of the latter work is a tale "in partibus
Cancie [i.e. Kent], temp. reg. Henr. iii". See further Hauréau, *Not. et
Extr.* vol. iii, p. 129.

[4] Inc. pars ii. (ed. *Ch. Hist. of Engl.* Ser. in Foxe, *Acts and Mons.*
vol. iii, pt. 1, p. 300).

[5] Cf. *Stans Puer ad Mensam, How the Good Wife taught her Daughter,
How the Wise Man taught his Son* (ed. Furnivall, E.E.T.S. O.S. no. 32;
Hazlitt, *E. Pop. Poetry of Engl.* vol. i; etc.), *Ratis Raving, The Thewis off
Gud Women* (ed. Lumby, E.E.T.S. O.S. no. 43), etc., etc. The same
literature would seem to have inspired the so-called 'Prodigal-son'
plays of the Tudor period, such as *The Disobedient Child, Nice Wanton,*
etc. (Cf. further below, p. 493.)

Such, then, is some of the evidence by means of which the medieval pulpit in England can rightly claim to have been a creative centre of literary Satire and Complaint. Through three long chapters we have traced its influence in a literature here and there crude and unpromising enough, representing, many will say, what is of least literary merit, of least beauty and inspiration in the work of the time. It may be so: but who shall deny that it was a potent and enduring influence? The dilettante man of letters may spurn it, if he like; the true historian of letters never. There is a picturesque saying about the poets of the Middle Ages to the effect that in gay youth they begin by singing of love and its delights; later, they choose to versify the anecdotes, histories and animal fables of their country; finally, in old age and infirmity they turn to sacred and philosophic themes.[1] If now for the word "poets" we substitute that of "poetry", our tale would represent, with some equal degree of truth, the main effect of the long struggle of religion to conquer and subdue the territory of secular and romantic verse. A sickness of body and soul at length turns our glittering troubadour into a grey friar: the Church has won a victory.[2] This impact of religion upon poetry produces in England no brilliant theological epic, no exquisite *Vita Nuova* with its tale of romantic love transfigured, become mystical, philosophic. But where we do recognise the voices of the churchmen dominating for a while, dictating terms to the vanquished, is in the Satire and Complaint of our later medieval poets. For the Faith itself this may have been indeed a barren victory. For English literature and for English institutions it is eloquent of mighty stirrings and pregnant resolves at the nation's heart. On the one hand, the impact led, as we have seen, to a new and ruthless realism, and a tragic as well as a comic sense of Life; on the other, to "the first recognisable steps on the road of political and religious liberty", taken with a grim determination. It helped therein to prepare the mind, to quicken the eye and strengthen the purpose of the coming generations that were to produce both a William Shakespeare

[1] A. Dinaux, *Les Trouvères du Nord de la France*, vol. iv, p. 51.
[2] Cf. here, Digby MS. poem, E.E.T.S. O.S. no. 117, pp. 756–7.

and an Oliver Cromwell. For, the pulpit of the Middle Ages first trained men, like the eaglets in one of its own favourite apologues, to gaze unflinchingly at the full noon-day sun of the world's heat and glare, its passion and its pathos. The kitchen-knave thus stood revealed in all his native weaknesses; the prince and the prelate appeared stripped of their finery, their dignities and pretensions, with now no sham-heroic veil of Romanticism to hide their grosser shame or their lighter follies. A "mirror" indeed had been lifted up to nature: and men looked and pondered freely. It was highly characteristic of this first stage on the road to social and literary emancipation that whatever was thus presented was, for all its new air of reality, still regarded as type rather than as individual. Nevertheless, the full emergence of the individual from the social group, with rights and features of his own, became inevitable from that day onwards. Sooner or later, in politics as in religion, the rule of "divers persons fearing God and of approved fidelity and honesty" would be tried as a substitute for that of ungodly prince and bishop; and the god-fearing at war with his sovereign would be as ready to fire his pistol at him as at any common offender against God and the realm. As for literary Satire and the Drama, henceforth in ever advancing degree—

> Like as the Preacher dooth discommend
> All vices living with mouth and wil,
>
> .   .   .   .
>
> Like so mine auctor dooth the same,
> No creature living spoken by name.[1]

[1] (*The Schole-house of Women.*)

CHAPTER VIII

Sermon and Drama

I N a brief footnote to one of his chapters on the French pulpit in the twelfth century, the Abbé Bourgain raises the interesting question of relations between the sermons and the mystery-plays.[1] Speaking solely for the place and period of his own particular study, he denies that either of them has influenced the other. Their early growth and development, he says, have been independent. The sermon Dialogues are anterior to the birth of liturgical drama, and therefore not derived from it. The Mysteries, for their part, were already fully developed by the end of the eleventh century with a history of their own—in the words of M. Léon Gautier—"des compositions entièrement originales, entièrement en vers".[2] Common sense, however, would suggest, at the outset, that the sacred plays of the Middle Ages, which so obviously "combined the moral and religious teaching of the homily with the exciting movement of the drama",[3] if independent in origin, at least must have had some subsequent points of contact with the sister art of the pulpit. Even the secular drama of modern times will easily outdo the sermon in its own task of purging and uplifting the listener, whenever it presents to him those "unspeakable Realities" which are perfectly expressed in the complex relations of life, but rarely or never in mere words alone. Where the glib phrases of the pulpit have left us cold, "κάθαρσις" in the modern drama of Tchekov as in the ancient drama of Euripides may well stir to the very depths of our being. For here, if anywhere,—to use the language of Goethe—"good thoughts stand before us like free children of God, and cry 'We are come!'" So it is that we begin to read without

---

[1] *La Chaire franç.* p. 232.
[2] *Le Monde*, Aug. 30, 1872, quoted in Bourgain, v.s.
[3] Courthope, *Hist. of Engl. Poetry*, vol. i, p. 239.

surprise, in M. Sepet's "epoch-making *Étude*",[1] that the
Mystère known as *Les Prophètes du Christ* is the "transformation pure and simple" of a Christmas sermon ascribed to
St Augustine, Bishop of Hippo; and that the Mystery and the
Sermon had at least a common place in the Offices for the
Feast of the Nativity. Similarly, as Professor Johan Vising
reminds us in a more recent study,[2] the chief source for the
twelfth-century *Mystère d'Adam*—probably an English work
—apart from the Bible proves to be the same pseudo-Augus-
tinian *Sermo contra Judaeos*. By M. Lecoy de la Marche we
are reminded further that in religious dramas of the thirteenth
century on the Continent the play was prefaced by a sermon,
and other sacred discourses of a like kind frequently punctuated
its course, continuing the original theme where last it had been
broken off.[3] In the later history of the stage, indeed, these
homiletic interludes were to suffer a strange fate, characteristic,
none the less, of the waning influences of religion. "N'est-il
pas curieux de voir", remarks the same archivist, "que les
intermèdes dramatiques, remplis aujourd'hui par la danse, con-
sistaient autrefois en sermons?" To some, doubtless, this
quaint link between dance and moralization will recall their
actual combination in the work of the ancient Greek chorus.
Finally, when we come to "le grand siècle des Mystères" in
France, early in the fifteenth century, we have the assurance
of M. Émile Roy, for example,[4] that the sacred dramatist
Arnoul Gréban not only knew the *Postilla* of Nicholas of
Lyra, but "followed them very closely" in the writing of his
plays. Likewise, M. Émile Mâle, who also refers to this fact
in his more recent study of Religious Art, has himself re-
emphasized the importance of the *Meditationes* of the pseudo-
Bonaventura in the same field,[5] another work which, as we

---

[1] *Bibl. de l'École des Chartes*, 28th yr. vol. iii, 6th Ser. esp. here,
pp. 14 and 25.   [2] See *Anglo-Norm. Lang. and Lit.* p. 45, § 27.
[3] *La Chaire franç.* p. 286 ("Commençons ou nous finasmes au matin!").
Cf. also, G. Duriez, *La Théol. dans le drame relig. en Allemagne*, 1914, p. 17.
[4] See *Le Mystère de la Pass. en France*, in *Revue Bourguignonne de
l'enseignmt. sup.* vols. xiii and xiv.
[5] *L'Art relig. de la fin du moyen âge*, cap. ii, esp. pp. 36–51. (Cf. p. 36:
"L'auteur des *Méditations*, en effet, a l'instinct du drame, et il se révèle

have seen, exercised a marked influence upon our English homilists.[1] With such initial justification, then, the stage is clearly set for some closer investigation of the links between sermon and drama. Indeed, one is left to wonder that they should so long have escaped the notice of learned editor and commentator, intent upon the task of tracing the beginnings of modern dramatic art in this country.

In the matter of our own native play-cycles written in the vernacular, we can hardly hope ever to determine the exact degree of their indebtedness to the English sermons now before us; nor how far the plays in their turn may have influenced the subsequent art of the pulpit. Certain general considerations at the outset, however, favour the first of these two hypotheses. In the first place, the age-long tradition of sacred oratory itself tends to support belief that it was the preacher who taught the dramatist, rather than *vice versa*. Assuredly, it was not from "the Miracles of foolish clerks" that proud and influential orators of the Church, like Bromyard who uses this scornful phrase,[2] first learnt to speak the common language and develop a common histrionic style. And no English preacher, we remark, however generous in his acknowledgment of other sources, ever deigns to mention the plays, save at the rarest moments and then in tones of contempt or at best of carefully qualified and condescending approval. Our verdict, therefore, if relationship can be established, is bound to be, as formerly in the case of sermons and "political poems", in favour of the older, more authoritative and widespread activity as parent source. Familiar association of the religious drama in its earliest stages with the Liturgy of the Church[3] hitherto seems to have blinded most scholars to the fact that in the pulpits, for centuries, the sacred episodes had been declaimed with a freedom and dramatic intensity unknown to mere liturgical

disciple accompli de saint François qui mimait ses sermons et jouait la scène de Noël....Les *Méditations* sont à la fois pittoresques et dramatiques, et c'est pour ces deux raisons qu'elles ont tant séduit les auteurs de Mystères....Ils y trouvaient surtout de l'imagination, de la poésie, de l'émotion, tout ce qui donne l'élan au drame".)

[1] See *Preaching in Med. Engl.* p. 288, etc.
[2] Cf. below, p. 480.   [3] But see below, p. 547, n.

recitation. To Sir Adolphus Ward, for example, English preaching is virtually non-existent by the close of the thirteenth century, which saw the rise of these same "Mysteries".[1] Neither Sir Edmund Chambers, nor Professor A. W. Pollard has a word to say upon its activities. Little wonder, therefore, that by others the influence of the pulpit has been so grossly overlooked! Professor Creizenach, on the other hand, does acknowledge "additions" to the later English dramas "taken over...from the sermons of enthusiastic preachers, whose brilliant imagery in its lofty flight brought before their audience all the different stages of Our Lord's life and Passion".[2] To this extent he has shown himself superior to most writers on the subject. But the element of naïve humour in the plays remains a fatal stumbling-block to him. He cannot conceive that anything of the sort could have been borrowed from "theological authors".[3] Consequently, like others again who have already recognized the influence of apocryphal matter from well-known homiletic sources such as the *Cursor Mundi*[4] or the *Legenda Aurea*,[5] he is never aware that *every* variety of expression to be found in the plays—canonical and un-canonical, serious and humorous, satiric and tragic—is of the very stuff and essence of the medieval English sermon. Instead, the student is left to imagine that the medieval play-writer was poring independently over the learned tomes of "Bona-venture" and "Doctor de Lira", or busily sketching for him-self the current life; whereas, in truth, he had to·go no further than the ordinary homilies and pulpit-manuals of the day for all this kind of matter. To take but a single example, that very reference in one of our plays to the words written by Christ upon the sand, which Creizenach traces to the *Postilla* of the aforesaid Nicholas,[6] we ourselves have had occasion to note

---

[1] *Hist. of Engl. Dram. Lit.* vol. i, p. 84, n. 1.

[2] See *Camb. Hist. of Engl. Lit.* vol. v, p. 42. This article I take to represent the mature opinions of the distinguished author of *Geschichte des neueren Dramas.*   [3] Ibid. p. 43; and *Gesch. d. n. Dr.* i, p. 197.

[4] Cf. here, e.g., Miss L. Toulmin Smith, *The York Plays*, Introd. pp. xlvii–ix.

[5] Cf. here esp. Miss Frances Foster, *A Stanzaic Life of Christ*, E.E.T.S. O.S. no. 166, Introd. pp. xx–xxviii.   [6] See art. as above, p. 50.

already in the sermons of an English preacher,[1] who, to complete the parallel, has actually apologized for his "sympull cunning" in the dramatist's own phrase.[2] If now the reader turns to a recent study of *British Drama* by Professor Allardyce Nicoll, he will see at once how far back into the old morass our study of the miracle-plays has tumbled. For here he is confronted again with the old familiar verdict of Messrs Ker and Waller upon Middle-English "political" verse.[3] The plays, we read, "in England as elsewhere", are "a form of art springing fundamentally from the lives of the people".[4] They are "distinctively the creation of the common people, with all the defects and virtues consequent upon that fact". Thence comes their naïveté of treatment—"a way of escape from piety in all manner of license", and so forth.[5] Oh, truly marvellous medieval sons of toil! Once more, then, scholarship has been sadly led astray by lack of acquaintance with another and a much despised literature which had already set forth in true and satisfying combination the colloquial, the proverbial, the jovial and the religious. Can we find, however, apart altogether from this particular *lacuna*, a further reason for the blindness of our scholars? We shall probably not be far wrong, if we place upon the well-known Tudor "Banes" of the Chester Cycle a good deal of the responsibility for this subsequent attitude. For here we have a source not only for Ward's belief concerning the death of vernacular preaching, but also for the view of others that the comedy of the plays must necessarily be a non-religious and secular growth. No lying chronicler of medieval times, no impudent sixteenth-century Reformer could better have deceived the modern literary savant. In both directions the statements of this ignorant or malicious ban-writer are at utter variance with the truth as we now know it. He is palpably wrong, as our evidence proves, when he speaks of—

These storyes of the Testament at this tyme, you know,
In a common Englishe tongue never read *nor harde*.[6]

[1] See above, p. 122. [2] See in my *Preaching in Med. Engl.* p. 22.
[3] Cf. above, p. 216. [4] *Brit. Drama*, p. 23. [5] Ibid. p. 27.
[6] *Chester Plays*, ed. Deimling, E.E.T.S. Ext. S. no. 62, p. 3, ll. 22-3.

He is wrong again, as we shall see shortly, when he says of the episodes of humour—

> Interminglinge therewith *onely to make sport*,
> Some thinge *not warranted by any writt*,
> Which to gladd the hearers, he woulde men to take yt.[1]

Such, indeed, was certainly never in the mind of the faithful "dan Heggenett" or whoever else may have been the original author of these Chester pageants. As for our ban-writer, he shows himself at least to be a good Protestant, if a bad introducer of miracle-plays. We recognize as one of his typical acquaintances that unknown Tudor gentleman who prefaces a fourteenth-century sermon, republished in Elizabethan days, with similar pleasantries upon those despised and bygone times, "when", as he puts it, "the worlde not slumbred, but routed and snorted in the deepe sleep of ignorance".[2] No one yet, so it seems, has relegated these Chester Bans to the place which they deserve. Fortunately, however, we can end our introductory account of miracle-play interpretation on a brighter note. The researches of Miss Frances Foster, in America, have now definitely linked sections of all the four great Cycles with two didactic poems which, as she rightly observes, are in the nature of typical verse homilies, framed "for the purpose of instructing the laity in matters of religion".[3] One of them, *The Northern Passion*, with close affinities to the *Cursor Mundi* and the so-called *South-English Legendary*, belongs to a "school" of such literature; and, in finding a place for itself in the *Northern Homily Collection*, "thus became part of the regular course of sermons delivered from parish pulpits".[4] The relation of these verse homilies to the wider range of

---

[1] Ibid. p. 2, ll. 12–14.

[2] See my *Preaching in Med. Engl.* pp. 361–2. Cf. further the banwriter's characteristic reference to "the fyne witt at this day aboundinge", which "at that day and that age had verye small beinge", with the prefacewriter's allusion to his own marvellous times, when men had crept out of darkness "and come forth to the hot shining Sunne of God's Word".

[3] See *The Northern Passion*, pt. ii, E.E.T.S. O.S. no. 147, esp. pp. 7–9 and 81–101, and *A Stanzaic Life of Christ*, E.E.T.S. O.S. no. 166, esp. pp. xxviii–xlii. Cf. further in my *Preaching in Med. Engl.* pp. 273–8.

[4] *The Northern Passion*, pt. ii, p. 81 (for dates, see pp. 1–5).

sermons in prose has yet to be worked out; and many gaps remain. But Miss Foster is at least able to state that "the plays are not isolated phenomena...detached from English literature; but...the dramatists, like the lyric poets, drew from the common store of English tradition"[1]—that tradition, indeed, which it has been our special task to examine in these pages. Here, then, we see already how "a poem written for use in the pulpit was carried out of the church and brought home to the people through a new medium, the stage".[2]

In his authoritative study of the Medieval Stage,[3] Sir Edmund Chambers has dealt with the "capital importance" of what he calls "the critical period for the religious drama"[4] from the middle of the thirteenth century to that of the fourteenth. This is the period of the "secularization of the plays", as he puts it, when the place of acting is transferred from the interior of the church to its precincts, to the surrounding graveyard or to the neighbouring market-place. The sung drama of the liturgies now gives way completely to the spoken drama of the greater cycles. Moreover, this "laicization" is "accompanied by a further development of the secular and even comic elements" in the plays. "A more human and less distinctively ecclesiastical handling became possible", we are told, when the actors quitted the sacred building. Thus, in the words of Dr Greg, "the plays from being ecclesiastical became human, from being Latin became vernacular, from being cosmopolitan became national".[5] The results of this transference are obvious enough; but the only explanation here given for the transference itself is that of mere "physical necessity", due to "the growing length of the plays" and "the increasing elaboration of their setting". Contact with the new environment was apparently responsible for the other changes. Now it is precisely at this point that we are faced, in the history of the

[1] Ibid. p. 101.
[2] p. 8. See also *A Stanzaic Life of Christ*, p. xliii, quoting Mrs Frank, "Vernac. Sources and an Old French Passion Play", in *Mod. Lang. Notes*, vol. xxxv, p. 268.
[3] See esp. vol. ii, pp. 79 et seq. and 147–8.   [4] Ibid. p. 96.
[5] W. W. Greg, *Bibliogr. and Textual Problems of the Engl. Miracle Cycles*, 1914.

pulpit, with a parallel development that would explain fully and far more profoundly how this apparently bold and original step came to be taken. It was *popular preaching*, we believe—an activity entirely overlooked by Chambers—that brought about the "secularization" of the drama. Every feature characteristic of this new presentation of the plays is familiar to us already in the methods of open-air preaching inaugurated by the friars.[1] Why, then, it may be asked, did the promoters of the sacred pageant venture to shift the scene of their activities from the church to the churchyard? Simply because the preachers had already shown them the way to that self-same place, we reply. How else, indeed, might clerical supporters hope to override that initial antipathy of their fellows to performances on the greensward or the highway, such as Robert Mannyng still expresses, without the help and guidance of some such precedent? The *scaffaldi* of these evangelists stood erect already among the crowded lay-folk assembled to hear popular sermons in the cemetery garth, before ever any actors' *scaffaldus* had arrived upon the spot. The pageant-producers merely followed the preachers' example, giving performances in the churchyard with a sermon retained as the Prologue. How did the free vernacular colloquy in the play come so easily to displace the more dignified liturgical Latin of the older drama? Our answer is clear: precisely because vernacular preachers were daily proving the efficacy of this kind of speech in sermons on a level with the thought and expression of popular audiences. If it is still possible to read that gross misstatement that miracle-plays led in the van of vernacular religious instruction in the Middle Ages,[2] we have only one more proof—if indeed that were needed—of the scandalous neglect into which these ancient monuments of our English pulpit have been allowed to fall. From the same source of inspiration sprang also the comic interlude of the new drama. The preachers with their merry satire and *exempla* interlarding the sermon, were themselves sometimes guilty of even worse profanities than the pranks of a rascally sheep-stealer, or

[1] See my *Preaching in Med. Engl.* p. 313 et passim.
[2] Cf. Ward, *Hist. of Engl. Dram. Lit.* vol. i, p. 84, n. 1.

Noah's troublesome wife.[1] The very devils, likewise, were already alive and prancing in their more lively discourses. Dominican and Franciscan orators had thus discovered a way by which they might hope to outbid the japes of the obscene juggler, the dancers' *cantilenae* and the equally profitless amusement of worldly *ludi*. If their comments were generally less vulgar, they could be no less scathing and mirth-provoking in their way. Furthermore, just as this new bid for popular favour on the part of the preachers provoked a reaction in due time against its own worldliness and vulgarity, so a strong body of opposition arose against the new plays, and orthodox opinion remained divided. Nor was the churchyard the only place whither the actors appear to have followed the steps of the preacher. Market-places and streets at length rang with the accents of both. The very association of the plays with the sacred procession, as, for example, that which took place at the Feast of Corpus Christi, may itself be derived from the part regularly played in such public events by the *Sermo in Processione*.[2] It is at any rate interesting to note that here the parallel is made complete. What thus holds good of place and manner may yet apply further to time. For there is some evidence to suggest that the normal hours of open-air preaching and of miracle-playing on the simpler scale must frequently have coincided.[3] Finally, what was said in a previous chapter upon sermon Allegory and Personification will have made it clear that in the work of the preachers may be found every element, in its older and more appropriate setting, which contributed at length to the emergence of the Morality as distinct from the miracle-play. Even, then, if the sacred liturgy must still be held responsible for the birth of the drama, to the *pulpit* would be due its native development and popularization.

We may well pause for a moment at this stage to enquire what attitude our later homilists adopted towards the religious stage of their own day. In the light of such fresh evidence as

---

[1] Cf. my *Preaching in Med. Engl.* p. 83, and above, p. 167.

[2] See ibid. cap. v, pp. 201 et seq.

[3] Cf. the Newcastle play-time, and others mentioned in Chambers, vol. ii, p. 129; also "apres mangers" in *Man. des Pechiez*, l. 4309.

their writings supply, it would seem that Chambers' view[1]—
that the opposition which it encountered after the thirteenth
century came solely from heretic preachers—will have to be
modified. Indeed, that same tone of mingled ridicule and
hostility which we saw directed against the minstrel, the juggler
and other threatening rivals, by quite orthodox preachers,
appears to apply to the fresh case in question. But here, again,
as over the thorny problems of Holy Poverty or Gracious
versus Denunciatory Preaching, the contemporary pulpit by
no means spoke with one voice. As Dr Coulton rightly
reminds us in other connections, the historian is far too apt
to see a complacent uniformity in the attitude of orthodox
churchmen to medieval questions of the day. Whereas, of
course, the two pulpit controversies just mentioned are in
themselves most striking evidence to the contrary; while in the
matter of clerical acquiescence in official decrees, we have only
to recall the testimony of no less an expert in Canon Law
than Bromyard, that wellnigh every non-lucrative Decretal
and Constitution of the Church is made but to be broken.[2]
Undoubtedly the most enlightening comment concerning the
plays in all this new literature falls from the lips of that same
highly-placed Dominican preacher and theologian of the fourteenth century, John Bromyard himself. He is discussing the
many worldly pre-occupations offered in his day as excuse for
non-attendance at sermon-time. And yet, in spite of these, he
goes on, nobody is hindered thereby from taking his regular
meals, even in the autumn,[3] or from leaving home to dine at
a friend's house when invited. "And few there are", he continues, "whose business keeps them from new shows [or
pageants—*novis spectaculis*], *as in the plays which they call
'Miracles'. Why, then, are they prevented by attending the
Miracles of foolish clerics?* Such men Chrysostom rebukes—
super Johannem, Homelia ix: 'On account of business', says

---

[1] *Med. Stage*, vol. ii, p. 102.
[2] Cf. above, p. 252, etc. It may be noted here that the *Glossa Ordin.*
to the *Decret.* (c. 1263) as quoted by Chambers, *Med. Stage*, vol. ii,
p. 100, n. 2, is given in the *Flor. Barthol.* of Jo. of Mirfield (De Ludis),
MS. Camb. Univ. Libr. Mm. ii. 10, fol. 258b.
[3] I.e. the busy harvest-time.

he, 'they excuse themselves from the hearing of sermons, and
at theatres and race-courses they spend the whole day!...'"[1]
There is no actual prohibition of the miracle-play in Bromyard's
comment, it is true, such as occurs in the case of the well-
known Wycliffite *Tretise of miraclis pleyinge*;[2] but the tone
of contempt and the significance of those other amusements
with which the plays are here linked are quite unmistakable.
A little earlier, in the same section of the work, he speaks of
the Devil and his evil members "leading away those who intend
to go and hear the word of God to the taverns *or to the
pageants*".[3] William of Waddington, it will be recalled, in his
Manuel des Pechiez had likewise scorned "les fols clercs",
authors of "un folie apert...qe *miracles* sunt apelé".[4] If we
are to accept Bromyard's use of the term *spectacula* as generally
embracing the miracle-plays of the day, we have a further
parallel to his criticism in a Latin sermon-collection of equally
indisputable orthodoxy. The unknown author of the Lollard
Tretise that has just been mentioned is loud in his complaints
of "the lustis of the fleyssh and the myrthe of the body", the
"veyne siȝtis of degyse, aray of men and wymmen", the
idle "felawschipe of glotenye and lecherie" and other "occasions of perverting", engendered "in sich dayes of myraclis
pleyinge". So now the orthodox homilist is found to complain of the encouragement they give to what modern homilists
would decry, perhaps, as the "gay week-end" habit. The
fashionable and flighty man of his generation he describes as
"garrulous and unstable, because at one moment he is in the
taverns, at another at the dances, and at the next *at the pageants*,
now hither, now thither".[5] It is not difficult to understand
how that stern, pessimistic outlook upon the world which
drove both orthodox and heretic to condemn its light-hearted
frivolity and carelessness in religious duties led also to this
condemnation of the miracle-play. Bromyard would declare
fearlessly that sermons are quite adequate for presentation of

[1] *S.P.* s.v. "Audire (Verbum Dei)". Cf. also s.v. "Chorea".
[2] MS. Add. 24202, fol. 14. Cf. Grossetête's well-known prohibition,
and the "inania" in the Hereford injunction of 1348, *Reg. Trillek.*
[3] Cf. here MS. Harl. 2276, fol. 37 (as quoted, ibid. p. 71).
[4] E.E.T.S. O.S. 119, p. 154.   [5] MS. Add. 21253, fol. 57 (15th cent.).

the Truth. Such plays, then, are clearly to be reckoned amongst the "vana, curiosa et jocosa" of religious instruction, things to be shunned and suppressed.

But secondly, the Dominican's comment is valuable because it reasserts the fact once more that the plays remain essentially a *clerical* and not a popular production. Our subsequent studies will show that this is true to the very core. Like the Lollard's own tirade, it bears witness to the fact that "alas, more harme is, pristis now on dayes most shrewyn hemsilf and al day" in busying themselves "aboute siche pleyis". Among clerics who lent their support in this fashion were not a few, no doubt, who made use of their very gifts of preaching and instruction to write "banis" like the Dominican Thomas Bynham,[1] or actual parts for new performances.[2] If the tradition is correct which makes the monk Ranulf Higden the author of the Chester Cycle, as Dr Craig believes, then we have at least one definite case where a clerical dramatist of note was also the author of a treatise on the Art of Preaching,[3] and other homiletic aids.[4] A well-known instance of the way in which the pulpit might lend its support—and, indeed, en- couragement—to such performances is that of the "certain very religious father William Melton, of the order of the Friars Minor, S.T.P.,[5]...and a most famous preacher of the word of God". Coming to the city of York, in the year 1426, at the time of the Corpus Christi pageants, he "in several sermons recommended the aforesaid play to the people, affirming that it was good in itself and very laudable". It is again worth noting that, in the case of these York performances, even so sympathetic a preacher has to complain "that the

[1] 1423. For the Beverley Corpus Christi Play see Chambers, vol. ii, p. 339.
[2] Cf. the well-known passage in Wycliffe's *De Officio Pastor.* (cap. xv): "And herfore freris hav tauȝt in Englond the Paternoster in Engliȝesh tunge, as men seyen in the playe of Yorke"; or the work of the ex-monk Fraunces (see Chambers, vol. ii, p. 349).
[3] MSS. Bodl. 5 and 316.
[4] E.g. *Speculum Curatorum* (cf. below, p. 515).
[5] See Drake's *Eboracum*, App. p. xxix (from York City Records, Bk. A, fol. 269); *York Memor. Bk.* Surtees Soc. 1914, vol. ii; and, for the cor- rected translation, G. G. Coulton, *Art and the Reform.* p. 393.

citizens of the said city, and other foreigners coming to the said Feast, had greatly disgraced the play by revellings, drunkenness, shouts, songs and other insolences, in no wise attending to the divine offices of the said day". Clearly, then, there were good grounds for the grievances of Lollards and the disdain of a Bromyard. English sermons of the fourteenth and fifteenth centuries give interesting sidelights upon the similar disorders which accompanied plays and revelry in the Christmas season. Medieval rustics and townsmen of England, let loose on the Holidays, were no more apt to control themselves than their brethren—clerical or lay—on the continent, whose excesses in church and cemetery at Feasts of Fools and Asses called down the fury of Lenten preachers, as *Quadragesimalia* still testify. "Pleyng at Cristmasse Heroude and the thre kynges, and other processe of the Gospel, bothe thanne and at Ester", so heartily approved by the author of *Dives et Pauper*,[1] often gave the wilder spirits too good a chance to relieve pent-up feelings. Says Bromyard, they offer to Christ at this Festival only "a feast of words, with dancing and ditties".[2] Of "these Cristemas halydays, that wer ordenyd in holy chyrch for greth solemnyte and the merytes of Cristes feyth", says another,

in the old tyme men and women wer ful glad for to make them clene in sowle from all maner of unclennes of syn. But now-a-dayes that solemnyte ys turnyd to syn and unclennes, not only yn pryde but all the vii dedely synnys, and in ou3thragyng, drynkyng, wakyng, pleyng veyn pleys with all rybawdry and all harlotry. And so he [that] can most rybawdry in spekyng or in syngyng, he [is] most sett by, and he ys callyd a joly felowe and a stowte revelour. Thus these holydayes of Cristemasse, that wer ordend to goddes worschyp now be turnyd to gret offence to almyghty God. Wherefor, our moder holy chyrche, seyng her chyldern thus drownyd with de[d]ly syn, as a kynde moder full of [com]passyon and forgevynes, sche hath ordenyd this day for them, and layde downe this day *Allya* [= *Alleluia*] and oder songes of melody and gladnes, as *Gloria in excelsis* and *Te deum*; and takyth forth tractes that be songes of mornyng and hevenes.[3]

---

[1] See Prec. iii, cap. xvii. [2] *S.P.* s.v. "Adventus".
[3] MS. Glouc. Cath. Libr. (unpaginated), Sermo Domin. i, Septuages. (cf. also Myrc's *Festial*, E.E.T.S. ed. p. 63). Similarly, a 13th-cent. sermon, in MS. Harl. 2345, fol. 50, condemns the worldly merriment over bonfires, "shameful and lawless plays", etc., at the Feast of St John the Baptist. For improper songs at Christmas, cf. again Gascoigne, s.v. "Nativitas Dom. nost. J.C." (*Loci e Libro Verit.* p. 144).

Apparently these "songes" of Holy Mother Church by most Churchmen were considered outlet enough for the emotions of the season. For another preacher speaks thus, in an Advent Sermon,[1] of "the tyme of [Christ's] blessid nativite; in the whiche tyme we owʒte to syng the songes of lawde and preysyng in honour and worchype of Cristes blessid burthe, and in the holydayes folowing, at the tymes of the devyne service of God". For the rest—"be well ware that ʒe syng not the songes of fowle rebawdry and of unclennes; for then ʒe do disworchip to the tyme of Cristes burthe". The Christmas play is here not so much as mentioned. But, on the other hand again, it is equally clear that the medieval cleric himself might produce one of the less ambitious "Crystmas games", which men delighted to "pleien...about the fier",[2] at that festive season. For an example is preserved for us in a "Cristemasse game made by Maister Benet, howe God almyghty seyde to his apostelys, and echen off them were baptiste, and none knewe of other".[3] His twelve stanzas of seven wretched doggerel lines apiece put into the mouth of the Almighty, who thus welcomes each of His Apostles in turn, would seem to offer little scope for acting, for amusement or, indeed, for edification of any kind:

> Come on, Petir, syt downe at my knee.
> Here is a place preparate for the!

But, along with this highly familiar, if not boisterous tone of address, we must supply in imagination the added attraction of appropriate costumes and "make-up", of dignified procession and solemn imitated ritual before the throne of the Almighty, all acted out with the bustle and excitement of a modern parlour "charade". For the 'game' is plainly one of many such naïve transmutations of secular *ludi*, which, like the pagan archetype of the *Danse Macabre*[4] and the medieval

[1] MS. Linc. Cath. Libr. A. 6. 2, fol. 23 b.
[2] MS. St Albans Cath. fol. 5 b (treatise on the Decalogue).
[3] MS. Harl. 7333, fol. 149 b (printed in T. Wright, *Christmas Carols*, Percy Soc. (1841), p. 28). Master Benet is supposed to be identifiable with Benedict Burgh, rector of Sandon, Essex (c. 1440), who died in 1483, author of several poems (see *Camb. Hist. of Engl. Lit.* vol. ii, pp. 208–9).
[4] Cf. Miss B. White in *The Dance of Death*, E.E.T.S. ed. p. xiii.

ancestor of our modern "Blind Man's Buff",[1] were carefully adapted by earnest "Maister Benets" of the day, to recall the sacred message in silent mummery, *cantata* or playlet at rustic festivals. Be this as it may, in the matter of the plays many English preachers of the fourteenth and fifteenth centuries clearly would have sided neither with the party of unqualified approbation, nor with that of extreme contempt. Following the good example of William Melton and the unknown author of *Dives et Pauper*[2], rejecting the disdain of Robert Mannyng and John Bromyard, they would approve with *Pauper* of "miracles, pleyes and daunces" done mainly for devotion, honesty and mirth, without ribaldry, taint of heresy, or indecency, and without keeping men from divine service, or "fro goddes worde hering". Otherwise performed, the plays were unquestionably bad, and worthy of the boldest pulpit denunciation. Those who ventured to condemn them all outright on patristic authority they would answer, precisely as we have already heard the iconoclasts answered:[3] Christian people, in the days of "Austyn", were "moche medlyd with hethen peple", and therefore especially prone to unhonest dances and the like. Hence the older prohibition. But nowadays they could certainly make mirth in seemly fashion without risk of misunderstandings or contamination from that quarter.

Before we make use of the material provided in the present work, we shall best begin our study of the relations between sermons and plays by considering first those more obvious evidences of homiletic construction which the latter supply in the light of the author's introductory volume. In England, indeed, where the golden age of vernacular religious drama coincides, so far as existing records suggest, with the golden age of vernacular preaching, the parallels between them are far too numerous and arresting to be mistaken for mere coincidences. Even when due allowance is made for the fact that both drew inevitably upon a common store of theological doctrine, there remain overwhelming similarities in the actual handling of the matter, the details of certain characters and topics, the very texture and language of the two classes of

[1] See below, p. 510. [2] Prec. iii, cap. xvii. [3] See above, p. 138.

composition. The generic varieties of "Miracle" and "Morality" themselves suggest to us at the outset two general types of sacred discourse. On the one hand, we have the *Sermones super Evangelia* and *Sermones de Sanctis* concerned like the former with episodes in the lives of Christ and His Saints; on the other hand, moral discourses devoted like the latter to *Credo, Paternoster*, or Commandments, along with special emphasis upon the character of Vices and Virtues. Looking closer at the plays, we observe how the mounted *Expositor* of the Chester Cycle[1] and the *Contemplatio* of the *Ludus Coventriae* continue from time to time to do the office of those homiletic commentators indicated by Lecoy de la Marche in connection with thirteenth-century French plays.[2] Nor has the introductory sermon wholly vanished from our sight. For, in the Corpus Christi Pageant of the Shearmen and Taylors at Coventry, for example, the prophet Isaiah performs this same task, with the unmistakable paraphernalia of sermon Invocation and Conclusion.[3] In some ways, perhaps, more striking still are the various sermonettes delivered from the body of the plays, without previous warning, by leading characters in the scenes. The course of the narrative may be actually held up for a time, or even a conversation interrupted, while the chosen speaker turns to pour forth an undisguised homily upon the audience. Thus in the Towneley Cycle,[4] and again in the Sixth Play of the *Ludus Coventriae*, Moses gives in epitome the regular pulpit exposition of the Decalogue which we already know so well, to be followed later in the Play by the corresponding Ten Plagues "for brekinge of the X commaundementis".[5] St Paul, in like manner, preaches a sermon

[1] For mounted preachers, see my *Preaching in Med. Engl.* pp. 210–11.
[2] This parallel has been overlooked by Ward (cf. *Camb. Hist. of Engl. Lit.* vol. v, p. 12).
[3] Cf. E.E.T.S. ed. Ext. S. no. 87, pp. 1–2 (and my *Preaching in Med. Engl.* pp. 317 and 330). In the Weavers' Pageant following (pp. 33 et seq.), the play starts with an introductory dialogue, but the formal sermon ending is retained (pp. 38–9).
[4] See E.E.T.S. ed. Ext. S. no. 71, pp. 57–9 (beginning—"Herkyns all, both yong and old...").
[5] Thus in MS. St Albans Cath. fol. 45 (sermon-treatise on the Decalogue. See further, *Lud. Cov.* E.E.T.S. ed. Introd. p. li (K. S. Block).

upon the Seven Deadly Sins in the course of the Digby Play of his *Conversion*. Most remarkable of all, however, is the address of Lazarus in the Towneley Play that bears his name, following upon his resurrection from the tomb at Bethany by Jesus.[1] For it is practically word for word identical to the smallest detail with Bromyard's sermon upon the fate of the dead.[2] The 'worm's meat', the decay of knightly garments, the roof of the new hall that "youre nakyd nose shall towche", the toads, the worms and the winding-sheet, the indifferent family, the unfaithful executors, all are here, as though directly transcribed from the homilist's pages. So, again, amongst minor homilies of the kind in this same Play-cycle, we have brief warnings against the follies of marriage from the mouths of Noah, the Second Shepherd and St Joseph,[3] and denunciation of—

Thise dysars and thise hullars	[dicers—lechers
Thise cokkers and thise bollars	[fighters—drunkards
And all purs-cuttars,—	

along with particular mention of the follies of gambling and the vagaries of Dame Fortune's Wheel, by the Torturers of the Passion Scene,[4] all of which will now be readily recognized as taken direct from some sermon manual or other. In similar fashion, we might go on to point out little tricks of the preachers' art which were certainly never invented by anyone else, least of all by those concentrating freshly and independently upon the production of a popular religious play. Such, for instance, are the Latin quotations from Scripture and the Fathers scattered in the Coventry and Towneley Cycles,[5] or the "saffron" of Latin phrases occurring in the speech of God

---

[1] E.E.T.S. ed. as above, pp. 390–2.
[2] *S.P.* s.v. "Mors", as sketched in my *Preaching in Med. Engl.* pp. 343–4. Notice also Lazarus' reference to himself as "youre myrroure" in the Play (l. 120).
[3] pp. 35 (and see further below, in the author's present chap. p. 492), 119 and 164, respectively. Cf. above, pp. 378–82.
[4] pp. 291–2. Cf. again, pp. 100–1. With this cf. above, pp. 239 and 372.
[5] Cf. further Dr A. W. Pollard on *The Towneley Plays*, E.E.T.S. ed. p. xxx, and Dr Hardin Craig's observation in *Two Cov. Corp. Chr. Plays*, E.E.T.S. ed. p. xviii.

Almighty that opens the First Chester Pageant, precisely in
the pompous manner of our more naïve vernacular sermons.[1]
Could anyone wish for a happier hunting-ground in which
to pursue the preachers' tracks? Like Isengrim the Wolf in
the sermon-fable, our homilist now turned play-writer is quite
unable to suppress his former habits and conceal his identity
from us. The clerical accent will out sooner or later, and never
more clearly than in those very passages which have been
supposed hitherto to exhibit the birth of a native dramatic
sense, struggling free of the old clerical traditions, uproarious
with a people's mirth, fresh, realistic and redolent of the soil.
Finally, the emotional high lights and shades of the sermons,
as sketched in the author's chapter on "Sermon-making",
are those of the miracle-plays also: on the one hand, the pathos
and pitiful appeal of the Nativity and Passion Scenes, or the
elaborate glorification of the Virgin Mother; on the other, the
unrelieved horrors of Hell, Doomsday, the cruelty of demons
or the relentless character of Death. And, interspersed amid
all these, again are touches of that curious, rollicking humour
which will best be studied in the fresh context to which we
now turn.

Every chapter in the present work thus far has had its own
story to tell of literary penetration. But, at the same time,
every one, if carefully re-examined, will be found to contribute
something to this other story of the way in which our vernacular
Play Cycles took their ultimate form. We must be thankful
to Professor Nicoll for having laid emphasis once again upon
what he is pleased to call "the realistic flavour" and "the
freshness" of the latter. "In origin the English Mysteries",
he says, "may have borrowed much from the French Plays
of a similar type, but fundamentally they breathed of the English
soil."[2] Here, then, we have clearly the fruits of that sermon
Realism which our First Chapter revealed, a Realism, indeed,
as widespread and international as the medieval pulpit itself,
at least as ancient and original as the naïve humour of Odo's

---

[1] See *Chester Plays*, E.E.T.S. ed. pt. i, pp. 9–10 (and *Preaching in
Med. Engl.* pp. 231–2, etc.). Cf. further, the Devil's 'new names' in the
Lud. Cov. (E.E.T.S. ed. p. 228) with p. 96, above.   [2] *Brit. Drama*, p. 40.

Fables, or the plain speaking of a Jacques de Vitry and a Berthold of Regensburg on the continent. As evidence of the connection, let the reader observe how even some of the very proverbs which we saw the preachers using in a religious context reappear in this other literature of sacred drama. "So long goys the pott to the water, men says, at last comys it home broken", exclaims Mak's wife again in the Towneley Shepherds' Interlude;[1] while the worldly monarch of the *Pride of Life* is made to excuse his indevotion with that familiar adage to the effect that the church will not run away.[2] The Second Chapter, it will be remembered, presented us with what we might now call certain conventional "properties" of the religious stage, namely, the Castle and certain Virtues and Vices in human form. To these must be duly added the general setting of the Doom Scenes and further fantastic individuals, such as *Mors* and the denizens of the under-world, all of which will be discussed at greater length in the pages which follow. In accord with what was said of the poet Langland's method of constructing his personalities from the impersonal statements of the homily-books, we shall also have occasion to see that this is precisely the manner in which the dramatist evolved his own dilatations of Scriptural characters. In its emphasis upon the preachers' "modernization" of the latter and their free rendering of Biblical scenes, the Third Chapter of our study has expressly prepared the way for appreciation of another trait in the English miracle-plays. For, the reader will now realize how naturally and inevitably the pulpit here contributed to a genuine dramatic feeling for the episodes of Holy Writ. The whole feudal array of tyrant-rulers and counsellors, Bishops of the Jews' Law, knights and peasants, patriarchs and saints, sir Noe, sir Lazarus and the rest reappear in their characteristic medieval dress. Furthermore, since both preacher and play-producer—like the artists of the period—are concerned pre-

---

[1] E.E.T.S. ed. p. 126, ll. 318–9 (cf. above, p. 43).

[2] This saying is noted by Creizenach, see art. *Camb. Hist. of Engl. Lit.* as before, vol. v, p. 53 (and above, p. 45). Cf. further, e.g., the 2nd Shepherd's reference to women as "cackling hens" in the second Towneley Shepherds' Play (E.E.T.S. ed. p. 118) with the same phrase in Lichfield's sermon, above, p. 387, and its sources.

eminently with the same great mysteries of the Church as celebrated at Christmas, Epiphany, Lent and Eastertide, the one in his pulpit, the other upon his scaffold, we shall hardly be surprised to find a similar correspondence in their choice of Gospel themes. Our Fourth Chapter, in presenting the homilist as a humorist with his witty tales of domestic folly, prepares us a step further for the so-called "native comedy" of the Plays. Just as the preacher introduced his anecdotes to lighten the theological solemnities of his address, thus making them more palatable to the common folk, so likewise does the play-writer with his comic interludes—"to plesen the puple", but always with an eye to their ultimate edification. A single phrase, therefore, originally applied to the *Vision of Piers Plowman*,[1] applies with equal force to the sermon and to the miracle-play. Each of them alike is "a long religious argument with comic interludes". As for the more serious type of *exemplum*, the Croxton drama of *The Sacrament* suffices in its turn to show how a favourite pulpit story setting forth the miraculous virtues of the Host could be dramatized once more direct from the preacher's note-book. Nor again are some of the favourite beasts of the Bestiaries missing, where, as in the Chester Play of the Deluge, the story of Noah's Ark provides an opportunity for their enumeration; nor again those curious *figures* constructed from natural phenomena, like the Sun and the Glass, which finds its place in the *Ludus Coventriae* as a simile for the doctrine of the Virgin Birth of Christ. It is in our most recent chapters, however, upon Sermon Satire and Complaint, where the pulpit has already proved itself to be an inspirer of verse of that kind, that we come upon the most striking revelations of all. Here, with the sermon-books in our hand, we can see, as in no modern editor's groping commentary, exactly how the more popular and lively additions to the earlier drama came to be incorporated. He who wishes to grasp within easy compass the significance of medieval preaching for the development of our native literature, and the advance in present knowledge which a study of it makes possible, need only consider the case of the Towneley Play-

[1] By Prof. W. P. Ker, in *Engl. Lit.: Mediev.* p. 196.

cycle. Hitherto deemed to be less homiletic than its fellows, it now proves itself in this sense to be the most typically homiletic of all. First, let the student begin by reading one of the earlier play-fragments; then Dr A. W. Pollard's scholarly Introduction to the Towneley Plays, observing, when he comes to it, this editor's modest, almost plaintive confession of the difficulty of "bringing literary criticism to bear" upon them.[1] Along with the latter, let him note with care the two leading observations that Dr Pollard makes upon the attitude of one whom he has here skilfully picked out as "the real genius of the Cycle". The first observation is to the effect that this poet's "sympathy with poor folk and his dislike of the 'gentlery men', their oppressors, seem something more than conventional"; the second that "his Satire is sometimes as grim as it is free".[2] Now let our inquirer proceed to read for himself the actual contributions of this dramatic genius to the Play-cycle in question, its Judgment Scene, for example, and the Shepherds' Complaints aforementioned, in the light of the new matter presented in our Sixth and Seventh Chapters. From them, if he wishes, he can turn to consider the satire of the Coventry Plays, flashing out now against extravagant costume, now against oaths, now against the Church Courts, now against the evil back-biter. He will at least agree, we think, at the end of his reading, that the pulpit has contributed something to the new realism and satire of the medieval stage, and that the poet's attitude is not so unconventional after all.

The suggestion has just been put forward that the sermons are responsible for those well-known excursions of the later religious drama, which carry it beyond the limits of Scripture and apocryphal legend into something approaching more nearly to a free dramatic interpretation of human life and conduct. It is time therefore to set about testing the truth of this remark by reference to some concrete examples. Let us begin with the character of Cain as portrayed in the Towneley *Mactatio Abel*. Putting aside the *purely* Biblical framework of the scene, we have here the portrait of a bad husbandman in an evil mood, who loses his temper with his plough-team and

[1] E.E.T.S. ed. pp. xxviii–ix.   [2] Ibid. p. xxx.

bullies his boy, curses and blasphemes God, blaming Him for
his bad harvests and general ill-fortune, above all a bad tither,
who not only objects to his duty, but further tithes dishonestly
—"making a jump" in the counting of his sheaves—and
giving of his worst, when compelled to give by the example
of his righteous neighbour. Finally, in a fit of envy he turns
murderer and slays his brother. The reader will not need to
be reminded that he has met this figure before.[1] It is, of course,
the preachers' portrait of the bad husbandman, a combination
of the special vices considered typical of his class, along with
one or two others of a more general kind, which help to
heighten its colour and expand its moral appeal. To that extent
and that only is Cain "an English peasant", drawn from the
life, certainly with nothing peculiarly characteristic of Yorkshire about him, as Ten Brink seems to have imagined;[2] for
he is little more than *a general pulpit type*. We turn next to
the yet more famous figure of Noah's wife. She has already
been revealed to us, indeed, as the offspring of a passage in the
Book of Proverbs.[3] But again her immediate foster-parent is
very clearly the native pulpit. She is of course the typical
shrew of the sermons. Of her evil garrulity we have evidence
both in the York and Chester Cycles, where she clamours for
the companionship of her favourite gossips.[4] We know that
she is a gad-about, if only from her remark in the York Play,
when ordered into the Ark by her long-suffering husband—

"Doo barnes, goo we and trusse to towne!"[5]

Finally, she is an example of the disobedient wife, a disturber
of domestic peace and charity. Well may Noah declare—

"Yee men that has wifis, whyle they ar yong
If ye luf youre lifis, chastice thare tong."[6]

[1] Cf. above, pp. 364–70, etc.
[2] See *Hist. of Engl. Lit.* vol. ii, p. 262. Cf. further Allardyce Nicoll,
Brit. Drama, p. 40 (Noah's wife a cursed shrew of some provincial
town, etc.).   [3] See above, p. 385 et seq.
[4] *York Pl.* ed. L. T. Smith, p. 49; *Chester Pl.* E.E.T.S. ed. pp. 56–7.
[5] p. 48.
[6] *Towneley Pl.* p. 35. (Similarly, of course, the Mary and Joseph
dialogues set forth the homilist's views of Married Life; also the Shepherd's
comments, pp. 118–19, in the lively manner of a Langland.)

If only we were privileged to see her upon the contemporary stage, we should find her costume and complexion eloquent of those remaining womanly vices of which the pulpit has so much to say. Does not the author of *The Book of the Knight of La Tour-Landry* tell us of the sermon which he once heard a learned bishop deliver against the evil finery of the Sex—in particular, their "highe hornes"—in which the speaker reminded his audience how "Noyis flode" was ordained as a punishment "for the pride and the disguysinge that was amonge women"?[1] Amongst other Old Testament types in this drama, the expanded parts of the Abraham and Isaac Plays can be shown likewise to be a dramatization of current pulpit themes setting forth the right and dutiful relations between parent and child. Isaac is the ideal medieval son alike in his willing obedience, in his filial respect, and in his readiness to receive punishment for any wrongdoing.[2]

And chyldern also owen to theyr parentes, to fader and moder and to theyr maysters, to obeye in folowynge Ysaac, the whiche obeyed in suche wyse to his fader that he was all redy to receyve the deth at his commaundement, as it appereth the xxii chapytre of Genesis; and yet he was at that tyme of the age of xxxii yere.[3]

Amongst characters of New Testament scenes which have suffered a like expansion at the play-writers' hands, Herod stands out before us as the feudal tyrant of the day. But those critics who regard him merely as the random product of some artless dramatist's pencil sketching the truculent bully partly from imagination, partly from real life, have missed the whole secret of his peculiar growth and fashioning. If the reader will now turn back to our preachers' sketches of the proud nobleman, themselves merely a vivid colouring of earlier phrases in thirteenth-century pulpit manuals, he will discover, not perhaps without surprise, one main source of the dramatist's inspiration. Here already is the future Herod of the miracle-

[1] E.E.T.S. ed. pp. 62–4.   [2] Cf. e.g., *Chester Pl.* pp. 73, 76, etc.
[3] From Caxton's translation (*The Book of Good Maners*, 1487, bk. iv, cap. iv: "Of the estate of yonge peple, and how they ought to governe themselfe") of *Le Livre de Bonnes Mœurs*, by the Austin friar, Jacques Legrand, 1410. Expansions of the early life-story of the Magdalene in *Magd. Plays* also seem to be indebted to such literature.

plays in broad general outline, as one who boasts of his might, of his personal beauty, of his sumptuous dress and array, of his noble ancestry, of his fame, his rich substance and his territory[1]—all those very gifts of Kind, Fortune and Grace which the preachers specified as the ground of Human Pride. He is further the "grett ffelowe" "among grett men and lordes" of the country, whom we saw[2] haughty and disdainful towards his inferiors, bitterly jealous of any possible rival, mean and oppressive to his subjects,[3] a terror to his servants,[4] much given to "braggynge" and "bostynge", a blasphemous swearer,[5] laughing at the thought of his own cruelty and expecting those who stand around him to sing his praises and flatter him for ever. From Herod we may well turn to his Knights. Here is the conventional picture of evil and decadent knighthood as drawn by the pulpit and now borrowed very naturally by the play-writer for the construction of his scene. Once again, he has merely to convert these general pulpit statements into the direct colloquy of individuals, and, apart from questions of rhyme and metre, his task is wellnigh done. Like the English knights of whom we read, Sir Waradrake and Sir Launcher of the Chester Plays are splendid boasters, but poor warriors. Their imaginary foes, like the distant Saracen whom their eye has never seen, are merely "those dogges":

> I slue ten thowsand upon a day
> Of kempes in their best aray
> There was not one escaped away
> My swoard it was so keene.

Indeed, "no man dare me abyde".[6] But when the summons

---

[1] See *Two Cov. Corp. Chr. Plays*, pp. 17–19; *Lud. Cov.* pp. 151–4 and 157; *Towneley Pl.* p. 141; etc. Cf. also in the *Towneley Pl.* the same boasting by Cesar Augustus and Pilate, pp. 79, 279, etc.

[2] Above, pp. 308–12.

[3] Cf. his idle promise to pay his knights "when he comes again", and his glorification over the reported slaughter of the Innocents, in the *Towneley Pl.*; and further, p. 168.

[4] Cf. ibid. p. 148; and further to his knights, p. 171, and his counsellors, p. 173.

[5] Cf. p. 169, l. 116, etc.

[6] Pt. i, pp. 194–5, etc. Cf. further *Towneley Pl.* p. 171, and Pilate's knights, pp. 224, 312, etc.

to fight comes—"in armowre full bright", their "best aray"—
as in the Towneley pageant of *Herod*, they are panic-stricken.[1]
As soon as they hear, however, that children are to be the
target of their lances, courage returns. Yet even the blows of
distaffs and the threats of broken-hearted mothers prove too
much for their mettle at the Slaughter of the Innocents. For
Secundus Miles wants to "ryn fote hote", before ever his task
is fully accomplished.[2] Back from the campaign they come,
therefore, with many a loud boast to their lord and master,
whose manners they love to ape, and upon whom they fawn,
like the knights of our preachers' story. Their avaricious eye
is already on the prizes that may await them—ladies, castles,
towers and a fat wage, yet more ground for foolish boasting.[3]
Could anyone have fashioned a wittier little scene, within the
framework of Scripture, out of the pulpit satires of a Bromyard?[4] The figure of Pilate we recognize next as our old friend
of the Civil Courts, the unjust Judge. We were introduced to
him by name in the sermon passage which told how "by
unjuste dred, one word acombers the jugges",[5] and again in
Brunton's strange comparison of English "justice" to the
situation at Christ's own trial.[6] In the opening of the Towneley
Conspiracy Play, Pilate himself proclaims his kinship, in un-
mistakeable terms, with the evil men of law in our homily-
books:

ffor I am he that may make or mar a man
Myself, if I say it, *as men of cowrte now can*;
Supporte a man to day, to-morn agans hym than.
On both parties thus I play, and fenys me to ordan the right. [feign]
Bot all fals indytars,
Quest mangers and Jurers
And all thise fals out-rydars
Ar welcom to my sight.[7]

[1] *Towneley Pl.* p. 174.　　　[2] Ibid. p. 178.
[3] p. 179. Cf. here with p. 552 below.
[4] Cf. further, the latter's comparison of the evil knights of his day
to the knights of the Passion, as above, p. 336.
[5] Above, p. 344. Similarly in Bromyard, *S.P.* s.v. "Falsitas" and
"Judices" (on injustice of contemporary lawyers and judges).
[6] Above, p. 339.
[7] *Towneley Pl.* pp. 204–5. Cf. again, pp. 243–4.

Later on in the Pageant of the *Flagellatio*, in a passage of more
than usual naïveté, the dramatist has actually forced him to
give us a clear hint of the place of his real origin:

> I am full of sotelty,
> ffalshed, gyll and trechery:
> *Therfor am I namyd by clergy*
> As mali actoris.[1]

From thence, he goes on to tell us, in the old familiar style,
how in the courts he cunningly inclines first to the right side,
then to the wrong, if he sees the chance of a better bribe. Of
his general avarice we have ample evidence in the undignified
way in which he grabs for himself the gown of the crucified
Jesus. When the Torturer, who has won it, will not part with
it as a favour, then the Judge uses threats until the wretched
man is forced to give way.[2] In Pilate's pompous Latin phrases
we have further echo of that learned "sotelty" which made
the law a bane for the poor and simple.[3] Even in the scene
of private life his conversation with his spouse in the York
Plays furnishes the dramatist with an opportunity to repeat
in satirical terms the old pulpit warning against kisses.[4] If
Pilate represents the Civil Judge, Caiaphas and Annas stand
for the evil Ecclesiastical Lawyer, dressed as "Bishops of the
Old Law" in mitre and rochet, hood and tabard, accompanied
by a host of lesser jurists.[5] Their presence here in the Play
offers our dramatist his sole chance to pillory the sins of churchmen. Like the good son of the pulpit that he is, the genius
of our Towneley Cycle goes at least as far as he dare in so
secular and undignified a place to fulfil the homiletic tradition.
For, Caiaphas proclaims to the world that "he gets more by
purchase than by land-rents",[6] and through his disgraceful
show of violence, calls down even the rebukes of his own

---

[1] p. 243.　　　　　　　　　　[2] pp. 286–91.
[3] Cf. ibid. pp. 279–80, and the characteristic "ergo" in the *Chester Pl.*
pt. ii, p. 291.　　　　　　　　[4] Cf. above, p. 382.
[5] Cf. *Two Cov. Cor. Chr. Pl.* App. ii, pp. 82, 86, 96–7; *Lud. Cov.*
pp. 230 et seq.; *Towneley Pl.* pp. 233, 237; etc.; and Myrc, as above, p. 116.
[6] *Towneley Pl.* p. 233.

clerical colleague, here speaking to him *in loco predica-*
toris:

> Sir, thynk ye that ye ar a man of holy kyrke.
> Ye shuld be oure techer, mekenes to wyrk![1]

So much, then, for the development of human character in
the miracle-plays.[2] We can hardly do better than conclude our
study of sermon influence upon them by considering in some
greater detail three of the outstanding scenes which they
present. In many ways that of the Nativity is for preacher
and for dramatist the most artistic of all. The first and greatest
of friars had himself given his blessing in a sermon, over that
primitive Manger-scene erected at Grecchio,[3] to what remained
perhaps as the most perfect expression in one common episode
of the common spirit of medieval preaching and medieval
drama. There can be no question here about the prior antiquity
of the pulpit tradition. For, a homily of the fourth century,
we are told,[4] exhibits those same tender and vivid little touches
which delight us still in English homilies upon this theme in
fourteenth- and fifteenth-century manuscripts. These latter will
repay our attention because they reveal not merely the spirit
in which the plays were fashioned, but also how their various
component parts were actually assembled and put together.
It is from the medieval chronicler, apparently, that first
preacher and then dramatist drew his special information con-

[1] Ibid. p. 234 (cf. further p. 237: "Sir, ye ar a prelate!"). Caiaphas
also laments that as a clerk he may not lay hands on Jesus (p. 238), and
curses his upbringing. Annas again has to rebuke him, though he assents
to the buffeting of Christ.

[2] Cf. further, with pp. 453–7 above, the *detractores* of the *Lud. Cov.*
(E.E.T.S. ed. pp. 124–34); pp. 314, 369, 410 above with the strutting
groom of the Digby *Conv. of Saul* (p. 31); etc.

[3] Cf. Thos. of Celano's 1st *Life of St Francis*, cap. xxx: "The Saint of
God stood before the manger, full of sighs, overcome with tenderness
and filled with wondrous joy.... Then he preached to the people who
stood around, and uttered mellifluous words concerning the birth of the
poor king and the little town of Bethlehem. And often, when he would
name Christ Jesus, aglow with exceeding love he would call Him the
Child of Bethlehem, and uttering the word 'Bethlehem' in the manner
of a sheep bleating, he filled his mouth with the sound...".

[4] Cf. *Biblioth. Sacra*, Oberlin, 1915, vol. 72, p. 506, and *Journ. of
Theol. Stud.*, Oxf., Jan. 1915.

cerning the circumstances and chief characters of the time immediately preceding the sacred Birth. Thus Octavian of the
Chester Plays, the "Cesar Augustus" of the Towneley Cycle,
is introduced to an English sermon-audience in the following
manner:

> For, as cronicalers sein,...it [the Nativity] was in the two and fourti
> ʒer of Octovian that was emperour of Rome, whych also was cleped
> August Cesar:...ffirst "August", that is, "echinge",[1] for he echede in
> his tyme moost the emperie of Rome; and "Cesar" he was clepid aftur
> Julius Cesar, a gret conquerour whiche was emperoure to-fore hym. This
> Octovian, what bi rial power, what bi gret wit, sujetide the more part
> of the world in his tyme to hym.

At the height of his glory, this monarch decides to tax his
Empire, continues the preacher. Consequently Syria is chosen
as the starting point, because as "the navele of the worlde"
it would offer a central example to other lands of what would
be applied to them in due course.[2] A sermon of the *Festial* and
exempla in other collections reproduce for us the story of
Octavian and the Sibyl, which figures again in the Chester
Nativity. In it "Sybyll the Sage", by means of a vision, fore-
tells Christ's birth; and the wise Emperor, to whom she
prophesies, at length himself offers sacrifice to the child "that
schuld be grattyr than he".[3] The Nativity scene, as we view
it with the eye of the medieval homilist, lies wrapped in a golden
mist of marvel.

> Many merveyls fell at this tyme of ys commynge, and dyvers myracles,
> as wittenes Innocentius Quartus, that xii ʒere afore Cristes burthe it was
> a generall pese thorough out all the world. And ther-fore the Romanes
> ordeynd a solempne tempull and a fayre, and called it the tempull of pese.
> Than thei wente un-to a mawmente[4] that thei had, that was called Appolyn,
> and asked hym how long that the temple shuld last, and he answered them
> and seid—"till a mayde have borne a child". And when thei herd this,
> thei seid that the tempull shuld last for evermore. Than thei wrote
> abowen on the tempull these wordes—"*Templum pacis est in eternum*",

[1] = increasing.
[2] MS. Add. 41321, fol. 41. Cf. also Myrc, *Festial*, p. 22; etc. and
Chester Pl. pp. 112–15, esp. ll. 201–18, 241–4 and 258–76.
[3] Myrc, p. 25. Similarly, MS. Roy. 12. E. i, fol. 146 (early 14th cent.);
MS. Add. 6716, fol. 12b (15th cent.); *Leg. Aurea*; etc. Cf. *Chester Pl.*
pp. 118-19 and 129-31. I.e. the Tiburtine Sibyl.
[4] = idol.

for thei trowed that it myght never have bene that a mayden shuld have consceyved and aborne a child and after hur burthe to have ben clene mayden. But that same ny3tht that Crist was borne, the tempull cleve on too and fell to now3the, and than thei beleved the prophecie. The beestes also that knew no reson fell on her knees and worshipped oure saviour. Truly this commyng restored us to oure heretage. ffor now we shall have the same joy in oure sowles as muche as herte can thenke and tonge can tell.[1]

This very marvel, strange to say, also has its place in the Chester *Nativity Play*,[2] between the final colloquy of Octavian and the Sibyl aforementioned and one further marvel preceding it, according to the dramatist's order,[3] which now claims our attention. This is the famous apocryphal incident of Our Lady's Midwives. Again it is to be found in sermon literature, notably among the discourses of John Myrc, who dwells in the neighbouring county of Shropshire. Two midwives, Zebell (or Tebel) and Salome, says Myrc, had been hastily fetched to the Virgin's bed-side by St Joseph. When they discover that "a mayden hath borne a chylde", Zebell is astounded, and "Salome would not leve[4] that, but busturly hondeled our lady; and therwyth anon hor hondes dryden up". However, a miracle of restoration follows: "Then come ther an angell, and bade hyr towch the chylde, and be hole. And soo scho dyd, and was hole".[5] This is the pulpit topic beloved of the ladies, which the author of the poem known as *Pierce the Ploughmans Crede* mentions as typical of Minorite efforts to win popular favour, when they preach "to plesen the puple" in the age of Chaucer.[6] Professor Skeat, who edited the poem in 1867, unacquainted with the use of this incident in English preaching, has probably been led astray by the poet's allusion here to "miracles of mydwyves". For, from the context, the phrase would seem to bear no reference to plays, as he imagines,[7]

---

[1] MS. Roy. 18. B. xxiii, fols. 168 b–9. Notice the preacher's mention of his source.

[2] pp. 127–9. (Here the dramatist says merely—"wee read in Cronycles", again, l. 585.) Cf. with the above account esp. ll. 629–44.

[3] pp. 123–6.   [4] = believe.

[5] *Festial*, p. 23. The Coventry Play version together with the source (*Protevang.*) will be found in Hone, *Anct. Mysteries*, pp. 67–72.

[6] E.E.T.S. ed. p. 4, l. 78.   [7] See his Note, p. 35.

but to the miracle itself as expounded in the friars' sermons.[1]
An interesting comment upon the subject as thus utilized by
the pulpit appears in a roughly contemporary manuscript of
homilies by one who is himself probably a Lollard and certainly
no friend of friars,[2] thus lending weight to our contention.
The speaker condemns all those who maintain this foolish
legend in church, and incidentally corrects a curious hagio-
logical confusion which sheds some fresh light upon the current
superstitions of Christmas-time:

> Ry3t so the hooli gost wrou3te bothe the conceyvynge and the birthe
> of this blesside chylde, with-oute wem of bodi or ani desese of the worthi
> maydenes bodi, his moder. And this proveth also wel that her nedide
> at that tyme no midwyves, ne non helpe to the birthe, as othere wymmen
> neden. And so thei dremen that seien that Anastase with creven hoondes
> was oure ladi[s] midewyif, and at that tyme sche was helid of her hondes.
> And this blynde evidence moueth hem, it seemeth, that on Cristemasse
> day at the seconde masse [at] the cherche seithe a memorie of her. But
> this evidence is to lewede. For, manye a 3eer aftur Crist suffride passioun,
> Anastase, on the same day that Crist was born, sche diede; and therfore
> the cherche maketh memorie of hir at that tyme.[3]

The reader who now looks back at the Chester *Nativity Play*
will see that we have covered practically every episode of
importance in it, with the exception of the opening Annunciation Scene, which he will find paralleled in due course by
another vernacular sermon-excerpt given later in our chapter.[4]
The greatest marvel of all, however, in the Christmas story
has yet to be mentioned—the Christmas babe itself. It was
into a typical feudal world, where outward pomp and splendour
still counted for so much among the great and influential of
the earth, that the homilist beheld Him born who was none
other than Heaven's King. For our homilist, though seldom
an artist, was, as we have said, above all a realist. How then
shall Heaven's King descend among men? "Ybore he was in
a pore hous that stode amydde the heye way", answers one

---

[1] Cf. l. 74: "And precheth..."; then later, l. 80, again: "Thei ne
prechen nou3t...". The reference to Our Lady's girdle refers, of course,
to the Images in churches, of which they preach, as above, pp. 145–8.

[2] Cf. below, p. 502, n. 1.

[3] MS. Add. 41321, fol. 45. (The reference is to St Anastasia.)

[4] Below, p. 539. (MS. Roy. 18. B. xxiii, fol. 139b.)

of them sweetly.[1] "As a pore childe, bonded in a cribbe betwix a nox and a nasse", says another.[2] In sermons of the period we find this a favourite theme, contrasting in vivid language the splendour of worldly monarchs with the poverty of the Christ-child. An unknown preacher thus dilates with eloquence and pathos upon the Divine Humility, "qwhan that thys kyng that is kynge of all kynges and lorde off all lordys wylffully forsoke worschip to be made pore ffor our sake". He bids the inquirer, who looks for some precious palace or high hall for such an occasion, note how that the Christ-child had for his chief chamber only a beast's bin, crib or manger. How for his retinue he had but an ox and an ass, for meat nought save the milk of his sweet mother's breast, for his garments only her own lap.[3] Closely similar is the declamation of yet another, whose fourteenth-century *Sermones de tempore* have only recently been added to the manuscripts of the British Museum:

Heere men may see, who-so biholdeth wel, gret poverte in the aray at this lordes birthe. And bothe pore and riche moun lerne heere a lessoun, the pore to be glad in her poverte and bere mekely hire a-staat, seynge hire lord and hir maker wylfully to ȝeve hem suche ensaumple; the riche also to be a-drad of misusynge of her richesse in lustis and lykyngis out of mesure, and lyttil or noȝt to departe of hem to Cristis pore brethreen.

Wher weren the grete castellis and hye toures, with large halles and longe chaumbres realli[4] diȝt with doseris,[5] costeris[6] and coscions, beddes and corteynes of gold and selk, able to the birth of so hiȝ an emperoure? Wher weren thoo rial ladies and worthi gentel wymmen to be entendaunt to this worthi emperise, and bere hire cumpenie at that tyme? Wher weren thoo knyȝtis and squieris to brynge service to this ladi of noble metes, costeli arayes, with hoote spices and deutevous drynkes of diverse swete wynes? In stude of the real castel arayed with riche clothes, thei hadden a stinkynge stable in the hyȝe wey. In stide of real beddes and corteynes, thei hadden non other clothes but suche as longede to a pore

---

[1] MS. Harl. 2398, fol. 21.   [2] MS. Roy. 18. B. xxiii, fol. 112.
[3] MS. Camb. Univ. Libr. Gg. vi. 16, fol. 36b. Cf. further, in Latin, e.g., Waldeby, MS. Caius Coll. Camb. 334, fol. 80 (as given in my *Preaching in Med. Engl.* pp. 346–7; Bromyard, *S.P.* s.v. "Adventus"; etc.). The whole conception is drawn from the *Medit.* of the *Pseudo-Bonav.* and kindred semi-mystical works beloved of the pulpit.
[4] = royally.   [5] = hangings, tapestries.
[6] Tapestry side-coverings for beds, tables or seats.

carpenteris wyif in pilcrimage. In stide of cumpenie of kny3tis and ladies,
thei hadden but pore Joseph her housbonde and two doumbe beestes.[1]

At this point we open our copy of the Shearmen and Taylors'
Pageant at the Coventry Corpus Christi Festival to discover
some of these very phrases there uttered in verses from a
Prophet's mouth:

> *ii Profeta:* Yett do I marvell
> In what pyle or castell
> These herdmen dyd hym see.
>
> *i Profeta:* Nothur in hallis nor yett in bowris
> Born wold he not be;
> Nother in castallis nor yet in towris
> That semly were to se;
> But att hys Fathurs wyll,
> The profeci to full-fyll
> Be-twyxt an ox and an as
> Jesus, this kyng, borne he was....[2]

This last outburst of the Christmas orators brings us very
close to the spirit in which those dramatic scenes were fashioned
which subsequent generations acclaim as the masterpieces of
our early religious drama. We refer, of course, to the Shepherds'
Plays. The character of that first embassage to the cradle-side
is in perfect keeping with the humility of its surroundings, the
poor stable in the highway, which many an ancient play-goer
must have been driven to contrast with the gaudy brilliance
of Caesar's and Herod's courts. Much of the secret of its
peculiar appeal to a decaying feudal age lay in the fact that it
cut boldly across the formidable barriers of class and privilege,
bringing the humble and the mighty together in happy union
under one roof. In secular verse of the period, the popularity
of this same theme is further reflected in numerous tales of the

[1] MS. Add. 41321, fols. 45 b–6. The fact that this preacher is probably
a Lollard, and therefore an enemy of miracle-plays, lends added interest
to the above parallel, and helps to establish the independence of the
pulpit tradition. He goes on here to attack the Friars: "Heere moun
feynide ypocrites be sore aschamed that seyn that thei folewen Crist in
poverte next of alle men heere in erthe, that seyn that Crist was born
in so pore a place, and thei dwellen in so rial placis of halles, chaumbris,
panteris, boteries, kechenes and stables, and alle othere housses of office,
real ynow for kyng, prince, or duke to holde hir housholdes jnne".

[2] *Two Cov. Corp. Chr. Pl.* p. 16.

peasant who entertains his sovereign unawares:[1] likewise, in
the popular vogue of Dekker's *Shoemakers' Holiday* and some
of Shakespeare's best-known love-romances in Tudor times.
If, however, we are to understand to the full why this episode
of the Shepherds called forth the finest efforts of the medieval
dramatist and some of the purest poetry of the plays, we must
again have recourse to our sermons for an explanation. For
years, indeed for centuries, the preachers, as we have seen, had
denounced the follies and oppression of the great, the extravagance of lords and ladies, the hollow vanity of riches. The
cry of the righteous poor was often upon their own lips.
Furthermore the pride, sloth and worldliness of the official
hierarchy of the day, the haughty prelate and the ignorant
village priest, had not escaped their fiercest denunciation. Here,
then, was a historic event, with all the authority of Holy Writ
behind it, which in a measure would anticipate the verdict of
God's last solemn Day of Reckoning. The shepherds' adoration of the Christ-child touched the heart and kindled the
imagination of English homilists, as did no other incident of
the Gospels save possibly that of the Passion, because in it
they saw revealed a justice and a human sympathy in the Divine
attitude for which a weary, corrupted Christendom was lan-
guishing. "Lord, thou hast heard the desire of the humble:
thou wilt prepare their heart." Above the *Pagina Pastorum*,
then, we set the homilist's message, how God openly chose
first poor men instead of rich and powerful "to his know-
lechynge".[2] "He schewede first his birthe to pore men of
semple craft,...to schewe that he is not acceptor of persones;
but that acceptable may be a pore scheperde ether another
poore man of any lefful craft ether ocupacion, ʒef he love God
and keepe his heestes, as the hieste man of degree in this world,
temporal ether spiritual."[3] How then should the play-writer,

[1] Cf. *King Alfred and the Shepherd*; *King Edward IV and the Tanner
of Tamworth* (or *Daventry*); *Rauf Coilʒear*; *John the Reeve*; etc.
[2] Cf. here, *Towneley Pl.* p. 138, ll. 701–2.
[3] MS. Add. 41321, fol. 47b. Cf. *Old Engl. Homs.* (12th cent.), 2nd
Ser. E.E.T.S. O.S. no. 53, p. 35. The Lollard goes even further, seeing
in it a sign "that God oftetymes scheweth his privetees of scripture to
semple men and of esi lettere which beth meke, and hideth it fro grete

who is probably himself only the homilist, embroider such a
theme in his own verses? He will emphasize the unhappy lot
of the shepherd, the lonely nights, the floods, "stormes and
tempest", the bitter inclement weather to which they are
exposed:

> Now in dry, now in wete,
> Now in snaw, now in slete.[1]

He will emphasize their weariness, the endless anxiety of their
flocks:

> For with walking wery I have me wrought,
> Beside the ssuch my sheepe I soughte.
> My tytefull tuppes are in my thought
> Them to save and heale
> From the shrewd scab it (?) sought,
> Or the rot, if it were wrought,
> Yf the cough had them caught,
> Of it I colde them heale.[2]

He will emphasize their ludicrous simplicities and ignorance,
and their poverty:

> I have nothyng to present with thi chylde
> But my pype....[3]

The "genius" of our Towneley Cycle, who has more of satire
in him than pity, prefers to emphasize still further the clumsi-
ness, the low cunning and coarse degradation of the class from
which these men were sprung. Some of them are clearly the
sons of Cain. Yet it is he who has told us most in the Plays
of their load of helpless suffering, the rents and taxes, the
ruthless exactions of "gentlery men", the borrowed wain and
plough, domestic trials and the rest, not to mention the trials
of an impudent hireling, or the thievish tricks of a comrade.[4]

---

clerkes and hiʒe litterid men that beth proude of her kunnynge". Though
this again is really but little removed from the anti-Lollards: cf. *Jacob's
Well*, pp. 276–7, and below, p. 573, etc.

[1] Cf. as here, *Towneley Pl.* pp. 116, 118, etc.; *Chester Pl.* p. 132; *Two
Cov. Corp. Chr. Pl.* p. 11 ("Wynd, ne sun, hayle, snoo and rayne"); etc.
For the sermons, cf. above, p. 303.

[2] *Chester Pl.* p. 133.

[3] *Two Cov. Corp. Chr. Pl.* p. 11. Similarly in the other Cycles.

[4] Cf. esp. pp. 100–2 (note here again, st. 8, the complaint of the
preachers, as given above, p. 369, etc.), and 117 et seq.

In the presence of the Saviour, however, all is forgiven and sorrow swallowed up in joy. The words of a master-homilist, again, declare to us "how sweteli the childe on thaim smylid, and with his loveli ien sweteli on thaim lokid".[1] It remained, therefore, but to translate the prose of his vision into the charming phrases of a shepherd's greeting in the Play:

> Lo, he merys;
> Lo, he laghys, my swetyng,
> A welfare metyng,
> I have holden my hetyng.

With a similar feeling for the charms of young children, John Myrc, in two short sentences of one of his sermons, has pictured dramatically the Massacre of the Holy Innocents: "For thay wern so ȝong that thay cowthe not speke, thay schewet hor love by open sygne. For thay dydden lagh on hom that slowen hem, and playde wyth hor hondes when thay seen hor bryght swerdes schyne".[2] That episode, too, was a favourite with the medieval dramatist.

The Nativity Pageant, however, was not to be without a touch of feudal splendour and stately pageantry amid its own humble surroundings. After the homage of the shepherds, there follows that of the three "gret prynces" of the East, known to us as the Magi. "To the shepherdes, Jewes, that were resonable of beleve", says our homilist, God "ordeynt angels, the wiche that ben resonable, to tell hem of is burthe". Now, by means of "an unresonable creature", that is, a star suited to the fact that they were "paynyms", God was to summon into the presence of his Son certain representatives of the world of privilege, wealth, and learning. The sermon of this same preacher, as quaint as it is informing, lets us into the mind of those who depicted upon the contemporary stage the marvellous entry of the Three Kings. In his accents, as here recorded, we seem to catch the actual query of some bewildered rustic onlooker at the play: "Explain to us, from the Gospel story, who these new figures may be!" To such an one the sacred

---

[1] MS. Arund. 507, fol. 61, here applied to the three kings. See Horstmann, *Yorksh. Writers*, vol. i, p. 149 (an Engl. version of the *Medit.* here attributed to Rich. Rolle). Cf. further the medieval English Christmas carols. [2] *Festial*, p. 29.

showman now makes reply, providing a running-commentary upon the scene which we, in company with the questioner, might well be beholding amongst the medieval pageant-crowd:

> But ȝitt, here myȝthe be resonable asshed a question—"Seth thise thre princes were kynges, as the comon glose seith, than qwy be thei called in the gospell *magi*, men of gret connynge, and not *reges*, kynges; seyn the name of kynges is of gretter dignite?" Here-to itt is answerd—and this is the cause, to shewe the grett connynge of thise thre princes, thei were called *magi*.... For like as the grettest clerces amonge the Grecceth [sic!] were called *philosophi*, "philisofres", and amonge the Jewes, "scribe", *scribus*, and amonge us Latyns, *magistri*, "maistres", ryght so were thei called amonge Perses *magi*. For it was more fittynge to grounde of oure feyȝth and beleve in tham undir the name of clergy, than undir the name of knyȝthod; and ther-fore were thei called in the gospell *magi*, men of gret connynge, and not kynges. All-be-it that thei were myghty princes in armes and men also of right gret letture.[1]

Two marvels, a greater and a less, excite comment from our homilist in connection with the Magi's visit. The first concerns "the wondirfull governaunce of this stere" which led them to their destination.

> For this ster was no fix stere in heven, nother no planete, as is mevynge shewed well; but it was a comete, *stella comata*, new made by the myghty powre of almyȝthy God. For as other steres be meved at the mewynge of ther speres[2] deferentes, other *Epicicles*, est other west, this ster was meved fro the est welnyȝ in to the sowthe.... Also, other steres, sawynge the sonne, clerely lyththens only by nyȝthe. But this stere shyned wondir clerely by day qwhils the sonne shyned, and also by nyȝthe. And thoȝ other steres be meved alwey to hur cours, this stere som tyme stode with-owte mevyng. And the fowrte cause, for ther-as other steres be meved in [orb?] of the hevens, this stere was meved alowe in the eyre; for els it myȝth not have been redely shewed to thise kynges the place of Cristes burthe.[3]

The "lasse marvel" of the Magi story is concerned with the method of "ther hasty commynge in xiiii daies from so farre countre. For, as Austyn, Jerom and Fulgentius seyn, thei reden uppon beestes that men callen *dromedus, dromedi, vel*

---

[1] MS. Roy. 18. B. xxiii, fol. 130.   [2] = spheres.
[3] MS. Roy. 18. B. xxiii, fol. 130. Cf. *Towneley Pl.* p. 146. (The star is also described as *stella comata*, in *Piers Plowman*, cf. C text, pass. xxi, l. 249.)

dromede in latyn, wiche as Ysodre seithe, *Ethymologiis, libro 21, capitulo primo,* thei ben beestes of so gret swyftnes, that on of hem will esely bere a man an C myle on a daye. And so thei toke there jornay directe to Jerusalem".[1] How closely the writer of miracle-plays can agree with the homiletic narrative is well illustrated when we compare this account with part of a conversation between two Magi before they set out, in the Eighth Pageant of the Chester Cycle:

> *Secundus Rex:* Yea sirs, I red us every one
> Dromodaryes to ride upon,
> For swifter beastes be there none;
> One I have, you shall see.
>
> *Tertius Rex:* A dromedary in good faye
> Will goe lightly on his way
> A hundreth myles upon a day,
> Such corsers now take we![2]

So much then for the scenes of Christmas. The earthly career of the Redeemer, which in its opening provided such rich material for pulpit and pageant alike, provided further scope for the emotions in the tragic circumstances of its close. Here, that debt to the pseudo-Bonaventura which M. Mâle has re-emphasized in the case of continental miracle-plays, is as patent in our English Passion Sermons as it was found to be in those dealing with the Nativity. Both therefore are in the line of a great living homiletic tradition. Sometimes a yet earlier debt to St Bernard is acknowledged in these same discourses,[3] thereby reminding us afresh that the plaintive realism of the pulpit is no recently imported growth. We have a right to believe, therefore, that from an early date, the English preacher, like his brother upon the continent, gave public utterance to the reflections of the mystics upon this solemn theme. In the fourteenth century, at all events, we find them reviving the agonies of the Passion in the burning speech of their predecessors. They kindle the lurid imagination of the people, not even hesitating to appeal to them, as from the very

[1] Ibid. fol. 130b. Notice mention of sources again.

[2] *Chester Pl.* pt. i, p. 164. The same appears in *A Stanzaic Life of Christ,* E.E.T.S. ed. p. 60. (Cf. also *Leg. Aurea,* ed. Leipzig, p. 89.)

[3] Cf. MS. Roy. 18. B. xxiii, fol. 83; Myrc, *Festial,* p. 113; *A Stanzaic Life of Christ,* p. 200; and Miss F. Foster in *The North. Pass.* pt. ii, cap. v.

Cross itself, in the accents of the Crucified. A few examples will
show that the dramatic intensity of their language in no way
lags far behind, let us say, the intensity of the Coventry
Passion Play,[1] or that of the well-known Norwich Retable
which depicts in line and colour the horrors of the Flagellation.
With almost a morbid delight in detail, the homilist now bids
his listeners "behold with their ghostly eyes the piteous
Passion of Christ":

> Byholde, thanne, that goede lord chyveryng and quakyng, al his body
> naked and bounde to a pyler; aboute him stondyng the wycked men,
> withouten eny resoun, ful sore scourgyng that blessed body, withouten
> eny pite. See how they cesse nouȝt fram here angry strokes, tyl they se
> him stonde in his blode up to the anclees. Fro the top of the hed to the
> sole of his fote, hole skyn saved they non. His flesch they rase to the
> bone, and for werynesse of hemself they him leevyd al-most for dede.
> Loke thanne asyde upon his blessed moder. Se what sorowe sche maketh
> for hure dere sone.... Turne aȝayne to thy lord and se....A garland
> of thornes they thrast on his heved, tyl the blode ran doun in his eyȝen,
> nose and mouth and eeren.[2]

Another will enrich his account with some further exaggeration of detail, ruthlessly adding horror to horror in his attempt
to heighten the realism of the scene:

> He was betun and buffetid, scorned and scourgid, that unnethis[3] was
> ther left ony hoole platte of his skyn, fro the top to the too, that a man
> myȝte have sette in the point of a nedil. But al his bodi rane out as a
> strem of blood. He was crowned with a crowne of thornes for dispite.
> And whanne the crowne, as clerkis seien, wolde not stik fast and iust
> doun on his heed for the longe thornes and stronge, thei toke staves and
> betun it down, til the thornes thrilliden the brayne panne.[4] He was naylyd
> hond and foot with scharp nailis and ruggid, for his peyne schulde be
> the more; and so, at the last, he sufferid moost peynful deeth, hanging ful
> schamefulli on the cros.[5]

[1] See also Ward, *Hist. of Engl. Dram. Lit.* vol. i, p. 88. Cf. further
the *Towneley Pl.* plays xxi and xxii.
[2] MS. Harl. 2398, fol. 186b. Cf. again, MS. Bodl. 95, fol. 54 ("Crystus
body was al nakyd, y-bowynd wyth a corde and y-bete wyth knotty
scorges ful wyth many wondys, the skynne in to the bone, that men myȝt
tel hys rybbys...").
[3] = scarcely.
[4] Cf. here *Towneley Pl.* p. 251, ll. 233–4; etc.
[5] MS. St Albans Cath. fol. 20 (= MS. Laud Misc. 23). Cf. Waldeby,
MS. Caius Coll. Camb. 334, fol. 80 (as quoted in my *Preaching in Med.
Engl.* p. 347); Wycliffe, in Arnold, *Sel. Engl. Works*, vol. iii, p. 107

The first-mentioned homilist goes on to discuss the actual process of the crucifixion step by step. First, "they hurle him forth to an hey hulle": then follows the stripping, the nailing, the stretching of the limbs, the spearing, and so on. Finally we are led to consider the anguish of the Virgin,[1] and "the teers of Maudelyn and of hure other frendes". To crown all, the stricken Saviour hanging from the crucifix may Himself be made to speak to the gaping throng beneath through the lips of these ardent spokesmen:

> Thow man for vanyte syngyst and rowtes; and I for the crye and wepe. Thou hast on thy hed a garland of flowres,[2] and I for the on my hed suffyr a wrethe of stynkynge thornes. Thou hast on thy hondys whyt gloves, and I for thy love have blody hondys. Thou hast thyn armes sprad on brode ledyng carallys,[3] and I for thy love have myn armes sprad on the tre and tachut wyth grete nayles. Thou hast thy clothe raggyd[4] and pynchyt smale, and I have my body for thy love full of gret walus. And, over thys, that grevyth me most, thou settyst no3t by my passyon that I suffryd for the. But by me horrybull swerys all day umbraydys me, sweryng by my face, by myn een, by myn armes, by myn nayles, by myn hert, by my blod, and so forth, by all my body. And soo thou marterys me by a foule use and custom of sweryng![5]

Master Rymyngton addresses the same kind of appeal to his audience of clergy *in synodo*:

> God Almighty Himself for thy redemption hung naked between two thieves upon the Cross, and of His own free will exposed his body to the Passion: yet thou dost refuse to wear for love of Him the garments ordained for thy use. He allowed his own head, for thy crimes, to be crowned with the sharpest thorns in infamy: and thou dost not allow the

---

(quoted in Workman, *Jo. Wyclif*, vol. ii, p. 213); MS. Worc. Cath. Libr. F. 10, fol. 46b; MS. Linc. Cath. Libr. A. 6. 2, fols. 41–2; MS. Salisb. Cath. Libr. 103, fol. 103 (unpublished *Jacob's Well*); MS. Roy. 18. B. xxiii, fols. 83–84b; MS. Add. 41321, fols. 54b, 80–80b; etc.

[1] Cf. further below, p. 541 (and the similar dialogues in the Plays).
[2] I.e. the chaplet of the holiday-makers. Cf. above, p. 393.
[3] = dances.   [4] Cf. above, p. 410, n. 3.
[5] *Festial*, p. 113. Similarly, MS. Linc. Cath. Libr. A. 6. 2, fols. 130–1 (as quoted in my *Preaching in Med. Engl.* pp. 347–8); Bromyard, *S.P.* s.v. "Passio Christi" (cf. "Tu in choreis brachia extendis in modum crucis ad vanum gaudium, et ego in crucem ad opprobrium"); MS. Bodl. 95, fols. 54–54b (in the 3rd person); *A Stanzaic Life of Christ*, pp. 200–1; poems in Chambers and Sidgwick, *E. E. Lyrics*, p. 116; and E.E.T.S. O.S. no. 15, pp. 190–8; etc. Cf. *Towneley Pl.* p. 380.

proper shaving of thine own head and beard as the appointed sign and honour of His service . . . ".[1]

From exhortations such as these, inspired by the preaching of St Bernard,[2] the English dramatist of the Middle Ages, then, must have received his first lesson in tragic declamation. One minor detail of the Towneley narrative now deserves our notice before the subject of the Passion is left. In the *Summa Predicantium* John Bromyard links together, in an argument against false counsellors, "the manner of the Jews who buffeted Christ when blindfold, saying—'Prophesy, who is it that smote thee?'",[3] and "the manner of those who, *in still playing that game*, smite someone on the head smartly while his face is hidden, but laugh at him, when he raises his head to see, as though they had done nothing to him".[4] The pastime here referred to is a well-known medieval variant of Blindman's Buff, known as *Qui fery?* or Hot Cockles, played stationary and without hoods.[5] Curiously enough, to prove the continuity of the idea in pulpit lore, we find the same two actions again identified in a sermon of the century following, thus:

A common game in use nowadays is that which the soldiers played with Christ at his Passion: it is called *the bobbid* game. In this game, one of the company will be *blindfold* and set in a prone position; then those standing by will hit him on the head and say—

"*A bobbid, a bobbid, a biliried*:[6]
Smyte not her, bot thu smyte a gode!"

And as often as the former may fail to guess correctly *and rede amys*, he has to play a fresh game. And so, until *he rede him that smote him*, he will be *blindfold stille and hold in* for the post of player.[7]

---

[1] MS. Bibl. Univ. Paris 790, fol. 116.
[2] Cf. Migne, *Patr. Lat.* vol. clxxxii, col. 1133, etc.
[3] See Luke xxii, 64.   [4] s.v. "Consilium".
[5] (*Hautes Coquilles.*) Cf. Thos. Wright, *Homes of Other Days*, pp. 243–4, and Strutt, *Sports and Pastimes of the People of Engl.* p. 501; also Halliwell, *Dict. of Archaic . . . Words*, vol. i, p. 190, s.v. Bob-and-Hit; etc.
[6] Corrected in the MS. margin to—"*a byrlyryhode*".
[7] MS. Bodl. 649, fol. 82 (c. 1420). This hitherto unpublished account, with its quaint couplet, should be of interest to students of folk-lore. For further reference to 'didactic' games, cf. above, pp. 484–5.

Turning now to our Towneley Pageant of the *Talents*, we
find that the dramatist has actually incorporated this quaint
pulpit tradition in the body of his dialogue, making one of
Christ's torturers thus responsible for the invention of the
game:

> (*Secundus Tortor*): I was at Calvery this same day,
>   Where the kyng of Iues lay,
>   And ther I taght hym a newe play,
>   Truly me thoght it right.
>   The play, in fayth, it was to rowne,
>   That he shuld lay his hede downe,
>   And sone I bobyd hym on the crowne;
>   That gam me thoght was good.[1]

The game itself is of ancient Greek origin.[2] But this adaptation
of it by the medieval homilist suggests another deliberate
attempt to ingraft upon the popular folk-diversions of Christ-
mastide a new religious significance.[3] At all events, in the
Play it would seem to be one more piece of evidence of our
"Towneley" dramatist's debt to pulpit influences.[4]

Our last selected scene is that of *The Judgment*. Here we
have to deal with certain characters hitherto left undiscussed,
whose treatment at the play-writer's hands has evoked a good
deal of inaccuracy in modern comment. Allusion has been
made already in our pages to the lively behaviour of the devils
in sermon anecdote and admonition. In the present author's
previous volume they were seen busily at work, plaguing the
devout at their orisons or at sermon-time, the aged on their
death-beds, and the damned in the underworld of Hell. In the
present work we have beheld them again infesting earth and
air, in a dozen curious shapes and functions.[5] Little need be
added, therefore, to point the connection between the demons

[1] *Towneley Pl.* p. 283.
[2] Cf. Strutt, *Sports and Pastimes*, pp. 499 and 501.
[3] A further reference to the game occurs above, p. 373.
[4] Note further, how, in this same dramatist's Play of the Talents, the
actual game itself as played between Pilate and the three Torturers
follows the regular line of the preachers' attacks on dicing and gambling
(apart even from the moralization at the end, pp. 291 et seq.). The game
leads to (*a*) cursing, and (*b*) quarrelling.
[5] See above, p. 112.

of the pulpit and those of the sacred pageant. So real and
vivid a person was the Prince of Darkness to both sets of
expositors, that their imagination conceived of him in a hundred
homely pranks and catastrophes, ceaselessly spying, scheming,
fighting against the sons of men with every ingenuity, almost
as one of their own flesh and blood, an arch-villain upon the
stage of daily life. Even God himself apparently set man an
example of how cunning in the fiend must be met by cunning
in the righteous opponent. For, Myrc tells us in one of his
sermons that Christ was driven to suffer circumcision in order
to evade the Devil, by tricking him into the belief that through
His share in "that penaunce" He must be the same as any
other sinful man begotten upon earth. "For, yf he [the Devil]
had knowen hym redely that he had comen forto by[1] monkynd
out of his bondam, he wold never have tysut[2] mon to have
don hym to deth. This was also the cause why oure lady was
wedded to Joseph, forto deseyve the fende, that he schule wene
that he was his fadyr and not conseyvet of the Holy Gost."[3]
In the Towneley Plays it is to be noted that Jesus, in his conversation with Satan at Hell-gates, alludes to the latter trick.[4]
Students of English literature, at the mercy of the text-books,
might well gather the impression that this rollicking, human
type of demon, this Mephistopheles of the market-place was a
characteristic product of the later religious drama and the antics
of human impersonators upon the "scaffold". The truth is, however, that, so far from remaining mere abstract spirits of evil
in serious exposition, the leading devils were already known
and even mentioned by their nick-names in pulpit manuals
from the thirteenth century onwards. Thus in the *Speculum
Laicorum*, for example, we are introduced to one, Colewin.[5]
But the favourite, as we might guess, is none other than Tity-
villus or Tutivillus, "the young infernal humorist"[6] of the
Towneley *Judgement-Scene* and of the Macro Morality known

---

[1] = buy.　　　　　　　　　　　　[2] = enticed.
[3] *Festial*, p. 46. Cf. further, p. 107, and below, p. 596.
[4] p. 310 (cf. also *Chester Pl.* p. 154, ll. 535–8).
[5] Ed. Welter, p. 15 (colesweyn).
[6] Ten Brink, *Hist. of Engl. Lit.* vol. ii, p. 263.

as *Mankind*. He makes his appearance before us in the popular sermons of Jacques de Vitry,[1] and in the *Dialogus Miraculorum* of Caesarius of Heisterbach,[2] both authors freely drawn upon by sermon-compilers in this country. In actual works of the kind by these latter, he is named in a collection of *Exempla* by an unknown Franciscan writing in the first quarter of the century following, and more than once in the *Summa Predicantium* itself.[3] His regular task, as Bromyard reminds us, is to gather up in sacks, with the help of his attendants, the fragments of Psalms slurred over or omitted by indolent clerks in their recitation of the Divine Offices.[4] Another colleague, the impudent Grisillus, concerned himself with similar weaknesses of the laity,[5] while a third, unnamed, keeps other folks at their labours outside the church. In addition, we have mention in the same work of Pokerellus, the infernal sacristan, of Drawsheet, the infernal chamberlain,[6] and three more fleet-footed little gentlemen who disturb the people when in church.[7]

[1] See *Exempla of J. de V.* ed. Crane (Folklore Soc. vol. xxvi), no. 19 and p. 141 (note).

[2] Dist. iv, cap. ix (here unnamed).

[3] MS. Add. 33956, fol. 26 (A.D. 1313–26: see Welter, *L'Exemplum*, p. 267); *S.P.* s.v. "Feriae seu Festa" and "Ordo Clericalis" ("...quasi gigas sacco pleno onustus...", etc.). Cf. similarly, MS. Arund. 506, fol. 46 (first half of 14th cent.), quoted in Wright, *Lat. Stories*, Percy Soc. p. 44; MS. Douce 104 (A.D. 1427) as quoted in Wright and Halliwell, *Reliq. Antiq.* vol. i, p. 257.

[4] Dr A. W. Pollard, in his edit. of the *Towneley Pl.*, does not seem to have recognized (p. 375) the first line of what he calls the "Latin gibberish" of Tutivillus. It describes, of course, regularly his special task, as in the sources given above, n. 3. ("Vir...ille de illo [demone] versus fecit, dicens—'Fragmina psalmorum Tutivillus colligit horum'....") A second line is added by Bromyard, *S.P.* s.v. "Ordo Cleric.": "In die mille vicibus se farcinat ille". See further, Wright, *Lat. Stories*, pp. 225–6.

[5] "Grisillus orantes laicos facit altitonantes." ("Ii omnes cum complicibus suis ad hoc confederati videntur ut Dei festa modis omnibus impediant.")

[6] See above, pp. 394 and 412.

[7] See in my *Preaching in Med. Engl.* p. 175. These are the three devils familiar in continental sermons, sometimes called Clocuer, Cloboche and Cloborse (Bromyard, *S.P.*, it will be noticed adds a fourth, Obturans-aures-et-os). Cf. Wm. of Mailly, *Abjiciamus*; Jo. Herolt, *Promptuarium*; etc.; etc. (See Hauréau, *Not. et Extr.* vol. iv, pp. 144 and 159.)

The Franciscan *Exemplarium* already referred to gives us the further diabolic names of Neptunus, Milleartifex and Rixewaldus.[1] Elsewhere we read of yet others that run around with cup and pitcher or grease-boxes, for ever up to some such mischief.[2] Here, then, are friend Tutivillus and his fellows of the Towneley Play, lugging their sacks,[3] and chatting furiously about their achievements, as we fall in with them on that fateful day when all roads lead to one place, the Judgment-seat of God.[4] The fall of Lucifer and his companions, which constitutes an episode of the Chester Cycle, is discussed from an English pulpit in equally naïve fashion. At length the speaker comes to the interesting question as to whether the once-fallen angels would really like to get back to heaven again. St Gregory, he informs us, actually put this question once to a devil of his acquaintance, who replied with an emphatic affirmative—'yes, even if he had to climb a fiery ladder to get there, hotter than "anny fyre in helle,...fro this tyme to the day of dome"'.[5] Questioned further, therefore, as to whether he would not like to petition God to grant him this favour at the last, he answers—"No certeyn! ffor sethen that I was bryghtest of all angels, I will not lowen mynselfe to aske forȝevenes". Pride was his fatal sin. Adam, on the other hand, who was prepared thus to sink his pride, we are told, was pardoned accordingly through the coming of Christ, and given his chance along with the rest of mankind.[6] The hosts of Lucifer, when deeply preoccupied with their dreadful task in the infernal regions, no

---

[1] MS. Add. 33956, fol. 83 b. Cf. another name—Gillebochat (French), in MS. Arund. 52, fol. 114 (14th cent.).

[2] See *Preaching in Med. Engl.* pp. 152, 174 and 176.

[3] The Devil's "great sack" of rolls is again referred to in Bromyard, *S.P.* s.v. "Consilium".

[4] Dr Pollard, *Towneley Pl.* p. 371, has made another slight error here (margin). The devils are not carrying "bags full of all kinds of sinners", but bags full "*of brefes*" of the various sinners. For Tutivillus as "roller", cf. in my *Preaching in Med. Engl.* pp. 176–7. Notice also how in Bromyard (s.v. "Feriae..."), Tutivillus is heard to "boast of his gains that day", as in the Towneley Scene.

[5] Cf. Caesarius of Heist. *Dial. Mirac.* dist. v, cap. x (and *Towneley Pl.* p. 303).

[6] MS. Roy. 18. B. xxiii, fol. 168 b (see also Myrc, *Festial*, p. 259).

doubt were wont to take themselves all too seriously. But once let out for a day off in the world, like the English "goddam" in Mr Bernard Shaw's masterpiece—"straight from hell", their roguish sense of humour clearly got the better of them:

> Rum tum trumpledum,
> Bacon fat and rumpledum,
> Old saint mumpledum
> Pull his tail and stumpledum![1]

The preachers themselves tell us how the fiends will pull faces at the churchfolk they love to torment,[2] grin and mock at the dying,[3] laugh at a colleague's discomfiture when he falls into the mud from off a lady's skirts,[4] and even cause laughter in a gospeller when another of their number is seen to bump his head inadvertently against a wall.[5] Ranulf Higden devotes a whole chapter of his *Speculum Curatorum* to the topic—"de ludificationibus demonum".[6] Shakespeare's Ariel and Puck,[7] then, are but merry medieval devils from the sermon-stories like him "of-a-thousand-tricks", first cousins to "the foul fiend Flibbertigibbet" serving better masters. Alike they will delight to "flame amazement" at the storm-tossed mariner or lure the drunkard into "filthy-mantled pools" only to mock him, lurk in a gossip's bowl or upset an ancient dame from off her perch; "and then the whole quire hold their hips and laugh".[8] If their magic is the magic of the fairies, their characters are those of impish schoolboys on holiday, the youthful impishness of the Middle Ages. The direct influence of all such grim homiletic devil-humour, therefore, upon the authors of miracle- and morality-play will need no further word of explanation.

[1] *Saint Joan*, Epilogue, p. 105.   [2] See *Preaching in Med. Engl.* p. 176.
[3] Cf. *Pricke of Consc.* p. 61, esp. ll. 2225–6.
[4] See above, p. 398.
[5] As in *Hand. Synne*, p. 291. Cf. *Preaching in Med. Engl.* p. 177; and the older versions in the *Exempla of J. de Vitry*, ed. Crane, as before, p. 239; also important references given by Herbert, *Cat. of Romances in B.M.* vol. iii, p. 19, esp. that of MS. Arund. 506, fol. 20.
[6] Unpublished. MSS. are B.M. Harl. 1004, Camb. Univ. Libr. Mm. i. 20, and Balliol Coll. Oxf. 77 (see *Stud. pres. to Sir H. Jenkinson*, p. 278).
[7] Cf. metr. homily in *O. Engl. Misc.* E.E.T.S. p. 76, l. 120; *Piers Pl.*; etc.   [8] *A Midsummer Night's Dream*, Act ii, Sc. i.

So rich is the endowment of the past, in tract and sacred discourse, that, had we no other possible sources to consider, the English Doom Scene in its most realistic state could well be accounted for by reference to this homiletic inspiration alone. Miniature and sculpture, wall-painting and window-glass, pulpit and stage, all in these later Middle Ages, however, must have constantly acted and reacted upon each other to produce a most lively sense of the last great episode of history. Sometimes the intimacy of the connection is illustrated in our manuscripts in quite a remarkable way.[1] From the point of view of the pulpit, English sermons themselves supply us with every detail of the Judgment, which even in far-off pre-Conquest times had provided the "Blickling" homilist with an impressive theme.[2] "Sirs," cries the enthusiastic preacher, "I counsell all maner of men fully to thenke on this dome."[3] We have already witnessed one great example of the kind, product of a Dominican pen.[4] The Fifteen "marvellus tokens" which usher in the Doom, as specified again, for example, in the Chester Play, were a frequent subject of discourse.[5] The dramatic form which they take is well set forth in the *Pricke of Conscience*,[6] with the usual familiar attribution to St Jerome. Where the dialogue of the plays may fail us, records of the stage properties in use go to prove how closely they conform to every detail in the homiletic account. Such, for example, was the "barrell" for the earthquake, and the "link" to set the

[1] MS. Linc. Cath. Libr. C. 4. 6 is a good example. Here, in the margin of fol. 34, we have a typical drawing (in colour) of the Doom Scene: another, on fol. 120, shows St Michael weighing a soul, with a devil trying to tip the scale. Here too are the so-called *Meditationes Sancti Bernardi, Elucid. Anselmi* (Hon. of Autun) and other homiletic matter dealing dramatically with kindred themes. The crude drawing on fol. 89 of the Devil and the Religious each trying to pull the layman a different way is in the same spirit.

[2] See E.E.T.S. ed. pp. 60, 92 et seq., etc. Cf. further, *Engl. Homs.* (12th cent.) E.E.T.S. ed. O.S. no. 137, p. 125, etc. (from MS. Bodl. 343).

[3] MS. Roy. 18. B. xxiii, fol. 57.   [4] As above, pp. 300–2.

[5] Cf. MS. Glouc. Cath. Libr. *Sermo de Adv. Chr. in judic.*; and others in my *Preaching in Med. Engl.* pp. 338–9; etc.

[6] Ed. Philog. Soc. pp. 108–10 and 127–34. Cf. the account of Antichrist here (pp. 110–25) with the Chester Play of that name; etc.

world afire.[1] Every little particular of time and place in the subsequent order of events seems to have been carefully sought out and published by the pulpit:

> But, peraventure thou arte a lewde man, thou wolde witt when is this commynge and when the day of dome shall be, and also where it shall be, in erthe, or in hevene, or els beneth the erthe. ffor sothe, ffrendys, where it shall be I shall tell ye, as holy writt seyth and also the Maister of Sentence. He seyth that itt shall be in the vale of Josaphate; and that vale is beside Ierusalem, welny3 by the place where owre ladie seynt Marie was buried, there shall be the dome. . . . But trewly, what tyme and when it shall be, and whether nyght or day, ther is no clerke in erthe, ne aungell, ne postell, ne seynt in heven that can tell that day. . . .[2]

In the *Narratio* of a Sermon for All Saints' Day John Myrc depicts the King of Bliss sitting in his majesty with a great multitude of angels about him. Enthroned beside him, in a chair of gold, is the Queen of Heaven, Empress of Hell, the Blessed Virgin, richly crowned and arrayed, with a corresponding company of holy virgins around her. Various groups of distinguished persons, standing apart, precisely in the manner of privileged Circles at some earthly Court, complete the picture. One clad in camel-skins is at the head of a great company of old men, presumably the prophets. Another, clad like a bishop (that is, St Peter), has a following of many others clad like himself. Finally, there is the general company— "like to knights of diverse peoples", comprising the martyrs, confessors and heroes of the Church.[3] To such an assembly, then, come the souls of men to be judged at the last. "ffor he schal deme every man affter he hath deserved, with-oute acceptinge of persones, both popes and kynges as the knaves of the kechene."[4] A sermon in a Cambridge manuscript describes

---

[1] See *Two Cov. Corp. Chr. Plays*, pp. 99–102. For the editor's remark—"First introduced in 1561" (p. 101), read—"First mentioned in Expense Lists in . . ."—a very different thing!

[2] MS. Roy. 18. B. xxiii, fol. 113. (Probably derived from the *Pricke of Consc.*; see pp. 140–1.) See also here, Bromyard, *S.P.* s.v. "Judicium Divinum" (quoting the "Magister Hist.", i.e. Peter Comestor (d. 1178), in *Histor. Scholast.*; etc.). "Mag. Sentent." (as above) = Peter Lombard.

[3] *Festial*, p. 268. Cf. again, p. 153 (the Angel courtiers).

[4] MS. Add. 41321, fol. 22.

the scene, in equally dramatic fashion, as it will present itself to the eyes of the guilty, in language as old as Chrysostom:

> Above hym shall be God, hys juge, to ȝeve redye sentence aȝense hym. Be-nethe hym shall be helle redye to receyve hym. On the ryghȝt syde shall be heyr awne synnes to accuse them, upon the lefft syde shall be inffenyte develes to drawe them to everlastynge peyne. Withinfforthe, heyr awen consciens shall gruge and ffrete them; and withowtefforthe shall be all the worlde brennynge all on ffyr. Thys shall be a dredffull dey off doome![1]

Such is the stage-setting, then, for the opening Act of this final drama. In their own special amplification of the theme, our English dramatists, for the rest, may be said to follow the example of preacher rather than of artist. For it is not so much "the chevalrie of heven",[2] the saints and the "ix ordres of aungels",[3] nor even God himself, but the damned aforesaid, who tend to loom largest in their picture. Here again the evidences of pulpit influence are sufficient to arrest our attention. If we begin with the Chester Judgment Play, it is easy to see how the author has set about the task of interpreting his chief characters to us and developing the dialogue of the scene within its prescribed framework. Let the reader compare once more the typical sermon diatribes upon society and the vices of its various members with the speeches of the damned in this Play.[4] First, we have the confession of an evil representative of the Churchmen, *Papa Damnatus* himself. He tells us how, although he was privileged to be a "cunning" clerk, covetousness has had him in thrall. Silver and Simony in fact

[1] MS. Camb. Univ. Libr. Gg. vi. 16, fol. 50b. Cf. again fol. 48 ("See warily beneath thee hell sinful souls perceiving. See above thee busily God, chief justice, all this world dooming"). Similarly, *Old Engl. Homs.* (12th cent.), 2nd Ser. E.E.T.S. O.S. no. 53, p. 173; *Pricke of Consc.* pp. 146–7, ll. 5404–21, and in my *Preaching in Med. Engl.* pp. 339–40.
[2] Alkerton's phrase, MS. Add. 37677, fol. 59 (see *Preaching in Med. Engl.* p. 340).
[3] MS. Roy. 18. B. xxiii, fol. 113 ("as clerkes seyn, ther buthn ix ordres of aungels..."). The nine Orders appear in *Two Cov. Corp. Chr. Plays*; see p. xxi. A detailed account of the Angelic Orders will be found in Bromyard, *S.P.* s.v. "Angelus" (cf. here, the third Order: "Tertius est Thronorum in quibus Deus residet et jocundatur sicut princeps inter speciales amicos").
[4] *Chester Pl.* pp. 433–40.

made him Pope. Now he must render account of the many souls whose damnation his evil conduct has caused. Next, *Imperator Damnatus* comes forward to lament his former proud possession of town and tower. He is guilty of manslaughter, covetousness, false dooms and misgotten moneys. Likewise, *Rex Damnatus*, who follows him, confesses how he had no pity for the poor or the sick in his lifetime, how he did wrong, robbed Religion, and committed acts of lechery and avarice. His Queen, *Regina Damnata*, speaks for the race of worldly Womanhood. Her lechery, her pearls, her pride and her rich wardrobe, like her former comeliness, are all now matter for idle tears, with no brave baron or knight to plead for her. *Justiciarius Damnatus* voices the special crimes of his class, the false causes that he has maintained at law, the favour bestowed upon barons and rich burgesses, the silver that he has sought, whilst troubling the poor and spoiling Holy Church. Finally, *Mercator Damnatus* adds his tragic tale in equally familiar strain. Marred by merchandise and the lure of land and fee, he has forced the poor to part with their inheritance and has fleeced them mercilessly. False purchase, false assize, false swearing, false tithing and usury are again in the list of his crimes.[1] One by one, then, each has now to acknowledge the truth of that indictment which we heard the oppressed deliver with such terrifying vehemence by the mouth of our Dominican prophet. As usual, however, it is to the Towneley dramatist that we must go for the most perfect revelation of the preacher's influence upon the drama. In this particular version of the Judgment, it is safe to say that there is no line that does not suggest an inspiration from that quarter. From the moment when the angelic trumpets first herald the Doom to that moment in which we behold the last sinner dragged ruthlessly from the stage into hell-mouth, we can follow the play-writer as he transmutes the homilist's narrative into the yet more lively dialogue of his own verses. The cries of four sinners are the first to greet the universal summons. These

---

[1] Cf. further in this Cycle (p. 203) the fate of the false tapsters carried off by demons to hell, with the sermon strictures upon them, as above, pp. 351 and 354, etc.

express in familiar language, that reminds us as much of the
Pricke of Conscience[1] as of our vernacular prose homilies, the
terror of the occasion. Thus, for example, the Second Evil-doer
repeats the warning that each must now answer for his own
misdeeds without help of legal cunning,[2] while the Third recalls the fact that by this Doomsman's verdict they will have
to abide,[3] and the Fourth, in concert with his companions,
shuddering at the thought of having to look Him in the face,
curses his own parents and the very day of his birth.[4] From
our knowledge of the sermons we recognize at once to what
Tertius Malus refers when he speaks of sacrificing to Satan
while others slept.[5] In order to acquaint us with the characters
of the damned by the natural expedient of conversation, our
dramatist next introduces us to the devils of the underworld
as they follow the footsteps of their charges Doomwards.[6]
Here all is ready to hand for him in the homily-books that lie
doubtless at his elbow. The diabolic conversation soon turns,
accordingly, upon the topic of the women-folk. A question
from the First Demon sets Tutivillus talking again later of
their vices in the usual style, their paint and finery, their ill-
temper and dissimulation, their horns, their gins and their
"spouse-breech".[7] Alas! as we have so often heard elsewhere,
the world grows worse, people and laws alike:

> ffaithe and trowth, maffay, has no fete to stande;
> The poore pepyll must pay, if oght be in hande.
> The drede of God is away, and lawe out of lande.[8]

From this very typical preachers' summary, with accompanying
hint of its source,[9] we proceed to the old complaints against
male finery and fashions, as exhibited, naturally, in the "new

---

[1] Cf. esp. pp. 144–7 and 190–200.
[2] *Towneley Pl.* p. 367 (cf. in my *Preaching in Med. Engl.* p. 339).
[3] Ibid. p. 368.
[4] p. 369 (similarly, *Sec. Malus*, p. 367; etc.).
[5] p. 368. The phrase is used of those who practise sorcery and witch-
craft. Cf. also the night gamblers, above, pp. 275, 444, etc.
[6] pp. 371 et seq.
[7] pp. 372 and 375–6.   [8] p. 373.
[9] Cf.— "Alle this was token domysday to drede.
   Full oft was it spokyn, full few take hede...".

gett" of the day.[1] This leads on to satire of the over-dressed
grooms and maid-servants who ape their masters and mistresses.[2] At length the whole pulpit gamut of evil-doers is let
loose upon us once more. With Hell's chief captain, we pass
in review the "fals swearars"—"mo than a thowsand skore",
"rasers of the fals tax" and the like, the "kyrkchaterars" and
whisperers, "barganars and okerars and lufars of symonee",[3]
then the well-known figures of Ire and Envy, Covetise and
Gluttony, the slothful "ale-sitters" and drunkards singing,
quarrelling and blaspheming all night, who hate church-going,[4]
even the "Janettes of the stewys" and their tragic rout, the
liars and thieves, the false jurors, "hasardars and dysars", the
slanderers and back-biters.[5] The faithful dramatist brings all
before our eyes, a preacher's *Castellum Diaboli* disgorging its
captives now upon their last trial.

The Trial-scene itself, the natural climax of the Play—and,
we may believe, of not a few sermons, opens, as in the *Pricke
of Conscience* and similar works, with a speech from Christ,
the Chief Justice. First, He sternly announces the purpose of
His coming to earth to deliver Judgment, for the wicked a day
of dread, for the righteous a day of rejoicing. He displays His
wounds and rehearses His former sufferings, then summons the
righteous to bliss, those who in their lives fed, clothed and
sheltered Him in the person of His poor and needy. There
follows for the guilty the awful exposure of their guilt, the
long public rehearsal of their crimes and follies to which we

[1] pp. 374 and 376 (cf. esp.—"Gay gere and witles, his hode set on
koket: As prowde as pennyles his slefe has no poket..."; with the
extracts above, pp. 406–11).

[2] p. 377 (cf. above, pp. 369–70).

[3] p. 376. (For the "kyrkchaterars", see in my *Preaching in Med. Engl.*
pp. 175–8, etc. and cf. further, Bp. Repingdon, MS. Jo. Ryl. Libr. Manch.
Lat. 367, fol. 274b, col. i ("scurrilitatibus et derisionibus seipsos et alios
culpabiliter scandalizant").)

[4] Dr Pollard, in his side-note (p. 378), has missed the connection of
the narrative here (drunkards slothful in church-going), as revealed above,
pp. 435–7.

[5] pp. 377–8. (Besides the sermon extracts given above, in chaps. vi and
vii, see also, for those slothful in church-going in my *Preaching in Med.
Engl.* pp. 172–3, etc.)

listened in the *Summa Predicantium*.[1] To these charges the demons next add their witness, claiming the wicked as their own rightful prey.[2] "And bot thou make dewly amendis, or that thou dies", says the preacher solemnly from his pulpit,

else thi cursed synne shall be oponlye knowon to all the world at the day of dome, before the Holy Trinite and the seyntes and angles of hevene, before all the feendes of hell. Than the cursed lord, the feend that thou haste served, shall ther accuse the pleynly, and reherse thi synnes afore thin own face, what tyme that thou synned and in what place, and klaminge the as for is servaund. And there-fore thu shalte goye with hym to the payne of hell, where that thou shalte have sorowe withouten ende.[3]

Master Richard Alkerton, preaching at St Mary Spital in London, in the year 1406, depicts, for his sermon climax, that awful moment when the Judge delivers sentence:

"Go, ȝe curselyngs, to evere-lasting fier, whiche is maad redy to the devil and to his aungels!" And sodeinly thei shuln be cast doun into helle with the devil and his aungelis, and the ȝates of helle shul be schut for evermore that thei go nevere out. And ther thei shul [be] bulyd in fyr and brymstone withouten ende. Venemous wormes and naddris shul gnawe alle here membris withouten seessyng, and the worm of conscience, that is grutching in her conscience, shal gnawe the soule....[4] Wepe ȝe nowe, and ȝelle!...Now ȝe shul have everlasting bittirnesse; ȝour pley is tornyd in to moorning, ȝoor lauȝing is turned in to sorwe, and ȝour wepyng schal be withoute conforte and everlastyng. This fyr that turmentith ȝou shal never be quenchid, and thei that turmentyn ȝou shul never be wery, nether dye.[5]

In similar language, it will be remembered, John Bromyard

[1] *Towneley Pl.* pp. 379–84; similarly, *Lud. Covent.* pp. 374–7. (Cf. *Pricke of Consc.* pp. 141–68; the Doom questions as put to all "kynges, princes, knyȝtes and squyers, justices, mayres", etc., in MS. Linc. Cath. Libr. A. 6. 2, fol. 219; a 13th-cent. metr. homily in *An Old Engl. Misc.* E.E.T.S. pp. 80–3; Wimbledon; etc.)   [2] Cf. below, p. 540.

[3] MS. Roy. 18. B. xxiii, fol. 85. This open publication of sins, referred to, e.g., in the *Lud. Covent.* p. 374 ("ffor all ȝour dedys here xal be sene / Opynly in syght..."), is regularly mentioned in the sermons, as above: cf. further, *Old Engl. Homs.* (12th cent.), 2nd Ser. E.E.T.S. O.S. no. 53, pp. 69, 173, 223, etc.; Bromyard, *S.P.* s.v. "Contritio"; Myrc, *Festial,* pp. 89 and 95; MS. Harl. 2398, fol. 45b; *Pricke of Consc.* p. 154; etc., etc.

[4] Cf. *Pricke of Consc.* p. 191, ll. 7088–9; *Old Engl. Homs.* as before, p. 69, etc.: also *Two Cov. Corp. Chr. Plays,* pp. 99–102.

[5] MS. Add. 37677, fol. 60b. For another elaborate description of the Doom in a sermon (unpublished), cf. MS. Add. 41321, fols. 21b et seq.

prophesied the fate of the rich and the mighty of this world.[1]
In similar language, the demons of the Towneley Play now
hail their victims, as "Harry Ruskin" and his companions are
hustled off to the infernal regions. Let them curse the day on
which they were born, cry the tormentors. Where are now the
gold and treasure they amassed, their "merry menee", the
"gay gyrdyls, iaggid hode, prankyd gownes; whedir"? Their
sins are about their necks,[2] their pride is fallen, their merriment
gone. They who once greedily "pouched their pennies",
sparing nothing for the needy, they who practised extortion
and broke their wedlock, they who chatted and laughed merrily
now quake and are dumb. They shall dwell for ever in pitch
and tar with endless sorrow. Vivid phrases like those of Bromyard which tell of the devils "who then shall run to meet them
with salutations of mocking laughter, dragging them to hell
with their cudgels",[3] enable us to complete the scene, far
better than any mere stage directions. The dramatists do not
lead us, like Dante or the visionary of St Patrick's Purgatory,[4]
into the gruesome underworld itself. But we may be sure that
those last lingering moments of the Play, showing the exodus
thither, were full of a lively significance and a quaint realism
for the serious onlooker. There, in hell-mouth "is stynke, and
ther is all derkenes.... There is horribull sygh3t off develes,
dragons, wormes and serpentys to turment them. Ther is
sygh3ynge and sorowynge, wepynge and weylynge, hideous
cryynge, grugeynge and murnynge, hunger and thyrste irre-
mediable, wyth gnagyng off tethe wyth-owte ende".[5] For,
"clerkys seyn that alle clerkys that evere were and schul be
cowde no3t ymagyn oo peyne thereof. For thei are so stronge
that alle the peynes of the wor[l]d is but as an oynement to
regard of tho peynes.... Seynt Austyn seyth,—'Lord, lete me
be brokyn and boyled here, that I be no3t dampnyd; for me

---

[1] See *Preaching in Med. Engl.* pp. 343–4, and further, below, pp. 527–8;
similarly, *Pricke of Consc.* pp. 190–1.   [2] Cf. above, Bromyard, p. 301.
[3] *S.P.* s.v. "Judicium Divinum" (again, s.v. "Executor").
[4] Quoted by Bromyard, e.g. s.v. "Mors"; *Spec. Laic.* cap. lxxiv; etc.
[5] MS. Camb. Univ. Libr. Gg. vi. 16, fol. 49b. For the cry of the
damned, cf. further, e.g., MS. Harl. 2316, fols. 2 and 9b; etc.

thynketh esy thi chastesing here'".[1] If any reader doubts the
dramatic power of the homilists when dealing with this theme,
let him read the relevant sections of that most popular of
pulpit "common-places", the *Pricke of Conscience*: notably
those which describe the hideous "dyn" of hell, the shrieks
of the tortured, the yells "and raumpyng of devels, the
dyngyng and dusching" of their glowing hammers, as the
close-packed mass of humanity sways this way and that under
their blows in the infernal oven, each fighting and scratching
at his neighbour's face like a grinning madman, or ripping off
his own flesh and gnawing away his own tongue with passion
indescribable.[2] The final word of the Play refers to that
equally astounding spectacle which awaits the righteous. So,
"ȝiff thou ende in good liff", testifies the homilist, "than thou
shalte to heven bothe bodie and sowle, even as thu arte here.
But thi bodye shall than be glorified. What is that thi bodie
that is nowe so hevy and so hoge, it shall be than as bright
as the sonne.... Than, when ther shall be mo bodies gadered
to-thether than is steeres on heven or graweyll in the see, and
everyche of hem so bright, than ther will be a glorious sight.
ȝut shall that be but as a shadow to the bryghtenes of Goddes
blessed face".[3]

What, then, are the final conclusions which we may be
entitled to draw from our analysis of these three scenes of
the English Miracle-Plays in the light of the sermons? One

[1] MS. Salisb. Cath. Libr. 103, fol. 103 (unpublished *Jacob's Well*).
[2] (The 14 Pains of Hell, etc.), pp. 175–202, esp. pp. 198–200. (Cf.
also the realism which describes how the tortured shall see the hideous
devils that madden them in the glow of the sparks which light up their
torture-chamber (p. 186).) On this favourite homiletic theme, see further,
Old Engl. Homs. (12th and 13th cents.), E.E.T.S. 1st Ser. O.S. no. 29,
pp. 41–3, 2nd Ser. O.S. no. 53, pp. 173, 224, 227–9, etc.; *Spec. Laic.*
(13th cent.), cap. xlv, and ed. Welter, p. 72 (on the terrors of Hell);
Bromyard, *S.P.* s.v. "Poena"; Myrc, *Man. Sacerd.* lib. v, cap. xix (*De
contemplatione penarum infernalium*); *Ayenb. of Inwyt*, pp. 71–3, 264–5;
and further in my *Preaching in Med. Engl.* pp. 336–8.
[3] MS. Roy. 18. B. xxiii, fol. 89 b. Cf. further, the "ioyes of paradyis"
as described in *Old Engl. Homs.* (12th cent.), E.E.T.S. O.S. no. 53,
pp. 230–2; Bromyard, *S.P.* s.v. "Gaudium"; MS. Salisb. Cath. Libr. 103,
fol. 103; *Ayenb. of Inwyt*, p. 75; and *Pricke of Consc.* pp. 209–52.

fact, at all events, has been definitely established. Their subject-
matter and the detailed manner of its treatment can no longer
be studied in the semi-isolated fashion of earlier critics. So far
from being bold and original essays of the dramatic genius,
striving independently, at an early stage, towards a popular,
vernacular presentation of religious truth, we have found them
to be surrounded on every side by a mass of kindred homiletic
material, itself bound up with a yet more ancient pulpit tradition, and at least as dramatic, as lively and forceful in the
handling as anything to be found in the plays.[1] In the case
of the Towneley "genius", we can say without hesitation
what has been said already in connection with our study of his
leading characters, that here the author has worked direct from
current sermon sources. In the case of the earlier Cycles, it
may be necessary to meet the argument that, where dramatic
parallels occur in the sermons, we are in reality witnessing
the effect of the drama upon preaching, and not *vice versa.*
That the miracle-plays in their turn must have reacted here
and there, like the work of artist and minstrel, upon a
sensitive pulpit, few, we think, will deny. The Shropshire
Festial of John Myrc, for example, may well reflect the
impressions of one who has been a spectator at neighbouring
Chester pageants. Nevertheless, when once the links between
contemporary pulpit and stage have been firmly established,
such concrete evidence as we possess points definitely to the
former as prime pattern and source. The sermons, as we
have seen, whether preserved in English or in Latin, are
themselves in the line of an unbroken tradition that links
them directly with the work of earlier expositor and legendary.
The vernacular plays, on the other hand, in so far as their
sources have been disclosed by modern scholarship, are shown
to have been constructed—not, indeed, unnaturally—from
actual sermon material. Finally, the new fact has now to be
borne in mind—that, throughout the period of the Middle
Ages, in England as elsewhere, it is the pulpit, not the stage,

---

[1] For the highly-developed dramatic element in 12th-cent. sermons,
cf. e.g. Bourgain, *La Chaire franç.* pp. 211–16.

that remains the major as it was the older of these two
clerical activities directed to a common end.

From the miracle-plays it is now high time to pass to the
Moralities. Here, at the outset, we are already on firmer ground
in making a similar claim for pulpit influence. Literary critics
and historians—in their most vague manner, it is true—have
at least pointed to the latter as a parent of that "allegorical
tendency" which led to the creation of this type of drama.
Some, indeed, have actually gone so far as to state, though with
the customary blindness to the dramatic element in medieval
preaching, that, "as the miracle play grew out of the Liturgy,
so the moral may be said to be a dramatic development of the
sermon".[1] In our present studies, however, we have been
enabled already to make more definite advance in this same
direction. For, in discussing the development of Allegory in
the sermons, we found that even such picturesque dramatic
features of the Moralities as the Besieged Castle, the Vices
personified, and the Disputation of the Four Heavenly Virtues
were commonplaces of the former:[2] likewise, yet more recently,
in the case of friend Tutivillus and his companions of the
Towneley Cycle. It only remains now, therefore, to clinch
the argument for pulpit inspiration by tracing back to this
source one other important feature which may be considered
characteristic of the morality-plays as distinct from the Miracle
proper. Courthope, indeed, in his account of their growth
from the latter, mentions as a further distinctive trait "the
imitation of actual nature in their satirical portraits".[3] Since,
however, the part played by preaching in the development
of this very realism has been fully emphasized and illustrated
in previous chapters, no further comment upon it is needed.
The preachers, we said, not the Classical Humanists, were the
pioneers of the great Return to Human Nature in literature.

---

[1] G. Crosse, *The Relig. Drama*, p. 99.
[2] I.e. in Chap. II above.
[3] *Hist. of Engl. Poetry*, vol. i, p. 425. On this subject of the transition
from miracle to morality-play, see also Chambers, *Med. Stage*, vol. ii,
pp. 155–6.

The remaining important feature, then, which calls for our attention is the dramatic treatment of human life and death in both morality-plays and homilies. Several pages of the author's *Preaching in Medieval England* were devoted, it will be remembered, to illustrations of the prominent place given to the subject of Death in pulpit oratory.[1] Tracts on the *Ars Moriendi*, lyrical verses like those of the celebrated Vernon manuscript repeatedly echoed its melancholy sentiments and warnings. "Hav mynd o thi last ende!"[2] In thus calling attention to the perils and woes of man's demise, therefore, the authors of *The Pride of Life* and of *Everyman* were merely performing a prescribed homiletic duty in their work for the religious stage.[3] But there is more even than mere pessimism and warnings in pulpit treatment of the theme. We found something approaching to a genuine tragical feeling—certainly more classic than Christian—when the preachers reviewed the lot of humanity trembling on the brink of the grave. Thus Bromyard, in a fresh passage not cited in our original study, contrasts the state of him who once "was strong as a boxer, who was once wont to fight, to smite, to leap, to raise the hand in dances and sing loudly ditties of inordinate love" with that of the same man now scarcely able to move his feet at the call of nature, lift hands to feed himself, drive away the flies from his mouth, or even turn from side to side in his own bed of weakness. "Qui insuper linguam fortem et potentem habere solebat atque velocem ad placitandum, ad jurandum, et ad mentiendum et detrahendum atque superjactandum, tunc non potest illam movere vel ad confitendum vel orandum, sed nec ad respondendum sacerdoti. . . ." So, too, with beauty and with worldly wisdom. He who formerly was plump and well-favoured, declares the Dominican, in view of the grave, would

---

[1] pp. 268, 341–4, etc. It is significant that Bromyard's chapter on "Mors" in the *S.P.* is one of the longest in the book (151 sections).

[2] MS. Worc. Cath. Libr. F. 10, fol. 49b. Cf. *Ayenb. of Inwyt*, p. 70.

[3] There is still no reason to doubt the judgment of Ten Brink (see *Hist. of Engl. Lit.* vol. ii, p. 302) that the *Elckerlijk* and other foreign versions are translations and adaptations of the original English *Everyman*, and not *vice versa*. Cf. here also Skelton's *Magnificence*, and such typical verses as *The Three Deid Powis* by Henryson, or Patrick Johnstone.

seem but to have been fattening his own flesh to feed the worms
more royally or to make the flames of hell-fire burn the
fiercer with his fat! Horses in the stable, money in the chest,
corn in the barn, clothes upon the perch, he goes on, all must
be left behind, when Death appears on the scene.[1] In the
"stynkyng dust" of the grave, "truliche seith this clerk
[Ambrose], 'I dar wel seie the schalt nat perseyve ther any
defference betwyx a begger and a kyng, nor betwyx a maister
and his knave'".[2] With a note of undisguised mocking yet
another English preacher taunts his audience thus: "Why
rememberiste thou no thyng of thi riches that thou browȝttiste
in to this worlde? Thou wottyste well i-nowȝe that nowȝte
thou browȝttiste into this worlde and nowȝt thou schalt bere
hens. Now thou hast worldly riches, and seyste all is thyne.
Why doyste not thou take it wythe the?"[3] If "Everyman"
then must needs be forsaken of his "Goods", so too must he
be forsaken of his earthly companions "Fellowship" and
"Kindred", at this juncture. As it is in the more famous
morality-play, so precisely is it in the sermons. The hollowness
of earthly friendships and the waning of family affection at
death are frequent melancholy themes upon homiletic lips.
Their testimony is abundant to the callous and selfish indifference of an age as greedy and calculating as our own,
which well-nigh a thousand years of Catholic Christianity had
failed to eradicate. A tale of the thirteenth-century *Speculum
Laicorum* tells how King Philip Augustus of France lies
groaning upon his death-bed, because all his boon companions
have left him to perish alone. Another tells how even children
forget their own father in the grave.[4] Bromyard speaks with

---

[1] *S.P.* s.v. "Mors". Cf. Odo of Cheriton (early 13th cent.) on riches
that stay in the world when their owner dies (see Herbert, *Cat. of Romances
in B.M.* vol. iii, p. 49); Bozon, *Metaphs.* cap. ci; *Pricke of Conscience*,
pp. 25-7; poems in E.E.T.S. O.S. nos. 117, pp. 761-2, and 24,
pp. 83-94; etc.   [2] MS. Worc. Cath. Libr. F. 10, fol. 48b.
[3] MS. Linc. Cath. Libr. A. 6. 2, fol. 101. Cf. MS. Camb. Univ.
Libr. Gg. vi. 16, fols. 49b-50 ("sent Bernarde in a sermonde that he
makythe...."); etc.
[4] cap. lii. The first is also in the earlier collection of MS. Roy. 7. D. i,
fol. 107 (A.D. 1270-9).

equal bitterness, more than once, of those who think only of what they can get for themselves out of the bequests of their relations, even going to the length of paying frequent visits to the dying in order that they may be remembered in their wills. When the latter have gone, the profuse promises made to them are allowed to dissolve likewise.[1] In another place, Bromyard compares picturesquely the departure of a visitor at some great man's court, escorted to the gate by a multitude of servants who then withdraw, to the case of the dying man led to the gate of death by a weeping family. There he discovers that they cannot accompany him further, but will return home as soon as he is laid in the grave. "All that remains to him then are his deeds and short-comings."[2] The words of a somewhat later vernacular sermon provide further interesting commentary in prose upon the equivalent lines of *Everyman*:

The while that a man hath for to dispende, in the mene tyme he shall have servantes and felowes makynge to hym grett solaces and murthes, preyinge hym to feestes and ledynge hym to taverne.... When that thei come to the acounte of dethe and shall rekene ther, everyman than taketh of other what that thei may stell, and hent away. And, anon, as thei be dede and passed owte of this worlde, than thei be putt owte of mynde. Than thei that be lefte, thei rennen to suche hem newe, and on the same wyze thei serve the laste as thei dud the firste.... But what 3eveth the worlde to mankeend after is dethe? In ys liff I wot wel the world granteth to many man ryches, mekell pompe,...and manys wurshippe therwith. But what...at the laste? And wold thu see trewly—nowth els but an olde shete to the erthe to wreppe hym in. This is a lewde frenshippe![3]

---

[1] Cf. *S.P.* s.v. "Amor (carnalis)", "Executor", "Mors", "Retentio", etc. Further, *Old Engl. Homs.* (12th cent.), E.E.T.S. O.S. no. 53, p. 183; Bozon, *Metaphs.* cap. lxxxii; MS. Harl. 45, fol. 66 ("ffalse executoures"); *Hand. Synne*, pp. 44, 202–9; etc. With such, cf. *Piers Plowman*, passim, on the guile and greed of executors.   [2] s.v. "Avaritia".

[3] MS. Roy. 18. B. xxiii, fols. 80–1. Later he goes on: " ...Fadere and modere, brothers and...sustren, is wiff and is children,...but what frenshippe sheweth thise unto hym?—wepen and cryon and weylon is dethe and bryngeth him to the grave; and ther thei leven hym, and, after that the moneth mynd is do, anon after, thei have forgett hym...". Cf. again, fol. 155 (when mishap comes, friends fly), and *Gesta Rom.* p. 131. It is significant that the very phrases of the Morality *Everyman* (cf. ll. 728 et seq. and 709 et seq.) devoted, as Dr Pollard points out (*Engl. Mir. Plays*, p. l), to the "exaltation of the priesthood", occur also in a sermon of the above MS. (Roy. 18. B. xxiii, fol. 146)—[The

"For the world laghes on man and smyles:
Bot at the last it him bygyles."[1]

Equally striking is the parallel afforded by a sermon in Latin,
delivered probably in the cathedral church at Worcester about
the same period, c. 1390 to 1410. The speaker has chosen for
his text a passage from the Canticle—"Nigra sum et formosa".[2]
At length he turns in sudden dramatic fashion to address, as
it were, the ghost of the departed with a bluntness of speech
more worthy of the stage than of the sacred rostrum. Then
follow some vernacular verses which might well stand as the
Epilogue of "Everyman's" wife:

Tell us, O lady *de blacworth*, what worth have worldly glory and the
aforesaid vanities, of which men are wont to make boast. Once you were
fair in body, gentle of blood, privileged with honours, abounding in
houses and wealth. All these things you possessed, and now of all you
can say thus—

"Now all men mowe sen be me,
that wor[l]dys Joye is vanyte.
I was a lady; now am I non.
I hadde worchepes; now it ys begon.
I was fayr and gentil both.
Now ich man wyle my body loth.
My frendys, my godes me hav forsake.
To wyrmes mete now am I take.
Of al the wor[l]d now haf I noȝth
bitt gode dedes that I wrogth.
Only tho schuln abyde wit me.
Al other thynges arn vanyte".[3]

office of the priesthood is above that of angels, etc.] "the wiche power
nother archaungell ne aungell myȝthe never atteyne....Ther is none
erthly powre egall to the powre of prestehod. The powre, seyth he
[i.e. "Seynt John Crisostyme"], of a kynge, other of a prynce temporall,
it goyth uppon the body and uppon worldely thinges, and no thinge
uppon the soule. But the powre that prestes have...it atteyneth to
mans soule and maketh it both fre and bounde, qwike and dede...", etc.
A parallel imitation of the general pulpit theme of Death and Everyman
will be found in Hoccleve's *Regement of Princes*, see E.E.T.S. ed. p. 26.
Cf. also Bertoldo's closing speech in Massinger's *Maid of Honour*,
Act iii, Sc. i ("...How like a prison is to a grave!"...).

[1] *Pricke of Consc.* ll. 1092–3 (cf. also ll. 1182–99).   [2] Cant. i, 5.

[3] MS. Worc. Cath. Libr. F. 10, fol. 208. Cf. the *exemplum*, in *S.P.* s.v.
"Mors",§ 145, "of Isabella, daughter of St Louis, King of France, formerly
Queen of Navarre" (wrongly quoted from the *Lib. de Dono Timoris* [of
Humbertus de Romanis]: see Herbert, *Cat. of Rom.*...p. 451).

One further point of resemblance occurs in connection with this subject, before we pass on. In *Everyman* again, in *The Pride of Life*, also in the Eleventh Play of the Coventry Cycle, "Dethe, goddys mesangere" personified, makes terrifying entry upon the stage.[1] Indeed, a modern editor of the *Ludus Coventriae* declares of this episode: "The most dramatic passage in the series is perhaps the unnoted entrance of Death in the midst of the revelry of Herod and his knights".[2] Now it is perfectly clear that, before ever the *Danse Macabre* had become widely popular in this country, it was the pulpit that strove to capture men's imagination by picturing the grim figure appearing in this fashion. Those were days of sudden disaster and little medical skill, when, as one aptly remarks, "ofte cometh deth amonges men. And they a man be in goede poynt at eve, happylyche he is ded by the morowe".[3] From the so-called *Meditations* or *Sayings of St Bernard*, in particular, a very favourite medieval source-book for sermons,[4] our English homilists seemed to have derived their conception of Death as a skulking, ghostly tyrant, who flits through all lands from place to place, sparing none, be he rich or poor, high or low, king or emperor, pope or prelate, religious or secular, a dread visitor whose coming is sudden, privy and unannounced:

> Forthi says Saynt Bernard in a boke:
> *Quid in rebus humanis cercius est morte;*
> *Quid incercius hora mortis invenitur?*

[1] See here E. K. Chambers, *Med. Stage*, vol. ii, p. 153; and cf. also the coming of Death in *Piers Plowman*, C text, pass. xxiii, ll. 100–5; B text, pass. xx, ll. 99 et seq.

[2] Miss K. S. Block, in E.E.T.S. Ext. S. no. 120, Intr. For the episode, see pp. 174–7 (cf. the usual references to Poverty, Worm's Meat, Hell, etc.).

[3] MS. Harl. 2398, fol. 46b ("they" = "though"). Cf. *Pricke of Consc.* ll. 2102–3.

[4] Ed. Migne, *Patr. Lat.* vol. clxxxiv, col. 485 (the work is sometimes described as *Tractatus de Interiori Homine*). Copies are exceedingly common in our sermon MSS. Cf. in Cathedral Libraries, MS. Linc. C. 4. 6, as mentioned above, p. 516, n. 1; MSS. Worc. F. 75, F. 117 and Q. 27; MSS. Heref. O. 3. xi, O. 6. vii and P. 3. iii; etc. Cf. similarly, e.g., Will of Roger Celle, chaplain at St Albans, 1446, in MS. "Stoneham" Reg., Somerset House, i, fol. 48 (as described in my art. in *Trans. of the Herts. Archaeol. Soc.* 1929, p. 188); etc. See further below, p. 596.

He says: "What es til man mare certayn
Than the Dede es that es swa sodayn;   [Death]
And what es mare uncertayn thyng
Than es the tyme of the Dede commyng?"¹

Apart from the author of the *Pricke of Conscience*, whose testimony to his main source is thus freely given,² at least three preachers of the fourteenth century, who are known to us by name, adopt the same language of dramatic personification. The Austin Friar, John Waldeby, speaks of the solemn moment "when Death, who is God's Bailiff, shall come to arrest" men.³ The Franciscan, John of Grimston, notes down in his sermon-encyclopaedia, completed about the year 1376, for future use amongst an assortment of vernacular verse on the subject of "Mors", some lines beginning—

Be war, man, i come as thef
To renne thi lif that is the lef....⁴   [snatch—dear to thee]

Twelve years later, Thomas Wimbledon, in his sermon at Paul's Cross, expatiates upon the Three Sumners ("other sergeauntes") who summon men to reckoning, of whom Death himself is the third.⁵ "And the condicion of him is that whan ever he come, first, other the second, other the last houre, he ne spareth neyther poure ne rych, aged ne yonge, ne he dreadeth no thretning, ne he ne taketh hede of no prayer ne of no gift, ne he graunteth no respit; but withouten delay he bringeth forth to the dome."⁶ It is probably the same orator who exclaims in another sermon— "How slely the deth schal robben ham: how apertely he schal a-teyn ham: how diversly he schal towche hem!"⁷ In the

¹ See *Pricke of Consc.* pp. 52 and 54, ll. 1865–89 and 1940–59. (Also, quoting "Saynt Austyn", ll. 1960 et seq.)

² Bernard is again quoted, ll. 1875 et seq.

³ MS. Caius Coll. Camb. 334, fol. 174b. So Shakespeare, *Hamlet*, Act v, Sc. ii: "As this fell sergeant, death, is strict in his arrest".

⁴ MS. Advoc. Libr. (now Nat. Libr. of Scotland), Edinb. 18. 7. 21, fol. 86b. Cf. dan Michel's sermon, E.E.T.S. O.S. no. 23, p. 264.

⁵ Ed. *Acts and Mons. of Jo. Foxe*, in *Ch. Hist. of England*, vol. iii, pt. i, pp. 300–2. Cf. here the Poem of the Vernon MS.—"Of thre Messagers of Deeth", E.E.T.S. ed. O.S. no. 117, pp. 443–8.

⁶ Cf. here Dethe's remarks in *Everyman*, ll. 115 et seq.

⁷ MS. Camb. Univ. Libr. Ii. iii. 8, fol. 160b, a *Latin* sermon, with English phrases. (Amongst the physical organs which Death is here said to "touch" are the legs—"per *gowte*".)

new century following, the English translator of the *Gesta Romanorum* speaks likewise of "Dethe, the whiche iugylithe and sleithe us alle".[1]

The shock of death, with the yet greater tragedy that might be in store beyond it, cast its shadow backward athwart the whole of human life, as with solemn eye the preachers reviewed it from cradle to grave. From St Bernard again they had learnt to speak of it in yet older phrases as a thing tragic and pathetic in its very beginnings. "Ich am a dedliche man, seith Salamon,[2] lich al other, of the kynde o him that was formed o the erthe; and e my modres wombe was a vowl lu[m]pe of fles, vyve monthes congeled togeder e my modres blod. And be the norschyng of slep ate last was browth forth into the wrecchid world and sorliche wepte, as al other don. And tus with miche kar and miche sorwe lyve forth a-mong other men."[3] Such is Shakespeare's "unaccommodated man".[4] Through that long dreary night of the European Middle Ages in which the Tragic Muse of the theatre slept, from the waning triumphs of Greek drama in a Graeco-Roman world to the dawn of Elizabethan Tragedy, it was the Christian pulpit, strange to say, that never ceased to keep alive her memory and her rite, a dim lamp burning perpetually before a moss-grown altar. While aristocratic bards might sing of the tragic deaths of their heroes, and rhyme-makers in Latin compose their mournful verses for equally limited circles, the preachers, on the other hand, from generation to generation, declaimed publicly to the masses, high and low alike, sometimes with moving eloquence, this story of universal human calamity and decay. It was they who taught ordinary men and women to see life as one continuous drama played out in a succession of Acts, all tinged with an ancient Hebrew melancholy—the helplessness and pathos of childhood, the folly of youth's strivings and ambitions, the empty vanity of middle-age, the end of all mortal effort and

[1] English version, E.E.T.S. ed. p. 135.   [2] See Wisd. vii, 1–3.
[3] MS. Worc. Cath. Libr. F. 10, fol. 49b. Cf. similarly, MS. Roy. 18. B. xxiii, fóls. 106b and 143b; MS. Harl. 45, fol. 11, etc. (as quoted in my *Preaching in Med. Engl.* p. 341, with further references in n. 2); *Pricke of Consc.* pp. 13–15; *Ayenb. of Inwyt*, pp. 130, 215–6; etc.
[4] Cf. here Prof. Dowden, *Shaksp. His Mind and Art* (7th ed.), p. 346.

of the restless excitement of human passions. Every medieval poem that deals with these topics breathes out to us the same direful homiletic spell.[1] Life on earth, according to these prophets of darkness, then, was one long unbroken tragedy. Its several stages might be reckoned as three, four, seven or ten, according to the whim of the moralist.[2] The end of the play was always the same: Man falling, falling, as the Wheel of Fortune completes for him its final revolution. One brief example out of many will suffice to illustrate both the pessimism and the charm of this peculiar type of sermon artistry:

Man's lyffe may well be figurde by roosis in iii degreis. ffyrst there is a bud, in the whiche the rosis ben closyd. And aftyr, owte of this bud spryngythe a feyre rose and a swete and a delicius. And sone aftyr, with wyndys and weders the levis fadithe a-wey to the grownde, and so turnethe to erthe.

So, in lyke wyse there is in every man and woman of the worlde iii degres of agys. The firste is chyldhode, in the whiche the flowre of man-hode and womanhode ben closyd in. ffor there is no man that can tell what schall falle of a chylde in tyme commyng, wheder he schall be riche or pore, good or bad, wise or unwyse. ffor hys flowre schall spryng, increce and growe aftyr governaunce. And, aftyr this, commythe ȝowthe; and then hathe he or sche lyȝtnes, swyftnes, wantonnes and many other ornamentes of kynde. But at the làste commythe age; and then schrynkethe hys flessche, then fadythe his colowre. Hys bonys ben sore; his lymmys wexythe febyll; his bake begynnythe for to croke downwarde to the erthe that he came of. And then his feyre flowris declynethe and fallyth a-wey to the grownde. And so man hathe no sure abydyng here.[3]

To another, less poetically inclined, Youth is but "a day *of drirines*, because *muche filth, care and soroo is in it*": Middle age is "a day *of besines*, because much toil and tribulation is in this middle-life": Old age is "a day *of hevynes*, because

[1] Readers unfamiliar with the mass of poetry of this description will find some excellent samples in Chambers and Sidgwick, *E. E. Lyrics*, Moral, pp. 163–200 (with Notes); *Vernon MS. Poems*, E.E.T.S.; etc.

[2] Cf. the allit. poem, *The Parlement of the Thre Ages*, c. 1350, ed. Gollancz, Roxburgh Club, 1897, and *Sel. E.E. Poems*, vol. ii, Oxford, 1915; the Three Ages again in the *Pricke of Consc.* p. 12 et seq.; a Treatise on the Four Ages, in MS. Add. 28260 (late 13th cent.) and in Ch.-V. Langlois, *La Vie en France...*, vol. ii, pp. 184–222; the Seven Ages in the Treatise *Ratis Raving*, E.E.T.S. ed. O.S. no. 43, pp. 57–74; etc.

[3] MS. Linc. Cath. Libr. A. 6. 2, fol. 5. For similar descriptions of Old Age in sermons, see in my *Preaching in Med. Engl.* p. 342; and for poetry, *Reliq. Antiq.* vol. ii, pp. 210–12; E.E.T.S. O.S. no. 24, pp. 71–81; etc.

great penalty, *soroo and seknes* is in this ultimate end".[1] By the
further statement that "these days the holy man Job compares
to a seiling schipp",[2] we are reminded afresh that the influence
of Old Testament Scripture looms large in all this pessimistic
sermon-utterance.[3] As for the antiquity of the tradition in
English preaching, the reader need only turn back to the early
twelfth-century homily known as the *Poema Morale* to find
the same melancholy ponderings set forth in verse.[4] Thence-
forward they are regularly repeated in such prose homily-
collections of early date as have hitherto been made accessible
in print.[5] The tradition, indeed, is strangely and persistently
continuous. Here, then, in this pulpit treatment of human
life and death lies the nucleus of what we may call the plots
of a group of English morality-plays, including *The Castell
of Perseverance, Mankynde*,[6] and *The Worlde and the Chylde*,
the earliest group of stage Tragedies in our language. From
them, leaping a century and more, we come to Shakespeare,
greatest of English tragedians, and listen again to the preacher's
familiar accents in the immortal speech of Jaques upon "the
Seven Ages of Man."[7] In form and substance alike it is as
clearly the fine fruit of medieval English preaching as Hamlet's

[1] MS. Bodl. 649, fol. 120b. (For the tragedy of Old Age, see further
fols. 121b-2.) [2] See Job ix, 26.
[3] It is worth observing, e.g., that in the MS. Camb. Univ. Libr. Kk. i. 5,
which furnishes us with the metrical treatise *Ratis Raving* (referred to
above), there appears along with it the *Dicta Salomonis*, a favourite
preachers' source, itself drawn from the Books of Ecclesiastes, Wisdom,
etc. and dealing with these same mournful themes.
[4] Ed. Morris, *Old Engl. Homs.* E.E.T.S. O.S. no. 34, 1st Ser. pt. ii,
p. 159. See also Ten Brink, *E. Engl. Lit.* vol. i, pp. 153–5.
[5] Cf. *Twelfth Cent. Homs.* ed. Belfour, E.E.T.S. as referred to in my
Preaching in Med. Engl. p. 344; *Old Engl. Homs.* ed. Morris, E.E.T.S.
O.S. no. 53, 2nd Ser. pp. 179–85; etc.
[6] Notice here how Old Age falls into the grip of Avarice (or Covetousness) as in *Ratis Raving* (pp. 64 and 71–2) and in the earlier sermon stories,
e.g. above, pp. 170–2.
[7] *As You Like It*, Act ii, Sc. vii. Cf. esp. with the *Ratis Raving* version
(as above, p. 534, n. 2), and again with such a remark as that of the
preacher in our MS. Roy. 18. B. xxiii, fol. 138: "ʒiff this world be an
interludie, as doctors ymagynne (I wote never who shall pleye the seynte
in our interludie)". See also in the latter connection, Douce, *Illustrations
of Shakesp.* pp. 184–5.

soliloquies upon the churchyard skull, or King Lear's briefer sermon upon the new-born babe.[1] The contribution of sermon to drama in respect of the morality-plays is indeed one of vital importance. We can best gauge its importance, perhaps, by listening to a recent verdict passed upon the plays themselves: "It is not fanciful here to see the beginnings of that tragic soul-struggle which later became so marked a characteristic of the Shakespearean drama. Men were taught here the secret of progression of character and the delineation of conflicting passions. And to these features...must be added the sense of construction and unity of form".[2] That, in brief, is precisely what we have just seen to be the specific contribution of the pulpit to the framing of these same Moralities.

In two further directions the technique of sacred oratory clearly left its impress upon the structure of the plays and helped to mould their characteristic lines of development. With a word or two upon these our chapter must end. Amongst the problems left more or less unsolved in the study of this dramatic literature is the part played by the earlier forms of Dialogue in the shaping of medieval Miracle and Morality. The connection between them, of course, has been vaguely realised for some considerable time. But so completely have scholars identified the history of religious play-acting with developments in the liturgy, and likewise the Dialogue itself, whether as *débat* or *estrif*, with the activities of secular minstrel and scholastic disputant, that the intermediary influence of the pulpit has again been overlooked. The subject is usually dismissed in the text-books with a passing glance at the familiar apocryphal poem known as *The Harrowing of Hell*, treated as though it were a lonely, isolated phenomenon "marking the transition from the older liturgical drama to the more popular miracle".[3] Where others have indicated, it is true, "the

[1] *King Lear*, Act iv, Sc. vi, "We came crying hither...". Cf. with the "wepynge babe" again in MS. Roy. 18. B. xxiii, fol. 143 b, as quoted above, p. 37; etc. The whole is derived from Wisd. vii, 3, and not as Douce imagined from Pliny (see *Illustrations*, p. 418).

[2] Allardyce Nicoll, *Brit. Drama*, p. 42.

[3] F. J. Snell, *The Age of Chaucer*, p. 79, referring to Pollard on this subject.

striking use" made of the Dialogue by such preachers as St Bernard, it remains for them merely to add that "the process by which these methods of instruction grew into the actual plays is obscure".[1] There is apparently no English pulpit tradition to bridge the gap. So much then for our first line of enquiry, for the moment. The second will be concerned with what so far as we know is the oldest class of Moralities, the *Paternoster* and *Creed Plays*, as performed at York and elsewhere.[2] As all students of the subject are aware, no actual version of this type of performance has come down to us. Consequently its character has provoked a good deal of conflicting speculation. A last look at our sermon-literature may possibly help even in this direction.

From quite early times a curious use of the Dialogue is prominent in Christian preaching, by means of which "extensive imaginary speeches" are put into the mouths of well-known Biblical characters, or of the angelic and diabolic disputants who argue for possession of the souls of men around the Judgment-seat of Christ. Amongst pulpit orators of the seventh and eighth centuries whose sermons offer us such examples are Andrew of Damascus, later Archbishop of Crete, and Germanus of Cyzicus, eventually Patriarch of Constantinople.[3] If we turn to a study of twelfth-century preaching in France, like that of the Abbé Bourgain which has been frequently quoted in these pages, we learn that, amongst all the forms of dramatic expression cultivated in sermons of the time, "the dialogue holds first place". Nor is it merely the matter of a few lively phrases constituting a rhetorical device intended to break through the monotony of the discourse. On the contrary, "it constitutes a true type of preaching", we are told, "authorized by frequent use and reserved for grand effects".[4] Having announced the subject of his Dialogue, the

---

[1] G. Crosse, *The Relig. Drama*, 1913, p. 99.

[2] On this subject see E. K. Chambers, *Med. Stage*, vol. ii, pp. 154, 378, 404–5, etc.

[3] See E. C. Dargan, *Hist. of Preaching*, vol. i, pp. 140–1 (based on R. Rothe, *Geschichte der Predigt*, §§ 57–63) and 116–17.

[4] *La Chaire Franç.* pp. 211–16 (examples are here given from Guerric

preacher proceeds to introduce the various interlocutors of the scene to his audience, and forthwith the sermon-dramatization begins in earnest, with the homilist himself in the rôle of a modern Shakespearean reciter. This quaint practice continues to survive in subsequent centuries. M. Hauréau publishes in full, for example, a typical specimen of the Doomsday disputation from a fourteenth-century manuscript in the *Bibliothèque Nationale*.[1] Where our knowledge of English medieval preaching, still in its infancy, points here and there to indications of the same kind of procedure, we have a right therefore to believe that these sermon-dialogues were once common enough in our own land and exercised a corresponding influence upon English taste. Here, too, the *Meditationes Vitae Christi* attributed to St Bonaventura would again give every encouragement to ambitious preachers of the day with a liking for *predicatio theatralis*.[2] Bourgain himself has discovered and published for us a homily of the kind of much earlier date, by Archbishop Anselm of Canterbury, dealing with the visit of Mary Magdalene to the Sepulchre.[3] By such distinguished adepts at the art, the practice, no doubt, would be introduced into this country.[4] So, of the early thirteenth-century homily in the vernacular known as *Sawles Warde*, Professor J. E. Wells is able to remark that—"the great amount of direct discourse gives the piece a dramatic quality approaching that of the much later Moralities".[5] In the *Speculum Laicorum*, later in

d'Igni (d. 1156) and Stephen of Tournay (1203), or Peter of Blois?). "Quelquefois ces discours dépassent de beaucoup les proportions du dialogue. Les personnages sont plus nombreux; on dirait qu'ils vont et viennent, entrent et sortent comme sur un théâtre, qu'il y a une mise en scène considérable, une représentation vivante avec des péripéties et un dénouement."

[1] No. 18216, fol. 94 et seq. (*Not. et Extr.* vol. vi, pp. 92–108).

[2] Cf. here M. Émile Mâle on the Pseudo-Bonav.—"Il a imaginé une foule de dialogues entre Joseph et Marie, entre Jésus et ses disciples, entre Jésus et sa mère. Tout parle dans son livre: Dieu, les anges, les vertus, les âmes...". (*L'art relig. de la fin du m. a.* p. 36.)

[3] *La Chaire Franç.* pp. 30, n. 1, 225, and 373–83.

[4] Cf. later, again, a typical Judgment-day Dialogue (between Satan and God) in a sermon preached in England by Peter of Blois (J. M. Neale, *Med. Preachers*, pp. 202–8); also Miss F. Foster in *The North. Pass.* pt. ii, p. 81.   [5] *Man. of Midd. Engl. Writings*, p. 273.

the same century, there appears a version of the Judgment
dialogue between Satan, Truth, Justice and the Blessed Virgin.[1]
Finally, although none too numerous, sufficient hints can be
found in English sermons of a date corresponding to that
of our earliest vernacular morality-plays to support the
theory that the Dialogue thus grew naturally into the native
drama from that same parent stock which had nurtured
its Satire, its Allegory and its humour. These later English
examples, as we should expect, often hark back directly
to the older models of continental preaching to which
reference has just been made. Thus Master Robert Rypon
of Durham borrows from a sermon of the celebrated twelfth-
century Master Peter Comestor, for one of his own, an
imaginary colloquy between the Holy Spirit and a celebrating priest, which introduces a typical moralization of
the Mass Vestments.[2] Another dialogue preserved in a
fifteenth-century vernacular discourse claims to be derived
from a sermon of St Augustine, "*de Annunciatione Dominica*".
God the Father prepares to despatch the angel Gabriel to earth
to announce to Our Lady the unique honour that awaits her.
A conversation ensues between the two former in the manner
of a naïve scene from some English miracle-play. Gabriel in
a speech to the Almighty at length asks Him for His "signett",
that he may convey it to the Virgin as tangible evidence of
His favour. The Almighty explains in reply that His signet is
His special grace, "the wiche I marke with my choson children.
...And it may well be called my signett; for itt is so secrete
that ther wote no man lyvynge with-owte revelacion whether
that he be signett ther-with or no". However, in the case of
the Mother of Christ, He is willing to grant the Archangel's
request. Presented with such a token, indeed, "she will
resceyve thee as she ow3th to do my messanger", He adds.
Gabriel then flies off to Nazareth upon his errand, and the
Annunciation Scene itself is pictured in much the same naïve

[1] See Herbert, *Cat. of Romances in B.M.* vol. iii, p. 395, and ed. Welter,
p. 74. Cf. another *excellent* example in dan Michel's sermon (E.E.T.S.
O.S. 23, pp. 264–8).

[2] MS. Harl. 4894, fol. 216 (*Cordule circa pectus, alba, manipulum, stola,
casula*, etc.).

fashion.[1] Another quaint little apocryphal conversation of the kind, between Adam and Eve and the Creator in the garden, will be found in a homily of the *Festial* series.[2] From such fragments of conversation as persist in our sermons, however, it is clear that the most popular occasion for these Dialogues remained that provided by the Doom-theme, in connection with which the fate of the sinner would be discussed and determined, as at the Last Day itself, by the witnessing parties of Heaven and Hell in the presence of the Supreme Judge. Thus in a homily upon Covetousness in *Jacob's Well* there is an echo of the dialogue from a well-known story told by Caesarius of Heisterbach in his *Dialogus Miraculorum*.[3] Four fiends and four angels argue with each other in turn, armed with texts of Scripture, for the soul of a rich man who died in an abbey.[4] Sometimes the wicked will receive the usual warnings in direct speech from the lips of the Judge, or dispute with Him the justice of their sentence.[5] The Devil, on the other hand, may venture to express his opinions to the President —"I turmented noon in helle but thoo that greveden thee: but these robbers robbide as wel the good as badde"; or the angels chime in with their fatal testimony—

> And say thus, "Our rede thai wald noght do;   [counsel]
> Bot agayne our wille foly thai wald use".

It is easy to picture with what telling effect a preacher of some histrionic ability would be able to recite and expand these

---

[1] MS. Roy. 18. B. xxiii, fol. 139 b. (Of the Annunc. proper, the preacher states, e.g., "When that he [Gabriel] seid that she was full of grace and blissed hur abowon all women, this aungell, as a wize messaunger, see that she was somdell trowbled; and therfore he spake to hur more famyliarly, callyng hur by hur name, seying on this wise,... 'Drede ye not, maide Mari!'".)   [2] pp. 67–8.

[3] Dist. ii, cap. xxxi (ed. Bland, *Broadway Med. Libr.* vol. i, p. 117).

[4] *Jacob's Well*, pp. 139–40. (In Caesarius, the rich man is a repentant usurer.)

[5] Cf. e.g. MS. Linc. Cath. Libr. A. 6. 2, fols. 8 et seq.; *Sermo in festo Corp. Chr.* (metric.), E.E.T.S. O.S. no. 98, p. 172; *Pricke of Consc.* pp. 141, 145, 149–50, etc. See also such independent examples as the *Disputatio inter Deum et hominem*, in MS. Add. 36983, fol. 275: others in MS. Add. 37049, fols. 28 b, 73 b, etc., showing also a drawing of the Scene, with appropriate remarks from each figure (fol. 19); *Vernon MS. Poems*; etc.

dialogues, with all the appropriate gestures and facial expression of the *mimus*. Our closing example, which is of a more tender nature, worthy alike of the pathos as well as the realism of the religious stage, comes from a Latin sermon in a manuscript preserved at Worcester, presumably of early fifteenth-century date. A transcription of the passages concerned appears in the official Catalogue of the Cathedral manuscripts.[1] But since the book is not accessible to many, and, moreover, since this particular transcript teems with minor errors,[2] we shall give the text here in full. The chosen theme is the Passion, as will be easily recognized:

> ...sub cruce, super quam mortuus est Christus, inventa erat fortis mulier, scilicet, beata virgo, ejus mater, quam tradidit Johannis custodie quando dixit—"Mulier, ecce filius tuus", etc. "A! blyssedful mayden and modyr! This is a wonderful change. The angyll behette[3] the that Kryst walde be thi sonne and dwel wyt the, and now he takys the a new son and gosse fro the.

> The angell sayde to the that the fruyt off thi body sulde be blyssyde;
> Ande now in the dome of the Iewys crist es a-cursede.
> At hys burth thu harde angels syngynge;
> Ande now thow seys hys frendis wepynge.
> At hys burthe kyngys and schiperdys dyd hym omage and wyrschyppe;
> And now al maner of men don hym despyte and schendschyppe.[4]
> At hys burth thow wantyd womanes wo.
> Bot, as thow wel fellys, now it ys noght so.
> Some tyme thou hadest cause for to synge lullay.
> Bot now thi songh ys all off wylaway.
> Somtym thou fed hym wyth thi sweet mylk to hys esse;
> Ande now the Iewys fedyn hyme wyt bitter gall to his dysesse.
> Som tyme thou fonde hym in the mydyl off the doctors in the temple;
> Ande now thou ffyndyst hyme hangynge in the mydyl of the Iewes on the krosse".

Crisostomus de planctu beate virginis ymaginat quod beata virgo, stans sub cruce, dixit filio suo sic—"Fili, agnosce matrem tuam; exaudi precem meam: decet filium audire matrem.

---

[1] Compiled by Rev. J. K. Floyer, edit. and revised by S. G. Hamilton, Fellow and Librarian of Hertford Coll. Oxford (Parker, Oxf. 1906, for the Worc. Hist. Soc.). See p. 6.
[2] I reckon approx. 40!   [3] = promised.
[4] = ruin, damage.

> A! son! Tak hede to me whas son thou was,
> And set me uppe wyt the on i crosse.
> Me her to leve, and the thus hense go,
> Yt ys to me gret kare and wo.
> Stynte now son to be harde to thi moder,
> Thou that ever was god to all other".

Et sic idem doctor ymaginat ibidem—filius matri conquerenti sic respondet—

> "Stynte now moder and wepe no more.
> Thi sorow and thi dyssesse grevysse me fule sore.
> Thow knowyse that in the I tok mannys kynde;
> In hyt for mannys syne to be the pynde.   [tormented]
> Be now glade, moder, and have in thoght
> That mannes hel es fondyne that I have soght.   [heal]
> Thow salt noght now kare what thow salt done.
> Lo! Ione thi kosyne sal be thi sone".

Et istud ostendit quando dixit—"Mulier, ecce filius tuus"....[1]

This fragment of dialogue serves to show how the English preacher would translate and expand an earlier sermon-dialogue in Latin of the kind that has just been described.

Whether or not the immediate relations between drama and sermon-dialogue have thus been satisfactorily established, we can hardly be in doubt as to the influence of preaching when we come to consider the further question of plays upon such familiar topics as *Paternoster* and *Credo*. In official decree after decree, their exposition by the parish clergy was enjoined, along with certain other prescribed essentials of the lay-folk's Faith.[2] Writers of vernacular tracts in prose and verse at length vied with the pulpits, during the two centuries preceding the Reformation, in their attempts to fulfil this urgent task. The special purport of the plays, therefore, will not be disputed by anyone. But the problem remains, in face of our complete ignorance of their contents—how exactly were these familiar expositions of doctrine dramatized? Apart from some lively and often satirical sketches of current society, there would

[1] MS. Worc. Cath. Libr. F. 10, fol. 25. With the above, cf. the Laments of the B.V.M. before the Cross, with Christ's replies, in the miracle-plays, e.g. *Towneley Pl.* pp. 267 et seq., *Lud. Cov.* pp. 300-1, etc.; in *Spec. of Lyric Poetry*, ed. T. Wright, Percy Soc. 1842, pp. 80-3; etc.
[2] Cf. in my *Preaching in Med. Engl.* pp. 46, 145-6, 282, etc.

seem to be little enough material in them for the requirements of the stage.[1] Canon James Raine the Younger, the well-known editor of *Fasti Eboracenses*, believed that the missing *Crede Play* of York "will, I think, be some day discovered" to be the metrical English version of Archbishop Thoresby's *Instruction* on the Creed, Commandments, and kindred homiletic matter prepared by John de Gaytrige, Garrick or Taystek, monk of that city, in the year 1357.[2] But dan Gaytrige's *Sermon*, as it is sometimes called, in spite of the fact that it is written in verse, presents no dramatic possibilities whatever; and the documentary evidence upon which the good Canon's theory was based lends him no real support. For, in his reading of it, he had been led, like others, to confuse the word "pagynes", meaning simply "writings",[3] with the word "pageants". Nor again does Dr A. W. Pollard's reference to the Contest of the *Psychomachia* help us any better.[4] For the statement which he quotes in its support, recording the character of the Play, is regularly used to describe the conventional sermon of the times[5]. Bernhard Ten Brink, for his part, wonders if the twelve articles of the *Crede Play* may have been represented by twelve pageants. If so, "were the contents of each article presented to view as a symbolic drama?... Or was the origin of each article referred to one of the Apostles, according to the well-known tradition? Or, finally, did each separate case treat of the wondrous recompense or punishment for belief or unbelief?"[6] Now, there is extant a work of the first years of the fifteenth century,[7] dealing, not indeed with

[1] Cf. Ten Brink, *Hist. of Engl. Lit.* vol. ii, p. 298: "The relations of such contents to the *Paternoster* can be at least partly imagined from medieval confession-books and moral tracts".

[2] See *Fasti Ebor.* vol. i, pp. 470–1; and *Test. Ebor.* vol. ii, p. 117. (The book of *Le Crede Play*, in the Will of Wm. Revetour.) Cf. also my *Preaching in Med. Engl.* pp. 53, 281–2, etc.

[3] Cf. Halliwell's *Dict.* s.v. "Pagyin". For the quotation in question see *Fascic. Ziz.* Rolls Ser. p. xiii.

[4] See *Engl. Miracle Plays*, p. xliii.

[5] Cf. my *Preaching in Med. Engl.* p. 322, n. 3. (The phrase is thus used in *Dives et Pauper*: "commende vertuis and despise vices"; etc.)

[6] *Hist. of Engl. Lit.* vol. ii, p. 291.

[7] See *Notes and Queries*, 11th Ser. iv, 321.

Creed or Paternoster, but with the sister topic of the Commandments, in the form of a homiletic tract completely in dialogue. This work, known as *Dives et Pauper*, which as yet has hardly attracted the attention that it deserves upon this one ground alone, occupies therefore a middle place in our study between the older sermon-dialogues and our extant Moralities proper. If, indeed, the latter were already developed when *Dives et Pauper* first appeared, we have only to believe that it was an unduly late example of a type of composition now superseded by works of a more advanced dramatic character. For, the literature of the later Middle Ages is strewn with such antiquated survivals. *Dives et Pauper*, then, would appear to give us an Interlude in the correct sense of that word[1]—or better, a series of Interludes—at once doctrinal and popular, designed to compete, in the interests of religion, with the coarse and improper interludes of street entertainers. Precept by precept, the Ten Commandments are expounded in conversation between two symbolic human characters of the times. The piece opens with what, though called "the firste chaptre", is really an introductory sermonette, put into the mouth of Pauper. This again is in keeping, as we have seen, with an old custom of the *Mystères*. A text from Holy Writ is given out in the usual pulpit style, first in Latin, then in the vernacular ("These ben the wordes of Salomon this moche to say in Englissh"); other typical quotations from Bede and from Scripture follow in the body of the discourse. Then the conversation proper opens with the second chapter. If the length of the work would seem, at first sight, to preclude its use in the manner suggested, it has only to be pointed out that each separate Precept would serve, in turn, for a complete performance in itself. The whole could thus be spread out at convenient intervals, like a typical series of sermons, or even one of the larger Play-cycles. Moreover, as Miss Toulmin Smith reminds us, we have some definite indication that the York *Crede Play* was also "of considerable length".[2] While all movement or plot of any kind is lacking in the piece, here

---

[1] Cf. Chambers, *Med. Stage*, vol. ii, pp. 183, 185.
[2] See *York Plays*, Oxf. 1885, p. xxx.

and there a certain picturesque liveliness in the conversation is manifest. Says *Dives* to *Pauper*—"Men preche these dayes ful welle ayens synne".

Pauper: Summe do so; but aȝens the grete synne that al the lond is entriked in—and al Cristendome knowth, and is open cause of oure myschefe—ayens that, no man precheth, but nighe al be aboute to mainten it.

Dives: Which sinne is that?

Pauper: Ofte have I tolde the: but thou beleveste me not. Go over the se, and there men shal tel it the, if thou axe....[1]

Along such lines, then, it would seem likely that the earliest writers of morality-plays proceeded. So long as the formal divisions of the particular subject of exposition were uppermost in their minds, their compositions would have little or no dramatic unity or action, no continuous plot to be unwound. Characters would come forward, recite their lines and disappear in monotonous succession as each dull, disjointed colloquy ended. We are back again to the stiff and formal days of the most primitive experiments in liturgical drama. Unity and continuity of form were only to come to the Morality, as we have seen, when some more living, human theme of the pulpits, like that of the successive "Ages of Man" or his life-long struggle with evil, was borrowed for it. *Dives et Pauper*, indeed, is at all events an excellent object-lesson in the need for such elements.

Here, alas! we must leave the story of our English stage, even on the very threshold to better things. For, the pulpit only weaves its spell directly over the more tentative, early efforts of the national art and literature, while they are still clumsy, prolix, often stiff and undignified, like the efforts of children. Nevertheless, our review of these English Miracles and Moralities in the light of the sermons can claim to have lifted them out of a comparatively narrow groove on to a new and wider plane, in which their true relations begin to appear. In this, we are but following a path, the approaches to which

[1] See in my *Preaching in Med. Engl.* pp. 207–208; and cf. ibid. p. 323, n. 2, and Bp. Brunton, MS. Harl. 3760, fol. 142b: "Non est natio sub celo ita de adulterio diffamata, sicut natio Anglicana...", etc.

have been noticed by previous scholars, who nevertheless, for
some reason or another, have been disinclined to explore it
for themselves. Thus Dr Pollard, for example, has remarked
with sure discrimination that any adequate study of the subject
will have to include within its purview the history of religious
thought and the contemporary literature "both at home and
abroad".[1] If Tutivillus at his advanced age is still capable of
laughter, we may be sure that he indulges in a peculiarly hearty
chuckle at the thought of how his old enemies, the preachers,
have been for so long robbed of their due. Our modern
men-of-letters may remark, of a pulpit so primitive and
remote, that no good could ever be expected to come nowadays
out of that poor, little Nazareth. Yet, the fact remains that,
through fresh contact with it, we can no longer regard the
sacred drama as pursuing, uninfluenced from outside, a course
of its own, developing boldly in comparative isolation from
a rigid, lifeless body of doctrine. Each little improvement
made in the plays will no longer be attributable, in the facile
manner of some critics, to the particular dramatic genius who
first happens to display it. For the hands and brains of others
are patent in his verse. Such were inheritors of another living
tradition, masters of the contemporary technique of sacred
oratory, themselves inspired by a message and a humanism not
born of any new Classical Renaissance,[2] well accustomed to

---

[1] See *Engl. Miracle Plays*, p. xl.

[2] Consider, again, for example, in the light of our sermon-evidence
upon the subject, such a comment as that of Prof. Allardyce Nicoll upon
Skelton's Interlude, *Magnyfycence*. This work, he says, "is particularly
interesting as showing the influence of humanistic thought upon this
form of drama, the didactic aim being not so much moral as calculated
to convey a truth emphasized by many classic philosophers—the folly
of expending money lavishly and trusting all to friends who may prove
false" (*Brit. Drama*, p. 44): or again, upon Lyndesay's *Satyre of the
three Estaits*—"with its biting realistic touches" (p. 44) and its satire of
the corruptions in Church and State (p. 45); etc. Our chapter proves
further the soundness of a recent criticism of Prof. Nicoll's latest book,
Masks, Mimes and Miracles, in the *Times Lit. Supplement* (Aug. 13,
1931): "Mr Nicoll seems to us on far less secure ground when he
suggests an over-riding influence of the mimetic stage upon the religious
plays." As for their origins in the Latin liturgy, it is interesting to note

present the old Scriptures in vigorous, homely phrases of their own. In scene after scene of the plays, we have found it possible to trace each dominant idea in the preacher's mind, his view of the world as well as of religion, his little mannerisms and tricks of speech, his own tears and laughter, the peculiar inflection of his voice over some favourite tragedy or comedy of the *Ars Predicandi*. Thus the expanded vernacular play itself often seems to be little more than a dramatized sermon or set of sermons. It is itself a product of the great homiletic revival of the thirteenth and fourteenth centuries. Incessantly it derives fresh life and matter from this wider source of supply around it. In other words, the medieval pulpit is a long-forgotten foster-mother of our modern stage.

that a reviewer of Mr Oscar Cargill's *Drama and Liturgy* (New York) in the *Church Quart. Rev.* about the same time (July, 1931, vol. cxii, pp. 335–7), is able to remark that "it is no longer possible to maintain that the Mystery Plays are the result of growth from liturgical sources. . . . The book's main case may be regarded as proved." However, the subsequent publication of Professor Karl Young's two learned volumes on the *Drama of the Medieval Church* may be considered to have settled the matter in a contrary sense. Nevertheless, it is still possible to suggest a sermon in dialogue as source in a particular case, in addition to the established example mentioned above on p. 472: see R. B. Donovan, *The Liturgical Drama in Medieval Spain*, p. 112.

CHAPTER IX

A Literary Echo of the Social Gospel

IN his last sketch of English Medieval Literature, the late Professor W. P. Ker put forward what apparently he considered to be an important argument for single authorship of the *Vision of Piers Plowman* and its three well-known versions. Of "the tone of thought in the poem", he remarks—

it is hard to believe that there were two authors in the same reign who had the same strong and weak points, the same inconsistencies, wavering between lively imagination and formal allegory, the same indignation and the same tolerance. *Piers Plowman* is one of the most impartial of all reformers. He makes heavy charges against many ranks and orders of men, but he always remembers the good that is to be said for them. His remedy for the evils of the world would be to bring the different estates— knights, clergy, labourers and all—to understand their proper duty. His political ideal is the commonwealth as it exists, only with each part working as it was meant to do; the king making the peace, with the knights to help him, the clergy studying and praying, the commons working honestly, and the higher estates also giving work and getting wages.[1]

Now, in the course of our study of Sermon Satire and Complaint against the ruling class we had occasion to note, strangely enough, another and a kindred suggestion of uncommon impartiality of view in social matters attributed to John Wycliffe by Professor G. M. Trevelyan.[2] That view, it will be recalled, proved, when we examined it in the light of the sermons, to be false in its limited application to the Reformer, but thoroughly true and typical if applied to medieval homilists *as a whole*. The present case is precisely analogous. So far from being in any way unique, this "tone of thought" in *Piers Plowman* appears, on investigation, to be in perfect accord with that of the most commonplace orthodox preaching of the times, indeed a perfect echo in every respect of the Church's message

---

[1] *Engl. Lit. Med.* (Home Univ. Libr.), p. 200. Cf. also on this subject, e.g., Courthope, *Hist. of Engl. Poetry*, vol. i, pp. 227–33 and 236.
[2] Cf. above, p. 289.

to the world. If in his final phrase here Professor Ker means
nothing more than "getting wages" in the figurative sense
of the Gospel Parable of the Husbandmen,[1] we may accept his
summary forthwith as an accurate statement of Langland's
constructive social gospel, and proceed at once to hear what
our preachers have to say upon the subject. The task should
make a fitting conclusion to our studies not only of the sermons,
but also of the great poem itself. For, we have already been
led to discover in the former the sources of its "formal
allegories", its "lively imagination" along with many of its
characters, and more recently still of its "indignation" and its
"heavy charges against many ranks and orders of men"
delivered with an impressive 'impartiality'.[2] Varieties of
interpretation still continue to pour forth unabated[3] and many
problems remain. But, with the due establishment of this
further point of indebtedness, we may surely claim that the
medieval pulpit helped to fashion much of the poet's fundamental thinking. Finally, for its own sake, the social
message of the pulpits deserves our closest attention. For here
we exchange the more rarified yet more familiar atmosphere
of the Schools, the inner chambers of eminent scholar and
learned jurist, for that of the platform and the street-corner,
for a political propaganda—if such it may be called—planned
and broadcast for the ears of common folk.[4]

A favourite *figure* used by the preachers to set forth their
political or social ideal is that of the Vineyard with its three
Orders of husbandmen.[5] Let us listen to Master Thomas
Wimbledon haranguing at Paul's Cross, the recognized national

[1] As below, p. 551. Cf. also below, p. 561.
[2] (Cf. Prof. Ker, as above) possibly also of the poet's "discursiveness"
(cf. above, p. 89).
[3] Cf. recent studies by Fr. T. P. Dunning, Miss G. Hort, Prof. R. W.
Frank, etc., and numerous articles and books listed in J. E. Wells,
Manual of Writings in M.E., Supplmts. 6 to 9.
[4] Those unfamiliar with the broad outlines of this doctrine in its
academic (Thomist, etc.) form should consult Ernst Troeltsch, *Die
Soziallehren der christlichen Kirchen und Gruppen*, cap. ii (Engl. transln.
by O. Wyon, 1931, *The Soc. Teaching of the Christian Ch.*).
[5] See Matth. xx, 1–16; etc.

platform for public discussion of all such questions of the day,[1] in language that probably owes much to St Anselm, and certainly beyond him not a little in the first instance to the *Republic* of Plato:[2]

For, right as ye see that in tilling of the materiall vine there ben divers labours—for some kutten awey the void branches, some maken forkis and railis to beren up the vine, and some diggen away the old earth fro the rote, and leyn there fatter; and all this offices ben so necessary to the vine that, if any of them faile, it shal harme greatly other destroy the vine; for but if the vine be kutte, she shall waxe wilde, but if she be rayled, she shall be ourgo with netles and wedis, and but if the rote be fatted with dong, she for feblenes shuld wax baraine—right so in the church beth nedefull these three offices, priesthood, knythode, and laborers. To priesthood it falleth to kut away the void braunches of sinnes with the swerd of her tong. To knighthode it falleth to letten wrongs and thefftes to ben done, and to maintaine Goddis law and them that ben techers thereof, and also to kepe the londe from enemies of other londes. And to labourers it falleth to travail bodelich and with their sore swete geten out of the earth bodilech lifelode for hem and other partes. And these states beth also nedefull to the church, that none may well ben without other. For if priesthood lacked, the people for default of knowing of Goddis lawe, should waxe wilde in vices, and deyen gostely: and if the knithod laked, and men to rulin the puple by law and hardinesse, theeves and enemies shulden so encres, that no man shuld live in peace: and if the laborers were nought, both knightes and priestes must become acre men and herdis, and els they shuld for defaut of bodily sustenance deye. And therefore, saith clerke Avicenne,[3] that every unreasonable best, if he have that that kind hath ordeined for him, as kind hath ordeined it he has suffisance to live by himselfe without any help of other of the same kind. And if there were but one horse, other one shepe in the world, yet if he had grasse and corne as kind hath ordeined for such beasts, he shuld live well enow. But if there ne were but o man in the world, though he had all that good that is therein, yet for defaut he shuld deie, or his life shuld be wors than if he were naught: and the cause is this, for that thing that kind ordeineth for a mans sustenance without other arraieing than it hath of kind accordeth nought to him. As though a man have corne as it commeth from the earth, yet it is no meate according to him, unto it be by mans craft chaunged into bread; and though he have flesh other fish, yet while it is rawe as kind ordeined it, till it be by mans travaile sodden, rosted, or baken, it corded not to mans lifelode. And, right so, wolle that the sheepe beareth mot

---

[1] Cf. below, p. 586.   [2] Cf. esp. bk. ii, etc.

[3] Avicenna, of course, the famous Arab philosopher and physician Ibn Sīnā (fl. 988–1037), a transmitter of the ancient Greek wisdom to the Medieval West, notably that of Aristotle.

by mannis divers craftis and travailes be chaunged, or it be able to cloth any man; and certis, o man by himselfe shuld never doo all these labours. And therefore, saith this clerke, it is neede that some be acre men, some bakers, some makers of cloth, and some marchaunts to fetch that that one londe fetteth from an other, as there it is plentie.

And certis, this shuld be a cause why every state should love other; and men of o craft shuld not despise ne hate men of none other craft, sith they be so nedefull everich to other; and oft thelke crafts that ben most unhonest might worst ben forbore. And o thing I dare well say, that he that is neither travailing in this world on studieng, on praiers, on preaching for helpe of the people—as it falleth to priests, neither ruling the people, mainteining ne defending fro enemies—as it falleth to knights, neither traveling on earth in diverse craftes—as it falleth to labourers, whan the day of reckening commeth, that is, the end of this life, right as he lived here withouten travaile, so he shall there lack the reward of "the penie", that is, the endles ioie of heaven. And as he was here living after none state ne order, so he shall be put than in that place that no order is in, but everlasting horror and sorrow, that is, in hell. Herfore everich man see to what state God hath cleped him, and dwell he therein by travile according to his degree.[1] Thou that art a laborer or a crafty man, do this truelly. If thou art a servant or a bondman, be suget and lowe, in drede of displeasing of thy Lord. If thou art a marchaunt, disceive nought thy brother in chaffering. If thou art a knight or a lord, defend the poore man and needy fro hands that will harme them. If thou art a iustice or a iudge, go not on the right hand by favour, neither on the left hand to punish any man for hate. If thou art a priest, undernime,[2] praye, and reprove, in all maner patience and doctrine. Undernime thilke that ben negligent, pray for thilke that bene obedient, reprove tho that ben unobedient to God. So every man travaile in his degree. For whan the even his come, that is, the end of this worlde, than everye man shall take reward, good or evill, after that he hath travailed here.[3]

Such, then, in brief is the whole Law and the Prophets in

---

[1] Cf. 1 Cor. vii, 20.

[2] = rebuke (not "instruct", as in ed. 1563: cf. 2 Tim. iv, 2).

[3] Sermon at St Paul's Cross, 1388 (ed. *Ch. Hist. of Engl.* Jo. Foxe, *Acts and Mons.* vol. iii, pt. i, pp. 293–4). MS. Linc. Cath. Libr. A. 6. 2, fols. 67 b–68 b is another example, where the above theme of Wimbledon has been incorporated practically verbatim in a late fifteenth-century sermon for Septuag. Sunday ("*Voca operarios et redde illis mercedem suam*"—Matth. xx, 8). Cf. further, MS. Add. 41321, fol. 65 ("Upon this gospel a man miȝte touche that, riȝt as in a bodili vineȝard ben thre maner of werk-folk with diverse occupacions, so in this gosteli vineȝerd beth also the same..."); Bromyard, *S.P.* s.v. "Compassio", etc.; Rypon, MS. Harl. 4894, fols. 187–8; Myrc, *Festial,* E.E.T.S. ed. p. 65; MS. Roy. 18. B. xxiii, fol. 129; etc., etc.

the Church's positive teaching upon the social question. The actual *figure* chosen to express it may change from the Vineyard to the Body and its Members,[1] to the edifice of the Church with its component architectural parts,[2] or even to the animals of the Farm:[3] the doctrine itself remains rigidly constant. Within the strict limits of each divinely-appointed Order a further elaboration of reasons and duties often follows. Thus Master Rypon, in his sermon, identifies the origins of Knighthood and the derivation of the title, in typical fictitious manner, with the work of King Romulus at Rome: "De institutione militie dicitur in principio quarto Historie Romanorum quod, condita civitate a Romulo, quam ex nomine Romam vocavit, mille pugnatores de populo elegit, quos a numero appellavit 'milites'. Dicitur, enim, 'miles', i.e. unus ex mille; et sicut 'miles' est nomen laboris, ita est nomen honoris. . . ". After explaining, from the *Policraticus* of John of Salisbury[4] and the *De Re Militari* of Vegetius, the significance of the knightly Oath and the special purport of their "election", he goes on to describe the necessary steps by which "Knights may ascend to heaven". First, there is the virtue of Fortitude, to be exhibited in bold and strenuous defence of Church and State. Secondly, there is Justice—"that they fight in a just cause, and do no injury or insult to any man"; thirdly, Prudence in action; fourthly, Moderation—"not only in food, indeed, but also in a rational appetite for wealth"—"that they be 'content with their wages',[5] and not plunderers and destroyers of their neighbours' goods". In honouring Holy Church, let them follow in the steps of Julius Caesar and Alexander the Great, who prohibited the

---

[1] Cf. Bromyard, s.v. "Caritas", etc.; Brunton, as quoted below, p. 587; Rypon, in MS. Harl. 4894, fol. 189; *Pricke of Consc.* pp. 160–1; *Ayenb. of Inwyt*, pp. 102, 146–9; etc. Cf. here the political poem—*The Descryvyng of Mannes Membres*, in *Twenty-six Pol. and other Poems*, ed. Kail, E.E.T.S. O.S. No. 124, pp. 64-6 (and Gratian's *Decretum*).

[2] Cf. Rypon, MS. Harl. 4894, fol. 188. An early example (The Three Props of the Throne) is given from the 10th-cent. MS. Cotton, Nero A. i, fol. 72, in Wright, *Pol. Songs*, Camden Soc. p. 365. See further above, p. 72 (The Ship and its parts).

[3] Cf. Bozon, *Metaphs.* cap. xviii (quoting St Basil?).

[4] Lib. vi. cap. v, as quoted by Rypon.   [5] See Luke, iii, 14.

spoliation of temples and spared the church.[1] Likewise the Agricultural Labourers, in their turn, are bidden by the same speaker to recognize their ancestry in Adam, "the first husbandman",[2] and his sons, and their special task—"to sustain the body of the Church, by preparing and yielding up the necessities of life. Therefore their office is to labour faithfully, bravely and usefully".[3] "These moun be understonde", explains a quaint vernacularist,

bi the lowist estaat of holi chirche, that is the comyne peple, whos ocupacions stondeth in grobbyng aboute the erthe, as in erynge and dungynge and sowynge and harwynge and other ocupacions that longeth to the erthe. And this schulde be do iustli and for a good ende, withoute feyntise or falshede or grucchynge of hire estaat.... ffor this was the first degree that longeth to alle men; and thus with hire tr[e]we labour thei schul bere up and susteyne the othere tweie parties of the chirche, that is kny3tes and clerkis.[4]

The unknown author of the English version of the *Gesta Romanorum* calls them "the lewde men" that "most holde up the laame men" of Holy Church, that "have not of hire owne to lyve with".[5] There is a tendency on the part of some preachers to recognize none but the three historic Orders, that have been mentioned, as the divinely-instituted Pillars of Society. In one or other of the three categories all men must find their place, their fundamental avocation, responsibilities, privileges and general outlook. God had no room or reason for more. Thus a sermon *exemplum* of earlier date, preserved in an English manuscript of the fourteenth century along with the *Alphabetum Narrationum*, remarks significantly of the rising

---

[1] MS. Harl. 4894, fols. 188b–189.

[2] Cf. MS. Glouc. Cath. Libr. Homs. as below, p. 555, n. 5: "for labour was the testament of Adam that he left to all his successorys".

[3] MS. Harl. 4894, fol. 189, et seq. (He adds: "Iste triplex modus laborandi pertinet tam ad cives quam ad agricultores".)

[4] MS. Add. 41321, fol. 65b. With all this cf. esp. *Piers Plowman*, B text, pass. vi, etc.

[5] E.E.T.S. ed. pp. 16–7. Cf. here Bromyard's defence, in *S.P.* s.v. "Civitas", of the position that clergy should not do *manual* labour, with arguments from Greek and Roman authors ("...Ista sunt contra illos qui improperant religiosis viris et ecclesiasticis, quod non prosunt rei-publicae, quia non laborant manualiter. Sed illi tamen, si boni sunt, plus prosunt consulendo, docendo, orando. Unde Seneca...").

middle-class that God made the Clergy, Knights and Labourers, but the Devil made the Burghers and Usurers.[1] Not even a conservative pulpit, however, could for long refuse a special place of honour in its discourses for those upon whose new wealth and enterprise the future greatness of kingdoms was to be built. Brunton, preaching in the heart of London amid evidences of such successful industry on every side, declares unreservedly that "merchants and faithful mechanics are the left hand" of the Body Politic, and "citizens and burgesses, placed as it were in the middle, are its heart".[2] So, the vernacular preacher in his turn, who has been discussing the three great traditional Orders of Society, finds, with Plato, a fundamental need and justification for the "merchauntes"—"for to sett in one londe that is not in a-nother londe, and so for to make plenty of all maner thing in tyme of nede".[3]

Bound up with this doctrine of the Body Politic, it will be seen, are certain important corollaries which receive their due emphasis in the social gospel of the times. First, there is the doctrine of Work for all. The preachers' ideal State provides no place for the indolent. Says our representative Dominican upon this point:

God has ordained three classes of men, namely, labourers such as husbandmen and craftsmen to support the whole body of the Church after the manner of feet, knights to defend it in the fashion of hands, clergy to rule and lead it after the manner of eyes. And all the aforesaid who maintain their own status are of the family of God. The Devil, however, finds a certain class, namely, the slothful, who belong to no Order. They neither labour with the rustics, nor travel about with the merchants, nor fight with the knights, nor pray and chant with the clergy. Therefore they shall go with their own Abbot, of whose Order they are, namely, the Devil, where no Order exists but horror eternal.[4]

[1] MS. Harl. 268, fol. 29. The same idea is expressed in a vernacular poem, *Von Wuocher*, by the early thirteenth-century German didactic poet Freidank (see *Deutsche Nat.-Litteratur*, Bd. ix (Didaktik), p. 275).

[2] As quoted below, p. 587.

[3] MS. Linc. Cath. Libr. A. 6. 2, fol. 69. Similarly, Wimbledon, as above, p. 551.

[4] *S.P.* s.v. "Accidia". Similarly, Wimbledon, as quoted above, p. 551, and cf. further Jo. of Mirfield, *Flor. Barthol.* s.v. "De Labore Manuum", MS. Camb. Univ. Libr. Mm. ii. 10, fol. 99b ("...Et ita omnes clerici ad operandum validi artificiosa et literas discant...").

Again, reference is made to the learned Avicenna on this point. For he argues that the man who has no laudable status in the community and obeys no master is useless to it, forfeits his birthright therein and should be expelled from it for his sloth and idleness. "If Saracens have made such ordinances in their States," exclaims the Dominican, "how much more should Christians do the same!"[1] Pulpit use of the word *labor* is apt to be ambiguous: sometimes it clearly refers to *manual* labour alone.[2] But English homilists alike of the twelfth and the fifteenth centuries leave us in no doubt that Adam's curse lies heavy upon us all: "*In sudore vultus tui vesceris pane tuo*".[3] "So did he first, and we all do so after. Every man in his way uses such labour as he is tied to: the cleric after his mode, the knight in his way, the husbandman in his, and such practice of each craft as he is tied to."[4] "For this ye may understonde that hit ys the wylle of Gode that every man and woman schuld labour besyly. For yf Adam and Eve had ben occupyed wyth labour, the serpent had not overcum them: for ydulnesse ys the devylles dyssyr. Wherfor ye may know well yt ys the wylle of Gode that we schuld labour and put our body to penaunce for to fle synne. Thus dyd Adam and Eve, to example of all tho that schuld come after them."[5] But human toil, though so unpleasant in its origins, might yet prove a blessing in disguise for the sons of Adam. In the preachers' eyes it had a salutary value in itself, even apart from the immediate spiritual condition of the toiler. "Per viam laboris pervenit ad mercedem consolationis."[6] For the reprobate, indeed, it might be considered the first step on the road to spiritual reclamation. "But natheles, thou3 werkes doon in dedli synne profiteth no3t to

---

[1] s.v. "Civitas".   [2] Cf. below, p. 569.

[3] Gen. iii, 19 (as quoted here: cf. also *Piers Plowman*, A text, pass. vii, ll. 219–20; etc.).

[4] *Old Engl. Homs. of the Twelfth Cent.* 2nd Ser. E.E.T.S. O.S. no. 53, p. 181. Cf. *Spec. Laic.* (13th cent.), cap. xlvii (ed. Welter, p. 69): "Laborant homines tripliciter: quidam vero laborant circa spiritualia . . ., quidam laborant circa temporalia ut habeant quibus se et suos sustineant, sicut boni activi. . ., quidam laborant circa delenda vicia, ut peccata puniant. . ."; Bromyard, *S.P.* s.v. "Labor" (14th cent.); etc.

[5] MS. Glouc. Cath. Libr. *Sermo de doctrina in Septuag.* (15th cent.).

[6] *S.P.* s.v. "Beatitudo". Cf. further, *Ayenb. of Inwyt*, p. 206.

encrecyng of blisse, ȝeet thei profiten to thre thynges: oon is
that the worldli goodes of suche men schul encrece the more;
another is that thei schullen the sunnere have grace to arise
ouȝt of here synne; another is, if thei schul be dampned, hire
peyne schal be the lesse. And therfore it is good evere to
wirche wel."[1] "For nothing in this life", says Bozon, "is
worth so much for body and soul as well-ordered work. As
to which Holy Scripture describes work in this fashion: 'Work
is the life of man and keeper of health. Work drives away
occasion for sin, and makes a man rest himself, is the relief
of languor, a stay to illness, safety of the people, sharpener of
all the senses, stepmother to idleness, duty to the young and
merit to the old'. Hence he who would give up the joy of
everlasting life takes care, says Scripture, that he does not work
at all in this life. Wherefore it is better to be an ass than a pig"
(as in the Fable following).[2] Finally, when the ordinary day's
work is over, there is no need or right for any to be idle: for
there are yet "merytory werkes" to be done, "and thu wilte
be perfite in the feyȝth".[3] While the rich man sets about his
various deeds of mercy, even labourers are expected by Rypon
—in the words of "Wallensis"[4]—"to pay their tithes and
offerings to the Church, and do alms so far as they can".[5]
When, in his turn, the Lollard preacher, driven to denounce
the supposed merits of pilgrimaging, reminds his hearers of
"the trewe labour that thei shulden do at home in help of
hemsilf and hore neȝeboris" in place of all such idle tasks,[6] we

[1] MS. Add. 41321, fols. 10b–11.

[2] *Metaphs.* cap. cxxi. The references to Scripture are erroneous.

[3] MS. Roy. 18. B. xxiii, fol. 97b ("good werkes"). Cf. *Gesta Rom.*
Engl. version (as before), pp. 249, 305; Bromyard, *S.P.* s.v. "Caritas";
etc. The typical list—clothing the naked, feeding the hungry, visiting
the sick and imprisoned, harbouring the stranger, burying the dead, etc.—
appears, e.g., in MS. Harl. 2398, fols. 24–6, including in addition—
"makynge of churches and of brigges and causyes and amendement of
perilous weyes in savyng of mennes lyves and eke of bestes".

[4] I.e. John Walleys, or Wallis, S.T.D. Franciscan (fl. 1260).

[5] MS. Harl. 4894, fol. 189. It is interesting to observe that in *S.P.*
s.v. "Intentio", Bromyard reckons Manual Labour as "sometimes"
worthy of a place amongst Good Works meritory of Eternal Life.

[6] MS. Add. 24202, fol. 27b (cf. further, fol. 28b).

ourselves are reminded of the honoured place which Work has continued to hold in Protestant faith and practice. Its subsequent achievements, alike in science and industry, art and philanthropy, when "meritory works" were finally discountenanced, prove once again our kinship with the past. The gulf of the Reformation is thus bridged once more,[1] and the spiritual continuity of our history maintained in the face of all such inevitable changes. Meanwhile, students familiar with the poem of *Piers Plowman* will not fail to recognize the profound influence of this medieval doctrine upon the poet's Vision.[2]

> Treuthe herde telle her-of, and to Peres he sent
> To taken his teme and tulyen the erthe,
> And purchased hym a pardoun *a pena et a culpa*
> For hym and for his heires for evermore after.
> And bad hym holde hym at home and eryen his leyes;
> And alle that halpe hym to erie, to sette or to sowe
> Or any other myster that miȝte Pieres availle,
> Pardoun with Pieres plowman treuthe hath ygraunted.
>
> .   .   .   .
>
> Forthi I conseille alle cristene to crye God mercy,
> And Marie his moder be owre mene bitwene,
> That God gyve us grace here, ar we gone hennes,
> *Suche werkes to werche,* while we ben here,
> That after owre deth-day Dowel reherce,
> At the day of dome, we dede as he hiȝte.[3]

From the doctrine which we have just considered it follows naturally that each man's first duty—be he knight or priest, workman or merchant—is to learn and labour truly in the things of his own particular calling, resting content therewith[4] and not aspiring to meddle with the tasks and mysteries of others. The social ranks and their respective duties, ordained by God for humanity, were intended to remain fixed and immutable. Like the limbs of the Body they cannot properly exchange either their place or function. "Some folk are good

---

[1] See here my *Preaching in Med. Engl.* p. 280.
[2] Cf. esp. A text, pass. vii and viii, and the equivalent in the other versions.
[3] B text, pass. vii, opening and closing passages.
[4] Cf. here above, pp. 314, 353, 370, etc.

for one function, others for others."[1] We have, indeed, seen already how Master Wimbledon bases upon the command of St Paul—"Let each man abide in the same calling wherein he was called"—a doctrine of social distinctions and barriers of this kind.[2] In the *Summa Predicantium* a pleasing *figure* is used to emphasize the same argument. Society Bromyard here compares to a delicately-stringed harp.

> The order of these various ranks in the community ought to be like the position of the strings upon the harp. Here it is essential for the purpose of good melody that each string should keep to its own place, the shorter in their appropriate place, those of medium length in the middle, and the taller in their own part of the instrument. So, in any community each man ought to keep to his own station—the lower in working and obeying, those who are called "ministers", the lawyers and the churchmen, in consulting, praying and speaking, the rulers in ruling and protecting, whose office is like to that of the harpist.

As long as the proper position and touch of the strings is observed, so long will the community give forth a sweet melody. As soon as the strings are disarranged, the melody jars, and the State or community and its internal peace are rudely confounded. Such is the case "when he who is unworthy in respect of manners, knowledge and wisdom is set in high position through favour, bribery or inordinate love. Behold the string out of its place which destroys the whole melody! Likewise, conversely, when he who for the merit of good life and learning should be set in high position is thrust down...".[3] The prime task of every individual in the State is well set forth for us in the warnings of a vernacular sermon:

> And so it were ryght fittyng that every man hold hym content to common maters of ys faculte, policy and governaunce. So that knythes and other gentils with hem shuld sett her besines abowte the good governaunce in the temporalltee in the tyme of pees, and also abowte duds [and]

---

[1] Bozon, *Metaphs.* cap. xviii.

[2] See 1 Cor. vii, 20, and above, p. 551. Cf. here the recent interesting correspondence in *The Times* by Mr H. A. L. Fisher and others over the statement in the Prayer-Book *Catechism* concerning "that state of life unto which it shall please God to call me". The present author suggested in the course of it, in the same columns (Aug. 11, 1928), that here the influence of this pre-Reformation social doctrine is still clearly traceable, in the sense in which Mr Fisher interprets the above phrase.

[3] s.v. "Civitas".

poyntes of armes in the tyme of werre, as the lawe and the cronicle techeth hem. For ther beth many sotell questions and conclusions in mater of warre and armes, as the phylo[so]fre declareth, *de Re Militari*....[1] Prestes shuld principally entermet[2] to lerne the lawe of Criste and law-fully to teche itt; and lower men shuld hold hem contente with here own occupacions, and not entremet farther than reson and lawe rewels to hem.[3]

Speaking of the social order beyond the grave, in terms of the Chessmen "when thei be put up in the poket" at the end of the game, our English *Gesta Romanorum* remarks consolingly —"Therfore let us not change of oure estatis": for "then hit is no charge who be above or who be byneth!"[4]

Class duties and class distinctions, however, do not exhaust between them all the important consequences which flow from this doctrine of the medieval pulpits. If the work and status of rulers and ruled, students and toilers, learned and "lewd" could never be confused or intermingled without harm to the Body Politic, at the same time it is equally true that all were designed for a common purpose. The members were differ-entiated, as we have already seen, the better to supply the needs of the one body of which they formed part: "And if we had no laborers, then prestes and knyȝtes muste nedes labor them-selffe [i.e., of course, *manualiter*]; and thei can not. And if that thei dyd labor, thei scholde peressche in a lityll tyme for defawte of sustynaunce".[5] The various types of husbandmen were all busy about the same vineyard. Each, that is to say, by doing his own work faithfully was serving a supreme com-mon good. Hence it follows that, although no single individual was to take upon himself the special work and concerns that belonged to another station, yet each and all were to be ever conscious of their relations to the whole and to one another in unity of spirit and disinterested service. Society, therefore,

[1] I.e. Vegetius. The preacher here may well have in mind the case of Sir John Oldcastle, as in Hoccleve's *Poem* addressed to the Lollard knight, advocating similarly the reading of "Vegece, of the aart of Chivalrie", etc. (*Minor Poems*, E.E.T.S. ed. Extr. S. no. 61, p. 14, st. 25.)
[2] = meddle, interpose.   [3] MS. Roy. 18. B. xxiii, fol. 129.
[4] E.E.T.S. ed. p. 71. Cf. Bromyard, *S.P.* s.v. "Mundus".
[5] MS. Linc. Cath. Libr. A. 6. 2, fol. 68b.

must be continually made to realize its corporate nature. "For", as Master Rypon observes, "the unity of the State exists not merely in its houses or its streets, but, as all the philosophers testify, in the agreement of its minds. Even among infidels it is so; therefore so much the more should it be among the faithful."[1] To convey this vital truth to the popular mind in an arresting way, the preachers make use of very varying imagery. Thus Bozon, for example, points to the habits of stags when seeking pasture across a stretch of sea. "Each of them puts his head on the other's rump", he says, "with the strong in front. When the leader weakened by toil withdraws, another puts himself in front; and so each is aided by the other. So ought it to be with us who are passing this perilous sea.... Each ought to aid and support the other, as the apostle Paul teaches us, 'forbearing one another in love'."[2] Bromyard, for his part, points to the mail hauberk, "in which all the rings are linked together and give mutual support". "With the snapping of a single ring, danger threatens the whole of the body, when its wearer is attacked....Wherefore, as mutual concatenation is essential for the protection of the outward man, so mutual support and fellowship are essential in universal human society."[3] It is this same fundamental idea which comes to the rescue, when our preachers have to wrestle with the age-long problem of Riches and Poverty. "The rich and the poor", argues Bishop Brunton, drawing upon a homily of Augustine,

although they may appear contrary, are nevertheless very necessary to each other. For, if all men were poor, there would be none to support the other. If all were rich, then no one would work; and so the world would at once decay. Therefore the rich man has been created for the benefit of the poor, and the poor man for the benefit of the rich.... Catholic doctors are in agreement upon that saying of the Gospel—"the poor ye have always with you",[4] etc., where they set forth the reasons why God has allowed the poor to remain amongst us, when nevertheless he is able to provide sufficient for all. First, because, just as a mother provides enough for her child when she gives sufficient to the nurse whence she can nourish both herself and the infant, so the Lord provides

---

[1] MS. Harl. 4894, fol. 182.   [2] *Metaphs.* cap. xxxviii (Isidore).
[3] *S.P.* s.v. "Justitia". Cf. further, s.v. "Compassio"; and *Spec. Laic.* cap. xiv (sheep; stars; cranes).   [4] Matth. xxvi, 11; etc.

enough for the poor while so much is bestowed on the rich whence they can supply food and drink to themselves and the poor also.... Secondly, the poor are allowed to exist in order that God may test the love of the rich.... Therefore He has willed that the poor should be in want, so that by this means He might prove what rich men are His friends and what His enemies. Thirdly, to increase the merit of the poor.... [1]

If we turn now to the sermons of Master Ralph of Acton, we find precisely the same argument employed upon a wider scale:

When God could have made all men strong, wise and rich, He was unwilling to do so. He wished instead that these men should be strong, those weak; these wise, those foolish; these rich and those poor. For if all were strong, wise and wealthy, one would not be in need of the other. Again, if all were feeble, foolish and poor, one would not be able to help the other. Therefore He willed these men to be strong and healthy, wise or rich, that they might save their own souls by helping others through love of them: those others He willed to be weak or foolish or in want, that they might save their own souls by enduring hardship in patience. [2] Hence God says—"The poor ye have always with you".... [3]

While Brunton points out, as the natural sequel to his argument, that "the rich man's duty is to dispense, [4] the poor man's to pray, inasmuch as he is obliged to pray for the rich as soon as he has received alms from him", so Bromyard, in his turn, declares that the rich have been deputed by God to be the protectors of the poor, as the tutor for the pupil; also because they live of their labours. For this guardianship they receive payment from God in the shape of townships, estates and rents. Thus, their subjects are bound to toil and serve them faithfully, while they themselves bestow honest government and payment for these services. [5] The rich, the wise and the strong are to

[1] MS. Harl. 3760, fol. 111b et seq.

[2] See further above, pp. 296–7.

[3] MS. Jo. Rylands Libr. Manch. Lat. 367, fol. 4.

[4] The reader who desires to make acquaintance with the patristic and later sources of this typical teaching may here be directed to an essay by Dr A. J. Carlyle, on "The Theory of Property in Med. Theology", in *Property, its Duties and Rights*, Macmillan, 1913, pp. 119–32, with important references, in connection with the above, to the works of Ambrose, Augustine and Aquinas, and the *Opusculum* of Peter Damian. Cf. further in our Engl. homil. literature, e.g., *Gesta Rom.* Engl. version, E.E.T.S. ed. p. 353 ("What is than for to do riche men?...Forsothe, that thei divide her temporall goodes to poore men, as it is written— 'yeve almesse'..."); etc.

[5] *S.P.* s.v. "Furtum".

aid the poor, the foolish and the weak, the first with his gifts, the second with his information, the third with his protection.[1] Once again, the parallel with Langland's doctrine in the *Vision* is manifest and illuminating.[2] Says the author of the *Pricke of Conscience* in the same strain:

> Ful many men lyfes here of tha
> That er halden for to do swa:
> Als he that gret and myghty es
> Es halden to defende tham that er les;
> And the ryche that mykel rychesces has,
> To gyf tham that here in povert gas;
> And men of laghe alswa to travayle
> And to counsaile tham that askes counsayle;
> And leches alswa, if thai wyse ware,
> To hele tham that er seke and sare;
> And maysters of thair science to ken
> Namly, tham that er unlered men;
> And precheours Goddes worde to preche
> And the way of lyfe other to teche.
> Thus es ilk man halden with gude intent
> To help other of that God has tham lent
> Frely for goddes luf, and for noght elles.[3]

From such an ideal, then, implanted by the medieval pulpit, however naïve and unsatisfying, have sprung in subsequent centuries the finest traditions of English manorial life, now alas! wellnigh perished from the countryside. The preachers' vision of the ideal Christian Commonwealth is that of a battle-line "constipata et compensata", in which no gap appears, but all stand shoulder to shoulder in a common love to God and to their fellows. For such was to be the bond between class and class. "And sothely this is the cawse that every man schold love other, for none of hem may be sparyd from other. And that crafte peraventure that semyth moste dishoneste[4] may the worste be sparyd."[5] As members of the one body, or as rays proceeding from the one sun, so each one benefits by his neighbour's good, "just as in a merchants' company, where, when one makes profit, all profit, and when one loses, all lose".

---

[1] S.v. "Justitia". Cf. *Ayenb. of Inwyt*, pp. 145–9, etc.
[2] I.e. notably, A text, pass. vii and viii; etc., as before.
[3] Ed. Philog. Soc. pp. 160–1.   [4] I.e. least respectable.
[5] MS. Linc. Cath. Libr. A. 6. 2, fol. 69. Similarly, above, p. 551.

"If", on the other hand, "love be wanting through the evil of discord, a gap yawns in the ranks."[1] Here the actual world facing our homilist compared all too ill with his ideal. "A division of parties and of hearts" had brought back the ancient curse of the builders of Babel[2]—ruin and infidelity. In the first place, local feeling and a growing spirit of national self-consciousness drove those whom Bromyard calls "citizens of the Devil's State" to "divide others from them on the score of country, race or language, provoking them in an attitude of wrath and tumult, saying—'You are a Northerner', 'You are a Southerner', or 'you are of such and such a nation', after the manner of that cursed maid of the guest-house who cried out at Peter, saying—'Thou art a Galilean, for thy speech agreeth thereto'".[3] Thus do they rend the Body of Christ limb from limb, contrary to that saying of Scripture—"There is no difference between Jew and Greek".[4] Secondly, as we have seen, of the several classes within the nation "ich on now-a-daies is besy to accuse other in exscusyng of hem-selfe".[5] Amongst these citizens of the modern Babylon, "the dividing-up of tongues" spelt a dividing-up of affections, and that in its turn "is cause of all ruin and impoverishment, in that one man does not help the other, as the members in the body. ...Thus in that Devil's State this division is the beginning of wars and distresses...".[6]

ffor we bid and preye iche day in holy churche—all maner of prestes and other men also—for to have pees. But the more harme is, we have evermore strives and debates, iche man wel nye with other, that ther is no pees in herte. For no man loveth other. And outwardly we may

---

[1] *S.P.* s.v. "Caritas".   [2] See Gen. xi, 1–9.   [3] Mark xiv, 69–70.
[4] Rom. x, 12. (Bromyard here, s.v. "Civitas", also emphasizes the hostility between townsmen and rustics. The former love to deceive the latter in their simplicities with false oaths, weights, measures and the like, when they come to market.) With the above, contrast the nationalistic type of preaching, as indicated above, pp. 225, etc.
[5] MS. Roy. 18. B. xxiii, fol. 167. See further above, p. 272.
[6] *S.P.* "Civitas", as before. Cf. further here: "Vide...contradictionem cordium, quia nullus alium diligit; vel linguarum, scil., inter advocatos et legistas; et inter nationes diversarum plagarum vel operum, quia quilibet nititur alium deprimere, et specialiter adventantes et pauperes qui vellent inter eos vivere".

knowe all that we ben in warre aȝeyns many londes on iche syde, and thei aȝeyns us.[1]

Everywhere, indeed, the world seemed torn by the hatred and envy which Master Rypon, like his fellows, declares to be the chief destruction of States.[2] The harp-strings were disordered; the harpists would not play correctly according to the rules of their art:[3] all was disharmony.

Unable to read aright many of the deeper signs of the times, the preachers strove nevertheless, not without real spiritual discernment within their limited sphere, to probe this evil to its roots, and rescue the community from imminent peril of disintegration. The social system itself was sound enough. No other was conceivable to them. Why, then, did its component parts refuse to function properly: why this current lack of charity, this disunity, this conflict? The answer must lie in the state of unregenerate human nature. Deadly sin, sins in the individuals who composed, like so many cells, the various limbs of the Body, engendered of worldliness, was the true explanation. Hence the volume of pulpit satire and rebuke that has engaged so much of our attention. In a sermon on the very theme—"*Quomodo stabit regnum?*",[4] one of our homilists insists, with profound truthfulness, that all sin has a social and

[1] MS. Roy. 18. B. xxiii, fol. 65.
[2] MS. Harl. 4894, fol. 182. Cf. further above, pp. 452–60.
[3] In illustration of this (cf. above, p. 558), Bromyard says: "sicut patet quando illa [chorda] quae debet tangi non tangitur, et alia ultra vires tangitur. Ita quaecumque communitas modo confunditur ex hoc—quod malefactores non 'tanguntur' nec puniuntur....[In the State] Latrones, homicidae et hujus modi propter sanguinis nobilitatem vel propter munera a suspendio liberantur. Duodecim enim latrones [i.e. jurors] liberant coram judice tredecimum. Ecce, chorda quae deberet tangi non tangitur, et hoc propter munerum perceptores! Et haec est causa quare tot sunt latrones et homicidae; quia in terra, ubi non est justicia, multiplicabuntur latrones et homicidae". Likewise in the Church, the "robbers of God" escape, lechers, adulterers, etc.—"quia citharedi ecclesiastici eos non tangunt sicut deberent, sed accipiunt munera, vel vident lupum et timent". Finally—"iterum pax in ista cythara impeditur ex hoc—quod una chorda plus stringitur et durius tangitur quam deberet", i.e. the poor ("chorda parva"): "Unus pauper modicum delinquens in curia mundi graviter et ultra justiciam amerciabitur . . .."; etc.
[4] Matth. xii, 26.

national as well as a merely individual significance. Says he—
"Each sinner in the realm is making for the destruction of that
realm in part or in whole". Take the gluttons for example.
They work not only for their own undoing, but for that of the
needy also, for whom they ought to provide sustenance. "The
proud, too, in our midst, threaten destruction to our realm,
because he who is proud desires to have no superior or equal,
and so, as far as in him lies, destroys all his superiors and
equals."[1] Most patent of all is the insatiable avarice of the
age. Upon this current selfishness John Bromyard remarks
significantly that, unlike the old Roman days, the rule of life
now is each one for himself: "Sed moderno tempore circa
honorem et commodum proprium quasi tota utatur intentio".[2]
For the rest, he sees the evil influence of the vicious spreading
rapidly, where men are always prone to copy the worst in
others. The World, the Flesh and the Devil had the mastery
over them. Thus, our Body and its Limbs are torn asunder;
and the ideal Society fashioned by God himself, according to
His good will and purpose, is about to perish through human
wickedness. Such, then, is the message not of our sermons
alone, but also of the "faire felde ful of folke" less fair than
their surroundings, to which Langland introduces us at the
outset of his famous Dream. It is the same company again,
so we read, that faces *Resoun*, when he goes arrayed "alle the
reume to preche", bidding them turn from their evil ways to
that particular work and service for the community which
Heaven had ordained for them.[3] In no other direction might
men arrive at the Truth—in things political or personal.

But finally, there is one further question to settle. Can we
find in this sermon-literature any traces whatever of Piers
Plowman himself? In an important chapter of his learned work
on *The Medieval Village*, Dr G. G. Coulton, discussing
"Church Estimates of the Peasant" on the European scale, has
delivered a verdict which will seem at the outset to discourage
any answer in the affirmative. On the other hand, our own

[1] MS. Camb. Univ. Libr. Ii. iii. 8, fol. 149b. Cf. *Ayenb. of Inwyt*,
p. 102; and above, in chaps. vi and vii, passim.
[2] s.v. "Civitas", as before.   [3] A text, pass. v, ll. 9–42; etc.

researches in the English section of this field have already
proved beyond doubt that there is still very much to be said
for the opposing view of MM. Guérard and Delisle that the
voice of the preachers "was a continual appeal to the emancipation of the people",[1] so far, at all events, as medieval England
is concerned. The passionate sympathy of John Bromyard,
for example, some of whose language Dr Coulton himself has
recognized as an inheritance from Jacques de Vitry,[2] needs
always to be set alongside the somewhat severer strictures of
other friars like Berthold of Regensburg and Alvarus Pelagius.
Similarly, we have seen that "the theoretical Socialism" of
Gower is no poet's fancy, but a regular part of the social
message of the pulpit:[3] likewise, again, its praise for the virtues
of honest toil, of which more will be said later.[4] No one who
has any real knowledge of the subject-matter will be inclined
to question either the validity of Dr Coulton's actual sources
or his own unrivalled mastery in the European field. But there
is a further important question of the kind of conclusions which
we are entitled to draw from such evidence as he produces,
of where, in the midst of so much apparently conflicting sentiment, the final emphasis should be laid. Here there is certainly
room for some difference of opinion. On the strength of it,
the present writer is compelled at this point to put forward
two criticisms in the light of what has gone before. First, we
may ask—is Dr Coulton really justified in making so radical
a contrast between what he appears to consider the lip-service
of "egalitarian rhetoric" and the innate "class-snobbery" or
aristocratic prejudices of these same clergy? We think not.
Once again our learned author, as in a previous case which
we discussed of clerical relations to Art,[5] seems to have discovered a definite confusion of mind as well as an insincerity
of speech in the Church's attitude, where none really exists.
A backward glance at the arguments of the present chapter
should be sufficient to show that, however fundamentally

[1] See here Coulton, *Mediev. Village*, pp. 231 and 238, and cf. above,
pp. 287–307.   [2] Cf. ibid. p. 20.   [3] See above, p. 292.
[4] See above, pp. 554–7 and below, pp. 568–9 (and cf. Coulton, ibid.
p. 233, etc.).   [5] See above, p. 49, n. 5.

gratuitous you please, there is nothing contradictory or illogical about her belief, stated again and again in expository literature, that, while in origins and at death all men are equal, during their career on earth God has chosen to ordain for them a graded "class"-system with varying privileges and duties.[1] Secondly, it is of the greatest importance to observe that most of the strictures and rebukes which Dr Coulton has quoted come from that part of a literature which is devoted exclusively to the task of moral *correction*. The same fact, of course, has a vital bearing on the censure of clerical vices. It is not merely a part of the business, it is the whole business of these moralists here to expose the various follies of the community, to criticize those whose moral welfare is thus at stake. They are not at the moment concerned with the distribution of praise. Thus, we ourselves have had occasion to note how the English peasant and labourer receive in their due turn that homiletic chastisement which falls without fear or favour upon every rank of society throughout Christendom.[2] None escapes that fate. "Omnes enim peccaverunt, et egent gloria Dei." So far, then, the peasant is in no way different from anybody else. We do gain from these indictments, it is true, much valuable information concerning the specific sins of the various classes. But it is unreasonable to expect to derive therefrom any direct comparative moral estimate of the classes as a whole, even where fervid oratory has cooled and solidified upon the manuscript page. These catalogues of vices, after all, are no carefully balanced statistical tables, from which we can reckon up, as it were, in modern currency, from the respective amounts of accusation allotted to each group in the literature concerned, the debit or credit balance of a spiritual account.[3] Where, however, in the present writer's judgment, it is possible to get a more accurate knowledge of the Church's current estimate is in the preacher's less conventional remarks, the frank comments and confessions scattered here and there in the body of his narrative, some casual observation made in the course of

[1] Cf. above, pp. 292 et seq., 528, etc.   [2] Cf. above, p. 361.
[3] Although I uttered this warning in my first volume (cf. p. 190), some of my reviewers appeared to be unaware of it.

an independent argument, or, better still, on that yet rarer occasion when the speaker himself ventures on a comparative class-estimate of his own.[1] Above all, we may learn much from any favourable comments which he may be willing to pass. Does our preacher ever bestow, we ask, some rare word of praise upon clergy or knights, merchants or labourers, and what is the comparative extent of his appreciations? Here, indeed, as we shall see, is a most significant test for "Church estimates of the peasant" in medieval England.

With the way thus cleared for fresh consideration of our problem, let us first return for a moment to the doctrine of Work in the sermons. "England", says the Dutch historian, Professor Huizinga of Leyden, "gave towards the end of the fourteenth century, the first expression to the sentiment of the sanctity of productive labour in that strangely fantastic and touching poem *The Vision of William concerning Piers Plowman*".[2] Professor Huizinga's lack of acquaintance here with medieval homiletic literature is no more extraordinary than that of the other scholars whom it has been our task modestly to combat, for the honour of the pulpit. But in this case his error is the less pardonable in that, more than forty years ago, that learned French *savant* M. Paul Meyer took the trouble to draw our attention to "the Canonization of Hard Work" in the sermon-stories of Nicole Bozon.[3] More recently, a fellow-countryman, M. Émile Mâle, in connection with his study of the illustrative Calendars of the Middle Ages, has pointed to the thirteenth-century *Speculum Doctrinale* of Vincent of Beauvais[4] as an important source of the same idea, for art as well as for letters.[5] This "Beatification of Manual Labour", as M. Mâle styles it, though not so clearly expressed, is none the less in keeping with the place of honour accorded to the "*boni activi*"—between the Contemplatives and the Destroyers of Vices—in our English *Speculum Laicorum*;[6] also in the *Summa*

[1] Cf. *Preaching in Med. Engl.* p. 130, n. 3; and above, pp. 259–60, 268.
[2] *The Waning of the Middle Ages* (Engl. ed. 1924), p. 162.
[3] *Les Contes Moral. de N.B.* p. xxvii.
[4] Pars I, cap. ix.
[5] *Relig. Art in France in the 13th cent.* (American ed.), pp. 64–5.
[6] See above, p. 555, n. 4.

Predicantium to the "craftsman, whoever he be, who ceases not
to labour in lawful pursuits".[1] Other homilists, like Master
Ralph of Acton, again leave us in no doubt as to the kind
of humble labour which is thus worthy to be "canonized":
"Labour of the hands confers four benefits. It destroys vices,
it nourishes virtues, it provides necessaries, it gives alms".[2]
There seems to be no place in our sermons for the sneers of
a William of Auvergne at *servilia opera*.[3] Clearly, then, the
doctrine of Langland in this respect is no innovation, but a
re-emphasis of the doctrines of the pulpit. But what now of
the honest toiling poor themselves? The very phrases of the
preachers already quoted spring at once to the mind, eloquent
of much: "simple working folk,...the righteous poor";[4]
"patientes pauperes";[5] "fideles simplices";[6] "the trewe pore
peple";[7] "goddes knyghtes", proved by "angres, tribulaciouns
and woo".[8] In a manuscript of the fifteenth century in the
Bibliothèque Nationale,[9] there is a miniature—assuredly the
very negation of what we find in Dr Coulton's *Medieval
Village*—setting forth for us pictorially and in retrospect, as
it were, in the most vivid fashion, one influence at work in
the history of our pulpit which helped materially to determine
the preachers' attitude to the humble toiler. On one side of

[1] s.v. "Labor". Here, at the end of a list of those who labour well,
with merit and subsequent reward (see § 4, etc.).
[2] MS. Jo. Rylands Libr. Manch. Lat. 367, fol. 190b. Cf. further, e.g.,
Jo. of Mirfield, *Flor. Barthol.* s.v. "De Labore Manuum", MS. Camb.
Univ. Libr. Mm. ii. 10, fol. 98b, et seq. (Manual labour shields men
from temptation, from sloth, and from vain and idle thoughts, etc.)
[3] See Coulton, *Mediev. Village*, pp. 233–4.
[4] Bozon, *Metaphs.* cap. xxiv (as above, p. 299).
[5] Brunton, MS. Harl. 3760, fol. 111b (as above, p. 296).
[6] Bromyard, *S.P.* s.v. "Ministratio" (as above, p. 296); s.v. "Passio
Christi" (as below, p. 573); etc.
[7] MS. Roy. 18. B. xxiii, fol. 142 (as above, p. 69).
[8] MS. Harl. 45, fol. 80 ("for a worldliche knyght may never be proved,
til he have be assayed by bataile and werre").
[9] MS. franç. 9608, fol. 11b: reproduced in É. Mâle, *L'Art. relig. de
la fin du moyen âge en France*, p. 308. M. Mâle's accompanying description does not quite bring out the full significance of the scene, as will be
recognized by the account following above.

the picture, there stands a feudal castle upon a hill, on the other a cottage with gaping roof. A path leads down from the former to the latter. In the foreground we behold four kneeling figures on the greensward: two are those of a peasant and his wife, presumably from the cottage adjoining. Both are clad in ragged garments: the woman, carrying a distaff, suckles an infant at her breast, while at her husband's side lies his own instrument of toil, the spade. Facing the peasant is a Franciscan friar, his book on the ground before him, emblem of his faithful spiritual labours. Beside him is a fellow Dominican. The eyes of the Greyfriar and the peasants are raised to heaven, where, in a parting of the clouds, the figure of God the Father appears, clothed with the symbols of that Majesty which will one day ensure that justice is done upon His righteous poor. The woman's hands are busy with her child; but the hands of the other two are raised in prayer and supplication. Meanwhile, the Friar Preacher, himself in a tunic full of holes, directs the attention of two ill-clad beggars to the same heavenly vision. It is a picture of the perfect union of Holy Poverty and Beatified Labour, Secular and Religious together, Active and Contemplative, peasant and preacher. Now our miniature may well be a full century later than Langland's own masterpiece; while, in the latter, already the corrupted and avaricious Mendicants and the faithful ploughman are many leagues asunder. Nevertheless, the fact remains that in the earlier days of Mendicant zeal, the poverty and sufferings which such layfolk endured in a spirit of patience and meekness did link them with those, whom Bozon calls "the folk that have put themselves into poor Religion for God", in bonds of sympathy and a common hope which no mere stern necessity of rebuking sin would weaken. Even when, at length, the Orders themselves to a large extent had degenerated, and in losing touch with the poorer masses now incurred the rebuke of their own faithful preachers,[1] we still hear expressed, as on the lips of Bozon and Bromyard, not merely that same sympathy with the righteous labourer's lot, but also a very definite belief that of such is the Kingdom of Heaven.

[1] See here in my *Preaching in Med. Engl.* pp. 90–1, etc.

With the French miniature still in mind, then, we turn to the pulpit orators of England. Once again let it be emphasized that, in keeping with the special character of their task, the actual references in their sermons to the virtues of the labouring poor are as few in number as their denunciations of the oppressors are many. Albeit, the references are there. Of the virtues of other classes we hear hardly a word. If we begin, early in the thirteenth century, with the Cistercian Odo of Cheriton, for example, here we find that important link between the Religious and the secular poor man to which allusion has just been made. In a sermon on the theme of Dives and Lazarus,[1] attacking the vices of the rich, Odo quotes a significant passage from St Ambrose: "The poor man in his hut, wealthy in conscience, sleeps safer upon earth than the rich man in his gold and purple". "Wherefore," the preacher continues, "when a certain hermit was asked why he dwelt in so tiny a hovel, he replied well in saying—'One can leap to heaven more quickly from a little hut than from the lofty palace of kings'."[2] The unknown author of our *Speculum Laicorum*, later in the same century, echoes similar sentiments from the *Speculum Historiale* of Vincent of Beauvais: "Poverty, as saith the philosopher Secundus, is a hateful good, the mother of liberty, a remover of cares, felicity without solicitude, faculty without difficulty". It should be embraced upon the threefold example of Christ, the Apostles and the Philosophers.[3] This is as near as ever we get in sermon-literature to that "classic praise of rustic life" which, as Dr Coulton observes, is so conspicuously lacking from the medieval moralist's pages. To the latter, indeed, all existence in the natural world proceeded under a cloud.[4] What, however, in respect of mere poverty, held good for the Religious, held good equally for

---

[1] Luke xvi, 19.   [2] MS. Arund. 231, ii, fol. 47b.

[3] cap. lxiv (ed. Welter, p. 87). The reasons given are—(1) "quia viatorem exonerat", (2) "quia a laqueis diaboli liberat", (3) "quia celestis regni divicias impetrat". Cf. *Piers Pl.* B Text, pass. xiv, l. 275, etc.

[4] Dr Coulton, however (*Med. Vill.* p. 234), is hardly justified in omitting this observation. Cf. Bromyard's typical plaint, s.v. "Mundus"— "Tempore moderno nec terra vel arbores vel aquae tantae sunt fertilitatis sicut esse solebant"—with *Piers Pl.* C Text, pass. xviii, ll. 88–9.

the rustic layman. For, be that state voluntary or involuntary, the purpose of God was, as we have seen, precisely the same in both cases.[1] Coming to friar Bozon, in the early years of the fourteenth century, we still find this association—to use the friar's own phrase—of "society in the world and in religion", where the merits of "poor folk who are the children of God" are being discussed.[2] Here, too, Holy Scripture[3] lends the full weight of its testimony in support of "the simple folk who know not covetousness, nor trickery, nor wish to learn it, to save their conscience", still the constant prey of injustice and oppression in the high places. Such, then, is he who, in the words of Isaiah, "departeth from evil" only to be spoiled thus;[4] "the poor innocents" of Jeremiah, whose blood is to be found upon the wings of cruel lords;[5] the poor man of the Book of Proverbs, "better...in his uprightness than he that is perverse in his ways, though he be rich";[6] even the very Lord of Heaven Himself "in the person of the poor man",[7] crying out against the spoilers in the passionate language of the prophet Micah—"I am as the grape gleanings of the vintage!"[8] It is in the *Summa Predicantium*, however, that vast storehouse of sermon-lore, that we catch the clearest glimpses of the *fideles simplices* of lay society, now no longer confused with their brethren in "poor Religion". We see them here still unspoiled by evil example or outrageous hardship in a world of avarice, pride, sloth and self-indulgence, living "content with their lowly and honest status", in spite of the sneers of their superiors.[9] "Now the honest and simple folk,

---

[1] Cf. above, pp. 297 and 561, and below, pp. 573–4. Again, Dr Coulton appears to have missed the point (see *Mediev. Village*, p. 241).

[2] Cf. cap. xi and cxxi.   [3] Cf. similarly, above, pp. 297–8.

[4] cap. iii (Isa. lix, 15).   [5] cap. vi (Jer. ii, 34).

[6] cap. xi (Prov. xxviii, 6).

[7] It is clearly this favourite transfiguration in the sermons that is the secret of the famous scene of *Do-bet* in *Piers Plowman* (cf. C text, pass. xxi), in which Piers becomes Christ himself wearing the Ploughman's "coat-armour". For another example of this association in our homilies, cf. above (Bromyard), p. 262. The whole conception clearly springs from the medieval system of interpreting Scripture, as described above, p. 60, in this case from the imagery of Matth. xxv, 35–40.

[8] cap. xii (Micah vii, 1).   [9] *S.P.* s.v. "Ministratio".

desiring to honour Christ, go to church, to mass, to sermons, to learn how they ought to honour Him; while the greater, richer and falser men, whom the Apostle [Paul] calls 'enemies of the cross of Christ' (Phil. iii), indulge in those things which are contrary to Christ, in taverns, assizes, traffickings and falsities, 'crucifying afresh the Son of God' (Hebr. vi)."[1] "So He is received in the souls of the poor rather than of the rich.... For the rich and noble offend Him with false oaths and vows at almost every word."[2] "The rich commonly are worse sinners than the poor and do less penance", etc.[3] We see them again, "the simple folk", who, "as frequently happens, receive beggars into their barns and the other confined little hovels where they live more willingly than the rich in their great palaces. (So Elias was granted hospitality by the widow rather than by the king—iii Reg. xvii)".[4] Again, be it noted, "in the art of the Soul", Bromyard declares that "clerics of the highest rank who are negligent about the soul's salvation are plunged into hell, where poor diligent lay-folk are saved".[5] "Moreover, to the humble He preached who says—'He sent me to preach the Gospel to the poor'"; and such humble folk "He chose to be His poor disciples".[6] Following a typical discussion upon the ethics of Riches and Poverty, the same homilist observes that "for certain we have great evidence from what we daily hear and read" that sinners and those abounding in this world's goods may well fear that they are no friends of God. For God allowed His own Mother and His Apostles, whom He called His friends, to be poor in this world, when He could have made them rich, if He had liked, thus to enrich them with spiritual

[1] s.v. 'Passio Christi" (Bromyard goes on to tell how these *inferiores* may be corrupted by their superiors). Cf. similarly the later vernacularist, MS. Roy. 18. B. xxiii, fol. 125: "Thus itt farethe be many men in this world, whils that thei are poure thei are meke and worshippeth God; but when that thei are riche, anone thei forʒete God". Cf. here *Piers Plowman*, B text, pass. xiv, ll. 207–20, etc.

[2] s.v. "Adventus". [3] s.v. "Eleemosyna".

[4] s.v. "Adventus". For further references to the "simple, honest folk", see, e.g., s.v. "Acquisitio Mala", "Advocatus", "Falsitas", etc.

[5] s.v. "Accidia". Cf. further Rypon, quoting Jo. Walleys, MS. Harl. 4894, fol. 189.

[6] s.v. "Humilitas" (see Luke iv, 18).

goods. So those who are born to a poor man's lot will one day thank their Creator for thus having rescued them from the flames of hell—like the poor man at Chartres who lacked even the necessary halfpenny to get a night's lodging, only to learn later that that very night the lodging-house had been burnt to the ground.[1] It may be true that the peasant class furnishes few saints to the Calendar.[2] None the less it is equally clear that there will be many of their number among the obscurer souls of the Redeemed in Paradise: "Nonne Deus elegit pauperes in hoc mundo divites in fide et heredes regni?"[3] In the *Summa* we behold these faithful sons of toil as the Pawn among the world's Chessmen. He, it is, "who moves only one square at a time. He is the simple or poor man, who in this world seeks the maintenance of life alone. Such an one always 'goes straight', save when he 'takes'; for, while he dwells in simplicity and truth, he lives in straightforward fashion and safety. Prov. x".[4] For, to the poor is vouchsafed the supreme hope and consolation of a happy conscience,[5] mitigating all their labours and hardships. The *Summa Predicantium*, like many another homily-book of its scope and learning, may well strike the reader as a queer assortment of ill-digested matter and shifting sentiment. Nevertheless, by now he will be able to recognize, emerging from its pages here and there, very dimly, very tentatively, the familiar features of a literary hero.[6] It is none other than our immortal PIERES THE PLOWMAN, he who by a stroke of poetic genius was one day himself to become the chosen prophet of the Gospel of Truth and Reconciliation.

Such, then, is the kind of sources from which Langland

---

[1] s.v. "Bonitas". Cf. *Jacob's Well*, p. 80 ("smale folk").

[2] Cf. Coulton, *Mediev. Village*, pp. 241 and 526–7.

[3] James ii, 5. Cf. here, *Ayenb. of Inwyt*, pp. 138, 150, 188, etc.

[4] s.v. "Mundus". Sim. *Gesta Rom.* E.E.T.S. pp. 460–1. Cf. also *Ayenb. of Inwyt*, p. 139, and above, p. 296, etc.

[5] s.v. "Conscientia" (cf. also "Discordia", "Ministratio", etc.). With this and the numerous other references to the virtue elsewhere in sermon-literature, cf. the part played by Conscience in *Piers Plowman*.

[6] Cf. also the virtuous *Plowman* of Chaucer's *Cant. Tales*, Prol. ll. 530–41 (as discussed above, p. 370).

drew the first great message of his *Vision*, its "heavy charges", its "remedy for the evils of the world", and its "political ideal". The messages of preacher and poet are fundamentally the same. Langland's "common-sense", as M. Jusserand styles it, his championship of justice for the oppressed, his sane admixture of respect for institutions with his rebuke for those who defile them, his gospel of mutual sympathy and work as contrasted with revolution, his stress upon good deeds and moral reform without theological subtlety, all these and more were being proclaimed unceasingly from the pulpits of the land. We hear them in the simpler accents of the *Ayenbite of Inwyt*, the *Metaphors* of Brother Bozon, the *Pricke of Conscience*, the expanded versions of Rolle's Psalter,[1] the *Myrour for Lewde Men*, the Book of *Catoun*, and the many vernacular homilies "compiled for the mass of the people, rather than for the exalted ones".[2] We hear them again in John Bromyard's *Summa Predicantium* and Bishop Brunton's sermons, with all that they represent of many noted preachers of the day at Paul's Cross or St Mary Spital, with their wider interests and more learned appeal, talking of leaders and public affairs in Church and State amid the bustling scenes of city life.

Professor Ker has not been the only critic who, through contempt for the medieval sermon, has failed to discover the one adequate clue to the poet Langland's treatment of social and political questions. Professor Skeat himself claimed, as we saw,[3] that "William's originality is most surprising". However, M. Jusserand's acute parallels to the statements of the *Vision*,

[1] It is difficult to understand Prof. R. W. Chambers' apparent surprise at Langland's "appeal to the Psalter, with a constancy which we cannot match elsewhere in great literature, save in Thomas à Kempis" (see *Essays and Studies by members of the Engl. Assoc.* vol. ix, p. 51). "Great literature" and Thos. à Kempis have really nothing to do with the matter. Langland is simply following here the general practice of the English homilists, writing and preaching under "the prevailing influence of Hampole". (See, e.g., my *Preaching in Med. Engl.* p. 291, etc.)

[2] (Jusserand, *Piers Plowman* (Engl. edit. 1894), p. 173.)

[3] See above, p. 228. But cf. also his comment on the additions of the B text, with some of which we are especially concerned in this chapter— "distinguished by great freedom and originality of thought" (Clar. Press S. ed. as before, 1886, p. x).

drawn from current Parliament Rolls, delivered a first serious blow at that idea from another quarter. They proved how completely Langland is at one with the feelings and opinions of the Commons of England as expressed in Parliament—"wanting what they wanted, hating what they hated".[1] But unfortunately, forgetful again of the pulpit, Jusserand makes his hero to be a kind of lonely *Vox Populi*, crying in the wilderness beyond Westminster—"an echo and a commentary", he says, "that they had nowhere else at that time".[2] To this claim Professor Manly replied in his article in *Modern Philology* for July, 1909,[3] by arguing that such views *must* have been "commonly held and discussed" when the *Vision* was being written. Yet even he has missed the real source of inspiration here, alike for poet and for people. One noteworthy little instance will suffice to show how deep an impression was left upon Langland's mind by the faithful political message of a contemporary preacher. It possesses an added importance from the fact that it seems to offer us some fresh interpretation of a famous passage in the Prologue of the so-called 'B Text'.[4]

Tyrwhitt, Skeat, Jusserand, Manly, all agree that this particular version of the work belongs to some date within the rough limits of June, 1376, and June, 1377. The former year had opened darkly enough. The old King Edward III was now under the disastrous influence of a mistress, his government impotent and discredited, his court rapidly becoming a scandal to the eyes of all good and loyal subjects. By the month of June matters were no brighter. With the death of the Black Prince,[5] the early promise of the Good Parliament was destined

---

[1] *Piers Plowman*, as before, pp. 71, 133, 176, etc.

[2] Ibid. p. 103 (see also p. 176).

[3] Reprinted in E.E.T.S. Ext. S. no. 139c (see pp. 3–5).

[4] The following section of the present chapter is an expansion of the author's article on "The *Angel* and the *Goliardeys* of Langland's Prologue" in the *Mod. Lang. Rev.* vol. xx, No. 3, July, 1925, pp. 270–9. (See Notices, etc., in A. H. Bright, *New Light on Piers Plowman*, Oxford, 1928, p. 30; Miss D. Everett, in *The Year's Work in Engl. Stud.* for 1925, Oxf. 1927, vol. vi, pp. 99–100, and for 1926, vol. vii, p. 97; and *Les Lang. Mod.* Paris, Mar. 1927, pp. 141–2.)

[5] June 8, 1376.

to be blighted and its work undone. The evils return. "Popular sympathy coupled together, as martyrs of the same cause, Wykeham, wandering homeless through his Bishopric like Lear through his Kingdom, and the Speaker of the House of Commons, fast in the dungeons of Nottingham Castle."[1] A year later the king himself follows his eldest son to the grave,[2] leaving but a boy of eleven in his place. Now to this short epoch and the dozen years following it, belongs at least one London preacher of particular distinction, no mere onlooker either, from outside, at these critical events for court and government. A clerk like Langland, living "in a little house in Cornhill, not far from St Paul's", himself a sermon-goer at the famous Cross[3] where the former sometimes preached, could hardly have been unacquainted with his reputation and his eloquence. This was Thomas Brunton, Bishop of Rochester.[4] Once a Benedictine monk at Norwich, he was destined to become a Royal Confessor, and, as a noted enemy of Wycliffe,[5] to take part in the famous Council at the London Blackfriars in 1382, which condemned the reformer's heresies.[6] Both the *Historia Anglicana* of Walsingham[7] and the *Liber Custumarum* among London Guildhall documents[8] make mention of the sermon delivered by him at Paul's Cross, *in processione*, on the day following King Richard II's coronation; and the former records his death in 1389, as though it were a misfortune of almost national dimensions. Of the literary remains of this once famous but now almost forgotten orator apparently all that we possess is the single manuscript of his Latin Sermons, preserved in the British Museum.[9] For the rest, it is the

[1] Trevelyan, *Engl. in the Age of Wycliffe* (1920 impr.), p. 35.
[2] June 21, 1377.
[3] See B text, pass. xiii, ll. 65–6; C text, pass. xvi, ll. 69–91.
[4] 1373 (?) to 1389. See my *Preaching in Med. Engl.* pp. 15–20, etc.
[5] See Workman, *John Wyclif*, vol. i, pp. 296 and 304.
[6] *Fascic. Ziz.* Rolls S. p. 286.
[7] vol. i, pp. 338–9, Rolls S. The sermon is wrongly ascribed by the editor here (Index) to Thos. Trillek, Brunton's predecessor, who had died in 1372.   [8] *Munim. Gild. Lond.* Rolls S. vol. ii, p. 481.
[9] MS. Harl. 3760 (see my *Preaching in Med. Engl.* as above). Bale, however, mentions *Sermones coram pontifice Romano* by him (*Script. Brit. Index*, Oxf. ed. 1902, p. 433), and elsewhere—"atque alia plura" (ibid. p. 51).

chronicler again who reminds us that in the anxious months of the year 1376, when the Good Parliament was determining to bring pressure to bear on the king's evil administration, Brunton was one of four Bishops singled out to give counsel in the emergency to the knights of the shires, who "on being informed by their advice would be able to reply the more circumspectly to the royal petitions".[1] During that same period, as Professor Trevelyan observes, the Bishops "rose to a height of popularity with the Londoners which they never attained again".[2]

Turning now from the background of the scene to Langland's celebrated expansion of his original Prologue in this B text, we are introduced first[3] to "a lunatik, a lene thing with-alle", who on bended knee offers to his sovereign a greeting and good wishes for his reign. "I have no doubt", comments Skeat, "that the *lunatic* is William himself." If this be so, it is only reasonable to suppose that subsequent figures looming mistily out of the same misty scene will be equally real and recognizable personalities of the day. Next, then, "in the eyre an hiegh, an angel of hevene lowed to speke in latyn".[4] It is none other, we believe, than the figure of Bishop Brunton of Rochester, bending from his London pulpit. The very words "in latyn" at the outset have about them a decidedly "unangelic" and topical ring. Few, we think, will be fully satisfied with Skeat's attempted explanation of them.[5] On the other hand, if the angel be really this saintly but very human orator of the

---

[1] See *Chron. Angl.* Rolls S. pp. 69–70. The others were London, Norwich and Carlisle. This event in Bp. Brunton's career has been overlooked by Dr R. L. Poole in his article ("Brinton") in the *D.N.B.* q.v.

[2] *Engl. in the Age of Wycliffe*, as before, p. 35.

[3] Prol. ll. 123–7.   [4] Ibid. l. 128.

[5] "The angel [or Conscience] descends and begins to speak, but only in Latin, since common people ought not to be told how to justify themselves; all who could not understand Latin or French had best suffer and serve" (ed. Clar. Press S. 1876, p. 100, note to l. 128, and E.E.T.S. O.S. no. 67, pt. iv, § 1, p. 20). The present writer suggests what seems to him the more natural and straightforward meaning of this sentence which begins—"for lewed men ne coude . . . " on p. 582, below. (The angel speaks, because the "lewd" *cannot* speak for themselves in their own defence.)

Church, Latin, it is to be noted, would be the appropriate language of his address for sermons before "Parliaments" of clergy.[1] Furthermore, if a sermon summary in Latin verse, such as follows in the poem, appears unfamiliar to the modern reader, we have only to point again to medieval parallels presented by an Abbot of St Albans and by other homilists who sometimes add such memoranda to their own extended prose homilies.[2] Thirdly, in support of the same theory, there is something at the least suggestive about the fact that the English Dominican, Thomas Walleys, in his *De Arte Predicandi*,[3] a treatise of the first half of the fourteenth century current in Langland's day, uses this very figure of "the angel—*de celo lapsus*" to illustrate his view of *the preacher's* ideal of deportment *in the pulpit*.[4] Finally, we may notice that in the C text of the poem the *angel* becomes *Conscience*, the preacher of *passus* v of the A text, speaking now explicitly "to clergie and to the kyng",[5] in further accord with our argument.

Now, Dr Gasquet[6] has already identified one sermon of the Brunton manuscript[7] with the period concerned, when the Good Parliament meets in April of the year 1376. References in it to the evil domination of Alice Perrers, to the woes of the realm now in the grip of such corrupt and avaricious ministers as Lords Latimer and Neville, to the hedge of wanton upstarts about the throne like Stury, Lyons, Ellis, Peachey and Bury, shutting out the wise and virtuous counsellors, all strengthen his contention:

Apparetne vobis regimen equitatis, si rex et filii per consiliarios ita sunt ducti quod ipsi sunt pauperes et eruptuosi quantocumque gradu, et

[1] See my *Preaching in Med. Engl.* pp. 223 et seq.

[2] *Reg. Jo. Amundesham*, Rolls S. vol. i, pp. 229–31; and in my *Preaching in Med. Engl.* pp. 260, 272, etc.   [3] MS. Harl. 635, fol. 6 b.

[4] Cf. here the woodcut of Wisdom as an angel in the pulpit, in Alex. Barclay's *Ship of Fools* (ed. Edinb. 1874, vol. i, p. 119), and below, p. 596.

[5] C text, pass. i, ll. 151–7. Cf. below, here, p. 587.

[6] *Old Engl. Bible, and other Essays*, chap. iii. The value for the serious student of this sketch of "The Forgotten Preacher", however, is considerably lessened by Gasquet's failure to give regular references to the MS. page, and the original Latin text. The sketch is *very* "scrappy" and inadequate, and its author sometimes mistranslates.

[7] I.e. Sermo 69 (MS. Harl. 3760, fol. 186, et seq.).

ipsi ductores ita habundant pecuniis quod, si quarta pars temporalium regni esset venalis, haberent omnia parata talia ad emendum?. . . Nisi enim regi et filiis in habundantia sit provisum, eos oportebit ecclesiam spoliare et populum devorare. Apparetne regimen equitatis quod persone indigni et bassi status habeant ingressum ad regem pro negotiis expediendis ut magnates et prelati, si ad portam veniant pro negociis ecclesiarum suarum necessariis, non introducantur, sed extra portam stare inter pauperes compellantur, ubi per ceteras personas a rege non missas positi ad questiones, sine responso utili revertuntur? Heu quod rex Francie ter in ebdomada popularibus plenam facit audientiam, et omnibus petentibus personaliter facit justitie complementum, ubi magnates Anglie non possunt habere justitiam, licet eam expetant toto posse! Item, si alienigene et precipue domini de Aquitania, qui pro jure regni Anglie perdiderunt dominia atque castra, si veniant in Angliam pro remedio in hac parte, non honorantur, nec confortantur, nec habent vadia, immo vix bonum vultum et bona verba. Item, estne regimen equitatis quod rex Francie habeat de consilio suo privato 60 et decem personas de omni mundo electas, de quorum consilio omnia ardua operantur; rex autem Anglie, licet habeat et officiarios prudentes et fideles, tamen in arduis per unius consilium tantummodo operatur, ut veniat id scripturae—"*Operatur unus?*"[1] Nec est decens vel tutum quod ad unius uxoris[2] cingulum pendere debeant omnes claves. Hoc regimen est contra consilium Jetro,[3] qui Moysi rectori populi consuluit in hunc modum. *Exod.* 18: "*Provide de omni plebe viros potentes et timentes deum in quibus sit veritas, et qui oderint avariciam*", etc.[4] Et bene debent esse consiliarii viri—non pueri, juvenes et lascivi; quia Roboam, relinquens consilium seniorum et adherens consilio juvenum, perdidit regnum suum;[5] non mulieres, que pro utilitate propria sunt sagaces, sed viri probitate, maturitate et sanctitate, quia "*impius facit opus instabile*", *Proverb.* xi. . . . [6]

Brunton's theme[7] is primarily a call to action, fearless downright action in the cause of justice, on the part of all holding positions of responsibility in Church and State. For, "Faith without works is dead":

[1] Presumably a reference to the influence of John of Gaunt.
[2] I.e. Alice Perrers.   [3] I.e. Jethro.
[4] Exod. xviii, 21.
[5] Cf. here Bromyard on the influence of evil counsellors, *S.P.* s.v. "Adulator" ("regulati adulatoribus et consiliariis et malis confessoribus et pueris dominium suum et seipsos et ecclesiam destruunt. Figura, *Judic.* xvi: de Sampsone ducto a puero domum concussit et seipsum et multos secum occidit. . . "); also "Mundus" and "Ministratio".
[6] v. 18 (fol. 190 of the MS.). Cf. further, *Rich. the Redeles*, E.E.T.S. O.S. no. 54, pp. 475–7, 490–5, 498, etc.
[7] Text—"Factor operis hic beatus" (Jas. i, 25).

Amore Christi, et ob defensionem regni, in tanto discrimine constituti non simus tantum locutores sed factores, et sic *"abjiciamus opera tenebrarum, et induamur arma lucis"*,[1] ut vita nostra emendetur et regnum in justitia reguletur.... Pro processu est notandum quod proverbialiter solet dici—*"Bene fac et bene habe!"*; et ad istam finem sit omnis sermo, ut discant auditores quomodo bene debeant operari, et juxta bona opera premiari.... Tamen constat evidenter quod regnum Anglie, quod olim divitiis habundavit, modo est pauper et impecuniosum; quod olim gratia radiavit, jam est ingratiosum et ignominiosum; quod olim se per justitiam regulavit, jam est sine regula viciosum. Ut quilibet vestrum, qui se divisit a deo per peccatum et mala opera, deo per bona opera reconsilietur, ...age penitentiam![2]

There follows after "the Angel's" plea for justice, a further plea for piety, precisely as in the verses of Langland:

...justus es, esto pius!
Nudum jus a te vestiri vult pietate....[3]

Says Brunton:[4]

Facienda sunt opera sanctimonie quoad deum. Hec opera consistunt in auditione missarum et sermonum, et in devotis processionibus. De primo patet exemplum de rege Anglie, Henrico tertio, et Lodowico, rege Francie....[5] Nam, quando temporales domini in talibus erant devoti, habebant gloriam et honorem et pacem....

Unde concludo quod, si rex vel princeps daret exemplum humilitatis, in processionibus exhibendo suam presentiam corporalem, glorificaret deum et esset in majori reverentia quoad mundum.[6]

The good Bishop makes it clear in this same sermon that most others of his rank and authority, temporal as well as spiritual, were keeping silence in the face of great abuses of State, through fear of displeasing the sovereign and those in power:

Tacent domini temporales; quia timent offensam regis, "trepidantes ubi non est verisimiliter trepidandum";[7] quia, si credibiliter veritatem dicerent, ita est tractabilis et ductilis quod talia [crimina] in regno nulla-

---

[1] Rom. xiii, 12.   [2] fol. 188.

[3] ll. 134–5. There seems no very good reason for following Skeat here in his translation of Langland's "pietas" as "mercy".

[4] fol. 189–189 b.

[5] The well-known *exemplum* of the preference of the one for hearing sermons, and of the other for hearing masses—a holy rivalry!—follows here (cf. the version in our 13th-cent. Engl. *Speculum Laicorum*, as above, p. 161, n. 3).

[6] See further in my *Preaching in Med. Engl.* pp. 215–16.

[7] See Ps. liii, 5.

tenus paterent. Tacent confessores, quia dum possint libere habere propria solacia, commoda et honores, non curant de animabus; et ideo non debent vocari confessores sed confusores, non doctores sed potius proditores.... Tacent predicatores; quia multi eorum, si ante hec tempora in sermonibus apud crucem vicia dominorum generaliter tetigerunt, statim isti, tanquam malefactores arestati, coram regis consilio erant ducti, ubi examinati, reprobati, banniti, vel a predicandi officio perpetuo sunt suspensi; ut sic ad concludendum istud verificetur de eis quod dicit Psalmus—"*Omnes declinaverunt, simul inutiles facti sunt: non est qui faciat bonum, non est usque ad unum*"....[1]

The Dominican Bromyard bears similar testimony to the fact that in the parliaments of his day the prelates and other advisers of the sovereign merely cry "Amen" meekly to whatever they recognize that their lords and masters wish done, no longer fearlessly denouncing their evil deeds.[2] No one dares, he says, to reveal the truth to the sovereign in parliament; to propose the removal of the king's worthless ministers, or put forward measures for greater economy in his household.[3] Now, therefore, Brunton stands forth boldly with his pulpit challenge, in defence of the suffering, toiling masses of the people, silent through no fault of their own:

> for lewed men ne coude
> iangle ne iugge, that iustifie hem shulde,
> But suffren and serven....[4]

He illustrates here in his discourse the kind of helpless disadvantage at which they lay in a world where, as Bromyard put it, the game of life was not fairly divided between them and their superiors: "Nam ubi mediocres et subditi penas sustinent in presenti per quas purgantur, domini tamen et consiliarii, quantascumque iniurias irrogant ecclesie et publice utilitati, evadunt communiter impuniti".[5]

The most curious and telling feature of resemblance in the effusions of preacher and poet, however, has yet to be mentioned. It is the renowned Fable of the Rat Parliament. M. Jusserand himself has discovered it twice already in English

---

[1] Ps. liii, 3 (fol. 187b of our MS.).
[2] *S.P.* s.v. "Consilium".   [3] s.v. "Rapina".
[4] *Piers Plowman*, B text, Prol. ll. 129–31.
[5] fol. 190. Cf. above, pp. 253–4, 268, 340–4, etc.; also *Rich. the Redeles*, as before, ll. 56–64, 139, 300–51, etc.

homily-books of the period, namely, those of Bozon and Bromyard.[1] But here in Brunton's sermon it greets us again, at the very crisis in national affairs of which Langland is writing in his new Prologue:

> With that ran there a route of ratones at ones,
> And smale mys myd hem, mo then a thousande,
> And comen to a conseille for here comune profit.
> For a cat of the courte cam whan hym lyked,
> And overlepe hem ly3tlich and lau3te hem at his wille,
> And pleyde with hem perilouslych and possed hem aboute.[2]

So Brunton pictures the scene: "Non sic, domini reverendi! Sed ne parliamentum nostrum comparetur fabuloso parliamento murium et ratorum, de quibus legitur...."[3] "Who will bell the Cat?" then, is the cry of the hour. Upon the impotency of "the rats and mice", Brunton has already commented, as follows:[4]

Inter opera cetera in regno Anglie a retroactis temporibus acceptata iam pendet in manibus opus arduum et excellens ex eo, quod ad parliamentum sunt vocati prelati, domini, et communes ad tractandum et declarandum de regimine bono regni. Sed quid proderit puncta parliamenti tractare et facta transgressorum publice declarare, nisi post declarationem sequitur penalis executio debita in hac parte, cum frustra sint jura nisi sint qui jura debite exequantur? Sed numquid est scitum et quasi undique predictum, quomodo singulares persone non virtuose, sed viciose et scandalose, per multa tempora habuerunt principale regimen huius regni? De quorum regimine, licet universaliter murmuremus et etiam obloquamur, ad correctionem tamen debite faciendam veritatem solidam dicere non audemus.... Sic moderni ductores regni, oppressores veritatis et etiam equitatis, volentes suos dominos deificare,[5] cum quomodo sciant, pusillanimem dicunt audacem, debilem fortem, stultum sapientem, adulterum et luxuriosum castum predicant atque sanctum. Et ad finem quod ipsi singularia commoda prosequantur et domini sui[5] in criminibus notoriis foveantur, curiam ingredientibus ponunt ydolum mundani

[1] It occurs also in Odo of Cheriton (early 13th cent.). See J. A. Herbert, *Cat. of Romances in B.M.* vol. iii, p. 36. For Bozon, see *Les Contes Moral. de N.B.* ed. Smith and Meyer, p. 144: for Bromyard, *S.P.* s.v. "Ordo Clericalis".

[2] B text, as before, ll. 146, et seq.

[3] A translation of the whole passage is given in Gasquet, as above.

[4] fol. 187.

[5] Trevelyan (*Engl. in the Age of Wycliffe*, p. 20) has unfortunately reproduced Gasquet's clumsy translations here (*Old Engl. Bible*, ed. 1897, p. 72) in his illustration of the Bishop's eloquence.

timoris, ut nullus cuiuscunque gradus vel status audeat contradicere vel corripere delinquentes.

Sed quorum interest in materia ista loqui?—Certe prelatorum, temporalium, confessorum et etiam predicatorum.

It is interesting to note that again Bromyard has the same complaint to make about Parliament in his *Summa Predicantium*:

Et ista infirmitas communiter sequitur parlamenta moderna, ubi multa dantur consilia sed nulla fit in opere executio. Ideo merito vocatum est nomen ejus "parlamentum", quia ibi multa loquuntur, sed in toto vel magna parte est postmodum mentitum quod ibi fuit locutum et ordinatum.[1]

Both Friar and Bishop agree, too, that for the future ecclesiastical influence should play a leading part in the cure. Says the former—"Clerus debet cum principibus consilium inire, et per censuras ecclesiasticas eos cogere ad consilium tendendum".[2]

If the "Angel" of the Prologue be Brunton, who then is the "Goliardeys, a glotoun of wordes", who next appears in the poem, "and to the angel an heiȝ answered after"?[3] No one reading Brunton's sermon and after it the complaints of Sir Peter de la Mare, spokesman of the Commons, as expressed

---

[1] s.v. "Consilium". Here then is Carlyle's "talking shop"!

[2] Ibid. Cf. further s.v. "Dominatio", where he adds that kings and feudal lords ought to consult the Church before imposing taxes and other inflictions on their subjects. A further point is worth noting here in connection with the Text which Langland takes for the theme of his new Prologue to the B text (cf. Skeat's ed. as before, p. x), from Eccles. x, 16— "Vae terrae ubi rex puer est!" Bromyard introduces it with the following comment: "Ve terre ubi rex puer est, et cuius maiores, qui terram defendere et regere haberent, pueriliter vivunt; et cuius principes mane comedunt antequam veniant ad consilium vel ad parliamentum, ut pransi et potati minus intelligant quod consulendum sit". This agrees precisely with Robt. Crowley's marginal interpretation of the Text, as it occurs in his sixteenth-century edition of *Piers Plowman*, thus—"Omnium doctissimorum suffragio, dicuntur hec de lassivis, fatuis aut ineptis principibus, non de etate tenellis: quasi dicat—'ubi rex puerilis est'". Skeat's "obvious reasons" for this added comment of Crowley, therefore, do *not* prove the latter to be a prevaricator (see above ed. p. 103, n. 191). Bromyard's remarks show that it was an ancient interpretation, and, doubtless, that which the poet himself had in mind.

[3] Prol. ll. 139–142.

in his speech "to the Kynges conseille" in the Good Parliament of 1376,[1] could fail to be struck by the remarkable agreement between them. Sir Peter then is undoubtedly the grieving "goliardeys" in question. Was ever a more appropriate and witty sobriquet chosen?—"Glotoun of wordes". He who is actually the first recorded Speaker of the lower house in English history, was described by the chroniclers as one peculiarly noteworthy for his "facundia sermonis", and his fearlessness in address. Idol of the London crowds, popular verses were composed and circulated in honour of this "goliardeys"; he was greeted with acclamation and with gifts; and a priest who once spoke ill of him was promptly set upon and beaten to death in the streets.[2] As in the poem, so then in the world of historic events, he "answers after" the angel, prompted, that is, by the prelate's courageous example. At his back, like a supporting chorus, stand "alle the commune", crying their "Precepta Regis sunt nobis vincula legis".[3] Their wistful hope and confidence in the strong personal rule of the monarchy is that of the old preacher who cries thus to his congregation on the Sunday:

Worschypffull ffrendys,...exsperiens schewethe that in the absens off a kynge, or ellys yff a kinge be not had in reputacion, ffavour, worchepe, and drede, lyke as [Scripture?] schewythe a sovereyn awethe to be, offtyn there growethe and encresethe myche malyce and wykkudnes; and schortlye to s[p]eke off, ffalshed, syn, and [un]trawthe have there grete dominacion. ffor than be spolyacions, robbryes, deseytes, tresons, and many wrongys doo wyth-owte correccion, and cawsethe offtyn tyme the pepull to be rebell, and ryse anenense the pees, as it had lyke ffor to have be in thys reem wyth-yn ffewe ʒeers, had not god schewed to us off hys good grace.[4]

Evidences of the influence of preacher upon poet, however, are not confined to any single utterance in this remarkable sermon-series of Brunton. In discussing Professor Ker's summary of the message of Piers Plowman to the world, we remarked that it was none other than the ancient preachers'

---

[1] See *Rot. Parl.* vol. ii, 323 (and Jusserand, *Piers Plowman*, p. 45).
[2] See *Chron. Angl.* Rolls S. pp. 72, 73, 124, 150 and 392 (App.); also art. in *D.N.B.* s.v. "De la Mare".   [3] Prol. ll. 143–5.
[4] MS. Camb. Univ. Libr. Gg. vi. 16, fol. 34. Again, in MS. Glouc. Cath. Libr. *Sermo Dom. i. Adv.* inc.

ideal of Priesthood, Knighthood and Labourers working in perfect harmony for the peace and welfare of Christendom. Langland's opening vision, and in particular the more optimistic passage inserted in the B text of his Prologue immediately preceding the appearance of the "lunatik"[1] show, none the less, some advance upon the homilist's original theme, ancient enough in his own day. There is now a more national, a more definitely English feeling in his appeal, as there is also a more careful and detailed attention to the many smaller groups and professions that make up the "felde ful of folke". The old generalizations upon feudal society, with their breadth, their simplicity, their vagueness here give place to a more concentrated, intimate treatment of the contemporary scene. Our poet's world cannot be lightly dismissed in the old threefold fashion. In its very shrinking to national dimensions he studies what he sees more closely. In the ordinary course of modern criticism this development will be—and indeed has been—attributed to the special genius of the writer. He is a poet and an artist, not a commonplace moralist of the pulpit, we shall be told.[2] But those who trouble to make themselves acquainted with the preaching of the great Bishop of Rochester and of others like John Bromyard, whom we have repeatedly quoted, will not be so inclined to accept the explanation. Thomas Brunton, too, has advanced in similar directions. Again and again in his sermons he is moved to leave the familiar beaten track for new and more independent paths of his own. Not content, for example, merely with the usual exhortation to fellow-prelates to preach faithfully in their dioceses, he urges them to preach also in London, because of its national significance. Let them think in terms of "all the churches of England", he says in effect, and act as voices of righteousness to the whole nation.[3] Discussing Knighthood on another occasion, as we have seen, he fearlessly turns the point of his argument against

[1] Prol. ll. 112, et seq.
[2] Cf. here Prof. R. W. Chambers' distinction, as applied to the poem, between what he calls "devotional treatise", and "satire in the strict sense of the word" (*Mod. Lang. Rev.* vol. xiv, p. 136).
[3] MS. Harl. 3760, fol. 60b (see my *Preaching in Med. Engl.* p. 208).

his own fellow-countrymen, the English knighthood of the day, with a characteristic—"Sed, ut veniamus ad exempla magis domestica...".[1] Likewise, he is equally outspoken in denouncing the sins of the magnates "in regno Anglie",[2] or the causes of "misfortunes, pestilences and wars", which have recently befallen her: "Item in Anglia fiunt tot furta....Tot in Anglia inundant homicidia...".[3] Finally, even in his treatment of the typical theme of the Body and its Members, there are signs that the social organism has been subjected to a fresh and more acute analysis, clearer still when he goes on to deal, like his contemporary Bromyard, with the separate vices and weaknesses of the age in detail. He is speaking with some authority of his own, not merely as the scribes. Change but a metaphor, and we are back to the ideal community of William Langland again:

Unum corpus multi sumus. Hujus mistici corporis multa sunt membra: quia capita sunt reges, principes, et prelati, occuli sunt judices, sapientes et veraces consiliarii, aures sunt religiosi, lingua doctores boni, manus dextra sunt milites ad defendendum parati, manus sinistra sunt mercatores et fideles mechanici, cor sunt cives et burgenses quasi in medio positi, pedes sunt agricole et laborantes quasi totum corpus firmiter supportantes. Et licet in omnibus membris istis, precipue in duobus principalibus sollicite veritas est servanda, viz. in capitibus discrete et juste ad regendum, in cordibus perfecte ad diligendum. Dixi primo quod in capitibus veritas est servanda discrete et juste ad regendum, quia capita et rectores tam temporales quam spirituales debent esse uni cum Deo per firmam adherenciam....Secundo, principes et rectores debent esse unanimes cum subditis, eos in periculis tanquam capita precedendo...", etc.[4]

Langland, the poet, may have come to regard the good Bishop as his spiritual guide, in yet earlier days, when the original *Vision* was still taking shape in his mind. Here was one worthy, then, to appear in his poem as "Conscience", a pulpit hero most fitted to direct the folk of that Field, which is the world

---

[1] Ibid. fol. 152 (see further above, pp. 331–2).
[2] fol. 142 b.　　　　　　　　　　[3] fols. 124 b, 142 b–143, etc.
[4] fols. 61–61 b (the *exemplum* which follows here illustrates the truth that the stronger should take the lead). Cf. similarly, the author of the *Pricke of Consc.* as quoted above, p. 562—mentioning lawyers, physicians, scholars and preachers; and Bozon, as above, p. 560.

of fourteenth-century England, to the courts of heaven, the "tour ther Treuthe is inne":

> Then sauh I muche more then I beofore tolde,
> For I sauh the Feld ful of Folk that ich of bi-fore schewede,
> And Conscience with a Crois com for to preche.
> He preide the peple have pite of hem-selve,
> And prevede that this pestilences weore for puire synne,[1]
> And this south-Westerne wynt on a Seterday at even
> Was a-perteliche for pruide, and for no poynt elles.
>
> .   .   .   .
>
> Of this Matere I mihte momele ful longe,
> Bute I sigge as I sauh, (so me god helpe!),
> How Conscience with a Cros comsede to preche.[2]

The suggested identification of this older passage with Brunton, however, may be merely the present writer's dream, not that of the poet. Some other preacher of the hour may here have furnished him with a model. Nevertheless, there remains good reason for the belief that in the new text of Langland's Prologue, prepared, doubtless, when the later sermon in question was on every intelligent Londoner's lips, we have an enduring and a worthy memorial of our Bishop's pulpit heroism. Preserved thus in the *Vision*, like some fossil-fragment in its rocky bed, the sermon has long outlasted even the very name and fame of its author. Therein lies a parable, meet for the ending of our survey, of the way in which the preachers' message lies enshrined in the literature and history of the nation. Yet, indeed, we do wrong to speak here of any relic of an extinct and lifeless antiquity. The influence of the medieval pulpit, could we but see and feel it, is part of the undying past that still lives in our letters, still pulses in our veins and throbs at the heart of many of our institutions. Of that long neglected oracle and its forgotten ministers, then, we have a right to say—"Si monumentum requiris, circumspice!" More than five-and-a-half centuries have rolled away since Langland first wrote his immortal poem. Many of the grosser abuses in State and Church which he and his fellow-homilists

---

[1] Precisely as in one of Bp. Brunton's own sermons. See my *Preaching in Med. Engl.* pp. 206–7, and cf. MS. ibid. fol. 124b, etc.

[2] A text, pass. v, ll. 9–23.

attacked so bravely are now happily banished from the realm of England. On the other hand, that Social Order in which he and they reposed so unhesitating a trust seems to-day crumbling before our eyes. Few, at all events, even among the most hide-bound, would care to defend it as God-given. Notwithstanding, there remains one simple but profound truth in the social message of poet and preacher, as vital for the present as for the past. Peoples and politicians nowadays, thinking themselves so much wiser than Plato and better than the old moralists, are inclined to put their trust in the instrument of social legislation and a general levelling of humanity to bring in the New Jerusalem. But, even under "enlightened" democracies, we begin to rediscover that men cannot be made good by Acts of Parliament. The vicious and covetous individual, to whatever party he may belong, still threatens to frustrate every serious effort towards a better social order, if better there be. For all its boasted enlightenment, its scientific achievements and its new-found liberties, then, our modern civilization cannot yet afford to dispense with the preacher of righteousness and "truth in the inward parts".

> The tumult and the shouting dies:
> The captains and the kings depart.
> Still stands Thine ancient sacrifice—
> An humble and a contrite heart.
> Lord God of Hosts, be with us yet,
> Lest we forget, lest we forget.

.   .   .   .

Among the many types of men which history presents to us, the sacred orator is one of the most unsubstantial and elusive. Eminent lawgivers, counsellors, politicians, soldiers, explorers and other leaders in action have definite triumphs and achievements to their credit writ large in its pages. The fruits of the successful toil of merchants and professional men of lesser fame we estimate by the growing wealth, health and prosperity of the State as a whole. Even the labourer of the countryside, reaping where he has sown, the factory-worker and the fisherman all receive their due recognition in the tale of harvests upon land and sea. Likewise, the accomplishments of the thinker, the eminent man of letters and the artist are regularly appraised and commemorated each in their turn. But the preacher seems to stand apart. He has no such solid triumphs to show. His own literary remains tend, for the most part, to be as ephemeral as the efforts of modern journalism. How, indeed, shall we measure, according to any material or even ethical scale, the extent of his achievement, where the moral progress of peoples is either itself a delusion, or else is so slight and so variable that the historian must often feel compelled to neglect it? Like the lonely seabird on the wing that utters its plaintive cry of warning as the traveller passes, or the merry skylark pouring forth into his ear its songs of praise as it mounts rapidly skywards, the medieval preacher will not abide. He rarely toils or spins in the way of other mortals: where he sows he does not reap. If harvest there be upon the earth as the result of his labours, "herein is that saying true—'One soweth, and another reapeth'". Like the birds, again, as a denizen of the skies, his vision of earth is that of one who is wont to survey it more often from above than from the ordinary ground level. At the sound of his voice men may cease from work for a moment or two, to follow his flight heavenward: then he vanishes, and they return to their earthly tasks again. Only scant memories of his song will linger. Nevertheless, if it be true that belief and motive play the decisive part in human affairs, we cannot afford to neglect these transient songsters of history. Thus, while perforce neglecting the more spiritual side of their influence, we have come to see in these pages how their very music has contributed to the music of poet and dramatist in our medieval England. We have traced their influence upon the early development of the language and the growth of a reading and a thinking public. We have had occasion to note how to the scenes and characters of everyday life, the trivial sayings of unlettered folk, the common objects of their tears and laughter, they gave a first literary significance, which led in due time to a revival of Realism amongst genuine men-of-letters. Further, while the scenes and characters of Scripture woke again to a new life upon the preachers' lips, we observed how Scriptural allegory in its turn gave birth under their spell to a whole fresh family of symbolic creatures, which likewise invade the territory of a wider and better-known literature. Upon the same bookless adult society, the pulpit bestowed also an entertaining Fiction, and the first smatterings of a knowledge of the world of nature, travel and antiquity that led to the demand for more. Its satire and complaint gave powerful ventilation to social wrongs, thus promoting the supply of popular "political" verse and helping to foster a national spirit. Finally, in its same shadow, we watched the emergence of a native school of vernacular comedy and tragedy, parent of our modern drama. All this, though not itself endowed with the qualities of a great literature, is no mean achievement. It serves at least to remind us that once the pulpit was a force to be reckoned with, alike in literature and politics as in religion. Moreover, it is prophetic of the greater literature to come. For these picturesque folk-themes of preaching, crude as they are, have that intense feeling for life and yearning for a moral order which are the necessary prelude to any noble and enduring art.[1] When the master-musician arrives, he will weave them into some grand symphony worthy of a free, enlightened people.

The student who comes fresh from a study of medieval homiletics to the greatest of the Elizabethans can hardly fail to be impressed by its twofold contribution to the realism and moral purpose of Shakespeare's maturer Stage.[2] It is now the dramatist's express aim "to hold, as 'twere, the mirror up to nature; to show virtue her own feature, scorn her own image, and the very age and body of the time his form and pressure".[3] That little mistake of Francis Douce to which reference has already been made,[4] where he attributes to the influence of

[1] I do *not* say—"necessary accompaniment of" the same. The great artist himself, however personally "immoral", yet works consciously or unconsciously under this very spell. Whether leading or led, indeed, the artist, after all, *is* the sensitive child of the age that produced him. I rejoice to see that Prof. Ernest Barker has recently reiterated, in discussing Goethe (*The Times*, March 29, 1932, p. 15), that—"there is no way of divorcing aesthetics from ethics." The fruits of such an attempt we are witnessing to-day in much 'modern Art'.

[2] For the latter, the reader may well refer again to Prof. Dowden's masterly study, *Shakspere, His Mind and Art*, esp. chap. v.

[3] *Hamlet*, Act iii, Sc. ii.   [4] See above, p. 536, n. 1.

Pliny what Shakespeare could draw from his own Bible, may be taken to represent the more general error of the critics who hitherto have ascribed to the Classical Renaissance much of that lively inspiration which the poet owed to our more modest preachers. As for their moral influence over him, we need look no further than to the play which presents us with the passage just quoted. To modern interpreters, even as to Edward Dowden and the many scholars of his day whom he calls to witness, the play of *Hamlet* is still somewhat of a "mystery", a "baffling vital obscurity". Obsessed with the traditional lore of the theatre, wise in its superficial stage-craft, but still strangely unfamiliar with the inner mentality of the times, they fail to see that the story of the Prince of Denmark is in reality the story which they learnt at their own mothers' knees. It is all so simple, we fear, so utterly at variance with modern fashions in the art, that, were the solution presented to them, they would laugh it out of court with a superior scorn. Nevertheless, the theme of Shakespeare here, be it said, is none other than the homely theme which has haunted us through all these pages—the hideous consequences of sin in human affairs. Let the guilty sinner strive as he may to hide his guilt and suppress its very memory, sooner or later that sin will out, poisoning society like a rankling plague, a rottenness in the very state of Denmark. In the play, therefore, it is to be seen blasting alike the guilty and the innocent, the old and young, the wise and the foolish. It destroys the brilliant promise of youth and thwarts the tender relations of man and maid, making one mad and another seeming mad in the unutterable bitterness of a barren grief. It breeds suspicions, discords, plots and idle vengeance. It puts the realm itself in turmoil:

> So shall you hear
> Of carnal, bloody and unnatural acts,
> Of accidental judgments, casual slaughters,
> Of deaths put on by cunning and forced cause,
> And in this upshot, purposes mistook
> Fall'n on the inventors' heads.

There is no "mystery" here: only a superb *exemplum* of an

old pulpit truth, elaborated by a master hand. Remove this moral significance from the play, and the tale of *Hamlet*, apart from the manner of its telling, sinks to the level of any idle narrative of the Renaissance wits, "full of sound and fury, signifying nothing". It is in such bankruptcy of spirit that modern critics have come to tell us that Shakespeare's many murder-scenes were just a trick to please the groundlings, not the inevitable issue of his own solemn theme. Such critical folly, indeed, is only to be matched by the recent attempt to derive autobiographic detail from a mathematical calculation of the poet's images. As we plunge farther into the plays, the reappearance of other pulpit themes becomes almost as startling as the ghost of Denmark's king. In *Macbeth* we behold again the insatiate Worm of Conscience, writhing its way through the tragic story of human covetousness: in *Macbeth*, too, and in *Antony and Cleopatra*, the dominating figure of Woman with her charms as man's fatal seducer. "The subject of *Coriolanus* is the ruin of a noble life through the sin of pride",[1] along with a social gospel that has been actually described as "uncompromising feudalism". *King Lear* is a gigantic picture of the tragedy and pathos of human existence on earth; while, in the satire of the Comedies, we perceive once more its "grotesque hieroglyph". Painful though it may seem, then, even Shakespearean scholarship may have something yet to learn from the despised literature of medieval preaching. "Utique, numquam legistis—'Quia ex ore infantium et lactentium perfecisti laudem'?"

> FLOR AND FRYTE MAY NOT BE FEDE [blighted
> THER HIT DOUN DROF IN MOLDEƷ DUNNE;
> FOR UCH GRESSE MOT GROW OF GRAYNEƷ DEDE,
> NO WHETE WERE ELLEƷ TO WONEƷ WONNE. [home brought
> OF GOUD UCHE GOUDE IS AY BY-GONNE;
> SO SEMLY A SEDE MOƷT FAYLY NOT.

[1] Dowden, as before (7th ed.), p. 317. (Cf. further here—"The greatness of Brutus is altogether that of the moral conscience".) See also the late Sir Israel Gollancz's Shakespeare Lecture before the British Academy, 1922, printed from shorthand notes in an *In Memoriam* volume, 1931, *Allegory and Mysticism in Shakespeare: A Medievalist on "The Merchant of Venice"* (privately printed).

ADDITIONAL NOTES

CHAP. I, page 4. Cf. also *Metrical Chronicle* of Robert of Gloucester, c. 1300, line 7543: "Ac lowe men holdeth to engliss and to hor owe speche ʒute ... " (ed. Rolls Ser., vol. ii, p. 544).

CHAP. I, pages 52–4. Apart from extended sermons proper, a series of references to classical pictures of this kind will be found in Holcot's *Moralitates* and in the illustrative extracts for sermons in MS. Harl. 7322 (xiv cent.), fols. 64 b, 78 b, 103 b, 104, 155 b, 157-8, 162 b, 163; also *amoris imago* in A. Carpenter's *Destructorium Viciorum*, pars. vii, cap. 12; etc. See now the learned and illuminating article by Miss B. Smalley on "Robert Holcot, O.P." in *Archivum Fratrum Praedic.*, xxvi, 1956, espec. pp. 65-82.

CHAP. II, page 94. Cf. the well-known tale of King Richard I capturing the warlike Bishop of Beauvais in battle and sending his cuirass to Pope Celestine III with the words: "Vide an tunica filii tui sit an non!" (Gen. xxxvii, 32).

CHAP. II, page 106. This particular development from the imagery of Esdras seems to bear little or no relation to the better-known Bridge of Souls in the so-called Vision of St Paul, the Vision of Tundale and St Patrick's Purgatory, dealing with the after-world. For these latter, which had their own vogue in English medieval homiletic literature, see T. Silverstein, *Visio S. Pauli* (Studies and Documents IV, 1935), espec. pp. 77-8 and 123-4; etc.

CHAP. III, page 125. This description of St James the Less is obviously taken from the *Legenda Aurea*. It derives from Hegesippus in Eusebius, *Hist. Eccles.*, ii, 23 (Loeb ed. vol. i, p. 170). Cf. F. C. Burkitt, *Christian Beginnings*, pp. 57-61; etc. In the ensuing case of St Clement here, likewise taken from the *Leg. Aurea*, Prof. W. O. Ross of Detroit has rightly warned us that even the preacher's own statement of his source-book is not always reliable.

CHAP. III, pages 137–43. With this discussion of Images, compare throughout Roger Dymmok, *Liber contra xii Errores et Hereses Lollardorum* (c. 1395), pars viii, edit. Rev. H. S. Cronin, Wyclif Soc. 1922, pp. 181-202, and for Patristic sources especially St John Damascene, *De Fide Orthodoxa*, lib. iv, cap. xvi (Migne, *Patr. Graec.* vol. xciv, cols. 1168-74) and St Gregory the Great, *Epist.* lib. ix, epist. cv (Migne, *Patr. Lat.* vol. lxxvii, col. 1027). For the Epistle of Epiphanius of Salamis (the prelate of the incident) to John of Jerusalem, referred to on page 139 of my text (and note 4), see St Jerome, *Epist.* li (Migne, *Patr. Lat.* vol. xxii, col. 526, §9)—

"a Hieronymo Latine reddita". The king of the legend referred to on page 140 is Abgar (Oukhâma) of Edessa. See art. "Abgar (La Légende d')", by H. Leclercq, in Dom. F. Cabrol, *Dict. d' Archéol. Chrétienne*, and compare Damascene, as above, col. 1173.

CHAP. V, page 227, note 2. For Lichfield's verse, see Carleton Brown, *Reg. of Midd. English Relig. and Didactic Verse*, vol. ii, no. 1672, and *Polit., Relig. and Love Poems*, ed. F. J. Furnivall, E.E.T.S. O.S. no. 15, ed. 1903, pp. 160 et seq. ("*Goddis Owne Complaynt*"). Cf. further, in the latter volume, a series of vernacular poems from another sermon-book, MS. Harl. 7322 (espec. pp. 249 et seq.).

CHAP. V, page 278. For Hugh of Fouilloy, see *De Claustro Animae*, lib. ii, cap. 23, "De irreverentia juxta altare. Abusio duodecima", ed. Migne, *Patr. Lat.* vol. clxxvi, col. 1085. For full discussion of authorship, etc., see B. Hauréau, *Les œuvres de Hugues de St.-Victo.*, 1886, pp. 155–64.

CHAP. VI, pages 328–9. See another typical complaint quoted in my *Destructorium Viciorum of Alex. Carpenter*, 1952, pp. 30-1.

CHAP. VI, page 334, line 7: *ailettes*. Readers will recall in this connection the description of Piers Gaveston's magnificent *alae*—"Les alettes garniz et fretter de perles"—in a List of his Jewels and Horses, c. 1312–13, in Rymer, New *Foedera*, vol. ii, pt. i, p. 204, and the emblazoned *alae* worn by Sir Geoffrey Luttrell in the well-known miniature of him in the *Louterell Psalter*, c. 1340. This mention of them by Bromyard is indeed a further indication that the *Summa Predicantium* belongs to the earlier rather than the later part of the same century, since they appear to have gone out of fashion in the latter period.

CHAP. VI, page 350. Cf. also the Franciscan *Fasciculus Morum*, as indicated in my art. "*Sortilegium* in Engl. Homiletic Literature of the 14th century" in *Studies presented to Sir Hilary Jenkinson*, p. 276. Sim. Bromyard, ibid. p. 291.

CHAP. VII, page 426. For the Fathers on the subject of "Ebrietas", see Migne, *Patr. Lat.* vol. ccxx (Indices, vol. iii), "De Gula", cols. 823-5.

CHAP. VII, page 430, lines 5-18. Readers of Prof. Eileen Power's English edition of *Le Menagier de Paris (The Goodman of Paris*, Broadway Mediev. Libr. 1928) will recognize here "the picture of the female glutton" in the Third Section, to which the Editor draws particular attention (pp. 5 and 84). As will be seen, Miss Power is mistaken in attributing it to the Ménagier, "with a charm that is all his own". For, like our own excerpt from MS. Harl. 45, it is drawn from the *Somme le Roi* (or *Somme des Vices et des Vertues*) of friar Lorens, with a mere change of sex: likewise, the passage on the Tavern as the Devil's Church, which immediately follows (and should be compared with p. 438 above). The *Somme* of Lorens, indeed, should be added to Jérôme Pichon's list of the Ménagier's sources on p. 312 of Miss Power's volume.

CHAP. VIII, page 512. For the oldest version of this legend of the tricking of the Devil, in the Epistles of Ignatius, A.D. c. 120, see F. C. Conybeare, *Myth, Magic and Morals*, p. 205; H. Lietzmann, *Beginnings of the Christian Church*, pp. 326–7; etc.

CHAP. VIII, page 531. M. Émile Mâle, it should be noticed, actually derives the *Danse Macabre* itself from the medieval pulpit, namely, from Mendicant *sermons mimés* on Death (*L'Art relig. de la fin du moyen âge en France*, p. 362).

CHAP. IX, page 579. Preachers are also likened to angels by Humbert de Romans in his *De Eruditione Predicatorum*, Richard of Thetford in his *Tractatus de Angelis*, John Bromyard in his *Summa Predicantium* and Alex. Carpenter in his *Destructorium Viciorum* (quoting "Guilelmus Parisiensis"). All interpret the seven angels of the Apocalypse in this sense.

INDEX

To both text and footnotes